ENGLISH PLACE-NAME SOCIETY. VOLUME XLIX
FOR 1971–1972

GENERAL EDITOR
K. CAMERON

D0082096

THE PLACE-NAMES OF
BERKSHIRE

PART I

ENGLISH PLACE-NAME SOCIETY

The English Place-Name Society was founded in 1924 to carry out the survey of English place-names and to issue annual volumes to members who subscribe to the work of the Society. The Society has issued the following volumes:

The volumes for the following counties are in preparation: *Berkshire* (Parts 2 and 3), *Cheshire* (Part 5), *Dorset, Kent, Leicestershire & Rutland, Lincolnshire, the City of London, Shropshire, Staffordshire.*

All communications with regard to the Society and membership should be addressed to:

THE HON. DIRECTOR, English Place-Name Society, School of English Studies. The University, Nottingham.

The publication of the first of the three volumes on *The Place-Names of Berkshire* celebrates the 50th anniversary of the foundation of the English Place-Name Society on 9 January 1923. To date, the Society has published forty-eight volumes and with the completion of those for Berkshire it will have surveyed the place-names of twenty-three counties.

For the future, work on Dorset has been completed and the volumes are being prepared for the press. Further, surveys are being carried out for Durham, Hampshire, Kent, Leicestershire and Rutland, Lincolnshire, The City of London, Norfolk, Shropshire, Suffolk and Staffordshire.

ENGLISH PLACE-NAME SOCIETY. VOLUME XLIX

THE PLACE-NAMES OF BERKSHIRE

By
MARGARET GELLING

PART I
COUNTY, DISTRICT, ROAD, DYKE AND RIVER-NAMES
THE HUNDREDS OF RIPPLESMERE, BRAY, BEYNHURST,
COOKHAM, CHARLTON, WARGRAVE, SONNING,
READING, THEALE, FAIRCROSS

CAMBRIDGE
AT THE UNIVERSITY PRESS
1973

Published by the Syndics of the Cambridge University Press
Bentley House, 200 Euston Road, London NW1 2DB
American Branch: 32 East 57th Street, New York, N.Y.10022

Library of Congress Catalogue Card Number: 72–75303

ISBN: 0 521 08575 6

Printed in Great Britain
at the University Printing House, Cambridge
(Brooke Crutchley, University Printer)

CONTENTS

PREFACE

THE preparation of this place-name survey has been protracted. It was started in 1950, when I was working in Cambridge as Research Assistant to the English Place-Name Society. The Society had a small nucleus of material for Berkshire, mostly put together by Lady Stenton in the course of making her much more substantial collection for Oxfordshire. It was felt to be desirable that after completing the Society's survey of Oxfordshire I should expand this small nucleus, with a view to producing the survey of Berkshire. The work of collection proceeded quickly, especially after the English Place-Name Society moved to University College, London, in 1951. During the two years in which I worked at the new headquarters I was able to spend a great deal of time at the Public Record Office and the British Museum, and to extract most of the necessary material from the main unpublished sources. My work in Reading Public Library and the Berkshire County Record Office was done at about this time.

After leaving the Society's employment and moving to Birmingham, I was able to concentrate on the working up of some of the material into a Ph.D. thesis, which was accepted by the University of London in 1957. After this, work on Berkshire occupied less of my time, mainly because it was apparent that many other volumes were to be published before this survey was required for inclusion in the English Place-Name Society's series. In 1967, when Professor Cameron became Hon. Director of the Survey, Berkshire was immediately assigned a firm place in the series, and it appeared worth while to make it once more my main academic occupation. This means that there has been a gap of about fifteen years between the assembling of the material and the final period of interpretation and presentation. I hope that this has not been entirely detrimental, and that the experience gained by working on other toponymical projects during those fifteen years has resulted in a more mature interpretation. An uneasy feeling remains that some things which might have been apparent while the process of collecting the material was fresh in my mind have been lost, and that my editing of my own material after a prolonged gap has the same sort of dangers as the editing of material collected by a stranger. As regards unpublished material, the abbreviations for sources, with their implied statements about what is not in print and what is uncatalogued, should be interpreted as reflecting the state of affairs in 1953.

This gap in the preparation of the survey also causes difficulties when I try to recall the names of people who have helped. Some obligations may well have been forgotten. Lady Stenton has already been mentioned as having assembled an important nucleus of material. This included a number of spellings recorded in the handwriting of Sir Frank Stenton, some from sources which do not relate primarily to Berkshire, and which would certainly have been missed if he had not recorded them. Also, Sir Frank's interest in and encouragement of the project must be recalled with deep gratitude. Professor Dorothy Whitelock (who is entirely responsible for my involvement in place-name studies) has shown a sympathetic and much-appreciated interest in the work. The late Professor Hugh Smith supervised and examined my thesis on *The Place-Names of West Berkshire*. I have not had a great deal of contact with residents in the county, but I had a long and particularly fruitful correspondence with the late Mrs G. M. Lambrick, who generously made available to me her unrivalled knowledge of the Hundred of Hormer. Mrs Shelagh Bond has more recently made important additions to the sections of the book dealing with Windsor and Clewer. Professor B. Dickins and Professor K. Jackson have read the proofs and made valuable suggestions.

One of the great advances of recent years in the work of the English Place-Name Society has been the meticulous editing to which the volumes are now subjected by Professor Kenneth Cameron. The privilege of being included in his team, and in particular his work on the typescript of the Berkshire volumes, are greatly appreciated. He is responsible also for persuading the Society's Hon. Vice-Presidents in Scandinavia, Professor Matthias Löfvenberg and Dr Olof von Feilitzen, to study the typescript and write detailed comments on names which were not adequately treated. To be able to draw on their expertise is again a great privilege.

Finally, I am much indebted to my husband for providing the conditions in which this work can be carried on, and for his advice on all matters requiring archaeological expertise or agricultural common sense; and it is doubtful whether my work would have been possible without access to the Library of Birmingham University, for which I am most grateful to the Librarian, Dr K. W. Humphreys.

MARGARET GELLING

August 1972
Birmingham

ABBREVIATIONS AND BIBLIOGRAPHY

ABBREVIATIONS printed in roman type refer to printed sources and those in italic to manuscript sources.

a.	*ante.*
Abbr	*Placitorum Abbreviatio* (RC), 1811.
Abingdon	*Chronicon Monasterii de Abingdon*, ed. J. S. Stevenson (RS), 2 vols., 1858.
AC	*Ancient Charters*, ed. J. H. Round (PRS 10), 1888.
acc.	accusative.
AD	*Catalogue of Ancient Deeds* (PRO), in progress.
AddCh	Additional charters in the BM.
adj.	adjective.
AE	Ancient Extents (PRO).
al.	*alias.*
All Souls	C. T. Martin, *Catalogue of the Archives in the muniment rooms of All Souls College*, 1887.
AN	Anglo-Norman.
Anderson	O. S. Anderson, *The English Hundred-Names, The South-Western Counties*, Lund 1939.
AnnMon	*Annales Monastici*, ed. H. R. Luard (RS), 5 vols., 1864–9.
AOMB	Augmentation Office Miscellaneous Books (PRO).
ArchJ	*The Berks, Bucks and Oxon Archaeological Journal* and *The Berkshire Archaeological Journal.*
ASC	*The Anglo-Saxon Chronicle*, ed. B. Thorpe (RS) 1861; *Two of the Saxon Chronicles Parallel*, ed. C. Plummer, 1892–9.
ASCharters	*Anglo-Saxon Charters*, ed. A. J. Robertson, 1939.
Ashmole	Elias Ashmole, *The Antiquities of Berkshire*, 3 vols. 1719.
Ass	Assize Rolls (PRO).
Asser	Asser's *Life of King Alfred*, ed. W. H. Stevenson, 1904, New Impression 1959.
ASWills	*Anglo-Saxon Wills*, ed. D. Whitelock, 1930.
ASWrits	*Anglo-Saxon Writs*, ed. F. E. Harmer, 1952.
AugOff	Augmentation Office Documents (PRO).
Ave.	Avenue.
Baker	Agnes C. Baker, *Historic Streets of Abingdon*, 1957.
Banco	*Index of Placita de Banco*, 1327–8 (PRO Lists and Indexes 32), 1909.
Barrington	Terrier of Lord Barrington's Lands, 1771.
Battle	*Custumals of Battle Abbey in the Reigns of Edward I and Edward II*, ed. S. R. Scargill-Bird (Camden Soc.), 1887.
BC	*The Boarstall Cartulary*, ed. H. E. Salter (OxHistSoc 88), 1930.

BCS	*Cartularium Saxonicum*, ed. W. de G. Birch, 3 vols., 1885–93.
Bd	Bedfordshire.
BdHu	*The Place-Names of Bedfordshire and Huntingdonshire* (EPNS 3), 1926.
Berks	Berkshire.
Bk	Buckinghamshire.
	The Place-Names of Buckinghamshire (EPNS 2), 1925.
Black Prince	*The Register of Edward the Black Prince* (PRO), 1930–3.
BM	British Museum.
BM	*Index to the Charters and Rolls in the Department of Manuscripts, British Museum*, ed. H. J. Ellis and F. B. Bickley, 2 vols., 1900–12.
BMFacs	*Facsimiles of Royal and other Charters in the British Museum*, 1903.
Bodl	Documents in the Bodleian Library, Oxford.
Bract	*Henricus de Bracton, Note Book*, ed. F. W. Maitland, 1887.
Brocas	Montagu Burrows, *The Family of Brocas of Beaurepaire and Roche Court*, 1886.
BT	*An Anglo-Saxon Dictionary* (based on the collections of J. Bosworth), edited and enlarged by T. N. Toller, 1898.
BTSuppl	*Supplement* to BT, by T. N. Toller, 1921.
Bucklebury	A. L. Humphreys, *Bucklebury*, 1932.
c.	*circa*.
C	Cambridgeshire.
	The Place-Names of Cambridgeshire and the Isle of Ely (EPNS 19), 1943.
Camden	W. Camden, *Britannia*, 1600 and later editions.
CartAntiq	*The Cartae Antiquae Rolls 1–10*, ed. L. Landon (PRS NS 17), 1939; *The Cartae Antiquae Rolls 11–20*, ed. J. Conway Davies (PRS NS 33), 1960.
cent.	century.
CH	Christ's Hospital Abingdon, Calendar of Documents 1165–1898, four volumes in RecOff.
Ch	*Calendar of Charter Rolls* (PRO), 6 vols., 1903–27.
Ch	Cheshire.
	The Place-Names of Cheshire (EPNS 44–7), 1970–2.
ChanProc	*Calendar of Proceedings in Chancery in the reign of Queen Elizabeth* (RC), 1827–32.
Chatsworth	Abingdon Abbey Cartulary in the Chatsworth Collection. (Forms from the late Mrs Lambrick.)
ChCh	*Cartulary of the Mediaeval Archives of Christ Church*, ed. N. Denholm-Young, 1931.
Chertsey	*Chertsey Cartularies* (SrRecSoc), 1915, 1928, 1932, 1958, 1963.
ChR	*Rotuli Chartarum*, ed. T. D. Hardy (RC), 1837.
Cl	*Calendar of Close Rolls* (PRO), in progress.
ClaudiusBvi, ClaudiusCix	The two versions of the Abingdon Chronicle in BM. These are printed in Abingdon, but some forms have been taken from the MSS.

ClR	*Rotuli Litterarum Clausarum*, ed. T. D. Hardy (RC), 1833–44.
Co	Cornwall.
Coin	Spelling taken from the legend of a coin.
CornAcc	*Ministers' accounts of the Earldom of Cornwall 1296–7*, ed. L. M. Midgley (Camden Soc.), 2 vols., 1942–5.
CourtR	Court Rolls in RecOff (Coleshill, Coxwell), PRO (Wootton, Bray), Bodleian Library (Cumnor).
Crawford	O. G. S. Crawford, *Archaeology in the Field*, 1953.
Ct	Court.
Cu	Cumberland.
	The Place-Names of Cumberland (EPNS 20–2), 1950–2.
Cur	*Curia Regis Rolls* (PRO), in progress.
	Curia Regis Roll for 1198, in PRS NS 31.
D	Devon.
	The Place-Names of Devon (EPNS 8, 9), 1931–2.
Darby	Stephen Darby, *Place and Field Names, Cookham Parish, Berks*, 1899 (for private circulation).
dat.	dative.
Db	Derbyshire.
	The Place-Names of Derbyshire (EPNS 27–9), 1959.
DB	Domesday Book.
Delisle	*Recueil des Actes de Henri II*, ed. L. Delisle and E. Berger, Paris 1916.
Dep	Depositions (PRO).
DEPN	E. Ekwall, *The Concise Oxford Dictionary of English Place-Names*, 4th ed., 1960.
dial.	dialect(al).
DInc	*The Domesday of Inclosures 1517–18*, ed. I. S. Leadam (RHistS), 1897.
DL	Records of the Duchy of Lancaster (PRO).
Do	Dorset.
Du	County Durham.
Dugdale	W. Dugdale, *Monasticon Anglicanum*, 6 vols. in 8, 1817–30.
e.	early.
E.	east.
ECR	Eton College Records. Forms for names in Clewer, Windsor, Stratfield Mortimer, Winkfield, Bray, Maidenhead and Cookham have been taken from typed calendars compiled by Mr H. N. Blakiston, of which a set is deposited in PRO.
ed.	edition; edited by.
Ed I, Ed 2 etc.	Regnal date, t. Edward I, t. Edward II etc.
EDD	J. Wright, *The English Dialect Dictionary*, 6 vols., 1898–1905.
Eden	Wm. Eden, *Map of Windsor Park and part of the Forest*, 1800.
EETS	Publications of the Early English Text Society.
EgCh	Egerton Charters in BM.
EHD	*Select English Historical Documents of the Ninth and Tenth Centuries*, ed. F. E. Harmer, 1914.

Ekwall Street-Names   E. Ekwall, *Street-Names of the City of London*, 1954.
el.   place-name element.
Elements   A. H. Smith, *English Place-Name Elements* (EPNS 35, 36), 1956.
Eliz.   Regnal date, t. Elizabeth I.
EnclA   Unprinted Enclosure Awards, chiefly in the County Record Office.
EPNS   English Place-Name Society publications.
Ess   Essex.
                      The Place-Names of Essex (EPNS 12), 1935.
et freq.   *et frequenter*; and frequently (thereafter).
et seq   *et sequenter*; and subsequently.
Eynsh   *The Eynsham Cartulary*, ed. H. E. Salter (OxHistSoc 49, 51), 1907–8.
f., ff.   folio(s).
FA   *Feudal Aids* (PRO), 6 vols., 1899–1920.
Faringdon   P. J. Goodrich, *Great Faringdon Past and Present*, 1928.
Fd   Field.
Fees   *The Book of Fees* (PRO), 3 vols., 1920–31.
Feilitzen   O. von Feilitzen, *The Pre-Conquest Personal Names of Domesday Book*, Uppsala 1937.
fem.   feminine.
FF   Unpublished Feet of Fines (PRO).
FF   *Feet of Fines 1196–7* (PRS 20), 1896; *The Feet of Fines for Oxfordshire, 1195–1291*, ed. H. E. Salter (OxRecSoc 12), 1930.
Finchampstead   W. Lyon, *Chronicles of Finchampstead*, 1895.
Fine   *Calendar of Fine Rolls* (PRO), in progress.
FineR   *Excerpta e Rotulis Finium*, ed. C. Roberts, 2 vols., 1835–6.
Fm   Farm.
f.n., f.ns.   field-name(s).
ForProc   Forest Proceedings (PRO).
Forsberg   R. Forsberg, *A Contribution to a Dictionary of Old English Place-Names*, Uppsala 1950.
France   *Calendar of Documents preserved in France* (PRO), 1800.
Frid   *The Cartulary of the Monastery of St Frideswide at Oxford*, ed. S. R. Wigram (OxHistSoc 28, 31), 1895–6.
FW   Florence of Worcester; *Florentii Wigorniensis monachi Chronicon ex Chronicis*, ed. B. Thorpe, 2 vols., 1848–9.
G   German.
Gaimar   *Gaimar, Lestorie des Engles*, ed. T. D. Hardy and C. T. Martin (RS), 2 vols., 1888–9.
gen.   genitive.
Gerv   *The Historical Works of Gervase of Canterbury*, ed. W. Stubbs (RS), 2 vols., 1879–80.
Gilbert Crispin   J. Armitage Robinson, *Gilbert Crispin, Abbot of Westminster*, 1911.
Gl   Gloucestershire.

	The Place-Names of Gloucestershire (EPNS 38–41), 1964–5.
GlastonCh	*The Great Chartulary of Glastonbury*, ed. Dom A. Watkin (SomRecSoc 59, 64), 1947, 1950.
GlastonFeod	*A Feodary of Glastonbury Abbey*, ed. F. W. Weaver (SomRecSoc 26), 1910.
GlastonInq	*Liber Henrici de Soliaco Abbatis de Glaston*, ed. J. E. Jackson, 1882.
GlastonRent	*Rentalia et Custumaria Michaelis de Ambresbury 1235–1252 et Rogeri de Ford 1252–1261 Abbatum Monasterii Beatae Mariae Glastonicae* (SomRecSoc 5), 1891.
Godstow	*The English Register of Godstow Nunnery*, ed. A. Clark (EETS, OS 129, 130), 1905.
Gor	*The Goring Charters*, ed. T. R. Gambier-Parry (OxRecSoc 13, 14), 1931–2.
GR	O.S. National Grid Reference.
Gray	H. L. Gray, *English Field-Systems*, 1915.
Grinsell	L. V. Grinsell, *White Horse Hill and the surrounding Country*, 1939.
Ha	Hampshire. Mr J. E. B. Gover has permitted the consultation of his unpublished typescript on the place-names of Hampshire.
HaRecSoc	Hampshire Record Society Publications.
HarlCh	Harleian Charters in the BM.
He	Herefordshire.
Hearne	*A Letter containing an account of some Antiquities between Windsor and Oxford*, T. Hearne, printed in Vol. v of Hearne's edition of Leland's *Itinerary*, 2nd ed. 1744.
HistAb	F. M. Stenton, *The Early History of The Abbey of Abingdon*, 1913.
HMC	(Report of) The Historical MSS Commission.
HMC Var Coll	*Historical MSS Commission, Report on MSS in Various Collections.*
Ho	House.
Holthausen	F. Holthausen, *Altenglisches Etymologisches Wörterbuch*, Heidelberg 1934.
Holtzmann	W. Holtzmann, *Papsturkunden in England*, 2 vols., Berlin 1931, 1935–6.
Hrt	Hertfordshire. *The Place-Names of Hertfordshire* (EPNS 15), 1938.
Hu	Huntingdonshire.
Hungerford	Walter Money, *An Historical Sketch of the Town of Hungerford*, 1894.
Hunter Fines	*Fines sive Pedes Finium*, ed. J. Hunter, 1835.
Hurley	F. T. Wethered, *St Mary's, Hurley, in the Middle Ages*, 1898.
Hy 1, Hy 2 etc.	Regnal date, t. Henry I, t. Henry II etc.
HydeR	*Liber Vitae, Register and Martyrology of New Minster and Hyde Abbey*, ed. W. de Gray Birch (HaRecSoc), 1892.
ib, *ib*	*ibidem.*

InqMisc *Calendar of Inquisitions Miscellaneous* (PRO), in progress.

Introd Introduction to *The Place-Names of Berkshire*, to appear in Part 3.

Ipm *Calendar of Inquisitiones post mortem* (PRO), in progress.

IPN *Introduction to the Survey of English Place-Names* (EPNS I), 1924.

Jackson K. Jackson, *Language and History in Early Britain*, 1953.

Jas 1, Jas 2 etc. Regnal date, t. James I, t. James II etc.

John of Worc *The Chronicle of John of Worcester 1118–1140*, ed. J. R. H. Weaver (Anecdota Oxoniensia), 1908.

Journal EPNS Journal, in progress.

K Kent.

KCD *Codex Diplomaticus Aevi Saxonici*, ed. J. M. Kemble, 6 vols., 1839–48.

Kelly *Kelly's Directory of Berkshire & Oxon*, 1911.

KPN J. K. Wallenberg, *Kentish Place-Names*, Uppsala 1931.

l. late.

L Lincolnshire.

La Lancashire.

Lei Leicestershire.

Leland *The Itinerary of John Leland*, ed. L. Toulmin Smith, 5 vols., 1907–10.

LHRS The Records of the Berkshire Branch of the Local History Recording Scheme, in the Central Library, Reading, and the BM.

Liebermann *Die Gesetze der Angelsachsen*, ed. F. Liebermann, 3 vols., Halle 1903–16.

LN *Liber niger Scaccarii*, ed. T. Hearne, 1728.

Lo Lodge.

Loder *Robert Loder's Farm Accounts, 1610–20*, ed. G. E. Fussell (Camden Soc.), 1936.

Löfvenberg M. T. Löfvenberg, *Studies on Middle English Local Surnames*, Lund 1942.

LRMB Land Revenue Miscellaneous Books (PRO).

Lyell The Lyell Cartulary, an Abingdon Cartulary in the Bodleian Library (forms supplied by the late Mrs G. M. Lambrick).

Lysons D. and S. Lysons, *Magna Britannia*, 1816.

m. mid.

Madox *Formulare Anglicanum*, ed. T. Madox, 1702.

Maitland F. W. Maitland, *Select Pleas in Manorial Courts* (Selden Soc. 2), 1889.

Margary I. D. Margary, *Roman Roads in Britain*, Vol. 1, 1955.

masc. masculine.

Mdw Meadow.

ME Middle English.

MemR *The Memoranda Roll of the King's Remembrancer for 1230–31* (PRS NS 11), 1933; *The Memoranda Roll*

	for the Michaelmas Term of the First Year of the reign of King John (PRS NS 21), 1943.
MinAcc	Ministers' Accounts (PRO).
ModE	Modern English.
Mon	Monmouthshire.
Moulton	H. R. Moulton, *Palaeography, genealogy and topography 1930 catalogue*, 1937.
MS, MSS	Manuscript(s).
Mx	Middlesex.
	The Place-Names of Middlesex (EPNS 18), 1942.
Myres	Documents relating to Kennington, Sunningwell, Radley and Abingdon in the possession of Dr J. N. L. Myres, The Manor House, Kennington.
N.	north.
Nb	Northumberland.
NCy	North Country.
NCPNW	B. G. Charles, *Non-Celtic Place-Names in Wales*, 1938.
n.d.	undated.
NED	*A New English Dictionary*, ed. J. A. H. Murray and others, 1888–1933.
Newbury	Walter Money, *A Popular History of Newbury*, 1905.
Nf	Norfolk.
NLC	*Newington Longueville Charters*, ed. H. E. Salter (OxRecSoc 3), 1921.
NoB	*Namn och Bygd*, in progress.
nom.	nominative.
NonInq	*Nonarum inquisitiones* (RC), 1807.
Norden	Norden's Survey of Windsor Castle and Forest, 1607 (BM Harl. MS 3749).
NS	New Series in a run of periodicals or publications.
Nt	Nottinghamshire.
	The Place-Names of Nottinghamshire (EPNS 17), 1940.
Nth	Northamptonshire.
	The Place-Names of Northamptonshire (EPNS 10), 1933.
O	Oxfordshire.
	The Place-Names of Oxfordshire (EPNS 23, 24), 1953–4.
ObAcc	*Accounts of the Obedientiars of Abingdon Abbey*, ed. R. E. G. Kirk (Camden Soc.), 1892.
OblR	*Rotuli de Oblatis et Finibus*, ed. T. D. Hardy (RC) 1835.
OE	Old English.
Ogilby	John Ogilby, *Itinerarium Angliae*, 1675.
OHG	Old High German.
Os	*Cartulary of Oseney Abbey*, ed. H. E. Salter (OxHist Soc 89, 90, 91, 97, 98, 101), 1929–36.
O.S.	Ordnance Survey.
OS	First Edition Ordnance Survey 1″ maps.
OS	Original Series in a run of periodicals or publications.
OSaxon	Old Saxon.

OxHistSoc	Oxford Historical Society publications.
OxonCh	*Facsimiles of early charters in Oxford muniment rooms*, ed. H. E. Salter, 1929.
OxRecSoc	Oxfordshire Record Society publications.
p.	page.
p.	*post.*
(p)	place-name used as a personal name or surname.
P	*Pipe Rolls* (PRS), in progress.
Padworth	*A Record of the Parish of Padworth*, ed. W. O. Clinton, 1911.
ParColl	Anthony à Wood and Richard Rawlinson, *Parochial Collections*, ed. F. N. Davis (OxRecSoc 2, 4, 11), 1920–9.
ParlSurv	Parliamentary Surveys (PRO).
Pat	*Calendar of Patent Rolls* (PRO), in progress.
PCC	*Wills proved in the Prerogative Court of Canterbury* (British Record Society), in progress.
Pemb	Pembrokeshire.
pers.n.	personal name.
P.H.	Public House.
Pk	Park.
pl	plural.
p.n., p.ns.	place-name(s).
PN Do	A. Fägersten, *The Place-Names of Dorset*, Uppsala 1933.
PN -ing	E. Ekwall, *English Place-Names in -ing*, 2nd ed., 1962.
PN He	A. T. Bannister, *The Place-Names of Herefordshire*, 1916.
PN K	*The Place-Names of Kent*, J. K. Wallenberg, Uppsala 1934.
PN La	E. Ekwall, *The Place-Names of Lancashire*, 1924.
PN NbDu	A. Mawer, *The Place-Names of Northumberland and Durham*, 1920.
PN St	*Notes on Staffordshire Place Names*, W. H. Duignan, 1902.
PN Wt	Helge Kökeritz, *The Place-Names of the Isle of Wight*, Uppsala 1940.
Pride	Thomas Pride, *A Topographical-Map of the Town of Reading and the Country adjacent to an Extent of Ten Miles*, 1790.
PRO	Public Record Office.
PRS	Pipe Roll Society publications.
PrWelsh	Primitive Welsh.
PubLib	Catalogue of Berkshire Deeds in the Central Public Library, Reading.
PubLib(Bray)	Documents relating to Archbishop Laud's property in Bray, in the Public Library, Reading.
PubLibDoc	Documents in the Central Public Library, Reading, which are not catalogued.
PubLib(Clayton)	Clayton MSS in the Central Library, Reading (uncatalogued).
Queen	*The Archives of The Queen's College, Oxford* (typescript in Bodleian Library).

QW	*Placita de Quo Warranto* (RC), 1818.
R.	River.
R1, R2, etc.	Regnal date, t. Richard I, t. Richard II etc.
RBE	*Red Book of the Exchequer*, ed. H. Hall (RS), 3 vols., 1896.
RC	Record Commission publications.
Rd	Road
ReadingA	Jamieson B. Hurry, *Reading Abbey*, 1901.
ReadingAlm	BM MS Cotton Vespasian E.v (*Cartularium Elemosinariae Abbatiae de Radingia* on spine).
ReadingC	Cartulary of Reading Abbey in the BM (Egerton MS 3031).
ReadingC(2)	Cartulary of Reading Abbey in the BM (Harley MS 1708).
ReadingC(3)	Cartulary of Reading Abbey in the BM (Cott. Vespasian E.xxv).
Reaney	P. H. Reaney, *A Dictionary of British Surnames*, 1958.
RecOff	Berks County Record Office.
RecOff	documents in RecOff.
RecOff Cat	Catalogues of documents in RecOff.
RecOff Map	Maps in RecOff.
Redin	M. Redin, *Studies on Uncompounded Personal Names in Old English*, 1919.
ref., refs.	reference(s).
RentSur	Rentals and Surveys (PRO).
RG	*The Metrical Chronicle of Robert of Gloucester*, ed. W. A. Wright (RS), 2 vols., 1887.
RH	*Rotuli Hundredorum* (RC), 2 vols., 1812–18.
RHistS	The Royal Historical Society.
Rix	Mary Bright Rix, *Boars Hill Oxford*, 1944 (with map of Wootton and Boars Hill dated 1796).
r.n.	river-name.
RN	E. Ekwall, *English River-Names*, 1928.
Rocque	J. Rocque, *A Topographical Survey of the County of Berks*, 1761.
RotLib	*Rotuli de Liberate ac de Misis et Praestitis regnante Johanne*, ed. T. D. Hardy, 1844.
RotNorm	*Rotuli Normanniae*, ed. T. D. Hardy, 1835.
RR	*Receipt Roll of the Exchequer for Michaelmas Term 1185*, ed. H. Hall, 1899.
RS	Rolls Series.
RSO	*Registrum Sancti Osmundi*, ed. W. H. R. Jones (RS), 2 vols., 1883–4.
Rutland	HMC Rutland Report, Vol. iv, 1905.
S.	south.
S	*The Sandford Cartulary*, ed. A. M. Leys (OxRecSoc 19, 22), 1938–41.
Sa	Shropshire.
s.a.	*sub anno*.
SaltSocColl	*Collections for a History of Staffordshire*, The William Salt Archaeological Society.
Sandred	Karl Inge Sandred, *English Place-Names in -stead*, Uppsala 1963.

Sar	*Sarum Charters and Documents*, ed. W. R. Jones and W. D. Macray (RS), 1891.
Saxton	Saxton's Map of Berkshire, 1574.
sb.	substantive.
Sc	Scottish.
SCD	Sunningwell Charity Deeds. Forms supplied by the late Mrs Lambrick from calendar of deeds found among notes of late Rev. C. Overy. Whereabouts of originals not known.
Sf	Suffolk.
sing.	singular.
Skeat	W. W. Skeat, *The Place-Names of Berkshire*, 1911.
s.n.	sub nomine.
Snare	*Snare's Map of the Country Ten Miles round Reading.* 1846.
So	Somerset.
SomRecSoc	Somerset Record Society publications.
SP	State Papers Domestic (PRO), in progress.
SpecCom	Special Commissions (PRO).
SpecComMap	Maps with preceding.
Speed	John Speed, *The Theatre of the Empire of Great Britain*, 1610.
Sr	Surrey.
	The Place-Names of Surrey (EPNS 11), 1934.
SR	Lay Subsidy Rolls (PRO).
SrRecSoc	Surrey Record Society Publications.
St	Staffordshire.
StJohnMap	Maps in St John's College, Oxford.
StJohnSurvey	Survey of Fyfield in St John's College, Oxford.
Stenton	F. M. Stenton, *The Place-Names of Berkshire*, 1911.
Stonor	*The Stonor Letters and Papers*, ed. C. L. Kingsford (Camden Soc.), 1919; *Supplementary Stonor Letters and Papers* (Camden Soc.), 1924.
Survey	Surveys (PRO).
s.v.	sub voce.
Sx	Sussex.
	The Place-Names of Sussex (EPNS 6, 7), 1929–30.
t.	*tempore.*
TA	Unprinted Tithe Awards, chiefly in Ministry of Agriculture (Tithe Redemption Office, London).
Templars	*Records of the Templars in England in the Twelfth Century*, ed. B. A. Lees (Brit. Academy), 1935.
Thame	*The Thame Cartulary*, ed. H. E. Salter (OxRecSoc 25, 26), 1947–8.
ThamesDic	*Dickens's Dictionary of the Thames from Oxford to the Nore*, 1880.
Throckmorton	MSS at Coughton Court, Alcester, Warw.
TRE	*tempore Regis Edwardi*, the DB term for 'on the day that King Edward the Confessor was alive and dead'.
TRMB	Treasury of the Receipt Miscellaneous Books. (PRO).
Turner	*Select Pleas of the Forest*, ed. G. J. Turner (Selden Soc. 13), 1901.

VCH	*The Victoria History of the County of Berkshire*, 4 vols., 1906–24.
VE	*Valor Ecclesiasticus*, ed. J. Hunter (RC), 6 vols., 1810–34.
W	Wiltshire.
	The Place-Names of Wiltshire (EPNS 16), 1939.
W.	West.
Wa	Warwickshire.
	The Place-Names of Warwickshire (EPNS 13), 1936.
Wallingford	HMC Rep. vi, Appendix, 572 ff. (Records of the Corporation of Wallingford).
WAM	Westminster Abbey Muniments.
WBR	Windsor Borough Records (forms for Windsor street-names supplied by Mrs Shelagh Bond).
WCy	West Country.
Wd	Wood.
Wherwell	BM Egerton MS 2104 (Wherwell Cartulary).
Winchester	*Chartulary of Winchester Cathedral*, ed. A. W. Goodman, 1927.
WinchesterPR	*The Pipe Roll of the Bishopric of Winchester 1208–9*, ed. Hubert Hall, 1903.
Windsor	Catalogue of Muniments, St George's Chapel, Windsor (unpublished copy in County Record Office). Material from this was extracted in 1951. The catalogue was later published as *The Manuscripts of St George's Chapel, Windsor Castle*, ed. J. N. Dalton, 1957.
Wo	Worcestershire.
	The Place-Names of Worcestershire (EPNS 4), 1927.
Wood	*The Life and Times of Anthony Wood*, ed. A. Clark, Vol. 1 (OxRecSoc 19), 1891.
WSax	West Saxon.
Wt	Isle of Wight.
YE	East Riding of Yorkshire.
	The Place-Names of the East Riding of Yorkshire and York (EPNS 14), 1937.
YN	North Riding of Yorkshire.
	The Place-Names of the North Riding of Yorkshire (EPNS 5), 1928.
YW	The West Riding of Yorkshire.
	The Place-Names of the West Riding of Yorkshire (EPNS 30–7), 1961–2.
*	a postulated form.

NOTES

(1) The county-name, some other district-names, road-names, dyke-names, and river-names are discussed first. After these, the place-names are treated inside the divisions of the old Hundreds. The Hundreds are dealt with in order from south-east to south-west, and then from north-west to north-east. Within each Hundred the names are arranged in the civil parishes of the Ordnance Survey Combined Index map (showing civil parishes and the Ordnance Survey maps). These parishes are treated in alphabetical order within the Hundreds. Within the parish, the parish-name is followed by names of primary historical or linguistic interest, arranged in alphabetical order. At the end of these sections, all the remaining names on the 1911 6″ O.S. map are listed, in alphabetical order, with such early forms and etymological comment as can be provided. The final section in each parish lists field-names, divided into modern (i.e. p. 1800), and earlier. The a.1800 names are printed in italic.

Street-names are given in a section immediately following the interpretation of a town-name. The treatment of street-names varies from town to town. All names which appear on the 1911 6″ map are included, but in some towns (e.g. Reading) street-names likely to be of nineteenth- or twentieth-century origin are in small print, and are not individually indexed. Similarly, if a parish (e.g. Sunninghill) contains a number of large houses, individually named on the 6″ map but likely to be of comparatively modern origin, these are listed in small print and not indexed.

(2) Place-names believed to be no longer current are marked '(lost)'. Such names are printed in italic when referred to elsewhere in these volumes and in the index. Place-names marked '(not on map)' are believed to be current locally.

(3) In explaining place-names and field-names, reference is made, by printing the elements in bold type, to the two volumes of *English Place-Name Elements* (EPNS 25, 26). In the case of place-name elements specially characteristic of Berkshire but not discussed in those volumes, a page reference is given, and a discussion of the element will be found on that page.

(4) Unprinted sources of the early spellings of place-names are indicated by printing the abbreviation for the source in italic. The

abbreviation for a published source is printed in roman type. Where two dates are given for a source, e.g. 1256 (l. 13th), the first is the date at which the document purports to have been composed, and the second is the date of the copy which has come down to us.

(5) When a letter or letters in an early place-name spelling are enclosed in brackets, this means that spellings with and without the enclosed letter(s) occur.

(6) Cross-references to place-names in other parishes are given either by page number, or by the name of the parish. The references *supra* and *infra* with no page number indicate a place-name in the same parish as the one in question.

(7) Putative forms of personal names and place-name elements which will appear asterisked in the analyses in Pt 3 are not always asterisked in the text, but the discussion will usually make it clear which are on independent record and which are inferred.

(8) The texts of all known Anglo-Saxon charter boundaries relating to Berkshire will be printed in Pt 3 with notes on the place-names. Names from charter boundaries are only cited in Pts 1 and 2 when they are required as documentation for place-names recorded in later sources.

BERKSHIRE

Berrocscire, Bearrocscire 893 (11th) Asser, *Bearrucscire* c. 900 (s.a. 860) ASC A, c. 931 (c. 1200) BCS 687, c. 954 (c. 1400) EHD, m.11th (s.a. 1006) ASC C, c. 1100 (s.a. 1006, 1011) ASC F, *Bearrocscire* c. 1000 (s.a. 860) ASC B, m. 11th (s.a. 1009, 1011) ASC C, *Barrocscire* m. 11th (late 11th) ASWrits, *Bearrucscira* 1045–8 (c. 1200) ib, *Bearrucscyre* m. 11th (c. 1200) ib, *Berroches-(s)cire* 1086 DB, *Bearrocsira* 1089 Gilbert Crispin, *Barrucscire* c. 1150 (s.a. 860, 1006) ASC E, *Berrochscr'* 1161 P, *Berochescr'* 1169, 1172 ib, *Berochscr'* 1170 ib, *Berroch'scr'* 1176, 1190 ib, *Berrucsire* 1179–82 Os, *Beroc sir'* 1185 RR, *Berucsyre, Berucsyra* 12th or e. 13th AnnMon, *Barrocscir'* 1208 P, *Barrokshyre* c. 1210 (c. 1280) Os, *Berwykschire* c. 1433 AnnMon

Berchesire, Berchesira 1086 DB, *Berchescira* 1130 P *et freq* with variant spelling *Berchesir* to 1164 ib, *Berksira* 1156 (13th) RBE *et freq* with variant spellings *Bercs(c)yre, Berchscir', Berksyria, Berksire, Berkshyre, Berkscir'*; *Berkesira* 1160–1 (13th) RBE *et freq* with variant spellings *Berkesire, Berkesc(h)ira, Berkescir(e), Bercke scr', Berkesyre, Berkeschire*

Barcssire, Barkssire c. 1300 RG, *Barkshire* 1600 Camden

The statement of Asser 'Berrocscire: quae paga taliter vocatur a Berroc silva, ubi buxus abundantissime nascitur' is supported by a reference to a wood of this name in a charter of King John, dated 1199, confirming to the nuns of Fontévrault the possessions of the nunnery of Amesbury, which had been granted to them in 1179 by Henry II. The charter of King John mentions *nemus de Barroc*, along with other places in Berks and W. This charter is a repetition of Henry II's charter of 1179, which is recited in later Inspeximus charters of Edward II, Edward III and Henry III, the name of the wood appearing in these as *Berroch', Berrochia*. It is safe to assume that the wood-name was current at least until 1179. These medieval references are fully discussed by W. H. Stevenson, *Asser*, 155–7. Another possible reference, dated 1203, occurs in Cur II, 239, where Maria, daughter of Richard and Odo *de Berkewod'*, is mentioned in connection with seven and a half acres in *Berkewod'*. The case is assigned to Berkshire by the marginal note *Berk'*, but no indication is given of the exact location of the land.

The position of the wood cannot be determined with certainty. King John's charter mentions Challow, Fawley, South Fawley, Rockley (in Ogbourne W) and Letcombe, and then gives details of rents to be obtained from the wood of *Barroc*, and from Chute Forest in W. This context clearly suggests that *Barroc* was in the south-western part of the county. H. J. Peake, in *Transactions of Newbury and District Field Club*, VII, 177–80, argued plausibly that it was 'on the clay lands between and including Enborne and Hungerford'.

Barroc is a Celtic name, derived from *barrǭg*, 'hilly' (Jackson 228). Barrock Fell (Cu 201) has the same origin, and Professor Melville Richards points out that there is a township called Barrog in Denbighshire and a river called Barrog in Montgomeryshire. The lost *Cum Barruc* near Dorston He (H. P. R. Finberg, *The Early Charters of the West Midlands*, p. 137) is not relevant, as Professor Richards informs us that *Barruc* is there a pers.n. It is possible that *Barroc* was originally the name of the Berkshire Downs, supplanted by OE *Æscesdūn* (2–4). Asser's statement about box growing abundantly in *Berroc silva* is perhaps gratuitous; it may possibly allude to a popular etymology which connected *Berroc* with the word **box**.

See further Introd.

DISTRICT-NAMES

ÆBBANDUN (lost). There are some grounds for thinking that OE *Æbbandun*, the source of Abingdon (Pt 2), was originally applied to an upland area of some extent, comprising the high ground between Abingdon and North Hinksey. This use of dūn would resemble that found in *Ashdown infra*. For a detailed discussion of the whole problem *v.* M. Gelling, 'The Hill of Abingdon', *Oxoniensia* XXII (1957), 54–62.

ASHDOWN (lost)

> (*be*) *Æscesdune* c. 900 (s.a. 648) ASC A, (*on*) *Æscesdune* c. 900 (s.a. 871) ASC A, *Æscesdun* 893 (e. 11th) Asser, (*æt*) *Æscesdune* c. 946 (12th) EHD, (*andlang*) *Æscesdune* 11th (s.a. 1006) ASC C *Asshedon'* 1284 *Ass*

Asshesdune 1299 Imp, *Aschesdone* 13th *ReadingC*(2)
Ayshe Downe 1548 *LRMB*

This was the OE name for the Berkshire Downs, *v.* Introduction. The etymology suggested by Asser, 'Æscesdun, quod Latine "mons fraxini" interpretatur', was firmly rejected by W. H. Stevenson in his edition of Asser (1904), pp. 234 ff., on the grounds that *Æsc* must be a personal name because it occurs in the genitive. Professor Dorothy Whitelock, in the 1959 edition of Asser, pp. cxxxiv–cxxxv, cites this as one of the few points at which Stevenson's notes on place-names require emendation; and the work on genitival compositions in place-names, which has caused Stevenson's statement to appear too categorical, is summarised in EPN **1**, 158–9.

Genitival compositions do occur with tree-names, as in Alresford Ha, Elmsworth Wt, Maplescombe K, but in none of these instances does the resulting name refer to a natural feature extending for over 10 miles. There is a close connection between *Æscesdun* and *Æscesburh*, the OE name for Uffington Castle, the most impressive of the Iron Age hill-forts on the Downs. If the hill-fort and the whole line of the Downs are both named from a single ash-tree, it must have been a very impressive one. Possibly æsc is here used in the same way as fearn in Farnsfield Nt 163, with a collective sense. In the last resort, however, it is impossible to say whether Ashdown and *Æscesburh* derive from the word æsc or from a formally identical pers.n. As a pers.n., *Æsc* is only on independent record as a variant of *Oisc*, the name of the son of Hengest, the conqueror of Kent.

Mention should be made of Ashdown Forest Sx 2, though the forms for that name are not early enough or consistent enough to provide a safe parallel, and of Ashey Wt 25 (*æsces hege* 982), for which Professor Kökeritz was unable to decide between the tree and a pers.n.

Stevenson was perhaps too positive in accepting Ashdown Park (Pt **2**) as a survival of the name *Æscesdūn*. Such early forms as have been found for that name do not support this theory. As to the exact location of *Æscesdūn*, it is generally agreed that the name was applied to the whole line of the Berkshire Downs. Stevenson quotes Francis Wise, writing in 1738, to the effect that in his day the shepherds still called the Downs *Ashdown*. References which give some help with the location are that in BCS 908 (955, in a MS of c. 1240) to land *æt*

Cumtune (i.e. Compton Beauchamp) *juxta montem qui vocatur Æsces Dune*, that in ASC C and D s.a. 1006, which records that the Danes went from Cholsey *andlang Æscesdune* to Scutchamer Knob in East Hendred (Pt 2), that in 1284 *Ass* 46m7 to an event which occurred *super Asshedon' in villa de Sperholt* (i.e. Sparsholt), and that in 1299 Ipm to pasture in Ginge upon *Asshesdune*.

BRUNINGMERE (lost), *Brunyggemere* ?1221–34 (m. 14th) *Lyell, (foresta de) Brunningemor, Bruningemer* (bis), *Bruningemer* 1222 Pat, *(foresta de) Bruningemer'* 1223, 4 ClR, *(pasturam de) Bruningemere* 13th *ReadingC(2)*. Apparently a lost -inga- name, probably meaning 'pool of Brūn's people', *v.* mere. The reference in ClR (1, 530) concerns Buckhold in Bradfield, and that in *Lyell* concerns land in Oare, so the forest extended at least six miles from east to west. The pasture mentioned in *ReadingC(2)* was in Frilsham. This is hilly country, and an alternative etymology could be obtained by regarding the first element as a hill-name, 'the brown one', as in Brown So, hence 'the pool of the *Brūningas* (the people who lived near *Brown*)'.

VALE OF WHITE HORSE, the vale of *Whithors* 1368 Cl, *the fruteful vale of White-Horse, the vale of Whit-Horse* 1542 Leland, from the figure on White Horse Hill (Pt 2).

WINDSOR FOREST: early forms for this are *Foresta de Windesores* 1086 DB, *Foresta de Windlesores* 1087 Madox, *Foresta de Windleshora* 1109–20 (13th) RSO, *Foresta de Windresores* 1146 (copy) Sar, *Foresta de Windresoris* 1157 P, *Foresta de Windelshora* 1158 (13th) RSO. *v.* Windsor 26–7. The bounds of the forest in 1300, as defined in Cl p. 383, included all the county east of the River Loddon.

ROAD-NAMES

DEVIL'S HIGHWAY, *Devils Highway* 1761 Rocque, *Divels High Way* 1800 Eden. This is the Berks section of the Roman road from London (LONDINIVM) to Silchester Ha (CALLEVA ATREBATUM); *v.* Margary 76–81 for a description of its course. The part which crosses the parish of Easthampstead is referred to as *La Longestret* 1342 Gor, and there was a family in Finchampstead surnamed *de Stonistrete* 1220 Fees, *de Stonstred* 1275–6 RH, probably another ME name for the same road, *v.* lang, stānig, strǣt.

ICKNIELD WAY, (*on*) *Icenhilde weg* 903 (c. 1200) BCS 601, (*to*) *ikenilde streate*, (*of*) *ikenilde strete* c. 931 (c. 1200) BCS 687, (*æt*) *ichenilde wege* 944 (c. 1240) BCS 801, *Ykenildeweye* c. 1220–30 *Queen*, *Ikelington'*, *Ikelinge* 1241–2 FF, *Ikelinge* 1241 *Ass*, *Ickleton Way* 1778 *EnclA* (Uffington). *v.* BdHu 4. Icknield is a pre-English name, of unknown etymology, treated as an OE feminine in -*hild*. The element strǣt in the reference to the Way in the bounds of Uffington (BCS 687) perhaps indicates that it was Romanised in that portion.

OLD STREET is (*to*) *strǣte* 948 (c. 1240) BCS 866, *Old Streetway* 1761 Rocque. This road, which is marked on the 1″ map from the east boundary of Farnborough parish to a point about 1½ miles east of Chieveley, is mentioned in Crawford (85). It is not clear in what sense the word strǣt was applied to it.

PORTWAY (the road from Rowstock in East Hendred to Wantage), *Portway(e)* 1607 *LRMB* (in East Hendred), *Ecleton or Port Way* 1761 Rocque. The road was probably so called because it led to the town of Wantage; *v.* port-weg. The road to Faringdon is similarly called *port wege* in the bounds of Longworth in BCS 1047. *Ecleton* in the reference from 1761 is probably due to confusion with *Icknield supra*. The Icknield Way runs parallel with this road about a mile to the south.

RIDGE WAY, (*on*) *hrycwæg* 856 (12th) BCS 491 (in Woolstone), (*on*) *hrucg weg*, (*of*) *hrucg wægæ* 944 (12th) BCS 796 (in Woolstone), (*oþ þone*) *hricg weg* 944 (c. 1240) BCS 801 (in Blewbury), *Ruggeweye* c. 1220–30 *Queen* (in Uffington), *The Ridge Way* 1761 Rocque, *v.* hrycg, weg. For a description of this famous prehistoric track *v.* Grinsell 27–8.

DYKE-NAMES

EAST DITCH (Lambourn). This earthwork is discussed in Crawford 112–13, where it is suggested that *Grynesdiche* c. e. 13th (c. 1425) Frid, a field-name in Bockhampton, refers to the ditch, and is an error for *Grymesdiche*, for which term *v. infra*.

GRIM'S BANK (Padworth), *Grimmer's Bank* 1840 Padworth; *v.* Grim's Ditch, *infra* 6.

GRIM'S DITCH. The course and nature of this long earthwork is discussed in Crawford, 114–17. Dr Crawford has traced it for 10 miles along the escarpment of the Downs, from Lattin Down 2½ miles S.E. of Wantage to a point N. of Streatley. It is a boundary ditch, not a defensive one. For part of its course, on Moulsford Downs, it is called Devil's Ditch. *Grīm* is a by-name for a supernatural power, probably Woden; *v.* DEPN 205 for other examples of ditches with this name. There are references to the earthwork in charter boundaries. (*on*) *grim gelege* c. 895 (c. 1150) BCS 565 in the bounds of Cholsey is on the line of the ditch. The meaning of this term is considered doubtful by Forsberg (76–7). BTSuppl suggests a term **gelegu* 'a tract of land', on the basis of four names in charter bounds, of which this is one. Further west, the term (*andlang*) *drægeles bæces* 944 (c. 1240) BCS 801 in the bounds of Blewbury refers to the same earthwork, as does (*to*) *drægeles bæce* in BCS 565 in the bounds of Hagbourne (which include the parish of Upton). The second element of this name is OE *bæc* 'back', is used in p.ns. to mean 'ridge'. Here it refers to the bank of the earthwork, just as modern dialect *back* is used of a ridge of earth thrown up from a ditch (EDD *back* sb³). *drægeles* is obscure. Dr O. von Feilitzen suggests a pers.n. *Dregl*, recorded on a coin of Edmund, which he considers a native derivative of *dragan* 'to draw'. He compares ON *dregill* 'ribbon, band', found as a byname. Alternatively, if we could postulate an OE noun **dregel*, derived from *dragan* and meaning something like 'ribbon', this would be an excellent name for Grim's Ditch. It is an unimpressive work, unlike the more common type of linear earthwork which divides one major territory from another by a bold straight line. It runs more or less east and west near the crest of the Downs, but makes sudden right-angle bends which bear no relation to the terrain, as if it were a local boundary taking account of small units of land-ownership.

RIVER-NAMES

AMWELL (affluent of Thames, in Cholsey and Aston Tirrold, not named on map), (*æt*) *amman welle*, (*on*) *west wylle þen on oþre naman hæt æt amman wylle* 944 (c. 1240) BCS 801, (*on*) *west welle* c. 895 (12th) BCS 565, *Amwell Furlong* 1841 *TA* (Cholsey). The name seems to have survived as that of a spring. Grundy (ArchJ 27, p. 200) says that Amwell is still used for the spring 'which rises in great volume ¼ mile east of Lollingdon Fm in Cholsey parish'. In the charter bounds, however, it appears to be applied to the watercourse along the parish boundary between Cholsey and Aston Tirrold. Assuming the name belonged originally to the spring, the meaning is 'Amma's spring'. For the pers.n., v. Gl, 1, 48. The alternative name means 'west stream', possibly to distinguish it from the parallel watercourse about 400 yards to the east.

BAGMORE BROOK (branch of the Ock, in Balking), cf. (on) baccan mor 931 (c. 1200) BCS 684, in the bounds of Shellingford, and 955 (12th) BCS 902, in the bounds of East Woolstone. 'Bacca's marsh', v mōr. Bagmere Barn in Charney Bassett, about four miles away, is named from the same extensive tract of marshland. W. J. Arkell (Oxoniensia vii, 9) says that its bounds 'coincide with a broad tract of alluvium (now lush meadows) between and on either side of the branches of the meandering Ock between Balking and Charney'.

BATTLE BOURNE (affluent of Thames, in Old Windsor), Battles Bourn 1729 LHRS, cf. Batelrydyng ?Ed 4 RentSur, Batelsbayly 1554 LRMB, bayliwicke of Battaile 1601 Dep, Battle Walke als Battles Bailiwick' 1628 ForProc. A family named Bataille is mentioned 1302 Fine as holding a bailiwick of Windsor Forest.

BLACKMOOR STREAM (affluent of Englemere Pond, in Winkfield), cf. (on þone) blacan mor, (of þam) blacan moran 942 (c. 1200) BCS 778, Blackmoor Park 1719 Ashmole. 'Black marsh', v. blæc, mōr.

BLACKWATER (affluent of Loddon), la Blakewatere c. 1300 ArchJ 46. 'Black water', in distinction to the Ha Whitewater, with which it unites on the county boundary, some 1½ miles before reaching the Loddon. Cf. Sr 2, where a somewhat earlier form is cited for the Sr portion of the river. The stream formed by the union of Blackwater and Whitewater is called Swalewe 1272 RN (in Ha), 1300 Cl. For this Germanic r.n., which occurs also in K and YN, v. RN 383–5 and swalwe[2]. The meaning is something like 'rushing water'.

An alternative early name for the Blackwater above its junction with the Whitewater was (on) duddan broc 973–4 (12th) BCS 1307, Wodebrok (sic) 1270 Turner, Dodekrok (sic) 1300 Cl, Dudbroke 1533 Finchampstead. This name, which means 'Dudda's brook' survives in Deadbrook Fm in Aldershot Ha, for which additional references are *Dodebroke, Dedebrok* 1298 *For, Dudbrooke, Dedbroke* 1567 Crondal Records (HaRecSoc 3), (ex. inf. Mr J. E. B. Gover).

THE BOURN (affluent of Thames in Bray), *Bourne* c. 1340 *RentSur* (p), 1372 *PubLib*(*Bray*) (p), *v.* burna. *Holebourne* 1316 Fine probably refers to this stream, *v.* hol² 'running in a hollow'.

THE BOURNE (affluent of Pang, between Bradfield and Englefield), *La Burne* 1271 AD, *The Bourne* 1609 *LRMB*, 1648 *RecOffCat*.

BOURNE DITCH (affluent of Thames, in New Windsor), *La Bourne* 1311 *ECR, La Burne* 1326 Brocas, *The Bourne* 1607 *Norden, v.* burna.

BRADFORD'S BROOK (Wallingford), *v.* Pt 2.

BULL BROOK (in Warfield), *v.* 117.

CASTLEWELL (lost in Abingdon), (*pratum de*) *Carswell* 1275–6 RH, (*watercourse of*) *Carswelle* c. 1275–1325 ArchJ 45, (*gurgite*) *Cassewell'* Ed 4 *RentSur, the Carswell, the Caswell* 18th ArchJ 45, *Castlewell* 1941 ib. 'Cress-stream', *v.* cærse, wella, and cf. the same name 44. For an account of this stream, which at one time supplied water for the dwellers in Ock St, *v.* ArchJ 45 pp. 37 ff, where A. E. Preston says that watercress was plentifully grown in the stream within his recollection.

CHILDREY BROOK (affluent of Ock), (*andlang*) *cille riðe* 940 (c. 1200), (*andlang*) *cilla riþe* 940 (c. 1240) BCS 761, (*be tweox eoccene and*) *cilla riðæ* 944 (c. 1200) BCS 798 (*on*) *cilla riðe*, (*on*) *cillan riðe* 947 (c. 1200) BCS 833, (*on*) *cyllan rið* 956 (c. 1240) BCS 949, (*on*) *cilla riðe*, (*on*) *cillan riðe* 958 (c. 1200) BCS 1034, (*on*) *cille riðe* 968 (c. 1200) BCS 1224, (*andlang*) *cyllriðæ* 1032 (c. 1200) KCD 746. For forms referring to the village *v.* Pt 2. A ME reference to the stream occurs in the field-name *Chilretheforlong* 1317 AD in West Hanney. The second el. is rīð 'stream'. Stenton (39) and Ekwall (DEPN) suggest that the first el. is a pers.n. *Cilla*, perhaps a short form of masculine names in *Cēol-*, as the recorded *Cille* is a short form of the feminine name *Cēolswīð*. This may well be the case, though it could alternatively be the fem. *Cille* itself. A similar problem is presented by other names such as Chilham (K PN 372). *Cēolswīð* or *Cille* was the sister of Hean, Abbot of Abingdon in the e. 8th cent., *v.* Hist Ab 9–10.

COLE (affluent of Thames). The bounds of Watchfield in BCS 675 (dated 931) run *on lentan,* clearly with reference to the stretch of the Cole which forms the west boundary of the parish and of the county. For other references to this early name of the Cole, which is probably allied to Welsh *lliant* 'flood, stream', *v.* W 5–6, RN 249–50. The modern name Cole is probably a back-formation from Coleshill (Pt 2). Field-name evidence (*v.* Pt 2) indicates that the name *Lynte* was known in Coleshill in 1551. The earliest instance of Cole which has been noted is 1761 Rocque, where Cole Common is shown on the right bank of the river.

DUDBROOK (lost), *v.* Blackwater *supra* 7.

DUN (affluent of Kennet), *v.* Dunmill in Hungerford, Pt 2.

EMM BROOK (affluent of Loddon, between Hurst and Woodley), *Embrooke* 1572 SpecCom, c. 1631 ArchJ 36, *Em Broke* 1619 SpecCom, *Emme Brooke* 1641 SP, *Emme Brook* 1761 Rocque. The forms are too late for etymology, but perhaps cf. RN s.n. Emel.

ENBORNE (affluent of Kennet)

    alaburna, (*andlang*) *alaburnan* 944 (c. 1240) BCS 802
    Aleburn 1221 Pat, 1233 *Windsor, Aleburn'* 13th *ReadingC,* 1284
    Ass, Aleburne 1335 AD
    Auborn River 1761 Rocque
    Emborne or Amburn 1911 Kelly

There are earlier forms for this name in some Ha charters, for which *v.* RN 148. These include (*on*) *alorburnan* 909 (12th) BCS 624, *alerburnan* 931 (12th) BCS 674, 943 (12th) BCS 787. Mr J. E. B. Gover adds the forms *Aneburne* (*n* for *u*?) 1256 *Ass, Auborn river* 1695 Camden. The etymology is probably 'alder stream', *v.* alor, burna, as in Alderbourne (Bk 242), though the first -*r*- has been lost very early in the Berks name. Enborne, which evidently came into use in modern times, is a back-formation from the village of that name, Pt 2, doubtless due to the similarity of the two names. Enborne is some distance from the river, but there are places named Enborne Street and Enborne Row much closer. Kelly's Directory, as late as 1911, seems not to connect the river-name with that of the village of Enborne.

FOUDRY BROOK (affluent of Kennet, at Reading), (*on*) *fulan Riþe* c. 950 (c. 1240) BCS 888, (*inter*) *Fulritham* (*et . . .*) 13th *ReadingC*, *Fulldry Dyche*, *Fullriche Diche* Ed 6 *LRMB*, 'foul stream', *v.* fūl, rīð. Simon *Foulrith*, mentioned 1371 Pat in connection with property in Reading, probably derived his surname from this stream; cf. also Richard *de Folrithe*, mentioned 1283–4 Battle, in Brightwalton.

GINGE BROOK (affluent of Lockinge Brook), (*iuxta riuulum*) *Geenge* '726–37' (c. 1200) BCS 155, (*on*) *Gæing broc* 956 (c. 1200) BCS 981. For forms referring to the village *v.* Pt **2**. The original form appears to have been *Gæging*, and Ekwall, PN -ing 208, suggests that this stream-name is a singular name in -ing, the first element of which is connected with OE *gægan* 'to turn aside'. Ginge is a similar formation to Lockinge, *infra* 13, the brook with which it unites. For the palatalisation of -ing in both names *v.* Introd. The 6″ map also applies the name Ginge Brook to part of the united stream in Steventon, but this was certainly called *Lacing* in OE times, *v. infra* 13. ·

HAKKA'S BROOK (affluent of Mill Brook, in West and East Hagbourne and South Moreton). It is possible that the naming of this stream on the O.S. map is an antiquarian revival rather than a genuine survival. In BCS 565 the stream is described as (*of*) *haccebroce* and (*on*) *haccaburnan*; it is (*on*) *haccan broc*, (*andlang*) *haccan broces* 944 (c. 1240) BCS 801, (*of*) *hacce broce*, (*on*) *hæcce broc* 964 (c. 1240) BCS 1143. The bounds of BCS 1143 (which are those of Aston Upthorpe) run (*on*) *hæcceleas dic* immediately before reaching the brook. This is the stream from which East and West Hagbourne are named, *v.* Pt **2**. The second el. is brōc, alternating with burna, but the first offers some difficulty. If it were a significant word, then *hæcceleas dic* in BCS 1143 would denote a ditch which lacked the object that gave name to the brook. In BTSuppl *hæcceleas dic* is noted as a possible combination of *hæcce* 'hatch, floodgate', or *hæcce* 'fence of rails', with -*lēas* 'less'. The connection with Hagbourne, however, makes it very unlikely that the first el. originally had -*æ*- and the OE form appears to have been *hacca*. If it were not for the universal -*cc*- in the charter forms, it would be possible to suggest derivation from *haca* 'hook', which is found in stream-names, e.g. Hawkwell (Ess 186), Hagbourne (W 274). Apart from this linguistic difficulty, however, it is probably too fanciful to imagine a 'hooked' stream in association with a 'hookless' ditch along the straight boundary of Aston Upthorpe between Blewburton Camp and the stream. There seems no satisfactory alternative to the suggestion in DEPN that the first element of Hagbourne and of *haccan broc* is a pers.n. *Hacca*, and that *hæcceleas dic* is the 'ditch of Hacca's lē(a)h'. Evidence for the pers.n. is slight, but *v.* Feilitzen 281; there is a *Hac(c)a* in the Exon DB.

HOLY BROOK (northern branch of Kennet, in Burghfield and Reading), *the Halowid Brooke* 1542 Leland, *Le Granators Broke als le Hallowed Broke* 1552 *LRMB, the Hallowed Brooke* 1596 *SpecCom,* 1700 *PubLibDoc.* The brook was presumably given this name because it flowed past Reading Abbey; cf. Holy Water Lane 172. The alternative name, *Granator's Brook*, occurs somewhat earlier in the forms *le Garenters Broke* 15th *ReadingC(2), Graniteresbrok'* 1441 *ReadingAlm.* A granator is 'one who has charge of a granary or grange', and the name presumably refers to the use of this stream for driving several corn mills; *v.* E. W. Dormer, ArchJ 41, 73 ff.

HUMBER. There are two instances of this common river-name in Berks. One is mentioned in the bounds of Harwell in BCS 1183 and 1292 (dated c. 960 and 973), which run *on humbracumb* immediately before reaching the Icknield Way. This valley (*v.* cumb) is that of a small stream which flows west through East Hendred to the brook known in the 10th century as *Lacing* (*v. infra* 13). The East Hendred *TA* refers to the valley as *Humberdean.*

The other Berks *Humber* is a stream about 4 miles W. of *humbracumb,* which rises in Charlton and flows into Letcombe Brook. This is called Humber Ditch on the 6″ map, but no early forms have been found.

Ekwall (RN 201–5) considers the name British, but Jackson (510) expresses grave doubts about a Celtic origin for it.

KENNET (affluent of Thames)

(*inter Tamesen et*) *Cynetan* 893 (11th) Asser, (*on*) *Cynetan* 944 (c. 1240) BCS 802, 956 (c. 1200) BCS 942, 984 (c. 1240) KCD 1282, 1050 (c. 1240) KCD 792, *Cynete* 984 (c. 1240) KCD 1282, 1050 (c. 1240) KCD 792
Kenete 1180–1200 (c. 1200) Thame, 1220 Pat
Kanet 1259 Cl
Kinete 13th Gerv

These forms refer to the Berks section, *v.* W 8 for W forms. Kintbury (**Pt 2**) and Kentwood in Reading (176) are named from the river. The name is British *Cunẹ̄tịū* of doubtful meaning, occurring in a number of river-names; *v.* Jackson 302, 331, and RN 225–8.

KIBBLE DITCH (affluent of Mill Brook between North Moreton and Mackney). This stream is referred to in two Winchester charters. BCS 810 gives the bounds of Brightwell, Sotwell and Mackney as running *and lang gybhilde*, and refers to part of the estate as 'locis palustribus quæ rivulus que Gybhild agnominatus circumcingit et fecundat'. BCS 864 says of Mackney in Brightwell 'Ðis synt þa fif hida æt Maccanige. þe gibhild seo lacu. eallan butan bælið on ælce healfe'. Ekwall (RN 230–1) assumes that the stream is probably also referred to in BCS 565, which gives the bounds of Cholsey as running 'on tibbælde lace. ðonon on maccan eige.' Forsberg (16) also assumes that *tibbælde lace* must be connected with *gybhild*. It seems clear from the boundaries, however, that *tibbælde lace* is a different stream, not named on the O.S. maps, which forms the northern half of the west boundary of Cholsey and flows into Mill Brook from the south.

The forms for Kibble Ditch are *Gybhild* 945 (12th) BCS 810, *Gibhild* 948 (12th) BCS 864, *Gebyll Dyche* 1529 ArchJ 18, *Gibble Ditch* 1571, 1597, 1600 ib. The name may be pre-English, in which case it has, like Icknield (5), been interpreted as a feminine in *-hild*, or it may be a jocular OE name for the stream. In the latter case, Ekwall makes the ingenious suggestion that it consists of an unrecorded OE *gybb* 'refuse, mud', combined with the ending *-hild*, common in feminine names, to mean something like 'the slattern, the dirty female'.

LAMBOURN (affluent of Kennet), *Lamburnam* 943 (c. 1240) BCS 789, 956–9 (c. 1200) BCS 996, (*on*) *lámburnan* 949 (contemp.) BCS 877, (*ut on*) *lamburnan* 956 (c. 1200) BCS 963, (*on*) *lam burnan* 958 (c. 1200) BCS 1022, (*on*) *lamburnam* 968 (c. 1200) BCS 1227, *Lamborn'* 1376–7 *RentSur*, *Lamborne* 1388 Cl, *Lambourn* 1441 Pat. Probably 'lamb-stream', *v.* Pt 2. The form from BCS 877 is the main evidence in favour of an alternative etymology 'loam stream'.

LAND BROOK (affluent of Ock, between Charney Bassett and Lyford), (*on*) *landbroc* 947 (c. 1200) BCS 833, (*on*) *land broc* 958 (c. 1240) BCS 1034, (*innan*) *lanbroc*, (*andlang*) *landbroces* 959 (c. 1200), (*innan*) *landbroc*, (*andlang*) *landbroces* 959 (c. 1200) BCS 1047, *landbroce*, (*andlang*) *landbroces* n.d. (c. 1200) *ClaudiusCix*. Possibly identical with Lambrook So, which Ekwall (DEPN) considers to have **land** as first el., but which Forsberg (54) discusses under the elements **lām**, **lamb**. Forsberg does not include the name *landbrōc*, although it is well evidenced in Berks charters. The meaning is probably 'boundary brook', *v.* **land, brōc**. Land Brook forms the boundary between Denchworth and Goosey.

LETCOMBE BROOK, *v.* Wantage *infra* 17–18.

LOCKINGE BROOK (affluent of Thames), (*be norðan*) *Lackincg* 868 (c. 1200) BCS 523, (*on*) *lacing*, (*on*) *ealdan lacing* 956 (contemporary) BCS 935, (*on*) *lacing broc* '956' (c. 1200) BCS 981, (*on*) *lacing* 958 (c. 1240), 960 (c. 1200) BCS 1032, 1058, (*on*) *lacinge broc* 964 (c. 1200) BCS 1142. For forms which refer to the villages of East and West Lockinge, *v.* Pt **2**. Ekwall, PN -ing 208, suggests that this stream-name is a singular name in -ing derived from OE **lāc** 'play', **lācan** 'to play', and this is likely enough. *v.* also Forsberg 1 ff. For the palatalisation of the second syllable *v.* Introd.

The charter boundaries are consistent in their application of the name. BCS 981 gives the bounds of Ginge as running *on lacing broc. Andlang broces eft on Gæing broc. andlang broces on þa æwylma*. This shows that *lacing broc* refers to the stream at present called Lockinge Brook and (a little later in its course) West Hendred Brook, and *Gæing Broc* to that named Ginge Brook which forms the present boundary between Ardington and West Hendred. These two streams unite west of Hill Fm in West Hendred to form a stream, variously named on the O.S. maps in different parts of its course, which is referred to in BCS 1032 (in the bounds of Drayton) as *lacing*, at a point fairly near its junction with the Thames. O.S. marks this portion as Mill Brook. That which forms part of the boundary between Steventon and East Hendred is called (*on*) *lacinge broc* in BCS 1142. In the bounds of Milton in BCS 935 the phrase *on ealdan lacing* suggests that the stream has changed its course slightly, cf. *Wantage infra* 17.

LODDON (affluent of Thames), *Lodena* 1190 (copy) Sar, *Lodene* 1227 Ch, 1241 Ass, *Lodona* 1300 Cl, *Lodyn* 1364 Pat. Ekwall (RN 258) suggests a British **Lutnā* 'muddy river', but Professor Jackson points out that this is quite hypothetical. There are other probable examples of the r.n. in Nf and He.

LULLE BROOK (affluent of Thames, at Cookham), *Lullebroch* 1186 P (p) *et freq* with variant spellings *Lullebroc, -brok*; *Lollebroc* 1284 *Ass* (p), *Lillebrok'* 1291–2 *FF* (p), *Le brooke voc Lollebrooke* 1608 *LRMB*, 'Lulla's brook'.

MYDELING (lost, in Drayton). The bounds of Drayton in BCS 1032 run from Mere Dike (Pt **2**) to *mydeling*, then to the stream known as *waneting* or 'old' *waneting*, for which *v. infra* 17. The name occurs with the same spelling in BCS 1058, the dates of the two charters being 958 and 960. Grundy (ArchJ 29, p. 99) identifies *mydeling* with a stream more or less on the line of the Wilts and Berks canal, and has found that a field on the line of this stream, near the north boundary of the parish, is called *Middlings*. *Midlinge* occurs 1815 *EnclA*. The probability is that this is another stream name of the same type as Ginge (10), Lockinge (13) and Wantage (17), but the etymology must remain uncertain. The word *mud* is not recorded till the 13th cent., but is certainly Germanic and may go back to OE. A derivative of this with the diminutive suffix *-el* would be a possible source for a stream name. More spellings occur in Steventon f.ns., Pt **2**.

NOR BROOK (affluent of Ock, in East Hanney), (*pratum de*) *Northbrok'* 1252–5 *FF*, 'north brook'; it forms the N. boundary of the parish.

OCK (affluent of Thames)

   (*on*) *æoccænen* 856 (c. 1150) BCS 491, (*on*) *æoccæn* 944 (c. 1150) BCS 796

   (*on*) *eoccen* 931 (c. 1200), 955 (c. 1200), 965 (c. 1200), BCS 684, 906, 1169, (*and lang*) *eoccen*, (*ut on*) *eoccan* 940 (c. 1200) BCS 761, (*Be tweox*) *eoccene* 944 (c. 1200) BCS 798, (*andlang*) *eoccenes* 955 (c. 1200), 956 (c. 1200), BCS 906, 924, (*to*) *eoccen* 956 (c. 1200) BCS 924, (*on*) *eoccene* 956 (c. 1240), 958 (c. 1200), 960 (c. 1200) 968 (c. 1200), 970 (c. 1200) c. 977 (c. 1200), BCS 977, 1032, 1058, 1224, 1261, KCD 1277, (*on*) *Eoccenne* 956 (c. 1200) BCS 949, (*innan*) *eoccen* 959 (c. 1200) BCS 1047, (*of*) *eoccan* 965 (c. 1200), 968 (16th), 970 (c. 1200), c. 977 (c. 1200), BCS 1169, 1221, 1261, KCD 1276, (*of*) *eoccen*, (*on*) *eoccan* 1032 (c. 1200) KCD 746

   (*betweox*) *Eccene* 944 (c. 1240) BCS 798, (*on*) *eccen* 955 (c. 1240) BCS 906, (*on*) *eccene* 958 (c. 1240) BCS 1028, (*innan*) *eccen* 959 (c. 1240) BCS 1047, (*of*) *Eccene* c. 977 (c. 1240) KCD 1277 (*on*) *occenes* (*gerstun*) 955 (c. 1200) BCS 906, (*on*) *ocenne wyllas* c. 955 (c. 1150) BCS 902, (*on*) *occenes* (*gærstun*) 956 (c. 1200) BCS 924

(*on*) *oeccene* 958 (c. 1240), 960 (c. 1240), 968 (c. 1240) BCS 1032, 1058, 1224

Eoche W I, Hy I (c. 1240) Abingdon

Ocke Hy I (c. 1240) Abingdon, 1241–2 *Ass*, c. 1540 Leland, *Okke* 1248 *Ass*, *Och*(*e*), *Ouke* c. 1540 Leland

Ock 1336 Pat

There is little to add to the discussion of this name in RN 307. It is from a derivative of the Celtic word for a salmon, for which Jackson (362) gives the British form **esāco-*. This may be a fanciful name for the stream, rather than a reference to the presence of salmon. cf. the Welsh use of animal names in r.n.s., e.g. *banw* 'pig' in R. Aman.

In charter boundaries the stream which rises near Woolstone is regarded as the source of the Ock. *on æoccænen upp and lang stremæs on þonæ æwulm* in BCS 491 and *on occene wyllas* in BCS 902 refer to this stream, *v.* Pt **3**.

OSSE DITCH (affluent of Ock, not named on map). The bounds of BCS 777 (dated 942) and of 1047 (dated 959) apply the term (*to, andlang*) *wasan* to the stream which forms the modern boundary between Appleton and Bessels Leigh. BCS 1222 (dated 968) applies (*on*) *wase*, (*of*) *wæse* to what is probably the same stream, and BCS 977 and 1221 (dated 956 and 968) refer to (*on, andlang*) *wasan* and (*on*) *wase*, (*of*) *wasan* in the boundaries of Fyfield, where the reference is quite certainly to the southern part of the same brook. Later forms are *La Wose* 1241 *Ass* (p, in Hormer Hundred), 1267–8 *FF* (position uncertain), 1316 (l. 14th) *Lyell* (in Cumnor), 1343 Ipm (p) (at Oxford), *Wose* 1412 FA (mentioned with Cumnor), *Ose Coppice* 1713–14 *Bodl* (in Cumnor), *Osse Ditch*, *Osse Field* 1828 *StJohnMap*. *Osse Field* is shown twice on *StJohnMap*, referring to land in the immediate vicinity of this stream, which also seems to be the 'river with no official name but locally always called the Os' mentioned in R. P. Beckinsale's *Companion into Berkshire* (London 1951), p. 13. There is a house called Osse Field at the southern end of Appleton village. There seems to be no doubt that Grundy is right in his identification of these charter forms with the stream which rises south of Cumnor and flows into the Ock south of Marcham, although Ekwall (RN 437 n.) is not prepared to admit that *wasan* is a stream-name or that it is connected with the modern name Osse Ditch.

There are two other occurrences of the name in Berks. One of these, in the bounds of Buckland, is *(to, of) wasan* 957 (c. 1200) BCS 1005. Grundy considers this identical with a stream called Ouse Ditch in the *TA*. The other is WOOSE HILL (in Wokingham Within), *Owse Hill* 1571 *PubLibDoc, Woosse Hill, Wosse Hill, Wos(e)hill* 1607 *RentSur, Woose Hill* 1846 Snare. In this case the name probably refers to a small tributary of the Emm Brook.

The evidence shows that OE *wasan* is a stream-name derived from *wāse* 'mud', which occurs three times in the county, surviving in one case as Os or Osse and in another as Woose, and in the third case occurring in a *TA* as Ouse. OE *wāse* occurs occasionally in stream-names in other counties, cf. Sx 6, Wa 4.

PANG (affluent of Thames), *(on) panganburnan* '956' (c. 1200) BCS 919, (water called) *Pangeburne* 1271 AD, *v.* Pangbourne *infra* 167. The earliest forms for the village name date from 843, and point to an OE **Pǣgingaburna*, which is difficult to reconcile with the earliest form for the r.n. Ekwall (RN 319) suggests that *Panganburnan* is a mistake for *Pangaburnan*, a contracted form of *Pǣgingaburnan*.

SANDFORD BROOK (affluent of Ock), *(andlang) lucringes* 959 (c. 1200, c. 1240) BCS 1047. Ekwall (RN 210) suggests that *-c-* is an error for *-t-*, and that **lutring* would be a derivative of *hlūtor* 'clear'. In support of this, Forsberg (163) points to the occurrence in one version of these bounds in *ClaudiusCix* of *totan* for the *coten* of *ClaudiusBvi*. It is perhaps safer to leave the name unexplained, although it deserves notice as a probable singular name in -ing applied to a stream, *v.* Introd. The modern name is from Dry Sandford, Pt 2.

SEVERN (?lost, in Hurley), *Severne* 1246–7 *FF*, Ed I, 1353 Hurley, *Seuerne* 1268, l.13th, 1341, 1344 ib, *Sauerne* Hy 3, Ed I ib, *le Severne* 1544 VCH III (148), *the Severne* 1673 *PubLib, Severn Meadow* c. 1840 *TA*. The contexts of two early forms (*campus qui jacet subtus Severne* 1246–7 *FF, usque ad Seuerne* 1268 Hurley) suggest that the name is that of a stream, presumably the one which flows into the Thames through Temple Park. A note in Hurley (p. 104) says that *The Severn* was the name of a meadow enclosed in Temple Park in

1876. This is a further example of the pre-English river-name Severn, for a discussion of which *v.* RN 360. There was a small stream in Bedford (BdHu 9) with this name, as well as the great West Midland river.

SHOVEL SPRING (in West Hagbourne), *Sobewell* 1199 *FF*, *Schobewell* 1408–9 *RentSur*. 'Sc(e)obba's spring', *v.* w(i)ella. The personal name is only recorded in place-names, *v.* Bk 128.

STUTFIELD BROOK (affluent of Ock), (*innan*) *Tealeburnan* 959 (c. 1200) BCS 1047, (*on*) *tealeburnan* 963 (c. 1200) BCS 1121, (*on*) *talleburnan* 953 (c. 1240) BCS 899. Ekwall (RN 389) considers this name to be identical with Tale D, Tala Water Co, D, which he derives from OE *getæl* 'quick, ready, active'. In D 13 it is stated, however, that Tale is sluggish in character. The modern name has probably been extended to the brook from Stutfield Bridge in West Challow (Pt 2).

SWALE (lost), *v.* Blackwater *supra* 7.

THAMES. For a discussion of this river-name *v.* M. Förster, *Der Flussname Themse* (München 1941) and RN 402–5. The name occurs in the boundaries of a number of Berks charters as *Temese*, which is its commonest OE form. The meaning is not known. *v.* **tamo-*.

WANTAGE (lost)

    (*on*) *wanotingc broc* 956 (c. 1240), (*on*) *wanontingc broc* 956 (c. 1200) BCS 949

    (*on*) *wanetincg* 958 (c. 1200), (*on*) *wanetinge*, (*andlang*) *waneting* 958 (c. 1240) BCS 1032, (*on*) *waniting*, (*andlang*) *waneting* 960 (c. 1200), (*on, andlang*) *waneting* 960 (c. 1240) BCS 1058, (*on*) *wanetingc broc* 964 (c. 1200), (*on*) *wanetinge broc* (c. 1240) BCS 1142, (*on*) *wanating*, (*on*) *ealden wanatiting* 968 (c. 1200), (*on*) *waneting*, (*on*) *ealden wæneting* 968 (c. 1240) BCS 1224

The forms have been given together here, although they refer to two separate streams, one of which gives name to Wantage, Pt 2.

Waneting is said in RN 143 to be the old name of Letcombe Brook, which rises in Letcombe Bassett and flows through Wantage, ultimately to the Ock. In fact only one of the references in the charter boundaries is to Letcombe Brook. BCS 949, in the bounds of East

Hanney, applies *wanotingc broc* to Letcombe Brook and (*on þone*) *ealdan broc* to the boundary between East Hanney and Drayton, formed by the course of a tributary of the Ock, part of which has been drained, but which must originally have run parallel with Letcombe Brook about a mile and a half to the E. Another version of these bounds in BCS 1224 calls this latter stream (*on*) *ealdan wæneting*. In the bounds of Drayton in BCS 1032 it is referred to as (*on*) *wanetinge*, and in those of Hendred in BCS 1142 it is called (*on*) *wanetingc broc*.

It is clear that both these streams were called *Waneting*, the eastern one being sometimes called 'old Wantage' or 'the old brook'. In p.ns. **eald** sometimes means 'disused', and it is not impossible that the drainage of the lower half of this brook had occurred in Anglo-Saxon times. One at least of the drainage ditches in the immediate vicinity, Mere Dike in Drayton (Pt 2), was there in the 10th cent.

Ekwall (RN 433) suggests that Wantage is a derivative of OE *wanian* 'to decrease', the immediate base being an abstract noun **wanot* 'decrease', or perhaps a verb **wanotian*. There was another stream so called in Do, recorded as *aqua de Wanetinge* 1244 *Ass*. As a careful reading of the Berks boundaries makes it clear that the name was applied to two Berks streams, it seems likely that it was a term which could be applied to any stream of varying volume.

For the palatalisation of the final syllable *v.* Introd.

WHITE BROOK (affluent of Thames, in Cookham), *Wythebrok* 1372 InqMisc, *Westwithbrooke* 1607 *ECR*, *Wide Brook* 1761 Rocque, 'willow brook', *v.* **wīðig, brōc**.

WILDMOOR BROOK (affluent of Ock, in St Helen Without, Abingdon), cf. *Willmorefurlonge* 1548 *LRMB*, *Wildmoor* c. 1840 *TA*: second el. **mōr** 'marsh'.

I. RIPPLESMERE HUNDRED

Riplesmer(e) 1086 DB, *Riplesmere* c. 1200 *ClaudiusCix*, 1242 P, 1391
    Ipm, *Ripplesmere* 1224–5, 1284 *Ass*, 1316 FA, 1327 *SR*, *Ryplesmere*
    1284 *Ass*, *Rypplesmer'* 1332 *SR*
Ripplemere 1184, 1195 P, 1225 *Ass*
Rippemere 1189 P, *Ripemere* 1190 ib
Rippesmere 1275–6 RH

'Pool of the *ripel*', *v.* mere. OE rip(p)el probably means 'strip',
corresponding to Norwegian *ripel*. It occurs in a number of p.ns. and
has been taken to mean 'strip of wood' (cf. He dialect *ripple* 'small
coppice or thicket') and 'tongue of land', the latter topographically
appropriate in the case of Ripple (Wo 158). The meeting-place of
Ripplesmere Hundred is not known, and pools are so numerous in
the area that there is little hope of identifying the one in question.
Cf. also YW **7** , 135, s.n. Ribble.
    Ripplesmere Hundred contained the lost DB manor of *Ortone*
('farm on a slope or river-bank', *v.* ōra[1], tūn); there is a lost *Overton*
in Windsor which may represent this with interchange of ōra and
ōfer.

Clewer

CLEWER

    Clivore 1086 DB
    Cliuewara 1156 P *et freq* with variant spellings *Cliueware, Cliuewar',*
        Clyveware
    Cliwara 1157, –8 P *et freq* with variant spellings *Cliwar', Clywar',*
        Clyware, Cliware; Clyeware 1284 *Ass*
    Clifwara 1159, –60, –67 P *et freq* with variant spellings *Clifware,*
        Clyfware
    Cliffewar 1242–3 Fees
    Cleware 1289, 1361 Fine, 1517 D Inc, *Cleuwar* 1361 Fine, *Cluwar*
        1401–2 FA, *Cluer* 1535 VE, *Clewar Brokas* 1604 *SpecCom.*

'The dwellers on a river-bank', *v.* clif. The same name occurs in
So, and the second el. is -ware 'inhabitants'. *Clewer Brocas* consisted
of lands held by Sir John Brocas in the first half of the 14th cent.
(VCH III, 71).

DEDWORTH, *Dideorde* 1086 DB, *Didewurth'* 1204 P, *Diddewurth'* 1204–5 *FF*, 1241 *Ass*, *Dydewrze* 1220 Fees, *Diddeworth'* 1224–5 *Ass*, *Didewurth* 1227–8 *FF*, *Didiwrth'* 1247–8 *Ass*, *Dydeworth* 1284 *ib*, *Diddewrþe*, *Dudewrth* 1294 *SR*, *Diddeworthe* 1316 FA, *Dideworthe* 1330 Ipm, *Didworthmauncel* 1334 Brocas, *Dideworth Maunsel* 1354 ib, *Dedeworth-Loryng* 1401 *Windsor*, 'Dydda's worð'. Ekwall (DEPN) gives an OE pers.n. *Dydda*, which he assumes to be a side-form of *Dudda*, as the first el. of this name, and of Dedham Ess and Tidenham Gl; *v.* also Gl **2**, 9. Peter de *Loring* held land here at the beginning of the 13th, and John *Maunsell* is mentioned in this connection in 1313 (VCH III, 74).

LOSFIELD (lost), *Losfelle* 1086 DB, *Losfeld* 1130 P, 1275–6 RH, 1302, 1320, 1330 Pat, *Losfeld'* 1219 Fees, *Lossefelde* 1554 *LRMB*. The second el. is **feld**, used of a clearing in Windsor Forest, cf. Leafield O 361, and the first probably **hlōse** 'pig-stye'. The chapel of St Leonard (*infra*) is stated 1320 Pat to be in Losfeld. There was also a *Losfeldeshath*, *Losfeldeshaith* 1279 HMC Var Coll I, *v.* **hǣð**.

RUDDLES POOL, *Rodelespole* 1286 Cl, *Bodelespole* 1340 (1711) Hearne, *Ridleys Poole* Eliz *RentSur*, *Riddel Pole* l. 16th Ashmole, *Rydles Poole* 1607 *Norden*, *Ridlespoole* 1640 *SpecCom*, *Ruddles Poole* 1640 *SpecComMap*, *Ruddlespole* 1711 Hearne. This is a pool in the Thames, and the second el. is **pōl** in the sense 'pool in a river'. The first may be an unrecorded pers.n. perhaps *Hrōdel*, with the diminutive suffix -*el*. Alternatively, Professor Löfvenberg suggests the gen. of a compound p.n. **Hrēodlēah* 'reed clearing'.

ST LEONARD'S, ST LEONARDSHILL (*Seynt Leonerds* 1548 *LRMB*, *St Leanerdshill* 1607 *Norden*, *St Leonards* 1761 Rocque, *St Leonards Hill and Lodge* 1800 Eden) are named from a hermit's chapel dedicated to St Leonard, for which *v.* VCH III, 76. It is first mentioned in 1215. THE HERMITAGE, in the same vicinity, presumably refers to the same chapel; cf. *Ermytescroft* 1365 Cl, *le Hermytage*, *Hermytage Grove*, *Armetriding' als the Hermetryding'* 1548 *LRMB*. The last name is identical with Armetridding (PN La 133), and means 'hermit-clearing', *v.* **ryding**.

SURLEY HALL ROAD, cf. *Surly Hall* 1800 Eden. This may be named from *Suthelee* 1333 Brocas, *South Ley* 1490 Brocas, *Sudley, Great and*

Litill Southley 1548 *LRMB*, 'south wood or clearing', *v.* sūð, lēah. Development of sūð to *Sur-* would be identical with that found in Circourt in Wantage.

ASH PLANTATION, cf. *Le Aysshe* 1548 *LRMB*. BELL FM. CLEWER COURT, *Cluer Courte* 1548 *LRMB*. CLEWER GREEN, 1761 Rocque, *Cluergrene* 1539 *Windsor, Cleworth Greene* 1573 *SpecCom*. CLEWER HALL, MANOR AND MEAD. CLEWER HILL HO. CLEWER NEW TOWN. CLEWER RD. DEDWORTH MANOR (*v.* 20). DEVIL'S GAP. FOREST PARK. GORDON RD. GREEN LANE. HATCH LANE, *Woodhatche Lane, Woodhatche Gate* 1548 *LRMB*, *v.* hæc(c). HIGH STANDING HILL, 1800 Eden, *v.* standing. HOUSE OF MERCY. KENTON'S LANE. MANOR HOUSE FM. MILL HO, *Mill Lodge* 1822 OS, cf *Le Mylle Mede, Milnemede, Le Myll Broke* 1548 *LRMB*. OLD HOUSE, *Clewer House* 1822 OS. NELSON RD. NEW RD. PARK CORNER. PARSONAGE LANE. QUEEN ADELAIDE'S BEECH AND RIDE. ROSES LANE. ST LEONARD'S DALE (*Leonards Dale* 1822 OS), LODGE AND RD (*v.* 20). SEFTON LAWN. SMITH'S LANE, *Smythislane* Hy 6 AD, from the surname *Smith*. SUTHER-LAND GRANGE. SWAN INN. THREE ELMS P.H. VALE FM. WHITE LILIES. WINKFIELD RD. WITHY COVER, cf. *Wythy Crofte* 1558 *LRMB*, *v.* wīðig.

FIELD-NAMES

The principal forms in (*a*) are 1839 *TA* except where otherwise stated; forms for which no date is given are 1548 *LRMB*, 1573, 1601, 1604 *SpecCom*, and 17th *PubLib(Clayton)*.

(*a*) Asket Bridge 1800 Eden; Brick Fd; Bridge Mdw; Clewer Park; Coppice Fd; Cross Oat Fd; Forest Hill 1848 *PubLibDoc*; Glassmoor (*Glasemore, v.* glæs², mōr); Great Pond Hill; The Hill; The Home Fd; Long Mdw; Sophia Farm 1800 Eden; Spinners' Fd; Sweetheads (cf. *Swete Crofte, v.* swēte); Taylor's Corner (cf. *Tayloreshale* 1384 Brocas, belonging to Thom. *Taylour, v.* halh); Ten Acres; West Mdw (*Le Westmed* 1413 *Windsor*, Le *Westmede*); Withy Close (*Withie Close* 17th).

(*b*) *Aysshenstubb'* (*v.* æscen, stubb); *Bataille Rudyng* 1384 Brocas (*v.* ryding, first el. possibly the surname *Batayle*); *Beaurepir* 1262 Pat (*v.* bel², repaire and Introd.); *Bek(e)s Crosse*; *Bewley Lane, Beawlewstile* (*v.* bel², lieu and Introd.); *Le Brache* (*v.* brēc); *Brocas Farm* 1554 *RentSur* (*v.* 19); *Brode Lane, Lease and Mede* (*v.* brād); *Le Broke Bridge and Grove, Brokefeld* 1548 *LRMB*, *Brookefeild* 1604 (*v.* brōc); *Broks Gate*; *Le Brome* (*v.* brōm); *Budginghame*; *Burdingbusshes*; *Burnette* 1573, *Burnetts* 17th (*v.* bærnet(t)); *Busshye Lease*; *Le Butte, Butridings* (*v.* butte, ryding); *Le Cawseye* 1604 (*v.*

caucie); *Chappell Croft* 1573; *Claremede, Clere Mede* (possibly 'Clewer mead'); *Clywaresthrop* 1384 Brocas, *Cluer Thorpe, vico voc' le Thorpe* 1548 *LRMB, v.* prop); *Cleypitts; Cokerey Mede; Connynge Yarde* (*v.* coninger); *Copped Hall'* 1548 *LRMB, Copthall* 1657 *PubLib* (*v.* coppede); *Cradlescrofte; Crallescroft* 1227–8 *FF; Cranfords* 1548 *LRMB, Cranford(e)s Lane* 1604 (possibly a surname); *Craule* 1333 Brocas, *Crawle* 1398, 1411 *Windsor, Crowley, Craule, Crawley* (*v.* crāwe, lēah); *Culuerhouse Lane* ('dovecot lane'); *Deulacresse* 1279 HMC Var Coll I ('may God increase it', a French name identical with Dieulacres St; the Berks name refers to an assart belonging to Salisbury Cathedral); *Don(n)crofte* 1548 *LRMB, Duncrofte* 1604 (*v.* dunn); *Fayrefurres* (*v.* fæger, furh); *Fernehill; Fishers, Fishers Mead* 1601; *Le Flotgond* (a ditch) 1295 *ECR, Flotgonges* 1298, 1307 *ib, Flotgong* (a ditch) l.13th–e.14th *ib., Le Flodgonge* 1426 *ib., le Flatgamesfeld* (the 1426 ref. appears to be to a mill-race, 'flood passage', *v.* flōd, gang); *Frogmyll Busshes; Fullyfare* 1501 *Windsor, Fullyforde Brige, Fullyfere Brige* (possibly OE *ful gefær* 'muddy going'); *Le Fyre* (probably OE *fyr from fyrh* dat. of furh 'furrow', cf. Löfvenberg 73–4); *Le Glede* (possibly glǣd[3] 'glade'); *Gonnecrofta* 1466 Brocas ('Gunna's croft', the same f.n. occurs O 55); *Le Gravellpitts; Haggebussh* 1490 *Windsor* (*v.* hagga); *Le Hale* 1333 Brocas, 1384 *ib*, 1399, 1411 *Windsor, Hales Sherde* (*v.* halh, sceard); *Le Hall Garden; Le Harvest Hawe* (*v.* haga[1]); *Hawe* 1327–8 *SR* (p); *Hertesgroue* 1323 *Windsor; Le Hethes* (*v.* hǣð); *Le Highe Garden; Highe Feld; Holmanstrowdes* (*v.* strōd, first el. the surname *Holman*); *Holme Strands* 1601 (possibly a corruption of preceding); *Homers Lane* 1573; *Hudewyneshale* Hy 3 *ECR* (*v.* h(e)alh, first el. a pers.n. or surname); *Hye Lande Plott* 1604, *Hylands Plott Comon* 17th; *Innyngs* (*v.* inning); *Kechyn Close* (*v.* cycene); *Kyngestyle* 1416 *Windsor, Le Kings Stile; Kytte Garden* 1548 *LRMB, The Kytt Wate Meade* 1573; *Langford* 1517 D Inc (*v.* lang[1], ford); *Longcroft; Longefere* (*v.* furh); *Lot Mede* (*v.* hlot); *Lullings Eight* 17th (*v.* ēgeð and cf. Thom. *Lullyng'* 1327–8 *SR); Market Crosse; Le Marshe* 1548 *LRMB, The Mersshe* 1573; *The Marshe* 17th; *Mayre Lane; Meane Meade* (*v.* (ge)mǣne); *Merewoode* 1605, 1628 *Windsor, Merewoods* 1662 *ib* (*v.* (ge)mǣre or mere); *La More* Hy 3 *ECR*, 1326 Brocas, 1548 *LRMB* (*v.* mōr); *Myddellrydings* (*v.* ryding); *Newe Mede; Nokefeld, Noke Benche* 1548 *LRMB, Oakefeild* 17th (*v.* atten, āc, and cf. Will. *atte Oke* 1327–8 *SR); Opcrofte* 1295 *Windsor, Upcrofte* 1298 *ib, Opefeld* 1274 Cl (*v.* upp); *Oxlease* (*v.* lǣs); *Pasted Strete* 1508 ArchJ 4; *Pensforde* 1548 *LRMB, Painshford* 17th; *Perrycroft* (*v.* pirige); *Philpeshawe* 1501 *Windsor, Phipps Hall, Fippshall, Phippishallfeld* ('Philip's enclosure', *v.* haga[1]); *Plumtreehedge* 1604; *Pockerds Gate; Purle Stanpitts, Purloshill,* (cf. Joh. *Porle* 1327–8 *SR); Le Reyemede* 1351 Brocas, *Raymede, Le Rye Broke, Rye Croft Oke, Le Rye Brige* 1548 *LRMB, The Ray Bridge* 17th (cf. Ray Court in Maidenhead 55; in VCH III, 72, The Rays is given as the name of the island on which the race-course is situated); *Le Riche* (possibly risc 'rush' used collectively, but it might be a scribal error for **Rithe, v.* rið); *Rowegrove, Rowgrove Mede* (*v.* rūh); *Le Royse; Ruyhersh* l.13th–e.14th *ECR, Ruerssh* 1344 *ib, Ryercherse Feld* (*v.* ryge, ersc); *Shepeclose; Sidlowe* (*v.* sīd, hlāw); *Small Eights* 17th (*v.* ēgeð); *Snapes Lane* 1380 *Windsor, Snapyslane* 1449 *ib* (cf. Will. *Snape* 1327–8 *SR); Le Stantputte* 1297 *Windsor, Le*

Stanhuttes 1326 Brocas, *Stampitts Sherde, Stanpitts, Le Stonpitts* (*v.* stān, pytt, sceard); *Sweynfurlong* 1401 *Windsor*; *Le Tadlocke*; *Toncrofte* m.13th AD (*v.* tūn); *Tylehall*; *Wallnuttree Close* 1604; *Le Warde* 1548 *LRMB*, *Westefeild als Wardshott* 1604, *Ward Shott and Mead* 17th (*v.* weard, scēat); *Welforde Brige*; *Westgate* 1384 Brocas; *Wheters, Whetehirste, Wheathorsley, Whetersshe* (*v.* hwǣte, ersc); *Wickers Dytche* 1604; *Wood Yates* (cf. Will. *Wodeyate* 1327–8 *SR*); *Wyganescroft* 1338 Brocas, *Wyganeslond* 1384 ib (first el. the Breton pers.n. *Wigan v.* La 103, Reaney s.n. *Wigan* and cf. 66); *Wyggenhill* and *Wygginham* m.13th AD, *Wiginghame, Whitingham, Wiggenhame, Wigginghamfelde, Wiggynhame* (probably 'Wicga's hill and hamm').

Easthampstead

EASTHAMPSTEAD

Lachenestede 1086 DB

Yezhamesteda 1167 P, *Yethamstede* 1176 ib (p) *et freq* with variant spelling *Yethamsted'*; *Yetzhamsteda* 1180 P, *Jezhamestede* 1185 RR (p), *Yeshamsted'* 1224–5 *Ass et freq* with variant spellings *Yeshamsted(e)*; *Yestamested'* 1224–5 *Ass, Yashamsted'* 1238 Cl, *Yashamstede* 1275–6 RH, 1294 *SR*, *Yeshampstede* 1331 Fine, 1342 Gor, *Yesshampsted* 1316 FA

Chesthamstede 1169 P

Hiecamesteda c. 1220 *AddCh 38976*

Essamested' 1216 Cl, *Eshamstede* 1284 *Ass, Esthamstede* 1284 *ib,* Ed 2 *Hurley, Estehampsted* 1535 VE

v. hāmstede. Probably, as suggested in DEPN, the prefix is *geates*, and the meaning 'homestead by the gate'. Ekwall also suggests that the gate may have been one leading to Windsor Forest, but Easthampstead was well within the area of the medieval forest, not on its boundary. geat occurs in forests in such names as Reigate Sr 304, which are considered to refer to fences with gaps to allow free movement to the king's deer. Such a gap in a fence may be the 'gate' of Easthampstead. The DB form is corrupt.

SOUTH HILL PARK, cf. *Suthull* 1234–5 *FF* (p), *Southille* 1455 *Windsor, Sowthill* 1607 *Norden, Southill Lodge* 1790 Pride, *South Hill Park and Star* 1800 Eden, *v.* sūð, hyll, the site is relatively high ground S. of Easthampstead and Bracknell.

THE TOWN, (field called) *le Toune* 1342 Gor. It is probable that this name and that of the nearby Wickham Bushes (*infra*) refer to the remains of a Romano-British village, for which *v.* VCH II, 206.

WICKHAM BUSHES, 1607 *Norden*, 1761 Rocque, 1800 Eden, cf. *Wikhamgate* 1329 Hurley. This is a piece of rough ground adjacent to The Town, where the 6″ map marks 'Roman Remains Pottery & Coins found'. VCH I, 206 gives an account of excavations in the 19th cent., which uncovered traces of houses, associated with Roman pottery and coins. It seems most probable that the two names, The Town and Wickham, refer to Roman remains.

The connection between OE **wīchām** and Roman roads and settlements is discussed in M. Gelling, 'English Place-Names derived from the Compound *wīchām*', *Medieval Archaeology* XI (1967), 87–104. *v.* also Wickham in Welford (Pt **2**) and Introd.

BEECHCROFT.   BIG WOOD.   BILL HILL, 1790 Pride, *v.* 142. BIRCH HILL.   BLACK HILL.   BOROUGH GREEN.   BRAMSHAW. BROOK HO.   BURNTHOUSE RIDE.   BUTTER HILL, BUTTER HILL BOTTOM, 1761 Rocque, 1790 Pride, possibly referring to rich pasture. CAESAR'S CAMP, *Windmill Hill Fort* 1607 *Norden*, *Cesar's Camp* 1761 Rocque, *Ceasars Camp* 1800 Eden, a name frequently given to Iron Age hill-forts.   CHURCHSTILE FM, *Church Stile Meadow* 1841 *TA*. CLAY HILL, CLAYHILL PLANTATION.   THE COTTAGE.   CUNWORTH COPSE, *Cunworth* 1629 VCH III, 78.   DOWN MILL, *Downe Mills*, *Downe Millne Lands* 1607 *RentSur*.   DOWNSHIRE ARMS P.H.   EASTHAMPSTEAD PARK, *Easthampsted Parke* Chas I *RentSur*. EAST LODGE.   FIRLANDS.   FROG LANE.   GORMOOR COTTAGES.   GORMOOR POND, 1761 Rocque, probably *Gall Moare* 1607 *Norden*, *v.* **galla, mōr**.   GORRICK WELL.   GRAVEL HILL, *Grauell Hill* 1607 *Norden*.   HAG THORN, *Hagthorne* 1761 Rocque. HANWORTH PLANTATION, *Hanworthes* 1342 Gor, (*pasture called*) *Hanworth* 1621 *PubLib*, *Hamsworth Hill Oak* 1800 Eden, *Harmsworth* 1816 OS, probably from a surname.   HOLLY COTTAGE.   HOME FM.   HUT HILL.   JENNETT'S HILL, *Jennings Hill* 1841 *TA*, cf. *Jeynkynnysgrene* 1463 Gor, *Jenkins Green* 1816 OS, 1846 Snare, the surname *Jenkin* was probably corrupted to *Jenning* and then to *Jennett*.   LAUNDRY FIRS AND RIDE (for Ride *v.* 34).   THE LODGE, cf. *Lodghill* 1607 *Norden*.   LONG LEAKE COPPICE. LONGSHOT LANE, *Longshot Lane Piddle*, *Longshot Meadow* 1841 *TA*. LOWER STAR POST, ROMAN STAR OR UPPER STAR POST.   MANOR FM.   MILL FM.   MILL LANE, 1761 Rocque.   MILL POND. NANCRY COPPICE, *Le Acrey* 1508 *Bodl*, *Nac(k)ry Field* 1841 *TA*, probably 'oak stream', *v.* **āc, rīð**, with N- from **atten**.   NEW

POND. NEW RD. NEWTON COTTAGE. NORTHERAMS. OAK-
DENE. OLD BRACKNELL FM AND HO. PARKSIDE. PARSONAGE
LANE. PEACOCK FM, 1846 Snare. PEACOCK LANE. PRIEST-
WOOD COMMON, 1761 Rocque, *Priestwood* 1573 *SpecCom, Preistwood*
1644 *SpecCom*. PRIESTWOOD HO AND CT. PUDDING HILL (*v.*
284). ROUND HILL, 1761 Rocque. SANDPITS. SKIMPED-
HILL LANE, *Skimpets* 1841 *TA*. SOUTH LODGE. STONEY RD.
STREETS LANE FM. TARMAN'S COPSE, *Tawmans* 1841 *TA*.
WAGBULLOCK HILL, *Wagbullocks Hill* 1800 Eden. WATERHAMS,
Waterhams, Waterhams Moor and Meadow 1841 *TA*. WELLINGTON
COTTAGES. WEST GARDEN, WEST GARDEN COPSE. WESTWICK.
WILDRIDINGS, *Wyderydyng* 1463 Gor, 'wide clearing', *v.* wīd, ryding.
WINDMILL STEM, 1607 *Norden*. WINDSOR RIDE. WOODEN HILL,
1800 Eden. WOODENHILL PLANTATION. WYKERY COPSE, *Wickary
Lane* 1800 Eden, *Wykery Meadow* 1841 *TA*. YEWTREE CORNER,
1761 Rocque.

FIELD-NAMES

The principal forms in (*a*) are 1841 *TA* except where otherwise stated;
early spellings dated 1607 are *Norden*, 1761 Rocque.

(*a*) Adams Piddle; The Alders; Ash Hill and Piddle; Bagshot Gate Fd;
Great Bars (*Barres Coppice* 1629 VCH III); Beedles Hill 1800 Eden (cf.
Bedellond Ed 3 Hurley, *v.* bydel); Birch Croft; Boulters (cf. possibly *Bowl-
sters Groue* 1607); Broad Croft; Brook Mdw; Bull Lane Piddle; Camp Fd;
Carrot Fd; Carters Close and Fd; Carthouse Close; Church Brook Mdw
(*Chyrchbrokemed* 1342 Gor); Church Brook Moor and Piddle; Clam Close
(*v.* Ch 3, 47); Cocks Moor and Mead; Coxs Green 1846 Snare (*Cockse Green*
1761, *Cox's Green* 1790 Pride); Coppice Close; The Crate (a form of croft);
Cressy Mdw; Down Hill Fm 1846 Snare; Duncotes; Easthampstead Plain
1800 Eden (1761, 1790 Pride); Estray Plat (*v.* plat²); Ferny Croft; Frogmoors;
Furze(n) Hill; Furze Moor; Garstons (*Garston'* 1327–8 *SR* (p), *Garston*
1341 NonInq (p), *Le Garstone* 1342 Gor, *Garston* 1588 *Bodl*, *v.* gærs-tūn);
Gorse Grove Close (*Gors Grove* 1761); Gravelley Close; Greet Fd (*Grete-
croft* Ed I Hurley, *v.* grēot); The Grove, Grove Fd; Gunston Mdw; Ham
Fd, Great and Little Ham (*Hamme Field* e.13th BM, *v.* hamm); Haw Brook
1816 OS; Heath Moor; High Plain Star 1800 Eden; Hill Fd and Ground
(cf. *Hill' Ende* 1521 *PubLibDoc*); Great Hollands; Hole Ground (cf. *Holmed*
1379–80 *Bodl*, *v.* hol, mǣd); Home Close and Ground; Hurst Close; Kiln
Ground; Lawham; Leaches Close; Lemoins Mdw; Lick Pots (*v.* 283);
Littleworth (*v.* 283); The Meadow; Mill Mdw; Minkerets; The Moor
(*Moor Corner* 1761); Mount Close; Mud Walls (cf. *Mudwalls Mead* 1839
TA for Wokingham); Natts; Northcotes; Oaken Coppice 1816 OS, 1846
Snare (*Oaken Cops* 1761); Oat Fd; Old Lane; Parsons Piddle; Patten Fd;
Pauls Acre Mdw; Piddle (here, and elsewhere in this parish, a variant of

pightel); Plat (*v.* plat²); Pond Mdw and Moor; Poors Land and Mdw; Puddle Dock Mdw (possibly identical with Puddle Dock Ess 135, earlier *Puddleduck*); Ragged Row Mdw; Reeds Hill; Rickyard Mdw; Ridings (*The Rudinge* e.13th BM, *La Rudinge* Ed 2 Hurley, *v.* ryding); Rye Fd; Little Saffron (presumably where the plant grew); Sheepridge; Stable Mdw; Stoney Ham; Swinley Road Slip (*v.* slipe); Thistley Close; Three Cornered Ground; Thrift Coppice 1816 OS (*v.* fyrhð); Town Fd; Triangular Piece; Trys Moor; Turf House Mdw; Two Veers Ground; Walldens Fm 1846 Snare (*Waldens Green* 1800 Eden, 1816 OS); Waste Ground; Winding Ground; Woodfield; Woodwells; Wren Park (*v.* Db 758); Yieldalls Moor (*cf.* Walt. *yhildhalle* 1327–8 *SR*).

(*b*) *Aldheghes* 1337 Hurley (*v.* ald, (ge)hæg); *La Benhahecroft* Ed I ib; *Brystetherudyngge* 1342 Gor ('Beorhtgÿð's clearing', *v.* ryding); *Bulstrode Grove* 1607–8 SpecCom, *Bullstred Grove* 1761; *Burchettes Grove* 1588 Bodl; *Covpershill'* 1521 PubLibDoc, *Coopers* 1761; *Crasislonde* 1455 Windsor (first el. probably a surname, cf. Reaney, *s.n. Crass*); *Crosherne* Eliz RentSur (*v.* cros, hyrne); *Felcroftes* Eliz RentSur; *Feldlonde* Ed 3 Hurley (*v.* feld, land); *Fishers Lodge* 1761; *Hallgroue* 1607; *Hogshead Hill* 1761, 1816 OS (from the shape); *Hurt Hedges* 1607; *Kitthollsbottome* 1607; *Lytylynnynge* 1463 Gor (*v.* lÿtel, inning); *New Cot Hill* 1761; *Northcroft* Ed I Hurley; *Northgrof* 1379–80 Bodl (*v.* grāf); *Odeslonde* Ed 3 Hurley (first el. possibly the surname *Oade, v.* Reaney); *Popes Stock* 1607; *Pound Green* 1790 Pride; *Queen's Meadows* 1629 VCH III, *Quenestanding Hill* 1607 (*Standing Hill* 1761, *v.* standing); *Rush-holls* 1607; *Sandy Hill* 1761; *Sarnsbroc* 1342 Gor (possibly scearn and brōc); *Shelbred Hills* 1607 (possibly scofl-brǣdu); *Stuttesgrof* 1379–80 Bodl (*v.* grāf, first el. probably a surname, *v.* Reaney s.n. *Stout*); *Suthparroc-croft* Ed I Hurley (*v.* sūð, pearroc); *Vylemoar* 1607; *Well Bottome* 1607; *Wellond* Ed 3 Hurley (*v.* wella, land); *Westworth* 1379–80 Bodl (*v.* west, worð); *Wythycrofte* Hy 3 Hurley (*v.* wiðig, croft); *Yelderns Green* 1790 Pride.

New and Old Windsor

WINDSOR, NEW AND OLD

Windlesoran mid 11th (l.11th) ASWrits, 1096 *et seq* ASC E, (*æt*) *Windles oran* 1061 ib, (*on þam*) *niwan Windlesoran* 1110 ib, (*to*) *Windlesofra* 1126 ib, (*on*) *Windlesoure* 1127 ib, *Windlesores* 1087 Madox, 1139–40 BMFacs (p) *et freq* with variant spellings *Windlesor'*, *Wyndlesore*, *Windlesor*, *Windlesour* to c. 1265 (c. 1450) Godstow, *Windleshora* 1109–20 (13th) RSO, *Wyndleshor'* 1139 (c. 1280) S (p), *Windelshora* 1158 (13th) RSO, *Windlessores* 1194 P, *Windelsores* l.12th (13th) Gerv, *Windelesor'* 1218–19 FF, *Windleshor'* c. 1240 (l.13th) S, *Wyndeles'* 1242–3 Fees, *Windleshouere* 1248 Cl, *villam regis de Windles' et... veterem Windles'*

1257 ib, *Windelesore, Windlshore, Winleshore, Windelsore, Windlesores* 13th Gerv.

Vuindisor 1072 HMC 5th Rep I, *Windesores* 1086 DB, 1130 P *et passim* with variant spellings *Windesoris, Windesor(e), Wyndesore, Wyndesor'* to 1600 Camden, *Windesoueres* Hy 2 Gaimar, *Windesouer'* 1204–5 *FF, Vet'i Windesores* 1212–13 *ib, Old Windeshour* 1251 Ch, *Old Wyndesore* 1281 Fine, *Wyndesouere* 1377 ib

Windresores 1146 (copy) Sar, 1172, 4 P, *Windresoris* 1157 ib, *Windresor'* 1160, 1176 ib, *Windreshor', Windr'hores* 1185 RR, *Windreshora* l.12th *ReadingC*

Winlesor' 1156 P, *Winlesores* l.12th (13th) Gerv, *Wynlesore* 1306 Ipm

Wildesores 1162 P, *Wildeshoram* a. 1170 (c. 1200) *ClaudiusCix*

Veteri Windsore, Nova Wyndsore 1316 FA, *Windsor* 1618 *SpecCom*

'River-bank with a windlass', *v.* **windels, ōra**. The forms show interchange of *l-n-r* (*v.* Pt **3**), and early confusion of ōra with ōfer.

There are six certain examples of this name, the other five being Broadwindsor and Little Windsor Do, Windsor Pemb and Wa, and Winsor D and Ha. Two more possible examples are Windsor (Cu 442) and *Windesore Mill* (Db 541). The Berks name should probably be dissociated from Windlesham Sr, about 7 miles away, which may (like *wyndelescumb* BCS 721 in D) contain a personal name *Windel.

New Windsor was the name given to the settlement which grew up near Windsor Castle, built in the late 11th cent.

WINDSOR STREET-NAMES

Castle Hill, 1662 *RecOff*, *Castle Street* 1796 *WBR*.

Church St, 1826 *WBR*, cf. *semita ecclesiastica* 1317 *ECR*, *Churche Lane* 1422 *Windsor*. Modern Church Lane is at right-angles to Church St. Church St. was earlier *Fysschestrete* 1340 *ECR*, *Fish Street* 1584 *Windsor*, 1644, 1700 *PubLib*, *Fish Market Street* 1658 *WBR*.

Datchet Rd, cf. *Dachet Lane* 1552 *LRMB*, *Datchet Lane* 1736 *Windsor*, 1761 Rocque.

Goswell Rd and Lane, cf. *Gosewelde* e.Hy 3 *ECR*, 1274 Cl, 1319 *Windsor*, *Gosewelde Diche* 1349 *ECR*, 1368 *Windsor*, *Goseweldebrug* 1383 *ECR*, *Le Goswell Diche* 1484 ib, *Le Gosewell, Goswell Mede, Gret and Litill Goswell* 1548 *LRMB*, *Goswell Meade* 1583 *Windsor*, *Goswell Mead* 1587, 1622 ib, *meadow called the Gorsewells* 1722 *PubLib*. Possibly 'goose stream', but the final *-de* occurs in all the earlier spellings, and while an excrescent *-d* is not uncommon after *-l*, it is not normally found in names containing w(i)ella.

HIGH ST, *Altus Vicus* 1398 *ECR, High Street* 1550 *Windsor,* 1627 *PubLib*;
also known as *Marchetstrete* l.13th–e.14th (*ex. inf.* Mrs Bond).
OXFORD RD, earlier *Cliware Strete* 1319 *Windsor* ('Clewer Street').
PARK ST, *Cuthorse Well Street, Cuthorse Well alias Pound Street* 1583
Windsor, Pound St 1764 *PubLib*. Earlier *Mor Strate* Hy 3 *Windsor et freq*
with variant spellings *La More Strate, Le More Strate, Le Morestrete, Moore
Street, More Street* to 1589 *Dep. v.* mōr 'marsh', but a family surnamed
de La More had property here e.Hy 3 *ECR*; they may be named from
La More in Clewer (22), and the street from them.
PEASCOD ST, *Puscroftestrete* e.Hy *ECR, Pusecroftestrate* Hy 3 *ib, Puscrofte
Strate, Pescrofte Strat* Ed I *Windsor*. Forms with -*croft* as second el. are *freq*
in *Windsor* from 1308–1421. Other forms are *Pesecodstrete* 1335 *ECR,
Puscodstret, Pescod Strete* 1368 *Windsor, Puscotestrete* 1374, 1379 *ib, Pusecod-
strete* 1387 *ib, Pusecost Stret* 1404 *ib, Pesecod Stret* 1405 *ib, Pusecod Strete*
1409 *ib, Pescod-street* 1603, 1610 Ashmole, *Peascod Street* 1800 Eden. It
seems probable that the original *peos-croft, 'croft where peas are grown',
was changed by popular etymology to *peas-cod* 'pea-pod'.
RIVER ST, earlier *Beer Lane* 1622 *PubLib*. Cf. also *Niwestrate, Neuestrate*
Hy 3 *ECR, Berelane alias Newstrete* 1535 *ECR*.
ST ALBAN'S ST, 1806 *WBR*. from a house of the Duke of St Albans, earlier
Prestestret 1379 *Windsor, Prestestrete* 1399 *ib, Prestistrete* 1444 *ib, Preste
Streete* 1573 *SpecCom, Preeste St* 1684 *Windsor, Priest Street* 1709 Moulton.
SHEET ST, *Le Shet Strette* 1296 *Windsor, Schetstrate* l.13th *ib. La Shete Strete*
1306 *ib, Shetestrete* 1326 Brocas, *Shete Strate* 1342 *Windsor, Le Shete Stret*
1408 *ib, Shete Stret* 1449 *ib, Shyre Strete* 1454 *ib, Sheer-Street* 1503, 1510
Ashmole, *Sheete St alias Shere St* 1593 *PubLib, Sheirestreet* 1677 *Windsor,
Sheir Street* 1710 *ib, Sheet Street* 1761 Rocque. The street is named from
one of the open fields called *La Shete* 1296 *Windsor et freq* with variant
spellings *Le Shete, Le Schete* to 1419 *ib. Shete* occurs as the name of a wood
1313 Cl. Cf also *Le Longeshete, Le Shorteshete* 1411, *Longeschete, Shorteshete*
1429, *Le Schetys, Le Schetes* 1454, *Shootes* 1552, *The Shoots* 1605, *The
Shutes* 1667, 1727, all *Windsor, Shoots Bridge* 1822 OS. The name is WSaxon
scīete, a variant of scēat 'corner of land, angle, projecting piece of land',
perhaps used in the sense 'projecting piece of woodland'. The el. is common
in W. Surrey, *v.* Introd.
THAMES ST, 1777 *et seq ECR*, cf. *Tamestrate* 1307 *ECR, Thamys Strete*
1552 *LRMB*. Mrs Bond informs us that the 1307 name may not be a genuine
antecedent of the modern one, and that the modern Thames St was
Bisshopesstrete 1312 *ECR, Bisshopistrete* 1548 *LRMB*, also *Brigstrete* 1526
ECR, Brigestrete alias Bisshop Strete 1535 *ib*.

No early forms have been found for the following Windsor street-names: ADELAIDE
SQUARE AND TERRACE, ALBANY RD, ALBERT ST, ALEXANDRA RD, ALMA RD, ARTHUR
RD, BARRY AVE., BEAUMONT RD, BEXLEY ST, BOLTON AVE., CRESCENT AND RD (from
a Mr T. D. Bolton c. 1888, the street was *Bone Lane* in the 19th cent., *ex. inf.* Mrs
Bond), BOURNE AVE. AND LANE, BROOK ST, BRUNSWICK TERRACE, CLARENCE
CRESCENT AND RD, CLAREMONT RD, DAGMAR RD, DEVEREUX RD, DORSET RD,
DUKE ST, ELM RD, FRANCES RD, GLOUCESTER PLACE, GROVE RD, HELENA RD,
JAMES ST, OSBORNE RD, PARK ST, QUEEN'S RD AND TERRACE, RUSSELL ST, ST

LEONARD'S RD (*v.* 20), ST MARK'S RD AND PLACE, SPRINGFIELD RD, TEMPLE RD, THAMES AVE. AND SIDE, TRINITY PLACE (c. 1840, from Holy Trinity Church), VANSITTART RD (the Vansittarts owned Clewer manor 1720–1859), VICTOR RD, VICTORIA ST, WILLIAM ST, YORK PLACE AND RD.

Lost street-names include *Groupecountelane* 1315, *Crepecountelane* 1340, *Gropelane* 1344, 1347 (all *Windsor*), *Gropecontelane* 1396 *ECR*, *Grope Lane* 1826, 1840 *WBR* (a common medieval street-name of obscene meaning, *v.* YE 289, O 40 *infra* 172). Cf. also *Bolestake* 1400 *Windsor*, 1437 *ECR* ('bull-stake', near the market-place). Some of these are clearly 19th cent.

New Windsor

FROGMORE, 1573 *SpecCom et freq*; cf. *Frogemer'* 1224–5 *Ass* (p), the surname of a man concerned with land at Winkfield. If this surname derives from the place in Windsor, the name means 'frog pool', *v.* frogga, mere, and there is later confusion with mōr 'marsh' in the second el.

SHAW FM, *Sages*, *Schage* 1191 P (p), *Saghes* 1241 Cl, *Chawes* 1278 ib, *Shagh(e)* 1281 Pat, 1361 Ipm, *Shaw(e)* 1321 Cl, 1363 *RentSur*, *Schawe* 1353 *Windsor*, *Farme of Shawe* 1573 *SpecCom*, *Shawfarme* 1631 *Windsor*. 'Small wood', *v.* sceaga, and cf. the same name 263. SHAWLANE PEN, cf. *venelle vocat' Shaw Lane* ?Jas I *RentSur*, *Shaw Lane* 1800 Eden.

SPITAL, *Le Spitell* 1535 VE, *Le Spittill'* 1548 *LRMB*, *the Spittle* 1573 *SpecCom*, *Spitall* 1761 Rocque. Cf. *Spitelesbrig*, *Spitelesbrugg* 1251 Ch; *Le Spitulstrete* 1351 *PubLibDoc*, *Spittlestrete* 1554 *LRMB*; *Spitelhulle* 1339 *ECR*, *Spytelhulle* 1418 *Windsor*, *Spittill Hill Medowe* 1548 *LRMB*, *Spittle Hill*, *Spittle Hill Meadow* 1573 *SpecCom*, *Spittle Hills* 1818 *ECR*. ME spitel 'hospital' from which were named a bridge, street and hill. This was the site of a hospital for lepers, *v.* VCH II, 101–2.

UNDERORE (lost), *Undesoura* 1156–7 ReadingA, *Hunderora* 1142–84 (l.12th) *ReadingC*, *Vnderore*, *Underhore*, *Vnderora* 12th (l.12th) *ib*, *Underore* l.12th *ib et freq*, *Windelesore Vnderhore* 13th *ReadingC*, *Windsor Underore* 1539–40 ReadingA, *Underower Manor* 1595 *Windsor*, *Underhoure* 1682 *ib*. 'Under the slope', *v.* under, ōra. In VCH III, 66, it is stated that this manor probably included the land lying between Windsor and Eton, N.W. of the Castle and extending down to the Thames.

UPNOR (lost), *Vpenore* 1172, 1175 P (p), *Vppenore* 1175, 1190, 1202 ib (p), *Uppenor'* 1203 Cur (p), *Hupenora* 1203–4 *FF*, *Wpenorr* 1220 Fees (p), *Upponore* 1359 *RentSur*, *Uppenor* 1361 Ipm, *Uppenore* 1363 *RentSur*. 'Upon the slope', *v.* uppan, ōra, presumably in contrast to the preceding name.

ALBERT COTTAGE.   ARKLOW COTTAGE.   BACHELORS ACRE (not on map), *Batchlers Acre* 1629 *ECR*.   BOURNE DITCH, *v.* 8. BROAD WATER.   BROMLEY HILL, 1800 Eden.   BROOK'S CORNER, *Brookes Corner* 1800 Eden.   CAMBRIDGE LODGE.   CASTLEMEAD. THE COBLER, an island in the Thames.   CUTLER'S AIT, *v.* ēgeð. DININGROOM CLOSE, *Dining Room Close* 1848 *TA*; the 6″ map shows a small copse with pools, possibly fish-ponds.   DOUBLE GATES, 1822 OS.   FIREWORK AIT, *v.* ēgeð.   HERNE'S OAK†.   HOG COMMON, 1798 *WBR*, *Hogg Common* 1822 OS.   THE HUT. JUBILEE MOUNT.   KING EDWARD VII AVENUE.   KINGSCOT. KINGSMEAD.   KINGS WALDEN.   LIME AVENUE.   NEW COVER. NORTH LODGE.   ORWELL COTTAGE.   PADDOCKHILL COPSE, *Paddock Hill* 1848 *TA*.   PALATINE GATE.   PARK RIDE.   PICKLE-HERRING POND.   PLAIN RIDE.   PRINCE CONSORT'S DRIVE. QUEEN'S ACRE.   QUEEN ANNE'S GATE, MEAD, AND RD.   QUEEN ELIZABETH'S WALK.   QUEEN VICTORIA'S WALK.   ROMNEY CASTLE, ISLAND AND WEIR.   ROSEMEAD.   ROUND ORCHARD PEN.   STAR CLUMP, *Star Field* 1848 *TA*.   WINDSOR CASTLE was built at the end of the 11th cent.

Old Windsor

CRIMP HILL, cf. possibly *Crintone Hedge* Hy 3 *ECR*, *Crinton* 1359 InqMisc, *Grynton'* 1359 *RentSur*, *Crymptonmed* 1361 Ipm, *Crimp Field* 1842 *TA*. The forms are too varied and late for a certain etymology.

HAM FIELDS, *La Hamme* Hy 3 *ECR*, *Le Hamme* 1298 *ib*, 1317 *Windsor et freq* with variant spellings *La Hamme*, *Le Hame*; *Le Hammefield* 1483 AD, *v.* hamm; the area is in a loop of the Thames.

SNOW HILL, *Snoudon* 1321 Cl, *Snowedon* 1365 ib, *Snowedon'* Ed 3 *RentSur*, *Snowdon Hill* 1607 *Norden*, *Snow Hill* 1761 Rocque. 'Snow hill', *v.* snāw, dūn, identical with Snowdon, Caernarvonshire

---

† The site of the tree which features in Shakespeares's *The Merry Wives of Windsor*. The oak fell in 1863 (Kelly 265).

(NCPNW 238). *Hill* was later added and subsequently the original second el. dūn was dropped. Note also Snowdon (D 294, 311) and Snowden (YW **5**, 61).

TILEPLACE COTTAGES, THE TILERY, *cf. Tywele* (p), *Tiwel'* 1214–15 FF, *Tigelee* (p), *Tygele* 1214 Cur, *Twyle, Tyule* 1241 *Ass* (p), and *Tylehous* 1451 AD. The early name means 'wood or clearing where tiles are made' *v.* tigel, lēah and is identical with Tiley (PN Do 200) and Tyley (Gl **2**, 258), the latter *on tigel leage* 940 (12th) BCS 764. Professor Löfvenberg observes that such spellings as *Tywele, Twyle, Tyule* are due to influence from OFr *tiule, tuile* 'tile'.

WALTON (lost), *Walenton'* 1212 Fees, *Waletona* 1219 ib, *Waleton* 1361 Ipm. Probably 'farm of the serfs or Britons', *v.* walh, tūn and cf. the same name in Pt **2**.

AMERICAN CLUMP. BAILIFF'S LODGE. BARTLETT FM. THE BATTERY. BATTLE BOURNE, *v.* 7. BEAR'S RAILS, 1842 *TA*, BEAR'S RAILS GATE, *Beers Rayles Gate* 1607 *Norden*, BEAR'S RAILS DEER PEN AND POND (ME *reille*, *v.* 281, the 6″ map shows an enclosure with an earth bank round it). BEAUMONT R.C. COLLEGE. BEE-HIVE HILL. BISHOPS GATE, 1800 Eden, *Bushops Gate* 1607 *Norden*, BISHOPSGATE, BISHOPS GATE HO (Partly in Sr, *v.* Sr 125). BREAK-HEART HILL (*v.* 283). BUCKHURST PARK. BURFIELD LODGE, *Burr Field* 1842 *TA*. CELL FM. CHAPLAIN'S LODGE. CHURCH RD. CLAYHALL COTTAGES AND LANE, *Clayhall* 1822 OS. CON-SERVATORY COVERT. COOKE'S HILL, *Cookes Corner* 1607 *Norden*. CORK CLUMP. CUMBERLAND LODGE. DARK PLANTATION. DARK WOOD, 1800 Eden. DEEPSTROOD, 1657 *RecOffCat*, *Deepstroode Lawne* 1607 *Norden*, 'deep marsh', *v.* dēop, strōd, launde. DEER PEN. THE DELL. DUKE'S LANE. THE ELMS. FIR PLACE. FOREST GATE. FRANK'S PLANTATION. THE FRIARY, FRIARY FM AND COTTAGES. THE GALLOP. GORE PLANTATION. THE GRANGE. GRAVEL HILL, 1842 *TA*. GREAT MEADOW POND. GREENBROOM COVERT. THE GROVE. HAREWARREN CLUMP. HENHOUSE COVERT. THE HERMITAGE. HIGH BRIDGE, *Highe Bridge Land* 1607 *RentSur*. HIGH FLYER'S HILL. HILTON'S COVERT. HOLLYBUSH COTTAGES, *Holly Bush Corner* 1842 *TA*. HOLLY DRIVE. HOLLY GROVE, 1800 Eden, *Hollie Grove* 1607 *RentSur*. HORSE SHOE CLUMP (*Horse Shoe Piece* 1842 *TA*, from the shape). ISLE OF WIGHT POND, *Ile of Wighte* 1607 *Norden*, *v.*

284.   JOHNSON'S POND.   LEIPER HILL, 1800 Eden, *Lippery Hill and Lawne, Lipperye Pond* 1607 *Norden, Lippery Hill* 1729 *LHRS.* LIDDELL PLANTATION.   LONG PLANTATION.   THE LONG WALK, 1761 Rocque.   LORD NELSON P.H., *Nelson* 1822 OS.   LYNDWOOD.   MANOR COTTAGES AND FM.   MANOR HILL, 1800 Eden, 1842 *TA*, MANORHILL COTTAGES AND PLANTATION.   MARCHIONESS OF HERTFORD PLANTATION.   MEZEL HILL, 1822 OS, *Mazel Hill* 1800 Eden.   MENZIES PLANTATION.   MILL BUILDINGS.   MILL COVERT AND POND.   MILLER'S LANE.   MILLHILL PLANTATION (*Mill Bottom and Hill* 1842 *TA*).   MOUNT PLACE.   NEWMEADOW DEER PEN.   NORFOLK FM, NORFOLK FM COTTAGES.   OLD COVERT.   OLD WINDSOR WD, *Olde Windsore Wood* 1607 *Norden, Old Windsor Wood Common* 1800 Eden.   OUZELEY LODGE.   OX POND.   OXSHED COVERT.   PARK PLACE, 1822 OS.   PELLING PLACE AND COTTAGE.   PETER'S HILL, 1842 *TA*, PETERSHILL COPSE. POETS LAWN, 1800 Eden.   PRIMROSE HILL, 1800 Eden, PRIMROSE-HILL COVERT.   PRINCESS BEATRICE PLANTATION.   PRINCE CHRISTIAN PLANTATION.   PRINCE CONSORT'S PLANTATION AND WORKSHOPS.   PRINCE OF WALES DEERPEN, POND AND PLANTATION. THE PRIORY, *Priory Meadow* 1842 *TA*.   QUEEN ANNE'S RIDE. QUEEN VICTORIA'S AVENUE AND PLANTATION.   QUELMANS HEAD, QUELMAN'S HEAD RIDE, *Upper and Lower Quelmans* 1839 *TA* (North Winkfield).   RANGERS LODGE, 1800 Eden.   RICHARDSON'S LAWN. ROSEMEAD.   ROUND OAK (*Round Oak Piece* 1842 *TA*).   ROYAL LODGE.   RUSH POND.   RUSSEL'S POND AND PLANTATION, possibly from the family of Simon *Russel*, whose son is mentioned 1344 AD in connection with land in Old Windsor.   SANDY ARCH. SEYMOURS PLANTATION.   SHEET STREET RD, *v.* 28.   SLANS HILL, 1800 Eden, SLANSHILL DEER PEN.   SMITH'S LAWN, 1800 Eden, 1842 *TA*.   SOUTH LODGE.   SPRING HILL, 1800 Eden. SQUARE COVERT.   STRAIGHT RD.   TAYLOR'S BUSHES RIDE. TEMPLE HILL AND COTTAGES, *Temple* 1800 Eden, *Temple Hill and Mead* 1848 *TA*.   TIMBERLODGE HILL, *Timberlodge Hill, Timberlodg Lawne, Timberlodge South Lawne* 1607 *Norden, v.* launde. TOWER RIDE.   TRAFALGAR PLACE.   THE VINERY.   WATCH OAK, 1822 OS, WATCHOAK PLANTATION.   WEEDEN'S FIELD. WILD BOAR ENCLOSURE.   WILDERNESS.   WINDSOR BRIDGE, *pons de Windesore* 1275-6 RH, *Windesore Bridge* 1607 *Norden*.   WINDSOR GREAT PARK, 1761 Rocque, *parcum de Windes'* 1243 Cl, *Wyndesore Park* 1293 Fine, *Park of Wyndesore* 1313 ib, *The Greate Parke* 1601

Dep; Norden's map (1607) shows *The Litle Parke* in New Windsor, cf. also *Littelparke* 1526 *ECR*. WITHY BED. WOODCOCK PEN COVERT. WOODSIDE, WOODSIDE FM.

FIELD-NAMES

The principal forms in (*a*) are 1842 *TA* except for those dated 1848, which are from the *TA* for New Windsor, and those dated 1800, which are Eden; forms in (*b*) dated 1607 and 1761 are *Norden* and Rocque respectively.

(*a*) Alesworth Fd (*Eldeswurth'* 1214–15 *FF*, *Eldesworth* 1363 *RentSur*, 1487 AD, *Eldsworth* 1483 ib, *Aylesworth Field* 1659 *Windsor*, 'Eald's worð', identical with Aldsworth (Gl 1, 23, Sx 56), Awsworth (Nt 137)); Barebones Close and Hospital 1848 (first el. possibly a surname); Barley Leys Mdw 1848; Bells Mdw; Belvedere Park; Blue Gate Piece 1848; Brick Ground; Bridge Piece; Brook Fd; Buket Hill 1800 (*Bucket Hill* 1761); Bullbrooks Orchard; Bushey Leys; Calves Close; Careless Mdw; Clay Pit Ground; Clays; Copse Fd; Cow Mdw; Cow Stall 1848; Crown Fd; Cumberlain Plain; Cut Bridge Fd; Dog Kennel 1800; Elm Cottage Mdw; Flat Bottom; Forked Piece; Front Fd and Mdw; Garlic; Gascons (possibly *Gertstoneshull* 1267 Ch, *Graston* 1363 *RentSur*, *Garstones* 1413–14 AD, *Garstons* 1451 ib, *v.* gærs-tūn); The Grove (*Le Grove Pece* 1552 *LRMB*); Hand Post Mdw (i.e. 'sign-post'); Hatton Hill 1848; Hawkley Hill; Heath Fd; Highgate Fd; Hilly Close and Fd; Hollow Rd; Home Fd (*Le Homefeld* 1363 *RentSur*); Horn Ware (*Hornedwere* 1356 Fine, *Horned Were* 1500 *ECR*, *v.* hornede, wer); Horse Bridge Fd; Hospital Mdw; Kiln Fd; The Lagg (*v.* lagge); Lamas 1848 (*v.* 281); Lamp Acre (*Lampe Acre* 1548–9 *RentSur*, *v.* 285); Lawn Mdw (*The Lawne* 1607, *v.* launde); Lea Fd and Mdw (*La Leye* 1317 *ECR*, *v.* lēah); Lion Paddock (*Lions Green* 1761, *v.* leyne); Lodge Mead (*Logge* 1328 AD, *v.* loge); London Rides; Long Lands (*Langlandes Lodge* 1607); Love Lane Piece 1848; Lucern Fd (from the plant *Medicago sativa*); Malthouse Corner; Manor Grounds; Mill Ditch (cf. *Mullebrok* 1364 *ECR*, *Mullane* 1365 ib, *Mylbroke* 1552 *LRMB*, *v.* myln, brōc, lane); The Moat (*Le Mote* 1452 *ECR*, *Le Motelond* Hy 6, Ed 4 *RentSur*, The Moate, Moate Parke 1607, 1666 Ashmole, *v.* mote); Mounts Corner; The Nap (*Le Knappe*, *La Knaprude* l.13th–e.14th *ECR*, *La Knaipe* 1335 Cl, *Le Knappes* 1344 AD, *Le Knaprude* 1355 *Windsor*, *La Knappe* 1365 Cl, *Knaphurst* 1386 *ECR*, *v.* cnæpp, (ge)ryd(d), hyrst); Nest Fd; Nursery Ground; Oak Tree Mdw; Old Orchard; Ox Close 1848; The Paddock; Paircoats; Pidgeon House Close; The Pightles 1848 (*v.* pightel); Pit Fd (*The Pittsfields* 1688 Ashmole, Mrs Bond informs us that this was another name for *The Worth* in (*b*)); Plum Tree Hill, Pond Fd and Piece; Poor Allotment; Queens Mdw; Robert Croft; Roman Fd; Rough Pasture and Ground; Roundabout Fd (*v.* 281); Saw Pit Close and Fd (*Sawpit Hill* 1607); Shaddocks Mdw; Shepherds Mdw; Shoulder of Mutton Fd (*v.* 284); The Slip (*v.* slipe); Spelters Fd (*Spelthurst* 1313, 1336 *ECR*, 1363 *RentSur*, probably identical with Speld-hurst KPN 76, for which there are some forms in *Spelt-*, and which is considered to be a compound of *speld* 'splinter, piece of wood' and hyrst); Spoil Bank; Spring Elms; Stag Mdw 1848; Stags Nest Fd; Stocks Grove Lane; Stumps; Three Cornered Piece; Three Sisters; Triangular Piece; Underdown; Vicars Fd; The Walls (*Le Walles* 1363 AD, *v.* wall); Welley Close.

(b) *Abbotesbury* 1369 *ECR* (*v.* burh 'manor', first el. possibly a surname); *Amberlond(e)* 1344 *ECR* (*v.* amore 'bunting', land); *Archeresryde* 1421 AD, *Archerryde* 1451 ib, *Archersryde* 1487 ib (*ryde* occurs in a number of names in Windsor, alternating with *rydynge* in the case of *Leeryde infra*; some of these have surnames, i.e. Archer, Shepherd and probably Bishop, as first el., and it is probable that *ryde* is here used of a division of a royal forest in the charge of a particular forester, a use not on record in ME, but *v.* NED *ride* sb[1] 1c and *riding* vbl. sb. 2b; this word may have been replaced by *walk*, which occurs in later names in Windsor Forest; *ride* 'a road through a wood' is also possible, but does not accord so well with the first elements of these names); *Ascroft* 1299 Cl (*v.* æsc, croft); *Asseresrude* 1359 InqMisc; *Assherugeshede* 1321 Cl, *Assheruggeslud* 1365 ib, *Asshenggeslad* Ed 3 *RentSur* (probably 'ash ridge', with an uncertain final el.); *Aylmerestrode* 14th VCH III ('Æðelmǣr's strōd'); *Barndestone* 1344 AD ('burnt stone', *v.* berned, stān); *Le Barredich* Hy 3 *ECR*, *v.* barre, dic, possibly, as elsewhere, referring to a defensive earthwork round the town); *Bencroft* l.13th–e.14th *ECR* (*v.* bēan, croft); *Benytestrete* 1365 Cl (*v.* strǣt, first el. probably the surname *Bennet*); *Bere* 1275–6 RH (*v.* bǣr[2]); *Berkele* 1248 Ch ('birch wood', *v.* beorc, lēah, identical with Berkeley Gl 2, 211–12, Berkley So); *Le Bernhawe* 1319 *Windsor* (*v.* bere-ærn, haga[1]); *Berneforde* 1327–8 *SR* (p); *Beterlake* l.13th *ECR*, 1326 Brocas, 1363 *RentSur*, 1431 *Windsor* (*v.* lacu, first el. possibly identical with that of Betterhale O 261–2, perhaps a bird-name); *Bissopesok* l.13th–e.14th *ECR* (an acre in Ham, 'bishop's oak'); *Blackheath* 1605 *SpecCom*; *Bolbacote ib*; *Bradelegh* Hy 3 *ECR*, *Bradley* 1473 *ib* (*v.* brād, lēah, a common name); *Brendebrigge* 1431 *Windsor* ('burnt bridge', *v.* berned, brycg); *Brocwod* 1274 Cl (*v.* brōc, brocc, wudu); *Brodeford* 1321, 1365 Cl (*v.* brād, ford); *La Brokhull* 1321 Cl (*v.* brōc, hyll); *Bullockesloke* 1322 *ECR* (*v.* loc 'river-barrier', first el. a surname); *Le Burgfeld* l.13th *ECR*, *Burghfelde* 1421 AD, *Burghfeld* 1487 *Windsor* (*v.* burh, feld); *Burrowstrood* 1607 (*v.* strōd); *Bushe Readinge* 1605 *SpecCom* (*v.* ryding); *Le Busshystrode* c. 1409 Brocas ('bushy marsh', *v.* strōd); *Le Butme* l.13th, 1426 *ECR* (a field in Ham, *v.* bytme); *Butter-Stoakes* 1510 Ashmole; *Byshoppisryde* 1451 AD (*v. supra*); *Cal(e)weshullesend* 1251 Ch (*v.* calu, hyll, ende[1]); *Catch Crofte* 1573 *SpecCom*; *Catelrydyng* Hy 6 *RentSur* (*v.* cat(t)el, second el. either ryding or the word discussed *supra*); *Le Cawsey Ende* 1552 *LRMB* (*v.* caucie, ende[1]); *Cherrie Close* 1631 *Windsor*; *Clapeshurst* 1319–20 *AE* (*v.* hyrst, possibly for *Knaphurst supra* 33, which is *Klaphurst* 1452 *ECR*); *Combery Hill* 1607; *Contowtesbreche* Hy 6 *RentSur*, *Buntowteysbreche* Ed 4 *RentSur* (*v.* brēc); *The Cote* 1548–9 *RentSur* (*v.* cot); *La Crikeledeock* 1321 Cl (final el. āc, cf. Cricklewood Mx, which has the same first element; the suggestion in Mx 58 of a participial adjective from the dialect *crickle* 'to bend, to give way' would be appropriate for this name); *Crippynges* 1400 *ECR*, *Crippinge* 1607 (probably from a surname); *Crokkerescroft* 1404, *Crockerescroft*, *Crockereshaw*

1413–14, *Crokkerscroft* 1451, *Crokkers* 1487 all AD (*v.* croft, haga[1], first el.
probably the surname *Crocker*); *Crucheputtes* 1323 ECR (*v.* crūc[3], pytt);
Daylese 1365 Pat ('dairy pasture', *v.* dey, lǣs); *The Deane* 1548–9 *RentSur*
(*v.* denu); *Dennyslond* Hy 6 *Rent Sur*(first el. probably a surname); *Depindale*
Hy 6, Ed 4 *RentSur* (possibly from dēop, in, dæl); *Doe Fall Hill* 1607; *La
Doune* 1326 Brocas (*v.* dūn); *Doueresfeld, Doverescrofte* l.13th–e.14th ECR
(*v.* croft, first el. a surname); *Eldelonde* 1348 ECR (*v.* (e)ald, land); *Eletewod'*
1270 Cl; *Elias's Spittle* 1719 Ashmole (a mineral spring, also known as
St Peter's Well); *Estcroft* 1270 Cl; *Esthurst* 1313 ib, 1412 *Windsor*, 1548–9
RentSur (*v.* ēast, hyrst); *Foulsong* 1365 Pat; *Fox Earthe Hill* 1607; *Gospoole-
hill* 1607; *Grayescroft* 1319–20 AE (first el. probably a surname); *Hadnes*
1607 *SpecCom*; *Haggeldern* 1306 ECR, *Hagelderne* 1312 ib, *Hageldern* 1315
ib (second el. possibly ellern 'elder-tree'); *La Hale* Hy 3 ECR (*v.* h(e)alh);
Halfe Hilles 1607 *SpecCom*; *Harewykesthorn* 1355 *Windsor*; *Le Haye* Hy 3
ECR (*v.* (ge)hæg); *Le Heghefeld* 1355 *Windsor*, *Hyfeld* 1359, 1363 *RentSur*
(*v.* hēah, feld); *Herne* 1327–8 SR (p) (*v.* hyrne); *High Grove* 1607; *Holecroft*
1321 Cl (*v.* hol, croft); *Holmes Hill* 1607; *Horsellrydes* 1451 AD (*v.* 34, a
family surnamed *de Horshull* appears 1315 ECR); *Le Hulle* 1398 ECR (*v.*
hyll); *Hunysled* 1264 Ch (*v.* slæd); *Le Hurte* (*cultura* called) 1353 ECR;
Hyrstlond Hy 6 *RentSur* (*v.* hyrst, land); *Islipps Hill* 1552 LRMB (Thom.
Islep appears in 14th-cent. deeds in ECR); *Key Close* 1605 *SpecCom*;
Kingesfrid Hy 2 (c. 1240) Abingdon, *Kyngefrede* 1365 Pat (*v.* cyning, fyrhð);
Kybescrofte Hy 3 ECR, *Kybescroft* 1326 Brocas (Wm. *Kibe* appears e.Hy 3
ECR); *Leeryde* 1417, *Leerydynge* 1421, *Lyryd* 1487 all AD (cf. *Archeresryde
supra*, first el. probably a surname); *Linghams Gate and Thick* 1607; *Loding-
pol* 1275–6 RH (*v.* pōl); *Langcroftes* 1330 ECR, *Longcroft* 1359 InqMisc,
1418 *Windsor*; *Longefur* 1321 *Windsor*, *Longe Fere, Shorte Fere* 1552 LRMB
(*v.* furh); *Lordes Wood* 1607 *SpecCom*; *The Lowe Ground* 1607; *Lydecroft*
1368 AD, 1378 Pat (*v.* hlid[1], hlid[2], croft); *Le Lymost* 1388 ECR, *Lymhostes*
1404, 1452 *ib* ('lime kilns', identical with Limehouse Mx 150); *Le Lynche*
1325 ECR (*v.* hlinc); *Madgrove* 1512 AD, 1659 *Windsor*; *Mantel* 1321 Cl,
Mancell c. 1409 Brocas (possibly *mantle* 'cloak' as in Freemantle Ha
(DEPN)); *Mapeldorerugge* 1321 Cl (*v.* mapuldor, hrycg); *Le Marchale* 1314
Windsor; *Margaret Acre* 1573 *SpecCom*, *Marget Acre* 1631 *Windsor*; *Marlyng-
pittes* 1363 *RentSur*, *Le Marling Pettes* 1429 *Windsor* (*v.* marling, pytt);
Marserude 1359 InqMisc, *Marsuryde* 1359 *RentSur* (*v.* mersc, rȳd); *Merhurst*
1351 Pat (*v.* mere, (ge)mǣre, hyrst); *La Mershe* 1314 ECR, *Le Mersshe* 1363
RentSur (*v.* mersc); *Middelhul* 1313 ECR ('middle hill'); *Minoll Woode*
1607; *Mistle Pond and Lawne* 1607; *Muchelehull* 1306 ECR (*v.* micel, hyll);
Munday Close 1666 Ashmole; *Nazeing* 13th VCH III; *Northfeld* 1363 AD,
1487 *Windsor*; *Northwode* 1369 ECR; *Nothurst* 1321 Cl, *Nuthurst* 1365 ib
(*v.* hnutu, hyrst, identical with Nuthurst La, Sx, Wa); *Le Oldhawes* 1392
ECR, *Old Hawes* 1449, 1684 *Windsor*, 1708 PubLib, *The Old Hawse* 1573
SpecCom ('old enclosures', with ME plural of haga[1]); *Olderuding* c. 1409
Brocas (*v.* ryding); *Outhlesham* 1346, 1410 ECR, *Poughtlesham* 1419 *ib*
(*v.* hamm); *Overton* 1345 *ib* (*v.* ofer, tūn, possibly DB *Ortone*, *v.* 19); *The
Parocke* 1607 (*v.* pearroc); *Perland* 1533, 1536 BM; *Pidwell* 1510 Ashmole;
Pinneshok 1251 Ch (Pinn's hōc'); *The Pleck* 1607 (*v.* plek); *Pokelane* 1310

ECR, Pukelane 1312 *ib, Powkenlane* 1449 *ib* (*v.* pūca, lane); *Portmanlese* 1313 *ECR* (*v.* lǣs, cf. Port Meadow O 22); *Pokepirye* 1345 *ECR* (*v.* pūca, pirige); *Porushe Lawne, Porush Hill* 1607; *Puckottsgate* 1552 *Windsor, Puckets-Gate* 1577 *ib, Puttock's Gate* 1604 Ashmole; *Pylle* 1392 Cl (p) (*v.* pyll); *Quenegraue* 1326 Brocas, *Quenegrove* 1354 AD (*v.* cwēn, grāf); *Rahurst* 1363 *RentSur* (*v.* hyrst); *Le Redhull* 1368 *ECR* (*v.* rēad, hyll); *Reineham* 1248 Ch (*v.* hamm, first el. possibly a pers.n. *Regna, v.* DEPN *s.n.* Rainford); *Ridyngmede* 1465 *ECR; Le Rowehulle* 1306 *ECR, La Rowehull* 1365 Cl (*v.* rūh, hyll); *La Rude* 1296, 1306 *ECR* (*v.* rȳd); *La Rudingge* Hy 3 *ECR, Le Rudyngg* 1328 AD, *Le Rudynge* 1359 *RentSur* (*v.* ryding); *La Rugge* 1235, 1238, 1240 Cl, *Ruges* 1275–6 RH, *The Rudges* 1607 (*v.* hrycg); *Rushie Lawn* 1607; *Ruttinge Place* 1607; *Sayesrudyng'* 1319–20 *AE* (*v.* ryding, first el. possibly the surname *Saye* (Reaney 284)); *Shepardesryde* 1451 AD (*v. Archeresryde supra*); *Schepgrove* 1392 *ECR, Shepgrove* 1439 *ib* ('sheep grove'); *Shirch* 1321 Cl; *Shopp Readinge* 1605 *SpecCom* (*v.* sc(e)oppa, ryding); *Skirrets Holl* 1607; *Le Skoleacre* 1375 *Windsor* ('school acre', perhaps a charitable endowment); *Sleyfeld* 1346 *ECR, Le Sleyghfeld* 1403 *Windsor, Slyfeld* 1466 *ib* (*v.* feld, first el. possibly slege, but cf. *Buttons Sleyes* in Blewbury 153); *Somerheyse* Ed 4 *RentSur* (*v.* sumor, (ge)hæg); *Sondheyse* Hy 6 *ib* (*v.* sand, (ge)hæg); *Sortebuttes* 1306 *ECR* (*v.* sc(e)ort, butte); *The Standinge* 1607 (*v.* standing); *Stanhill'* 1241 *Ass* (p), *Stonhull* 1326 Brocas (*v.* stān, hyll); *Stihelhalfaker* l.13th–e.14th *ECR* (*v.* stigel, healf, æcer); *Stonilonde* 13th *ECR* (*v.* stānig, land); *Le Stonputte* Hy 3 *ECR, Le Stanputtes* 1305 *Windsor* (*v.* stān, pytt); *Stubhalnaker* 1342 *ECR* (*v.* stubb, healf, æcer); *Suthcroft* 1214–15 *FF* (*v.* sūð, croft); *Trinitie Close* 1573 *SpecCom; La Valeye* 1299, 1325 *ECR, Valeye* 1365 *ib* (*v.* valee); *West Hawe* 1607 (*v.* haga[1]); *Westhurst* 1313 Cl (cf. *Esthurst supra*); *Wodebere* 1275–6 RH, *La Wodegrene* 1281 Pat, *Wodehawe* 1409 Dugdale (*v.* wudu, bǣr[2], grēne[2], haga[1]); *Woodbridge-lane* 1666 Ashmole, 1737 *WBR; Le Worthe* 1278 *et seq Windsor,* 1359 InqMisc, *The Worth* 1727 *Windsor, Worth* 1777 *ECR* (*v.* worð, this was an open field, there were also places called *Estworth* and *Northworth* in *Underore* which were distinct from *The Worth,* cf. *Est Woerthe* 1301 *ECR, Astworthe, Northworthe* 1339 *ib*); *Wowefurlong* 1306 *ECR* (*v.* wōh); *Wydestrode* 1267 Ch, *Widestrode* 1275–6 RH (*v.* wid, strōd); *Wyntefen* 1267 Ch (*v,* fenn, first el. possibly the pers.n. *Winta*); *Wythiham* 1359 *RentSur* (*v.* wiðig, hamm).

Winkfield

Winecanfeld 942 (c. 1200) BCS 778
Wenesfelle 1086 DB
Winicfelda, Wecenesfeld Hy I (c. 1200) *ClaudiusCix, Winegefeld'* 1167 P, *Wineche(s)feld'* 1176 ib (p), *Winekefeld* a. 1170 (c. 1200) *ClaudiusCix, Wynekfeld* 1316 FA
Wenegefeld' 1171 P, *Wenekefeld* 1220 Fees (p), 1224–5 *Ass,* 1294, 1327 *SR*

Wenkefeld 1185 RR, *Wenckefeud* 1249 Ch, *Wenkefeld* 1284 *Ass*
Winkefeld 1224–5 *Ass, Winkefeud, Wynkefeld', Wynkefeud'* 1284 *ib*,
   Wynkefeld 1347 Pat, 1359 Fine, 1517 D Inc
Wunekefeld' 1242–3 Fees
Wekenefeld' 1263 Cl
Wymekefeud 1275–6 RH
Woenekfeld 1329 AD
Wyngefeld 1359 Pat, *Wyngfield* 1601 *Dep*
Winkfield 1685 *Windsor*

'Wineca's open land', *v.* feld. DEPN suggests that this pers.n.,
which would be a diminutive of *Wine,* occurs also in Winkton Ha
and Winkleigh (D 373).

BUNTINGBURY (?lost), *Bontyngbury alias Bentyngbury* 1359 Pat,
Buntyngbury 1491 *PubLib(Bray),* Hy 8 *RentSur, Buntingbury Brocas*
1548 *LRMB, Buntingbury* Jas I *SpecCom,* c. 1840 *TA.* Probably
'Bunta's fortified manor-house', *v.* -ing-, burh. This OE pers.n. is
suggested as the first el. of Benton (D 30) and Buntingford (Hrt 182),
and evidence for a strong name *Bunt* is discussed Sx 271. Alternatively,
the first el. might be the bird-name bunting, which DEPN suggests
as the first el. of Buntingford. This would give a compound like those
discussed in Elements **I**, 61. For *Brocas* cf. VCH III, 74, 'The estate
known as Buntingbury...also formed part of the estate of Sir John
Brocas and is still annexed to the manors of Clewer Brocas and
Dedworth'.

CHAWRIDGE MANOR FM, *(on) ceawan hrycges (hagan)* 942 (c. 1200)
BCS 778, *Charriage Lane* 1800 Eden, *Chawridge Mead* 1839 *TA.*
'Ceawa's ridge', *v.* hrycg. For the pers.n. *v.* Challow, Pt **2**.

CRANBOURNE, CRANBOURNE CHASE (latter in New Windsor), *(riuulus
de) Crampeburn'* 1279 HMC Var Coll I, *Cranbourn* 1337 Pat, *Chasee
de Cranborne* 1554 *LRMB, Wood called Cramborne Woode, Chase
called Cramborne Chase, Cramborne Lodge* 1601 *Dep, Cramborne
Shace, Cramborne Woode* 1607 *SpecCom, Cranburn Park and Wood*
1761 Rocque, *Cranbourne Park and Chase* 1800 Eden. 'Brook
frequented by cranes or herons', *v.* cran, burna. The same name
occurs in Do and Ha.

FOLIEJON PARK: cf. *Folye Jon* 1315 Pat, *Foly Johan* 1317 ib *et freq*
with variant spellings *Folye Johan, Folie Johan;* (park of) *Foliejohan*

1359 Pat, (manor of) *Folyjon* 1367 ib, *Folly John Park* 1525 *Windsor*, *Folli-John Parke* 1591 Ashmole. There is nothing to add to the discussion of this name in Wa 385. Land here was granted to John de Drokenesford, Bishop of Bath and Wells, in 1302, and in 1315 the estate was taken into the king's hands as security for the discharge of the Bishop's debts. It seems fair to conclude that *folly* is here used of an extravagant building, perhaps one on which John de Drokenesford spent money.

In the first reference (1315 Pat) the manor is described as 'the manor of — *Belestre*, — commonly called Folye Jon'. This early name is identical with Bellister Nb. It is a French name, probably meaning 'pleasant sojourn', from bel² and the infinitive *ester* 'to stand, to stop, to stay', a type of formation paralleled by Belvoir Lei, from *bel* and the infinitive *vedeir*; v. M. Gelling, 'The Place-Name Bellister', *Namn och Bygd* 45 (1958), pp. 170–1. DEPN (4th ed.) suggests that the second el. is not the infinitive *ester*, but the noun *estre* 'place'.

HIREMERE (lost), *Hyremere* 1315, 1317 Pat, 1318 Cl, 1359 *RentSur*, *Hiremere* 1318 Pat, 1321 Cl, 1359 Pat, Fine, InqMisc. The second el. is **mere** 'pool'; the first looks like OE hȳr 'hire, wages', which might be used in a p.n. in the sense 'payment contracted to be made for the temporary use of something' (BTSuppl). This may be the first el. of Harbottle Nb. *Hiremere* is associated with Foliejon (*supra*) in most of these references. It is stated in VCH (III 87) to be mentioned in the bounds of Winkfield in the 10th cent., but the pool which occurs there is called *hrytmes mere*, and it is very doubtful whether the two can be identified.

SANDPIT GATE, 1607 *Norden*, cf. *San(d)puttes* 1279 HMC Var Coll I, *Le Sandpittes* 1363 *RentSur*, self-explanatory, v. sand, pytt.

STROOD FM AND LANE, cf. *La Brodestrode* 1321, 1365 Cl, *Ruysshirstrod'*, *Le Brodestrod'*, *Brodestrode* 1359 *RentSur*, *Brodestrod* 1374 *ECR*, *Rysschestrode* 1416 *ib*, *Russhystode*, *Broodstrodes*1587 *Dep*, *Rushyestroode Meade*, *Rushystrode* Jas I *SpecCom*, *Long and Broad Strouds* 1839 *TA*, v. brād, strōd; *rushy*, in the sense 'covered with rushes', is first recorded in NED c. 1586.

SWINLEY LODGE AND PARK, (æt) *Swin lea* 942 (c. 1240) BCS 778, *Swinleia* a. 1170 (c. 1200) *ClaudiusCix*, *Swinele* 1224 Cur, *Suinesl'*

1224 (c. 1250) Bract, *Swynlegh'* 1284 *Ass, Swinley Lodg* 1607 *Norden, Swinley Lodge Star* 1800 Eden. 'Pig-wood', *v.* swīn, lēah.

ABBEY FM. ABURY LANE. ALLSMOOR LANE, *Alsmore Enclosure* 1800 Eden. ANAVON. ASCOT COTTAGE, GATE, PLACE AND PRIORY, ASCOTGATE COTTAGE, *v.* 88–9. ASH PIT. BADGERS BRIDGE, BADGERSBRIDGE RIDE. BARNHILL, *Barn Mead* 1839 *TA.* BARTON LODGE. BISHOP'S LANE, 1729 *LHRS.* BLACKMOOR STREAM, *v.* 7. BLACKSMITH'S HILL. BLANE'S ALLOTMENT, FM AND RIDE, *Blanes* 1848 *TA.* BLUE LION P.H. BOG LANE, *Bug Lane* 1848 *TA.* BOWDEN'S RIDE. BOX FM. THE BRACKENS. BRACKNELL BRIDGE. BRANTS BRIDGE. BRAZIER LANE. BRIGHT'S ALLOTMENT. BROCKHILL HO, *v.* Brock Hill in Warfield. BROOK FM, *Brook Field and Meadow* 1839 *TA.* BROOM COVERT. BROWN'S FM. BURLEIGH, *v.* Burley Bushes in Sunninghill 89. BUTTERSTEEP ALLOTMENT, BUTTERSTEEP HILL, *Buttersteepe* 1607 *Norden, Buttersteep Hills* 1800 Eden. CHAVEY DOWN, 1761 Rocque, *Chavey Down Lodge* 1800 Eden, CHAVEYDOWN COTTAGES, FM, POND, RD, CHAVEY LAWN. CHAWRIDGE BOURNE, GORSE ¦AND LANE, *v.* 37. CHILSTON. CHURCH LANE. COACH RD. COOPER'S BRIDGE. CRANBOURNE COURT AND HALL, CRANBORNE CORNER, *v.* 37. CRISPIN P.H. CROUCH LANE, 1761 Rocque, *Croutch Lane* 1800 Eden, CROUCHLANE FM; cf. *Croyslan* 1462 *ECR, v.* crois, crūc³. CUCKOO PEN, *v.* O 438. DAIRY FM. DEADMAN'S TREE, 1729 *LHRS.* THE DELL. DENE COPSE. DEVIL'S LANE, *Devels Lane* 1761 Rocque. DUKE'S HILL, DUKESHILL ALLOTMENT AND NURSERY. EARLYWOOD, *Early Wood* 1761 Rocque, cf. Erlwood Ho in Sr, less than a mile away, which was *Early Wood* 1823 (Sr 154), EARLYWOOD CORNER, FM AND LODGE. EAST LODGE. ELM LODGE. EMMET'S WD. ENGLE-MERE POND, *Inglemoare Pond* 1607 *Norden, Englemoor Pond* 1761 Rocque, 1800 Eden. FERNHILL, FERNHILL COTTAGE AND FM, *Fernehill* 1607 *Norden, Fern Hill* 1761 Rocque. FERN HILL, FERNHILL ALLOTMENT (these two are not near preceding places). FLEUR DE LIS P.H. FORESTER'S HILL. FOREST FM AND LODGE. FOUNTAINS HILL. FOX COVERT. GOATERS HILL, *Goathurst Hill* 1816 OS, *v.* gāt, hyrst. GOLD CUP HOTEL P.H. GOOD-WIN'S FM, William *Godwyne* appears 1327–8 *SR.* GORSE PLACE. THE GRANGE. GRAVELPIT RIDE. GREEN LANE, 1839 *TA.* GREEN RIDE. THE GROVE. GROVE LODGE (not near preceding place). HANDPOST FM, *Hand Post Meadow* 1839 *TA*, referring to a sign-post. HARMANS WATER, 1761 Rocque, 1848 *TA*, *Hermans Water* 1800 Eden. HATCHET LANE, 1761 Rocque (*v.* hæcc-geat). HAWKSHILL WOOD, *Hawkes Hill* 1607 *Norden.* HEATH COTTAGES. HEATHERDOWN. HEATHFIELD. THE HERMITAGE. HIGH CHIMNEYS. HODGE LANE, 1729 *LRHS.* THE HOLLIES. HOLLOW OAK. HOLLY WALK, 1761 Rocque. HOME FM. HORSE AND GROOM P.H. HORSEGATE RIDE. HURSTLEIGH. ICEHOUSE HILL. IRON COVERT (possibly hyrne). KILBY'S FM. KILN COVERT, *Kiln Field* 1848 *TA*. KINGSLAND. KING'S RIDE, KINGSRIDE. LAMBROOK. THE LARCHES. LAVENDER FM, *Lavender Field* 1848 *TA*. LAWN HILL, cf. *The Lawne* 1607 *Norden*, *v.* launde. LILYHILL FM, *Lillyhill Park* 1848 *TA*, cf. *Lillilond* 15th *LHRS*. LIME AVENUE. LOCKS RIDE. LONG GROVE COPPICE. LONG HILL, 1761 Rocque, *Longe Hill* 1607 *Norden.* LOVEL DENE, LOVELHILL, LOVELHILL FM, *Lovelshill*, *Lovels Lane* 1800 Eden, the grant of 18 acres in Winkfield to Henry *Luvel*, the queen's cook, is recorded 1249 Ch. MAIDEN'S GREEN, 1839 *TA*, *Maiden Green* 1761 Rocque, 1800 Eden. MARTIN'S HERON, *Martins Herron Park* 1800 Eden, *v.* hyrne. MARTIN'S LANE. MEADOW BANK. MEADOWSCROFT. MILL POND. MILL RIDE. MILTON'S FM. MONTAGUE COTTAGE. MUSHROOM CASTLE. NEW COVERT. NEW ENGLAND HILL, 1761 Rocque, 1790 Pride (*v.* 284). NEWINGTON HO. NORTH LODGE (3 examples). NORTH STREET, 1800 Eden, *North Streete, North Strete* Jas I *SpecCom.* NORTHSTREET BRIDGE. NUT COVERT. OLD GROVE. ORCHARD LEA. PADDOCK WD, 1839 *TA*. PARK FM, *Park Mead* 1839 *TA*. PARKER'S LANE. PARSON'S RIDE. PASSMORE'S COTTAGE AND PLANTATION. PENNY HILL, 1607 *Norden*, 1800 Eden. PIGEONHOUSE LANE, *Pidgeon's House Lane* 1761 Rocque, *Pigeon House Close* 1839 *TA*. PLAISTOW GREEN, PLAISTOWGREEN FM, *Le Pleistoue* 1331 *ECR*, *Plastow Green* 1839 *TA*, *v.* pleg-stōw 'sport place'. PLANNERS FM. POPLARS FM. POPLAR VIEW. PRINCE CONSORT'S GATE. PRINCE OF WALES P.H. PUMP ROOM, PUMPROOM COPSE. PUMP ROUGH (not near preceding places). QUEEN'S DIAMOND JUBILEE PLANTATION. QUEEN VICTORIA'S TREE. RALPH'S RIDE. RAMSLADE, 1761 Rocque, *Ramslades* 1658 *PubLib.* RANELAGH SCHOOL. RAPLEY FM AND LAKE, *Rapleys Bottom and Farm* 1800 Eden. RED LODGE. ROSY BOTTOM, *Rosey Bottom* 1842 *TA* (Old Windsor). THE ROUGH (2 examples). ROUND

Copse. Row Fm. Royal Hunt P.H. Running Horse P.H. Ryemead, 1839 *TA*, Ryemead Lane. St. Ronans. School Allotment, School Allotment Ride. Scott's Hill. Skewball Arch. Slade Pond. Somerton Ho and Lodge, Sym. *Somerton* appears 1327–8 *SR*. South Forest, South Forest Cottage. Springhill. Squirrel P.H. Starch Copse. Stella Lodge. Surrey Hill, *Surry Hills* 1800 Eden, *Surry Hill* 1816 OS (on the county boundary). Tally Ho P.H. Thornhill Allotment. Tower Hill, 1761 Rocque, 1790 Pride, *New Towre* 1607 *Norden*. Tower Court. Tow's Bourne, *Tows Bone Piddle* 1839 *TA*. Vale Lodge. The Warren (2 examples). Westfield Lo. Weycroft Copse and Cottage, *Wycroft Mead* 1839 *TA*. Whitmoor Bog, *Whitemoare Woode* 1607 *Norden*, *Whitmore Bogg*, 1800 Eden, cf. Blackmoor Stream 7. Whitmoor Bog Cottages. Windsor Hill, 1839 *TA*. Windsor Ride. Winkfield Lodge and Place. Winkfield Plain, 1761 Rocque, 1800 Eden, *Winkfield Plaine* 1685 *Windsor*, this is a road on the boundary of Windsor Forest; for plain in the sense of open ground adjoining a forest *v*. O 389. Winkfield Row, 1761 Rocque, 1790 Pride. Winkfield Street, 1761 Rocque, 1800 Eden, *Wynkefeldstret* 1432 *ECR*. Winklands. Wishmoor Cross, *v*. Sr 155. Wood End, Woodend, Woodend Ride. Woodside, 1839 *TA*, Woodside Ho. Woodstock. Worlds End, 1848 *TA*, this is near the western edge of the parish, but not actually on the boundary. Worldsend Bridge and Hill.

FIELD-NAMES

The principal forms in (*a*) are 1839 *TA* (for North Winkfield), except for those marked S, which are 1848 *TA* (for South Winkfield); forms dated Jas I are *SpecCom*, 1607 *Norden*, 1729 *LHRS* and 1761 Rocque.

(*a*) Baiting Fd (possibly referring to good pasture); Barrow Moors; Barrow Fd S; Bears Moor S; Bee Mdw; Belle Fd; Berry Croft; Black Lands; Bog Fd S; Brank Fd S; Brick Close; Broad Lane Mead S; Broad Mead S; Broadleys; Brockbridge; Brock Hill, Brook Hill; Burt Fd S; Burywell; Bush Fd S (cf. *Wynkfeldbussehes* 1538 *RentSur*, *v*. busc); But Fd S; Clay Pieces; Common Hill; Coppice Ground S; Corporation; Court Fd (cf. *Courtnoll Heathe* 1607, *Courtmill Heath* 1729); Cowhouse Ground; Cuckoo Nest (*v*. 282); Dancer's Piece; Dane Fd S; Deer Paddock S; Drying Ground; Durden; Farr Mdw S; Five Ponds (also 1761); Folds, Folds Lane, Old Folds; Fry Fd S; Furze Hill S; Furzy Piece S; Game Fd S; Garden Fd S; Gaskers Hill (*Garstoneshull* 1374 *ECR*, *Gastons Hill* Jas I, cf. Thom.

de la Garston, 1327–8 *SR*, *v.* gærs-tūn); Gilbert Mdw S; Green Fd; Grove; Hatches (cf. *Cristina de Hecca* 1327–8 *SR*, *v.* hæc(c)); Heathinnings Close (*v.* hǣð, inning); Heath Pasture; Herriott; Hilly Ground; Holly Grove (cf. *Hollylayes* Jas I); Homefield S, Home Mdw S; Horselease, Horse Mdw; Howell Close S; Howells Fd; Hurleywick; Kiln Ground and Pightle (*v.* pightel); King's Breeches (*Breeches* 1729, *v.* brēc); Knee Fd S; Lands Down; Laneways; Law Haw S; Lodge Hill; Long Slip (*v.* slipe); Mill Fd; Mowed Mdw; Mutton Fd S; My Lady's Mdw; Nest Fd S; Nettle Hill (*Net(t)elyhull'* 1359 *RentSur*, *v.* hyll; *nettly* is not recorded until 1825); Newlands (Jas I); No Man's Land (*v.* 284); Northbrook Mdw (cf. Southbrook Mdw *infra*); North Croft; Nursery; Old Sarah (a dialect name for the hare); Oxford Mdw; Parsonage Close; Pear Tree Ground; Picked Innings (*v.* pīced, inning); Ploughed Fd and Closes; Pond Close and Mead; Postern Hill (cf. *Blinde Posterne* 1607, *v.* blind); Readings (*v.* ryding); Roman Down S; Rough Ground; Round Close; Rust Fd S; Rye Ditch; Sandy Fd; Sawpit Fd; Saxon Fd S; Sheepcroft; Shepherd's Mead (cf. *Shepparde Lane* Jas I); Slang S (*v.* Db 758 and J. McN. Dodgson in *Notes and Queries* April 1968); Southbrook Mdw (cf. Northbrook Mdw *supra*, probably 'north and south of the brook'); Standing Hill (cf. *The Stande* 1607, *v.* stand, standing); Stream Fd S; Stubbings, Lower S (*v.* stubbing); Swan Fd S; Thew Ground; Town Fd; Tuck Fd S; Vault Mead; Webb Fd; Well Fd; Wheatley Close; Whirl Lane Close; Wood Mead.

(*b*) *Ascotteplayne* 1457 *ECR*, *Ascot Playne* 1607 (*v.* plain and cf. Winkfield Plain 41); *Le Beanebrooke als Millbrook* Jas I; *Bound Tree* 1729; *Bray Gate* 1607; *Chauntrygrove* 1640 *Windsor* (*v.* 285); *Coblers Hole* (a bog called) 1792 *RecOffCat*; *Conductheads* 1607, *Le Conduit Houses* Jas I (*v.* conduit); *Coxlane* 1729; *The Dog Kennel* 1729; *Frythlaan* 1462 *ECR*, *Freelane* 1607 *Norden*, 1685 *Windsor* (*v.* fyrhð, lane); *Gundrichesforde* 1327 ArchJ 36 (probably identical with *Gunredesford* 942 (c. 1200) BCS 778, 'Gunrǣd's ford'); *Hagthornes* 1607; *Holme Meade* Jas I (*v.* hamm, mǣd); *Inffeilde* Jas I (*v.* infeld); *Jerdelea, Virdelæ* c. 1240 Abingdon (this should possibly be connected with *gyrdford* 942 (c. 1200) BCS 778, of which the first el. is gerd, gyrd 'a short tender shoot, a twig, a rod, a spar', but it is difficult to see in what sense this could be combined with ford and lēah); *Linchefeild* Jas I (*v.* hlinc); *Litillond* 15th VCH III (*v.* lȳtel, land); *Ludo* 1331 *ECR* (p), *Le Lude Lane* 1367 *ib* (*v.* hlȳde); *Le Market Place Ground* Jas I; *Mereyrud(d)e* 1359 *RentSur* (*v.* rȳd); *Merryfeilde* Jas I (*v.* myrge); *Mognode Meade* Jas I; *Monylane* Jas I; *Mershefelde* 1587 *Dep* (*v.* mersc); *Morefeld* 1359 *RentSur*, *Moore Lands* 1657 *PubLib* (*v.* mōr); *Newelane* 1356 *ECR*; *Newemarledride* 1359 *RentSur* (marlede means 'fertilized with marl', and in this context -ride is probably from rȳd 'clearing'); *Newname* Jas I; *Le Parrok* 1359 InqMisc (*v.* pearroc); *Preste Crofte* Jas I; *Salters Hall* 1607; *The Straites* 1607 (Norden shows a long narrow strip, cf. O 440); *Stretehend'* 1359 *RentSur* (*v.* strǣt, ende[1]); *Three Stakes* 1729; *Twidaneslond* 15th VCH III; *Wicchemere* 1349 AD, 1359 Pat, *Wichmere* 1359 Pat, *Wychemere* 1359 Fine, 1365 Pat (*v.* wice, mere); *Le Wodegrene* 1416 *ECR*; *Woodley Corner* 1607; *Wood Pond* 1761.

II. BRAY HUNDRED

Brai 1086 DB, *Bray* 1184, 1193 P, 1275–6 RH, 1316 FA, *Braye* 1241, 1261, 1284 *Ass*

v. Bray *infra.* Berkshire east of Reading was divided into seven hundreds in the 12th and 13th centuries, and these are referred to as the seven hundreds of Cookham and Bray, or the seven hundreds of Windsor. In the 13th cent. they had some degree of administrative unity, which they maintained throughout the medieval period. Their history is discussed by H. M. Cam in *Historical Essays in Honour of James Tait* (Manchester 1933), 19–20. She points out that the district only contained four Domesday hundreds, and that it may represent a pre-Conquest district similar to the four and a half hundreds of Bensington just across the river in O. It is interesting that this east-Berkshire group of hundreds corresponds very closely to the probable area of the district which in the 7th cent. was called the *provincia* of Sonning (132–3).

Bray

BRAY

Braio, Brai, Bras 1086 DB, *Brai* 1156 P *et passim* with variant spelling *Bray*; *Braya* c. 1160 (13th) RSO (p) *Brai Regis* 1167 P, *Braye* 1220 Cur, 1234–5 FF, 1247 Cl, 1316, 1428 FA

This name is explained in DEPN and in Elements as OE **brēg** 'brow (of a hill)'. The complete absence of spellings with -*e*- is against this etymology, and the topographical objections to it are serious. Bray occupies ground of exceptional flatness beside the Thames. For an area of two square miles round the village the O.S. spot heights vary between 72 and 97, and the view from the village and its outskirts gives only the slightest impression of ground rising away from the river. The etymology must be left open. In France and Belgium there is a common p.n. Bray(e), derived from an Old French word known from the 12th cent. which means 'mud'. It has not been possible to obtain an authoritative opinion on the origin of this, and it is probably rash to postulate any common root going back to pre-English times; but it is perhaps just possible that Bray is a post-Conquest p.n., derived from the French word. The appearance of a

French p.n. in DB can be paralleled by Montgomery in Wales, though the two cases are not analogous, as one is the name of a castle, the other a topographical term. Malpas Ch is first recorded in c. 1125, however, which suggests that some French names descriptive of the site did become established fairly early in the Norman period. Cf. also Boulge Sf, which DEPN derives from OFr *bouge*, and which occurs in DB.

The forms for Bray D (D 57) are very similar. It is not certain whether that name was originally applied to the River Bray, or to the village of High Bray, but in either case the topography is quite different from that of the Berks place. High Bray is on the side of a marked hill, and the river is not a marshy one. The Devon names, and the two Cornish ones mentioned D 57, should probably be regarded as distinct from the Berks name, and may well derive from Celtic *brigā 'hill'.

CRESSWELLS FM and LITTLE PHILBERDS (the latter name is shown on the 2½″ map, but not on the 1″ or 6″), *Creswell'* 1242–3 Fees, *Creswelle* 1249 Ipm, 1295 *Windsor, Cres(s)ewell', Kerswell'* 1284 *Ass, Cressewell* 1285 *FF, Cresewelle* 1327 *SR, Carswelle* 1340 *PubLib(Bray)* (p), *Crassewell* 1352 Cl, *Mannor of Craswells als Philberts* 1604 *SpecCom, Cresswells alias Filberds* 1650 *RecOffCat*. 'Cress stream', a common name, *v.* cærse, w(i)ella and cf. 8. Land here belonged to the family of *Sancto Phileberto* in 1208 (VCH III, 100); cf. *manerium de Sancto Fileberto in Cressewelle* 1401–2 FA, *Filberts* 1675 *Windsor, Manor of Philberds alias Cresswells* 1674 *PubLib*.

CRUCHFIELD Ho

Kerchesfeld 1185 RR
Cruchesfeld Hy 3 *RentSur*, 1251 Ch, *Curchesfeld'* 1241 *Ass, Crucchesfeld* 1247–8 FF, *Cruchesfeld'* 1284 *Ass*
Cruchefeld' 1230 P *et freq* with variant spellings *Cruchefeld(e), Cruchefeud'* to 1345 Hurley
Crichefeld 1256 Ch, 1255–8 FF, 1319 Pat, *Crychefeld* 1255–8 FF (p)
Crussefeld 1275–6 RH
Crukesfeud 1286 Cl
Crecchefeld 1351 Pat
Crutchfeild, Crutchfyld 1604 *SpecCom*

Cruchfield Ho is just below the top of a pear-shaped hill, the name of which was probably PrWelsh *crūg 'hill'. The second el. of Cruchfield, feld 'open land', was added to the OE genitive of the hill-name. The same name occurs in Sr (*v.* Sr 281–2).

FIFIELD, *Fifhide* 1316 Fine, 1385 *PubLib(Bray)*, *Fifhyde* 1324, 1395 *ib*, *Fyfyde* 1416 *Windsor*, *Fyfhede* 1491 *PubLib(Bray)*; cf. also *Fyfhydestrete, Fyfhydeslane* 1316 Fine, *Fifhidestrete, Fifhideslane* 1325 Cl, *Fifhydefeld* 1396 *PubLib(Bray)*, *Fyfhedefeld* 1491 *ib*, *Fyfeelde Greene* 1573 *SpecCom*, *Fifeild Feild* 1636 *PubLib(Bray)*, *Fyfield Green and Lane* 1800 Eden. 'Five hides', a common p.n.

GAD BRIDGE, *La Gatebrug* 1308 *Windsor*, *Le Gatebrugge* 1319, 1333 *ib*, *Gatebrug'* 1354 *PubLib(Bray)*, *the Gatebrege* 1427 *Windsor*, *the Gatebrygge* 1442 *ib*, *Gadbridge* 1641 *SP*, 'goats' bridge', *v.* gāt, brycg.

THE HATCH, *Hech'* 1220 Fees (p), *Hec* Hy 3 *RentSur* (p) *Hetche*, *Hatche* c. 1298 *RentSur*, OE hæc(c) 'gate', sometimes used of a flood-gate.

HAWESHILL, cf. *Halsescroft* 1254 Cl, *Halsushurst* 1288 *PubLib(Bray)*, *Halseleshull, Halseshull, Halsieshurst, Halseshurst, Halseslan(e)* 1316 Fine, *Halseshull, Halseslane* 1324 Ipm, *Halsishull, Halsehull, Halsel(l)ane, Halsesburgh* 1325 Cl, *Halsehille* 1449 AD, *Halsescroft* 1364 *Windsor*. The first el. of these names appears to be a place-name *Hals, from OE h(e)als 'neck', used in p.ns. to mean 'ridge, narrow neck of land'. To the gen. of this have been added croft, hyll, hyrst, burh and lane, the last el. (which is rare, except in street-names) having presumably its usual sense of 'narrow road'. A greater and lesser *Halseslane* are mentioned in the references of 1316 and 1324.

HAWTHORN HILL, *Horethorn'* 1327 *SR* (p), *Horethorne* 1494 Ipm, *Hothorne* 1573 *SpecCom*, *Hoe-thorne* 1607 *Norden*, *Hawthorne* 1790 Pride, *Hawthorn Hill* 1800 Eden. The place is on the parish boundary, and the meaning is probably 'boundary thorn', *v.* hār, þorn.

HOLYPORT, *Horipord'* 1220 Fees, *Holyport* 1395 *PubLib(Bray)*, 1525 *Windsor*, *Holyporte* 1522 BM, *Holliporte, Hollyport* 1586 *RentSur*, 1704–5 *PubLib*, 1761 Rocque, 1790 Pride. Cf. also *Holyportfeld* 1491

PubLib(Bray), *Hollyporte Feild* 1631–2 *Bodl*, *Hollyport Green* 1674 *PubLib*. Probably 'muddy market town', from **horig** and **port**, in which case the alteration of the first el. may, as suggested in DEPN, be due to a local desire for a pleasanter name. Cf. Holyford D 622.

MOOR FM, *Mora* 1207–8 *FF* (p), 1220 Fees (p), Hy 3 *RentSur* (p), *La More* c. 1298 *ib* (p), 1355 *PubLib(Bray)*, *More* 1341 NonInq (p), 1380 Fine (p). 'Marsh', *v.* **mōr**.

OAKLEY COURT AND GREEN, *Aukelay*, *Aukeley* 1220 Fees (p), *Accle* 1224–5 *Ass* (p), *Acle* 1241 *ib* (p), *Ocle* 1352 Pat, 1370 Fine, *Oclee*, *Okele* 1381 Pat, *Estocle* 1416 *Windsor*, *Okelemede* 1439 *PubLib(Bray)*, *Ocley Grove* 1498–9 *Bodl*, *Okeley Fielde* 1573 *SpecCom*, *East Ocleye* 1586 *RentSur*, *Okeley Greene* 1607 *Norden*, *East Okeley Greene* 1641 *SP*, *Oakley Green* 1790 Pride, 1800 Eden. The forms are not very early, and the 13th-cent. ones are all from pers.ns., but it seems probable that this was originally OE *āc-lēah* 'oak wood or clearing', which is a common p.n. There is another reference to oaks in Ockwells *infra*. This would be a possible location for the battle *æt Aclea* described in ASC s.a. 851, when Æðelwulf defeated the Danes. The Chronicle account might be held to imply that the battle was in Sr, but Oakley is less than 5 miles from the Sr border. *v. infra* 49 for early spellings of Water Oakley.

OCKWELLS, *Ocholt* 1260–1 InqMisc, 1268 Pat, *Okeholt* 1286 *Ass*, *Ockeholt, alias Ockholt, alias Ocole, alias Norrys, alias Ffetyplace* 1582 ArchJ 24, *Ockolles* 1586 *RentSur*, *Ockholts* 1642 *Bodl*. 'Oak wood', *v.* **āc, holt**, cf. Knockholt (PN K 27) and Occold Sf (DEPN). For the families named Norreys and Fettiplace, *v.* VCH III, 103.

PUCKMERE (lost), *Pukemere* 1283 Pat, 1300 Cl, 1316 Fine, *Pokemere* 1321 Pat, 1386, 1395 *PubLib(Bray)*, *Pokemer'* 1397 *ib*, 'goblin pool', *v.* **pūca, mere**. VCH (III, 101) equates this place with Foxleighs (48).

SHORTFORD (lost), *Sorteford* Hy 3 *RentSur* (p), *Shʋrteford* 1270 Pat (p), 1275 Ch, 1279 Cl (p), 1324 Ipm (p), (*aqua de*) *Schortford'* (*in villa de Bray*) 1286 *Ass*. Cf. also *Shortefordemore* 1395 *PubLib(Bray)*, *Shortfordemore* 1397 *ib*. 'Short ford', an unusual name which contrasts with the common Langford, Longford. There was also a '*Shortford* marsh', *v.* **mōr**.

STROUD FM, *Lestrod'* 1220 Fees (p), *La Strode* 1340 *PubLib*(*Bray*), *Strode* 1395 *ib*, 1416 *Windsor*, *Strode Grene* 1491 *PubLib*(*Bray*), *Strowde Grene* 1572 *ib*, *Stroode Greene* 1575 *ib*, *Stroode* 1586 *RentSur*, *Little Stroode, adioyninge Strood Greene* 1629 *PubLib*(*Bray*), *Stroud Greene* 1641 *SP*, *Stroud Green* 1761 Rocque, 1790 Pride, 1800 Eden, *v.* strōd 'marshy land overgown with brushwood'.

THRIFT WOODS, *Frith, Frith'* 1206 Cur (p), *La Frith'* 1235 Cl *et freq* with variant spellings *La Frythe, Le Frith, Le Fryth* to 1394 Fine, *Fryth* 1396, 1415 *Windsor*, *Frythe* 1457 *ib*, *Frithis* 1478 *ib*, *the great Frithe* 1542 Leland, *The Friathe* 1573 *SpecCom*, *The Thrift* 1843 *TA*, from OE fyrhð 'wood', which frequently becomes *Thrift* in modern names.

TOUCHEN-END, *Twychene* 1274–5 *RentSur* (p), 1353 Cl, *Twichene* 1314–15 *MinAcc*, 1316 Fine, *La Twichene* 1316 ib, *La Tuychene* 1338 Ipm, 1339 Fine, *Twechene* 1401–2 FA, *Twechen* 1426–7 *Court R* (p), *Towchinge* 1586 *RentSur*, *Tutcham Lane* 1641 *SP*, *Tutchin Lane End* 1711 Hearne, *Tatchin Lane* 1761 Rocque, 1790 Pride, *Tatchen Lane* 1800 Eden, from OE twicen(e) 'fork of a road, cross-roads'. Touchen-end seems to result from a shortening of *Tutchin Lane End*. The hamlet is situated at the fork of a road.

ARKLEY. ASHMORE LANE. BANHAM'S FM. BARTLETT. BISHOP'S FM AND LODGE, Robert *Busshop* is mentioned 1586 *RentSur*. BLACKBIRD, BLACKBIRD LANE, *Blackbirds Lane* 1800 Eden. BODING LANE. THE BOURN, *v.* 8. BOURNE BRIDGE, *Bornebridge Close* 1650 *RecOffCat*. BOURNE LANE. BRAY BRIDGE, *Braye Bridges* 1629 *PubLib*(*Bray*). BRAY COURT, PADDOCK AND RISE. BRAY MEAD, 1635 *Bodl*, 1761 Rocque, *Bray Mede* 1491 *PubLib*(*Bray*). BRAY MILL, *molendinum de Bray* 1206 OblR, *Braymyll* 1457 *Windsor*. BRAY TOWN (lost), cf. 'hamlet of Braye called *Brayeton*'' 1388 *Bodl*, *Brayeton*' 1442 *PubLib*(*Bray*), *Braytowne* 1497 *Windsor*, *Braie Towne* 1586 *RentSur*, *v.* tūn. BRAY WICK, 1739–40 ArchJ 19, 1761 Rocque, *Wyke* Hy 3 *RentSur*, *Wyke in Braye* 1384 *Windsor*, *Bray Wyk* 1491 *PubLib*(*Bray*), *Braie Wecke* 1586 *RentSur*, *v.* wīc. BRAYWICK LODGE AND GROVE. BRAY WOOD, 1573 *SpecCom*, 1761 Rocque, 1790 Pride, *Bray Woodes* 1607 *SpecCom*. BRAYWOOD FM. BRAYWOODSIDE, *Braye Wood Side* 1644 *SpecCom*. BROOK LEYS. BROOKMEAD, 1843 *TA*, *Brooks Meadowe* 1629

PubLib(Bray).   BROOM FM, possibly *Bromes* 1586 *RentSur.* BUILDER'S CROSS AND WELL.   BULLOCK'S HATCH BRIDGE, *Bulloke-strete* 1337 Pat, *Bullukfur* 1390 *Windsor*, *Bullock(e)s* 1586 *RentSur*, *Bullocks Hatch* 1600 *PubLib*, *Bullocks Manor* 1606 BM, *Bullocke Veere* 1629 *PubLib(Bray)*, *Bullocks Hatch, Meadow and Ayts* 1640 *SpecComMap*, v. strǣt, furh, hæc(c), ēgeð and VCH III, 102, for a family called Bullock in Bray in the 14th cent.   CANNON HILL, cf. *Canon' Mede* 1491 *PubLib(Bray)*, *The Canon* 1625 *Bodl*, *Canon House* 1790 Pride, the manor was granted in 1133 to the Abbey of St Mary of Cirencester (VCH III, 107).   CHAUNTRY Ho. CHUFFS, *Chuffes* 1650 *RecOffCat*.   CONINGSBY FM.   CRUTCH LANE, *Crutchfeild Lane* 1604–5 *SpecCom* (v. 44–5).   THE CUT. DARKHOLE BRIDGE AND RIDE.   DOWN PLACE, 1790 Pride, *Downe Place* 1586 *Rent Sur.*   DRIFT RD.   FAIR VIEW.   FIFIELD Ho (v. 45).   FIRFIELD.   FLEDBOROUGH HALL.   FORBE'S RIDE. FOREST GREEN.   FOXLEIGHS, *Foxles* 1586 *RentSur*, *Foxleys* 1639 Ashmole; *Foxley Green* is shown 1761 Rocque, 1790 Pride, 1800 Eden; a family surnamed *de Foxle* is mentioned in connection with Bray c. 1298 *RentSur*, 1324 Ipm, and there is a reference 1344 Pat to the park of Thomas *de Foxle* at Bray; in VCH III, 101–2, this estate is said to be the one earlier known as *Puckmere* (46).   FOXLEIGH GRANGE.   FOXLEY'S FM.   FURZE GROUND.   GADBRIDGE FM (v. 45).   GAYS Ho.   GREAT ELM.   THE GREEN.   GROVE Ho.   HARE AND HOUNDS P.H.   HAWTHORN HILL RACE COURSE (v. 45).   HEADPILE EYOT, *Headpile Eiot* 1636 *SpecCom*, v. ēgeð.   HENDENS MANOR, *Hyndens, Hendens* 15th *Bodl*, *Hendons* 1566 *PubLib(Bray)*, *Hindens Howse* 1586 *RentSur*, from the family of William of *Hynedone*, holding in Cookham in 1321 (Darby 42). HIND'S HEAD P.H.   HOGOAK LANE.   HOLLIDAY'S PLAIN (v. plain and cf. O 389).   HORNBUCKLE FM.   THE HUT, cf. *Hutt Mead* 1843 *TA*.   JESUS HOSPITAL.   JOLLY GARDENER P.H. KIMBER'S Ho, *Kembers* 1586 *RentSur*, *Kimbers Lane* 1800 Eden; Robert *Kember* is mentioned 1439 *PubLib(Bray)*.   LEDGER FM. THE LODGE.   LONG LANE, 1607 *Norden*, 1800 Eden.   LORD-LANDS FM.   LOWBROOK FM, *Lowbrooks* 1586 *RentSur*, *Lobrooke* 1599–1600 *PubLib*, *Low-Brook-Lane* 1711 Hearne, *Low Brook* 1761 Rocque; named from a family from Lulle Brook in Cookham (82), v. VCH III, 104.   LITTLE LOWBROOK FM.   MEADOW VIEW COTTAGE.   MONEYGROW GREEN, *Money Rowe Greene* 1641 *SP*, *Money Row Green* 1800 Eden.   MONKEY ISLAND, 1790 Pride.

MOUNT SCIPETT FM, *Mountskippet Lane* 1800 Eden, *Mount Sciputt* 1822 OS; this name is somewhat widespread; there are four Mount Skippitts, in Ramsden O, Aconbury He, Owermoigne Do, Kidderminster Wo (VCH Wo II, 297), one Mount Skeppet, in Penn Bk, one Mount Skep, south of Galashiels in Selkirkshire, one *Mount Skippett* (1838), in Almondsbury Gl (Gl 3, 109), three places called Mountskip, in Crossmichael Galloway, Tintwistle Ch, and Mobberley Ch (1839), two places called The Skippets, in Whitchurch O and Painswick Gl, one called Skippets Ho near Basingstoke Ha, and a Lower and Higher Skippet 3 miles W. of Dorchester Do; no etymology can be suggested, and no spellings have so far been noted earlier than the 19th cent.   NEW LODGE, 1607 *Norden*.   NEW-LODGE FM.   NIGHTINGALE CORNER.   NOBBSCROOK.   OAKLEY GREEN, OAKLEY PLACE FM (*v.* 46).   OLD HARE AND HOUNDS P.H.   PHILBERDS FM (*v.* 44).   PIGEONHILL EYOT.   PRIMROSE LANE.   QUEEN ANNE'S TREE.   QUEEN CHARLOTTE'S TREE.   QUEEN'S EYOT, *Le Queenes Eiot* 1636 *SpecCom*, *Queenes Eyot* 1637 *SpecCom*, *v.* ēgeð.   QUEEN'S HEAD P.H.   REDSTONE FM, *Red-Stone* 1711 Hearne.   ROYAL FORESTER P.H.   ST LEONARD'S FM (*v.* 20).   SHEPHERD'S HUT P.H.   SHORTLANE FM.   SHRUBBERY COPSE.   SMITH'S FM.   STUD GREEN, 1761 Rocque, 1790 Pride.   STUD-GREEN FM.   TARBAY FM.   THE TEMPLE.   THRIFT LANE (*v.* 47).   TITHE BARN.   WATER OAKLEY, 1761 Rocque, 1790 Pride, *Water Ok(e)ley*, *Water Ockley* 1572 *SpecCom*, *Waterocley* 1592 *PubLib(Bray)*, *Walter Okeley* 1598 Ashmole, *Walter Okely* 1607 *Norden*, *v.* 46.   THE WILLOWS.   YATE'S FM.

FIELD-NAMES

The principal forms in (*a*) are 1843 *TA*, except those dated 1800, which are Eden; forms dated 1207–8 are *FF*, 1286 Cl, 1607 *Norden*, and 1620, 1639, 1663 and 1690 ArchJ 24; all other forms for which no source is given are *PubLib(Bray)*.

(*a*) August Mdw; The Balance; Barge Piece; Barn Close; Brick Close; Bridge Mead; Brockwicke (possibly *Blewyxe* 1505 ArchJ 4, which may be named from Nich. *Blokyswyk*, mentioned 1381); Brook Lease; Buds Lane Piece (*Buddeslane* 1374 *Windsor*, *Budds Lane* 1566, *Buds Lane* 1800, Henry *Budde* is mentioned 1374 *Windsor*); Budy Mead; Clay Lease; Clays, Long and Short; Clenners Mdw (*Clenhurst* 1316 Fine, 1324 Ipm, *v.* clǣne, hyrst); Comps, Great and Little (*v.* Introd.); Coppice Fd; Dove Fd and Mead; The Downs (cf. *Dounemed*, *Dounemedesfur* 1338 *ECR*, *Dunnemede Vorlong* 1370 *Windsor*, *Dounemed'* 1374, *Dune Mead* 1593 *Windsor*, *v.*

dūn, mǣd); Ferry Grove; Genissis Grove; Gods Lane 1800; Grandmother's Mead; Hacken Hole; Hampshire Lane 1800; Handmore; Hangings (v. hangende); Harford Mead; Lower Hawses (possibly connected with *Aldhawes* in (b)); High Fd; Hills; Hog Common; Horseleys; Horse Pasture; 100 Acres; Key Havens; Mill Close and Fd; Mogmers; Mucks Corner; Nags Head Lane 1800; North Croft (*Northcroft* 1332 *Windsor*); Old Orchard; Park, Great and Little, Park Mead (cf. *Parkhills* 1639); Peacock Lane 1800 (cf. *Peacocke Tarrs* 1636 *SpecCom*); Pouten Lane 1800; The Rays (cf. Ray Court in Maidenhead 55); Readings, Broad and Home (cf. *Estrudyngge* 1362 *Windsor*, *Westeruydyng'* 1390, *Nestredyng* 1498–9 *Bodl*, v. ryding); Ridge Lane 1800; Rockalls; Sandy Lease; Long Slipe (*Long Slip* 1620, v. slipe); Slough Bridge Lane 1800; The 10 Acres (*Tenacris* 1332 *Windsor*, *Tyneacre* 1388, *Tenacres* 1436, *lez Teneacris* 1438, *Teneacr'put* 1439, *le Tenn' Acres* 1566, *The Tenne Acres* 1629); Whites Corner (cf. *Whyteslonde* 1390, *Whites Londes* 1395, *Whyteslondes* 1397).

(b) *Adelystre* 1286, *ad Elystr'* 1340 (1711) Hearne (possibly 'Æðel's tree', v. trēow; the ME fem. pers.n. *Adeliz* is also possible); *Aldhawes* 1346 (the same name occurs in Windsor 35); *Alcot* 1321 *ECR*, *Alecot* 1324 *Windsor* (v. eald, cot); *Ascroft* 1300 Cl, 1394 Fine, *Asshecroft* 1396 *Windsor*, *Assecroft* 1445 *ib*, *Nashecroft* 1531 *ib* (v. æsc, croft); *Assherugge* 1491 (v. æsc, hrycg); *Bailliesmere* 1417 *Windsor* (v. baillie, mere); *Bash Reding Copy* 1607; *Le Beane Close* 1572; *Beche Hill* 1607; *Bedemede, Bedemedelake* 1438, *Bedmeade* 1611 *SpecCom* (first el. possibly byden); *Bellehek'* 1434, *Le Ballehacche* 1442 (v. hæc(c)); *Bellfield* 1620, *Belfield* 1639 (v. 285); *Betime* 1442 (v. bytme); *Blakebuttes* 1429 *Windsor* (v. blæc, butte); *Borden Bridge* 1607 (first el. the obsolete adj. *boarden* 'made of boards'); *Braches* 1620 (v. brēc); *Brademer'* 1207–8, *Bradmer'* 1439 (v. brād, mere); *Bradenebrugg* 1286, *Bradenbrugg* 1340 (1711) Hearne ('broad bridge'); *Braibrok* 1328 Fine, *Braybroke* 1475 *Windsor*, *Brayforlong* 1370 Fine, *Braye Furlonge* 1629, *Bray Grene* 1548, *Braylok* 1252 Abbr, *Braye-rige* 1370 *Windsor* ('Bray brook, furlong, green, lock and ridge'); *Brayneste, Brayneyst* 1491 (second el. uncertain); *Bray Slade* 1641 *SP* (v. slæd); *Bramble Veere* 1629 (v. furh); *Brendemulle* 1316 Fine, 1324 Ipm (possibly identical with *molendinum combustum de Benetfeld'* (i.e. Binfield) in 1254 Cl, v. berned, myll); *Bridge Acre* 1586 *RentSur*; *Brodaker* 1207–8 (v. brād, æcer); *Brode Croft, Brode Lane* 1572; *Brokesland'* 1439; *Brundelhewe* a. 1290 *ECR*, *Brendelewe* 1337 *ib*, *Brundelewe* 1345 *Windsor*, *Brendelewe* 1363 *ib*, *Brendlewe* 1426 *ib* (apparently 'burnt mount', v. berned, hlǣw); *Le Burgeys* 1316 Fine; *Bylrewell* 1337, *Bylderwell'* 1388, 1491, *Bildirwellefur, Bildirwellemede* 1438, *Bylderwelmede* 1439, *Bylderwell' Downe* 1491, *Bilderwell Oke* 1607 (v. billere, a term for several water plants, w(i)ella, and cf. Wa 334); *Bytwenestret'* 1337 (v. betwēonan, strǣt); *Cherleia* 1207–8, *Cherley, Estcherley* 1438 (v. ceorl, lēah, identical with the p.n. Chorley); *Cherry Ayt* 1640 *SpecComMap* (v. ēgeð); *Chirchesfeld* 1310 Cl (v. cirice, feld); *Ci'sdeshull* 1207–8; *Cokkuls* 1442; *Conyfeild* 1608 *Windsor*; *Cornesmed'* 1207–8, 1339, *Cornes Mede* 1439 (v. corn², mǣd); *Le Costouwe* 1318, *Costowe* 1438, 1491 (v. cot-stōw); *The Court Howse* 1586 *RentSur*, *Le Cort Howse* 1611 *SpecCom*; *Cowbriggeforde*

1439; *Cowleys, Cowleys Ayt* 1640 *SpecComMap, Cowe Lease, Cowelease Eight* 1640 *SpecCom* (*v.* cū, lǣs, ēgeð); *La Crondle* 1332 *Windsor*, 1338, *Le Crundle* 1336 (*v.* crundel); *Cruchifur* 1315 *ECR, Le Crouchfer* 1337 *ib* (*v.* crūc³, furlang); *Cuncroft* 1207–8; *Le Dewlonds* 1442 (*v.* dēaw, land); *Le Diche Acres* 1442 (*v.* dīc, æcer); *Eldefeld* 1316 *ECR, Eldefelde* n.d. InqMisc (*v.* eald, feld); *Le Eldelond* 1324 *ECR* (*v.* eald, land); *Eldernestubbe* 1370 Fine (*v.* ellern, stubb); *Estcroft* Hy 3 *RentSur* (*v.* ēast, croft); *Estei* 1207–8, *Estheye* 1337, 1384 *Windsor, Esthey* 1438, 1442, *Easthey als Neasthey* 1611 *SpecCom* (*v.* ēast, (ge)hæg); *Estlongefur* 1324, *Astlongfur* 1408 ('east long furlong', *v.* furh); *Estringebrog, Estbrokesmed* a. 1290 *ECR, Astyngbrokesmed* 1330 *ib, Asbrokemede* 1454 *ib*; *Estwede* 1220 Fees (p), *Estewod* n.d. InqMisc (*v.* ēast, wudu); *Eye* n.d. ib, *Eastfurlonge als Eiefurlonge* 1611 *SpecCom* (*v.* ēg); *Fairesfure* 1337 (*v.* furh); *La Fayr(h)ok* 1286, *La Fayrhok* 1340 (1711) Hearne (possibly 'fair oak', *v.* fæger, āc, identical with Fairoaks So, this name may be antithetical to *fulan æc* 'foul oak', in the bounds of Abingdon discussed *Oxoniensia* XXII, 61, which is the probable source of the f.n. *Fullock* noted O 446, and the names probably refer to rotting and sound oaks); *Felling Ayt* 1640 *SpecComMap* (*v.* ēgeð); *Fordacr'* 1207–8 (*v.* ford, æcer); *Furmefourlong, Formiforlong* 1370 Fine; *Gerstune* ?13th, *La Garston'* 1346 (*v.* gærs-tūn); *Gentilcorsfeld* 1384 *Windsor, Gentilcorffeld* 1448 *ib* (Reginald *Gentilcorp* appears 1347 *ECR*); *Gongefure* 1396 (*v.* furh); *Gorefere* 1384, *Le Gerefur'* 1442 (*v.* furh); *Le Grasse Hill* 1636 *SpecCom, Grasshill Eyott* 1637 *SpecCom* (*v.* ēgeð); *The Greene Lane* 1641 *SP*; *Grymesdych* 1316 Fine (*v.* Grim's Ditch 6); *Hacche Buttis* 1442 (*v.* hæc(c), butte); *Hachtrewe* 1286, *Hethtrewe* 1340 (1711) Hearne (*v.* trēow); *The Hale* 1438, *The Hale Corner* 1705 *PubLib* (*v.* h(e)alh); *Le Hay* 1370 Fine (*v.* (ge)hæg); *Herethenie* 1639; *Hertesheld* 1337; *Le Hertestrete* 1316 Fine, *Le Hurtestrete* 1324 Ipm (*v.* heorot, strǣt, the road is mentioned also in f.ns. in Cookham 86); *Le Hethe* 1429 *Windsor* (*v.* hǣð); *The Hides* 1636; *Le Hillond* 1349 Cl; *Hoacr'* 1207–8 (cf. Hoo in Cookham 83–4); *Holstrete* 1321 *ECR* (*v.* hol², strǣt); *Holyndene* 1370 Fine (*v.* holegn, denu); *Homcroft'* 1346; *Horneyard or Horniyard Tarr* 1636 *SpecCom* (Darby notes a number of Cookham names in -Tarr, all islands in the Thames; the word is not in NED or EDD); *Hungerhull* 1370 Fine (*v.* hungor, hyll); *Inwood* 1618 *SpecCom* (*v.* in); *Islake Eiot* 1636 *SpecCom, Iselake Eyott* 1637 *ib* (*v.* ēgeð); *Iwhurst* 1316 Fine (*v.* īw, hyrst); *The Kanonboke* 1445 *Windsor, The Kanonoke* 1458 *ib* (*v.* āc, and cf. Cannon Hill 48); *Kenells Close* 1715 *PubLib*; *Kinges Crofte* 1586 *RentSur, Kingesgrof* Hy 3 *ib, Kyngesdon'* 1384 ('King's croft, grove and hill'); *Le Kynggesokes* 1427 *ECR* ('King's oak-trees'); *Lyttell Kyppyngs, Le Greate Kyppyngs* 1566; *Langifur* 1207–8 (probably 'long furlong'); *Lay Close* 1620 (*v.* lǣge); *Lestaneswyk* 1337 Pat (*v.* wīc, first el. the OE pers.n. *Lēofstān*); *La Linche* 1345 *Windsor* (*v.* hlinc); *Locklands* 1568 (cf. *Braylock supra* and Thomas *de La Loc* a. 1290 *ECR*); *Lokehawe* 1385, 1388 (this was a garden, the name is identical with Locko Db, Locka La and Lockwell Nt, from loc(a) and haga¹, evidently an enclosure which could be locked); *Longedole, Longmed* a. 1290 *ECR* (*v.* lang, dāl, mǣd); *Le Longe Ver'* 1439, *Longveere* 1629 (*v.* furh); *Long Meade Tarr* 1636 (cf. *supra*); *Lez Lyghfieldys* 1449 AD; *Martynesaker* 1385 ('Martin's acre', possibly from a surname, *v.* æcer);

Maydewell 1316 Fine (*v.* mægden, welle, there are several examples of the name in other counties); *Maystreffure* 1370 Fine; *Medulfur* 1429 *Windsor* (probably 'middle furlong', *v.* middel, furh); *Le Merefur* 1344 *Windsor*, *Merefere* 1384 *ib* (*v.* mere, (ge)mǣre, furh); *Merkfur'* 1438; *Middilmede* 1438 (*v.* mǣd); *Moresplace* 1446; *Mucchys Plase* 1438 (*v.* place, Will. *Mouch* is mentioned 1323); *New Rewe* 1491 (*v.* rǣw); *Nomans Eight* 1636 *SpecCom, Nomans Eyott* 1637 *SpecCom* (*v.* 284, ēgeð); *Okledeime* 1370 Fine (first el. Oakley 46); *Orodelaker* 1207–8; *Osannehurne* 1386, 1397, *Osenehurne* 1390, *Osanneshurne* 1395, *Osenherne* 1439 (*v.* hyrne, first el. probably the ME fem. pers.n. *Osanna*); *Picked Meadow* 1620, *Picked Mead* 1639 (*v.* pīced); *Pykeslane* 1343 *ECR, Pigge Lane* 1572; *Pirstoub* 1339, *Pyristob* 1390 *Windsor*, *Peristubbe, Shortpurystubbe* 1439 (*v.* pirige, stubb); *Portebrugge* 1337 Pat (*v.* port, brycg); *Pratteshull* 1316 Fine, 1324 Ipm, *Le Pratts Lande* 1566 (Ric. *Prat* witnesses a deed of 1340); *Quenes Lesse, The Quens Water* 1586 *RentSur*; *Round Mead* 1639; *Round Moore Mead* 1620; *Le Rythe* 1396, *Rytheie End, Rithey End* 1629 (*v.* rīð, rīðig); *Shaffield Pond* 1620; *Shepecote Croft* 1438, *Slepecote Croft* 1491, *Sheepcot Lane* 1761 Rocque; *Shirecroft* 1346 (John *Shyre* is mentioned), *Shyrecroft* 1438; *Shortebutts* 1548 *LRMB* (*v.* butte); *Shortefure* 1396, *Shortefere* 1436 (*v.* furh); *Sireduscroft* 1422 (first el. probably the surname *Sired*); *Sixacres* 1370 Fine; *Sledbrugge* 1337 Pat (*v.* slæd, brycg); *Smithelee* 1207–8 (*v.* lēah, first el. apparently smið or smiðõe); *Sparrborowes* 1639; *Sparre Bridge* 1641 *SP* (*v.* spearr); *Spratts Croft* 1639; *Spratwell Ayt* 1640 *SpecComMap* (*v.* ēgeð); *Stanpuhur'* 1370 Fine, *Stampitfurlong* 1439, *Stonpitts* 1629 (*v.* stān, pytt); *Sterte* 1207–8 *FF*, (*v.* steort); *Le Stompe* 1374 (*v.* stump 'tree-stump', but Professor Löfvenberg points out that there was a form *stamp); *Stontescroft'* 1346 (first el. probably a surname); *Le Suthlongefer* 1337 *ECR, Suthlongeuer* 1370 *Windsor* (*v. Longe Ver'* supra 51 and sūð); *Suthrey* a. 1290 *ECR*; *Tamesemanneslond* 1349 *Windsor* (Geoffrey *atte Tamese* is mentioned); *Toncroft* 1332 *Windsor* (*v.* tūn); *Tothull'* 1338 (*v.* tōt-hyll); *Townsend Pitts* 1629; *Trippescroft* 1339 (first el. the surname *Trip*); *Le Twentie Acres* 1566; *Twotayles* 1634 BM (*v.* tægl); *Tygherdes* 1439; *Le Tylehowsse Closes* 1572, *Tilehowse* 1586 *RentSur*; *Venne* 1394 (p) (*v.* fenn); *Wadeslane* 1316 Fine, 1324 Ipm (Henry *Wade* is mentioned in the second reference); *Walwort* 1438; *Warehouse Ayt* 1640 *SpecComMap, Wearehouse Eight* 1640 *SpecCom* (*v.* ēgeð); *Wast Wyke* 1491 (*v.* wīc); *Le Way* 1592; *Weldon* 1370 Fine; *Wellingcroft* a. 1290 *ECR*; *Wenkleswyke* 1371 *Windsor, manerium de Wencles* 1395 Brocas, *firma de Wincles* 1592 (*v.* wīc, first el. a surname); *Westcroft'* 1322; *Le Wete Veare* 1566, *Wettveare* 1629 (*v.* furh); *Wetingcroft* 14th; *Whitefoote Stile* 1607; *Wicchins Grove* 1438, *Whicchynsland* 1439 (Rob. *Whicchyn* is mentioned 1348); *Wickfield* 1663, 1690; *Woluinesfur'* 1207–8 (probably 'Wulfwine's furlong', *v.* furh); *Wood Bridg* 1675 Ogilby; *Woodmandowne* 1629; *Le Wykemede* 1442, 1445 *Windsor*, 1458 *ib* (*v.* Bray Wick *supra* 47); *Wymmullefur'* 1355 *Windsor* ('windmill furlong', *v.* furh); *Wynegodespol* 14th ('Winegod's pool'); *Le Yerdole* 1439 (*v.* geard, dāl).

Maidenhead

MAIDENHEAD

Maideheg' 1202 P, *Maydehuth'*, *Maydeheth'* 1241 *Ass* (p)
Maidenhee 1202 P, *Maydenhus* 1241 *Ass* (p), *Maydenhith'* 1262 Cl,
Maydenhach 1286 ib, *Maydeneth* 1297 Pat, *Madenhethe* 1384
Fine, *Maydenhith* 1402 ib, *Maidenheth* 1404 ib, *Maidenheued,
antiq. nom. South Ailington* 1542 Leland

'Landing-place of the maidens', *v.* mægden, hȳð. The spellings
show the alternation of *maiden* with the shortened form *maid* which
is found in some other p.ns., such as Maidford Nth 41, Medbury
BdHu 71. The precise meaning of mægden in p.ns. is always difficult
to determine. In this instance the reference is not likely to be to
ownership, which would be appropriate in the case of Maidencourt
Pt 2. It could be either to the convenient nature of the landing-place
on the Thames, or to its being a place where girls were in the habit
of assembling. The figurative uses of the adj. *maiden* are first
recorded in the 16th cent., otherwise 'made or used for the first time'
might be relevant. The use of *maiden* in Maiden Castle (Cu 256–7)
does not seem appropriate. There has been association with the word
maidenhead.

The name of the landing-place on the river replaced the earlier
name of the settlement, which was *Elintone*; *v. infra*. VCH ii, 36,
quotes a letter of 1325 in which the Bishop of Salisbury refers to a
chapel 'in villa de Southelyngton quae Maydenhath vulgariter
appellatur'.

Maidenhead was made a distinct civil parish in 1894 (Kelly 117).
Before that, it was in the parishes of Bray and Cookham.

MAIDENHEAD STREET-NAMES

ALBERT ST. ALEXANDRA RD. ALL SAINTS' AVE. ALWYN RD. ATKIN-
SON'S ALLEY. AVENUE RD. BATH RD. BELL ST. BELMONT RD AND
VALE, BELMONT PARK AVE. AND RD. BLACKAMOOR LANE. BOYNDON RD.
BOYN HILL AVE (*v.* 56). BRIDGE RD, ST AND AVE. BROADWAY BROCK
LANE. CAMDEN RD. CASTLE HILL. CHAUNTRY RD. CHURCH RD.
CLARE RD. CLIVEDEN MEAD. COLLEGE AVE, GLEN, RISE AND RD. COOK-
HAM RD. CORDWALLES RD AND ST. COURTHOUSE LANE. THE CRESCENT.
CROMWELL RD. DENMARK ST. DEREK RD. EAST RD. EAST ST.
FAIRFORD RD. FIELDING RD. FISHERY RD. FORLEASE RD. (from
Forleaze Acre, v. 57). FRANCES AVE. FURZE RD (*v.* 56). GORDON RD.
GRENFELL AVE, PLACE AND ROAD. GROVE RD. HARGRAVE RD. HARROW
LANE. HAVELOCK RD. HIGH ST. HIGH TOWN RD. KING'S GROVE.

King St.   Laburnham Rd.   Linden Ave.   Market St.   Marlow Rd.   Moffatt St.   Mossy Vale.   Murrin Rd.   Norfolk Rd. North Rd.   Northtown Rd (*v.* 56).   Oldfield Rd (*v.* 56).   Park St. Penyston Rd.   Portlock Rd.   Powney Rd.   Queen St. Ray Lea Rd, Ray Mead Rd, Ray Mill Rd, Ray Park Ave and Rd, Ray St (*v.* 55). Raymond Rd.   Risborough Rd.   Rutland Place and Rd.   St Ives Rd (*v.* 57).   St Luke's Rd, St Luke's Rd North.   St Mark's Rd.   South Rd. South St.   Spencer Rd.   Sumerleaze Rd.   Victoria St.   Waldeck Rd. Wellington Rd.   Westborough Rd.   Westmorland Rd.   West Rd. West St.   Woodhurst Rd.   York Ave and Rd.

Altwood Bailey and Ho, *Altewode, Altewude* 1241 *Ass* (p), *Altewode* 1258 Cl, Hy 3 *RentSur*, 1316 Fine, 1327–8 *SR* (p), 1341 NonInq (p), *Altewod'* 1265 Cl, *Altwood* 1573 *SpecCom*. The second el. is **wudu**. Altmore in White Waltham, for which no early forms have been found, may contain the same first el., in which case this was originally the name of an area. The places are roughly a mile apart. Alt La is derived by Ekwall (La 29) from Celtic **alto-* 'hill', the source of Welsh *allt* 'hill-side, hill, cliff, woodland'. Altwood and Altmore are on the slope of a gentle hill, but *allt* would only be used of a striking geographical feature. It is perhaps just possible that the ridge of high ground which runs from Remenham and Wargrave on the west to Cookham and Maidenhead on the east had this name, but that it only survives in names of places on the S.E. edge of the area. There may be another trace of the name in a f.n. in Hurley (adjacent to White Waltham), for which the forms are *Altesora* Ed I, *Altesore* 1346, *Alteshore* 1360 all Hurley. This appears to have **ōra** 'slope', added to the genitive of an earlier name. (Cf. Cruchfield 44–5 for this type of formation.) There was also a field called *Altridings* (1620 ArchJ 24) in Ockwells, a part of Bray adjacent to Maidenhead and White Waltham. This is *Altriding alias Altwoodriding* 1639 ArchJ 24, so may be only another occurrence of Altwood.

Elington (lost), *Elentone* 1086 DB, *Helintonia* c. 1160 *AddCh 22011*, *Elinton'* 1167 P *et freq* with variant spellings *Elynton', Elintona, Elynton* to 1336 Hurley (p), *Elenton'* 1199 Hunter Fines, 1241 *Ass* (p), *Ellynton', Ellintun'* 1220 Fees (p), *Ellenton'* 1241 *Ass* (p). Possibly a compound of -ingtūn with a pers.n. Ellington Hu, which has similar forms, is derived BdHu 239 from *Eli*, but Feilitzen (247) considers that there is no safe evidence for this pers.n. The absence or rarity of forms with -*ll*- for the Hu and Berks names makes derivation from the common *Ælla, Ella* (found in Ellington NRY 231) improbable, and if this is to be regarded as a name in -ingtūn the

first el. must be left uncertain. Professor Löfvenberg suggests a
compound of the OE plant-name *elene, eolene,* elecampane (*Inula
helenium*) and tūn.

The manor of *Elinton* contained South Elington, later Maidenhead, and North Elington in Cookham (VCH III, 137). North Elington was sometimes called *Knight Elington* (*Knyghtelynton'* 1291–2 *FF*,
Knyghtelynton 1306 Ipm, *Knyght Elyngton* 1554 *LRMB*, *Knight
Ellington* 1606 *SpecCom, woodland called Knight Ellington* 1608–9,
1806 *Bodl*). Darby (31) suggests that this prefix is from the Knights
Templars, who had other property in Cookham. Cf. also *Northelyn-
tone* 1428 FA, *Southealington hodie Maidenhead* 1600 Camden, and
v. supra 53. The name is perpetuated by Ellington Park, which
appears on the $2\frac{1}{2}''$ but not on the 6″ map.

MAIDENHEAD THICKET, *boscus de Thicket de Cokham* 1284 *Ass, Le
Thikket by Maydenhithe* 1370 Pat, *le thickett in parochia de Cookham,
le Thicket* 1606 *SpecCom, Maidenhead Thickett* 1661–2 *ib*, cf. also
boscus q.v. Chiker 1275–6 RH (this is in Cookham Hundred). OE
þiccett 'thicket'. Cf. Leckhampstead Thicket 254.

RAY COURT AND MILL, RAYMEAD, *Reye* 1342 Cl (p), 1346–7 *Bodl* (p),
1392 *ib*, 1412 FA, *Reyemulles* 1347, 1392 *Bodl, Reyemulnes* 1351 *ib*,
La Reye 1381 *Windsor, Ryemelles* 1419 *Bodl, Reymilles* 1431 *ib, Lez
Rey Milles* 1439–40 *ib*, Rey, *Lee Rey Laak* 1491 *PubLib(Bray)*, Ray
1517 DInc, *Cookeham Rey, Rey Mill* 1573 *SpecCom, Ray Mills*
1608–9 *Bodl*, 1761 Rocque, 1790 Pride, *Meadow called the Raye* 1611
SpecCom, the Raye Brooke 1629 *PubLib(Bray)*. 'At the island', OE
æt þǣre ēge, ME atter eye. This has become Rye in Sx (Sx 536),
but there is another example in K (Ray Wood PN K 390) in which
the development has been identical with that of the Berks name. The
name may have been applied originally to the island in the Thames
on which Ray Mill is situated, or it may always have denoted the land
between the Thames and the brook which rises S.W. of Maidenhead
Court. This brook is probably the *Rey Laak* mentioned in 1491 (*v.*
lacu), and the *Raye Brooke* of 1629.

SHOPPENHANGER'S MANOR, *Sobehang', Sobbehangr'* 1202 P (p),
Sobbelangl' 1202 Hunter Fines (p), *Sobehengr'* 1220 Fees (p),
Shobenhangre 1328 Banco (p), 1340 *PubLib(Bray)* (p), *Schobenhangre*
1339 Cl (p), *Shoppenhangers* 1586 *RentSur*, 1761 Rocque, 1790 Pride.

The second el. is **hangra** 'wood on a slope', and the first the pers.n. *Sc(e)obba*, for which *v.* Shovel Spring (17).

AMBERLEY COTTAGE.   AMBLER HO.   BATTLEMEAD.   BELLA VISTA.   BOULTER'S LOCK, *Bolters Lock Close* 1609 Darby, *Bolters Lock* 1761 Rocque, *Boulter Lock* 1806 Darby, cf. *bo(u)lter* NED 'one who sifts meal'.   BOYN HILL, 1791 *RecOffCat*, *Boynhyll* 1534 *RentSur*, *Boynehill* l.16th Ashmole.   BOYNINGS, BOYN GROVE, BOYN VALLEY, all near Boyn Hill.   BROOKWOOD.   CALDER LODGE.   CAMLEY.   THE CEDARS.   CELLINI.   CHALLOW COURT. CLAREFIELD.   COLCHESTER LODGE.   THE COPPICE.   CORD-WALLES COTTAGE.   THE COTTAGE.   THE COURT.   COX GREEN. CRAUFURD COLLEGE, HALL, HO, VILLAS, a Mrs Craufurd appears in the list of residents in Maidenhead in Kelly's Directory (1911). CURLS LANE, *Curles* 1586 *RentSur*, probably from the surname *Curl*. DARLING'S LANE.   DITTON HO, *Dytton* 1505 Darby, possibly connected with Benedict *de Ditton*, mentioned 1352 Cl in connection with a chantry at Maidenhead.   DOGKENNEL LA.   DUNWOOD HO.   EASTSTREET COTTAGES.   ELINDENE.   FERNHURST.   FERNLEY. THE FIRS.   FISHERY ESTATE.   FORESTERS' ARMS P.H.   FRATONS. FURZE CROFT AND PLATT, *Furze Hill, Piece and Platt* 1899 Darby. THE GABLES.   GARDEN COTTAGES.   GLANDWR.   GOLDEN HARP P.H.   GREEN LANE.   GRENFELL PARK.   GRINGER HILL. HARTWELLS, Richard *Hartwell* is mentioned 1570 Darby.   HARVEST HILL, HARVEST HILL RD.   HAVEN OF REST.   HEATH COURT. HEATHFIELD, 1609 Darby.   HETHEL HO.   HIGHWAY, HIGHWAY FM, *Highway Farm Homestead* 1899 Darby.   HINDHAY FM, *Hindhay or Langtons* 1899 Darby.   THE HOMESTEAD.   ISLET. KALYIS HO.   KIDWELLS PARK, 1899 Darby.   LAGGAN HO. LARCHFIELD FM.   LEOMANSLEY GARDENS.   LONGWOOD.   MAIDEN-HEAD COURT, MAIDENHEAD COURT PARK.   MEADOWBANK.   MONEY-CROWER.   THE MOOR, MOOR ARCHES.   NEW HALL.   NEW-LANDS.   NORDON FM.   NORTH TOWN, 1628 *PubLib*, *Le Northton* 1379 *ECR*, *Northtounfeld* 1426 *Windsor*, *The North Towne Feilde* 1573 *SpecCom*.   OLDFIELD, *The Oulde Feilde* 1573 *SpecCom*, *Olde Field* 1640 *SpecComMap*.   OLNEY LODGE.   PARK CORNER. PINKNEY'S GREEN, 1790 Pride, *Pigneys Green* 1761 Rocque, named from the family who held *Elington* (54–5) from the 12th cent.; in Hunter Fines (I, 104) there is a fine of 1199 relating to *Elenton'* between two parties both surnamed *de Pinkeni*, William *de Pinchingny* has land here 1220 Fees, and in 1432 Fine there is a reference to a manor called *Pynkeneysplace*, the property of Arnold *Pynkeney*. PLOUGH P.H. THE POINTS. PUNT HILL, 1899 Darby. RAY LODGE, RAYMILL HO, *v.* 55. REDRIFF. RIVER BANK. RIVIERA HOTEL. ROBIN HOOD'S ARBOUR, a fanciful name applied to a prehistoric earthwork, *v.* M. Aylwin Cotton, 'Robin Hood's Arbour: and Rectilinear Enclosures in Berkshire', ArchJ 59; Mrs Cotton notes that the name is first recorded in 1861. RUSHINGTON COPSE. ST ANNES. ST IVES COTTAGE, *Ivees* 1441 *PubLib(Bray)*, *tenement' vocat' Yves* 1461 *ib*, *Ives Place* 1761 Rocque, *Ive Place* 1822 OS, from the surname *Ive*, *St* being preferred by popular etymology. SAWKIN'S BRIDGE. SHEEPHOUSE FM, 1761 Rocque, 1790 Pride, *Shiphouse* 1609 Darby. SHIRLEY. SOMERLEA. SPENCER'S FM, *Manor of Knight Hillington, commonly called Spencer* 17th *PubLib*; John *le Despenser* of *Knight Elynton* is mentioned 1306 Ipm, 1341 Cl. STAVERTON LODGE. THATCHED COTTAGE. THICKET GROVE, *v.* Maidenhead Thicket 55. TITTLE ROW, 1822 OS, *Tittlebackrow on Maidenhead Thicket* 1727 *PubLib*. THE WALNUTS. WOODHURST. WOODSIDE.

FIELD-NAMES

A number of names listed under Bray and Cookham probably fall within the boundaries of Maidenhead, which is a parish of modern formation, but it has not been possible to ascertain the position of the numerous f.ns. recorded in the older parishes. Except where otherwise stated, the principal forms in (*a*) are 19th Darby. Early forms for which no source is given are Darby.

(*a*) Eastmore Hill Mdw (*Eastmore Hills* 1609, 1650, 1683, *Little Eastmore-Hill* 1719 Ashmole); Folly Fd and Hill (*The Folly* 1761 Rocque, 1790 Pride, *v.* folie); Highway Fm 1822 OS; Holman Leaze, Omman Leaze (*Homanne-lese, Homanlesefure* 1347 *ECR*, *Homanlese, Homannyslese* 1389 *Windsor*, *Holmeleys* 1488, *Holman Leaze* 1609, *v.* lǣs, first el. the surname *Holman*); Lavellys (*Le Lauermore* 1346 *ECR*, *Lavermore* l.16th Ashmole, *Laverleaze*, *Lavermore* 1609, *v.* lǣfer, lǣs, mōr); Old Bury Close 1806 Bodl (*Aldebury* 1324, *Oldebury* 1415, *The Olde Bury* 1608–9 Bodl, *v.* (e)ald, burh); Peaked Close and Piece (*Picked Close* 1658 ArchJ 24, *v.* pīced); Reading Pond 1822 OS; Vines Hill 1822 OS (1790 Pride).

(*b*) Babham Bucke(*s*) 1633 *SpecCom* (cf. Babham's End in Cookham 85); Brokefere l.16th Ashmole (*v.* brōc, furh); Clay Pitts 1629 *PubLib*; Delfurlong 1370 *ECR* (*v.* dæl); The Eighth l.16th Ashmole (*v.* ēgeð); Forlesemed a.1290 *ECR*, Forleaze Acre 1650, Fforleaz 1658 ArchJ 24, Foreleys 1719 Ashmole (*v.* fore, lǣs, mǣd, Forlease Rd is named from this); Forgmore (marsh called) l.16th ib (cf. 29); *Fulpolmed* 1403 *Windsor, Fulpole Mede* 1505 ArchJ 4, *Fullpool Mead* 1609 (*v.* fūl, pōl, mǣd); *Gaston Meadow* 1640 *SpecComMap* (*v.* gærstūn); *Halleplace* 1383 *PubLib*(*Bray*) (*v.* h(e)all, place); *Hatche* 1586 *RentSur* (cf. *Northeche, Sutheche* a. 1290 *ECR, v.* hæc(c)); *Horwoode* 1586 *ib*; *Inwode* 1275–6 RH, *Inwood* 1573 *SpecCom, In Wood* 1658 ArchJ 24 (*v.* in, wudu); *Kings Grove* 1586 *RentSur*; *Litulmour* 1379 *ECR* (*v.* lytel, mōr); *Le Longeleshe* 1362 *PubLib*(*Bray*); *Lude* 1319 *ib* (p), 1334 Cl (p) (*v.* hlȳde, but the family may be from Winkfield, *v.* 42); *Monkedons* 1609, *Munkington* 1712, *Munkendons* 1719 Ashmole (possibly from a family from *Monkeden* in Hurley 63); *Poddyngescroft'* 1362 *PubLib-* (*Bray*), *Puddynguscroft* 1405 *ECR, Puddyng Crofte* 1449 AD (first element the surname *Pudding*); *Le Pytaker* 1375 *Windsor* (*v.* pytt, æcer); *La Schortefur'* 1370 *ECR* ('short furlong'); *Schorting-dene* 1345 *ib, Shortynden* 1375 *ib* ('short valley', *v.* sc(e)ort, denu, cf. *Langenden* in Cookham 84); *Thrickholt* 1586 *RentSur*; *Westhull* 1317 *ECR* (*v.* west, hyll).

III. BEYNHURST HUNDRED

Beners, Benes 1086 DB, *Beners* 1180 P, 1224–5, 1247–8 *Ass, Benerse* 1224–5, 1261 *ib, Benhers* 1224–5 *ib, Benhersh, Benherse* 1241 *ib, Benerste* 1275–6 RH, *Benersh', Benhyrst, Benherch, Benherth'* 1284–5 *Ass, Benersshe* 1316 FA, *Benerhs* 1327 SR, *Bynerssh* 1332 *ib,* 1442 Pat, *Bernershe* 1402 FA, *Benersh* 1432 Fine, *Bernersh* 1610 Speed.

There is nothing to add to the discussion of this name in Anderson (203). It means 'bean field', from bēan and ersc. The site of the meeting-place has not been located.

ersc, which is common in Sr, is found in several names in east Berkshire but has not been noted in the west of the county (*v.* Introd.).

Bisham

BISHAM

Bistesham 1086 DB
Bistelesham 1152–4 (15th) Templars, *Bistlesham* 1199 P *et freq,* *Bystlesham* 1236 Cl, *Bistlisham* 1260 ib, *Bistellesham* 1275 ib (p), *Bistelsham* 1311 Fine
Bustelesham c. 1155 (15th) Templars, 1275–6 RH (p), 1284 *Ass,* 1327 SR, 1339 Pat, *Bustlesham* 1185 Templars (p), 1194 Cur *et freq, Bustlisham* c. 1240 (late 13th), S, *Bustelusham* 1330 Fine, *Bustlesham Mountagu* 1339 Ch, 1345 BM, *Bustellesham* 1517 D Inc
Bixlesham 1189 Templars, *Byxtlesham* 1225 Cl
Betlesham 1206 Cur
Bustnesham, Bestnesham 1224–5 *Ass*
Bestlesham 1230 P, 1241 *Ass,* 1308 Fine
Brustlesham 1284 *Ass,* 1322 Fine, 1337 Cl, *Brustelesham* 1334 Fine
Bristlesham 1322 Fine, *Bristlesham Mountague* 1535 VE
Butlesham c. 1337 (14th) Winchester, 1535 VE
Byssam 1535 VE, *Bissham* 1573 SpecCom, *Bissome* 1651 PubLib, *Bisham als Bustleham Montague* 1746 ArchJ 17
Bustleham 1573 BM

The second el. is hām or hamm, and the first a pers.n. Ekwall (DEPN) suggests OE *Byssel,* a derivative of **Byssa,* with -*t*-

developing as in Basildon (Part 2). *Byssa* is probably found in *byssan broc* KCD 1309. The forms with *Br-* suggest association with the word *bristle*.

William Lord Montagu obtained the manor of Bisham in 1337 (VCH III, 146).

BIGFRITH, *Bigefrithe* 1247–8 *Ass* (p), *Bigefrid* 1275–6 RH (p), *Byggefrith*, *Biggesryth* 1284 *Ass* (p). Probably 'Bicga's wood', *v.* fyrhŏe; for the pers.n., which is recorded in DB and occurs as a by-name earlier in the 11th cent., *v.* Redin 73. The adjective *big* (not recorded before the 13th cent. but considered by Redin to lie behind the personal name) is perhaps less likely as a first el., since micel is generally employed in this sense in p.ns.

THE HOCKETT, *le Nockett* 1606 SpecCom, *Hockett or Rockett* 1609 Darby, *Knockett* 1661 SpecCom. Probably from āc 'oak', and the collective suffix -et. Names of this type are particularly common in Sr (Sr 358–9), where there is another example with āc (*la Okette* 1294). Cf. also Robert *atte Okette* of Winchfield Ha, mentioned 1328 Cl, and Hockett Wood in Bucklebury, for which no early forms have been found.

LEE FM may be identical with *La Lieghe* 1372 InqMisc, a place in Cookham where an inquisition was held. The Fm is about ¼ mile from the boundary of Cookham. *v.* lē(a)h. John *atte Lee* witnesses a grant of lands in this part of the county 1364 AD.

APPLEHOUSE FM, 1822 OS, 1846 Snare, cf. *Apple House Field and Hill* 1850 *TA*.   APPLETREE HILL.   BEENHAM.   BISHAM ABBEY, 1790 Pride (the 13th-cent. preceptory of the Knights Templars forms the nucleus of the house).   BRADNAM WD, *Bradnam* 1850 *TA*, possibly 'broad river·meadow', *v.* brād, hamm.   CARPENTER'S WD.   CROSS ROADS.   CROWN INN.   DRY COTTAGE.   DUNGROVEHILL WD, *Dungrove Hill* 1850 *TA*.   FULTNES WD.   GOULDING'S WD.   THE GRANGE.   HARDING'S GROVE, *cf. Hardings Green Close* 1850 *TA*.   HIGH WD, 1850 *ib.*   HYDE FM, *Hyde Barn Farm* 1822 OS, *Hyde Field, Great Hyde* 1850 *TA*, *v.* hīd.   INKYDOWN WD, cf. *Inky Down* 1850 *ib.*   PARK FM.   PARK WD, *Bisham Park Wood* 1822 OS.   PINKNEY'S CT, *v.* 56–7.   PRINCESS ELIZABETH'S WELL.   QUARRY CT AND WD.   RED LION P.H.   SPEEN HILL.   STONEY WARE, *Stoney Veer* 1850 *TA*.   STUBBINGS

Ho, 1790 Pride, AND MANOR, *Stubbings* 1822 OS, *Stubbings Close* 1850 *TA*; Stubbings was made into an ecclesiastical parish in 1856 (Kelly 227). TEMPLE HO, 1790 Pride, FM, LOCK AND PARK, cf. *Temple Mills* 1761 Rocque, 1790 Pride (from the Knights Templars, who had a preceptory here; VCH III, 148, says *Temple Mills* and *Temple Lock* are mentioned in 1544). TOWN FM, *Town Fd* 1850 *TA*. WOOD SIDE.

FIELD-NAMES

The principal forms in (*a*) are 1850 *TA*; early forms for which no date or source is given are 1534 *RentSur*.

(*a*) Abbey Eyot (*v.* ēgeð, as elsewhere in the f.ns. of this parish); Ash Croft; Beaks, Great and Little (*v.* beak); Bean Close (*Bene Place*, *v.* bēan); Brick Close; Bucks Bits; Butwells, Great and Little; Camley Fd; Chalk Pit Fd; Church Mdw; Coppice Ground; Copthorn, Great (*v.* coppod 'pollarded'); Ditch Fd; Dubious Eyett; Fern Close; Garden Fd; Gravel Pit; Great Eyott; Great Walk; Hale, Upper, Middle, Lower and Good (*Hale* 1327 *SR* (p), 1341 NonInq (p), *v.* h(e)alh); Hog Trough (*v.* 283); Home Fd and Ground; Home Reach, Great and Little; Hop Garden; Horseleaze (*v.* lǣs); Lawn Piece (*v.* launde); Lion Close and Mdw (*v.* leyne); Little Eyott; Long Mdw; Lucern Ground (*v.* 282); Lucys; The Meadow; Mihills; Moor; Mulberry Close; Net Eyott; Newfoundland (*v.* 284); Pit Close (*La Putte* c. 1337 (14th) Winchester, *Pytt Lond*, *v*, pytt); Plot, Upper and Lower; Pond Close; Pound Mdw; Quarry Eyott; Rick Yard Ground; Rope Walk Mdw (probably where ropes were made); Rough Ground; Sand Pit Close; Shatley Heath; The Slip (*v.* slipe); South Close; Southery Mdw; Standing Hill (*v.* standing); Great Stoney Down; The Swilly (*v.* EDD *s.v.* swally; this and the variant *swilly* are used of a hollow place); Troys, Hither and Further; Two Croft; Twothorn; Under the Hill; Upper Mdw; Violets Hill; Well Reach; Wilderness; Winches Standcroft.

(*b*) *Le Covent Garden* Ed 6 *LRMB* (probably 'convent garden' belonging to the Templars, cf. Mx 167); *Davys Hayse*; *Daye Howse* (possibly 'dairy house', *v.* dey); *Hare Howse*; *Harte Place*; *La Hethe* c. 1337 (14th) Winchester (*v.* hǣð); *Hollywellfette*; *Lane Place*; *Laners More*; *Norysfylde*; *Pysbyche*; *Sheparde Close*; *Le Stonehouse* 1544 VCH III; *White Place*.

Hurley

HURLEY

Herlei 1086 DB, *Herleia* 1130 P, c. 1135–40 *et freq* Hurley
Hurleya, *Hurleia* 1086 Gilbert Crispin *et passim* with variant spellings *Hurlea*, *Hurleg*, *Hurle(e)*, *Hurl'*; *Hurlega feodi comitis Willelmi*, *Hurlea Prioris* 1167 P

Hurnleia 1106–21 Hurley, *Hurnly* 1218–19 *FF*, *Hurnley* 1241 *Ass* (p), *Hurnle* 1242–3 Fees, 1248 *FF*, Hy 3 Hurley, *Hurnl'* 1248 Cl, *Hurnlye* Ed 2 Hurley
Hernleia 13th Gerv

'Wood or clearing in a recess in the hills', *v.* **hyrne**, **lē(a)h**. There is a curve in the high ground south of the village, which is probably the feature referred to in the first el. The same name occurs Wa 18. The Priory was a cell of St Peter's, Westminster.

BURCHETTS GREEN, *Birches Green* 1761 Rocque, 1790 Pride, *Burchetts Green, Birchetts Green* 1843 *TA*, *Burchess Green* 1846 Snare. Simon *de Byrchet* and William *de Brichet* are mentioned 1284 *Ass* in connection with proceedings in Cookham Hundred. They may have come from one of seven places in Sr (Sr 341 *s.v.* **biercet**), but it is equally probable that the place in Hurley was the origin of their surnames, and that it is another example of the p.n. which is derived from **birce** 'birch', and the collective suffix *-et*, cf. The Hockett (60).

In Hurley and VCH Burchetts Green is identified with *Birchehurst* Ed I Hurley *et freq* with variant spellings *Byrec(h)hurst, Birchurste, Burchehurst(e), Byrchurst, Birchestre* to 1491 Hurley. On the whole, however, it seems likely that this is a different name, from **birce** and **hyrst** 'wooded hill'.

CHANNY GROVE, CHANNERS PLANTATION, *Chaderhangra* 1176 P (p), *Chedehengr'* 1220 Fees, *Chadelhengre* 1231 Hurley, *Chadhangre* 1236–7 (c. 1250) Bract, *Chadhangre* Hy 3, Ed I Hurley, *Chaddehangre* 1242–3 Fees, *Cheldenhanger* 1246–7 *FF*, *Chadenhang'* 1275–6 RH, *Schadelhangre, Chalenhangere* 1284 *Ass*. Apparently identical with Chadlanger W 158–9 and Chaddlehanger D 185, though the forms for the Berks name show the confusion between *l-n-r* which is so common in this county. The etymology 'Ceadela's wooded slope' given in D and W is probably correct, though the coincidence of **hangra** occurring three times with the same unrecorded pers.n. naturally arouses suspicion. There is good evidence in other p.ns. for this pers.n., however. It appears in Chadenwick W 178–9, Chadlington O 339, Chillington D 332 and another Berks name, Chaddleworth (Pt 2).

KNOWL HILL, 1761 Rocque, *La Cnolle* 1299 Hurley *et freq* with variant spelling *La Knolle*; *Knoll Hyll* 1536 ib, *v.* **cnoll** 'knoll, hillock'. A district with this name was made into an ecclesiastical parish in 1842 (Kelly 109).

LEE FM HO, *La Leghe* c. Hy 3–Ed I Hurley, *la Lehe* Ed I ib, *La Leye* 1323 ib, *v.* lē(a)h.

MUNGDEN WOOD, *Little, Middle and Upper Mungdens* 1843 *TA*, and probably *Monckesdon* Ed I Hurley, *Munkenedoune* 1353 ib, *Monkeden Field* 16th VCH III 153, 'monks' hill', *v.* munuc, dūn. The monks were presumably those belonging to the Priory.

RIDINGS, 1843 *TA*, *la Rudyng* 1292–3 Hurley, *La Rudinge* Ed 2 ib, from ryding 'clearing'.

ASHLEY HILL, 1761 Rocque, 1846 Snare, *Ashley Hill Wood* 1790 Pride. BARE REDDINGS, *v.* ryding. BARTLETT'S FM, *Bartletts Hill* 1843 *TA*. BLACK BOY P.H., *Black Boy Meadow* 1843 *TA*. BOTTLE LANE (leading to BELL AND BOTTLE P.H.), *Bottle Field and Ground* 1843 ib. BUTES. CALVES LEYS, *Calvesleaze* 1641 VCH III 154. CHALKPIT FM (1822 OS, 1846 Snare) AND COPSE. CHOSELEY HO. COCKPOLE GREEN, 1607 *LHRS* (bounds of Wargrave), 1846 Snare; the 1607 bounds mention *Cockpole* as well as the Green. DEAN PLACE FM, *La Dene* 1341 Hurley, *Dean* 1761 Rocque, *Dean Place* 1790 Pride, 1846 Snare, *v.* denu. DELLARS COPSE. DEWDROP P.H. DODSLEY CLOSE. FROGMILL FM, 1664 VCH III 154, 1846 Snare. FURZE HILL, cf. *Furze Piece* 1843 *TA*. HALL PLACE, 1762 Rocque (court of the lord of) *la Halle* 1334 Hurley, (manor of) *Halle* 1372 ib, *Halleplace* 1412 FA, *v.* h(e)all. HALL-PLACE FM. HIGH WD. HODGEDALE FM AND WD. HOLLO-WAY. HONEY LANE (this and Pudding Hill *infra* probably had sticky soil). HURLEY BOTTOM, 1790 Pride, 1846 Snare. HURLEY HO, LOCK, MILL HO (*v.* Mill Lane in f.ns.). KNOWLHILL FM (*v. supra*). LADYE PLACE, 1558 VCH III 155, built on the site of Hurley Priory, and named from the dedication of the Priory to the Virgin. LOT FM AND WD, *Lott Fm* 1846 Snare. MANOR HO, 1846 ib. MITCHELL'S FM. THE PARK, *Hall Place Park* 1843 *TA*. PARK WD, 1790 Pride. PINNOCKS WD. PROSPECT HILL, 1843 *TA*, 1846 Snare. PUDDERS FM, *Podgers* 16th–17th VCH III 154, *Pudder Fm* 1846 Snare. PUDDING HILL, 1843 *TA*, 1846 Snare. ROSE HILL, 1790 Pride, 1843 *TA*, 1846 Snare. ST

MARY'S PRIORY.   SCOTLAND FM, 1846 ib, *Scotland* 1822 OS, possibly referring to its position on the parish boundary.   SEVEN STARS INN, *Seven Stars* 1846 Snare.   SPEEN HILL, *Speen Hill Field, Spin Hill Field* 1843 *TA*.   SPRINGFIELD.   THE SQUARES. STAR LANE (leading to Seven Stars Inn).   TEMPLE PARK, *Temple Meadow* 1843 *TA*, referring to the Templars' preceptory at Bisham, *v.* 61.   TITHE BARN.   WARREN ROW, 1729 *PubLib*, 1761 Rocque, 1790 Pride, *The Warren, Warren Row Ground, Warren Meadow* 1843 *TA, Warren Row Common* 1846 Snare.   WHEAT SHEAF P.H.

FIELD-NAMES

The principal forms in (*a*) are 1843 *TA*, except where otherwise stated; those from *LRHS* are 20th; early forms for which no source is given are Hurley.

(*a*) Bank(e)y Piece; Bargeman's Fd (*Bargeman's Field* 1664 VCH III); Bay Rid(d)ings (*v.* ryding, possibly identical with Bare Reddings *supra* 63); Beachampton *LHRS* (*Bechamtone* 1316, *v.* bēce², hām-tūn); Beringer's Fd *LHRS* (*Beringeresfeld, Berengeresfeld* Ed I, *Bargentesfeld* 1487, *Beringer* is a ME pers.n.); Bigmoor *LHRS* (*Bikemere* Ed I, 1316, *Bykemerefield* 1348, *Bignore* 1673 *PubLib*, *v.* bic, mere); Bishops Mdw; Black Flat Ground, Black Hat Ground; Brick Kiln Fd; Broad Oak Fd *LHRS* (*La Brodehok* 1292–3, *La Brodeok* 1390, *Le Brodeokefeld* 1493, *v.* brād, āc, and cf. Broadoak in Reading 177); Bucks Mdw and Island; Bulls Pins; Burtless Coppice Fd; Bushy Leys; Butts (*v.* butte); Calves Close; Camp *LHRS* (*Compe* 1292–3, *Compefelde* 16th VCH III 153, *v.* camp and cf. Ruscombe 127); Castle Pond *LHRS* (*Le Castel* 1325, *Le Castelcroft* 1344, Castle Green Ground, *LHRS* states that there are no remains and no tradition of a castle); Chalk Grap; Chapel Fd (*Chappell Felde* 16th VCH III 153); Cherry Walk; Clam, great and Little (*v.* Ch 3, 47); Clays *LHRS* (*Le Clay* 1475, *v.* clǣg); Clemence Fd *LHRS* (*Clemencehulle* 1295, *terra Clemence* 1304, *Clemencefeld* 1320, Clements Field, *v.* hyll, feld, first el. the ME feminine pers.n. *Clemence*); Cold Harbour Pightle (*v.* Sr 406–10); Common Lea (Hurley, p. 157, says modern Common and Great Lea are *La Laye* 1323, *v.* lēah); Costers (*v.* cot-stōw); Cow Close; Cow Plat (*v.* plat²); Cox Setters (*Kocsete* Hy 3, *Cocsete* Ed I, *Cocsette* Ed 2, *Coksete* 1348, identical with Coxett PN K 290; the elements are cocc² and (ge)set, and the term may denote a place where a great many woodcock are found); Dog Kennel Ground; Double Ground; Down Hill; Dry Mdw; Farthings Leys; Furze Gibb; Gibb, Little; Golders Fm 1846 Snare (also 1654 VCH III 154, cf. *Goldorne Hurlefield* 1420); Good Herrings *LHRS* (also *TA*, from Ric. *Godherynge* mentioned Ed 2); Gravelly Close; Great Goings Out (*v.* 283); Great Ground; Green Lane; The Halfpenny; Handsome Acre; Hatch Gate Fd (*v.* hæcc-geat); Hill Close and Ground (*Le Hulle* Ed I); Hitchenden Fd; Home Dean; Hop Garden; Horse Leys and Mdw; Jacques Mdw; James Mdw; Janes Dean Fd; Jordans Fd (Ric. *Jordan* is mentioned 1280–90); Junipers; Kidneys Fd; Kiln Ground;

Limekiln Fd (cf. *Limekiln Lane* 1790 Pride); Lipscomb Fd; Lock Mdw (*Lockmede* 16th VCH III 153); Lodge Lane Close; Mangles Mdw; The Mews; Mile Stone Ground; Mill Lane *LHRS* (*Melnestrete* c. 1300); Mill Mdw; Old Grass Ground; Old Orchard (cf. Rob. *atte Orecharde* 1327–8 *SR*); Parish Mdw; Pigeon House Fd (*Pidgeonhouse Field* 1664 VCH III 154); Pightle, Little (*v.* pightel); Pit Fd; Plaster Hill Fd (possibly pleg-stōw); Poor Corner Fd; Postern Fd; Poyson Ducks *LHRS*; Pugdown Hill; Reddings Fd (*v.* ryding); Rick Yard Mdw; Round Hill; Rush Mdw; Rushy Grove; Sandy Ground; Slip (*v.* slipe); Slow Croft; Sparrow Pightle; Square Pightle; Stand Hill; Strads; Sutton Fd *LHRS* (*Soddone* 1292–3, *Suddon* 1323, 'south hill', *v.* sūð, dūn); Townsend Close; Vetchington Fd; Well Croft; White Close; Whitents; Witcats; Worleys; Youngs Copse Ground; Youngs Mdw.

(*b*) *Le Aldeheyes* 1320 (*v.* (e)ald, (ge)hæg); *Altesora* Ed I, *Altesore* 1346, *Alteshore* 1360 (*v.* 54); *Bernardestreth* 1292–3; *Le Bournehacche* 1317 (*v.* burna, hæc(c)); *Brodappeldure* Ed I (*v.* brād, apuldor); *Brodecroft* 1320, *Bradecroft* 1327, *Brodefeld* 1344 (*v.* brād, croft, feld); *Buckenhull* Ed I, *Bukenhull* 1348, *Bokenhyll* 1390 ('Bucca's hill' or 'hill of the he-goats', *v.* bucca); *Bychenden* 16th VCH III 153; *Byrlotesworthy* 1344, *Le Burlettys* 1493 (*v.* worðig, first el. probably a surname; in Hurley this is identified with a modern farm called Bartletts, but the names are not certain to be identical); *Le Calwefeld* 1343 (*v.* calu); *Chelescroft* e.Hy 3 (from a tenant named Geoffrey *Chele*); *Conyngre, Conyngherthes* 16th VCH III 153 (*v.* coninger, coning-erth); *Copidhall* 1594 BM (*v.* coppede); *Crockeresrowe* 1320, 1329, *Crockaresrewe* (*vico. q.v.*) 1322, *La Crockerewe* 1323, *Crokbernerewe* 1354 (*v.* croccere, rāw); *Crouchstrete* 1340, *Le Crouchecroft* 1343 *Cruchefeld* 1345 (*v.* crūc³, croft, feld); *Custescroft* 1284 *Ass* (possibly from fem. pers.n. *Cust*, short form of Constance); *Denesfeld* 1299, 1303, *Denfeld* 1345, *La Denehacche, Denestrete* 1353 (*v.* denu, feld, hæc(c), strǣt); *Dick Farm* 1664 VCH III, 154; *Donuellde* Ed I (*v.* dūn, feld); *Dunmere* 1246–7 *FF*, *Donmere* 1323 (*v.* dunn, dūn, mere); *La Eldedene* Ed I, *Oldedene* c. 1280–90 (apparently 'old valley', *v.* denu); *Estfeld* 1268, 1318, 1353, 1497; *Fating Leaze* (pasture called) 1664 VCH III, 154 (probably *fatting* referring to good pasture, *v.* O 443); *Frilistret* Ed I; *Grashogeshous* 1288; *Le Groscroft* c. 1280–90; *Hamondeslond* 1322 (first el. the surname *Hammond*); *Le Hangingegrave* 1318 (*v.* hangende, grāf); *Hardyngescroft* 1353 (first el. the surname *Harding*); *Le Hechynge* 1322, *Le Hechyn* 1497 (*v.* heccing); *La Heghegrove* 1323 (*v.* hēah, grāf); *Le Heyestret* (*v.* hēah, strǣt); *Le Homcroft* Ed I, Ed 2, 1340 (*v.* 93); *La Hose* 1304, (*venella voc.*) 1352, *Le Hose* (*vico q.v.*) 1325, 1342, 1347 (*v.* Hose Hill in Burghfield 205); *Hudestret* Ed I, *Le Huthestrete* 1326; *Hurlond* Hy 3 (*v.* hyrne, land); *La Innynge* Ed I (*v.* inning); *Kitchen Eyott* 1761 *PubLib-*(Clayton) (*v.* ēgeð); *Knollestret* 1352 (*v.* Knowl Hill 62–3); *Langcroft* 1303 (*v.* lang, croft); *Lauerehemere* e.Hy 3, *Lauerchemere, Lauerkemere* Ed I (*v.* lāwerce, mere); *Lock Eyott* 1761 *PubLib*(Clayton) (*v.* ēgeð); *Mareysdoune* 1295 (*v.* dūn); *Merkedich* 1323 (*v.* mearc, dīc); *Middelmed(e)* Ed I (*v.* middel, mǣd); *The Two Minnydons* 1664 VCH III 154; *Neweslonde* 1396; *Nuþerecroft* Ed I, *Nythercroft* 1318, *Nethercroft* Ed 2, *Nedurcroft* 1330, *Netherecroft*

3

1339 (*v.* neoðera, croft); *Northcroft* 1304; *Okdon* 1323 (*v.* āc, dūn); *Overcroft* Ed I; *Owde House Groundes* 17th VCH III 154; *Oxhaye* 1246–7 *FF* (*v.* oxa, (ge)hæg); *La Pennynggestret* 1333 (*v.* pening, strǣt); *Reynaldesdoune* 1334 (*v.* dūn); *Ruycroft* 1304 (*v.* ryge, croft); *Samareslond* Ed I ('Sǣmǣr's land'); *Santgath* 1292–3; *Sheephouse Field* 1664 VCH III; *Skynnesput* 1318 (*v.* pytt, first el. 'skinner', which may be a surname); *La Smalestret* 1305 ('narrow street', *v.* smæl); *Smalhangerden'* 1246–7 *FF*, *Smalhangredene* Hy 3 (*v.* smæl, hangra, denu); *Southfeld* 1353; *La Stamphulle* 1338 (Cristina *de la Stompe* is mentioned Ed I Hurley 141, *v.* stump 'tree-stump', hyll and cf. 52); *Standon, Standun* Hy 3, *Standone, Standune* Ed I, *Staundone* 1295, *Standens* 1487 (*v.* stān, dūn, a fairly common name); *Le Stonhous* 1344, 1355 ('stone house'); *Strode* 1261–6 *FF* (p) (*v.* strōd); *Suthhache* Ed I (*v.* sūð, hæc(c)); *Le Upstrete* 1348; *La Vortye* 1303, *La Vorteye* 1353 (*v.* forð-ēg); *Waterslade* 1246–7 *FF* (*v.* wæter, slæd); *La Westcroft* 1305, 1312; *Westfeld* Ed I, Ed 2; *Westmede* 1318, 1324; *La Westrethe* Ed I, *Le Westret* 1343, 1348; *Whetcroft* 1311, *Wetcroft* 1327, *Whetcrofte* 1333 (*v.* hwǣte, croft); *Widmerpole* 1475 (cf. Widmerpool Nt 257–8); *La Widyelonde* 1292–3 (*v.* wiðig, land); *La Windgate* Ed I (*v.* windgeat); *Wodefeld* Ed I (*v.* wudu, feld); *Le Wodesyde* 1372 (*v.* wudu, sīde); *Wrdi* Ed I, *Le Worthy* 1487 (*v.* worðig); *Wyca* 1254 (*v.* wīc); *Wydenhey* 1322 (*v.* wid, (ge)hæg); *Wygayneslond* 1343 ('Wigan's land', cf. 23); *Wytham Eyot* 1761 *PubLib(Clayton)* (*v.* ēgeð).

Remenham

REMENHAM

Rameham 1086 DB

Remenham 1086 Gilbert Crispin, 1224–5 *Ass*, 1227–8, 1309–10 *FF*, 1316 FA, 1327 *SR*, 1517 D inc, *Remnam* 1535 VE, *Remnham* 1655 BM, *Remenham alias Remnam* 1697–8 *Bodl*

Remeham 1167 P *et passim*

Ramenham 1227–8 *FF*, 1310 BM, 1326 Cl, 1502 AD, *Rampnham* 1450 BM

Rummenham 1241 *Ass*, *Rumenham* 1284 *ib*

Rumeham 1268 *Ass*

The second el. is hām or hamm; there are no spellings in -*mm*, but hamm would be perfectly appropriate in the meanings 'land in a river-bend' or 'water-meadow'. Ekwall (DEPN) suggests rima 'border', or a dialectal variant *rioma*, for the first el. and this would give excellent sense, the meaning being 'village by the river-bank', with reference to the position of the place immediately beside the Thames. The spellings with -*e*- and -*u*-, however, are more consistent with late OE -*eo*- (-*a*- in some forms would be a Norman spelling for

-e-); and while *reoma* is a possible dialectal variant of *rima*, it should be noted that the el. occurs in several p.ns. (Rimington YW, Rimpton So, Rimside Nb, Ryme Do), the spellings for which do not suggest any other form than *rima*. Dr O. von Feilitzen points out, however, that back-mutation of the vowel is not to be expected in stem-compounds such as *Rimingtūn*, *Rimtūn*, so *reoma*, dialect variant of *rima* 'border', is a possible first el. of Remenham.

Another possibility is OE *rēoma*, only recorded in the sense 'membrane, ligament', but perhaps having earlier meanings which would make possible a transferred sense such as 'narrow strip of ground'. Professor Löfvenberg points out that *rēoma* corresponds to OSaxon, OHG *riomo*, G *Riemen* 'strap, thong'.

ASTON, *Estun'* 1220 Fees (p), *Eston'* 1247–8 *FF*, *Aston* 1761 Rocque, 'east farm' (i.e. east of Remenham), a common name, *v.* ēast, tūn.

MARSH MILL, *la Merse* 1220 Fees (p), *Mersh* 1341 NonInq (p), *Marsh Mills* 1664 *PubLib(Clayton)*, 1670 *PubLib*, 1846 Snare, *v.* mersc.

ANGEL P.H.   ASTON FERRY AND FM, *v. supra*.   BIRD PLACE, *Bird Garden* 1840 *TA*.   THE ELMS.   FLOWER POT HOTEL. ISLAND TEMPLE, *The Temple* 1846 Snare.   IVY GATE.   PARK PLACE, 1761 Rocque, possibly a corruption of *Pecks Place*, for which *v.* VCH III, 162.   PARKPLACE FM.   REMENHAM LODGE, 1846 Snare.   REMENHAM FM, HILL, PLACE AND WD.   THAMESFIELD. TOWER LODGE.   UNDERWOOD.   WHITE HILL, 1698 *Bodl*, 1846 Snare.   WILMINSTER COLLEGE AND PARK.   WOODLANDS.

FIELD-NAMES

The principal forms in (*a*) are 1840 *TA*.

(*a*) The Bins (*Great Been* 1698 *Bodl*); Blandfords; Blandys Mdw; Bottom Piece; Bottom, Long and Short; Brick Fd; Brittain, Great and Little (*v.* 284); Bury Pit; Bush Ham; The Common; Cow Pasture; Dry Ground; East Mead; Forked Piece; The Gaskins; The Grove; Ham Bottom, Great and Little Ham (*v.* hamm); Hanging, Great and Little (*v.* hangende); Heading Ridge, Headings; Hillim Side; Holly Bush; Home Close; Horseshoe Common (1822 OS); Lady Moor; Lerchings; Lion Mead (*v.* leyne); Lockers Pightle; Lodge Fd; Marvels Cross; Milestone Fd; Mill Pits Mdw; Mill Tail Mdw; The Moors; Oaks Hill; Park Wood, Piece and Several; The Peaks, Picked Croft (*v.* pīced); Pit House Mead (*Pitthouse Mead* 1698 *Bodl*);

Pit Several (*v.* 282); Rackshaws Mead; The Roundabout (*v.* 281); Round Hill; Small Mdw; Sollars (*Sollers* 1439 BM, *Sallars* 1664 *PubLib(Clayton)*); Summer Leys; Turpins Mdw; Vine Fd; Vines Hill; The Warren; White Severals; The Winch Mdw (*v.* O 64); Wood Fd.

(*b*) *The Dene* 1484 AD (*v.* denu); *Eyte* 1697–8 Bodl (*v.* ēgeð); *Marle Hill, Marleshill Field* 1698 *Bodl*; *The Rodd Eyotts* 1670 *PubLib(Clayton)* (*v.* O 463); *The Slade* 1698 *Bodl* (*v.* slæd); *Smertis Pytyll* 1484 AD (*v.* pightel, first el. the surname *Smart*).

Shottesbrooke

SHOTTESBROOKE

> *Sotesbroc* 1086 DB, *Sotesbroch aurifabrorum* 1167 P, *Schottesbroc* 1187 ib, *Schottesbroch* 1189 ib, *Sotisbroc* 1261 Cl, *Sotesbrok* 1275–6 RH, *Shotesbrok* 1278 Cl, 1338 Pat, *S(h)otesbrok'*, *Sothesbrok'* 1284 *Ass*, *Sot(t)esbrok*, *Stotesbrok* 1297 Ipm, *Sotesbroke* 1316 FA, *Shottesbrok* 1400 Fine, *Shotysbroke* 1401–2 FA
>
> *Schotebroch* 1187 P (p), *Scotebroc* 1189 ib (p), *Scottebr'* 1195 ib (p), *Schottebroch* 1196 ib, *Sottebroch* 1196 ib *et freq* with variant spellings *Sotebroc(h)*, *Sottebroc(h)*, *Sotebrok'*; *Shcotebroc* 1202 P, *Shotebroc* 1214 Cur, *Sutebroch'* 1220 Fees (p), *Shotebrok'* 1241 *Ass* (p), *Schotebrok'* 1284 *ib* (p)
>
> *Shotbrok* 1338, 1341 Pat

Forms with and without -*s*- are about equally numerous. The former suggest the etymology 'Scot(t)'s stream', *v.* brōc, while the latter are consistent with Ekwall's derivation (DEPN) 'trout stream', from OE sc(e)ota. This may be the original name of the stream which flows through Warfield, Binfield, Shottesbrooke, Waltham St Lawrence, Ruscombe and Twyford to the R. Ock.

The manor was held in 1086 by Alward the goldsmith, whose father had held it TRE, and in the 12th cent. it was held by the serjeanty of furnishing charcoal to the king's goldsmith (VCH III, 164), hence *aurifabrorum* in 1167. The Berkshire goldsmiths are also discussed in VCH I, 291–2.

BRICK BRIDGE, 1641 *SP*, 1711 Hearne, 1761 Rocque, 1790 Pride. CHALKPIT BRIDGE, 1822 OS, 1846 Snare.   COLD HARBOUR, 1843 *TA* (*v.* Sr 406–10).   GREAT WD, *Shottesbrooke Great Wood* 1846 Snare.   LONG WD.   NEW ENGLAND WD, on the parish boundary, *v.* 284.   PITLANDS FM, *Pittlands* 1680 *PubLib(Clayton)*, perhaps from the family surnamed *de Laput'* 1220 Fees, *de la Pitte* 1252 Cl, *de La Putte* 1252, 1261 ib, *v.* pytt.   POND WD, PONDWOOD FM.   PUNDLES LANE, *Pundall's-Farm* 1711 Hearne.   ROUND WD, GREAT AND LITTLE.   SHOTTESBROOKE FM AND PARK, 1846 Snare.   SMEWINS, 1606 BM, *Smewyns Inninges* 1467 Cl (*v.* inning), *Smewyns,* now *Ripons* 1494 Ipm, *Smewyns Farme* 1680 *PubLib-(Clayton), Smewin's House* 1711 Hearne, *Smewing Fm and Bridge* 1846 Snare (the family from which this is named is traced back to the late 12th in VCH III, 174–5, cf. Walter *Smewyn* 1247–8 *FF*). SOUTH WD.

FIELD-NAMES

The principal forms in (*a*) are 1843 *TA*; early forms for which no date or source is given are 1680 *PubLib(Clayton)*.

(*a*) Abbotts; Alebutts or Whit Fd; Ash Copse Mead (*Ashen Copse*); Beadley; Blackmoor and Cusmoor Mdw; Bread Croft (*Bradecroft* 1349 AD, *Bradcroft* 1497 Chertsey, *Breade Croft* 1549 VCH III, *Bredcroft* 1711 Hearne, *v.* brǣdu); Burringham; Calves Lease (*The Calves Lease*); Care Fd (possibly *Cane Field*); Chambers Fd (*Chambers* 1680 *PubLib(Clayton)*, *Chambers Farm* 1790 Pride, a family surnamed *atte Chambr'* is mentioned 1341 NonInq); Constable Piddle (a variant of pightel); Copper Fd (*Coopers Field*, possibly *Coppe Hall Feld* 1551 *LRMB*, *v.* coppede); Cow Leaze (*Cowelese* 1467 Cl, *The Cow Lease*, *v.* lǣs, as elsewhere in this parish); Cox Close; The Down; Earlslow Down; Foster's Plat; Foxholes (*Foxwelles* 1467 Cl); Hill Plot or Plat; Holles Hill; Home Close and Mdw; Horse Pastures (cf. *The Horse Plott*); Kiln Plot; Mantes; Marsh Down; Mattingley's Plat (*Mattingleys Plott*); Oat Ash (*Otcherssh* 1467 Cl, *Otearshe* 1494 Ipm, *Oteershe* 1497 Chertsey, *Oaterish* 17th VCH III, *v.* āte, ersc and Introd.); Ox Leaze (*The Oxe Lease*, *v.* lǣs); Pear Tree Close; Pigmoor, Pinkmores, Pinks Fd (*Pinckmore Coppice* 1612 VCH III, *Pinckmoor, Pinkes Corner*); Rook Hill (*Rookshill*); Sandy Fd (*Sandefeld* 1551 *LRMB*); Shears Close; Slowfield; Spoil Heap; Temple Fd (*Hither and Further Temple Field*); Terriers (*Tyrries, Terresynnyng* 1497 Chertsey, *Terris Land* 1629 Windsor, *Terris Lane* 1697 *ib*, *Terresh Close and Garden* 1711 Hearne, from the surname *Terry*); The Triangles; Walkfield; The Warren; Well Croft (*Wellcroft*); Westley (*Westley* 1680 *PubLib(Clayton)*, *Westlowe* 1711 Hearne, cf. Westley Mill 78); Wise Plat; Woodhouse Fd, Great and Little (*possibly The 2 Woodwards Fields*); Wood Mdw.

(*b*) The Barton (*v.* bere-tūn); *Bradley* 1467 Cl, *Bradby* 1626 *Windsor, Bradley* 1697 *ib* (*v.* brād, lēah); *The Brick Plott; Burroughe Croft* 1626 *Windsor; Clovergrasse Peece; Costow* 1422 *Windsor, Costow(e)hegge* 15th Chertsey, *Corostores* 1626 *Windsor, Cowstone* 1697 *ib* (*v.* cot-stōw); *Culverhouse Lane* 1663 *ib* ('dove-cot' from OE **culver-hūs*, cf. Löfvenberg 44); *Gobcroft* 1626 *ib, Cob Croft* 1697 *ib; Kings Coppice; La Lee* 1248 *Ass*, 1276–7 *FF* (p), *The Lee Plot, The Great and Little Lee* (*v.* lēah); *Merchams Plott;*

The Mill Peece; *Newfield Wood*; *The New Ground*; *Norrington Field*; *Pidgeon Holes* 1680 *PubLib(Clayton)*, *Farm called Pidgeon-Holes* 1711 Hearne; *Shiteangrecroftes, Shitehangercroftes, Shitehangrecroftes* 1337 Pat ('wood on a steep slope', identical with Shuthanger D 551 and Shuthonger Gl 2, 72, *v.* Löfvenberg 187); *Westhersshe* 1467 Cl, *Westherse* 1663 Windsor (*v.* west, ersc and Introd, for the *-h-* cf. *Oakhurst* Herts 68).

White Waltham

WHITE WALTHAM

> (*on*) *Waltham*, (*into*) *Weltham* 'c. 1050' (13th) KCD 844, *Waltham* 1086 DB, 1242–3 Fees, *Waltham abbatis de Certeseia* 1167 P, *Westwaltham* Ric I (1246) Ch, *Wautham* 1214 Cur, *Wytewaltham* 1242–3 Fees, *Blaunche Wautham, Blaunche Wauttam, Alba Wautham* 1284 *Ass*, *Waltham Abbatis* 1316 FA, *Qwyt Waltham* 1346 Hurley, *Whyte Waltham* 1381 BM, *Whitwaltham* 1468 Fine, *Waltham Abbatis* 1535 VE, *White Waltham* 1557 *PubLib-(Bray)*

v. Waltham St Lawrence 112, from which this place is distinguished as 'white', probably with reference to the chalky soil which occurs in parts of the parish.

As explained in Part 3, the name *Wealtham*, in 940, appears to have denoted the whole area of the three modern parishes of Waltham St Lawrence, White Waltham and Shottesbrooke. By the 11th cent. the two Walthams are separate land-units, but the picture is complicated by the existence of two estates in White Waltham. One of these belonged to Chertsey Abbey, and this is the estate referred to in KCD 844 (a spurious writ of King Edward, discussed ASWrits 205 n.1), and in a number of spurious Chertsey charters (BCS 39, 1195, KCD 812). The other had belonged TRE to the Abbey of Waltham Holy Cross in Essex, and they held it also after the Domesday Survey. This is called *Westwaltham* in a spurious charter relating to the possessions of the Essex house (KCD 813), and t. Ric I (CartAntiq); and it included Heywood *infra* 72. Since Heywood is in the east of White Waltham parish, *West-* may be for distinction from Waltham Ess. It is sheer bad luck that Waltham Holy Cross had the same place-name, thus making it even harder to describe the history of the Berks estates clearly.

BURYCOURT FM, cf. *Burigrofe* 15th Chertsey, *Buriynnyng* 1497 ib, *Berry Farme* 17th *PubLib(Clayton)*, *White Waltham al. Berry Manor*

with Berry Farm 1657 BM, *Manor of Berry* 17th *PubLib, Berry Grove*
1789 Gough's Camden (Additions). *v.* grāf, inning. This is the old
manor-house of the estate belonging to Chertsey Abbey (VCH III,
171), and the first el. is burh in the sense 'manor'.

HOLLICKS (lost), (*to*) *heal wicum* 940 (c. 1240) BCS 762, (wood of)
Halewik 'c. 1060' (13th) KCD 844, (wood of) *Haleuuike*†, *Haleuuyke*
1256 Dugdale, *Halewyk* 1497 Chertsey, *Halwicke's-Wood* 1711
Hearne, *The Hollicks* 1816 *LHRS, Hollicks, Hollocks* 1843 *TA.* The
1711 reference is from Hearne's account of the bounds of White
Waltham, and this enables the wood to be located with some preci-
sion. It occurs between *Westlowe-Mills* (Westleymill in Binfield 78)
and Brick Bridge (in Shottesbrooke 68), and these two places are
about ¾ mile apart, on the S.W. boundary of the parish.

The name means 'farm in a nook of land', from healh and wīc.
Five more examples of this compound have been noted in other
county surveys. These are Holywick Bk 179, Holliwick BdHu 121,
Halewick Sx 202, Hollick Sr 110, Halliwick Mx 100. Most of these
have been rendered 'holy wīc', with occasional alternative suggestions
of 'dairy-farm belonging to a hall', and 'wīc in a healh'. The Berks
example is crucial, as it is the only one with a reliable OE spelling.
Hollick Fm Sr is *Haleuuik* in BCS 563, but a number of spellings
from this charter show post-Conquest influence. The Berks spelling
heal wicum is consistent with derivation from healh; and the medial
-e-, -i-, -y- which occur in ME and ModE spellings for all the names,
and which had led to rejection of healh and association of the first el.
with the word *holy*, are probably intrusive vowels. Such vowels can
be shown to develop between a consonant and a following *-w-* in
words like *periwinkle, pollywog, pilliwinks, periwig.*

The situation of these six places is important for the precise interpretation of the compound. Unfortunately, it cannot be ascertained
in all the examples, as the Bd and Mx instances are only known as
street-names, and are not on the 1″ map. Of the four which can be
located, three are in the corner of a parish. The Berks place is in the
S.W. corner of White Waltham, Holywick Bk is in a pointed projection at the N. end of Medmenham parish, and Hollick Fm Sr,
which was demolished for Brooklands motor-track, was in the S.E.
corner of the parish of Chertsey. It is possible, therefore, that these

† Dugdale gives *Halcuuike,* but the form has been checked in the MS (Cotton
Vitellius A xiii), and the correct reading is *Haleuuike.*

are examples of *healh* used of land in the angle of an estate. Other instances of this usage are given under Bracknell 116. Halewick near Lancing Sx is more likely to contain *healh* in the sense 'valley'.

HEYWOOD FM AND LODGE, *Heiwude* 1190 CartAntiq, *Heiwodewaltham* 1242–3 Fees, *Haywode* 1275–6 RH, 1354 (15th), 1497 Chertsey, *Heywode* 1284 *Ass*, *Heywood* 1339 Cl, 1761 Rocque, *Haywood* 1790 Pride, *Heywood Lodge* 1846 Snare, 'enclosed wood', *v.* (ge)hæg, wudu. The sense of the first el. may be 'part of a forest fenced off for hunting'. The Abbey of Waltham Holy Cross was given permission to enclose the wood t. Ric I (CartAntiq, Rolls 11–20, pp. 44–8). The name occurs in a number of counties.

LITTLEFIELD GREEN, *Lutlefeld'* 1238 Cl (p), *Littelefeud* 1286 ib (p), *Luttlefeld* 1318 *PubLib(Bray)* (p), *Lutlefeld* 1324 *ib*, *Littlefeud* 1340 (1711) Hearne, *Lytilfelde Grene* 1494 Ipm, *Litylfeld* 1497 Chertsey, *Littlefield Green* 1790 Pride, 'small piece of open land', *v.* lȳtel, feld.

LITTLEWICK GREEN, (wood of) *Lidlegewik* 'c. 1060' (13th) KCD 844, (wood of) *Lidleuuike* 1256 Dugdale, *Lidlewyk* 1340 Pat, *Lit(t)ylwik*, *Litylwike*, *Littilwike*, *Littilwykegrove*, *Littilwyk Hacch* 1497 Chertsey, *Little Wick Green* 1761 Rocque, *Littlewick Green* 1790 Pride. The bounds of BCS 762, which include White Waltham, Waltham St Lawrence and Shottesbrooke, run *to hild leage* shortly before the phrase *to wulfa leage*. *wulfa lēah* is Woolley (73), and it seems impossible to avoid the conclusion that *hild lēah* is the 13th-cent. *Lidlege-*. The later confusion of the first element with lȳtel was perhaps aided by the occurrence in the same parish of Littlefield (*supra*).

hild-leage is considered by Forsberg (111) to be a mistake for **hlid-leage*, 'wood or clearing with a gate', *v.* hlid². Dr O. von Feilitzen also considers hlid² to be the likeliest first el. Professor Löfvenberg suggests hliŏ, hlid¹ 'slope' as preferable. Both these commentators reject the literal interpretation of *hild-leage* as 'battle-clearing', from the poetic OE word *hild*.

wīc was added to the original name, possibly to the gen. since lēah is frequently fem. in p.ns.

PADDOCK WOOD. Hearne's account of the bounds of White Waltham in 1711 mentions *a Wood or Coppice called White-Paddock* between

Heywood House (*supra* 72) and *Payley-Street* (*infra*). This is clearly identical with Paddock Wood. An earlier reference occurs t. Ric I (CartAntiq, Rolls 11–20, pp. 44–8), when the monks of Waltham Holy Cross were given the liberty of enclosing their woods of *Witeparroch* and Heywood with a hedge and ditch. It is impossible not to identify this with (*on*) *hwitan pearruc*, (*of*) *hwitan parruce* 1007 (c. 1240) KCD 1303, but this landmark appears to be on the E. boundary of Waltham St Lawrence (*v.* Part 3). Paddock Wood, now on the E. boundary of White Waltham, may be the remnant of a much larger wood which extended right across the parishes of White Waltham and Shottesbrooke. The name means 'white enclosure', *v.* hwīt, pearroc, and cf. the parish name 70.

PALEY STREET, *Payley-Street* 1711 Hearne, *Paly Street* 1761 Rocque, *Paley Street* 1790 Pride. *Pailehirst* 15th Chertsey was near Paley Street. The forms are too late for certain etymology, but may go back to OE **Pǣgan lēah*, '*Pǣga's* clearing', to which hyrst has been added in the earliest form. For *street* used of a hamlet cf. Winkfield Street 41.

WOOLLEY GREEN, (*to*) *wulfa leage* 940 (c. 1240) BCS 762, *Wluelethe* 1224–5 *Ass* (p), *Wluelye* 1241 *ib* (p), *Wolveleye* 1286 Cl, *Wolvele* 1324 Ipm, 1325 Cl, *Woluele* 1327 *SR*, *Wolueleghe* 1340 Hurley, *Wolfle* 1428 FA, *Woolley-Green* 1711 Hearne, *Woley Green* 1761 Rocque, *Woolly Hall and Green* 1790 Pride, 'wolves' wood', *v.* wulf, lē(a)h, and cf. the same name, Pt 2. *Wolligate* ('Woolley gate') is mentioned 15th Chertsey.

ALTMORE, *v.* Altwood in Bray 54. BACK LANE. BUCK FM AND BRIDGE. CANNON LANE. CHERRYGARDEN LANE. CHET-WODE. COACH AND HORSES P.H. THE CUT. FEENS FM, *Fenys* 1497 Chertsey, *Fienles* 15th Chertsey, *Manor and Farm of Feens* 1682 *RecOffCat*, *Manor of Feines, alias Woolfeines, alias Wooleyfeines, alias Woolnefeines* 1700–1 *Bodl*; this was held by a family named *Fiennes* in late 14th and 15th, *v.* VCH III, 172; some forms have the name Woolley (*supra*) prefixed. GREEN LANE, *Green Lane Ground* 1843 *TA*. HORSE AND GROOM INN, *Horse and Groom Meadows* 1843 *ib.* HOW LANE, 1790 Pride, *Le Holelane, Howlane* 1497 Chertsey, *v.* hol² 'hollow'. HOWLANE BRIDGE, 1846 Snare, where *Howlane Wood* is also shown. LANE FM, *the Lane-House* 1711 Hearne. OLD FM. PAYLEYSTREET FM,

v. 73.   POPE'S FM.   SHEEPCOTE LANE, *Shipcotecroftes* 1497
Chertsey, *Shipcott Lane* 1641 *SP, Shipcott-Lane* 1711 Hearne.
STRATTON'S COPSE.   VINE COTTAGE.   WAKE'S FM, *Wiakkes-
mede* 15th Chertsey, *Wiakes* 1497 ib, Thomas *Wyakes* is mentioned
in the second ref.   WALTHAM GROVE.   WALTHAM PLACE,
1761 Rocque, 1790 Pride, *The Hill Farm or Windsors, Windsors alias
Walthams (or Waltham) Place* 1612 VCH III 174, *The Hill House,
formerly Waltham-Place* 1711 Hearne; the estate was owned by the
Windsor family until 1589, *v.* VCH III, 174.   WOOLLEY HALL
(1790 Pride), FM AND FIRS, *v.* 73.   WHITEHOUSE FM, *The White
House* 1729 *PubLib(Clayton)*.

FIELD-NAMES

The principal forms in (*a*) are 1843 *TA*, except for those dated 1816, which
are *LHRS*; early forms for which no source is given are Chertsey, except
for those dated 1711, which are Hearne.

(*a*) Barn Croft or Bean Croft; Bedwell Grove; Berry or Bury Northcot,
Berry Norcot (*Berry Norcott* 1682 *RecOffCat*, for *Berry v.* Burycourt *supra*
70–1); Binfield's Close (*Benfeldes* 1497) Bog Bottom; Bogget Fd (also 1816);
Botany Bay (*v.* 284); Broad Close; Bucketts (*Boketeslonde* 1456, *Beketeslond,
Bokettes Croft* 1497, first el. probably the surname *Buckett*); Calden Fd ((*to*)
cawel dene 940 (c. 1240) BCS 762, *Caweldon* 1349, *Cawden* 1550 VCH III,
'colewort valley', *v.* cāl, cawel, denu); Calves Close; Canden; Church Mead;
Coppice Close; Dial Close (*The Dyall Close* 1606 *LRMB, v.* dial);
Dod(d)ingley (*Doddyngly* 1497, *Doddinglegh* n.d. (15th), *Vodingley* 17th
VCH III, possibly 'Dodda's clearing', *v.* -ing-, lēah); The Down (*Nether-
downe* 1497, *v.* dūn); Drying Close; Finland (*v.* 284); Foster's Plat (possibly
Forestereslond 1497); Garden Piece and Close; Gassons (possibly identical
with *Ebbengegerstone* in (*b*)); The Green; The Grove, Grove Fd and Mdw
(cf. *Le Groffur'* 15th, *Groveveire* 17th VCH III, *v.* grāf, furh); The Half
Acre; Hand Post Fd (*v.* 281); Harpen Lay; Haynes Crofts; Hill Close and
Plat (*v.* plāt[2] and cf. *Hilleende* 15th, *v.* ende[1]); Home Close and Mead;
Honeycombe; Horse Pasture; Hurst Lane Ground; Inlands (*v.* inland);
Innings (*Innings* 1612 VCH III, *Inings Grove* 17th ib, *v.* inning); Joan Croft;
Jone's Mdw; Kiln Fd; Kitchen Close; Ledingham or Lidingham; Lee Plat;
Lindlands or Linlands (*Le Lyndelond, Lynlond* 15th, *v.* līn, land); Marlege;
Mosses; New England Piece (*v.* 284); Nokes (*Nokedowne, Lee Nokegrofe,
Lee Nokhacche* 15th, *The Nokes* 1711, *Nokes Wood* 1790 Pride, *v.* atten,
āc, dūn, grāf, hæc(c)); Norcutt; Oxmoor; Paddock; The Pightle (*v.*
pightel); Pit Ground, The Pits, Pitfield (*Pittfield* 1550 VCH III); Poor's
Plat; Ramsey; Ramsley or Ramsleaze (*Ramsley* 1550 VCH III); Redcrofts
(*Le Redcrofte* 1550 VCH III); Redstone; Ridings (*v.* ryding); Rough Ground;
Sawyers (also 1550 VCH III, cf. *Sawyerescroft* 1349, *Sawierescrofte* 1456,
Sayerescroft 1497); Seechem Shaw 1816; Shackells, Shackle's Fd; Shep-

pard's Croft (*Shepherd's Croft* 1612 VCH III); Slipe (*v.* slipe); Sow Moor; Steppers (a cottage named from some stepping stones, ex inf. Mr R. Cripps); Stone Mdw; The Stone; Stripe; Trunkwell; Turpler or Turplow; The Walk; Walnut Tree Close (*Walnut-Tree Plot* 1711 Hearne); Waltham Common; The Warren; Well Close; Wheat Close; White Fds; Wilding Croft; Wortley; Wotash (*Wotarshe* 1550 VCH III, *Wote Ershe* 1551 *LRMB*, *Watash* 1711 Hearne, possibly identical with Oat Ash in Shottesbrooke 69, with excrescent *W-*).

(*b*) *Ankerhawe* 1497, *Anker Hall, Old and New* 1578 VCH III (*v.* ancra, haga[1]); *Aylewardesbrigge* 15th (*v.* brycg, first el. probably the surname *Aylward*); *Beanclose* 1551 *LRMB*; *Boye* 1550 VCH III; *Bradecroft* 1349, 1456 (*v.* brād, croft); *Brode Mede* 1551 *LRMB*; *Budewell* 1349 (*v.* byden); *Clachyngham* 1349, 1362, *Chagyngehame* 1456, *Chaggynham* 1497 (*v.* ceacga, hamm; (*to*) *ceaggan heal* 940 (c. 1240) BCS 762 is in this vicinity); *Chestfeild* 17th VCH III; *Cokshet* 15th, *Cock-shott Bridge* 1711 (*v.* cocc-scyte; this may be *Cox's Bridge* 1822 OS); *Currescroft* 1497 (first el. a surname); *Dorne Acre* 15th; *Ebbengegarstone* 15th (*v.* gærs-tūn); *Egeleng'* 1200 (15th); *Eyllbudds Lane* 1711 (cf. 51); *Forde* 1497 (p); *Fowlyngehill Corner* 15th (*v.* fuglung); *Frithe* 1497 (p), *Frithecroft* 15th (*v.* fyrhð); *Le Galwes on le common* 15th (*v.* galga); *Godestyll* 1497, *Godestisele* n.d. (*v.* gōd[2], stigel); *Haiwod Marlepite* 15th ('Heywood (72) marlpit'); *Halecroft* 15th (*v.* h(e)alh); *Hatch* 1341 NonInq (p), *Hacchis* 1497 (*v.* hæc(c)); *Hegg* 1341 NonInq (p) (*v.* hecg); *Hengstescroft* n.d.; *Hethe House, Litill Hethe* 1551 *LRMB, Le Hethynnynges* 1400 Fine, 1403–4 Bodl, *Hethenynge, Hetheynyngs* 15th (*v.* hǣð, inning); *Homestall Close* 17th VCH III; *Le Knolle, Knollehille* 1497 (*v.* cnoll); *Lecroft* 1342; *Lepeffeldescrouch(e)* 15th (*v.* crūc[3]); *Longcroft* 1497; *Maistslond* 1497; *Maldecroft* 1342; *Malmyngehames* 1497; *Marshe Feld* 1551 *LRMB*; *Mauditys* 1497, *Mauditiscrofte* 15th (first el. a surname); *Merelanende* 15th (*v.* mere, lane, ende[1]); *Merlin Pitts* 1711; *Middilhege* (*v.* middel, hecg); *Mixtenham, Myxtenham* 15th (*v.* mixen, hamm); *Le Mylne House* 1551 *LRMB*; *Le New Pasture* 1550 VCH III; *Nutherndon, Nuthernden* 1342; *Okelees* 1497 (*v.* āc, lēah); *Palmerslond* 1497; *Powles Lane* 1573 SpecCom; *Redentzeuche* 15th; *Shere Wesland* 1497; *Souteresgrof'* 15th (*v.* sūtere, grāf); *Stert* 1497 (p) (*v.* steort); *Stonepitts* 1551 *LRMB*; *Stoutesgroft, croft named Stoute* 15th (cf. Ric *le Stoute* 1349); *Stroode* 1497 (p) (*v.* strōd); *Suthwode* 1256 Dugdale, *Suthewode* n.d. (*v.* sūð, wudu); *Thorne* 1341 NonInq (p) (*v.* þorn); *Tigheleheld* 15th (*v.* tigel, helde); *Westcascroft* 15th; *Westwanbrigg* 15th (possibly a third bridge on the same stream as Wom Bridge 115 and Wane Bridge 117, it appears to have been near Westleymill) *White-House* 1711; *Wolfeldes* 1456; *Wolueleslond* 1497 (*v.* Woolley 73); *le Worthy* (field called) 1342, *Le Wordyffeld* 15th, *Worthy Field* 17th VCH III (*v.* worðig); *Wylystrowde, Wilstrids* 1551 *LRMB* (possibly *Wylkestrecche* 1349 AD, which may contain strecca).

IV. COOKHAM HUNDRED

Cocham 1190, 1194 P, 1275–6 RH, *Chokeham* 1192 P, *Cokeham* 1193 ib, 1413 Fine, *Kokam* 1241 *Ass*, *Cogham* 1275–6 RH, *Cokham* 1284 *Ass*, 1310 Fine, 1316 FA, *Coukham* 1327 *SR*, 1339 Fine.
Named from the royal manor of Cookham (79–80).

Binfield

BINFIELD

Benetfeld' c. 1160 OxonCh, 1220 Cur, *Benetfeld* 1176, 1208 P (p),
    1224–5 *Ass*, 1400 Fine, *Benetfelde* 1336 Ipm, 1339 Fine, 1378
    BM, *Benettefeld* 1339 Cl
Benefeld 1185 RR (p) *et freq* with variant spellings *Benefeld'*,
    Benefeud to 1380 Fine; *Benifeud* 1217 Pat, *Benyfeld* 1447 Fine
Binefeld 1224–5 *Ass*
Bunetfeld' 1241 *Ass* (p)
Bentfeld' 1241 *Ass* (p), *Bentefeld* 1284 ib, *Bentfeld* 1297 Ipm (p)
Bunefeld', *Bunefeud'* 1284 *Ass*, *Bunefeld* 1302 Cl (p)
Benfelde 1388 Fine
Bynfeld 1517 D Inc

'Open land where bent-grass grows', *v.* beonet, feld and cf. Ess 533, O 65, for other examples of the same name.

COKELEY, cf. *Colecaimed* ?13th *PubLib*(*Bray*) (endorsed *Colcaye Mede*), *Calcrey Mede* 1552 LRMB, *Cockery(e) Meade* Jas I *TRMB*, *Cocrye Meade, Cookrye* 1606 LRMB, *Cockery Meadow, Cokery Four Acres* 1837 *TA*. The forms are too diverse for etymology.

ALBEN RD. ALLANBAY PK. AMEN CORNER, 1846 Snare, near the parish boundary, possibly from prayers during beating of bounds. APPLEPIE GREEN. ARTHURSTONE. BENHAMS COPSE. BILLINGBEAR FM, *v.* 112. BINFIELD CT, GROVE AND LODGE. BINFIELD GROVE FM. BINFIELD HO, 1790 Pride, 1800 Eden, 1846 Snare. BINFIELD PK, PARK FM, *Park, Great and Little Park* 1837 *TA*. BLACKMAN'S COPSE. BLADE BONE P.H. BLOSSOMFIELD. BRIDGE HOUSE P.H. BROOKLANDS, *Brook Meadow* 1648 VCH III,

1837 *TA*. BUCKHOUSE FM, cf. *Buckhurst Hill* 1837 *TA*, possibly named from Buckhurst in Wokingham. CABBAGE HILL, 1790 Pride, 1846 Snare, cf. *Cabbage Close and Field* 1837 *TA*. CABBAGE-HILL FM. CHURCH HILL (the name of the road leading to All Saints' Church). CHURCH MEAD. COKELEY BRIDGE, 1846 Snare *v*. 77. COPPIDBEECH LANE, *Copid Beech Lane* 1761 Rocque, *Coppid Beech Lane* 1790 Pride, 1846 Snare, *v*. coppod. THE COTTAGE. COVE'S FM. CRESSEX LODGE. CRIX COTTAGE. EAGLEHURST. EGMONT. ELM GROVE. ELM LODGE. EMMET'S NEST. FARLEY COPSE. FARLEY MOOR, *Farlinge Moore* Jas I *SpecCom* (this name occurs also in Swallowfield (111), with spellings *Farlingmore* c. 1300, *Farlyngmor* 1348). There is a place called Farley in Swallowfield (109), and there was probably another example of this common p.n. in Binfield, represented by Farley Copse, for which there are no early forms. *Farlinge Moore* in Binfield and *Farlingmore* in Swallowfield are probably 'marsh connected with Farley', from two independent examples of the name Farley, connective -ing- and mōr. FELIX FM. FOREST HO, LODGE AND RD, *Forrest* 1837 *TA*. GARDENER'S COPSE. GOLDEN BALL, *Golden Acron* 1761 Rocque, *Golden Acorn* 1822 OS. THE GORSE. GOUGH'S BARN. THE GRANGE. THE GROVE, Jas I *TRMB*. GUY'S COPSE. HAWLAND'S COPSE, *Upper and Lower Haw Lands* 1837 *TA*. HAZELWOOD COPSE AND FM, *Haselwood* 1608 *SpecCom*, *Haselwoode, Hazell Wood* Jas I *TRMB*, *Hasel Wood* 1761 Rocque, *Hazelwood Common* 1790 Pride, *Hazel Wood Green* 1800 Eden. GREAT AND LITTLE HAZES, *Ha(y)zes, Furze Hayzes* 1837 *TA*. HILL FM, *Hill Close, Ground and Field* 1837 *TA*. THE HOOKS. JACK OF NEWBURY P.H. JOCK'S COPSE AND LANE, *Jocks Field* 1837 *TA*. JOLLY FARMER P.H. LEVER'S PIECE. LONG COPSE. LONG GROUND. MANOR FM. MANOR HO, *Binfield Place* 1822 OS. MOOR CLOSE, 1837 *TA*. MURRELLHILL FM. NORTHWOOD. PICKED POINT, *Picking Poynte* (coppice called) Jas I *TRMB, Pickinge Poynts* 1606 *LRMB*, *v*. pīced. PITT'S BRIDGE. POCOCK'S COPSE. POINT COPSE. POLLARDROW COPSE, *Pollard Rows* 1837 *TA*. POPE'S WD, 1790 Pride, 1822 OS, *Popes Bridge* 1846 Snare, *Popes Cottage, Popes Wood Cottage* 1846 ib (Alexander Pope, 1688–1744, spent most of his boyhood at Binfield). POPES-WOOD, POPESWOOD LANE. PRIMROSEHILL. RAMSTED HO. RED ROSE. RIGGS COPSE. RIVERMEAD PLANTATION. ROSE FM. ROSE HILL. ROUNDS HILL, ROUNDSHILL FM. RYEHURST LANE,

Ryhurst Green and Field 1837 *TA*; cf. *Rye Arsh* 1647 VCH III, 123, *v.* ryge, ersc.   SHOULDER OF MUTTON INN, 1846 Snare.   SPINNING-WHEEL LANE, *Spinning Wheel Ground* 1837 *TA*.   THE TERRACE. TILEHURST LANE.   TINKERS COPSE.   UNDERWOOD COTTAGE. WESTCOTT GORSE, cf. *Northcot infra* (f.n.).   WESTLEYMILL, *Westney Myll* 1522 *LRMB*, *Westlowe-Mills* 1711 Hearne, *Westley Mill Bridge*, *Westley br. Lane* 1800 Eden, *Westley Bridge* 1846 Snare. WHITEHOUSE FM.   WICK'S GREEN, 1837 *TA*, 1846 Snare, *Wixies* 1635 *RentSur*.   WILSON'S COPSE.   WINDMILL COTTAGE.   WINTON CROFT.   WOOD LANE.   WOODLANDS.

FIELD-NAMES

The principal forms in (*a*) are 1837 *TA*, except for those dated 1800, which are Eden, and 1846 Snare; early forms dated Jas I are *TRMB*, 1552 and 1606 *LRMB*.

(*a*) Angells Mead; Barn Close, Fd and Mdw; Beacher; Bear Mdw; Biddle's Fd; Brewhouse Piece; Brick Kiln Fd; Bridle Hill; Broad Mdw (*Broadmead* Jas I); Broad Water 1800; Budging Hame (*Budginggame Meade*, *Litel Budgginggam' Pastur* 1606); Burgess' Mdw (*Burgesses Meade* Jas I, *Burgis Meade Pidle* 1606); Church Fd; Clog Weeds (cf. *Clubweed* Jas I); Clover Fd; Common Piece; Coppice Fd, Mdw, Moor and Ground (*The Coppice*, *Coppice Close* Jas I); Dockwell; Duke of York Piece; Foot Path Ground; Frontage; Fuel Allotment; Further Ground; Garden Mdw; Gascoigne Mead; Gensis Mdw; Goldridge (*Goleridge* 1606); Grassy Hook; Green Lane Allotment; Grove Grounds; The Half Acre; Half Moon (cf. 283); Hamblins Mead; Ham Corner (*Hamme* 1606, *v.* hamm); Hand Pightle (*v.* pightel); Hawthorne; Hickems; High Fd; High House Close; Hobble Close; Hog's Trough; Great Hogwell (*Hogewells* 1606); Home Mdw and Fds; Hop Garden; House Mdw; Innings, Long, Short, Great and Little (*Inninge* 1605 *SpecCom*, *Longe Inninges* 1606, *v.* inning); Intake (probably newly enclosed ground); Jack Ground and Mdw; Killing Grove (*Killing-groue* 1606); Kitchen Fd (*Kitchinfeild* 1606, *v.* cycene); Lane End (cf. *Lanecroft* 1520 *Windsor*); Lea Barn Mdw; Longcroft (*Langcroft* 1605 *SpecCom*); Long Slip (*v.* slipe); Merrills (*Merry Hills* 1605 *SpecCom*, *v.* myrge, hyll); Mill Bridge 1800; Mill Green; Millers Close and Fd; New Croft; Northcot; Nursery; Oak Pightle; Old House Mdw; Orange Hill 1846; Paradise Mdw (*v.* 283) Pear Tree Close; Pickles, Pickle Close, Pightle (cf. *Puddles als Pyddles* Jas I, *v.* pightel); Pond Mdw; Potatoe Ground; Pramslade Pightle; Ramslade; Readings (*Redings* 1552, *Redinges* Jas I, *Ridinges* 1606, *v.* ryding); Rookery; The Rows; Stackpool (*Stakpole-mede* 1552, *Stakepole Meade* Jas I, *Stakepoole Meade* 1606, *v.* staca, pōl); Stubb's Stile; Tippets Lane 1800 (also 1761 Rocque, *Tippit Lane* 1790 Pride); Trumplets; Turnpike Mdw and Fd; White Hill House 1846 (also 1672 *Bodl*); Winding Fd and Ground; Woo Croft, Further and Hither.

(b) *Avyd Croftes* Jas I; *Bargherst* 1230 Ch (possibly beorg and hyrst, Professor Löfvenberg suggests OE *bearg* 'pig' as first el.); *Benetfeldesheth* 1337 Pat ('Binfield heath'); *Birds Lane* 1552; *Blackpitt* 1644 *SpecCom*; *Bonelake* Jas I; *Bradecroft* 1349 AD (v. brād, croft); *Bucket Hill* 1761 Rocque, *Buckets Hill* 1790 Pride (possibly identical with Bucketts in White Waltham 74); *Culvercrofte* 1606 (v. culfre); *Depers Manor* 1538 BM, *Diapers* 1606, *Diphurst* 1608 *SpecCom*, *Diapers als Deepers* Jas I, *Depars Farme* 1635 *RentSur* (the history of the manor is discussed VCH III, 121, but none of the recorded owners is surnamed *Diaper*, so this may be a p.n., v. hyrst); *Downemead* 1606; *Durneford* 1528 *Windsor*, *Dunford Pidell* 1606 (v. d(i)erne, ford, a common name); *Esteam'* 1606; *Estgrove* 1348 Cl; *Feldams Coppice* 1606; *Foxlease* Jas I (v. lǣs); *Frengecrofte* 1606; *Le Furson* 1552 (a dial. form of *furze*); *La Giggehurne* 1348 Cl (v. hyrne; first el. possibly *gig* NED sb¹4 'a flighty girl'); *Hadnes* 1586 Moulton, *Hadnest Hurst* 1608 *SpecCom*, *Hadden Hurst*, *Haydenys Wood* Jas I, *Had(d)enhurst Wood*, *Hardenhurst* 1644 *SpecCom*, *Hadneys Wood als Hadneys Hurst Wood* 1661–2 *SpecCom*; *Le Halle Place* 1348 Cl, *Hallgroveclose* 1552 (v. h(e)all); *The Harpe* 1635 *RentSur* (this is a common f.n. in Gl, referring to shape); *Hawe Hatch* 1606 (v. hæc(c)); *Hawks Wood* 1761 Rocque; *Hazel Hatch* 1647 VCH III (v. hæc(c)); *Howbrook Lane* 1761 Rocque; *Lackynnynge Lande* 1598 Moulton; *Lamas Piddell'* 1606 (v. 281); *Leegrove Coppice* 1606; *Lees, The Leases* 1606; *Longstrete-lane* 1528 *Windsor*; *Le Marshe* 1552, *The Marshes* Jas I, *Short Marshe, The Three Marshes* 1606; *Myllponde Meade* 1598 Moulton, 1606; *Pease Croft* 1655 VCH III; *Pennymershe* 1606 (v. pening); *Pookepidell* 1606 (v. pūca, second el. a variant of pightel); *Priestwood Common* 1719 VCH III; *Redhurst* 1278 Ch (v. rēad, hyrst); *Roughgrove* 1348 Cl, *Rowgrove Meade, Pidel and Coppice* 1606 (v. rūh); *Runnall Gate* 1606; *Strodemede* 1527 *Windsor*, *Stroud Meade, Strood Pidell* 1606 (v. strōd); *Suthale* 1278 Ch (v. sūð, h(e)alh); *Welstrode* 1506 *Windsor* (v. w(i)ella, strōd); *Westenham Mill* 1550 BM, *Westerham Mill* Jas I, *Westman Hill* 1688 *PubLib*; *Wickham Greene* Jas I; *Wood Close* Jas I; *Woodrow* Jas I, *Woodrowe* 1670 Moulton; *Wydecrofte* 1552, *Wydcrofte* 1606 (v. wid, croft); *Wythemedegrove* 1348 Cl (v. wiðig, mǣd, grāf).

Cookham

COOKHAM

Coccham 798 (late 13th) BCS 291, (æt) *Coccham* c. 971 (12th) ASWills

(*to*) *Cócham* probably 997 (contemporary) ASWills, *Cocham* s.a. 1006 (12th) FW

Cocheham 1086 DB, 1157, 1164 P, *Cockeham* 1175 ib, *Cokeham* 1265 Ipm *et freq*

Cocham 1156 P *et passim* with variant spellings *Chocham, Cokham, Kocham*; *Coca'* 1185 RR, *Koka'* 1205 OblR, *Cokam* 1212 Fees *Coukham* 1327 *SR*, 1361 Cl, *Cookham* 1399 Fine

There are several names in -ham by the Thames in this part of the county, for which it is impossible to say whether the second el. is hām or hamm. In the case of Cookham, the situation is appropriate to hamm, but as there are three OE forms without -*mm*, hām should probably be preferred.

As regards the first el. the earliest spellings are not consistent. ASWills XVI (2), which is a contemporary parchment, gives *Cócham* as the name of the place where King Æthelred was holding his council. There is no reason to doubt that this is the royal manor of Cookham, and the later spellings, particularly *Coukham* 1327, *Cookham* 1399, support the -*ō*- of *Cócham*. The form *Coccham* occurs, however, in two ME copies of OE charters. The later of these references, from ASWills IX, seems certain to refer to Cookham, as it occurs with other places in Berks and the estate is left to the King. The identification with Cookham of *Coccham* in BCS 291 seems virtually certain on historical grounds which are discussed in Pt 3 (Introd). It seems necessary to assume that the 12th- and 13th-cent. scribes of ASWills IX and BCS 291 substituted *Cocc*- for *Coc*- owing to cocc[1] 'hill' and cocc[2] 'cock' being fairly common in p.ns. whereas *cōc* is possibly unknown except in this name.

The etymology appears to be 'cook village'. This would be an unusual type of p.n., but might perhaps be compared with Harpham 'harp village' YE 89–90, both names referring to a village noted for a particular activity.

Cock Marsh *infra* is probably not connected with the parish-name.

BRADLEY (lost), *Bradeleg'* 1220 Fees (p), *Bradelegh* 1317 *ECR*, *Bradele* 1347 Ipm, *Bradelegh* 1361 ib, *Little Bradley Greene* 1608 *LRMB*, *Great and Little Bradley* 1699 *PubLib*, 'broad wood or clearing', *v.* brād, lē(a)h, there are several instances of this name in Berks. The manor of Great Bradley lay on the north side of the road from Cookham Dean to the station, near the railway (VCH III, 128).

CANNONCOURT FM, *Cannon Court* 1541 VCH III 128, 1597 ChanProc, *Canon Farm* 1761 Rocque, *Cannon Farm* 1790 Pride, cf. also *Cannon Down* 1609 Darby, *Cannon Downe Feilde* 1627 *PubLib*(*Clayton*), so named from the Augustinian Canons of Cirencester, who were given the estate by Henry I and retained it till the Dissolution.

COCK MARSH, *Cokmerhs* 1317 *ECR*, *Cokmersh* 1344 *ib*, *Cokmarshe*, *Cokmershgate* 1608 *LRMB*, *Cockmershe Tarrs* 1636 *SpecCom*. First el. cocc^2 'wild bird' or cocc^1 'hillock, heap'. The second el. could refer to the tumuli on the low ground by the R. Thames. *Cockden Grove*, for which early forms are given *infra* 85, may be a related name, and here again it is impossible to say whether cocc^1 or cocc^2 is more likely. Previous authors (DEPN, Elements 1, 104) have connected *Cocdun* with Cookham, but, as explained *supra*, Cookham has a first el. cōc, and the two names discussed here seem more likely to derive from *cocc*.

ODNEY, *Odeney'* c. 1270 *Ass* (p), *Odenaie* a. 1290 *ECR*, *Odney* 1609 Darby, 'Oda's island', *v.* (ī)eg; the land is surrounded by streams.

SHAFTSEY (?lost), *Sceaftesige* 911–19 (c. 1025, 1562) Burghal Hidage, *Sefteseya* 1220 Fees (p), *Shafteseya* 1241 *Ass*, *Shetefley* 1275–6 RH, *Shaftseys Eight* 1899 Darby (*v.* ēgeð). For the identification with the place in the Burghal Hidage, and the exact location of the island in the Thames, *v.* Brooks and Gelling, *Medieval Archaeology* VIII (1964), 74–90. The name means either 'Sceaft's island', or 'island of the pole', *v.* sceaft, (ī)eg.

SLOW GROVE, (meadow called) *Slograve* 1252–5 FF, *Slogroue* 1633 *SpecCom*, *Slouegrove* 1637 *ib*, *Slogrove Mead* 17th *PubLib(Clayton)*, *v.* grāf 'grove'. The name is applied on the 6″ map to some marshy islands in the Thames, and the first el. could be slōh 'mire' or slāh 'sloe'.

BEECHING-GROVE WD, *Beechen Grove* 1609 Darby.   BEECHWOOD. COOKHAM BRIDGE (cf. *Bridge Close* 1609 Darby), COMMON, END AND RISE.   COOKHAM DEAN, 1761 Rocque, 1790 Pride, cf. *Le Dene* 1344 *ECR*, *Le Deane*, *Deanefeild* 1608 *LRMB*, *The Deane*, *The Deane House* 1699 *PubLib*; Osb. *de la Dene* had land in Cookham 1220 Fees, *v.* denu.   COOKHAMDEAN COMMON.   COOKHAM FERRY, 1633 *SpecCom*, 1739–40 ArchJ 19.   COOKHAM MILL, *molendina de Cokeham* 1270 Cl.   THE COPPICE.   DEAN CROFT AND FM, *v.* Cookham Dean *supra*.   DIAL CLOSE, 1843 *TA*, *Dyall Close* 1609 Darby, *v.* dial.   ENGLEFIELD HO.   FIRCROFT.   FORMOSA PLACE, *Formosa Island* 1790 Pride.   FURZE PLATT.   THE GROVE, *Graua* 1241 *Ass* (p), *The Grove or Cookham Grove* 1899 Darby. HARWOOD, *Harwoode* 1606–7 *SpecCom*, *Harwoods* 1609 Darby, near the parish boundary, *v.* hār^2.   HAZELDENE.   HILLGROVE FM

AND WD (*Hill Grove* 1609 Darby).   HILL HO (cf. names in hyll *infra* 83).   HINDHAY FM.   HURST.   KING'S COPPICE FM, *Coppice Farm or King's Coppice Farm* 1899 Darby.   LADY FERRY, cf. *Lady Mead* 17th *PubLib*(*Clayton*), *Lady Close* 1899 Darby, v. hlǣfdige.   LONG COPSE.   LULLE BROOK, LULLEBROOK MANOR, *Lollebrookes* 1622 *PubLib*, *Manor of Lollybrooks als Lillybrooks* 1752 ArchJ 15, v. 14.   MALDERS LANE, 1899 Darby.   MANOR HO. MAY BANK.   MELMOTH LODGE.   THE MOOR, MOOR HALL, *Mora* 1241 *Ass* (p), *Cookham Moor* 1609, 1899 Darby, *Moorhall Meadow* 1843 *TA*, v. mōr.   MOUNT FM AND HILL (1899 Darby), THE MOUNT, v. mont.   NOAH'S HO (only on 2½″ map), cf. *Noahs Ark* 1899 Darby, v. 283.   PIGEONHOUSE WD, *Pigeon House Coppice* 1843 *TA*.   POUNDCROFT, POUND FM, cf. *Poundfeild* 1608 *LRMB*. RONDELS, *Randalls* 1609 Darby.   ROUND COPSE.   ROWBOROUGH, 17th *PubLib*(*Clayton*), *Rowborowe, Rowboroe* 1608 *LRMB*, 'rough barrow', v. rūh, beorg: Darby says that Anglo-Saxon remains were found here.   SHEEPHOUSE FM.   SPADEOAK FERRY.   STER-LINGS.   STONE HO, *Stonehowse* 1633 *SpecCom*, *StonehouseEiot als Eight* 1636 *ib* (v. ēgeð), Darby says this was so named in 1532, when it belonged to the Prior of Bisham.   STRAND WATER, STRAND OR FLEET DITCH, YE STRAND CASTLE, *Strand, Strond* 1609 Darby, *Stronde Close* 1650 *ib*, *Strand Reach* 1843 *TA*, v. strand.   SUNNY-BANK.   SUTTON LODGE, *Sutton* 1386, 1719 *ECR*, *Comon Feild called Sutton* 17th *PubLib*(*Clayton*), *Sutton* 1609 Darby, *Sutton Field* 1843 *TA*, immediately S. of Cookham, v. sūð, tūn.   TYTHE BARN. WESTMEAD, 1627 *PubLib*(*Clayton*), *Westmeade* 1609 Darby, *The West Meade* 1648 *PubLib*(*Clayton*), W. of Cookham.   WHITEBROOK COMMON (WIDBROOK COMMON on 6″), *Widbrooke Pasture* 1649 Darby, *Widebrook Common* 1790 Pride, *Whitbrook Common* 1822 OS.   WHITE BROOK, v. 18.   WHITE HART P.H.   WHITE PLACE, 1609 Darby, *White Place Lawn* 1843 *TA*.   WIDBROOK FM, v. White Brook *supra*.   WINDMILL SHAW, *Windmill Coppice and Field* 1609 Darby.   WINTER HILL, 1899 *ib*, *Winter Hill Common* 1843 *TA*.   WINTERHILL FM AND HO.   WISPINGTON HO. WOODLANDS FM.

FIELD-NAMES

The principal forms in (*a*) are 1899 Darby except where otherwise stated; those marked *TA* are 1843 *TA*; early forms for which no source is given are Darby; those dated 17th are *PubLib*(*Clayton*). Information about landowners and topography is from Darby.

(a) Back Lane; Bald Steys; Barn Close and Stitch (*Barn Close and Park* 1609); Barney, Great and Little, Barney Hedge Shot; Bartle Mead, Great Bartles *TA* (*Bartelmede* 1523, *Bartle Mead* 17th, *Battlinge Mead* 1650); Bass Mead (*Bast Meade* 1548–9 *RentSur*, *Basse Mead* 1609); Beggar's Shaw; Bell Acre (*v.* 285); The Berrys (*Le Byres* 1498, *Le Bury* 1515, *Berry* 1609, perhaps byrig, dat of burh, with a ME plural in -*s*); Birds Close; Black Butts (*Le Blakebouttes* 1315 *ECR*, *Black Buttes* 1353 *Windsor*, *Black Bottes* 1524, *v.* blæc, butte); Blackamore Lane and Mdw (*Blakemore* 1477, *Blackmoore Lane* 1609, from a family); Bowden's Green (from a family); Bradcutts (*v.* 281); Brick Close *TA*; Broad Mead *TA* (also 1609); Bughazels (*Bugh Assils*, *Bughavills* 1609, William *de Buggehesel* is said in VCH III, 126, to have held land in Lullebrook e.13th); Bullocks (*Bullox Lee* 1609, from a family); Bulls Piece (*The Bulls*, *Bulls Close End* 1609); Burial Road; Bush Hill Slade (*Bush Hill* 1609); Butcher Dick's Mdw; Butt's Piece; Calves Ley (*Calves Leaze* 1609, *Calves Leaze Close* 17th, *v.* læs); Carter's Fd (*Carter's Farm* 1650, *Carter's Slade* 1664); Carter Shed, Carthouse Close (*Cart House Shed Meadow TA*); Castle Hill; Cat Moor (Darby says this is identical with *Catseyfeild* 16th VCH III, *Catsey Field* 1609, *v.* cat(t), (ī)eg); Chalk Pit Kents, Chalk Pit Shot; Choke Lane; Churchfield (also 1609, glebe land of the Abbey of Cirencester); Cocks Burrow, Coxborow; College, Great and Little (formerly belonging to Eton College); Coney Close (also 1609); Coney Coppice (cf. *Coney Close Grove* 1609); Court House Lane (*Court House Close* 1609); Cow Pasture; Cranefield, Great; Crooked Close; Crutchfield Corner (from a family); Curby Close *TA*; Dabstone Lane and Shot; Dickerleys Mdw and Hill (*Dickerleaze Hill Close* 1609, *v.* dicor, læs); Dismals, Long (*Dismarks* 1502, *Disners* 1609; John *Disners* witnesses a deed in Hurley 1322); Dollys Fm and Hill (possibly *The Doules* 1696); Driftway *TA* (*v.* 281); Dry Close, Dry Wells, Drying Ground; The Elms; Fag End; Farm Coppice (also 1509); Feens Shaw Close and Moor (*Ffynes More* 1488, *Fynesmore* 1523, *Feens Moor* 1609, *v.* mōr, first el. a surname); Fern Close; Fishery Mdw; Gayhole Furlong; Geldings (*Geldon's Close* 1609); Gibraltar Close and Wood (*v.* 284); Giles (also 1609); Gladman's Eyott (*v.* ēgeð); God's Close (*Gods Barne* 1573, *v.* god¹); Goose Mdw (cf. *Le Goosacres* 1386 *ECR*); Gravelly Close; Gravel Pit Close (also 1609); Great Fd; Great Leys, Greatley Fd *TA*; Great Orchard; Greenhill Lake; Green Lane Furlong and Pightle; Green Leys *TA*; Greenway *TA* (*La Grenewey* 1358 *ECR*, *Greenways Lake Close* 1609); Hall Dore, Hall Dore Shot (*Halldore* 1609, *Hall Doore Field* 17th, perhaps 'field at the hall door'); Ham Fd (also 1609, *Ham* 1649 *Windsor*, *v.* hamm); Hamerton's Elms (from a family); Harrow Lane and Mdw (from a Public House); Head Piece *TA*; Headington Coppice; Hemmings (*Hemyngs* 1609, from *Heming de Biggefrith* (in Bisham 60) mentioned 1284); Hill Fd and Close (*Hulle* 1218–19 *FF*, *La Hull'* 1220 Fees (p), *La Hulle* 1288 (p), *The Hill*, *Hill Close*, *Hilfield* 1609, *v.* hyll); Hog Close; Hog Trough (from the shape); Hollybush Close (*The Hollybush* 1609); Home Close; Home Fd (also 1609, cf. *Home Leys* 1412); Horton Grange; Howfield, Great (*Ho* 1207 Hunter Fines, *La Ho* 1220 Fees (p), 1241 *Ass* (p), (*boscus de*) *Ho*, (*villa de*) *Ho* 1241 *ib*, *Ho* 1278 Ch (p), 1280 Cl (p), *Hoo*

1324 ib (p), 1495, 1526, *Le Hoo* 1356, *La Hoo* 1366 *Windsor*, *Le Hoo-croft* 1477 ib, *Howe* 1485, *Howefields* 1609, *Howe Close* 1706 ArchJ 24, *v.* hōh); Ice Lake; The Ince (formally this could be identical with Ince Ch, La, from PrWelsh inis 'an island', but there are no early forms to support this conjecture); Islip Eiott (*v.* ēgeð); Kentish Down Bottom; Kiln Platt Mdw; The Lakes (*Long Lakes Close* 1609); Landgrove (*Lancroftefure* 1345 *Windsor*, *Langrove* 1609, *Longrove Close* 17th; if the names are identical, the second el. is croft, corrupted to *grove*, and the first is probably lang); Lawn Fd (*v.* launde); Leapfrog Mdw; Ley, Great and Little (*La Leyhe* 1371, *Legh* 1410, *Le Lee* 1477 *Windsor*, *Lea Farm* 19th, *v.* lēah); Leys Green; Lightlands (*Lichtwud'* 1205 RotChart, *Lichtwud* 1208, *Lichtlond* 1248 Ch, *Lithtlond* 1341 Pat, *The Light Land* 1553, *Lightlands* 1614, 19th, 'light-coloured wood and land', *v.* lēoht, wudu, land); Linkey Down Bottom and Shot (*Langinden* a. 1290 *ECR*, *Langyndon* 1309 *Windsor*, *Langedene* 1389 ib, *Langdene* 1426 *ib*, 1527, *Langdon*, *Longdown* 1609, *Lankey Down Bottom TA*, 'at the long valley', *v.* lang, denu, cf. *Shortynden* in Maidenhead 58); Lion Mead (*v.* leyne); Little Mdw (*Little Mead* 1609); Lock Mead (also 1609 and 17th); Long Ground; Long Mead (also 1609); Long Mead Hill; Lot Acre (also 1609, *v.* hlot); Lousy Hill (*v.* 283); Love Lane; Maberley, Great and Little, *TA*; Mead Hill; Miles Plat (*v.* plat²); Minson Mdw (*Michen Meade* 1609, cf. (meadow called) *Munchenelesse*, *Munechenelese* 1294 *ECR*, *v.* myncen 'nun', lǣs); Moor Lane Piece (cf. The Moor *supra*); Mossy Hill; My Lady Close *TA*; Navelling Pits (*Napkin Pitts* 1609, possibly *Kapden Pitt* 1617); Neats Crops; The New Inclosure *TA*; North Moor; Oaken Grove (also 1609); Oakley Close (*Oakley Hedge Closes* 1609); Oxen Close; Oxneys Mead; Parsons Croft (also 1609, 1634); Partridge Mead; Patches Close and Wood (*Patches Grove* 1609); Pauls Foot, Pauls Leg (possibly *Powle Acre* 17th, *foot* and *leg* referring to shape); Penling Close; Perrycroft (also 1609); Peter's Close; Picksfield Close (*Pixfield* 1581, 1609, *v.* pīc, cf. *Pixhill Yeate* 1494 *ECR*); Place Orchard; Plastows (*Plaisters* 1609, *Plasters* 1731, possibly pleg-stōw); Pond Mead; Poor Man a Peny (*v.* 283); Popes Lane; Press Meade Furlong (*Priest Meade* 1609); Pudding Acre (*v.* 284); Puntalls Coppice; Punt Hill; Ragaback Close (the ground is rugged); Ricksfield; Ridings (*La Rydynges* 1389 *Windsor*, *Le Rudyng* 1477 *ib*, ryding); Road Furlong; Rookhill; Rough Mead (*Rowmede* 1511, 1609, *v.* rūh, mǣd); Sand Grove *TA*; Sandhill Close and Fd; Shackles Moor; Shearland Close, Shearlings (*Sherlings* 1609); Shepherds Close (also 1609); Shortcrops, Lower and Upper; Shot, Cross and Long (*v.* scēat); Shoulder of Mutton Piece *TA* (*v.* 283); Shrew; Sydenham Mead (*Sidenham* 1609, *Sidnam* 17th, 'spacious river-meadow', cf. O 465); Slades (*Slade* 1320 *ECR*, 1420 ib, 1426 *Windsor*, *Slade Meadow and Shot*, *Slade TA*, *v.* slæd); Slipe (*v.* slipe); Small Meade (*Smalmed* 1471, *Small Meade* 1609, *v.* smæl, mǣd); Soanes (so named 1609, *Soons* 1543); Southey Close, Lower and Upper Southey (*Southey* 1574, *Southie* 1609, *v.* sūð, (ī)eg); Spike Orchard; Spots Mead; Spring Close *TA*; Staple Close *TA*; The Stich (*Stich* 1609, *v.* sticce¹); Stoney Leys (*Stoney Lee*, *Stoney Croft* 1609); Stubbings (*v.* stubbing); Summerhouse Mead; Summer Leaze (*Soomerleaes* 1573 SpecCom, *Somerleaze*, *Somerclose* 1609, *v.* sumor, lǣs); Sun Paddock *TA*; Swinsead Homestead (*Swineshead* 1470,

Swineshead Stile 1609, apparently identical with Swineshead BdHu 20); Tarr, Great and Little, Tarr Buck, Tarr Cockmarsh, Tarr Horneyarde, Tarr Longmead, Tarr Oozie, Tarr Peacock, Tarr Round, Tarr Willows (*Buck Tarr* and *Round Tarr* are mentioned 1636 *SpecCom*; these are all islands in the Thames, and the word *tarr*, which is not in any dictionary, is presumably a local term for an island); Terrys, Great and Little, Terrys Coppice (*Terrys* 1451, *Terris Close, Terrors Grove* 1609, from a surname, cf. John *Terry* 1387 *ECR*); Thumps; Tile Copice, Tilers Coppice; Townsen Close and Wood; Tugwood Common; Turners Close (*Turners Mead* 1633); Warpole Furlong and Gore; Wasdell Shot; Waterbutts Mdw; Waterloo Close (*v*. 284); Watery Butts; Well Coppice (cf. *Wellondes* 1469, *Well Close* 1609); Wellhouse Fd (*Welhouse Fielde* 1573 *SpecCom, Woolhouse Field* 1609); Wettons Mdw and Moor; Whirlpool Shot; Whittlea, Whiteley (*Whiteley Close and Gate* 1609, *v*. hwit, lēah); Wix Pightle; Woodmancuts (*Wdemenechoc*' 1220 Fees (p), *Wodeman(e)cote* 1241 *Ass* (p), *Wodemancote* 1340 Cl, 1361 Ipm (p), *Woodmancotes* 1545, *Woodmancutts* 1609, possibly a surname derived from one of the places called Woodmancote in Gl, Ha, Sx, Wo, but a deed of 1401 in *ECR* refers to land of Nicholas de *Wodemancote* at *Wodemancote* in Cookham); Workhouse Mdw; Worthy, Lower and Upper (*v*. worðig); Yanks.

(b) *Aluedemed* 1346, 1419 *ECR* (*v*. mǣd, first el. possibly a fem. pers.n.); *Andreshames* 1536 (*v*. hamm, first el. possibly the surname *Andre*); *Appesmede* 1386 *ECR*, *Aps Mead* 1609, 1696 (*v*. æspe, mǣd); *Archery Butts* 1509; *Asschforlong* 1309, 1352 *Windsor* (*v*. æsc); *Assheheit* 1634 (*v*. æsc, ēgeð); *Babeham* 1220 Fees (p), *Babham* 1346 Pat (p), *Babhams End* 1600 Camden, *Babham-End* 1719 Ashmole (there is an account of the Babham family in VCH III, 129, the surname is probably derived from a f.n. in Cookham meaning 'Babba's meadow', *v*. hamm); *Bardel Down* 1609; *Bare Leaze* 1561 (*v*. lǣs); *Barley Close* 1609; *Barrett Fere* 1609 (*v*. furh); *Bassemere* 1333 *ECR*; *Beanleaze* 1634 (*v*. lǣs); *Belton's Barn* 1609, *Biltons Barne* 1650; *Berendemulle* 1329 Darby, 1337 Cl ('burnt mill', *v*. berned, myll); *Bokeland* 1483 (*v*. bōcland); *Borrowland* 1573; *Bradelhuth* 1394 (*v*. hȳð); *Bradwell* 1480 (*v*. brād, w(i)ella); *Brambyburye* 15th VCH III (*v*. burh); *Broadcrofts, Broadleaze* 1609 (*v*. lǣs); *Brokfurlong* 1346 *ECR*, *Brokeforlong* 1354 *Windsor*, *Brokforlonge* 1358 *ib*, *Le Broke* 1532 (*v*. brōc); *Bromehill* 1609, *Broomehill* 1649 (*v*. brōm, hyll); *Buffine* 17th; *Bushie Plott Close* 1609; *Bydells* 1524; *Camley Close* 1609; *Checker Fere* 1609, *Chequer Acre* 1650 (*v*. cheker, furh); *Cocdun*' 1220 Fees (p), *Cocdon', Cockdon*' 1241 *Ass* (p), *Cockden Grove* 1609 (*v*. supra 81); *Cokdonse* 1403, 1527, *Cokdonsee* 1451 ('Cockdon fee'); *Cocksfarme* 1609, *Cook's Farm* 1615; *Cokewell* 15th VCH III (this may have the same first el. as Cookham 80); *Collingbourne* 1463; *Common Down* 1609 (cf. Cookham Common supra 81); *Comynslane* 1514; *Cooksbred* 1609; *Cookham Stone* 1506 (according to VCH III, 125, this stone was re-erected in Cookham village 1909; Darby, who says it was known as *Tarry Stone* in the 19th, describes it as a boundary stone of the Abbot of Cirencester's property); *Coppice Close* 17th; *Copyns* 1515; *Corn Close* 1609; *Costallo* 1609; *Le Cowclose* 1608 *LRMB*; *The Creke* 1636; *Cuigate* 1609;

Culver Close 1609 (*v.* culfre); *Curteys Lane* 1506; *Dedeman's Lane* 1456; *Deneslonde* 15th VCH III; *Devenyshe House* 1359 (Robert *Devenische* appears 1321 *ECR*); *Dovehouse Close* 1609; *Eastmorehills* 1650; *Edmundeslonde* 15th VCH III ('Edmund's land'); *Elderstubb* 1609 (*v.* ellern, stubb); *Eldfield Hatch, Eldfield Hill* 1609, *Alville Hatch* 1680 (*v.* hæc(c)); *Elven Close* 17th; *English Heyes* 1523; *Eyrome* 1609; *La Felde* 1220 Fees (p), *Epheldhuse* a. 1290 *ECR*, *La Feldhous* 1381 *Windsor* (*v.* feld); *Ferthynges* 1389 *Windsor*, *Ferthinges* 1403 *ib*, *Ferthynges*, *Fyrthyngisfeld* 1477 *ib*, *Farthings* 1609, 50, *Farthings* 1706 ArchJ 24 (cf. Thom. *Ferthing*, mentioned 1369); *Flaxhawe* 1317 *ECR* (*v.* fleax, haga[1]); *The Folly* 1761 Rocque (*v.* folie); *Forland* 1387, 1389 *Windsor* (*v.* fore, land); *Foxhullehegge* 1386 *ECR* (*v.* fox, hyll, hecg); *Fulpolmed* 1403 *Windsor* (*v.* fūl, pōl, mæd); *Ffinpole* 1517; *Fountain Mead* 1609; *Gasgate, Gargate* 1609; *Gentle Close* 1609; *Ginger Hill* 1609; *Gledingore* 1511; *The Grange* 1482; *Grassehill* 1672; *La Grene* 1247–8 FF (p), *Greene* 1608 LRMB (*v.* grēne[2]); *La Grenegore* 1315 *ECR*, *Le Grenerore* 1389 *Windsor* (*v.* grēne[1], gāra); *Gyrons Lane* 1488; *Hanbedd* 1609, *Vanbedd* 1633; *Hanses Water* 1700; *Hardegrepys* 1488; *Harpaire* 1609; *Haslenutts Coppice* 17th; *Hawkehill* 1573 *SpecCom*; *Hayes* 1706 ArchJ 24; *Henyswyke* 1502, *Haynswyks* 1512, *Hainswick* 1609 (*v.* wic, first el. probably a surname); *Le Hethe* 1353 *Windsor*, *Heathfield* 1608 *LRMB* (*v.* hǣð); *Henknol* 1321 *ECR* (*v.* cnoll); *Le Hyvehous* 1365 *ECR*, *Le Heyhouse* 1608 LRMB; *Hitcham Field* 17th; *Hitchendon* 1649; *Hogesfotescroft* 1388 *ECR*; *Hoggelder* 1609 (cf. *Haggeldern* in Windsor 35); *Le Horkell* 16th VCH III; *Horse Leaze* 1609 (*v.* lǣs); *Le Houleput* p. 1290 *ECR* (*v.* pytt); *Hurtestrete* 1325, *Hurtestreet Furlong, Hurstreet, Horstreet* 1609 (apparently 'hart street', *v.* heorot, strǣt, the same name occurs in Bray 51, probably referring to the same road); *Inwode* 1388 *ECR* (*v.* in, wudu); *Jurdans* 1493, *Jordans Leaze* 1609 (from the surname *Jordan*, which occurs *freq ECR*, and lǣs); *Kakesmeade* 1609 (a family surnamed *Cake* appears *ECR*); *Kitefaire, Kitefeare, Kites Acre* 1609 (*v.* furh); *Landspitt* 1609; *Lanesleaze* 1482, *Lanes Leaze* 1609 (*v.* lǣs); *Lawrencelondes, Laurencelande(s)* 1518 *Windsor*, *Lawrences Farm* 1718 *ib* (a family surnamed *Lawrence* appears *ECR*); *Layfield* 1609 (*v.* lǣge, feld); *Legg Croft* 1609 (*v.* Db 757); *Litelake Close* 1609; *Little Grove* 1609; *Lixton Hill* 1609; *Le Longecroft* 1305 *ECR*, *Long Croft, Longleaze* 1609 (*v.* lǣs); *Longfore* 1426 *Windsor* (*v.* lang, furh); *Marfield* 1609; *Le Markwey* 1333 *ECR*; *Marlston* 1536; *Mereworth* 1456 (*v.* mere, worð); *La Mersshe* 1372 InqMisc, *Mersshemede Acre* 1510, *Le Marsh Mead* 1608 LRMB, *Marsh Meadow* 1609, *The Marsh* 17th (*v.* mersc); *Milkhegge* 1456 (*v.* meoluc, hecg); *Morecroft* 1649, *Le Moreforlong* 1379 *ECR*, *Le Morefer* 1381 *Windsor* (*v.* croft, furh and The Moor *supra*); *Moris Lane* 1514; *La Morstret* 1331 *Windsor* (*v.* mōr, strǣt); *Mulleytes* 1322 (*v.* myln, ēgeð); *Munkeams* 1514; *Mushhorn* 1711; *Myllegarden, Myllemede* 1483, *Mill Close* 1609, *Le Mill Pond* 1636 *SpecCom* (cf. Cookham Mill *supra*); *Netherfonthey* 15th VCH III; *Newehouse* 1668 Moulton; *Niddon* 1477, *Litle and Greate Naddons* 1608 LRMB; *La North Hethe* 1331 *Windsor* (*v.* hǣð); *Nunpitts Fere* 1608 LRMB, *Nunpitt Fere* 1609 (*v.* furh); *Olde House Green* 1609, *Old House Green* 1706; *Olde Leys* 1488; *Orchard Mead* 17th; *The Park* 1609; *Picked Close and Fere* 1609 (*v.* pīced, furh); *Platt* 1609 (*v.* plat[2]);

Priors Leze 1561, *Pryors Leysues* 16th VCH III (*v.* lǣs, lǣswe); *Quangins Oak* 1609; *Queens Common* 1524; *Redishes Farme* 1600 *Bodl* (cf. James *atte Rededyche* 1371 *Bodl*, *v.* rēad, dīc, and cf. Redditch Wo); *Rock Close* 17th; *Salisbury Quarry* 1502, *Salsbury Pitt* 1636 *SpecCom*; *Saracens Head* 1563, 1609; *Schringing Oke* 1554; *Le Sharpende* 1477 *Windsor*, *Sharpes Heire* 1706 ArchJ 24 (*v.* scearp, ende[1]); *Shawes Water* 1609; *Shepecoteforlong* 1388 *ECR*, *Sheepcott*; *Sheepleaze* 1609 (*v.* lǣs); *Short Doll* 1609 (*v.* sceort, dāl); *Smith Close* 1609; *Smythmede* 1540; *Souter* 1609; *Sowllaze* 1609; *Stanlinche* p. 1290 *ECR*, 1294 *ib*, *Stanlynche* 1305 *ib* (*v.* stān, hlinc); *Le Stonde* 1322, *Le Stond* 16th VCH III (this was a pond, and is referred to in BCS 762, A.D. 940, in the phrase *at þære standan*, which gives the location of meadow attached to Waltham; Forsberg (112, n. 2) suggests that *standan* is the oblique case of a noun, OE *stande*, probably meaning 'pond'); *Swede Meade* 1609; *Till Close* 1609; *Totehill Style* 1488 (*v.* tōt-hyll, stigel); *Tryndle Acre* 1503 (*v.* trendel); *Tuggins Lane* 1609; *Wall Notte Tree Close* 1505 ArchJ 4; *Waterdells* 1608 *LRMB*; *Wessenham Lane* 1410 (probably leading to *Wassenham* in Waltham St Lawrence 117); *Wheatley Field* 17th; *Le Wheitcroft* 1305 *ECR* (*v.* hwǣte, croft); *Winchmeade* 1609, *Winches Mead, Winch Mead Acre* 17th (*v.* O 64); *Worth End Gate* 1574 (*v.* worð); *Wykelonde* 1414 *ECR* (*v.* wīc, land); *Wynslowe* 1481 (*v.* hlāw).

Sunningdale

The ecclesiastical parish of Sunningdale was formed in 1841 from portions of Old Windsor, Sunninghill, and the Surrey parishes of Windlesham, Egham and Chobham. It was made into a civil parish in 1894 (Kelly 229). Eden (1800) shows a place called *Sunning Hill Dale* in this area. *v.* Sunninghill *infra* 88.

SUNNINGDALE STREET-NAMES

BEDFORD LANE.   CHURCH LANE AND RD.   COWORTH RD (*v. infra*).   DALE RD.   HIGH ST.   PARKSIDE RD.   RISE RD.   SANDY LANE.   SONNING AVE.   WARDOUR RD.

BROOMHALL, *Brumhala* 1158 P, *Bromhale* 1204 ib *et freq* to 1262 Ch, *Brumhal'* 1206 P, 'broom corner', *v.* brōm, h(e)alh. The places so named are on the borders of Berks and Sr, and the name is discussed Sr 154, but with somewhat later forms. h(e)alh probably refers to land in the corner of a parish, *v.* Bracknell 116.

COWORTH PARK, *Cuwurth'* 1219 Cur, *Cowurth'* 1221 ib, *Cowurthe* 1255 Ipm, *Coworthe, Coworth Hill or Warren Hill* 1607 *Norden*, *Coworth* 1758–9 ArchJ 14, *Cow Worth* 1761 Rocque, 'cow enclosure', *v.* cū, worð.

THE BELT.   BROADLANDS.   BROOMHALL FM AND LANE, *v.* 87. CHARTERS, *Charters Pond* 1822 OS.   DEVENISH RD.   FIREBALL CLUMP.   FROSTFARM PLANTATION. GRAVELPIT CLUMP.   KILN LANE.   KING'S BEECHES, *King's Beeches or Blackwick Hill* 1761 Rocque, *Kings Beech Hill* 1800 Eden.   MOUNT PLEASANT.   THE RISE.   ROSE MOUNT.   SUNNINGHILL PK.   WHITMORE LODGE AND LANE.   WORLDSEND GATE, 1761 Rocque, 1800 Eden, WORLDSEND COTTAGE (on the county boundary, *v.* 284).

The following names of large houses appear on the 6″ map: AIRTH, CALLALY, CHARLCOMBE, CRAIGMYLE, CROFTON, THE DENE, DUNCROFT, GREENWAYS, KNOLE WD, LULWORTH, LYNWOOD, OAKFIELD, PARK LODGE, PINECOTE, ST BRUNO, SCOTSWOOD, WARDOUR LODGE.

FIELD-NAMES

(*a*) Blackwick Hill 1761 Rocque; Cracks Hole 1761 ib; Tinley House 1800 Eden.

Sunninghill

SUNNINGHILL

> *Sunigehill'* 1185 RR (p), *Sunniggehill'* 1199 Hunter Fines, *Sunigehull'* 1246 Cl
> *Sunningehull'* 1190 P (p), *Sunningehulla* 1193 ib (p), *Sunningehell'* 1221 Cur
> *Sunninghull'* 1191 P (p), *Sun(n)inghull* 1275–6 RH, *So(u)nnynghulle* 1327 SR
> *Sonynghull'* 1241 Ass (p), *Sonygehull'* 1294 SR
> *Shunigehull* 1255 Ipm
> *Suni(n)ghull'*, *Sunnynhull'*, *Sunnygeshull'* 1284 Ass
> *Sondynghill* 1447 Fine

'Hill of the *Sunningas*', *v.* hyll and 132–3.

ASCOT, SOUTH ASCOT AND SUNNINGHILL STREET-NAMES

BAGSHOT RD.   BROCKENHURST RD.   CHURCH LANE.   DALE RD. HIGH ST.   KENNEL SIDE (near *Kings Dog Kennell*, 1800 Eden, 1816 OS). LA TOUR RD.   ORIENTAL RD.   SONNING AVE.   STATION RD. SWINLEY RD.   VILLAGE RD, LOWER AND UPPER.

ASCOT, *Estcota* 1177 P (p), *Ascote* 1269 FineR *et freq*, *Astcote* 1348 BM, *Askote* 1359 Fine, 'east cottage(s)', *v.* ēast, cot(e). The name is a common one; this settlement is perhaps called 'east' from its position in relation to Easthampstead.

COOMBE GRANGE, MEADOWS AND LODGE, *Cunbe* (sic) 1220 Fees (p) *Combe* 1327 *SR* (p), *Comb Wood* 1816 OS, *v.* cumb 'valley'.

TITTENHURST, TITNESS PARK, *Tetenhurst* 1228, 1239 Ch, *Titness Park* 1848 *PubLibDoc, v.* hyrst. The first el. is probably a pers.n., perhaps the OE fem. *Tette* or a masc.n. *Tetta.* Cf. Tedburn D 451.

ASCOT HEATH, 1761 Rocque, *Ascott Heath* 1618 SpecCom, *v. supra.* BEGGAR'S BUSH, 1796 *PubLib, Beggers Bush Heath* 1800 Eden, *Beggar's Bush Common* 1812 *PubLib, v.* 283. BIRCH COPSE. BLACKNEST, 1816 OS, BLACKNEST GATE, *Blacknes Beeches* 1607 *Norden, Blackness Bridge* 1800 Eden. BOULDISH FM. BOW-LEDGE HILL, 1800 Eden. BREWER'S POND, *Brewers Ponde* 1607 *Norden.* BRICK KILN FM. BROAD POOL, BROADPOOL COTTAGES. BROOK HO AND LODGE. BROOKSIDE, BROOKSIDE HO. BUCK-HURST PK, *Buckhurste Posterne or Wynckfeyld Gate* 1607 *Norden.* BURLEY BUSHES, Jas I *SpecCom*, BURLEIGH LODGE AND WD. CAS-CADE BRIDGE. CHEAPSIDE. CHINA ISLAND, *Chinese Island* 1816 OS, *China Island Mead* 1842 *TA* (Old Windsor). THE DAWREY. ENGLEMERE, ENGLEMERE POND (*Englemoor Pond* 1816 OS) AND WD, ENGLEMERE WD COTTAGE (it is unfortunate that no early spellings have been found for this name, which may be of similar significance to Englefield 211). FAIRFIELD COTTAGE. FIREBALL HILL. FROGNAL. GREAT POND. GUNNES'S BRIDGE. HANCOCKS MOUNT. HAREWOOD LODGE. THE HATCH. HATCHET LANE, HATCHETLANE FM, *v.* hæcc-geat. THE HERMITAGE. HURST-CROFT. KEEPS CORNER. KING'S WICK, 1749 *RecOffCat* (for the history of the original house, which may possibly be identifiable with a hunting lodge built by Hy 8, *v.* VCH III, 135). KING'S WICK PLANTATION. LARCH AVENUE. LOWER FM. MAN'S COPSE. MILL LANE. THE MOUNT. NASH'S COPSE. PEMBERTON LODGE. PEMBROKE LODGE. PENSLADE BOTTOM. PLATT'S FIRS. POND HEAD. QUEEN'S HILL. RISING SUN P.H. ROOME'S FM. SANDY RIDE. SILWOOD PK, *Sillwood Park* 1812, 1813 *PubLib.* SMITH'S GREEN. SOLDIER'S PILLAR, 1816 OS. SOUTH ASCOT. SUNNINGHILL LODGE, *The Lodge, Lodge Hill* 1607 *Norden.* SUNNINGHILL MILL. SUNNINGHILL PK, *Sonninghill*

Parke 1601 *Dep*, *Sunninge Hill Parke* 1607 *Norden*.   SUNNINGHILL
WELLS, 1816 OS, *Sunninghill Well* 1761 Rocque, *The Wells* 1800
Eden (this is a chalybeate spring, 'formerly much frequented', *v.*
VCH III, 134).   TETWORTH.   THATCH TAVERN.   TITNESS
PK FM, *v.* 89.   WHITE HART P.H.   THE WILDERNESS.

The following names of houses appear on the 6″ map in Ascot and South Ascot:
ARMITAGE CT, ASHURST LODGE, BANGOR LODGE, BEECHCROFT, BERYSTEDE HOTEL,
BLYTHEWOOD, BRAESIDE, BURNSIDE, CARMEL, THE CEDARS, CISSBURY, COVERDALE,
ELIBANK, FIRGROVE, FOREST VIEW, THE FRIARY, THE GABLES, GREY FRIARS,
HEATHEND, HEATHERWOOD, HILLSBOROUGH, HOLMWOOD LODGE, HUNTINGTON,
KENEGIE, KENILWORTH, THE LINKS, LLANVAIR, MARYLAND, MOORLANDS, OAK-
HURST, ORCHARDWOOD, ORMIDALE, PINEHURST, QUEENSHILL LODGE, RAVENSBURY,
RAVENSPOINT, RAYSCOURT, ST MICHAEL'S, SHENSTONE HO, SILCOTE HO, SWINLEY
BIRCHES, THE TOWER, UDIMORE, WOODCOTE, THE WOODLANDS, WOODLEIGH.

FIELD-NAMES

Forms dated 1800 are Eden, 1607 are *Norden*.

(*a*) Crown Hill 1800; Hodge Lane 1800 (also 1729 *LHRS*); Sunninghill
Bog 1816 OS.

(*b*) *Arber Hill* 1607; *Bullocks Gate* 1607; *Causeway Pond* 1607; *Culuer
Hill* 1607 (*v.* culfre); *Foxhill* 1607; *Heathfelde Gate* 1607 (*v.* hǣð, feld);
The Manor 1607; *Newebrugge* 1246 Ch (*v.* nīwe, brycg); *The Parocke* 1607
(*v.* pearroc); *The Rayles* 1607 (*v.* 281); *Le Redhacche* 1358 Pat (*v.* rēad,
hæc(c)); *Rededich'* 1383 *PubLib(Bray)* (p), *Rededich* 1430 *Windsor* (p),
Reditche Gate, *Redi(t)che Wood* 1607 (*v.* rēad, dīc, the same name occurs 87
and Wo 364–5); *South Gate* 1607; *Sunning Howse* 1607; *Windesore Hill*
1607 (*v.* Windsor 26–7).

V. CHARLTON HUNDRED

Cerledone 1086 DB, c. 1200 *ClaudiusCix, Cherledon'* 1180, 1186 **P**
et freq with variant spelling *Cherledon*; *Cheorledona* c. 1180 (13th)
Abingdon, *Cherldon* 1332 *SR, Charlton* 1610 Speed.

'Hill of the peasants', *v.* ceorl, dūn. This was presumably the name
of the meeting-place, which has not been located.

Barkham

BARKHAM

(*æt*) *Beorchamme* 952 (16th) BCS 895
Beorcham 952 (c. 1240) BCS 895
Bercheham 1086 DB, *Berkeham, Berkehem* 1220 Fees, *Berkeham*
  1242–3 ib, 1517 D Inc
Berkham 1220 (13th) RSO, *Bercham* 1242–3 Fees *et freq, Berkham*
  1242–3 Fees (p) *et freq*
Bergham 1248 Fees (p)

'Birch-tree meadow', *v.* beorc, hamm. There are two copies
of BCS 895, one in the later version of the Abingdon Chronicle,
and the other in MS C.C.C.C. cxi (p. 145). In the latter MS
the charter has the heading 'ðis is þara þreora hida landboc æt
beorchamme – '. In view of this, the second element can probably
be identified as hamm rather than hām. Several small tributaries
of the R. Loddon flow through the parish. Barkham Sx 345 is
identical.

BCS 895 gives the bounds of this estate, but none of the places
mentioned can be identified. On account of the directions *andlang
stræt to loddera stræt* Grundy thought that the area described was
outside the parish of Barkham, probably the part of Finchampstead
north of the Devil's Highway (4), which he thought would be one
of the roads referred to as a stræt. It is much more probable, however,
that the bounds describe the modern parish of Barkham. The estate
referred to in the charter is one of 3 hides, and this is the hidage
assigned to Barkham in DB. There are other instances of the term
stræt in Berkshire charters in contexts which make it impossible to
identify the road with a known Roman one.

BARKHAM COMMON, 1844 *TA*.   BARKHAM HILL (*Hill Ground and Piece* 1840 *TA*) AND RIDE (*v*. 34).   BARKHAM SQUARE, *The Square* 1816 OS, 1846 Snare.   BEARS COPSE, *Beers Coppice* 1733 *PubLib-Doc*.   BIGNELLS COPSE, *Bignolds* 1840 *TA*.   BROOK FM. BULL INN.   CHURCH FM AND LANE.   COMMONFIELD LANE. THE COOMBES, *Coombs Grounds and Hill* 1840 *TA*.   COPPID HILL, 1846 Snare, *v*. coppede.   EDNEY FM, *Edneys Hill* 1840 *TA*. ELLIS'S FM.   HANDPOST FM, *Hand Post Piece* 1840 *TA*, *v*. 281. KEEPER'S COTTAGE.   KIDGEM COPSE, *Great and Little Kedgham* 1733 *PubLib(Doc)*, *Kidgham Coppice* 1816 OS, *Kitcham Copse* 1846 Snare.   LANGLEY COMMON, 1733 *PubLib* (*Doc*), 1761 Rocque, 1790 Pride, *Langley Heath* 1607 *Norden*.   LANGLEYCOMMON FM, LANGLEYPOND FM.   MANOR HO.   NASH GROVE, NASHGROVE LAND AND RIDE.   ROOK'S NEST FM, 1846 Snare.   SPARKS FM.

FIELD-NAMES

The principal forms in (*a*) are 1840 *TA*.

(*a*) Back Piddle; Barkham Piddle; Barn Close; Bear Pigs; Biggs Lane; Bistley Piddle; Bottoms; Boundary Piddle; Brick Close; Buffs Piddle; Bull Ground; Church Piddle; Common Close; Common Lands; Coppice Close, Mdw and Piece; Cottage Piddle; Culverst Close; Driftway Close (*v*. 281); French Close; Furzeney, Furzeny Mead; Graphage Ground (cf. Graffadge Grounds in Waltham St Lawrence 115); Great Ground; Green Close; Halls Bottom; Harriet or 3 Acre Mead; Heath Ground; Home Ground and Close; Inhams (*v*. innām); James Mdw; Kiln Close; Langley Pond Piece (*v*. *supra*); Leg of Mutton (probably referring to shape, like the common Shoulder of Mutton); Long Mdw; Longmoor; Long Piddle; Lucerne Piddle (*v*. 282); Milking Plat (*v*. plat^2); New Ground; New Inclosures; New Mead; Nomans Land (*v*. 284); Northern Mead; Old Cock Lane; Old House Ground; Orchard Close; Park; Parsonage Mdw; Parsons Green; Piddle (here, as elsewhere in this parish, a variant of **pightel**); Pins; Pond Close; Pound Ground; Ray Bridge (possibly the r.n. Ray, *v*. ēa); Rockinghams (also 1684 *PubLib*); Rudley 12 Acres; Sandpit Piece; Shoulder of Mutton (cf. Leg of Mutton *supra*); Southern Mead; Sunderland Close; Three Corner Piddle; Townsend Piece; Tucker, Long and Street; Upper Mdw; Wallens Piddle; Whitehall Mdw; Whitfield; Woking Moors; Wood Close, Ground Mdw and Piddle; Yard Close.

(*b*) *Burley Heath* 1607 *Norden*; *Endinge* 1573 *SpecCom*; *Langenhurst* c. 1330 *LHRS* (*v*. lang, hyrst); *The Moors* 1733 *PubLibDoc*; *La Synderbergh'* 1252–3 *FF* (p) (probably a compound of sinder and beorg, which might describe a pile of slag from smelting; there is probably no connection between this name and Sunderland in (*a*)).

Earley

EARLEY

Herlei 1086 DB, *Erlega* 1177 (p) *et passim* with variant spellings
Erleia, Erley(e), Erleg', Erle(g), Erlegh', Erleg(h), Erlee; Herleg'
1197 *FF*, 1220 Fees
Arle 1297 Ipm, 1428 FA, *Arlegh* 1535 VE

The p.n. Arley occurs in a number of counties, and in two cases
(Wa and Wo) where there are OE forms it can be proved to derive
from OE *earn-lēah* 'eagle-wood'. Earnley Sx means 'eagles' wood'.
The Berks name is very probably another example of the compound
earn-lēah, though it is impossible to be certain without OE forms.
Ekwall (DEPN) suggests OE *ēar* 'gravel', as a possible alternative
first el.

FOXHILL, 1840 *TA*, cf. *Foxele* 1309 Cl, which means 'foxes' wood or
clearing', *v.* **fox, lēah.** The latter name may be a corruption of the
earlier one.

WHITEKNIGHTS, (manor of Earley called) *Whitknythes* 1401–2 FA, *Le
Whiteknyghtes* 1412 ib, *Whyte Knyghtes* 1491 Ipm, *White Knights*
1638 BM. WHITEKNIGHTS PARK, *White knights Park* 1846 Snare.
Johannes de Arle dictus Whythknyght is mentioned 1428 FA, and the
manor is so called from this nickname.

BEECH LANE, *Beech Hill, Beach or Beech* 1840 *TA.* BROKEN
BROW, 1830 OS, *Brokenbrow* 1846 Snare. THE COPPICE, COPPICE
FM, *Coppice Ground* 1840 *TA.* CULVER LANE, cf. *Culuerhey(e)*
Ed 4 *RentSur*, 'dove enclosure', *v.* **culfre, (ge)hæg.** DREAD-
NOUGHT P.H. EARLEY LODGE. EARLEY RADSTOCK FM. EARLEY
WESTCROFT. ERLEIGH COURT, *Erley Sancti Barth'i otherwise called
Erley Leycourt* 1502 Ipm, *Early Court* 1761 Rocque; this was one of
the manors of Earley, called *Sancti Barth'i* from the chapel of St
Bartholomew *infra.* ELM FM. ELM RD. HOME FM, cf. *Le
Homfeld* 1329, 1343 *Queen*, Ed 4 *RentSur*, *Home Close, Ground,
Paddock and Pightle* 1840 *TA*; the first el. is *home*, denoting land near
the farmstead. HOMEFARM COTTAGES. KILN FM. LONDON
RD, cf. *Londoneweye* Ed 4 *RentSur*. LOWER EARLEY FM, COTTAGES
AND VILLA. LOWERWOOD FM, cf. *Earley Lower Wood Common,*

Earley Upper Wood Common 1840 *TA*.   MAIDEN ERLEGH, *Erley Maydens* 1502 Ipm, *Maiden Early* 1761 Rocque; this was an estate formed out of Earley Whiteknights in the 14th cent.; the reason for the name appears to be unknown.   OAK WD.   RED-HATCH COPSE.   RUSHY MEAD.   ST BARTHOLOMEW'S CHAPEL, this is mentioned 1220 RSO, and its history is described VCH III, 224.   SHEPHERD'S HO.   SHRUBLANDS.   SIDMOUTH GRANGE. THE SPINNEY.   TRELAWNEY.   UPPERWOOD FM, *v.* Lowerwood Fm *supra*.   WHITEKNIGHTS LAKE, *v.* 93.   THE WILDERNESS, *Wilderness* 1846 *Snare*.   WOODBINE COTTAGE.   WOODLEYHILL.

FIELD-NAMES

The principal forms in (*a*) are 1840 *TA*; early forms dated 1309 are Cl, Ed 4 *RentSur*; forms for which no source is given are *Queen*.

(*a*) Apple Tree Ground; Barn Close, Fds, Ground and Pightle (cf. *Berneye infra*); Bolt Platt; Brisling Coppice; Broad Fd and Mead; Browns Piddle; Bunters Pightle; Chalk Ground; The Chantilly Gardens; Charity Three Acres; College Fd; Common Allotment; Common Piece and Pightle; Comps, Lower and Upper (*v.* camp and cf. Ruscombe 127); Conygree (*v.* coninger); Corner Close; Culver Fd (*v.* culfre, cf. Culver Lane *supra*); Earley Heath and Mead; Fodder Close; Foot Path Fd; Furze Close; Garden Pightle; Gravelly Ground; Gravel Pit Ground; Great Ground; Ham, Lower and Upper (*v.* hamm); Hatch Close (*v.* hæc(c)); Hatch Field Close; Hattons Platt; Heath Close; High Hill Grove; Hill Lane; Horse Close; Hospital Close (cf. *Spytelhegge* Ed 4, *v.* spitel, hecg); Ivey Lake Mead; Larkins Piddle; Links, Lower and Upper (cf. *Lynchefurlonge* Ed 4, *Linch Feild* 1669 ArchJ, 31, *v.* hlinc); Loddon Close, Eyott and Mead (*v.* ēgeð); Mace Holes (*Mace Feild* 1669 ArchJ 31); Mans Ground; Marsh Coppice Ground; Mays Pightle; Moor; New American Garden and Grounds (near Foxhill and so in the northern corner of the parish, *v.* 284); No Mans Land Close (*v.* 284); North East Park, North West Park (near Erlegh Park); Old Drift Road (*v.* 281); Old Pond Pightle; Old Water Lane; Pack Piddle; Park Field (*Park Feild* 1669 ArchJ 31); Pasture Piece and Plot; Pepper Lane; Perkin's Piddle; Picked Close and Fd (*v.* pīced); Piddle (a variant of pightel, which is also common in this parish); Pigeon House Fd; Pigwash, Pigwash Close (*pigwash* is recorded in NED from 17th–19th meaning 'kitchen swill given to pigs'); Pit Fd; Pitt Mead; Pitts Close, Ground and Pightle; The Platt (*v.* plat^2); Pond Close; Pond Head Ground; Pound Close; Rick Piddle; Rick Yard Fd; Roundabout (*v.* 281); Saint Johns Close; Sand Piddle; Shaw Green; Sheep House Fd; Shoulder of Mutton Mead (*v.* 283); South East Park, South West Park (near North East Park *supra*); South Pasture; Spring Pightle; Stoke Lays; Stockwell Close; Tiggels Acre; Watercut; Wells Close; White Close; Withy Coppice Ground; Wood Hill, New and Middle

(*Wodehull* 1309 (p), *v.* wudu, hyll); Woodlands, First and Upper; Wood wards, Woodwards Ditch Mead; Worlds End Ground (*v.* 284).

(b) *Ailwardesham* 1309, *Aylwardeshamme* 1319, 1343, *Aywardesham* Ed 4 ('Æðelweard's hamm'); *Berneye* 1309 (*v.* bere-ærn, (ī)eg); *La Breche* 1309 (*v.* brēc); *Brodeweye* Ed 4 (*v.* brād, weg); *Le Brumcrofte* n.d. AD (*v.* brōm, croft); *Buchurstesmore* n.d. AD (*v.* mōr; possibly marsh land attached to Buckhurst in Wokingham Without 143); *Burham* c. 1185 (14th) *ReadingC*(3), *Burgham* 1309, Ed 4 (*v.* burh, hamm); *Le Chaddelond* 1309 (possibly identical with *Haddelond* in the same list); *Crundul* Ed 4 (*v.* crundel); *Denefelde* 1343, *Deneforlonge* 1336, *Denefurlonge* Ed 4 (*v.* denu); *La Dwolemede* 1309 (*v.* mæd; this was part of *Burgham supra*, and was perhaps a lot meadow, *v.* dāl); *Eliotes Innome* 1309 (*v.* innām); *Erlinguelde* 1341 (probably 'Earley field'); *Gilotesmore* 13th VCH III (*v.* mōr, first el. the surname *Gillett*); *Hawthorne Feild* 1669 ArchJ 31; *Herwardeslond* 1344 ('Hereweard's land'); *Le Heybern* 1309 ('hay barn'); *Le Knygtes Croft* 1335 AD; *Lechemore* 13th VCH III (*v.* læc(c), mōr); *Levegares-acre* 1309 ('Lēofgār's acre'); *Long Aker* 1326; *Lotemede* Ed 4 (*v.* hlot, mæd); *Loycroft* 1309; *Mene Crofte* Ed 4 (*v.* (ge)-mæne); *Myddelfurlonge* Ed 4; *Nethulle* 1327, 1330, *Le Neethulle* 1343, *Nethylle* Ed 4 (*v.* nēat, hyll); *Neweweye* Ed 4 (*v.* nīwe, weg); *Olde Flecceheyys*, *Oldeflecceheyse* Ed 4 (*v.* eald, (ge)hæg, *Flecce-* may be from an OE *fleca* 'hurdle' suggested in DEPN as first el. of Fleckney Lei, Flecknoe Wa); *Paradis* 1309 (*v.* 283; VCH III, 217, says this name was still known in 1912); *Pericroft* n.d. AD (*v.* pirige, croft); *La Pilparc* c. 1270–80 (*v.* pīl, park); *Ponyngeslond* 1309; *Rakeweyoslond* 1344 (*v.* hraca, weg, land); *Red Lane* 1790 Pride; *Le Rythe* Ed 4 (*v.* rīð); *Sheetehegge* Ed 4 (*v.* scīete, hecg); *Shepacrs* Ed 4, *Shepcroft* 1309 (*v.* scēap, æcer, croft); *Le Slade* Ed 4 (*v.* slæd); *Le Smalwey* 1309, *Smaleweye* Ed 4 (*v.* smæl, weg, and cf. *Brodeweye supra*); *Spillemannesbrome* 1309, *Spylmanysbrom'* Ed 4 (*v.* brōm, first el. the surname *Spillman*); *Le Stonicroft* n.d. AD (*v.* stānig, croft); *Swylyngholme* Ed 4 (a compound of swelgend 'whirlpool, deep place' and ME holme 'river meadow'); *Symons Feild* 1669 ArchJ 31; *Thre Thornys* Ed 4; *Tulleslane* Ed 4; *The Wharfe Feild* 1669 ArchJ 31; *Werdolkesmore* 13th VCH III; *Le Westfelde* 1344, *Westefelde* Ed 4; *Le Wokgeforlong* 1342, *Woghforlong* 1344 (*v.* wōh); *La Worthe* 1309, *Worthe* Ed 4 (*v.* worð); *La Wyteyate*, *La Whyteyat* 1309 (*v.* hwīt, geat).

FINCHAMPSTEAD

Finchampstead

Finchamestede 1086 DB, *Finchamstæde* s.a. 1098 (12th) ASC E, *Finchemsted'* 1220 Fees *et passim* with variant spellings *Finchamsted'*, *Finchhamstede*, *Finchamstude*, *Fynchamsted(e)*, *Finchamstede*; *Finhamstede* 1224–5 Ass, *Finghamsted'* 1242–3 Fees

Heamstede s.a. 1103 (12th) ASC E, *hamstede* c. 1300 RG

'Homestead frequented by finches', *v.* finc, hām-stede.

DODSWELL'S WELL, the following forms are given in Finchampstead 16 ff. – *Dozells* 1638, *Doswells* 1783, *Dodswell* 1871. The adjoining field is shown on the *TAMap* of 1841 as *Well Dorsell's Field*. Lyon, writing in 1895, says that the well was accidentally destroyed about 1872, by deepening the ditch on the roadside. It is marked on the $2\frac{1}{2}''$ map, however. The water is said to have had marvellous curative properties, especially for eye diseases, and Lyon suggests that the name was originally 'St Oswald's Well'. ASC E, s.a. 1098, 1100 and 1103, refers to blood bubbling out of a pool or out of the earth at Finchampstead, and there may be some connection with this well. For other references to the phenomenon, under the years 1029 and 1164, *v*. AnnMon IV 371, 381.

GREAT THRIFT, cf. *The Frithe Ponds* 1602 Finchampstead, *Finchamsted Fryths* 1607 *Norden, The Littell Frith* 1638 Finchampstead, *Little Frith Coppice* 1699–1700 *Bodl, Little Fryth Coppice* 1783 Finchampstead, *v.* fyrhð.

ARMHOLES.   BANISTERS, BANISTERS COPSE, *Lower and Upper Bannisters* 1844 *TA*, from the family surnamed *Banastre* who had land here 1220 and 1242–3 Fees, for the history of the manor *v*. VCH III, 242–3.   BARNECOURT.   BIGG'S FM, OLD BIGG'S FM. BULLOWAY'S FM.   CHURCH FM, near the church, cf. Churchams etc. *infra* 98.   CLAYPITS.   COLESHILL, 1844 *TA*.   COMMON-FIELD LANE, *Common Field* 1844 *TA*.   COPPICE GROUND PLANTA-TION, *Coppice Ground* 1844 *TA*.   CRICKET HILL, *Crickett Hill* 1844 *TA*.   EAST COURT, *East Courte* 1559 *Bodl*, 1591 Finchamp-stead, *East Court Manor* 1595 BM, cf. West Court *infra*.   EFT MOOR PLANTATION.   FIR GROVE.   FISHER'S COPSE, *Fishers Field and Meadow* 1844 *TA*.   FLEET COPSE AND HILL, FLEETHILL FM, *the common wood called the Fleete* 1589 *Bodl, Great and Little Fleet, Fleet Hill and Meadow* 1844 *TA*, *v.* flēot, which apparently means 'stream' in this name, as in Fleet Ha, some 6 miles S. FURZE HILL, FURZEHILL PLANTATION, *Furze Hill, Furze Hill Pit* 1844 *TA*.   GREAT COPSE.   GREYHOUND P.H.   HAGATES, HAGATES COPSE AND MEADOW, *Agates Meadow* 1844 *TA*.   HALL'S FM, *Hall Howse Land* 1623 Finchampstead, cf. Gunilda *de Aula*, who held land in Finchampstead 1275–6 RH.   HEATH POND, *The Heathe* 1573 *SpecCom, Heathes* 1623 Finchampstead, *Finchampstead Heath* 1654 *Bodl*, cf. Hen. *de Bruario* 1275–6 RH, *v.* hǣð, bruiere.

HILL RISE. HOGWOOD FM AND SHAW, *Hogwood Field, Pightle and Scrubbs* 1844 *TA*, possibly *The Hogshead Pightle* 1786 Finchampstead (*v.* pightel). HOLLYBUSH RIDE. JACK'S COPSE. KEEPER'S LODGE. LEA FM AND COPSE, *The Lee* 1668, 1699 Finchampstead, *The Lea Common* c. 1711 ib, *v.* lēah. THE LEAS, *Finchamstead Leas* 1761 Rocque, *Finchamstead Leys* 1790 Pride. LITTLE COPSE. LONG MOOR, 1761 Rocque, *Longemoor* c. 1605 *RentSur. Longe Moore Howse* 1623 Finchampstead, *Long Moore* 1684 *PubLib*, *v.* lang, mōr. LONGMOOR BOG AND LAKE. LONG-WATER LANE, 1829 Finchampstead. MANOR HO AND FM. MOORGREEN FM, *Moregrene* 1533 Finchampstead, *Moor Green* 1736 ib, cf. The Moor *infra* 98. MORLAIX FM. NEW INN. NEW MILL, 1790 Pride, *Newe Mill* 1641 *SP*. NORTH COURT, cf. East Court *supra*, West Court *infra*. PALMERS COPSE. PARK LANE, cf. *The Park, Park Pightle* 1844 *TA*. PIE HILL, *Pye Hill Row* 1708, c. 1711 Finchampstead. PIGS FM. PITHER'S FM. THE POOR'S COMMON. POOR'S COPSE. PORRIDGE BOTTOM, *v.* botm and 284. QUEEN'S OAK P.H. RIDGE FM, 1829 Finchampstead, RIDGE COTTAGE. THE RIDGES, *Finchampstead Ridges* 1816 OS. THE RISE. SHEERLANDS, 1844 *TA*, this is on the N.W. parish boundary, *v.* scīr[1](3). SHEPPERLANDS COPSE AND FM, *Shippardland Copse* 1651–2 *Bodl*. SOUTH COURT. SPOUT POND. SUNNYSIDE. THE WARREN (near Long Moor), *Warren Ho* 1816 OS. THE WARREN (near Banisters), 1844 *TA*. WARREN LODGE. WEST COURT, 1623 *PubLib*, 1761 Rocque, *Westcourte* 1456, 1467 Finchampstead, cf. East Court *supra*. WESTWOOD FM, *Weswood* 1607 *Norden*, *Westwood* 1651–2, 1654 *Bodl*. WESTWOOD COPSE, *West Wood Coppices* 1661 Finchampstead, *Hither and Further Westwood Coppice* c. 1711 ib. WHEAT-LANDS MANOR. WICK HILL, *Upwicks Hill* 1816 OS, WICKHILL FM, WICK VALE FM. WISE HILL, 1844 *TA*.

FIELD-NAMES

The principal forms in (*a*) are 1844 *TA*, except where otherwise stated; F = Finchampstead; early forms for which no source is given are *Bodl*.

(*a*) Acrey (*Akery* 1558, *The Great Ackree* 1602 F, *The Little Acrey* 1615 F, *The Great Acrey* 1654, *The Great Acre* 1699–1700, identical with Nancry Coppice in Easthampstead 24); The Acre, Acre Pightle; Ambletts (*Amletts Land and Well* 1736 F); Ashen Pightle; The Bag; Barn Fd, Close and Pightle (cf. *Barne Moore* 1623 F, *Barn Close* 1783 F); The Bear; Beehive;

Behind Granary; Bell Platt (cf. Joh. *atte Belle* 1341, *v.* Reaney for this sur-
name); The Big Mdw; The Black Croft (*Blackcroft* 1654, 1699–1700, *The
Black Croft* 1786 F); Blacksmiths Pightle; Blackwater Rails; Bone Gutter;
Bottom Close; Bottoms (*v.* botm); Brick Kiln (*Brickills* 1638, 1786 F,
Brickcill Coppice 1651–2, *Brickhales* 1661, *Brickhills* 1728–9, *Brickells* 1783
F); Broad Mdw (*Broad Meade* 1623 F); Brocklands (*Brooklandes* 1623 F);
Broom Close (*Broome Close* 1661); Brown Close; Burchells; Burnmoor
Mdw (*Burnt Moore* 1661); Bush Close; Canes Mdw; Carmoor or Charmoor
(*Charmor* 1654); Carpenters Pightle; Carrot Croft (possibly *Carry Crofte*
1558, 1594); Carroty Close; Carters Close; Castle Mead Pightle; Chalky
Moor; Cheery; Churchams (*Churchams* 1558, *Church Hames Piddle* 1623
F, *Church Hamms* 1786 F, *v.* hamm); Church Fd; Church Hill Piece;
Church Pightle; The Clumps; Cobhall (*Copped Hall* 1558 Bodl, 1615 F,
1728, *Coppyd Hall* 1609 PubLib, 1786 F, *Copthill Hill* 1675 ib, *v.* coppede);
Common Bit, Piece and Slip (*v.* slipe and cf. Commonfield Lane *supra*);
Coppice Moor; Copse Pightle; Corn Close; Cow Crib Pightle; Cowhouse
Ground and Mdw; Cowley; Cowstall Park Fd; Cricketting Fd; Cross Lane
Pightle; Culver Close (also 1638, 1783 F, *v.* culfre); Darlings Wood;
Deer Pens; Ennox Coppice 1829 F, Ennex (possibly inhōc); Fair Green
1829 F; Fallow Ground; Footpath Mead; Fuel Allotment; Furzey Close,
Furzy Bit and Moor (cf. *Furzen Close* 1683 F); Gammons (*Gamon Grene*
1558, *Gam Ham(m)es* 1623 F, *Gamon Greene* 1654, possibly 'sports' green',
v. gamen, grēne²); Gassons (*Gaston Coppice* 1602 F, *Gason Ground* 1778,
v. gærs-tūn); Goose Acre (*Gooseacre* 1661, *Goose Acre* 1786 F); Great
Ground; The Gut (*Gutt Meade* 1558, *Long Gutte Meade* 1594, *Longut
Mead* 1642 F, *The Guttmead* 1668 ib, 1699 ib, *The Gut* 1783 ib, from NED
gut sb 5 a. 'a channel — of water' or 5 c. 'a narrow passage or lane'); Hare
Moles; Hartmoor; Hatch Ground, Mdw and Pightle (*Hatchys* 1553 F,
Hatches 1558, 1594, *Hatch-Mead, The Hatch Pightle* 1786, *v.* hæc(c)); Haw
Bridge (cf. *La Hawe* 1275–6 RH (p), *v.* haga¹); Heath Ground and Pightle
(cf. Heath Pond *supra*); Hedge Croft; Highfield; High Grove; High Read-
ings (*Readinges* 1617, *v.* ryding); Hill Close (*The Hill Close* 1661, *Hill Close
Shaw* 1783 F); Hillfield; Hillicks; Holly Mdw; Home Fd, Ground, Mdw,
Pasture and Pightle; Innes Croft; Innhams (*v.* innām); Inward Mdw;
Kenell Mdw; Kiln Pightle; Lea Slip (*v.* slipe and cf. Lea Fm *supra*);
Long Croft (*Longe Crofte* 1596, *Longcroft* 1621 PubLib, 1783 F); Long
Ground; Long Slip; Ludlows Wood Fd; Mashall(s); Mill Fd; Mills; The
Mirks; The Moor (cf. *Mora* 1275–6 RH (p), *More* 1327 SR (p), *Moor Howse*
1602 F, *Moorehouse, The Moors* 1654, *Moorhouse* 1686, *The Moors* 1786 ib,
v. mōr); New England (*v.* 284); New Meadow and Ground; Nine Mile
Drive; North Lands; Nut Ground (cf. *Nutclose* 1558, *Nuttclose* 1699 F);
Nutkins; Oak Mdw; Old Kiln Yard; Old Shotford; Old Womans Pightle;
Orchard Ground and Pightle; Paddocks Pightle; The Paddock; The Park;
Park Ground and Pightle; Parsonage Mdw (also 1783 F); Peaked Croft
(*Picked Croft* 1623 F, 1686, *v.* pīced); Peartree Close and Mdw; The Pightle
(*v.* pightel, and freq. elsewhere in this parish); Platts, The Platt (*v.* plat²);
Pleasure Grounds; Pond Close, Fd, Piece and Pightle (cf. *Pond Mead* 1786
F); Pooks or Pucks; Pound Fd (cf. *The Pound Pightle* 1786 F); Rail Piece

(*v.* 281); Red Barn Fd and Pightle; Redgates; Rough Piece; Royal
George; Rush Platt; Sawpit Piece and Fd; Service Close; The Shaw (*v.*
sc(e)aga); Short Moors (*Shortemore* 1569, *Shortmore* 1654, *Shortmoor
Ditch* 1736 F, *Short Moor* 1786 F); The Slip (occurring also in several f.ns.
in this parish, *v.* slipe); Slutts; Smither Mead; Sones Moor; Sops; South
Pightle; Spring Pightle; Stable Close and Fd; Stony Pightle (*Stoney Piddles*
1699 F); Tare Fd; Tenets; The Three Oaks; Three Corners; The Wallet
(*v.* 285); The Water Mdw; Weir Ground and Mdw (*Weare Meade* 1623
F, *Ware Meadow* 1783 ib); Well Close; West Moor Fd and Lands (*Westmoore*
1608 F, *Westmore* 1638 F, *Westmoor* 1697–8); Winding Shotts; Wood Close
(*The Wood Close* 1786 F); Woodmore.

(*b*) *Aldermore* 1581–2 *PubLib*, 1699 F, *Aldermoor* 1621 *PubLib*, *Aldermer*
1642 F; *The Bathe* 1602, *The Bath* 1623, *Hubbard's Bath* 1675, *Bath Lands*
1699 all F (*v.* bæð, perhaps in the sense 'pool'); *Bedellys More* 1553 F,
Byddelsmor 16th VCH iii (*v.* bydel, mōr); *Borsey Meade* 1602 F, 1661
(Professor Löfvenberg suggests that *Borsey* is an adjectival derivative of the
OE plant-name bors); *The Breach* 1654 (*v.* brēc); *Bromfield* 1786 F (*v.*
brōm); *Burchat Coppis* 1650–1 (*v.* bircet(t)); *Cadish House* 1654; *The Cuttar
Close* 1786 F; *Damasyn Deanes* 1661, *Damson Deames* 1786 F; *The Downe
Close* 1608 ib, *The Downe* 1638, *The Down* 1783 F (*v.* dūn); *Fane Mede* 1553
ib, *Fanne Meade* 1556–7 ib, 1569, *Fan(ne) Meade* 1558 (*v.* fenn, and cf.
Sr xxiii); *Fearne Hills* 1623 F, *Gord Close* 1699 ib; *Hagville Farm al.
Bolsingham Farm* 1728, *Hagvill als Bolsingham Farm* 1786 F (*v.* 141); *Hangers
Ford* 1602 ib; *Hawkes Hilles* 1558, *Hawkehilles* 1594, *Hawkeshills* 1661 F;
Hyllcrofte 1558; *James Cross* 1686; *Lacambrooke* 1589; *Leasedown Shaw*
1783 F; *Longmeade* 1569; *Ludge Meade* 1623 F; *Mollefen or Mollefantes*
1608; *Mulsham* 1553 F, *Melsham* 1556–7 ib, 1558, *Moulsom Meadow* 1783 F
(*v.* hamm); *Mylwardes Meade* 1558; *Newhouse* 1736; *Newe Lane* 1558;
Peasedons 1661, *Peasedown* 1786 F; *Rushy Meads* 1786 ib; *The Sheare
Streame* 1558 *Bodl*, 1641 *SP* (this was on the county boundary and may contain scīr[1]); *Stony Close* 1617, *Stonie Close* 1642 F; *Wall Close* 1783 ib;
Westinhames 1623 ib (*v.* hamm); *Wheteles* 1575 ib; *Whitesfarme* 1602 ib,
White's Meade 1608 ib; *Wynnebusshe* 1455, *Wynbusshe* 1533, *Winbushes* 1623
all F, *Windbushes* 1654, 1676, 1698 (apparently a compound of winn
'pasture', and busc 'bush').

St Nicholas Hurst

HURST

Herst 1220 (13th) RSO, 1254 Cl, *Hurst(e)*, 1224–5 *Ass et passim*,
    La Hurste 1242 Fees, 1375–6 ObAcc, *La Hurst* 1316 FA

v. hyrst 'wooded hill'. There was a chapel of St Nicholas here,
built in the late 11th cent. and referred to as *capella de Herst, de sancto
Nicholao* in 1220 (RSO). The present church is dedicated to St
Nicholas. For a detailed description of the chapel as it was in the
13th cent., *v.* RSO i, pp. 280–1.

HINTON HO, FM AND LODGE, *Hentona comitis Patricii* 1167 P, *Henton'* 1182 ib (p), 1185 RR, 1224–5 *Ass* (p), *Heanton'* 1183, 1184 P (p), *Henton' comitis Saresb'* 1198 ib, *Henton* 13th *ReadingC*, 1362 Cl, *Heynton'* 1255 ib, *Hentone Ode, Hentone Pipard* 1332 *SR*, *Hynton* 1400 Cl, *Henton' Ody, Henton' Pypard* 1453 *SR, Brodehenton* (in the parish of Hurst, co. Wilts) 1479 *Pat, Hinton House* 1846 Snare, '(at the) high farm', cf. Hinton Waldrist, Pt **2**. Hinton in Hurst is not on high ground, however, so hēah[1] may mean 'important' in this instance. *Pipard* and *Ode* are family names. The manorial history is discussed in VCH III, 235–6, where it is stated that the three Hintons, Broad Hinton, Hinton Peppard and Hinton Hatch *infra*, were tithings of the Earl of Salisbury's hundred of Ashridge (142), which was a detached portion of Wiltshire. It is confusing that one of the Berks places should have been known as Broad Hinton, as there is another Broad Hinton in W (W 296).

HINTONHATCH CORNER, *Hacche* 1332, 1334 *SR, Hache* 1377, 1453 *ib, Hach* 1487 *ib, v.* hæc(c) 'gate'. All the early spellings are from Wilts Subsidy Rolls, where the tithing of *Hache* etc. regularly follows Hinton in the lists.

LEA HEATH AND LEA COTTAGE, LEA FM (in Winnersh), *La Legh* 1329 Cl, *La Lee* 1365 ib, *Le Lee* 1603–4 *Survey, Le Lee Parke* c. 1605 *ib, Leeheath* 1607 *Norden, Lee Heath* 1641 *SP*, 1790 Pride, *Leas Heath* 1761 Rocque, *Lea Heath Cottage* 1846 Snare, *v.* lē(a)h, hǣð.

WHISTLEY GREEN, WHISTLEYCOURT FM, WHISTLEYMILL FM

(*æt*) *Wisclea* 968 (c. 1200), (*æt*) *Uuiscelea* 968 (c. 1240) BCS 1226, *Wiscelea, Wisceleie* a. 1170 (c. 1200) *ClaudiusCix, Wiscelet* Hy 2 Gaimar, *Wiscelea* c. 1200 *ClaudiusCix*
Wiselei 1086 DB, *Wisselea* 1167 P, *Wiselega* 1185 ib (p), *Wyssel'* 1238 Cl, *Wysele* 1281 Abbr
Wistle 1185 RR
Whissheley 1378 Pat, *Whisley* 1758 ArchJ 14
Whistley Mills, Whistley Court 1659 *Bodl, Whistley Green* 1761 Rocque

This name derives from wisc 'marshy meadow' and lēah 'clearing' (later 'meadow'), a compound which is rather common in p.ns. Other instances are: *Wysshelegh'* (f.n.) Ch **1**, 159, Westley Fm D 502,

Wisheley (f.n.) Gl 4, 188, *wiscleageat* BCS 625 (A.D. 909) in the bounds of some woodland in north Ha, Whistley Fm Nth 60, Wisley Sr 155, Wistlers Wood Sr 340, Whistley Fm W 246 (where reference is made to f.ns. Whistley Leaze, Whistly Mead, Whistly Bottom, Whistle Mead). The related word *wisse* is probably the first el. of Wistley Hill Gl 1, 153, and a similar compound is found in Westley Sa, *Wesseley, Wasseley* 1230 P, with first el. *wæsse* 'swamp'.

This part of St Nicholas Hurst parish is described in VCH III, 247, as 'a narrow strip of alluvial meadow land bordering the river and liable to floods'.

BROAD COMMON, 1761 Rocque, 1790 Pride. BROADCOMMON FM AND RD. BROADWATER, 1761 Rocque, 1790 Pride. BROAD-WATER LANE. CAMERON'S COPSE. CASTLE INN. CHURCH FM AND LANE, cf. *Church Field and Meadow* 1841 *TA*. CHURCH-MANS FM, *Churchmans Meadow* 1841 *TA*, cf. *Antichurchmans Field infra* 102. DAVIS ST, *Davis Close, Davis's Ground* 1841 *ib.* DORNDON. DUNT LANE, DUNTLANE FM, *Duntland Farm* 1659 *Bodl.* ELEPHANT AND CASTLE P.H. ELLIOT'S GREEN, *Elliots Field* 1841 *TA*. FERREL BRIDGE. THE FURZE. FURZE COVERT. GREEN LANE, *Green Close and Lane* 1841 *TA*. GREEN MAN P.H. HAINESHILL, 1761 Rocque, 1790 Pride, *Haines Hill House* 1846 Snare. HAINESHILL FM. HATCHGATE FM, *Hatch Gate Field* 1841 *TA*, v. *hæc(c)-geat*. HOGMOOR LANE. HURST COURT, HO AND GRANGE. HURST GROVE, 1790 Pride. ISLAND-STONE LANE AND POND, *Island Town Grove* 1841 *TA*. JOLLY FARMER P.H. KAYERS BRIDGE, KAYERSBRIDGE FM, *Kersbridge Fm* 1846 Snare. KEBBLES FM. NELSON'S LANE, *Little Nelson, Nelson's Pightle* 1841 *TA*. NORTH OCKETT WD (v. 60). OLD CROWN P.H. OLD RIVER. THE ORCHARDS, *Orchard Meadow, Ground and Piddle* 1841 *TA*, v. pightel. POUND LANE, POUNDLANE FM, *Pound Field, Pound Field Enclosure, Pound Lane Ground* 1841 *ib.* QUEEN'S ARBOUR. SOUTHCOT DITCH. STOW BRIDGE, *Stowe-bridge* 1607 *RentSur*, v. stōw, perhaps referring to the chapel of St Nicholas. THE STRAIGHT MILE. TAPE LANE. TOWNS-END'S POND, *Townsend Field* 1841 *TA*. WARD'S CROSS. WARREN-HOUSE FM, *Warren, Little Warren* 1841 *TA*. WHEELWRIGHT'S ARMS P.H. WHISTLEY BRIDGE, PARK AND FM, v. *supra*. WOOD-LANDS, 1841 *TA*.

FIELD-NAMES

The principal forms in (*a*) are 1841 *TA*, and some of the names from this source may belong to fields in Winnersh and Newland.

(*a*) Acre Piddle and Staff (*staff* is recorded in NED sb[1] 17a, as a term for pasture ground; a quotation from 1786 refers to 'a Ham or Staff of rich meadow ground' in Kelmscott O); The Alders; Allwrights Piddle (a variant of pightel, very common in this parish); Antichurchmans Fd; Arability; Arms Thread Ground; Back Mdw; Bakers Piddle; Barn Fd, Ground, Mdw and Piddle; Benhams Green and Piddle; Bens Ground; Bentleys Brook Mdw; Bernards Common and Green; Berry Eyot, Croft and Fd (cf. *Beryegrove Cop'* 1538 *RentSur*, *Berry Croft More* 1603–4 *Survey*, *Berry Groue* 1607 *Norden*, *Berry Lands* 1659 *Bodl*); Bill Hill Park (*v.* 142–3); Blakes Piddle; Blanches Piddle; Blue Lion Mdw; Bottom Bridge Ground and Mdw; Boundary Fd; Bowling Green Fd; Brick Fd and Kiln; Broad Wings; Brookfield; Brookhouse Mdw; Broom Close; Brush Ground; Buckram Grove (*Buckhorn Grove* 1538 *RentSur*); Bullock Fd; Bulls Piddle; Burn Barn Piddle; Burn Ground; Bushey Lane; Calcutta Fd (*v.* 284); Cart House Mdw; Caskings Fd and Mdw; Castle Piddle (possibly near Castle Inn *supra* 101); Chairs; Chalket Mdw; Chandlers Piddle; Charcoal Piece; Cherry Tree Fd; Close Fd; Cold Bridge; Common Piece and Bit; Coopers Piddle; Coppice Barns and Close; Copse Grove and Pightle; Corderoy Garden; Corner Bit and Piece; Cottrell Piddle; Courer Fd; Cover Fd; Danes Wood; Dicks Devil; Dipping Hole Mdw; Drying Ground; Drying House Mdw; Dues Hill; Egertons Top; Ellis Hill; Elm Ground; Envy Pightle; Eton Fd; Feeding Ground and Piece; Ferney Piddle; Fidget Piece; Five Acre Coombs; Five Crates (*Crate* is possibly a dialect form of croft); Flys Lane; Fox Pightle; Frost Grove Lane; Garden Fd; Gardeners Mdw; Garningham Mdw; Good Acre; Goose Dubbs and Mdw (*v.* dubb 'a pool'); Gowers Grove; Great Ham (*v.* hamm); Greenwoods Piddle; Grey Lane Piddle; Grove Mdw and Land; Hail Mdw (*Hale* 1248 *Ass*, 1341 NonInq (p), *v.* h(e)alh); Hall, Hall Piddle; Hand Post Piddle (*v.* 281); Harbourer; Hay House Fd; Heath Close; Hell Mdw; Higgs Piddle; Highcut; Highway Piddle; Hill Piece; Hogshead Hill (*v.* 283); Holly Bush; Home Close, Brook, Pasture, Mdw and Fd; Hop Ground Mdw; Horns Mdw; Horse Pit Fd; Hurst Fd; Icehouse Ground; Icemans Land and Mdw; Inundation Mead; Iscott; Josh Mdw; Keeps Close; Kiloirge Fd; King Andrews Plot; King Sheet Fd (possibly for King Street 137); Lags (*v.* lagge); Lake Mdw; Lampers Pool; Lancers or Music Lane; Lane Grove; Leakstyle; Least; Linding Fd; The Lines (also 1822 OS, *v.* leyne); Loaders Copse and Piddle; Loddon Close; Lodge Fd; Longstaff (*v. supra*); Louse Close; Maiden Fd; Manyends; Marlow Mdw and Piddle; Marsh Close; Mary's Fd and Ground; Matts Piddle; May Piddle; Meadow Fold, Land, Plat, Plot and Piece; Medslips; Merrell Green Piddle (possibly identical with Merryhill Green in Winnersh 138); Mesums; Mickle Riggs (*v.* micel, hrycg); Mile Mdw; Mole Mdw; The Moor (cf. *The Little Moore, Middle*

More 1659 *Bodl*); Narrow Fd; Newfoundland, New Found Land Park
(*v.* 284); New Moor; North Croft Common; Oat Mead; Old Barn Close;
Old Bridge; Old Bridge Mdw; Old Mansion House Fd; Oriental Ground;
Out Close; Paddock; Pamphlets; The Park, Park Corner, Fd and Piddle
(cf. *The Little Parke, Old Park* 1659 *Bodl*); Pasture Piece and Ground; Pear
Tree Piddle; Pepperage Piddle; Petter Pool; Pheasant Piddle; Piccadilly
Lane, Great Piccadilly (*v.* 284); Pigeons Close; Pigs Mdw; Pinspool; Piper
Close; Piratical Fd; Plain Lyes; Plat, Plats Mdw (*v.* plat²); Pond Fd; Pond
Head Mdw; Pond Mdw, Pightle and Piddle; Ponies Mdw; Potato Piece;
Pump Mdw; Railway Piece; Remnant; Reynards Pightle; Rice Lands; Rick
Yard Close, Field and Piddle; Rod Pits; Round Mdw; Rowney; Ruggens;
Ruggerston Hill; Rushey Mdw; Sandeberry; Sawpit Piddle; Scotch Piddle;
Scrubbs; Sheep House Fd; Shepherds Piddle; Slade Fd and Mdw (*v.* slæd);
Slip, Slip Mdw (*v.* slipe); Small Mdw; Southay Mdw (*Southy* 1607 *LHRS*);
South Common; South Croft; Square Close; Stanaway Piddle; Stanpool;
Strident; Style Ground; Sutton Close; Swan Pond Mdw; Tenth Mdw;
Thicket Fd; Three and odd (*v.* 285); Three Cornered Fd; Toad Pightle;
Trapless; Triangle; Turnip Fd; Twinlock; Vale Ground; Victoria Fd and
Mdw; Walnut Tree Mdw; Wars Mdw; Water Piddle; Weldams; West Boun-
dary; West Lands; Wheel Mdw; White Hall Fd; Winding Ground, Mead,
Piece and Sheet; Worm Ground; Yard Gate Ground; Yard Fd and Mdw.

(*b*) *Ganlennesfeld, Galnnesfeld* Hy 3 *RentSur*; *Lye Place* Jas I *SpecCom*;
New Innings 1659 *Bodl* (*v.* inning); *South Meadows* 1659 *ib*; *Thistley Eyatt*
1659 *ib* (*v.* ēgeð).

Shinfield

SHINFIELD

Selingefelle 1086 DB

Sunningefeld 1155–8 Delisle, *Shuningefeld* 1224–5 *Ass*, *Sunnygge-*
feld 1284 *ib*, *Shuningefeld'* 1310–11 *FF*

Schiningefeld' 1167 P, *Shinningesfeld* 1168 ib, *Shiningefeld* 1254
Pat, *Shynyngfeld* 1324 Cl, 1349 (c. 1444) BC (p), *Sheyningfold,*
Shynnyngfold Jas I *SpecCom*

Scenegefeld' 1190, 1191 *HarlCh* 83 *A4*, *Schenynggefeld* 1221 (copy)
Sar, *Seningefeld* 1224–5 *Ass*, *Sennigefeld'* 1252 Cl, *Shenyngefeld*
1275–6 RH, *Schenigfeld', Schenigefeud', Chenigfeud, Shenigfeld',*
Shenygefeud' 1284 *Ass*, *Scheniggefeld'* 1294 SR, *Shenyngfelde*
1316 *FA*, *Schenyngefeld* 1327 *SR*

Singgesfeld' 1200 Cur

Cheningefeld' 1218–19 *FF*

Shenefeld 1324 Fine, 1474 Stonor

'Open land of Scīene's people', *v.* -inga-, feld. The pers.n. *Scīene,*
Scēne is found also in Shingay C 65. The spelling in DB shows the

confusion of -*l*- and -*n*- which is common in this county. The DB form *Soanesfelt*, given under Shinfield in DEPN, is very much more likely to refer to Swallowfield (108)'

SHINFIELD STREET-NAMES

FAIRMEAD RD.   OATLANDS RD.   THE SQUARE (in Spencers Wood).
WYCHELM RD.

DIDDENHAM FM, *Dinheham* c. 1190, *Didenam* 1195, *Didenham* c. 1195, *Dideham* c. 1200 all HMC 9th Rep 1, *Dideham* 1224–5 *Ass* (p), 13th *ReadingC*, *Didenham* 1224–5 *Ass* (p), 1345 Cl, *Dydeham* 1248–9 *Ass* (p), *Dydenham* 1294 *SR* (p), 1349 Ipm, *Didenham Fm* 1761 Rocque, *Diddenham Manor Fm* 1846 Snare. The second el. is probably hamm, as the farm is on low ground near Foudry Brook. For the first, the forms clearly suggest a pers.n. *Dida*, but no such name is on record; the name **Dydda* is well-evidenced in Gl (Gl **2**, 9), and the recorded *Dudda* occurs in Didcot (Pt **2**).

HARTLEY COURT

Hurlei 1086 DB

Hurtlea 1167 P, *Hurtlegh'* 1220 Fees, 1241 *Ass*, *Hurtleg'* 13th *ReadingC*(2), *Hurtley Batayle*, *Hurtley Du'mer'*, *Hurtleye Pelitot* 1294 *SR*, *Hurtleghe* 1316 FA, *Hurtlebatayl* c. 1346 InqMisc, *Hurtleye Amys*, *Hurtleye Dommere*, *Hurtleye Peletot* 1361 BM, *Hurtele Dunimere* 1428 FA

Hertlega 1167 P, 1185 RR *et freq* with variant spellings *Hertlea*, *Hertleg(h)'*, *Hertley* to 1490 *RentSur*, *Hertelega* 1177, 1185 P (p), *Herthlegh'* 1284 *Ass*, *Hereteley* 1409 BM, *Herteley* 1412 ib, 1515 *RentSur*, *Hertele Donimere* 1428 FA

Herleg' 1198 P

Hartley 1517 D Inc, *Harteley Amys*, *Hartley Domar* 1552 *LRMB*, *Hartley Court* 1659, 1661, 1670 *PubLib*, *Hartley Battell*, *Hartley Dommer*, *Hartley Ownys*, *Hartley Pollicotts* 1752 ArchJ 15, *Hartley Dammer* 1801 Census

'Hart wood or clearing', *v.* heorot, lē(a)h. The same name occurs in Do, Ha, K and So.

The complicated manorial history of the place is discussed in VCH III, 262–3. There were various manors: Hartley Dummer (where

Richard *de Dunmere*† held one hide in the first half of the 13th),
Hartley Battle (also one hide, held Hy 3 by the Abbot of Battle),
Hartley Amys and Hartley Pellitot (one hide here was held by Amys
de Peletot Hy 3, and another by a kinsman of his). *Hurlei* 1086 DB is
assessed at 2 hides, and may represent these last two holdings,
although the rubric puts it in Reading Hundred.

LAMBWOODHILL COMMON, *Lomwode* (p), *Lomwde* e. 13th ArchJ 2,
Lambwude 1241 *Ass* (p), *Lambewode* 1409 BM, (*communia vocata*)
Lambewodhill 1542 *MinAcc*, *Lombewood Hill* 1552 *LRMB*, *Lambwood
Hill* 1761 Rocque, 1790 Pride, *Lambwood Common* 1846 Snare; 'loam
wood' is perhaps more probable than 'lamb wood', but confusion
with **lamb** has taken place at an early date. *v.* lām, wudu.

RYEISH GATE AND GREEN, *Ryessth* 1369 *RecOffCat*, *Ryershe*, *Ryershe
Yate*, *Ryershe Grove* 1550 *LRMB*, *Ryeish Field and Pightle* 1838 *TA*,
'rye field', *v.* ryge, ersc. Ryarsh PN K 149–50 is an identical name.

BADGER FM.   BLACK BOY P.H., *Black Boy* 1846 Snare.   BRIDGE-
WATER FM, *Bridgewaters* 1838 *TA*.   BROOKER'S HILL, *Brookers
Hill, Pightle, Great and Little Meadow* 1838 *ib*.   BROWN'S GREEN,
1846 Snare.   CHURCH LANE AND FM.   CLARESGREEN FM.
COSTRILLS COPSE, *Coterells Place* 1550 *LRMB*, the surname *Coterell*
'cottager'.   CROCKERS FM (HILLSIDE FM on 6″).   THE CROFTS.
DUCKETT'S FM.   THE ELMS.   FOUDRY BRIDGE, *Fowdry Meadow*
1838 *TA*, *Foundry Bridge, Foundry Bridge Fm* 1846 Snare, *v.* 10.
GEORGE AND DRAGON P.H.   GOODREST.   GRAVELLY BRIDGE,
Gravel Bridge 1761 Rocque, *Gravelly Bridge Mead* 1838 *TA*.
GRAVELLYBRIDGE FM, 1846 Snare.   GRAZELEY, GRAZELEY CT, *v.*
166.   GROVELANDS.   HARTLEYCOURT FM, *v. supra*.   GREAT
LEA COMMON AND FM, 1846 Snare, *Lee Common* 1761 Rocque, *Great
Lea Common Piece* 1838 *TA*, *v.* lēah, other names in *Lee- Lea-, Lye,
infra* 107, may refer to this area.   HIGH COPSE, *High Coppice* 1846
Snare.   HIGHLANDS.   HILLSIDE NURSERY.   HITCH HILL, *Hitch
Hill and Meadow* 1838 *TA*, *v.* hiche.   HOLLOW LANE.   THE
HOMESTEAD.   HOPKILN FM, 1846 Snare, *Hop Kiln Seven Acres*
1838 *TA*.   HYDE END, *Hyde End Green and Ground* 1838 *ib*,
Hyde End Fm 1846 Snare.   KYBES LANE, 1838 *TA*, Ralph *Kibe*
is mentioned in connection with Hartley and Lambwood e.13th

---

† The surname is probably from Dunmore in Chaddleworth, Pt 2.

ArchJ 2; *Kybestrode* 1241 *Ass* (p) may have been named from the same family, *v.* strōd, and cf. Windsor f.ns. 35.   LANE END HO. MANOR HO, 1790 Pride.   MAY'S FM AND HILL, *Mays Hill Close* 1838 *TA*.   MEREOAK LANE, *Meer Oak Field and Street* 1838 *ib*, *Meir Oak Lane* 1846 Snare, *v.* (ge)mǣre.   MILLWORTH LANE, *Le Myllworke, Myllworthe, Millworthe More, Myllworthefeld* 1550 *LRMB, Millworth Field, Meadow and Moor* 1838 *TA*, *v.* myln, worð, the name may refer to a mill on the R. Loddon, of which O.S. maps show no trace.   MOOR COPSE, cf. *Le Litill More* 1550 *LRMB, The Moors* 1838 *TA*, *v.* mōr.   NORES HILL, 1838 *TA*, *Nowers* 1550 *LRMB*, 1838 *TA*, *Norrs Hill Copse* 1846 Snare, *v.* atten, ōra¹. NULLIS FM.   NURSERY CORNER.   OAKBANK.   OLDHOUSE FM, 1846 Snare.   PARROT FM, MAGPIE AND PARROT P.H.   PEAR-MAN'S COPSE AND LANE.   PLOUGH P.H.   POUNDGREEN, 1846 Snare; the pound is marked 1761 Rocque, 1846 Snare.   POUND-GREEN FM.   ST JOHN'S COPSE, *St Johns Land* 1550 *LRMB*, possibly from the family named *Sancto Johanne*, mentioned in con-nection with Shinfield 1245–52 *FF*, 1316 FA.   SCHOOLGREEN, 1790 Pride, 1846 Snare, for the school, which was built in 1707, *v.* VCH III, 261.   SHEPHERDTON LANE.   SHINFIELD GRANGE, GROVE AND LODGE.   SHINFIELD GREEN, 1846 Snare, *Le Grene, Shynfeld Grene* 1550 *LRMB, Shinefield Green* 1761 Rocque, 1790 Pride, *v.* grēne².   SIX BELLS P.H.   SPENCERS WD, 1761 Rocque, *Spencers Wood Common* 1790 Pride, *Spencers Common* 1846 Snare. STANBURY.   STAR P.H., *Star Close* 1838 *TA*.   STUD FM. SUSSEX LODGE, *Sussex Grene* 1550 *LRMB*.   SWAN P.H.   TANNER'S COPSE, 1846 Snare.   THREEMILE CROSS, 1761 Rocque, 1846 Snare, a cross-roads 3 miles from Reading.   UNIVERSITY COLLEGE FM. WARRENGATE FM, *Warren Gate Green* 1846 Snare.   WEATHERCOCK COTTAGES.   WHEAT SHEAF P.H.   WHITEHOUSE FM, 1846 Snare. WILDERS GROVE FM.   WOODCOCK LANE, 1761 Rocque, from a family first mentioned in Shinfield in 1424 (*LHRS*); George *Wood-cock* had land in Hartley Dommer 1566 AD.   WYVERN.   YEW-TREE FM.

FIELD-NAMES

The principal forms in (*a*) are 1838 *TA* except where otherwise stated; early forms for which no date or source is given are 1550 *LRMB*.

(*a*) Alder Moor(s); Barley Close; Barlands, Bar Mead; Barn Close and Pightle (*v.* pightel, very common in this parish); Bartholomew Reads

(*Barthelmewe Reades* 1566 AD, cf. Reads *infra*); Beech Lands; Biles Pightle; Black House Fm 1846 Snare; Black Lake; Blind Lane (a common name for a cul-de-sac); Blundens Pightle; Bonds Pightle; Bottoms Pightle; Breeches Piece; Bridge Close and Mdw; Broad Croft (*Brodecroft*); Broad Fd; Brook Leaze (*v.* læs), Mead and Pightle; Broom Close; Bushy Coppice Ground; Byefield; Calces Leaze Mdw; Cart House Ground; Casters (*Costowe(s), v.* cot-stōw); Chalk Ground and Pightle; Chandlers Pightle; Chapel Pightle; Charity Pightle; Cherry Tree Pightle; Chitterlane Moor 1846 Snare (*Chitling Moor* 1761 Rocque); Chub Hole Mead; Church Acre, Lands and Pightle (*Churchfelds, Churchelands*); Clay Pightle, The Clays (*Le Cley*); Coppice Close and Ground; Corner Fd, Ground and Pasture; Corn Leaze; Cow Slip Mdw; Critchers Pightle; Crooked Croft: Cross Mead and Pightle; Crown Furlong; Culvers (*Culluer Crofte, v.* culfre); Cut Bush Fm 1846 Snare; Diddicks; Drain Swarth; Duck Mead; East Meadow (*Estemede*); Elm Row; Fir Tree Fd; Flat Ground; The Folly (*v.* folie); Footpath Ground and Close; Fox Hill; Frogmore; Garden Close; Garstons (*v.* gærs-tūn); Gate and Stile Ground; Glaziers Pightle; Glebe Orchard; Gravelly Ground and Piece; Gravel Pit; Green Fd and Lane; Grove Close (*Le Grove Plot*); Gungins Plat (*v.* plat[2]); Ham Mdw (cf. *Est Ham* 1566 AD, *v.* hamm); Handkerchief Piece in East Meadow (*v.* 284); Hartley Fd and Moors (*v.* 104); Hatch Ground and Close (*v.* hæc(c)); Hatchet Ground; Heading Close (*Hedingcrofte*); Higgs Pightle; High Fd; Hill House Farm 1846 Snare; The Hill, Hill Close, Fd and Ground; Hiscocks Pightle; Hobley Mead; Home Close, Fd and Ground (*Le Home Close, Le Homegrounde, v.* 93); Honey bans; Hop Ground (cf. Hopkiln Fm *supra*); Horse Leys; How Land Mdw (*Howland Mead* 1733 *PubLibDoc*); Hide Croft; Ilbury Fd and Pightle (*Ilbury*); Ivy Lake Mead; Kepple Whites Closes; Ketts Pightle; Kiln Close and Ground; Ladys Fds (*Ladyfelds, v.* hlæfdige); Langley Mdw (*Langley, Langeley Mede, v.* lang, lēah); Lea Pightle and Close, Lee Croft (*Lee House* 1766, 1781 *PubLib v.* Great Lea Common *supra*); Leasing Hands; Leightons Pightle; Lock Mdw; Long Slip (*v.* slipe); Lords Mead (*Le Lords Mede*); Lucy Green Mead (*Lucy Green* 1761 Rocque); Lye Croft, Close and Mead (*Lyfeld, v.* Great Lea Common *supra*); Lyons (*v.* leyne); Marlow Green; Marlows Pightle; Marsh Pightle; Mead (*Le Mede, Mede Grove*); Mene Mead (*v.* (ge)mæne, mǣd); Milking Hayes; Moorhouse; Netherlands; Normans Land and Shaw (*Nomans Lande, v.* mann and 284); Norths Pightle; Orchard Brewerton; Orchard Close and Pightle; Paddock (cf. *Pattokks Perte* in (*b*)); Palmers Pightle; Park Close; Peacocks Pightle; Pear Tree Ground and Pightle; Perry Croft; Petty Croft; Picked Pightle (cf. *Le Pyked Crofte, v.* pīced); Pigeon Close; Pig Wash Fd (*v.* 94); Pile Croft Vicarage Land; The Pits (*Le Pitts*); Plates; The Plat(t) (*v.* plat[2]); Pond Close and Fd; Potatoe Ground; Rail Fd (*v.* 281); Readings (*v,* ryding); Reads Bridge 1846 Snare; Reads (cf. Reads Lane in the adjacent parish of Swallowfield 110); Rickyard Fd; Round Mead; Rushy Piece; Seagroves Pightle; The Shaw Close (*v.* sc(e)aga); Sheets; Small Mead (*Smale Mead* 1566 AD, *v.* smæl); Smith Field Mdw; Sorrell Close; Spectacles (*v.* 283); Spring Close; Square Shines; Stoney Croft (cf. *Stonyclose*); Tooveys Green 1846 Snare (*Tovey's Green* 1761 Rocque); Toovey's Mead; Upping Stocks;

Vere; Walk Ground; Wallis's Hill; Wares Pightle; The Warren Ground
(cf. Warrengate Fm *supra*); Waterloo Fm 1846 Snare (*v.* 284); Water Pightle;
Way Fd; Well Close (cf. *Well Crofte, Le Well Piddell*, and variant of pightel);
Whitegate Hill; Wicked Pightle; Wickets Pightle; Winding Ground; Withey
Eyott (cf. *Withies, v.* ēgeð); Woo Croft; York Pool Bridge 1828 *PubLib.*

(*b*) *Athelardesford* e.13th ArchJ 2 (*v.* ford, first el. a pers.n. in *Æðel-*,
probably *Æðelheard*); *Botteland* 1369 *RecOffCat* (*v.* butte); *Botulphus
Puddellez* 1433 AD ('Bōtwulf's enclosures, *v.* 197 for the second el.);
Brodley (*comen of*) 1566 AD (*v.* brād, lēah); *Butlers Yate* (*Towneyate voc.*)
1550 *LRMB, Butlers* 1673 *PubLib*; *Lez Butts* (*v.* butte); *Courtise Close*; *Le
Estefeld*; *Firson, Furson* (*v.* fyrsen); *Le Gores* 1369 *RecOffCat* (*v.* gāra); *Le
Highecrofte*; *Inholmes, Inhomes* (*v.* innām); *Litill Bedle*; *Le Longe Crofte*;
Le Longe Mede; *Oldhams* 1673 *PubLibDoc*; *Olde Mead* 1566 AD; *Pattokks
Perte* (first el. possibly the name Paddock in (*a*)); *Purchase Lande*; *Pye Lyes*
1550 *LRMB, Pyleys* 1673 *PubLibDoc*; *Le Rewen, Le Reowen in Le Lords
Mede* (possibly the dat.pl. of rǣw); *La Rudmed* e.13th ArchJ 2 (*v.* (ge)ryd(d)
mǣd); *Le Rye Mede*; *Sauceresland* 1369 *RecOffCat* (from the ME byname
Saucer 'one who makes or sells sauces', also found in a f.n. in Wargrave 122);
Sellcroft; *Shortecrofte* 1550 *LRMB, Shortcroft* 1673 *PubLib*; *Shynfeld
Estende, Shynfeld Weste End*; *Southefeld*; *Les Swathes* (*v.* O 468); *West
Beooreham* 1566 AD; *Westecroft*; *Whittofte*; *Woodcroft* 1369 *RecOffCat.*

Swallowfield

SWALLOWFIELD

Soanesfelt, Solafel, Sualefelle 1086 DB
Sarefeld 1155–8 Delisle
Sualewesfeld' c. 1160 OxonCh
Sualewefeld' 1167, 1176 P *et freq* with variant spellings *Swalewe-
    feld', Swalewefeld; Swalwefeld'* 1252 Cl, *Swalwefeld* 1361 Fine
Swalefeld' 1168 P *et freq* with variant spellings *Sualefeld, Suale-
    feld', Swalefeld; Swalfeld* 1275–6 RH
Swalofeld 1220 Fees, *Swalufeld'* 1241 *Ass, Swallowfelde* 1316 FA,
    Swalowefeld 1436 Fine
Swalfeld 1377 Pat

'Open land by the river *Swealwe*', *v.* feld; the river-name is discussed *supra* 7. The forms from DB and Delisle show the common
confusion between *l, n, r.*

BEAMY'S CASTLE, *Beaumys* 1265 Ch *et passim* with variant spellings
Beaumes, Beaumis, Beaumeys, Beaumees; Beamys 1322 Cl, *Beames*
1515 ArchJ 4, *Biem's* 1532 ObAcc. Identical with Beamish Du and
Beaumetz in France, a French name, from **beau** 'beautiful', and **mes,**

which latter term is translated by Godefroy (*Dictionnaire de l'ancienne Langue française*) as 'maison de campagne, ferme, propriété rurale, habitation, demeure'.

FARLEY FM

 Ferlega 1167, 1190 P, 1185 RR (p), 1224–5 *Ass*
 Farlea 1169 P, *Farlega* 1224–5 *Ass*, *Farlegh* 1332 *SR*, 1345 Cl
 Fernlega 1176 P (p)

 'Fern clearing', a fairly common name; *v.* fearn, lē(a)h.

RISELEY FM AND COMMON (latter in Ha), *Rysle* 1300 Cl, *Riselee* n.d. AD, *Rysle* 1572 *SpecCom*, *Riseley, Riseley Common* 1761 Rocque, 1790 Pride, *Riseley Common* 1827 *PubLib*, 'brushwood clearing', *v.* hrīs, lē(a)h; the same name occurs in Bd, Db and La.

SHEEP BRIDGE, *Shepreg'* 1224–5 *Ass* (p), *Siprugge* Hy 3 AD, *Scheperugge* c. 1240 (13th) ReadingA, *Sheperuge* 13th *ReadingC*(*2*), *Sheprige* n.d. (14th) *ReadingC*(*3*), *Little Sheperuge* 1332 Cl, *Sheprigge* 1345 ib, *Sheprugge Magna* 1365 BM, *Great Shupperugge* 1422 Fine, *Sheperidge* 1580 AD, *Sheep Bridge* 1760 Rocque, *Shepperidge* 1766 *PubLib*, 'sheep ridge', *v.* scēap, hrycg. The name was that of a manor, for the history of which *v.* VCH III, 271–2. The second el. was presumably interpreted as 'bridge', and the name transferred to an actual bridge over the Loddon.

STANFORD END, *Stanford* 1227 Ch, 1300 Cl, *Stamford* 13th *ReadingC*, *Standford End, Stanford Green and Mill* 1761 Rocque, *Stanford End* 1790 Pride, 'stone ford', *v.* stān, ford, a very common name which occurs several times in this county.

WYVOLS COURT, *Wyfalde* 1224–5 *Ass* (p), *La Wifaude* Hy 3 AD (p), *Wyvolde* 1327 *SR* (p), *Wyfold, Wyfold Crofte* 1550 *LRMB*, *Wifold*, *Wyfolde* 1607 *RentSur*, *Wye Field* 1846 *TA*. There are three occurrences of this name in Berks, *v.* Pt. 2.

ANGEL INN P.H. BACK LANE. BAILEY'S FM (UPPER FM on 6″). BARGE LANE. BETHEL CHAPEL. BODYS FM. BOW-YER'S FM. BRIDGE HO, *Swallowfeld Bridge* 1550 *LRMB*. THE BROADWATER BULL INN AND LANE. BUNCES SHAW. BUNGLER'S

HILL, *Bonglers Hill* 1550 *LRMB*.   CHILL HILL, 1846 *TA*, possibly
referring to an exposed situation.   CHURCH LANE, CHURCHLANE
COPSE.   CLARKS FM.   CLAY HILL.   COCKSETTERS, 1846 *TA*,
Coksetters Lande 1550 *LRMB*, first el. the surname *Coxeter*.
COLLINS COPSE.   COURT FM.   CROWN P.H.   CUCKOO PEN (*v.*
O 438).   DRUMHEAD.   DUNNING'S HOLE, 1787 *PubLib*, 1846
TA, *Donnings Hole* 1735 *PubLib*.   ELM LODGE.   EMMS COPSE,
Emes Lande 1550 *LRMB*, *coppice and land called Emmes or Immes*
17th *PubLib*, *House and land called Emmes* 1708 *ib*, *Emmes Coppice*
1714, 1715 *ib*, *Emms* 1846 *TA*, first el. probably the surname *Emm*.
FARLEY CASTLE.   FARLEY HILL, 1550 *LRMB*, 1654 *Bodl*, 1790
Pride, *Fareley Hill* 1607 ArchJ 36, *Fawley Hill* 1761 Rocque, *v.* 109.
FARLEYHILL CT AND PLACE.   FEATHERLANDS COPSE, *Featherlands*
1846 *TA*, *v.* 284.   FIR GROVE.   FORD LANE.   FOX AND
HOUNDS P.H.   FOX GORSE.   GEORGE AND DRAGON P.H.
GREAT COPSE.   GREAT WD.   HANDPOST FM (*v.* 281).   HIGH-
GROVE COPSE, *Highgrove Coppice* 1817 OS.   HOLLOWAY'S FM.
HOLLY CORNER.   HORNES COPSE.   THE ISLAND, *Island Meadow*
1846 *TA*.   JOULDINGS FORD AND LANE, *Jouldins Ford* 1761 Rocque,
Jouldens Ford 1817 OS.   KILNCLOSE POND.   KILN COPSE AND
HILL.   KING'S BRIDGE, 1761 Rocque, *Kingesbrige* Hy 3 AD,
Kingesbrigge n.d. ib, self-explanatory. There was a royal manor here
in 1086.   KINGSBRIDGE HILL.   KING'S COPSE.   KNIGHT'S
FM.   LAMB'S FM AND LANE.   LODDON CT.   LOWER FM.
MALES FM.   MAY'S HILL.   NEWBARN FM.   NEW PLANTA-
TION.   NOAH'S ARK, a small building.   NUTBEAN FM AND LANE.
NUTTER'S LANE, *Nuthurste* 1550 *LRMB*, *Nutters Mead* 1756 *PubLib*,
v. hnutu, hyrst.   PARKSIDE, this may be named from *Bluntespark*
1368 Ch (in Sheep Bridge).   PARSONS FM.   PART LANE.
PICKET'S COPSE, *v.* pīced.   PINK'S COPSE.   RAGGETT'S LANE,
Racketts, Great and Little Raggots 1846 *TA*.   READS LANE, *Reed's*
Seven Acres, Reed's Eight Acres 1846 *ib*.   ROWE'S FM, *Rows Six*
Acres, Rows Moor Piece 1846 *ib*.   RUSSELL HALL.   ST LEGER'S
COPSE.   SALTER'S BRIDGE, *Salters Meadow, Pightle and Seven*
Acres 1846 *TA*.   SANDPIT FM AND LANE, *Sand Pit Hills* 1846 *ib*.
SHEEPBRIDGE MILL, *Skipperidge Mill* 1607 Norden, *Shepperidge Mill*
1820 *PubLib*, *v.* 109.   SPRING GALLS FM, *v.* galla.   SPRING
LANE.   STANFORDEND FM AND MILL, *v.* 109.   SWALLOWFIELD
PK, 1761 Rocque, there was a park here in 1323 (VCH III, 270).
SWALLOWFIELD WEST.   TANNER'S FM, *Tanners* 1550 *LRMB*.

TAYLOR'S LANE.   TROWE'S LANE, *Trolls Lane* 1550 *ib.*   WAT-
MORE FM, *Watmores Pightle* 1846 *TA.*   WHEELER'S COPSE,
Whelers alias Greys 1550 *LRMB.*   WHITE'S GREEN, 1761 Rocque.
THE WILDERNESS, *Wilderness* 1846 *TA.*   WOODBURY.

FIELD-NAMES

The principal forms in (*a*) are 1846 *TA*; early forms dated 1550 are *LRMB.*

(*a*) Aspen Pightle (*v.* æspen and pightel, the latter common in the f.ns.
of this parish); Backdoor Fd; Balcombs; Barn Close, Paddock and Pightle;
Choseley Fd; Church Hills; Common Mdw (*Le Comon Mede* 1550);
Cowstail Pightle (probably from the shape); Cross Farm Pasture; Dairy
Ground; Decoy Ground; Delaware; Doctors Pightle; Duncans; Five
Cornered Fd; Fludyers Mdw; Footpath Mdw and Piece; Ford Hatch
Allotment; Fork Mdw; Furze Cover, Fd and Mdw; Garden Close and
Pightle; Greengate Ground; Hatch, Hatch Pightle (*v.* hæc(c)); Hill Ground
and Fd; Home Close and Park; Hop Garden; Hopkins's Pightle; Hungry
Mdw; Kennington's Pightle; King's Pightle (*Kinges Piddle* 1660 Moulton,
v. King's Bridge *supra* 110); Lock Mdw; Lodge Four Acres; Lug Close;
The Moor, Moor Mdw and Pightle (*La More* c. 1270 AD, *Moremede* 1550,
v. mōr); New Pasture; Parish Fd; Pasture Pightle; Pike Mdw (*v.* pīc¹);
Poors Pightle; Priests Pightle; Rickyard Fd; Rodd Piece (*v.* O 463); Round
Mdw; Rounds Land; Scotlands (*v.* scot); Shaws Pightle; Shaw Ground;
Sheep Walk; Sparkes Pightle; Thatchers Mdw and Pightle; Three Cornered Fd (possibly identical with *Threhurn* 1348 Cl, 'three corners', *v.*
þrēo, hyrne); Well Pightle; Wood Fd; Workhouse Pightle.

(*b*) *Le Banke* 1550; *The Bounds* 1761 Rocque; *Bowfeis Banke* 1710
PubLib; *Brodemed* Hy 3 AD (*v.* brād, mǣd); *Bromwell Hill* 1607 *Norden*;
Broome Close 1670, 1752 *PubLib*; *Church End* 1790 Pride; *Le Churchehouse*
1550, *Church House* 1648 *PubLib*; *The Corner Piddle* 1660 Moulton (a
variant of pightel); *Dedwater* 1550; *Dimmings Dale* 1647, 1676, 1703, 1707,
1709 *PubLib* (this p.n. occurs in Db, St, YW and D; it is discussed Db 169,
YW 6, 108, *v.* also 282); *Farlingmore* c. 1300 ArchJ 46, *Farlyngmor* 1348 Cl,
Fareley Moarr 1607 *Norden* (*v.* 77); *Forlese* 1348 Ipm, 1349 Cl (*v.* fore,
lǣs); *Foxhull* 1348, 1365 ib (*v.* fox, hyll); *Gardiners Land* 1348 ib; *La Grave*
1301 Pat (p) ('pit' or 'grove', *v.* græf, grāf); *Haymede* 1550, *Hay Mead*
1670–1 *PubLib*; *Horsleys* 1550; *Junonie* 1348 Cl; *Laggelee* c. 1270 AD ('marsh
clearing', *v.* lagge, lēah); *Lethennardesyate* c. 1270 ib (*v.* geat, the same first el.,
clearly a pers.n., occurs in two Ch f.ns., *v.* Ch 1, 125, 3, 158); *Le Olde Myll*
1550; *Patriks Forde* 1550, *Patrickes Ford* 1706 *PubLib*; *La Pleyok* n.d. AD
(p) (*v.* plega, āc); *Pookerige Lande* 1550, *Puckeridge's* 1735, 1739 *PubLib*
(first el. probably a surname from Puckeridge Hrt); *Port Lane* 1761 Rocque;
Swallowfeld Strete 1550; *Wales, Muchel and Litel* 1348 Cl (these were hays,
and the name may be a ME plural of walu 'ridge', used of the banks round
the hays, *v.* micel, lȳtel); *Westmede* 1348 Ipm, 1349 Cl; *Whitefeld* 1348 ib
(*v.* hwīt).

VI. WARGRAVE HUNDRED

Weregraue 1241, 1248 *Ass*, *Weregrave* 1275–6 RH, 1316 FA
v. Wargrave *infra* 119.

Waltham St Lawrence

WALTHAM ST LAWRENCE

(*æt*) *Wuealtham*, (*to*) *Wealtham* 940 (c. 1240) BCS 762, (*æt*)
Wealtham 1007 (c. 1240) KCD 1303
parva Waltham, *Waltam* 1086 Gilbert Crispin, *Waltham* 1086 DB,
parua Waltham 1169–89 Hurley, *Wautham* 1212 Fees, *Waltamia
Sancti Laurencii* 1224–5 *Ass* (p), *Wautham Sancti Laurencii* 1284
ib, *Waltham Sancti Laurencii* 1294 *SR*, *parva Waltham* l.13th
Hurley, *Lutelwaltham* 1315 ib, *Waltham Sancti Laurentii* 1316
FA, *Waltham Seynt Laurens* 1400 Fine, *Laurence Waltham* 1535
VE, *Larrance Waltham* 1606 BM, *Lawrance Walthum* 17th
PubLib(Clayton)

'Homestead in a wood', *v.* w(e)ald, hām. For other examples of this
name, and for a discussion of the OE forms, *v.* DEPN and Sx 77.
Ekwall's explanation that weald became *wealt* before the *h-* of hām
has been generally accepted. This place is called 'small', 'St Lawrence' (from the church dedication) for distinction from White
Waltham (70). The charters disposing of land at Waltham are discussed in Pt **3**. BCS 762 probably refers to both the Walthams and
Shottesbrooke (which is situated between them), and KCD 1303
probably refers to Waltham St Lawrence only.

BILLINGBEAR PARK, cf. *Pillingebere* 1208 WinchesterPR, 1275–6 RH,
Le Pyllingeber' 1238 Cl, *Pillingebir'* 1239 ib, *Pillinber'*, *Pillingber'* 1240
ib, *Peningber'* 1241 ib, *Pillingber'* 1261 ib, *Pollingebere* 1263 ib, *Pillingbere* 1275–6 RH, 1284 Ch, *Pullingbere* 1275–6 RH, *Pellingebery*,
Pillyngebery 1284 PontReg, *Pillyngbere* 1288–9 *RentSur*, 1339 Cl,
1401–2 FA, *Billings Bare* 1761 Rocque, *Billingbear* 1790 Pride,
Billingbear Park 1846 Snare. In several of the early references the
name is said to be that of a wood. The second element is probably
bǣr² 'swine pasture', and this is combined with **-inga-** and an un-

certain first el. If this were a pers.n. it could be an OE *Pilla, a hypocoristic form of the pers.ns. in Pīl-. But bǽr is not a usual final el. in a p.n. formed from a pers.n. and -inga-. Ekwall's suggestion (DEPN) that there was a lost place called Pilley ('wood where piles were got'), and that the people who lived there were called *Pillingas, is plausible. Alternatively, the people of the neighbourhood might have been called *Pyllingas, from the small stream which traverses this part of the parish; v. O 462 s.v. pyll. This would accord better with the occasional -e- and -u- of the forms. The change of P- to B- is evidently modern, and may have been helped by the comparative proximity of Bill Hill (142–3).

DOWNFIELD LANE, cf. Down Field 1761 Rocque, 1790 Pride. Possibly named from La Doune 1288–9 RentSur, The Downe 1697 Windsor 'hill', v. dūn.

SHURLOCK ROW, 1761 Rocque, 1846 Snare, Southlake Row 1790 Pride; cf. Surlock Street Ground 1839 TA. This and SOUTH LAKE HO (Southlake 1839 TA, 1846 Snare) are named from a place called Suthelak 1242–3 Fees, Suthelak' 1260–1 FF, Suthlake 1347 Pat. 'South of the stream', v. sūðan, lacu. The stream is Ruscombe Lake (128). For the development to Shur-, cf. Surly Hall (20–1) and Circourt (Pt 2).

WEYCOCK HILL, cf. (to) weg cocce 940 (c. 1240) BCS 762, Little Weacocke 17th PubLib(Clayton), Weycock 1711 Hearne, Waycoak Field 1761 Rocque, Waycock Field 1790 Pride, 1846 Snare. The els. are weg 'way', and cocc[1] 'hillock'. The point mentioned in the charter bounds (for which v. Pt 3) is on the west boundary of Waltham St Lawrence. There is no sharp ascent here, and it seems possible that cocc refers to some artificial feature, such as a tumulus, which, if it were situated by the wayside, would be a likely thing to be mentioned in charter bounds.

ANNSCOT.   BAILEY'S LANE, Baileys Mdw 1839 TA.   BEAR FM. BEARS FM AND COPSE.   BEENHAM'S FM AND HEATH, Beenham's, Beenham's Heath 1711 Hearne, Binham's Heath 1761 Rocque, Benhams Heath, Benham Fm 1846 Snare; John de Benham is mentioned 1260–1 FF in connection with land in Waltham; the family also had land in Beenham (150), whence their surname derives (VCH III, 180).   BELL INN.   BIRCH PLANTATION.   BORLASE'S.

BROADMOOR LANE, *Broadmoores* 1839 *TA*.   BROOK LANE, *Brook Lane Piece and Meadow* 1839 *TA*.   BRUNCKETTS, BRUNCKETTS FM, *Brunchetts* 1846 Snare.   BURRINGHAM WD, *Brummingham* 1626 *Windsor*, *Burringham* 1839 *TA*.   BUSHY LEES.   CALLIN'S BRIDGE AND LANE, *Callins Mead* 1839 *TA*.   CHARITY WD, *Charity Fm* 1822 OS, 1846 Snare.   CHURCH FM, 1846 ib.   CROCKFORD'S BRIDGE AND COPSE, *Crockfords* 1822 OS, *Crockfords Meadow and Pightle* 1839 *TA*.   DARVILLS LANE.   THE DENE.   DOWN- GROVE COPSE, *Dungrove* 1839 *TA*.   DOWNSHIRES FM.   FERREL BRIDGE OCKETT (the Bridge is in St Nicholas Hurst parish, for Ockett *v.* 60).   FOX AND HOUNDS.   GLADE, UPPER AND LOWER.   GOOSENEST FM, *Goose Nest* 1839 *TA*.   THE GRANGE.   THE GRAVELPITS, *Gravel Pit Mead* 1839 *TA*.   GUNSBROOK, 1839 *ib.* HALLS FM (1846 Snare) AND LANE, *Great and Little Hall Field, Halls Pightle* 1839 *TA*.   HAMMOND'S WD, *Hammonds Woodfield* 1839 *ib.* HEATH FM AND LODGE.   HONEYS.   HORSEPASTURE COPSE, LOWER AND UPPER.   HUNGERFORD, HUNGERFORD LANE, perhaps transferred from Hungerford (Pt **2**).   IDLICOTE.   KILN COPSE, *The Kiln* 1839 *TA*.   MALTHOUSE, OLD MALT HOUSE.   MANOR HOUSE.   GREAT MARTINS, *Great and Little Martins* 1839 *TA*, *Martins Green* 1846 Snare.   MILLEY FM, BRIDGE AND RD, *Milley* 1839 *TA*.   MIRE FM AND LANE, *Mire Mead* 1839 *ib.*   NUT LANE.   PARADISE, *v.* 283.   PARK FM, 1790 Pride.   PENN BUSHES.   THE PLANTATION.   RED COTTAGE.   THE ROUND PIECE.   ROYAL OAK P.H.   SILL BRIDGE, *Sil Grove, Little Sil Ground* 1839 *TA*.   SPRING COPSE.   STAR P.H.   STRAIGHT MILE.   SURRELLS WD.   TEMPLE GROVE, *Temples Mead* 1839 *TA*.   UNCLE'S LANE.   WARREN COPSE.   WEST END, *West End Mdw* 1839 *TA*, *West End, West End Bridge* 1822 OS, 1846 Snare.   WHITE HART P.H.   WHITFIELDS FM.   WICKS LANE.

FIELD-NAMES

The principal forms in (*a*) are 1839 *TA*; forms in (*b*) are Hurley.

(*a*) Abdys; The Alders; Armshill; Badcock; Barn Close and Fd; Black Hall Mead; Bookers Corner and Hill; Book Innings (*v.* inning); Bottom Ground; Breaches (*v.* brēc); Brickbatts (possibly a field where fragments of bricks were found); Broad Common; Brook Stile; Brookes Hill; Buckets Mead; Bulls Close; Butchers Mead; Butter Pightle (*v.* butere and pightel, common in the f.ns. of this parish); Charles, Little and Dead (Dead Charles might be from *Dedecherle*, for which *v.* O 439); Cherry Orchard; Clayhearne (*v.* clæg, hyrne); Common Piece; Coombs Fd; Coppice Ground; Costers Mire; Cranwells Pit; The Croft; Davisons Pightle; Deer Park; Emmetts Pightle; Footbridge Mead; George Ground; Giles Innings (*v.* inning); Gillitts Mead; Graffadge Grounds (*graffadge* is a dial. term for a sort of fence used at the junction of two ditches, or where a ditch abuts on a road); Green Close; Greeners Mead; Green Hill Fd and Mead; Haines Hill and Mdw; Hawkins Pightle; Hill Piece; The Hills; Holly Wood Fd; The Holt Ground (*v.* holt); Home Close; Horsenails (cf. Brickbatts *supra*); Kent Fds; Lappets; Last Fd; Lay Close; Lee Mdw; The Long Walk; Marlow Mead; Mawlands; Mead Bottom; Micklams Meads; Mill Bridge Pightle; Mill Fd and Piece; Moneys Mdw; Moot Ground; Mowing Park; Napbrooks; Newlands Mdw; No Man's Mow (*v.* 284); Orchard Ground; Pigeon House Close; Plum Pudding Fd (perhaps referring to sticky soil); Pond Ground and Piece; Pout House; Powneys Mead and Pightle; Pundells Corner and Mdw; Rey Ground; Rickyard Mead; Rowgrove; Saw Pit Mead; Shaw Fd; Sorry Bargain (*v.* 283); Spring Fd; Stavel Ground; Street Close; Sues Piddle (a variant of pightel); Three Cornered Piece and Pightle; The Three Meads; The Waste; Watering Place Ground; Well Close; Westcrofts; Whitneys (possibly identical with *Widney* 1607 *LHRS*); Wild Duck Mead; Windmill Fd; Wombridge (Wom Bridge 1822 OS, north-east of Beenham's Heath, on the boundary between Waltham St Lawrence and Shottesbrook; it is possible that *Wom* represents the *wassan hamme* of BCS 762, KCD 1303, for which *v.* Pt 3; the OE name means 'meadow of the marsh', *v.* wæsse, hamm).

(*b*) *Le Cnollecroft* 1315 (near Knowl Hill in Hurley 62–3); *Hesperuck-croft* Ed I; *Homcroft* Ed I (first el. hamm or hām); *Perpountstrete* 1315 (*v.* stræt, first el. the surname *Pierpoint*); *Ruycroft* Ed I (*v.* ryge, croft); *Suthcroft* Ed 2 (*v.* sūð, croft); *Thuuelheker* Ed I (*v.* æcer, first el. possibly þyfel 'bush, thicket').

Warfield

WARFIELD

Warwelt 1086 DB
Warefeld' 1171 P (p), 1212 Fees, 1284 *Ass*, *Warefeld*, *Warfeld'* 1176 P (p), *Warfeld* 1263 Cl, *Warefeld* 1275–6 RH, 1293 Fine, 1347 Pat, *Warrefeld* 1303–4 FF, *Warefelde* 1316 FA
Werrefeld' 1186 P, *Werrefeld* 1228 Cl

The second el. is feld 'open land', the first probably wer, wær, 'weir, river-dam, fishing enclosure in a river'. Cf. Wargrave 119. Warfield lies beside a stream. DEPN suggests that the first el. of Warfield is a contraction of *wernan wille* in the charter bounds of Winkfield, but although the two parishes adjoin, *wernan wille* is not near Warfield, and a connection between the names does not seem probable, *v.* Pt 3.

BRACKNELL, (*on*) *braccan heal*, (*of*) *braccan heale* 942 (c. 1200), (*on*) *braccan heal*, (*of*) *brachan heale* 942 (c. 1240) BCS 778, *Brackenhale* 1185 RR (p), *Brakehal'* 1224–5 *Ass* (p), *Brackenhal'* 1241 *ib*, *Braken-hal(e)* 1284 *ib*, *Brakenhale* 1285 Pat, (*de*) *Vetere Brackenale* 1463 Gor (p), *New Brecknoll, Old Brecknoll* 1607 *Norden, Bracknall, Old Bracknall* 1790 Pride, *Bracknell, Old Bracknell* 1800 Eden. Apparently 'Bracca's nook', *v.* healh. The possibility of there being such a pers.n. in OE is discussed Bk 83, Nth 49.

Bracknell is situated in the south-west angle of Warfield, and may be one of a group of names in which healh refers to land in a projecting corner of a parish. This sense is well evidenced near the Berkshire-Surrey border. Broom Hall (Sr 154) is in a narrow, projecting corner of Windlesham with Bagshot, Portnall (Sr 122–3) is in the southern projection of Egham, and Michen Hall (Sr 198) occupies a projecting corner of Godalming. Bracknell is recorded in 942, which might be thought early for this meaning of healh, but another possible instance in a name recorded in the 10th cent. is Lopshill (W 401), which occupies the southern projection of the parish of Damerham, which is also a projection of W into Ha.

It would be difficult to explain Bracknell as a topographical name, as it is not in a valley, but occupies a spur of land.

BRACKNELL AND BULLBROOK STREET-NAMES

ALBERT RD.	BINFIELD RD.	CHURCH RD.	HIGH ST.	HONEYMOON
RD.	LONDON RD.	NEW RD.	ROCHDALE RD.	SEARLE ST.	STANLEY RD.
STATION RD.	STONEY RD.	WOKINGHAM RD.

BROCK HILL, 1790 Pride, *La Brokhull* 1321 Cl. Probably 'brook hill', *v.* brōc, hyll; the site overlooks the junction of three streams.

GARSON'S LANE (*Garsons* 1841 *TA*), cf. *La Garston'* 1241 *Ass* (p), *La Garstone* 1261 Ipm (p), *La Garston* 1300 *ib* (p), in this part of the county, and Walter *atte Garston* 1344 *LHRS*, whose fellow-witness is William *atte Nuptown* (*infra*). The surname derives from the place-name gærs-tūn, of which there is an example in the adjacent parish of Bray 51.

NUPTOWN, *Nupton Greene* 1607 *Norden, Upton Green* 1761 Rocque, 1822 OS, *Nupp Town* 1790 Pride; William *atte Nuptown* witnessed a deed of 1344 (*LHRS*), and he may be identical with William *de Optoune*, who appears 1327 *SR*. 'Higher farm', *v.* atten, upp(e), tūn.

QUELM LANE, *Quelmys* 1462 *ECR*, *Quelmys*, *Quelmes* 1538 *Windsor*, QUELMES 1607 *Norden*, *Quelms* 1841 *TA*. O.S. maps show two streams rising in the vicinity. The name is probably the pl. of an OE cw(i)elm 'well, spring', discussed in Löfvenberg 160.

WANE BRIDGE is probably *Wambridge* 1841 *TA*. The bridge is on the stream which flows through the parishes of Binfield and Waltham St Lawrence to join the Loddon south of Twyford. There was a *Wom Bridge* lower down it, for which v. 115, and a less-well-recorded *Westwanbrigg* 75. Land near this stream is referred to as *wassan hamme* in the bounds of BCS 762, KCD 1303 (discussed in Pt 3). It is possible that this OE name, which means 'meadow of the marsh' (*v.* wæsse, hamm), was transferred from a tract of meadow to the stream, and lies behind the 19th-century forms *Wam* and *Wom*. Later names for this stream are discussed 128.

WICK HILL, 1790 Pride; cf. *Wyke* 1330 Cl (p), 1341 NonInq (p), *v.* wīc.

BAY RD.   BERRY LANE, *Berry Croft* 1841 *TA*.   BIG WD. BISHOP'S LANE.   BOOT P.H.   BOTT BRIDGE, *Bat Bridge* 1790 Pride, *Bot Bridge* 1800 Eden.   BOTTLE LANE.   BROCKHILL FM, BRIDGE AND COTTAGE (*v.* 116).   BUCKLE LANE, BUCKLELANE FM, *Bookehill* 1606 *LRMB*, *Buckle* 1837 *TA* (Binfield), *Buckle Pightle* 1841 *TA*; *v.* bōc¹, hyll.   BULL BROOK, BULLBROOK, BULLBROOK FM AND BRIDGE, *Bull Brook* 1790 Pride, 1816 OS.   BULL LANE, *Bull Meadow* 1841 *TA*.   THE CEDARS.   CHURCH FM.   CLINTON'S HILL.   COCK'S LANE.   COPPED HALL, *v.* coppede. CRICKETERS P.H.   DROWN BOY POND, *Drown Boy Ground* 1841 *TA*.   FAIRCLOTHES FM.   FOLDER'S LANE.   FOREST LODGE. FOUR HORSESHOES P.H.   GILNOCHIE.   GOUGH'S LANE.   HALEY GREEN FM, *Haly Green* 1761 Rocque, *Haley Green* 1790 Pride; it is stated in *LHRS* that the house was known as *Heathley Hall* in the 17th cent., *v.* also VCH III, 185.   HAWTHORNDALE, HAWTHORNDALE FM.   HAWTHORN LODGE.   HIGH ELMS.   HILL COPSE. HOGOAK LANE, *Hog Oak* occurs 1729 *LHRS* in some bounds of Winkfield.   HOLLY SPRING.   HOME FM, *Home Close, Croft and Meadow* 1841 *TA*.   HONEYWOOD FM.   JEALOTT'S HILL, *Jealous-Hill* 1711 Hearne, 1790 Pride, 1800 Eden, 1841 *TA*, *Jealots Hill* 1846 Snare.   JEALOTTSHILL FM.   JIG'S LANE.   KINGSCROFT LANE,

King's Croft 1841 *TA*.   LACKMAN'S HILL.   LAUREL COTTAGE.
LILYHILL.   MALTHILL FM.   MOSS END, 1790 Pride.   MOSS-
END FM.   NEWELL GREEN, 1800 Eden, *Newwell Green* 1761
Rocque.   NEWELL HALL.   NEW INN.   NEW LEATHERN BOTTLE
P.H.   NUPTOWN FM (*v.* 116).   NUTCROFT VILLA, *Nut Croft*
1841 *TA*.   OSBORNE LANE, *Osborns Lane Pightle* 1841 *ib*.   OSBORNE-
LANE FM AND BRIDGE.   PARK FM AND RD, *The Park, The Little
Park, Park Mead* 1740 *Bodl*.   PENDRY'S LANE.   PENFURZEN
LANE AND COVERT, *Pen Furz* 1790 Pride, *Penfurzen Green* 1800 Eden.
PIDWELL COPSE.   PRIESTWOOD FM, *Prestwood Meadows* 1841 *TA*,
from Priestwood in Easthampstead 25.   THE PRIORY.   RECTORY
HO.   SHEPHERD'S HO P.H.   SHEPHERD'S LANE, 1800 Eden.
STROUD'S COPSE, *Strouds Ground and Pightle* 1841 *TA*.   TICKLE-
BACK ROW.   WARFIELD COTTAGE, DALE, HALL, GROVE (1822 OS),
PARK AND STREET.   WELLER'S COVERT.   WELLER'S LANE, *Wel-
liers Lane* 1800 Eden.   WEST'S COPSE.   WEST END, 1790 Pride.
WESTEND FM.   WESTHATCH CORNER, *v.* hæc(c).   WHITEGROVE
COPSE.   WHITELOCK'S FM.   WICKHILL FM AND HO (*v.* 117).
WINDMILL HILL, 1841 *TA*.

FIELD-NAMES

The principal forms in (*a*) are 1841 *TA* except where otherwise stated.

(*a*) Angers; Aylands; Barn Close; Barnetts; Beards Green 1800 Eden;
Beeches, Little; Bell Mdw; Black Lands and Croft; Blackwells; Bloodlakes;
Bottom Green 1800 Eden; Brants Mdw; Bread Croft (*v.* brǣdu); Brickers
Fd; Broad Oaks; Brook Mdw (*Brookmead* 1740 *Bodl*); The Brooks; Brush
Close; Burgess Land; Busthill; Butter Croft (*v.* butere); Cabbage Lane 1800
Eden; Carters Mdw; Cart House Pasture and Pightle; Cherry Mead; Clover
Ground and Mdw; Coopers Cross and Hill; Coppice Ground; Cottage
Ground; Cotton Green 1846 Snare (also 1790 Pride); Covers Pightle; Down
Croft; Dunse Lane 1800 Eden; Edmunds Green Close (*Edmond Green* 1761
Rocque, *Edmunds Green* 1790 Pride); Fell Grove (*Fellgrove* 1740 *Bodl*);
Foldens Mdw; Fry Lane 1800 Eden; Gentles Mdw; Golds Mdw; Gores;
Green Lane 1800 Eden; Gylley or Gilley Lands; Hatch Close (*v.* hæc(c));
Hawkins Fd; Hay Oak Fd; Hill Close, Ground and Mdw; Holdshotts;
Holly Green 1800 Eden; Homestead Pightle; Inward Fd; Kiln Plat;
Kitchen Close (*v.* cycene); Lags (*v.* lagge); Leech Fd; Little Johns Grove
1846 Snare; Mallbridge; May Fd; Mays Pightle; The Moor; Nash Croft
(*v.* ætten, æsc); Old Lands; Ox Lays; Pasture Ground; Pear Tree Mdw;
Perry Fd; Picked Ground, Picketts (*Pick-croft alias Picketts* 1740 *Bodl, v.*
pīced); The Pightle (common in f.ns. in this parish, *v.* pightel); Pile Well;
Pit Fd; Pond Close; Potatoe Ground; Rose, Roses Ground; Rough Pasture;

Round Close; Rubbetts, Rubbletts; Ryeland Lane 1800 Eden; Sawpit Mdw; Scotchleek; Scotland(s) (*v.* scot); Slaughters Lane 1800 Eden; The Slip, The Slipe (*v.* slipe); Stiffs Mdw; Stony Cross Mdw; Thistly Ground; Thornhills; Trindles Ground; Turfhouse Close; Wases; Well Fd and Mead; Whites Lane; Wicketts, Little; Woodcocks Pightle; Woodhill; Woodwicks Ground (*Woodwicks alias Woodway* 1740 *Bodl*); Yew Tree Close; Younger Pightle.

(*b*) *Brembeltheye* n.d. AD (possibly identical with Brambletye Sx 328 'bramble enclosure', *v.* brēmel, tēag); *Bromhullesdene, Litelbromhulle* (*v.* brōm, hyll, denu); *Cattheslonde* n.d. AD (*v.* cat(t), land); *Church Field* 1790 Pride; *Colessunes Land* n.d. AD (first el. the surname *Coleson*); *Ferris Hill* 1510 Ashmole; *Five Ponds* 1790 Pride; *Ffrythe* 1420 *PubLibDoc* (p) (*v.* fyrhð); *Gatewicks* 1740 *Bodl*; *Gotelade* n.d. AD (*v.* gāt, (ge)lād); *Pechestrete* n.d. ib (*v.* strǣt); *Sandstrete* n.d. ib (*v.* sand, strǣt); *Siggeslond* n.d. ib (first el. a surname, *v.* Reaney s.n. *Siggs*); *Sloeland* 1608 Moulton; *Smithevelde* n.d. AD (possibly 'smooth field', *v.* smēðe[1]); *Stanrugg'* 1239, 1240 Cl, *Stanrig'* 1243 ib, *Stererugge, Sterhugg'* 1275–6 RH, *Stanrygg'* 1453 *PubLib(Bray)* ('stone ridge', *v.* stān, hrycg, in the last reference it is said to be a tithing in Warfield); *The Warren* 1790 Pride; *Wheat Close* 1740 *Bodl*.

Wargrave

WARGRAVE

Weregrauæ '1061–5' AS Charters, *Weregrave* 1086 DB, *Weregraua* 1154 BMFacs *et passim* with variant spelling *Weregrave* to 1316 FA, *Werregraua* 1162, 1163, 1191, 1194 P, 1241 *Ass, Weregraua Regis* 1167 P

Weresgrave 1137, 1190 (14th) Winchester, 1202 Cur

Wergraua 1157, 1158 P, *Wergrave* 1243 Cl *et freq* to 1401–2 FA, *Wergreve* 1280 Abbr

Warag' 1165 P, *Waregraua* l.12th *ReadingC*

Wellegraua l.12th *ReadingC, Wallgrove* 17th *PubLib(Clayton)*

Wargraue 1517 D Inc

Probably 'grove by the weirs', *v.* wer, grāf(a). The single form with -*greve* suggests, however, that the second element might be grǣfe 'grove, thicket' or grǣf 'pit, trench'. These three elements are always difficult to distinguish between.

WARGRAVE STREET-NAMES

BRAYBROOKE RD.   CHURCH ST.   DARK LANE.   FERRY LANE.   HAMIL-
TON RD.   HIGH ST.   SCHOOL LANE.   SILVERDALE RD.   VICTORIA RD.

BEAR GROVE AND PLACE, BEAR ASH, BEAR HILL, *la Bere* 1318 Pat (p), 1341 Cl (p), *Bare Plase, Bare Innings* 1580 *RentSur, Bear Ash, Hill and Place* 1790 Pride, *Bear Grove and Innings* 1840 *TA*, *Bear Place* 1846 Snare. Probably bǣr² 'swine-pasture'. *Innings* is from inning 'piece of land taken in or enclosed'.

CULHAM COURT, UPPER, MIDDLE AND LOWER CULHAM FM

Culnham (freq), *Culnam* 1208 Winchester PR, *Culnham'* 1242 Cl
Culeham 1242 Cl, *Culham* 1242–3 Fees, 1401–2 FA, *Culham Court,
Upper and Lower Culham* 1761 Rocque, *Culham Court, Middle
and Upper Culham* 1790 Pride
Kilham, *Kilham'*, *Kilkham'* (p), *Kylk(h)am* 1284 *Ass*, *Kylham* 1286–7
FF, *Kilham* 1655 BM, *Kilham Court* 1670 *PubLib* (*Clayton*)
Kellham 1695 BM

The first el. is cyl(e)n 'kiln', and the second could be either hām or hamm.

THE HOLT (1607 *LHRS*, 1846 Snare) may be *Rocholt* 1275–6 RH, *La Rachoke* 1288–9 *RentSur*. 'Rook-wood', *v.* hrōc, holt.

WORLEY'S FM (*Worsley Fm* 1846 Snare); in 1286–7 *FF* there is mention of land in *Horleye* owned by Will. *le Hore de Kylham*. If *Horleye* be an early form for Worley's Fm (which is quite near Culham), the name would appear to be identical with Wharley BdHu 69, from horu 'dirt' and lē(a)h 'clearing'. The similarity of the surname is probably coincidental.

THE ARCHES.   BOTTOM BOLES WD, *Boles More* Eliz *RentSur*, *Bules* 1840 *TA*, possibly ball 'rounded hill', there are small, round hills in the area.   BOWSEY HILL, 1790 Pride.   BUCK ISLAND.   CAMPS PUDDLE.   CANHURST FM, *Canthurst Field and Lane* 1840 *TA*. CAPE FAREWELL, *v.* 284.   CASTLEMANS, 1846 Snare, CASTLEMAN'S FM.   CHILTERN TOWERS.   THE CROFT.   CRAZIES HILL, 1846 Snare, *Crazes Hill* 1822 OS.   THE CRAZIES.   DEANPIT FM, *Deane Pitt* 1787 *PubLib* Dean Pit, 1840 *TA*, cf. *The Dean* 1607 *LHRS Dean Grounds* 1840 *TA*. *v.* denu.   THE DRUID'S TEMPLE, *Druids Temple* 1790 Pride; this is a megalithic monument transported from Jersey in 1785 (VCH III, 192).   THE ELMS (2 examples).   ENDALL'S FM, *Endalls* 1846 Snare.   FACEBY LODGE.   FAIRMAN'S WD, LITTLE FAIRMAN'S WD, *Fairmans* 1840 *TA*.   GIBSTRUDE FM, *Gibstrood Gate* 1607 *LHRS*, *Gebstrode Fm* 1790 Pride, *Gibstrude* 1840 *TA*, *Gibstroud* 1846 Snare, *v.* strōd, first el. the surname *Gibb*.

THE GRANGE. HARE HATCH, 1607 *LHRS et freq v.* hæc(c). HATCHGATE FM, OLD HATCH GATE, *Hatchgate Field* 1840 *TA, v.* hæcc-geat; *Cockpole Hatch* 1607 *LHRS* probably refers to the same gate, for Cockpole *v.* 63. HENNERTON, 1846 Snare. HIGH-COCKETT, *High Cock Hutt, High Cock Hut Lane* 1816 *LHRS*, perhaps 'cocked hat' used as a descriptive field-name, cf. Cockedhat Copse O 320. HIGHFIELD FM, 1790 Pride, *Highfield* 1580 *RentSur.* HIGH KNOWL WD. THE HILL. HOLLY CROSS, 1846 Snare. HORNS INN. KENTON'S FM, *Kenson Fm* 1822 OS. KILN GREEN, 1816 *LHRS*. KING'S FM, *Lower, Upper and Middle Kings* 1840 *TA*. LINDEN HILL, 1846 Snare. LINDENHILL WD. THE LODGE. MAPLE CROFT, 1840 *TA*. NEW INN. PENNY'S LANE, *Penny's, Penny's Hill* 1840 *TA*. QUEEN ADELAIDE P.H. RATS' ISLAND. ROSE HILL WD, *v.* 63. ROSEWELL COTTAGES. SCARLETTS, SCARLETTS FM AND WD, *Skarlettes* 1620 *PubLib, Scarlets Farme* 17th *PubLib(Clayton), Scarletts* 1790 Pride. SHEEPLAND, *Sheeplands* 1607 *LHRS*, 1840 *TA*. TAG LANE. TEMPLE COMBE, *v.* Druid's Temple *supra.* THATCHED HOLM. WAKE-FIELD. WARGRAVE COURT, HILL (1790 Pride), LODGE (1846 Snare), MARSH (ib), UPPER WARGRAVE. THE WILLOWS. WOODCLYFFE. WOODSIDE, *Woodside Fm* 1846 Snare. YELDHALL MANOR, *Yeld-halles Gate* Eliz *RentSur*; 'guild-hall' does not seem altogether appropriate as the name of a manor-house, and the first el. may be h(i)elde 'slope', with loss of *h-* and development of *y-*. YORK FM.

FIELD-NAMES

The principal forms in (*a*) are 1840 *TA* except where otherwise stated; forms dated Eliz and 17th are *RentSur* and *PubLib(Clayton)* respectively; early forms for which no date or source is given are 1607 *LHRS*.

(*a*) Alders; Backridge; Backside Deans; Barn Fd; Bearfoot's; Best's Mdw; Bigtree (*Bigfrey Common* 1790 Pride); Bincot Fd; Binlands (*Bene Lands* Eliz, *Bean Lands, v.* bēan); Blakes Lane 1816 *LHRS* (*Blake's Lane*), Blake's Fm 1846 Snare, Blake's; Bovetown, Buffdown, Buffton Mdw (possibly 'above the hill', *v.* bufan, dūn); Breach Mdw (*Breaches* 17th, *v.* brēc); Broom Close; Bushy Lees; Bycrofts; Cannons; Chalk Hill; Chalk Pit Piece; Chalky Lane 1816 *LHRS*; Chamberlains (*Chamberlains Cottage* 1816 *LHRS, Chamberlain's Fm* 1822 OS); Chinese House 1846 Snare; Cooks Hill; Copse Pightle; Copyall Mdw; Cottage Garden Piece; Cowleys Mdw (*The Coules* Eliz, *Cow Lease Acre* 1607, 'cow pasture', *v.* cū, lǣs); Crouch End 1846 Snare (possibly crūc[3]); Cutts, Little (*v.* 281); Dairy Ground; Dedicatts; Down Fd (*Downfield*); The Down; Ducks Puddle (*v.* 26);

Eastlands (*East Lands*, *v.* land); Ford House 1822 OS (*Ford House*); Frizes; Gaunt House 1848 *PubLibDoc*; Gays (*Gayes Corner*); Gosbirds Mdw; Grass Piece; The Great Fd (*Great Field*); Grove Cott; Grubbs (*v.* 281); Hand Ground; Heath Fd (*Heath Field*); Hedgebirds; Henditches; Herberts Fd; Highleys Moors; High Piece; Hill Farm Lane 1816 *LHRS*, Hill Fm 1846 Snare, Hill Pieces; Hogstrough (*v.* 283); Home Mdw; Hop Garden (*The Hop Garden* 17th); Horsall Gate; Hundred Acres; Hyems Hill; Kind Fd (*South Kind Field*); Kirby Fd; Knapps Fd; Knives Mdw; Laggs (*Laggs* 17th, *v.* lagge); Lake Fd (*La Lake* 1208–9 WinchesterPR (p), *The Lacke Close*, *The Lake House* Eliz, *v.* lacu, but the name may contain ME *lake* 'pool'); Langham's (*Langham*); Lavender Fd and Hill; Lawrence Fd; The Lea; Ley Bottom and Cuts (cf. Cutts *supra*); Little Bell Lane 1816 *LHRS*; Lords Mdw (*Lord's Mead*); Milk Platt; Milley (also 1790 Pride, *Milly Field* 1761 Rocque); Mill Green (*Mill Field*); Moor Fd (*The Greate More* Eliz, *v.* mōr); Mount Pleasant (*v.* 283); Mumberry, Mumbery Pightle, Mumbry Hill (*Mumbery Field*, *Mumbury Barn*); Norcutts (cf. Cutts *supra*); Oxley's Mdw; Park Piece, The Park (*The Park*); Parsons Pightle; Peat Fd; Penville; Pigotts Fm 1822 OS (*Piggotts Way*); The Pightle (*v.* pightel); Pit Pightle; Plantation Piece; Platts (*v.* plat²); Pond Close (*Pondclose*, *Pontes Close* Eliz); Pond Piece; Porters Cross 1816 *LHRS* (*Porter's Cross*); Roper's Mdw; Royal Hill; Rushy Platt; The Sandhills 1816 *LHRS*; Saucers (*Saucers Lane* 1816 *LHRS*, cf. *Sauceresland* in Shinfield 108); Shaddles; Shepherd's Hill; Silvers Moor; Slaymakers; Sloping Piece; Spring Close and Mdw; Stable Fd (*Stable Field*); Stamfords Mdw (*Stanford's Meadow* 1816 *LHRS*); Stirt (*The Start*, *v.* steort); Stubbings Fd (*v.* stubbing); Sully of Sunning (*Suller Sunnings Pond* 1816 *LHRS*); Thicketts Mdw (*Est Thicketts* Eliz); Tickle's Pightle; Townsend Fd; Trendils Fd; Upcrofts (*Upcroft* Eliz *RentSur*, 1607 *LHRS*); Vicarage Close; Waggs Platt; Weedon Hill (*Weedon Hill*; it is unfortunate that no form earlier than 1607 has been found, as the name may be identical with Weedon Bk, Nth, for which *v.* wīg); Westcots; Will Fd; Woodlands; Wood Pightle; Worsleys Hill (*v.* Worley's Fm 120); Wyvils; Wywalds.

(b) *Astons Lane*; *Bear Cross*, *Bear Croft* (*v.* Bear Grove 119); *Black Innings* Eliz (*v.* inning); *Body Crofts* 17th; *Bysshopes More* Eliz; *Callons* (grove called) 1572 *SpecCom*; *Churche Grove* Eliz; *The Clay, Clay Corner*; *Clivers Hedge*; *Culver Field* (*v.* culfre); *Frida* 1208–9 WinchesterPR (p), *Frythe* 1341 NonInq (p) (*v.* fyrhð); *Green Inning* Eliz (*v.* inning); *Hatch Croft* (*v.* hæc(c)); *Hemp Garden* 17th; *Higgins Hole*; *Inyngs Grove* Eliz (*v.* inning); *The Lees* (*v.* lēah); *Lime Kiln Lane*; *London Highway*; *Long Neck* (probably from the shape); *Lott Mead* (*v.* hlot); *Lomewood* 1572 *SpecCom*; *New Cross*; *No Man's Green* (*v.* 284); *Northcroft Hatch Gate*; *Old Fd*; *Pinfield*; *Powers End Field*; *Puells Pytte* Eliz; *Purfield*; *The Raye* Eliz, *Ray Close* (probably identical with Ray in Maidenhead 55); *The Rudgeway* ('ridgeway'); *Scopier's Bank*; *Sheephouse Hill*; *Stanwell Hill*; *Strode* 1208–9 WinchesterPR (p) (*v.* strōd); *Suffolk More* Eliz; *Swan Wood*; *Vine's Coppice* 1607 *LHRS*, *Vines Place* 1790 Pride; *Wellhouse Orchard* 17th; *Whit Hill Wood*.

VII. SONNING HUNDRED

Suningis c. 1180 HMC Var Coll 1, *Suninges* 1224–5, 1261 *Ass*, *Sunninges* 1241 *ib*, *Sunynghes, Suni'gg', Sunin'ge, Suniges* 1275–6 RH, *Sunnynge* 1284 *Ass, Sonnynge* 1316 FA

v. Sonning 132–3.

Arborfield

ARBORFIELD

Edburgefeld c. 1190 (13th), 1220 (13th) RSO
Erburgefeld, Erbergefeld 1222 (13th) RSO, *Erburgefeld* 1224–5 *Ass*, *Erberghefeud'* 1241 *ib, Erburgefeld'* 1242–3 Fees, *Erberghefeld'* 1247–8 *Ass* (p), *Erberwefeld* 1284 *ib, Erburghefelde* 1316 FA, *Erborghefeld* 1327 *SR, Erburghfeld* 1345 Ipm, *Erboroghfeld* 1369 Cl (p), *Erburghfelde* 1390 ib
Hereburgfeld' 1230 P, *Hereburgefeld* 1254 Pat, *Hurberfeld'* 1284 *Ass* *Erburfeld'* 1284 *Ass, Erberfeld* 1380 Fine, *Erberfild, Herberfeld* 1535 VE
Arburfeld 1535 VE

v. feld 'open land'. For the first el. DEPN suggests *Hereburh*, fem. pers.n., or eorðburg 'earthwork'. Forms without *H*- are the more numerous and the earlier, and this may mean that eorðburg should be preferred. Dr O. von Feilitzen, who is of this opinion, suggests that the *Hereburg*- forms are due to association with herebeorg. On the other hand, other names containing eorðburg show some spellings with *Erd*-. Harborough Banks Wa 289 is *Erdbyr'* 1220, and Arbury Wa 79–80 has numerous forms in *Ord-, Erde-, Erth-*. Such spellings are not represented for the Berks name, unless the two *Edburgefeld* forms are considered to belong to this category. Also, the forms for Harbury Wa 170, which is *Hereburgebyrig* 1002 so must be derived from the fem. pers.n., include some which closely resemble those for Arborfield. No final choice is possible between eorðburg and the pers.n. No earthwork appears to be known in the vicinity.

ARBORFIELD BRIDGE, 1817 OS, *Arborfeild Bridge* 1641 *SP.* ARBOR-FIELD CT, GRANGE, FM AND HALL. BARTLETT'S FM, 1846 Snare. BOTTOM COPSE, 1846 ib. BOUND OAK. BRAMSHILL HUNT P.H. CHAMBERLAIN'S FM, *Chamberlins Hill and Pightle* 1841 *TA*.

CROSSLANES FM.   DUCKSNEST FM.   GREENSWARD LANE.   LONG
COPSE, *The Long Copse* 1846 Snare.   LONG POND, *Long Pond
Meadow* 1841 *TA*.   MAGGS GREEN, *Mag Green* 1841 *ib*, 1846
Snare.   MILKINGBARN LANE, cf. *Milking Fm* 1846 ib.   MOOR
COPSE, *Moor Coppice* 1846 ib.   NEW FM, 1846 ib.   POUND
COPSE.   PUDDING LANE, 1846 ib, *Pudding Lane Ground* 1841 *TA*
(probably referring to sticky soil, *v.* 284).   ROBINHOOD COPSE,
Robin Wood Ground 1841 *ib*, cf. Robinhood Lane in Winnersh 138,
and Little Johns Grove in Warfield 118.   ROUNDS COPSE, *Round
Coppice* 1846 Snare.   ROUNDS ISLANDS.   SPRING COPSE.   WEST-
LAND'S COPSE, *Westlands Field* 1841 *TA*, *West Land Copse* 1846 Snare.
WHITEHALL COPSE AND FM, 1846 ib, *Whitehall Fm* 1817 OS, *White
Hall Meadow and Pightle* 1841 *TA*.   According to VCH III, 201,
this property was known in the 16th as *Wyfolde* or *Whytehall*; the
first form suggests confusion with Wyvols Ct in Swallowfield (109).
WHITE'S FM.   WOKINGHAM LANE.

FIELD-NAMES

The principal forms in (*a*) are 1841 *TA*; all early forms are ArchJ 46.

(*a*) Back Fd; Barn Close and Fd; Bean Fd; Blackwell; The Bottoms (*v.*
botm); Brants Orchard; Brewhouse Close; Bridge Fd; Broom Close (*v.*
brōm); The Bull Ground; Bunces Hill; Burnt Platt (*v.* plat²); Carrot Close;
Causeway Pightle; Church Close; Coldrums; Common Mead; Coppice Close
and Pightle (*v.* pightel, as elsewhere in this parish); Corner Pightle; Cow-
pasture; Dicks Croft; Double Five; Double Vere Ground; Droveway (*v.*
drāf); Elisha Mead; Eyot Mdw (*v.* ēgeð); Finches Platt (*v.* plat²); Footpath
Fd; Fore Fd (*v.* fore); Four Hurdle Hill; Free Ground; Front Pasture;
Green Close; Greenaways Fd; Greenfields; Handkerchief Ground (*v.* 284);
The Harborfield; Haylands; Home Close and Pasture; The Hop Garden
(*v.* hoppe); Hurdle Pightles; Lice Lands Pightle; Little Cool Oak Pightle;
Little Lock Mead; Little Mead and Pasture; Lodge Fd; Long Coppice Hill;
Long Furze; Long Hill; Long Pightle; Lords Mdw; Middle Hill; Mill
Close and Mdw; New Mead; Nineaways Orchard; Nortons Pightle; Olivers
Pightle; The Orchard; Ox Fd; The Paddock; Parish Furze Ground; Park
Ground and Fd; Parsonage Pightle; Peacocks Pasture; Picked Close (*v.*
pīced); Pipers Platt (*v.* plat²); Plannus Pightle; The Rances; Roundabout
(*v.* 281); Roundabout Furze; Rushy Mead; Short Hill; Short Lands (*v.*
land); Sloe Fd; Sparrow Close; Square Close; Stable Ground; Thackhams
Hill; Thorns Close; Titchings; White Well Hill Fd, White Well Pightle (cf.
Blackwell *supra* and *Goldenwell infra*); Winding Ground; Workhouse Pightle.

(*b*) *Le Birchet* 1420, *Byrchett* 1508 (*v.* bircet(t), and cf. Burchetts Green in
Hurley 62); *Bourdlond* 1508, *Boorde Landes* 1606–7 (cf. the same name in

Appleford, Pt 2); *Goldenwell Lane* 1518; *Heimeda* c. 1200 (*v.* hēg, mǣd); *Henmede* 1518; *The Hilles Cotte* 1606–7 (*v.* cot); *Hinutherudinge* c. 1250 (*v.* ryding); *Le Nethere Leyghton* 1350 (*v.* lēactūn); *Lokyngecrofte* 1482, *Lokyncroft* 1518 (perhaps an enclosure which could be locked, *v.* croft and cf. Locko Db 606, the first el. might be the past participle *locen* 'closed' suggested in DEPN for Lockton YN); *Moremede* 1518 (*v.* mōr, mǣd); *Pila* c. 1200, *Le Pylryche* 1347, *Pylryth Grene* 1518 (*v.* pyll, rīð); *Poureslond* 1420 (possibly land used for charity, *v.* 285); *Sotford Brydge* 1508; *Terrestrete* 1356 (*v.* strǣt); *Walis Oke* 1454; *La Wierdhoc* c. 1250 (p), *Werdek* c. 1300 (p); *Whetlond, Whetlondlane* 1407 (*v.* hwǣte, land).

Crowthorne

CROWTHORNE

Crowthorne 1607 *Norden, Crow Thorn* 1761 Rocque, 1790 Pride

The name is applied on Norden's map to a solitary tree at the junction of the Bracknell and Wokingham roads. An account of the growth of the hamlet after the arrival of Wellington College and Broadmoor Asylum is given in ArchJ 22 (85). Formerly in Sandhurst, the place was constituted a separate ecclesiastical parish in 1874, and a civil parish in 1894 (Kelly 71).

CROWTHORNE AND OWLSMOOR STREET-NAMES

ADDISCOMBE RD.   THE AVENUE.   CAMBRIDGE RD.   CHURCH RD.   CHURCH ST.   CIRCLE HILL RD.   DUKE'S RIDE.   ELLIS RD.   FOREST RD.   GRANT RD.   HEATH HILL RD.   HIGH ST.   KING'S RD.   NAPIER RD.   OWLSMOOR RD.   PINEHILL RD.   PINE WOOD AVE.   RAVENSWOOD AVE.   STATION RD.   VICTORIA RD.   WATERLOO RD.   WELLINGTON RD.   WILTSHIRE AVE.   WOKINGHAM RD.   WOKINGHAM NEW RD.   YEOVIL RD.

BROADMOOR ASYLUM, BOTTOM AND FM, *Broad Moor, Broad Moor Bottom* 1761 Rocque, 1790 Pride.   CIRCLE HILL.   LODGE HILL, 1761 Rocque, 1790 Pride.   MIRK BOTTOM, cf. *Mirk Field* 1842 *TA* (Sandhurst).   OWLSMOOR, 1842 *ib* (Sandhurst). PINE HILL.   POPPY HILLS.   WELLINGTON COLLEGE.   WERG HILL, *v.* wīðig.   WHORTLEBERRY HILL.   WISHMOOR BOTTOM (on the county boundary, *v.* Sr 155).

The following house-names are shown on the 6″ maps in Crowthorne: BARRACANS, BROUGHAM HO, CROWTHORNE TOWERS, THE FIRS, HEATHCOTE, HEATHERLY, HEATHERSIDE, HILLSIDE, OAKLANDS, ST ENEDOC, UNDERWOOD, WHITE CAIRN.

Newland

NEWLAND

La Newelond 13th *AddCh 38650* (p), *Newelong* 1284 *Ass, Nywelonde*
1294 *SR* (p)
Newland 1755 *PubLib*

'New land', *v.* DEPN for other examples. In this instance, as in
Gl (Gl **3**, 236), the name refers to land cleared for cultivation in a
medieval forest. The liberty of Newland was included in Bishop's
Bear Wood (*infra*), which was a chase of the Bishops of Salisbury
(VCH III, 250).

ARBORFIELD CROSS, *Alpheldecrouch* 1347 ArchJ 46, *Awfeildcross* 1607
Norden, Aufeild Crosse 1607 *RentSur, Awfieldcross* 1670 *PubLib,
Arborfield Cross* 1790 Pride. The second el. is **crouche** 'cross',
replaced by *cross*. The first el. might be a fem. pers.n., possibly
Ælfhild, but there has been confusion with the element **feld**, and later
with the name of the nearby village of Arborfield.

BEAR WD, *Bissopesbir'* 1256 Cl, *Le Busschopesber, Le Bishopesber* 1300
ib, *Le Bisshopesbere* 1331 ib, *La Bere* 1445 ArchJ 46, *Berewood, Bere
Wood, The Bearewood* 1572 SpecCom, *Berewood* e.17th *Survey,
Beare Wood* 1607 *Norden, Bishops Beare Wood Walke* m.17th *ForProc,
Bare Wood Common* 1761 Rocque, *Bear Wood Park* 1846 Snare.
v. **biscop, bǣr²**. This was a chase of the Bishops of Salisbury,
appurtenant to their manor of Sonning (VCH III, 253). The second el.
which means 'swine pasture', may have been applied to the wood
before it was made into a chase.

BARRETT'S LANE, *Barretts Piddle* 1841 *TA*.   BEAR LANE, 1841 *ib*.
BEARWOOD LAKE (*v. supra*).   BETTY GROVE, 1841 *TA, Berry Groue*
1607 *Norden*.   CARTER'S HILL, *Carters Hyll'* ?Eliz *RentSur*.
CARTERSHILL FM.   COLE LANE, *Collane Ground and Meadow* 1841
TA.   THE COOMBES, COOMBES LANE.   ELLIS'S HILL.   THE
GORSE.   GRAVELPIT HILL, LAND AND WOOD, *Gravel Pit Hill and
Field* 1841 *TA*.   THE GROVE.   HAZELTONS COPSE, *Haseldon
Copse* 1607 *Norden, Hazelton Coppice* 1733 *PubLibDoc*.   HOLLO-
WAY'S LANE, *Holloways Slipe and Pightle* 1843 EnclA *v.* **slipe, pightel**,
first el. probably a surname.   THE HOLT, *Holt Common* 1841 *TA*.
HUGHES GREEN, *Hew Greene* 1607 *Norden*.   JUKES LANE.

LANGLEY LANE, *Langley Meadow* 1841 *TA*. THE LARCHES. LOADER'S COPSE AND LANE, *Loader's Farm* 1755 *PubLib*. MOLE P.H., *The Mole* 1846 Snare. NEWLAND FM, 1755 *PubLib*. NEWLANDS, 1846 Snare. PARKCORNER LANE. STAG ISLAND. TARGETS FM. TEMPLE ISLAND. UPPER ISLAND. WOOD LANE.

FIELD-NAMES

The principal forms in (*a*) are *LHRS*.

(*a*) Bear Lane Mdw (cf. Bear Lane *supra*); Church Gate Paddock; Great Newland; Home Ground; Long Mdw; Planner's Mole Mdw (cf. Mole P.H. *supra*).

(*b*) *Barelands Cops* 1607 *Norden* (first el. possibly bǣr², *v*, Bear Wood 126); *Busley Heath* 1607 *ib*; *Gates and Crips Copses* 1607 *ib*; *Langenhurst* 1373, 1399 ArchJ 46 (*v*. lang, hyrst); *Waremundespudel* (*pudel* called) 1373 ArchJ 46 (*v*. pightel, first el. probably the ME surname *Waremund* from OE *Wǣrmund*, cf. John *Waremund* 1275 RH in Berks, quoted Reaney 343 s.n. *Warman*).

Ruscombe

RUSCOMBE

Rothescamp 1091, 1220 (both 13th) RSO, *Rotescamp* 1167 P, 1220 (13th) RSO, *Rothescampe* 1223 (13th) ib, *Rotescomb* 1226 (13th) ib *Roscamp* 1241 *Ass* (p), *Roscompe* Ed I Hurley (p), 1327 *SR*, *Ruscompe* 1284 *Ass*, *Roscombe* 1316 FA, *Roscomp* 1368 Pat, *Ruscombe* 1535 VE, 1601 Moulton *Rushcombe* 1596 Ashmole

'Rōt's enclosed land'. A pers.n. *Rōt*(*a*), from OE *rōt*, 'cheerful', has been generally accepted as the first el. of a number of p.ns. including Rooting PN K 395 and Rottingdean Sx 311, *v*. DEPN *s.n.* Rutland. The el. camp, which 'fell into disuse generally at an early period' (Elements **1**, 79), occurs also in f.ns. in Earley (94) and Hurley (64), both in the east of the county; *v*. Introd.

NORTHBURY FM and SOUTHBURY FM, *Ruscombe Southbury prebenda, Ruscombe Northbury prebenda* 1535 VE, *Northbury, Southbury Fm* 1846 Snare. The estate was apparently divided into two halves, known as 'north manor' and 'south manor', *v*. burh.

BOTANY BAY COPSE, *Botney Bay* 1840 *TA*, this is on the parish boundary, *v*. 284. CASTLE END FM, *Castle End Fm and Green*

1846 Snare.   EAST LANE.   GARTHING LANE, GARTHINGLANE
BRIDGE.   GIRDER BRIDGE, 1822 OS.   THE GORSE.   MIDDLE
COPSE.   THE RHODODENDRONS.   RUSCOMBE LAKE, 1822 OS,
this is now the name of a low, marshy tract, and in VCH III, 203, it is
considered to refer to an actual lake which has disappeared. It is,
however, possible (as suggested in Crawford 130) that Lake is from
OE lacu, and that the name referred originally to the stream here, cf.
Shurlock Row 113. The VCH article gives the modern name of this
stream as River Broadwater (cf. Broadwater and Broadwater Lane in
St Nicholas Hurst). A possible earlier name is discussed 117.
RUSCOMBE TURN (this is the junction of the Twyford and Ruscombe
roads).   STANLAKE PARK, 1846 Snare, *Stanlake* 1761 Rocque,
Stanlake Down 1840 *TA*; this may also contain lacu, with reference to
the stream discussed *supra*.   WINDSOR AIT, *v.* ēgeð.   WING-
WOOD COPSE.

FIELD-NAMES

The principal forms in (*a*) are 1840 *TA*.

(*a*) Balls Piddle or Orchard (Piddle, which occurs several times in this
parish, is a variant of pightel); Barn Close; Beefapple; Bow Cross; Church
Close and Land; Common Garden; Coppice Pightle (*v.* pightel); Cutlass;
Entrance Piddle; Foot Path Ground; Furze Common; Fuscott; Glade;
Gravel Pit Fd; Ground Mdw; Grove Plat (*v.* plat²); Hatches Ground;
Hawkets; Heath Close; Horse Pit Fd; House Plat; Lake Fd (*v.* Ruscombe
Lake *supra*); Lay Ground (*v.* lǣge); Manney Croft; Mans Acre; Morter Yard;
Mowing Mdw; Pear Tree Close; Picket Down (*v.* pīced); Pond Close; Poors
Garden (*v.* 285); Queens Mdw; Ruscombe Green and Lane; Rye Close;
Shoulder of Mutton Fd (*v.* 283); Sparrow Hawks (*Sparhawkes* 1575 *PubLib*);
Spoil Bank; Spring Plat (*v.* plat²); Summer Croft; Summer House Ground;
Tithe Barn; Trusham, Trusham Piddle; Waistcoat, Waistcoat Piddle (*v.* 283);
Whites Garden; Wilkinson; Wingroves; Withey Plat (*v.* wīðig, plat²).

(*b*) *The Eight* 1596 Ashmole (*v.* ēgeð); *West Croft and West Hall* 1607
LHRS.

Sandhurst

SANDHURST

San(d)herst 1175 P, *Sandh'st* 1185 RR (p) *et passim* with variant
spellings *Sandhurst, Sandherst*

'Sandy hill', *v.* hyrst; the settlement is on a low promontory
overlooking the Blackwater River. The same name occurs in Gl and K.

SANDHURST STREET-NAMES

ALBION RD. BRANKSOME HILL RD. THE BROADWAY. COLLEGE RD. GREEN LANE. LONGDOWN RD. NEW RD. PARK RD. RICHMOND RD. THIBET RD.

BLACKWATER BRIDGE (1575 Finchampstead, on county boundary) is on the site of (*on*) *brydanford* 973–4 (c. 1150) BCS 1307, *Brodesford'* 1270 Turner,† *Bredeford* 1300 Cl, *Brydeford* 1327 Pat, *Broad Ford* 1641 *SP*. The bridge is called *Blackwater or Brodforde Bridge* 1607 *Norden*. *Brydanford* could consist of ford added to the gen. of a river-name. A formally satisfactory source would be an OE *brȳde* 'gushing or surging stream, welling spring' postulated in Löfvenberg 26–7. This may be the first el. of several names in Gl, *v*. Gl **3** xi, **4** 107. If the el. be a stream-name, the reference can hardly be to the Blackwater, which in this stretch of its course was known as *duddan broc* (*v*. 7–8); but it could be to the stream in Wishmoor Bottom, which forms the boundary between Berks and Sr and which joins the Blackwater at this point.

CRISSELS STAR, HIGH CRISSELS, *Cristeshull'* 1241 *Ass* (p), 1348–9 *FF* (p), *Cristeshulle*, *Cristhulle* 1327–8 *SR* (p), *Crishillys* 1517 D Inc, *Cresselles Mede* 1533 Finchampstead, *Moor called Cryselles* 1553 ib, *Cresshulles Meade* 1572 ib, *Creswell's Meade* 1602 ib, *High and Low Crishill* 1842 *TA*. The surname appears later as *Creshull* 1533, *Crysell* 1553 Finchampstead. As the earliest forms are from a family-name, it is not certain that the hill called 'Christ's hill' was in Sandhurst. The p.n. does not appear to be on record elsewhere, however, so it is on the whole probable that the family took its surname from a p.n. here. There may have been a crucifix from which the hill was named, cf. Cressage Sa, 'Christ's oak', and *v*. cristel-mæl, mæl[1].

AMBARROW, AMBARROW HILL AND FM, *Amboro Hill* 1607 *Norden*, *Ambro Hill* 1739 ArchJ 24, *Amburrow Hill* 1761 Rocque, 1816 OS, *Ambarrow Fm* 1796 ArchJ 24. ANTRUM FM, earlier *Rackstraw's Fm*, *v*. ArchJ 22, p. 122. BEECH HILL, *Beche Hill*, 1549 *LRMB*. BREACH COPSE AND FM, *Le Breche* 1549 ib, *Breach Farm* 1796 ArchJ 24, *Breach Field, Moor and Pond, Upper Breach* 1842 *TA*, *v*. brēc. CAVES FM, Henry *Cave* was the tenant in 1809 (ArchJ 22, p. 122).

† This form is identified Sr 118 with Broadford in Chobham, but it seems more likely to belong here.

CHURCH FM.   COALPIT COPSE, *Coal Pit Close* 1842 *TA*. †   COCK-A-DOBBY, a fir plantation on a hill-top.   COLLEGE FM, *College Horse Pasture* 1842 *TA*.   THE DEVIL'S POUND, this type of name sometimes refers to a prehistoric enclosure, but nothing is marked here on O.S. maps.   EDGBARROW, EDGBARROW COTTAGE, LODGE AND HILL, EDGBARROWHILL STAR, *Edgeboro Hill* 1607 *Norden*, *Edgeburrow Hill* 1761 Rocque.   FORT NARRIEN.   GROVES FM, 1796 ArchJ 24, from a family surnamed *atte Grove* who lived in Sandhurst in the 13th cent. (ArchJ 22, 116).   HARRYSMOOR COPSE, *Harremore, Harrys More* 1549 *LRMB, Harries Moor Mead* 1739 ArchJ 24, *Harry Moor* 1842 *TA*, *v*. mōre, first el. the surname *Harry*.   THE HARTS LEAP.   HURTS HILL.   LONG DOWN, 1761 Rocque, *Longdowne* 1607 *Norden v*. dūn.   OAK GROVE.   PERRY'S BRIDGE, *Pyryclose, Le Piremore* 1549 *LRMB, Perry Moare Cops* 1607 *Norden*, *Perry Meadow* 1842 *TA*, *v*. pyrige 'pear-tree'; Joh. *atte Pirye* 1327–8 *SR* may have derived his surname from the same tree.   ROSE AND CROWN P.H.   SANDHURST FM AND LODGE.   LITTLE SANDHURST.   SNAPRAILS, SNAPRAILS FM, *Shape Rayles* 1613 ArchJ 22, *v*. 281.   WATTS FM.   WELLINGTON ARMS P.H.   WHITE SWAN P.H.   WILDMOOR BOTTOM.   WINDSOR RIDE LODGE (on a road through the Forest called Windsor Ride, *v*. 34).   WOODMAN'S LODGE.

The following house-names are shown on the 6″ maps in Sandhurst. BROADWAY HO. EAGLE HO. FOREST END. GOTHIC COTTAGE. RIVERMEAD. RYEFIELD. ST HELENS. SUNNY REST. UPLANDS. THE WARREN.

FIELD-NAMES

The principal forms in (*a*) are 1842 *TA*, except where otherwise stated; early forms dated 1272–1307, 1739 are ArchJ 24, 1498 Chertsey, Eliz *RentSur*, and those for which no date or source is given 1549 *LRMB*.

(*a*) Alexander's Fd (*Alysaunders*); Apple Croud (*Aple Close*); Aps Platt (*v*. plat[2]); Arbarana 1817 ArchJ 22; Ash Crate (*Asshe Crofte*); Barn Close (*Le Barne Close*); Bean Croft; Berrys Mdw; Black Croft (*Blacke Crofte*); Brickfield; Bridge Mdw; Broom Fd (*v*. brōm); Bucketts; Buckhurst (*Bukehurst* 1498, *Bukhurst* 1510–11 ArchJ 120, *Buckhurst* 1557 ib, *Buckhurst Mead* 1613 ArchJ 22, cf. the same name in Wokingham 143, both names may refer to the same wood); Butter Steep e.19th ArchJ 22 (the same name occurs in Winkfield 39); Calves Mdw (*Calves Leaze* 1613 ArchJ 22); Checker Mdw (*v*. cheker); Clay Fd; Collins Mead and Pightle (*Collins, Collyns Mede*); Common Allotment; Coxeys (*Cokkys, Cokkisplace* 1498, first el. the surname *Cock*); Crouts (*Crouts, Crutts*, probably from croft, *v*. Sr 357); Dawney

† Probably a pit for charcoal-burning.

Mdw (*Dorneymede*); Deep Mdw (*Depemede* 1549 *LRMB*, *Deep Mead* 1739, *v.* dēop, mǣd); Dipland Green (*Dipnell Green* 1817 ArchJ 23); East Mill Lane e. 19th ArchJ 23 (the mill is said to have been there in 1282); Ell Pightle; Engine Mdw; Footpath Fd; Fords Close (*Fordelondes* 1498, *Le Forde* 1549 *LRMB*, *Forde* Eliz, *v.* ford); Gills Mdw (cf. *Geal's Land* 1739); Grass Platt; Gravel Pit Fd; Greenlands e. 19th ArchJ 23 (*Grenelonde* 1498, *Le Grenelande*); Green Pightle; Grub Mdw (cf. *Grublyngs* 1613 ArchJ 22, perhaps a mistake for *Grubbyngs*, *v.* 281); Hall Grove e. 19th ArchJ 23 (*Le Hall Groue*, cf. *Will. atte Halle* 1327–8 *SR*); Halls Mdw; Hankum (*Hankhams* e. 19th ArchJ 23); Harbors Fd; Hawleys (*Hally*, *Le Hawley*); Heathy Close; Hiff Green 1817 ArchJ 23; Hill Moor (*Hillmore*); Home Close, Mead and Pightle (*Le Home Mede*, *Le Homefeld*, *Le Home Close*); Hone, Hone Hill and Pightle (*Le Honour* 1498, *Honeride* 1549 *LRMB*, *Hones Lane* e. 19th ArchJ 23, *v.* hān 'stone', *-ride* may be the word discussed 34, but cf. *Feld-Rede infra*); Honey Close (*v.* hunig); Horse Fd and Plat; Inhams (*v.* innām); Innords (possibly identical with *Inwood Mead* 1738 ArchJ 23); Kellers Hall; Kiln Ground; Lady Mead (*Ladymede*, *v.* hlǣfdige); Land Acres; Large Moor; Ley Mead (*v.* lēah, mǣd); Lime Mdw 1817 ArchJ 23; Long Vere 1817 ArchJ 23; Lurie Mdw 1817 ArchJ 23; Mill Mdw (*Le Myll Mede*); The Moors, Moor Mdw, Moor Lands (*Moreland* 1498, *The More* Eliz, *Moorland's Mead* 1739, *v.* mōr); Nip Lands (*Nepelonde* 1498, *v.* nēp); Nipple Green Pightle; Oaken Hole; Oatlands Close; Old Farm Mdw; Park Fd; Parsonage Fd and Pightle; Penny or Pinny Moor (perhaps a mistake for Perry Moor, *v.* Perry's Bridge 130); Perks; Plain (*v.* O 389); Pond Close (*Le Pondeclose*); Poors Mdw (*The Poor's Land* 1739); Post Fd and Mdw; Pot Piece; Pound Close and Pasture; Rack Close; Rainbow (*v.* 281); Rickyard Pightle and Platt; Rushy Moor; Scotland Common or Fd (*v.* scot); Small Brook (*Smallbrook Moore* 1607 *Norden*, *v.* smæl, brōc); Street End Pightle, Street Fd and Mdw (*Strete More*, *Stretemede* 1549 *LRMB*, *Strete More* Eliz, *Sandhurst Street* 1707 *PubLib*, *v.* strǣt, ende, pightel); Sues Pightle; Three Corner Pightle; Tumbling Bay Mdw; Valdery (*Feld Rede* 1549 *LRMB*, *Veldry Corner* e. 19th ArchJ 23, *v.* feld, rȳd, ryde); Walking Close; Ware Fd (*Were Mede v.* wer); Water Bars and Splash, Waterlands (*Le Waterlond* 1498, *The Waterland* 1549 *LRMB*, *Water Croft* Eliz); West Moor e. 19th ArchJ 23 (*Westmore Mede* 1549 *LRMB*, *West More* Eliz); White Hill e. 19th ArchJ 23 (*Whitynhulle* 1498); Whitings Mdw (*Whitings* 1739).

(b) *Absaundeslonde* 1498; *Adhams More* 1549 *LRMB*, *Addams More*, Eliz, c. 1605 *Survey*; *Ayllardes Piddel*, *Mede* and *Grene* Eliz (first el. probably a surname, *Piddel* may be the variant of pightel); *Brodemede*; *Bromhulle* 1327–8 *SR* (p) (*v.* brōm, hyll); *Le Butts* 1549 *LRMB*, *Butts* Eliz, 1613 ArchJ 22 (*v.* butte); *Le Byne Croft*; *Chapmannys Lond* 1498, *Chapmans More*, *Chapmans* (cf. Walt. *le Chapman* 1327–8 *SR*); *Chauldwell More* (*v.* c(e)ald, w(i)ella, mōr); *Churche Feld* 1549 *LRMB*, *The Churche Fyld* Eliz; *Clerkyslond* 1498; *The Comdellclose* 1549 *LRMB*, *Conydells*, *Conny Delles* Eliz, *Condy Dell* c. 1605 *Survey*; *Copes Groue*; *Frilonde* 1498; *Fysshcrofte* 1498; *Le Fryssen* (*v.* fyrsen); *Garston* 1272–1307, *Garsten Wood* Eliz (*v.* gærs-tūn); *Gosholde, Gosholde Groue*; *Gravell Close* 1613 ArchJ 22; *Le Hale* 1498 (*v.* h(e)alh); *Harecroft* (*v.* hara, croft); *Hethplot* 1272–1307 (*v.* hǣð, plot); *Hinctis Acre* 1498; *Hoggescroftes* 1498 (first el. probably a surname); *Hulle* 1327–8 *SR* (p), *Hullecroft* 1498, *Hullemede* 1425, 1442 VCH III (*v.* hyll, croft, mǣd), *Hullerslond* 1498 (held by Nich. *Huller*); *Le Lane Acre*; *The Litill House*; *Longcroft* 1498; *Long Grove* 1607 Norden; *Long Mead* 1613 ArchJ 22; *Longmore*; *The Lords More* Eliz; *Le Lotte Acre* (*v.* hlot); *Middilmore* 1498; *Morelane*; *Le Mylne Ponde*; *Mill grove* 1613 ArchJ 22; *Netherwell* 1498; *Northgrove* 1498; *Ouergrove* 1498; *Ouerhull, Le Ouerhillhouse*; *Perysnotherwelleghton* 1498 (*v.* lēactūn); *Pon Craft* Eliz (*v.* croft); *Redelak* 1498 (*v.* hrēod, lacu); *Risshparke, Risshgrove* 1498 (*v.* rysc); *Roundabout* 1787 ArchJ 23 (*v.* 281); *Spring Close* 1613 ArchJ 22; *Skeloslonde* 1498; *Stanrewemede, Stanry Lane* (*v.* stān, rǣw); *Stopeshulle, Stoppesaule* 1498, *Stipsells, Stipsallsmede* (Wm. *Stoppeshulle* 1498 probably took his name from the place, *v.* stoppa, hyll); *Sutheye* 1327 *SR* (p) (*v.* sūð, (i)eg); *Trupphallond* 1498; *Twycheners* 1498, *Tutchen House* 1606–7 AugOff, *Tutcham Bridge* 1641 *SP* (cf. Will. atte *Twychene* 1327–8 *SR*, Thomas *Twychene* 1498, *v.* 47); *Versye Hille* Eliz; *Wadelands*; *Whitmoare Woode* 1607 Norden, *Whitemore Copse* 1613 ArchJ 22 (*v.* hwīt, mōr); *Wildemede* (*v.* wilde, mǣd); *Woodley Corner* 1607 Norden; *Le Wooplote* 1498 (*v.* wōh, plot); *Wyde Mede* Eliz; *Wyfordeleighton* 1498 (*v.* lēactūn and cf. *Perysnotherwelleyton supra*, the first part of both names might be a surname or an earlier p.n.); *Wyndenersshe* 1498, *Wydnershe Feld, Wynershefeld* 1549 *LRMB*, *The Wyde Norst Fylde* Eliz (*v.* wid, ersc).

Sonning Town

SONNING

> *Soninges* 1086 DB, *Sunnings* 1146 (copy) Sar, *Sunningas* 1146 (15th) Holtzmann, *Sunninges* 1167 P *et passim* with variant spelling *Suninges*; *Sunningis* 1176 P (p), *Sunnigges* 1198 ib, *Suniges* 1185 RR (p)
>
> *Sunninches* c. 1180 (c. 1240) Abingdon
>
> *Sunning* c. 1200 (13th) RSO, *Suni'g, Sunni'g* 1275–6 RH, *Sonning, Sunninge* 1284 AnnMon, *Sonnynge* 1316 FA, *Sonnyg* 1327 *SR*, *Sunnyng* 1339 Pat

'Sunna's people', *v.* -ingas. The pers.n. is only recorded in p.ns. For a lost place called *Soninges* in K *v.* PN-ing 15. The Berks name occurs as that of a district in BCS 34, the earliest charter of the monastery at Chertsey Sr, which must have been drawn up before 675 (Sr xvi). This charter states that the land of the monastery extends 'usque ad terminum alterius prouinciae quae appellatur Sunninges'. The people called *Sunningas* have given name to Sonning and to Sunninghill (88), and it is possible that their 'province' included the whole of Berkshire east of Reading (v. Stenton, *Anglo-Saxon England* 298, and Introd.).

The earliest mention of the place is in a charter of 964 in Hickes Thesaurus (I, p. 140), one of the signatures to which runs *Osulf Sunnungnensis episcopus.*† 'Florence of Worcester' (I, p. 236, c. 1225) has a list of bishops headed *Nomina præsulum Sunnungnensis ecclesiæ*, and it is possible that this unusual form is derived from the charter in Hickes, which is a Worcester document. For the bishopric, v. Introd.

BOROUGH FM, BRIDGE, LAKE AND MARSH, *Burwey, Burwey Marsshe, Borewe Marshe* 1577 *SpecCom, Burway, Burway Marshe, Barway-feelde, Burrow Marshe* c. 1605 *RentSur, Burway, Burway Marshe* 1607 *ib, Burrow, Burrow Marsh* 1761 Rocque, 1790 Pride, *Borough Lake, Fm and Marsh* 1846 Snare. A much earlier form is found in RSO I 285–6, in the surname of two men mentioned in a list of tenants at Sonning dated 1220. The tenants are called *Rogerus Burgeia* and *Willelmus de Burgeia*. The name, a compound of burh and (ī)eg, is identical with that of Laleham Burway in Chertsey Sr (Sr 110), and probably with Burroway in Bampton (O 304), in spite of the suggested etymology 'way to or from a borough' given in O. All three places are beside the Thames and near an ancient settlement, and the meaning is probably 'island meadow belonging to the borough', rather than 'island with a prehistoric camp' as suggested in Sr. A fourth example is Burway near Ludlow Sa, which is *Burgeia* 1194 P.

BROADMOOR LANE, *Broadmere Lane* 1846 Snare. BUCK AIT, *v.* ēgeð. BULL HOTEL. CHARFIELD, CHARVIL LANE, *v.* 146–7. THE DELL. THE ELMS. GOGS, BIG AND LITTLE, *v.* gogge 'bog'. HALLSMEAD AIT. HOLME PARK, HOLME PARK FM, *The Home Parke* 1572, 1583 *SpecCom, Le Home Parke* 1575 *ib, Home Parke, The Holme Parke* 1585 *Dep*, 1617 *SpecCom, Home Parke* 1658 *ib, Holme Park, Holme Park Fm* 1846 Snare, probably 'home park', later associated with dialect *holme* 'river-meadow', because of its position by the Thames. THE LYNCH, cf. *eytes* (*v.* ēgeð) *called Linchedith* c. 1605 *RentSur, v.* hlinc, possibly referring to banks round the island. MANOR HO. PEARSON'S HALL. POUND LANE, 1846 Snare. RED HO. ST. PATRICK'S BRIDGE AND STREAM. SONNING BRIDGE, *The Great Bridge at Sonning, Sunning Bridge* 1658 *SpecCom*. SONNING GROVE AND HILL. SONNING

† The text in BCS 1134 reads *Osulf Sunningensis*.

LOCK, *Suning Locke* 1617 *Spec Com.*   SONNING TOWN, *Sonning Towne* 1607 *Rent Sur.*   THREE CORNER FIRS.   WHITE HART HOTEL.

FIELD-NAMES

Forms dated Eliz are Gray; those dated 1572, 1575, 1577, 1583, 1586, 1617, Jas 1 and 1658 are *SpecCom*; 1603–4, e.17th and c. 1605 *Survey*; 1585, 1606–7 and 1607 are *Dep, AugOff* and *RentSur* respectively.

(b) At Deane Corner Eliz (*v.* denu); *Balles More* e.17th; *Baly* 1220 RSO; *Barne Close* 1603–4; *Bedmans Ashe* 1603–4, *Bedeman Cornellis* e.17th, *Bedmans* 1658 (from the surname *Beadman, v.* Reaney 26); *Bedmershe* 1603–4; *Better Lease* 1603–4; *Bonnishe Feild* 1603–4, *Bonnishefield* e.17th; *Boswelle* c. 1605, *Boswells* 1606–7; *Bramleye* Eliz, *Bramley* 1603–4 (*v.* brōm, lēah); *Le Broadclose* 1603–4; *Brodcroft* e.17th; *Brodemeade, Broadmeadegate* 1603–4, *Broad Mead* 1658; *Le Brome Close* 1603–4, *Broome Lawne* 1617 (*v.* brōm, launde); *Brookspiddle* Eliz (*piddle* is a variant of pightel); *Bushie Grove Plott* 1603–4, *Bushydane, Bushy Close, Bushey Moore* c. 1605; *Chaforn Meade* 1603–4; *Charcrofte* 1603–4; *Chirkecrofte* e.17th; *Cherey Eyte* c. 1605 (*v.* ēgeð); *Le Churche Close* 1583; *Cobbs More, Cobbes Piddle* 1603–4; *The Cote Orchard* 1586; *Le Covet House* c. 1605; *Cranes Meade* 1603–4; *Cressfell* Eliz, *Croswell Crofte* 1603–4; *Crowehers Court and Wood* Jas 1; *Crowslowe* 1603–4, *Croslowe* e.17th; *Culver Close* 1603–4 (*v.* culfre); *Ye Deanes* 1585 (*v.* denu); *Demys Field* Eliz; *Dame More* e.17th; *Doleriver* 1603–4; *Dovehouse Pidle* 1583; *Dover Lands* Jas 1; *Downefield* (*als Stonyfield*) 1577, *Downefeld* 1603–4, *Le Downe, Downfeeld* c. 1605, *Downemyll* 1606–7, *Downe Myllande* e.17th, *The Downe* Jas 1 (*v.* dūn); *Drove Gate* 1577 (*v.* drāf); *Elme Landes* e.17th; *Fillis Crofte Pightell, Filliclose Yeate* 1603–4, *Filliclose* 1606–7 (the first el. might be identical with Phyllis Court O 75, *Filettes* 1341, which may contain f(i)ellet); *Fulling-mill Stream* 1603–4; *Fursey Hill* c. 1605; *Galmore* c. 1605 (*v.* g(e)alla, mōr); *Gadresse* 1603–4; *Garden Eyet* c. 1605 (*v.* ēgeð); *Le Garny Leise* 1603–4, c. 1605; *Goose Pidell* 1603–4; *Gorwayes More* 1603–4; *Gravely Close* 1603–4; *Greene Close* 1603–4; *Greenhills* Eliz, c. 1605; *Grove Plottes* 1603–4; *Gunhole Eyat* 1583, *Gonylete* 1586 (*v.* ēgeð); *Hall Place* 1603–4; *Hasill Field* Eliz, *Hasle Parke* 1572, *Hasell Park* 1603–4, *Haselwood* Jas 1 (*v.* hæsel); *Hawes, Hawe Close and Bridge, Hawe Mead Coppice* 1603–4, *Hawes Meade* 1606–7 (*v.* haga[1]); *Heathy More* 1603–4; *Higgmore* 1603–4; *Le Hoked More, Hooke More als Hoocked More* 1583, *Hokedmore* 1586, *Hooke or Hooked More* 1603–4, *Hooked More* 1607 (*v.* hōcede, mōr); *Le Horselease, The Horselease Meade* 1575, *Le Horse Lease* c. 1605 (*v.* læs); *Horsenayles* 1603–4 (perhaps from the finding of horseshoe nails, *v.* 285); *Idellstartes* 1603–4 (*v.* īdel, steort); *Ingrove Ende* e.17th; *Inhams* 1603–4 (*v.* innām); *Kings Bent Grove* Jas 1; *Le Kinge Oke Lawnes* c. 1605, *Kinge Oake Lawne* 1617 (*v.* launde, *King* may be a surname); *Lande Meade* 1585; *Lez Launds* 1575 (*v.* launde); *Langnes Meade* 1603–4; *The Lockeheise* 1585; *Longcroft* 1603–4; *London Way* 1575; *Longedole* 1603–4 (*v.* dāl); *The Lordes Meade als Sonninge Meade*; *Lotinge Meade* 1603–4; (*eights called*)

Lyons, Lyon Streame 1603–4, *Lyon Grove* e.17th (*v.* leyne, ēgeð); *The Mannor Gate* 1577; *Marecroftes* 1603–4; *The Marsh, The Marsh Greene* Jas 1; *Mathews Green* e.17th; *Mayes Greene* 1572; *Mewplandes* 1603–4; *Missie Crofte* 1603–4; *The Moore* Jas 1 (*v.* mōr); *Neplands* e.17th (*v.* nēp); *Neteslandes* 1603–4; *Northcroft* 1603–4; *Little Odney, Lyttle Udney* 1577, *Le Udney* c. 1605 (possibly another example of the name Odney which occurs in Cookham 81); *The Olde Bancke, The Old Ditch* 1617; *Old Gallows* 1779 *RecOffCat*; *Old Meade* 1603–4; *Olde Orchard Field* Eliz, *Oldorchard* 1603–4, *Old Orchard* c. 1605; *Oredes Croft* 1603–4; *Oxfordsheiremeade* 1575 (possibly on the county boundary); *Parke Feere* 1577, *Parkevere* 1603–4, c. 1605, *Parkfere* e.17th, *Parkworth* Eliz, *Parkeworthe* 1603–4, *Parkeworth* c. 1605, *Perk Corner Close, Perke Piddle* 1603–4, *Parke Corner Close* c. 1605 (*v.* park, furh, worð); *Picked Meade* 1603–4, *Pickle Mead* e.17th (*v.* pīced); *Pillmead* 1603–4 (*v.* pyll, mǣd); *Prestesmede* 1220 RSO (*v.* prēost, mǣd); *Procession Waye* 1603–4 (this refers to the annual beating of the parish bounds); *Great Puckewell* Eliz, *Pucknell* 1603–4; *Pudbrockes Hole* 1603–4; *The Rocke Holde als The Racke Heise, Le Rackhoulde als le Rackheyase* 1583, *The Roukhold, The Rockehould* 1585, *Le Rockhols als Rackhaise* 1603–4, *Le Rockall, Le Rockholes als Rackhayse* c. 1605, *Rockholdes* 1607, *Ruckholds* 1617 (the forms are too diverse for safe etymology); *Raynarde* (ground called) 1572, *Raynoldes* 1603–4; *Redinge, Rydings* Eliz, *Rydinges* 1603–4 (*v.* ryding); *Ridges, Rudges* Eliz, 1603–4; *Rockeridge Landes* Jas I; *Rouse* 1603–4; *Rowgrove* c. 1605, 1658, *Roughe Groue* 1607 (*v.* rūh); *Le Rufe Lawne* c. 1605, *Ruffe Lawne* 1617 (*v.* rūh, launde); *Rypon Lane* 1577; *Saffron Close* 1603–4; *The Sandes* 1575; *The Shepehouse* 1577, *Shepehouse Close* c. 1605; *Shoulke* 1606–7; *Shurbridge* e.17th; *Le Sluce Meade* 1603–4; *Le Sowth Meade* c. 1605; *Spring Well* e.17th; *Stacye Wildes als Stacye Wold* 1603–4, *Stacy Wildes* e.17th; *Statfeeld Moore, Stertfales* 1603–4, *Stutfalls* e.17th (*v.* stōd-fald); *Stonye Field, Stonyham* Eliz, *Stonye Feild* 1603–4, *Stoney Feeld* c. 1605; *Tangles Land* e.17th; *Upfeld* 1603–4, *Upfeild* c. 1605 (*v.* upp, feld); *Vernelle* Eliz, *Le Vernhille* c. 1605, *Fern(e)hill* 1658 (*v.* fearn, hyll); *Wasinghille* 1603–4; *Wearley* c. 1605; *Le Weare Plotte* 1583, *The Weare Plott* 1585, 1617, *Weres Plott* c. 1605 (*v.* wer); *Wexhill* 1603–4; *Le Wheatclose* 1603–4; *Whites Grove* 1572; *Wilbrams Hawes* 1606–7 (*v.* haga[1], first el. probably a surname from Wilbraham C); *Le Woodground* c. 1605, *the grownde called Woodlande* Jas I; *Wyldens Coppices* 1603–4.

Twyford

Twyford

Tuiford' 1170 P, *Thuiforde* Hy 2 Gaimar, *Twiford'* 1224–5 *Ass* (p),
Twyvorde 1327 SR, *Twyfold* 1332 *ib* (p), *Twyford* 1332, 1334 *ib*,
Twyforde 1377 *ib*, *Twhiford* 1430 Fine

'Double ford', *v.* twī-, ford, a common name, for some other examples of which *v.* DEPN. The road from Reading has to cross two branches of the R. Loddon here.

TWYFORD STREET-NAMES

BROOK ST.   HIGH ST.   LONDON RD.   STATION RD.   WALTHAM RD.
WARGRAVE RD.

LODDON PARK FM: a wood and a park *super Lodenam* are mentioned
1190 Sar, and in 1227 Ch there is a reference to 'where the *Lodene*
falls into the Thames under the park of *Suninges* which is upon the
Lodene'. For R. Loddon, *v.* 13.

BRIDGE HO.   GROVE HALL.   THE HERMITAGE.   HURST RD
(leading to St. Nicholas Hurst 99).   STANLAKE FM, *v.* Stanlake
Park in Ruscombe 128.

FIELD-NAMES

The principal forms in (*a*) are 1812 *EnclA*.

(*a*) Alders Green; Butchers Pightle (*v.* pightel, as elsewhere in this parish);
Calves Leaze Mdw; Clacks Pightle; Handycroft; Lorgs; Northcroft;
Obridge Hill and Pightle (possibly identical with Old Bridge in St Nicholas
Hurst); Ozon's Pightle; Palmers Green; Pound Fd (also 1790 Pride);
Rogaston Hill; Starvell's Pightle; White or Upper Croft (*White Craft* Jas 1
SpecCom).

(*b*) Twyford Bridge 1658 *SpecCom*; *Twyford Eye* c. 1605 *RentSur*, 1716
PubLib (*v.* (ī)eg).

Winnersh

WINNERSH

> *Wenesse* 1190, 1194 P, *Weners* 1247–8 *Ass, Wenhyrsc, Wonnersh'*
>   1284 *ib, Werenssh* 1397 AD
> *Wymerch'* 1327 SR, *Wimish* 1607 *Norden*
> *Winnersh* 1617, 1651 *PubLib*

The second el. is ersc 'stubble-field, ploughed field'. For the first,
Ekwall (DEPN) and Smith (Elements) give winn[1], wynn 'meadow,
pasture'. The phonological development is uncertain, as -*e*- in the
early forms may be miscopied for -*o*- and vice versa. If *Wen-* is
correct, the development may be compared with that in Windridge
(Hrt 92, considered by the same authorities to contain this el.), Winch
Nf (DEPN) and Winford PN Wt 173–4, which have ME forms in
Wen-. ME forms in *Won-* occur in Wonford and *Womberford* D 441,
625. Assuming the etymology to be correct, it is still difficult to

attach a precise meaning to a compound of **winn** and **ersc**. It might describe an estate where there was an unusually low proportion of arable land to meadow. Roughly half the area of the parish consists of flat ground in a bend of the R. Loddon.

SINDLESHAM, *Sindlesham* 1220 (13th) RSO, 1241, 1284 *Ass*, 1620 *PubLib*, *Sinesham* 1241 *Ass* (p), *Scindlesham* 1242–3 Fees, *Syndlesham* 1256 Cl, 1284 *Ass* (p), 1294 *SR* (p), 1383 Fine, *Syndelesham* 1284 *Ass*, 1397 AD, *Sillesham or Syndelysham* 1500 Ipm, *Silsham als Sindlesham* 1674 *PubLib*(*Clayton*), *Sinsham* 1761 Rocque. The final el. may be **hām**, but **hamm** is topographically suitable. Sindlesham village and Sindlesham Fm (the latter, so named 1620 *PubLib*, is in Woodley and Sandford parish) are on either side of the River Loddon, in low-lying ground. The first el. is uncertain. Ekwall (DEPN) suggests a pers.n. **Synnel* from *Sunna*, with *Synnles-* becoming *Syndles-*. Alternatively, if the *-l-* were a Norman spelling for *-r-* (as is quite frequently the case in this county), the first part of the name might be a p.n. **Syndor* 'apart', cf. Cinders Wo 84, from **sundor**. With regard to both these suggestions, however, it should be noted that there are no spellings with *-u-*, and this suggests that the base had *-i-* rather than *-y-*. Professor Löfvenberg comments that the absence of spellings with *-u-* renders it virtually certain that the first el. had OE *-i-*, and that if the p.n. were a ME formation a Continental pers.n. such as **Sindel* connected with OG *Sindilo* might be considered. Neither **hām** nor **hamm** is likely as the second el. of a post-Conquest compound, however, and the first el. must be regarded as obscure.

ARBOR COTTAGE, *The Arbor* e.17th *Survey*, *The Harbour* 1843 *EnclA*, *v.* Robinhood Lane *infra*. BEAR WD LODGES. BLACK BRIDGE, *Black Bridge Paddock* 1841 *TA* (St Nicholas Hurst). COLTS BRIDGE. FOREST LODGE AND RD. GIPSY LANE. HATCH FM. HIGH CHIMNEYS, *High Chimney* 1846 Snare. HOME FM. KELBURNE LODGE. KING STREET, 1761 Rocque, *Kingstret* 1603–4 *RentSur*, *Kinges Street Close* e.17th *Survey*, probably dialect *street* 'a straggling village' with the surname *King*; cf. Davis Street in St Nicholas Hurst. KINGSTREET COPSE, GORSE AND FM. LEA FM, *v.* Lea Heath 100. LODDON BRIDGE, bridge of *Loden* 1263 Pat, *Lodenebrugg* 1379 BM, *Lodden Bridg* 1607 *Norden*, named from R. Loddon 13. LODDONBRIDGE FM (there is another Fm with this name ½ mile W. in Woodley and Sandford). LODGE WD.

MERRYHILL GREEN AND BRIDGE, *Merrihill* 1603–4 *RentSur*, *Merry Hill* 1607 *Norden*, *Merrie Hill Bridge* 1641 *SP*, *Merril Green* 1790 Pride, *Merry Hill Green* 1822 OS, 1843 *EnclA*, *Merrill Green* 1846 Snare, v. myrge, hyll.   MERRYHILLGREEN FM.   MILL LANE.   MOORE'S FM.   MUNGELLS FM AND LANE, *Mungells Meadow*, *Munguls Ground* 1843 *EnclA*.   POPLAR LANE.   POULTER'S LODGE.   ROBIN-HOOD LANE, *Robin Hoods* 1841 *TA* (St Nicholas Hurst), *Robin Hoods Ground* 1843 *TA*, cf. *Robynpriserber* 1579 *SpecCom* and Arbour Cottage *supra*, which is near the Lane; perhaps 'Robin Hood's arbour', cf. the same name in Maidenhead 57.   THE ROUNDABOUT, *Small Roundabout* 1841 *TA* (St Nicholas Hurst), *Roundabouts* 1843 *EnclA*, this is a piece of land almost surrounded by lanes.   SADDLER'S LANE.   ST CATHERINE'S.   SIMON'S LANE.   SINDLESHAM HO AND LODGE (*v.* 137).   TOUTLEY BRIDGE AND HALL, *Towtley Heath* 1572 *SpecCom*, *Towley or Towtley* 1603–4 *RentSur*, *Toutley Hall* 1761 Rocque, *Toutly Common* 1790 Pride.   WALTER ARMS P.H. WATMORE'S LANE.   WINNERSH FM.   WINNERSH GROVE, 1843 *EnclA*, *Wimish Groue* 1607 *Norden*, *Winersh Grove Coppice* 1674 *PubLib*(*Clayton*).   WINNERSH LODGE, 1846 Snare.

FIELD-NAMES

The principal forms in (*a*) are 1843 *EnclA*; early forms dated 1387, 1445, 1487 and 1518 are ArchJ 46, and those for which no date or source is given e.17th *Survey*.

(*a*) Berry Grove; Binhams, Binhams Green; Blaunches Pightle; Bottom Bridge Ground; Bottom Pightle (*v.* pightel, as elsewhere in this parish); Brook Barns; Chosely Fd; Cold Ridings (*Goldrydinge* e. 17th *Survey*, *Cole Readings* 1658 *SpecCom*, *v.* col[1], ryding); Cole Pightle Shaw; Collins Pightle; Coppice Close and Piddle (Piddle is a variant of pightel); Corner Pightle; Cottage Garden Piddle; Crows Fd; Crutwells; Culvers Close (*v.* culfre); Dean Close; Duce Hill; Emm Brook Mdw (*v.* 9); Feeding Pasture; The Four Closes; Garsons (*v.* gærs-tūn); Graftage Mdw (perhaps for *Graffage*, *v.* 115); Great Mdw; Green Lane Ground; Greenwoods Piddle; Grove Mdw; Gwingham or Gwiningan Mead (*Grymingham Mead*); Hales Mdw, Inner Hales, Outer Hales (*Hayles*, *Inward Hales* Eliz Gray, possibly the plural of h(e)alh); Hall, Little and Great; Ham Mdw and Fd (*The Hammes*, *v.* hamm); Hand-Post Pightle; Hay House; Holly Bushes; Home Fd; Hopeless Ground (*v.* 283); Ivy Pightle; Jacobs Pightle; Katch Gate Fd; Keeps Mdw; King Andrew's Plot; Kingess Ground and Mdw; Lane Piece; Leek Hill, Leek Stile Slipe (*v.* slipe); Loddon Mdw; Long Fds; Long Grove; Long Mdw; Maples (*Maples*); Matts Pightle; May Piddle; Meadow Plott; Muddy Close; Music Lane Ground; New Mdw; Nightingale Close; Nocutts (possibly *cut*, 'lot', *v.* 281); Oat Mdw; Orchard Piddle; Pasture Piece; Pheasant Piddle; Piccadilly Common and Pightle (*v.* 284); Pond Close; Popes Pightle; Pound Fd or Pond Fds; Red Pit Ground; Rod Eyott and Pits (*v.* O 463); Round Mdw; Rushy Mdw; Sawpit Piddle; Shepherds Ground (*Shepperdes*); Slipe (*v.* slipe); Smiths Croft (*Smyth Crofte* 1397 AD, *Smythe Crofte* c. 1605 *Survey*, *v.* smið, croft); Snake Mdw (*Snakemead*); Square Close; Stroud Green and Piece (*v.* strōd); Style Ground; Three Corner Close; Walnut Tree Pightle; Water Lane Mead and Pightle; West Lands; Wildairs; Winding Mdw; Woodside Ground and Close; Worm Ground.

(*b*) *Assot Mead*; *Ayoitemead* (*v.* ēgeð); *Bagworth Acre, Boggworth* (probably identical with Bagworth in the adjacent parish of Woodley and Sandford, *v.* 148); *Birge Mead* e.17th *Survey, Burge Close* 1603–4 ib (*v.* brycg); *Buckmeade*; *Burnedhoke* (possibly 'burnt oak'); *Busheham*; *Callyce*; *Danelands*; *Edgemead, Edishe or Edice Mead* e.17th *Survey, Edge Mead, Edish Meade* 1603–4 *ib* (*v.* edisc); *Edmereham*; *Elsam Field*; *Gernish* 1675, 1689 *PubLib*; *Goldie Croftes*; *Goldsmithes Piddle*; *Corner Close*; *Gosswell Field* e.17th *Survey, Gosnell Feild* 1603–4 *ib*; *Greate Turning Corner*; *Grubbinge Mead* (*v.* 281); *Harwick* (possibly heorde-wic); *Haukeslade* 1387, *Hawkeslade* 1445, *Hawkslade* 1487, *Newmans Hawkslade* 1518 (*v.* hafoc, slæd); *Heath Crofte* (*v.* hǣð); *Hedgemore*; *Herses Acre*; *Hornewaye*; *Innyngis* 1487, *Innynge* 1518, *Jenkyn Inninges* (*v.* inning); *The Lacked Land*; *Little Grove* 1674 *PubLib*(*Clayton*); *Londeslond* 1658; *Malamyn*; *North Groves* 1674 *PubLib*(*Clayton*); *Parkemeade*; *Pattens Meadow*; *Payneslane* 1445 (first el. *Pain*, pers.n. or surname); *Penyam Field, Penyon Field*; *Perytree Close* (*v.* pirige); *Sewers Meade, The Sewes*; *Stoneycroft*; *Thesteham*; *Watery Close*; *West Rydinge* (*v.* west, ryding); *Whetershe Mead, Whetereshe, Wheterishe, Wheteridge* (*v.* hwǣte, ersc); *The Wythye* (*v.* wiðig).

Wokingham, Within and Without

WOKINGHAM

Wokingeham 1146 (15th) Holtzmann, 1219 (13th) RSO, 1227 Ch, 1227–8 FF, *Wockngeham* c. 1170–80 (c. 1280) S (p)

Wokingham 1146 (copy) Sar, 1241, 1284 *Ass, Woukingham* 1241 *ib*, *Wokkyngham* 1284 *ib* (p), *Wokyngham* 1339 Pat

Okynham 1517 D Inc, *Okingham* 1600 Camden

'The homestead of the people of *Wocc*', *v.* -inga-, hām. This place is probably named from the same group of people as Woking Sr 156; *v.* Introd.

The area was divided into two parishes, named 'Within' and 'Without', in 1894 (Kelly 281).

WOKINGHAM STREET-NAMES

BARKHAM RD.   BROAD ST.   CAREY RD.   COCKPIT PATH.   CRESCENT
RD.   CROSS ST.   DENMARK ST, *Down St*, 1639, 1738 *et freq PubLib*, *Down St
now Denmark St* 1868 *PubLib*.   EASTHAMPSTEAD RD.   FINCHAMPSTEAD RD.
FREDERICK PLACE.   GLEBELAND RD.   GOODCHILD RD.   HAVELOCK RD AND
ST.   HOWARD RD.   LANGBOROUGH RD.   LONDON RD.   LUCKLEY PATH.
MARKET PLACE.   MILTON RD.   MURDOCK RD.   NORTON RD.   OSBORNE
RD.   OXFORD RD.   PARK RD AND AVE.   PEACH ST, *Peche al. Peach Street*
1368 BM, *Peache Streate* 16th VCH III, probably from the surname *Petch*, Reaney
249.   READING RD.   RECTORY RD.   ROSE ST.   SCHOOL RD.   SEAFORD
RD.   SHUTE END, *Shute* 1815 *Bodl*, probably dialect *shoot* 'steep slope' found in
several instances of the name White Shute in the W. of the county.   SOUTH
DRIVE.   SOUTHLANDS RD.   STURGES RD.   WATERLOO RD.   WELLINGTON RD.
WESTCOTT RD.   A lost street-name is *Le Rothe Street* 1417 BM, *Rothstreat* 16th
VCH III, possibly from roð(u) 'clearing'.

Wokingham Within

BECHES, (tithing of) *Bech'* 1332, 1334 *SR*, *Beche* 1453 *ib*, *Beches* 1481–
2 *RentSur*. It is difficult to say whether this is a genuine p.n., or is
manorial in origin. Geoffrey *atte Beche* was living in Wokingham in
1327 (VCH III, 229). *v.* bēce² 'a beech-tree'.

LUCKLEY, *Luckley*, *Luckly Green* 1595 Finchampstead, *Luckly House*
1761 Rocque, *Luckley House* 1790 Pride, 1846 Snare. The forms are
insufficient for an etymology, but the final element is probably
lē(a)h.

THE THROAT, *Le Throte* 1498 Chertsey, *The Throat Bolsingham* 1786
Finchampstead, *The Throat* 1846 Snare. OE þrote 'throat', which is
found in several names in Sr (Sr 131, 366), and one in Db (Db 361).
The precise sense, which is presumably a transferred topographical
one, has not been determined. O.S. maps place the Berks name at a
junction of several roads, and its use may have been similar to that of
modern *bottleneck*.

WOODCRAY MANOR FM, *Wodetri* 1176 P, *Wudecrie* 1180 ib (p),
Wudecride 1228 *FF* (p), *Wodecrithe* 13th *AddCh 38646* (p), *ib 38649*,
Wodetrich'e 1294 *SR* (p), *Wodekrith* 13th *AddCh 38647*, *Wodecriz*
13th *ib 38650*, *Woodcrye* 1573 *Bodl*, *Woodcree* 1761 Rocque, 1790
Pride, *Woodcray Fm* 1846 Snare. As the only distinctive feature of the
topography is a tiny stream, the second el. is probably rīð. This
means that the *-c-* is part of the first el. and derivation from wudu is

impossible, but Professor Löfvenberg suggests an OE *wuduc* 'small wood'. The only other suggestion which can be offered is a pers.n. *Wuduca*, from the recorded *Wuda*.

ASHRIDGE FM (*v.* 142, this is *Belfound* 1816 OS, *v.* f.ns. 145). BARKHAM LODGE.   BARK HART.   BATTY'S BARN.   BEANOAK FM, *Land called Beenoak* 1715 Ashmole.   BLACKGROVE'S FM AND LANE.   BOB'S COPSE.   BOTTLE COPSE.   BUCKHURST FM (*v.* 143).   BUDGE'S COTTAGES.   CANTLEY.   CHAPEL GREEN, 1761 Rocque, a chapel is marked 1816 OS just N. of the Green.   CHAPEL-GREEN FM.   CLAVE COURT.   CLAY LANE.   DOLE'S FM, HILL AND LANE, *Doales Grove besydes Okingham* 1572 *SpecCom*, *Doles Woode* 1607 *Norden*, *Doles Barn* 1846 Snare.   DOWLESGREEN, 1846 ib, *Dowls Green* 1790 Pride.   DUCKETT'S LODGE.   EASTHEATH, 1761 Rocque, *Le Eastheath* 1571 *PubLibDoc*, *East Heath Fm* 1816 OS, 1846 Snare, *v.* hǣð.   EMMBROOK HO, *v.* 9.   FOLLY COURT AND FARMHOUSE, *Folly Fm* 1846 Snare, *v.* folie.   FOX HILL, 1839 *TA*.   FROG HALL, 1761 Rocque, *Frogshall* 1846 Snare, *v.* 142. FROGHALL GREEN, 1761 Rocque.   GIPSY LANE.   GLEBELANDS. GREAT MEAD, *Great Meadow* 1839 *TA*.   GULLY COPSE, *Gully Hole* 1839 *TA*.   HAGVILLE FM (given on 6″ to farm called WOOD-CRAY MANOR FM on 1″), *Hagfield Heath* 1761 Rocque, 1790 Pride, 1839 *TA*, *Hagville Farm al. Bolsingham Farm* 1728 Finchampstead, *Hagville Heath* 1816 OS, *Hagwell Fm* 1846 Snare.   HIGHCLOSE. HIGHFIELD.   THE HOLT, 1816 OS, *Holt House* 1790 Pride, *v.* holt. HOLT COPSE AND LANE.   HUTT'S FM.   KEEP HATCH, *Keepe Hatch* 1607 *RentSur*, *v.* hæc(c).   KEEPHATCH FM, 1816 OS. LANGBOROUGH RECREATION GROUND, *Langborough* 1684–5 *PubLib*, possibly from a tumulus, *v.* lang, beorg.   LIMMERHILL, 18th VCH III, 1846 Snare.   LUCAS'S HOSPITAL, *Lucas Hospital* 1846 Snare, founded under the will of Henry *Lucas*, dated 1663 (VCH III, 226).   MATTHEWSGREEN, *Mathews Green* 1761 Rocque, possibly connected with William *Matheu* of Wokingham, mentioned 1341 Cl. MATTHEWSGREEN FM.   MERTONFORD.   MOLLY MILLARS LANE. MONTAGUE HO.   NORRIS BARN, *Norrises* 1619 *SpecCom*; in the 16th cent. the family of *Norreys* had an estate in Wokingham known as Norreys Manor (VCH III, 231).   OAKFIELD.   OAKHURST. OLD LEATHERN BOTTLE P.H., *Leather Bottle* 1790 Pride, *Leathern Bottle* 1846 Snare.   PLOUGH LANE.   RANCES LANE.   ROUND HILL.   SANDY BOTTOM AND LANE.   SCOT'S FM, 1846 Snare.

STARLANE CROSSING, STARMEAD.   TAN HO, 1790 Pride, *Tan House Bridge* 1846 Snare (the Tannery is marked on the 6″ map). THATCHED COTTAGE P.H.   THREE FROGS P.H., near Froghall Green *supra*.   TITHE BARN.   TRENCH'S BRIDGE.   TWO POPLARS P.H.   WHITE HOUSE.   WILTSHIRE FM (1816 OS) AND RD, these names refer to the parish's ancient connection with Wiltshire, *v. infra*.   WINDMILL POND.   WOODLANDS.   WOOSE HILL, *Wose Hill* 1816 OS, WOOSEHILL LANE, *v.* 16.

The following names of houses are shown on O.S. maps in Wokingham Within: ABERFOYLE. BATTENHURST. BELMONT. EASTHEATH VILLA. EASTLEIGH. HOLMEWOOD. IVYDENE. MONTGOMERY LAWN. OAKHURST. PENVENTON. QUISISANA. RATHALDRON. RUSSLEY. SOUTHLANDS. WHITE HOUSE. WYLDECROFT.

Wokingham Without

ASHRIDGEWOOD, (wood of) *Hasherugg'* 1284 *Ass, Asserigge* 1285 Pat, *Assherugge* 1299 Cl, 1359 *RentSur*, 1365 Pat, *Ashrigge* 1318 ib, *Ashrigge als Ashridge* 1618 *SpecCom, Ashridge* 1619 *ib, Ashridge Wood* 1790 Pride, *Ashridge Copse* 1846 Snare. 'Ash-tree ridge', *v.* æsc, hrycg.

   Portions of Sonning and Charlton Hundreds, which were appurtenant to the manor of Amesbury in Wiltshire, were organised under the name of Ashridge Hundred, the court being held at Ashridge, alternatively known as *Hertoke*. The history of this hundred (which appears to be first mentioned 1397 Cl) is discussed in VCH III, 228–9. The only reference to *Hertoke* which has been found is that quoted in VCH III, 228, which states that the manor court was held there in the late 15th cent.

BIGSHOTTE RAYLES AND SCHOOL, *Bygshotte Walke* and *Rayles* l.16th ArchJ 36, *Bigshott Walke* 1607 *Norden, Begshot Walk* 1700 Finchampstead, *Bigshot Rails or Bagshot* 1761 Rocque, *Bigshot Lodge* 1790 Pride. The second el. is scēat 'projection of land'. The first might be the personal name *Bicga, v.* Bigfrith (60). For Rayles cf. *Rayles Lane infra.*

BILL HILL *Bollinghull'* 1241 *Ass* (p), *Bylhill, Bill Hill* 1572 *SpecCom, Bill Hill* 1761 Rocque, *Billhill* 1790 Pride. BILLHILL, *Billhill House* 1619 *SpecCom*. There is another Bill Hill in Easthampstead (24) for which no early forms have been found. The spelling in 1241 *Ass* (which has been checked) precludes the association of this name with

Billington La, Billingsley He, Billingshurst Sx, Billing Hill YW and Billinge Hill Ch, La, all or some of which may contain an OE hill-name *Billing*. A hill-name **Bullinge* was suggested by Wallenberg (PN K 494) as the source of a lost name *Bolling', Bulling* in Whitstable. The Berks and K names may, however, be identical with Bolinge Hill Ha (PN *-ing* 231), which derives from OE *bufan hlince* 'above the bank'. The Ha name was *Buvelynche* 1288, *Bullynge* 1310–20. The contraction might have taken place earlier in the Berks name owing to the addition of hyll to the compound. The Berks name is that of the western tip of the ridge referred to in Ashridgewood *supra*. Bolinge Hill Fm Ha (in Buriton, near Petersfield) has a similar situation.

BUCKHURST, *Bochurst* 1178 P (p), 1224–5 *Ass* (p), 1241 *ib* (p), 1281, 1321 Cl, *Bocurst* 1220 Fees (p), *Bokhurst* 1332 SR, *Boukhurste* 1334 *ib*, *Bokhirst* 1341 Cl (p), *Bokehirst* 1351 Pat (p), *Buchurst* 1342 Gor (p), *Bukhurste* 1552 LRMB, *Buckhurst Farm* 1790 Pride, 'beech wood', *v.* bōc, hyrst. The same name occurs in Ess (Ess 53–4), and there are several examples in Sx. BUCKHOUSE FM in Binfield is probably named from the same wood.

EVENDON'S FM, *Yhenedon', Yenedon', Yendon', Hynenedon', Yeningdon'* 1241 *Ass* (p), *Yeuedon, Ythengdone* 1284 *ib*, *Yenedon'* 13th *AddCh 38646* (p), *Yenenon'* 13th *ib 38648* (p), *Yenendune* 13th *ib 38649* (p), *Yhenindone* 13th *ib 38650* (p), *Yevingdon* 1293 Ipm, *Yendon'* 1294 SR (p), *Yeveden* Ed 1 BM, 1481–2 *RentSur*, *Yeuyndon* 1316 FA, *Yevyndon* 1341 Cl (p), *Manor or Farme of Evendens or Indens* 1602 Finchampstead, *Evendens Farme* 1607 *RentSur*, *Inden Farm* 1761 Rocque, *Indens Farm* 1790 Pride, *Evendons Farm* 1846 Snare. The final el. is dūn 'hill', sometimes weakened to *-den*. The spellings show a great deal of variety, but the first el. may be efen 'flat, level'. The farm is on the edge of a narrow ridge formed by the 200' contour. A prosthetic *Y-* is fairly common in names beginning with *E-*. Professor Löfvenberg considers that in view of the persistent *Y-* in the early forms the first el. is more likely to be a pers.n. *Geofa*, as in Evington Gl 2 83, Yeaveley Db 619, Yeoveney Mx 19, Jevington Sx 412.

THE APIARY.   ASHRIDGEWOOD FM. (*v.* 142).   BEECH WD. BIRCHEN INHAMS, *v.* bircen[2], innām.   BOG COTTAGE.   BRITTON'S FM, *Brittons* 1846 Snare.   CALIFORNIA, *v.* 284.   CALIFORNIA LODGE.   CARTER'S HILL, 1761 Rocque.   CARTERSHILL PLAN-

TATION.   CASWALLS.   CHAPEL ALLOTMENT.   CROOKED BILLET
P.H.   CROWTHORNE FM.   EDGCUMBE MOUNT.   FERNSIDE.
FOREST RD, 1790 Pride.   FOXLEY FM, *Foxleyes* c. 1620 VCH III,
Thomas de *Foxle* held land in the adjacent parish of Finchampstead
1428 FA.   GARDENERS GREEN, 1790 Pride, *Gardiners Green* 1761
Rocque.   GENISTA.   GORRICK WELL, 1816 OS, 1846 Snare,
Gorickwell 1761 Rocque, *Garrick Field and Moor* 1839 *TA*, *Gorrick
Lane End* 1846 Snare.   GORRICK PLANTATION.   GREEN LANE.
HAM BRIDGE, 1846 Snare, *v.* hamm.   HAMBRIDGE COTTAGE.
HEATH LAKE.   HEATHLANDS.   HOLME GREEN, 1761 Rocque,
Hones Green 1790 Pride, 1846 Snare.   HOLME GRANGE.   HONEY-
HILL, *Honey Pightle* 1839 *TA*, *v.* hunig.   JACK'S BRIDGE, *v.* King's
Bridge *infra*.   JERRYMOOR HILL, *Jerome Hill* 1839 *TA*.   KILN
SQUARE, *Kiln Field* 1839 *TA*.   KINGSCOTE, in the north of the
parish, the manor of Ashridge near here belonged to the crown
(VCH III, 228).   KING'S BRIDGE, 1761 Rocque, *Kings Bridge and
Cross* 1846 Snare, KING'S LODGE AND MERE, these names, Queen's
Bridge and Mere, and Jack's Bridge are close together.   LOCK'S
HO, *Locks Ferme* 1553 *PubLibDoc*, *Locks Farm* 1846 Snare.   MANOR
FM.   MARCHFIELD HO.   THE MOORS, *Mor* 1341 NonInq (p),
Moor 1839 *TA*, *v.* mōr.   NINEMILE RIDE, *Nine Mile Road* 1846
Snare.   OAKLANDS.   PEARCE'S FM.   PEBBLESTONE COPSE,
Pebblestone Coppice 1846 Snare.   PIKE'S FM.   POND WD,
PONDWOOD COTTAGE.   THE POPLARS.   QUEEN'S BRIDGE, 1846
Snare.   QUEEN'S MERE.   RADICAL FM.   RANDALL'S FM,
1846 Snare.   RAVENSWOOD.   REDLAKE.   ROUSE'S FM AND
POND.   RUSHTON'S FM.   SILVERSTOCK BOG, 1846 Snare.   STOKES
FM.   SWAIN'S COPSE.   TARGETS FM, *Targetts Fm* 1846 Snare.
TIPPEN'S WD, *Tippens Hill* 1822 OS, 1846 Snare.   WARREN HO
P.H., *Warren House* 1761 Rocque, *The Warren, Warren House Field*
1839 *TA*.   WATER HILL.   WATERLOO CROSSING (a railway
crossing) AND LODGE.   WATLEY'S COPSE.   WHITE HORSE P.H.
WIXENFORD.   WOOD'S FM.

FIELD-NAMES

(Wokingham Within and Wokingham Without)

The principal forms in (*a*) are 1839 *TA*; early forms dated 1553, 1571,
1597 and 1609 are *PubLibDoc*, 16th, c. 1620 and 18th VCH III, 1619 and
1658 *SpecCom*, and 1761 Rocque.

(a) Acre Down Close; Adder Pightle (v. pightel, as frequently in this parish); Arch Fd; Bachelors Acre; Back Lane Mdw; Barnacles; Barn Ground, Fd and Mead; Bean Ground Mdw; Belfont (Belfound 1816 OS, v. Ashridge Fm 141); Bell Close, Mead and Plat; Birch Mead; Bloomnights, Great and Little; Boarded Gates; Bottom Slip (v. slipe); Boundary Fd; Bran Oak; Breaches (v. brēc); Brew House Mead; Bridge Mdw; Brimpton or Bumpton Fd; Broad Croft; Brook Close and Mdw; Broom Close, Broomfield (v. brōm); Buck Hill (also 1761); Burnt Mead; Bursfield; Bushy Heighs; Calves Close; Causters, Short, Costers Common Fd (v. cot-stōw); Chalk Close; Chalky Fd; Charity Piece; Charnel Fd; Cherry Close; Church Lane, Mead and Fd; Clay Close and Pightle; Clay Pit Fd; Cockridge; Common Piece and Ground; Copped Row (v. coppod, rāw); Coppice Close, Mdw and Fd; Cowstall Mdw; Dial Fd (v. dial); Diamond Close; Drakes Mdw; Dry Ground; Ducksbridge Fd; Englishes Mead; Faggot Pile Mdw; Fair Hill; Fir Ride Fd (v. 34); Fuel Allotment; Furzey Close; Garstons, Flat and Great (v. gærs-tūn); Gravel Allotment; Gravel Pit Fd; Great Down (v. dūn); Green Broom (v. brōm); Green Pightle; Grove Close and Pightles; Gruffidge Ground (v. Graffadge Grounds in Waltham St Lawrence 115); Hagistons Fd; Half Moon Piece (v. 283); Ham Hill; Hatchet Fd (v. hæccgeat); Hawks Coppice; Hay Croft; Heath Fd; Highgate; Hill Moor; Hill Pightle; Holly Bush; Home Ground and Mdw; Homestall Mdw (Homestall is sometimes used in TAs instead of Homestead, v. Sandred 68 n. 2); Hop Garden and Ground; House Mdw; Inner Pightle; Lady Well (v. hlǣfdige); Lane Fd; Lee Pool; Lemon Close; Lone Barn Fd; Long Ground; Long Moor; Mill Moor; Moat Lane, Moor and Pightle; Monk Mdw; Moss Land; Mutton Mdw; Old Mdw; Ooze Fd (v. Woose Hill 142); Ox Leys (v. lǣs); Parchment; Peaked Close, Moor and Piece (v. pīced); Pease Furlong; Peat Moor; Pig Fd; Pond Mdw and Pasture; Poor Pightle; Rack Close; Reading Hill Fd; Roadfield; Rough Mdw, Park and Piece; Roundabout (v. 281); Rushy Ground; Shoulder of Mutton (v. 283); Slade Close; The Slip (v. slipe); Sloe Pightle; Slough (v. slōh); Sorrel Close; Sour Leys Pightle (v. sūr, lǣs, pightel); Spratley; Spring Pightle; Stable Ground; Stanbridge Mdw; Stoney Hill; Stout Mead; Stumps Fd; Tangley Moor (Tangly Farm 1761, Tangleys 1790 Pride); Temple Stile; Thistley Close; Three Cornered Mdw; Thrift (Frithland 16th, v. fyrhð); Town Fd; Triangle Mead; Well Pightle; Wheat Fry; Withy Close; Woodfield; Wood Ground.

(b) Bardhouse 16th; Baylieslade 1607 Norden (v. slǣd, first el. probably a surname); Billes Piddle, Long Billes 1619; Blare Close c. 1620; Broodmeade, Broode Mead 1609 (v. brād, mǣd); Carolls Bushes 1619; Coslowe 16th; Downe Bridge 1658; Godewykelane 13th AddCh 38649 (first el. probably a surname); Hancoks Oke 1607 Norden; Hayfield 1571; Herne c. 1620 (v. hyrne); High Bridge 1658; Highill 1619; Hooke Meadow 1619 (v. hōc); Inninge, Broade and Upp 1619 (v. inning); Keepings Hill 1790 Pride; Le Little Downe 1571 (v. dūn); The North Corner 1641 SP; North Grove 1553, 1597; Pipers Closes 1641 SP, Pipers Close 1761; Pond Cops 1761; Rayles Lane 1641 SP (ME reille 'fence, railing'; v. 281); Reynoldes Wood 1607 Norden; Rowgrove c. 1620; Rylands c. 1620; Sellgrove c. 1620; Sheetham 1571

PubLibDoc, Shetham 16th; *Southeye* 13th *AddCh 38649* (*v.* sūð, (i)eg);
Uppeynges 16th (possibly identical with *Upp Inninge* 1619, *v.* upp, inning);
Yieldhall Green 1761 (*v.* gild-hall).

Woodley and Sandford

WOODLEY

> *Wodlegh'* 1241 *Ass*, *Wodleyhe* 1341 NonInq (p), *Woodley* 1761
> Rocque

Possibly 'meadow by the wood', *v.* lēah, wudu, and cf. Lea and
Whistley in St Nicholas Hurst 100–1. The three names are in flat
ground on either side of the Loddon, and they may be of relatively
late origin and contain lēah in its final meaning 'meadow'.

SANDFORD

> *Sandford'* 1241 *Ass* (p), *Sanforde* 1402 Fine, *Sandforde* 1607
> *Norden*

'Sand ford', cf. Dry Sandford, Pt **2**. The ford, a crossing-place on
Old River (a branch of the Loddon), is marked on the 1″ map.

BULMERSHE COURT, *Buleneirs* (*bis*) c. 1180 HMC Var Coll I, *Bul-*
merssh 1412 FA, *Bulmershe Courte* 1596 *PubLibDoc*, *Bulmersh* 1607
RentSur, *Bulmarsh* 1658 *PubLib*, *Bulmarsh Heath* 1761 Rocque,
Bulmarsh Park 1840 *TA*, *Bulmershe, Bullmershe Court, Bullmershe*
Court Fm 1846 Snare. The first el. is bula 'bull'. The second is
probably mersc 'marsh', in spite of the earliest form. It should,
however, be noted that the manor is referred to as the 'manor of
Belvershale called *Bulnassh*' in 1448 Cl, and the form from HMC
Var Coll could possibly be a misreading for *Buleueirs*, which might
give the first part of the name *Belvershale*. It is perhaps improbable
that the place should have two distinct names which resemble each
other in this way, and both the forms given 1448 Cl should probably
be disregarded.

ALDER MOORS, 1840 *TA*.   BEGGARS HILL, *Beggars Close, Beggar*
Hill Ground 1840 *ib*, *v.* 283.   THE BIRCHES.   BULL AND
CHEQUERS P.H.   BUTTS HILL, *Butts Hill Pightle* 1840 *TA*, *v.*
butt[1], butt[2], butte.   BUTTS HILL BRIDGE.   CHALK BRIDGE.
CHARVIL FM, 1822 OS, *Char Field* Eliz Gray, *Charfeld* 1603–4
RentSur, *Charfeeld* c. 1605 *ib*, *Charfeild* 1658 *SpecCom*, *Charval*

Field, Upper and Lower Charval 1840 *TA, Charville Fm* 1846 Snare, probably identical with *Charfield* Gl **3**, 26–7, *v*. **feld**, first el. **cert** 'rough ground' or **cearr(e)** 'bend, turn'.   CHARVIL HILL. CHEQUERS P.H., *The Chequers* 1846 Snare.   COBBLER'S CITY (only on 6″ map, the name of a row of small houses bordering a road E. of Woodley village, *v*. 284).   COLEMAN'S MOOR, 1761 Rocque, *Colmans Moore, Colmons Moore* 1603–4 *RentSur, Colemans Moore* 1607 *ib, v*. **mōr**, first el. probably a surname.   COLEMANSMOOR FM, 1846 Snare.   COPPER BRIDGE, COPPERBRIDGE BROOK.   CROCK-HAM WELL, *Crockham Well Pightle* 1840 *TA*.   DAVIS'S FM. DEAN CORNER, *Ye Deanes* 1585 *Dep, Dean Pightle* 1840 *TA, v*. **denu**. DENMARK COTTAGES.   DUFFIELDS BRIDGE.   DUMPLING'S CLUMP. EARLEY STATION.   EAST PARK FM, 1846 Snare, *Est Parke of Sonnyng* 1520 ArchJ 5, *East Parke* 1658 *SpecCom*.   ELEVEN ELMS. FOSTER'S LANE, *Little Fosters* 1658 *SpecCom*.   GIDDY BRIDGE, 1603–4 *RentSur*, 1840 *TA, Guydie Bridge* 1603–4 *RentSur, v*. **gydig**, which may here refer to an unstable bridge, or may possibly be a stream-name.   GINGER TERRACE.   GIPSY LANE.   HEADLEY RD, *Hedlye, Hedley, Hedly Piddle* 1603–4 *RentSur, Hadley Crofte* e.17th *Survey, Hadleigh Heath, Moor, Mead, Ground and Pightle* 1840 *TA*, probably OE *hǣ ð-lēah 'clearing overgrown with heather', a common name.   HIGH WD.   HOGSBRIDGE, *Hog Bridge Close, Hog Moor* 1840 *ib*.   HOLINEMOOR COPSE.   LITTLE HUNGERFORD, 1846 Snare, *v*. Hungerford, Pt **2**.   LAKE, NORTH AND SOUTH. LAND'S END P.H.   LANDSEND LANE.   THE LARCHES.   LODDON-BRIDGE FM AND COPSE, *Lodin Bridge Meade* 1603–4 *RentSur, Loddon Bridge* 1790 Pride, *Loddon Fm and Bridge* 1846 Snare.   LUND'S FM.   MARSH FM.   MARSH LANE.   MARTIN'S CORNER.   MILL LANE.   MUSTARD LANE, *Mustard Lane Pightle* 1840 *TA*.   NORRIS'S GREEN AND COPSE.   PARK LANE, *v*. East Park *supra*.   POND HEAD WD.   RAG CASTLE, *Ray Castle Field* 1840 *TA*.   SAND-FORD FM AND MILL, 1846 Snare, *Sandforde Mill* 1607 *Norden*. SANDFORDMILL COPSE.   SANDPIT COPSE, *Sandpittes* 1603–4 *Rent-Sur*.   SINDLESHAM FARM AND MILL, *Sindsham Mill* 1674 *PubLib-(Clayton), Sinsham Common and Mill* 1790 Pride, *Sindlesham Mill and Bridge* 1846 Snare, *v*. 137.   SKINNER'S COPSE, 1846 ib, *Skynners* 1603–4 *RentSur*, probably from a surname, cf. Foster's Lane *supra*.   SOUTHLAND WD.   SPOIL BANKS, *Spoil Bank* 1840 *TA*, these are on either side of the railway line.   TIPPINGS LANE. WAINGEL COPSE, *Wengell* Eliz Gray, *Wangell, Wangell More*,

Waingell Moore 1603–4 *RentSur*, *Wangel-field* 1697 VCH III, *Wangel Field and Moor* 1840 *TA*. THE WARREN. WESTERN AVENUE. WHEELER'S GREEN. WHITE BRIDGE. WINDMILL PLANTATION. WOODLEY GREEN, 1761 Rocque, *Woodley Greene* 1603–4 *RentSur*. WORKHOUSE MOOR.

FIELD-NAMES

The principal forms in (*a*) are 1840 *TA*; early forms for which no date or source is given are c. 1605 *Survey*; 1603–4 *Survey*, and 1658 *SpecCom*.

(*a*) Alton Pightle; Bagworth Close (*Bagworthe* 1603–4, also mentioned in Winnersh, *v.* 139); Beech Mead; Black Innings (*Black Inninges*, 1603–4, *v.* inning); Breach Ground, Little (*The Brech* Eliz Gray, *Breaches* 1603–4, *v.* brēc); Broad Mead; Burrough Eyott (*v.* ēgeð); Bush Pightle (*v.* pightel, as frequently in this parish); Cain Mead (*Canemeade*); Calves Pightle; Clay Pightle; Coach Way Fd; Conny bury ('rabbit warren'); Conneygree, Conneygrove (*v.* coninger); Coppice Close; Crabtree Mead; Currough Fd; Dawn Mead; Day Pightle (*Daye Pidell* 1603–4, *v.* dey, 'dairy', pightel); Dry Close; East Croft (*Eastcrofte* 1603–4); Ellsome (*Elsham* 1603–4); Gosmoor Common, Meads and Waste (*Gosmore* 1603–4, *v.* gōs, mōr); Grass Moor; Great Grove; Great Mead; Green Pightle; Grub Ground (*v.* 281); Hatch Close; Heath Allotment (*Heath Pidells* 1603–4, *Le Heath Lane* 1606–7 *AugOff*, *The Heath* 1658, *v.* hǣð); Herne Mead (*Hernmeade, Hernmeade Eyte, v.* hyrne); High Mead; Hill Ground; Home Fd and Ground; Hop Ground (*Le Hope Garden, v.* hoppe); Horse Close; Hyde Mead; Jonathan Mead; Linny Close; Long Mead and Moor; Mill Mead; The Moor (*The Moore* Jas I *SpecCom, v.* mōr); New Lands Close; New Pond Pasture; North Grove; The Oziers; The Park Mead; Pen Crooks; Pound Pightle; Rays; Rushway Moor and Pasture (*Rushway* 1658 *PubLib*); Salt Close, Salt Hill Moor (*Salte Grove, Salthill* 1572 *SpecCom, Saltehille Grove, Le Salthide, Salte Close* 1603–4 *Survey, Salthill* 1758 ArchJ 14); Sand Pightle; Sellery Close and Pightle (*Shellerye* e.17th *Survey*); Shear Close; The Slip (*v.* slipe); Sluice Mdw; Sonning Lane End Ground; Star Close (*Stere Close*); Welsh Harp Piece (*v.* 283); Westland Mead (1658); White Moor (*Whitemoore*); Great Wold Mead.

(*b*) *Ashen Moore*; *Bushey Moore*; *Buthip Grove* 1658; *Church Feeld*; *The Corner Meade*; *Ford, Great and Little*; *Greenfull Pightell* 1658; *Hagstye* c. 1605 *Survey*, *Hogstie Grove* 1658; *Hoswell Feild* 1658; *Howlett* 1658; *The Long Mead* 1658; *The Old Orchard* 1658; *Pondeclose*; *Pottland Moore*; *Sawpittmoore*; *Stonie Fild* 1658; *Streetemore* (*v.* strǣt, mōr); *Waterclose*.

VIII. READING HUNDRED

Redinges, *Radinges* 1086 DB, *Redingia* c. 1125 Anderson, *Rading'*
1169 *et seq* P, 1220 Fees, *Radinge* 1186, 1188 P, *Rad(d)ing* 1275–6
RH, *Radyng'* 1316 FA

Named from Reading *infra* 170. The Domesday Hundred of
Reading consisted of Reading and Pangbourne and the present
Hundred of Theale. Theale Hundred (198) was formed between 1220
and 1241, and after that the name of Reading Hundred was applied
to a number of scattered vills belonging to Reading Abbey. These
include Blewbury and Cholsey (territorially in Moreton Hundred,
Pt 2) and Bucklebury and Thatcham (territorially in Faircross 231).
Three 1-hide estates at *Burlei* are listed under Reading Hundred in
DB; this has not been identified, the name is probably identical with
Burley Db; Ha etc., 'lēah belonging to a burh'. The 1-hide estate at
Lonchelei, which DB gives under Reading Hundred, may be Langley
in Tilehurst 194.

Beech Hill

BEECH HILL, *Le Bechehulle* 1384 MS at Stratfield *penes* the Duke of
Wellington, *ex. inf.* Mr J. E. B. Gover, *Bechehyll* 1572 PCC,
Beachill 1603 Finchampstead, *Beeche Hills* 1607 *Norden*, *Beach Hill*
1761 Rocque, *Beech Hill* 1817 OS, 1846 Snare

v. bēce[2] 'beech-tree', and hyll 'hill'. The parish was formed in
1868 out of the Berkshire portion of Stratfield Saye parish, the rest of
which is in Ha (Kelly 39). DEPN gives a form from 1335 under this
name, which actually refers to Beche in Aldworth (Pt 2).

TRUNKWELL HO

Tromkewull' 1190, 1191 *HarlCh 83A4*, *Trumqnulle* e.13th ArchJ 2
(p), *Trumkewell'* 1224–5 *Ass*
Trunkewelle e.13th ArchJ 2 (p), *Truncwell'* 1220 Fees, 1241 *Ass* (p),
Trunkewell', *Trulkewell'* 1241 *ib* (p), *Truncwelle* 13th *ReadingC*,
Trunkewell' 1268–72 FF, 1284 *Ass* (p), *Troncwelle* 1294 *SR*,
Trouncwell 1316 Ipm, *Trunkwelle* 1339 Cl, *Trunkwell* 1532
ObAcc, *Trunkewell* 1552 *LRMB*, *Trunkwell House* 1846 Snare

The second el. is w(i)ella. The first may be an OE pers.n., perhaps a diminutive in -uca, -ica or -eca of a name *Trum, from OE trum 'firm, strong, vigorous', found as the first el. of the compound pers.ns. Trumhere, Trumwine etc.

BEECH HILL COVERTS AND HO.   BROAD WAY.   CANNON BRIDGE. CLAPPERS FM.   CROSSLANE FM.   HOME FM.   LITTLE COPSE. MISSELS BRIDGE.   THE PRIORY, 1817 OS, 1846 Snare, PRIORY COPSE AND FM.   QUEEN'S HEAD P.H.   TROWE'S LANE.   WOOD LANE.

Beenham

BEENHAM

> Benham 1142–84 (l.12th) ReadingC, c. 1195 AddCh 7502 (p), 1284
>   Ass, 1312–13 FF, 1316 FA
> Beneham 1242–3 Fees, 1552 LRMB
> Bienham 13th ReadingC, ReadingC(2)
> Binham 1275–6 RH
> Beenham (Field and Farm) 1761 Rocque

The first el. is bēan 'bean'. The second is either hām or hamm, hām being perhaps more appropriate to the site of the village, which is on relatively high ground, over a mile from the River Kennett.

AWBERY'S FM, Abury Farm 1817 OS, Auberys Meadow 1839 TA, Aberry's Fm 1846 Snare; Alburystreet 1408 Bucklebury (161) could be an earlier ref.   BEENHAM GRANGE.   BEENHAM HILL, 1817 OS.   BEENHAM HO, 1790 Pride.   BEENHAM LODGE, 1846 Snare. BEENHAM STOCKS, STOCKS FM, latter 1846 ib, the 6″ map marks remains of stocks.   BELLA'S COPSE.   BUTLER'S FM, 1846 Snare. CLAYHILL FM.   EIGHT ACRE GULLY.   FERRIS'S FM, Ferres Farm 1817 OS, Ferriss Farm 1839 TA, 1846 Snare.   FIELD BARN, 1846 ib.   FODDERHOUSE COPSE, Fodder House Coppice 1814 EnclA. GRAVELPIT COPSE.   GRAVELPIT FM.   GREYFIELD WD, Greyfield Copse 1817 OS, 1846 Snare.   HAG PIT, 1840 Padworth, probably a peat-pit, v. Padworth 174 and O 69.   HALL PLACE FM.   HARE AND HOUNDS P.H., 1817 OS, Hare and Hounds or Halfway House 1790 Pride.   HIGH WD, 1817 OS, HIGHWOOD GULLY.   HILL FOOT FM.   JENNING'S COPSE, 1846 Snare.   KEAL'S COPSE. KITCHEN COPSE, 1846 Snare.   MALTHOUSE FM AND GULLY. MOUNTSION COPSE, Mount Sion, Mount Sion Shaw 1814 EnclA, v.

283.   NORTHLANDS, 1814 *ib, v.* land.   OLD COPSE, *Old Coppice*
1814 *ib.*   PARK FM.   PIGEONHOUSE GULLY.   RIDGE'S BELT,
shown on 6″ map as a narrow belt of conifers.   RINGS COPSE.
ROOKERY COPSE, 1814 *EnclA.*   SEVEN ACRE COPSE.   SHRUB
WD, 1814 *EnclA.*   SIX BELLS P.H.   SUMMERHOUSE COPSE,
Summer House Coppice and Pightle 1814 *EnclA.*   WHITE'S LANE.
WITHY COPSE.   WOODCOCK GULLY.

FIELD-NAMES

The principal forms in (*a*) are 1814 *EnclA*, except those dated 1846, which
are Snare.

(*a*) Bar Fd; Barn Close; Bourne Ground, Further and Hither; Bourne
Pightle (*v.* burna); Bowling Close; Broom Close, Broom Close Pit (*v.* brōm);
Bullers Wd; Church Ground, Lower and Upper; Clay Pightle (*v.* pightel,
as elsewhere in this parish); Coach House Ground; Coomb Bridge, Little
and Long, Comb Bridge Gutter Piece, Comb Bridge Shaw; Comb Lands
(*v.* cumb); Coney Coppice; Coppice Ground and Pightle; The Croft; Deans
Coppice and Bellows; Dunston Fd; East Mead; Fish Pond Piece; Foxhills;
Furze Ground; Furzehills; Great Ground, Hither and Further; Great Hill;
Great Wd; The Grove; Gull Acre, Gull Acre Shaw; The Hanging (*v.*
hangende); Hay Croft; High Pightle; Horse Leaze; Hunt Fd, Lower and
Upper; Inglefield; Kiln Ground; Langfords, Little and Great; Little House
Ground; Little Mead; Lye, Upper, Middle and Lower, Lye Furlong, Lye
Moor (probably from lēah); Mead Plot; Nuthook Pightle; Owley; Pains
Hills; Paradise (*v.* 283); Pasture Plat; Pear Tree Mead; Picked Ground (*v.*
pīced); Pordage Fm 1846; Pound Close; Round Hill; The Spring; Stable
Pightle; Stones; Thackum; Towney Mdw 1846 (Towney Mead *EnclA*, from
Towney in Padworth 214); Trenley; Vicarage Mdw; Wake Piddle (a
common variant of pightel); Wash Pond Close; Water Mdw; Well Close;
Wharf Fd; Wheathams; Wigley; Wild Goose Pightle; Workshop Mead.

(*b*) *Coley Place* 1703 *PubLib*; *Moorhouse* 1719 *ib, Moorhouse alias Cordery's
Fm* 1725 *et seq ib*; *Norþmed'* 13th *ReadingC*(2) (*v.* norð, mǣd); *Pond House*
1671 *PubLib*; *Rokesham* 1252–5 *FF*, 13th *ReadingC*(2) (probably 'Hrōc's
hamm'); *Southend* 1740 *PubLib*.

Blewbury

BLEWBURY

Bleoburg, (to) bleobyrig 944 (c. 1240) BCS 801, *Bleobirie* 1144 (13th)
    RSO, *Bleoburia, Bleoberia* late 12th *ReadingC*, *Bleoberiam* 1202
    (1227) Ch, *Bleobir'* 1218–19 *FF*, *Bleobury* 1380 Fine
Blidberia, Blitberie 1086 DB
Bleubiri 1091 (13th) RSO

Bleberiam 1144–7 BMFacs *et passim* with variant spellings *Blebiri,*
Bleberi(a), Blebir', Blebire, Blebyr', Blebiry, Blebirre, Blebyry,
Bleber(y), Blebur(y), Blebyre to 1377 Fine
Blieberia 1191 P, *Bliebiri* 1193, 1194 ib, *Blieberi* 1195 ib, *Blieburc*
1214 ib
Blubir' 1212 Fees, *Blubery* 1401–2 FA, 1535 VE
Blybiry 1230 P
Blewbery 1519 AD, 1535 VE, *Blewberry* 1830 OS

The place is named from the hill-fort on the parish boundary, on
the hill now called Blewburton Hill, which is (*ofer*) *bleo byrig dune* 964
(c. 1240) BCS 1143, *v.* dūn. Blewbury is a compound of OE *blēo
'variegated' and burh 'fort'. In *Antiquity* 23 (1949), 208–11, it is
suggested that Blewburton is a corruption of *Blewburdon* from *bleo*
byrig dun; and the hill is in fact called *Bluberdon* in Gough's edition of
Camden's *Britannia* (1789). The article in *Antiquity* also suggests
that the creamy-white chalk soil would have a variegated appearance
when the hill was under cultivation. Bleadon in So has the same first
el. compounded with dūn.

ALDERS FM.　ASHBROOK FM AND HO.　BARLEY MOW P.H.,
Barley Mow 1839 *TA.*　BERRY LANE, cf. *Berrymore* 1548 *LRMB,*
Berry Moor Ayte 1839 *TA*, probably byrig 'manor', referring to the
moated site of Blewbury Fm, *v.* mōr, ēgeð.　BESSEL'S WAY.
BLEWBURTON (*v. supra*).　BLEWBURY BARN, HILL AND MILL.
BLEWBURY DOWN, 1761 Rocque, *Le Downe* 1548 *LRMB.*　BLEW-
BURY FM, *Blewbery Farme* 1591 *SpecCom.*　BOHAM'S FM AND RD.
BRIDUS WAY, *Bridus Furlong and Meadow* 1839 *TA.*　LOWER AND
UPPER CHANCE FM.　CHURN FM AND HILL, cf. *Blewbury Churn*
1761 Rocque, *Churn Park and Hill* 1839 *TA*, and possibly *Churden*
Downe 1548 *LRMB*, 1591 *SpecCom.*　THE CLIEVE.　CURKNELL
PIT.　GREATTREE FM.　GRIM'S DITCH (*v.* 6).　HUNT'S
GRAVE, 1839 *TA.*　ICKNIELD WAY.　LID'S BOTTOM, 1839 *TA*,
AND PLANTATION.　LOAD OF MISCHIEF P.H.　LONDON ST.
MILL BROOK.　NEW BUILDINGS.　NEW INN.　PARSONAGE
FM, cf. *Parsonage Orchard* 1839 *TA.*　ROSE COTTAGE.　SALT-
BOX FM.　SHEENCROFT FM AND COTTAGES, *Shenescrofts, Shene-*
crofte 1550 *LRMB*, *Shene Croft, Sheenecrofte, Shynecroft* 1576
SpecCom, Shincroft 1761 Rocque (first el. possibly scēne 'beautiful').
WATT'S LANE AND SPRING.　WESTBROOK ST.　WHITE SHOOT,

Whiteshoot Piece 1839 *TA*, this minor name occurs several times on the Berks Downs referring to a trackway, *v.* EDD *shoot* sb. 11 'a steep hill; a precipitous descent in a road; a steep, narrow path'.

FIELD-NAMES

The principal forms in (*a*) are 1839 *TA*; early forms for which no date or source is given are 1548 *LRMB*.

(*a*) Above Town Piece; Beer Hill; Blackmans Orchard; Blewberton Piece, Under Blewberton (*v. supra* 152); Buttons Croft and Mdw (*Buttons Close, Crofte, Mylls and Sleyes* 1548 *LRMB, Buttons Sleyes, Mylnes and Londes* 1576 *SpecCom*, probably from a surname; for *sleyes* cf. O 168, Professor Löfvenberg considers the meaning of this f.n. el. to be 'sheep pasture (run)'); Castles Orchard; Char Croft (*Chalcrofte Lande* 1548 *LRMB, Chalke Crofte* 1576 *SpecCom*); Church Moor (*Churche Moare* Jas 1 *TRMB*); Close Orchard; Colts Paddock; Coway Piece; Disons Croft; Down Lands; Green Bench Piece; Greenoughs, Great and Little; The Grove (*La Graue, Graua* 13th *ReadingC, Groves Felde, Le Grovelandes, Grovelande* 1548 *LRMB, Grove londes, Grovelande* 1576 *SpecCom, v.* grāf); Hall Barn Close; Hedgewell Piece; Hop Garden (*v.* hoppe); Horse Croft Mdw (*Horsecrofte, Horssecrofte*); Horseleys Mdw; Lady Croft (*v.* hlǣfdige); Long Alden; Long Mere Downs; Lower Farm Close; Manorial Allotment; Mead Piece; Middle Mead (*Midle Mede, Mydle Mede*); Midsummer Acre; Mill Croft, Orchard and Piece; New Mdw; New Orchard; North Brook Mdw (*Northbrok'* 13th *ReadingC, v.* norð, brōc); Picked Piece (*v.* pīced); Play Close; Pound Furlong; Quakers Croft, Quakers House Croft; Rinous; Robin Hill; Salcom Bottom; Sheards Piece; Shoots Homestall (*Shotts* 1604 *SpecCom*, for Homestall *v.* 145); The Slades (*v.* slæd); Smoke Acre Piece (*v.* 282); Tadcom (*tottencumbe* 'c. 895' (c. 1150) BCS 565, *totan cumbe* 944 (c. 1240) BCS 801, 'Tot(t)a's valley', *v.* cumb); Tan Yard; Thorn Croft Mdw (*Thornycroft*); The Twelves; Water Mdw; Whitlocks; Winterbrook; Woohedge Furlong (possibly 'crooked hedge', *v.* wōh).

(*b*) *Aschesdone* 13th *ReadingC*(2), *Ayshe Downe* (probably referring to the Downs, *v.* 2–4); *Ayssheheys al Aysshencleyse* (*v.* æsc, (ge)hæg); *Barneleygh* (*v.* bere-ærn, lēah); *Barnesplace; Barth Plot; Bedeland* 1199 *FF* (*v.* bydel, land); *Bothe Lands; Brodemede* (*v.* brād, mæd); *Canesmede; Clements Sley* (for *sley* in Blewbury f.ns. *v. supra*); *Le Comen Downe; Cotshutle Mede, Cossettell Mede, Cos(s)etle Mede* (*v.* cot-setla); *Le Courte, Courte Sleys* (*v.* court); *Dame Agnes* 1548 *LRMB, Dame Annis* 1604 *SpecCom; Dingdongs* Jas 1 *TRMB; Donnesden, Donesdens, Donnsdens Furlong; Le Estefelde* 1548 *LRMB, East Feild* Jas 1 *TRMB; Le Free Acr'; Gutterige; Horsfelde, Horssemede; Indune* 13th *ReadingC*(2) (*v.* in, dūn); *Kingesmede, Kingeswod'* 13th *ReadingC*(2), *Kings More, Kynges More* (*v.* mæd, wudu, mōr, Blewbury was a royal manor); *Litle Garden; Longorcherd; Manderheyse* (probably a surname and the pl. of (ge)hæg); *Maylands* 1722 *Bodl; Midlebroke; Newelease; Northegrove; Nottingham Fee* Jas 1 *TRMB; Ouergrove Felde; Popple*

Mede, Puppole Mede, Pup(p)le Mede (*v.* popel, mæd); *Le Shepehouse*;
Sheringhayse (cf. *Manderheyse supra*); *South(e)grove*; *Walters Lake, Waters-*
lake (*v.* lacu, *Water* is a form of the pers.n. *Walter*); *The Warren* 1591
SpecCom; *Welheyse* (*v.* w(i)ella, (ge)hæg); *Le Westefelde*; *Weyre Close*;
Wolverhoke; *Wycheles*.

Bucklebury

BUCKLEBURY

> *Borchedeberie, Borgedeberie, Borcheldeberie, Borgeldeberie* 1086 DB
> *Burchildeburia* 1142–84 (l.12th) *ReadingC, Burchildeberi* 1176 P
>   (p), *Burchildebire* c. 1218–25 (copy) Sar
> *Burchildesbir'* 1198 P, *Burghildesbir'* 1284 *Ass, B(o)urghuldesbury*
>   1340 Cl
> *Burghildebur'* 1217 ClR *et freq* with variant spellings *Burghyldebir'*
>   *Burghildebir', Burghuldebur', Borgheldebir, Burghildeburg, Burg-*
>   *hildebury* to 1316 FA
> *Burhildebur'* 1212 Fees, *Burhildebyry, Burwaldebury* 1260 Ipm
> *Burghilbyr'* 1284 *Ass, Burghullebury* 1307 Ipm, *Burghulbury* 1571
>   *SpecCom*
> *Broghlesbury* 1348 Cl
> *Boucilbury* 1409–16 BM, *Bookylbury* 1544–5 Bodl, *Buckelbery* 1556
>   *ib, Bugglebury* 1651 *ib*

'Burghild's fortified place', *v.* burh; *Burghild* is a woman's name.
Cf. Buckle Street (Wo 2).

HAWKRIDGE

> (*Nemus uocabulum*) *heafochrycg* 956 (c. 1200) BCS 919
> (*boscus de*) *Hauechrugge* 1185 *et seq* P *et passim* with variant spellings
>   *Hauecrugge, Hauecrug', Hauekrig(e), Hauecryg* to 1292 Ipm,
>   *Hauekerigge, Hawekerugg'* 1241 *Ass, Aukerugg'* 1275–6 RH,
>   *Hauekerugge* 1284 *Ass* (p)
> *Hawcredge* 1571 *SpecCom, Hawkeridge* 1744 ArchJ 16, *Hawkridge*
>   1761 Rocque

'Hawk ridge', *v.* h(e)afoc, hrycg. The name occurs also in So
(DEPN).

MARLSTON

> *Verleston'* (sic) 1220 Fees
> *Marteleston'* 1241 *Ass* (p), 1327 *SR, Marteleston* 1275–6 RH, 1316
>   FA, *Martalleston'* 1284 *Ass*

Erleston' *Martel* 1241 *Ass*
Martelston (Richard *Martel's* manor of) 1264–5 InqMisc, *Martils-
tan'* 1391 *RecOffCat*, *Martleston* 1412 FA
Marleston 1571 *SpecCom*
Marston 1535 VE, 1761 Rocque

'Martel's estate'. The place is not mentioned by name in DB, but
it is stated VCH III, 292, to be probably identical with 4 hides in
Bucklebury held by the Count of Evreux, who gave all his lands in
England to a monastery at Noyon. The first recorded sub-tenant of
the manor was Geoffrey *Martel*, mentioned in a document of 1189–99.
Gilbert *Martel* was the tenant in 1240.

The forms from 1220 Fees and 1241 *Ass* might have been considered to indicate an original 'earl's tūn', but as there is no support
for this in the manorial history they are best regarded as erroneous.

RAMSBURY CORNER AND WOOD. There is a hill-fort here, not marked
on the O.S. maps, but discovered by means of an air photograph in
1948, and described in *Transactions of the Newbury District Field Club*,
IX, 2–4, 1951 and ArchJ 60, 49–50. The name is a fourth example of
Ramsbury, 'raven's fort', applied to hill-forts in Berks and east W;
v. Pt 2 for the others. *Totterdown Meadow* in the *TA* (*infra* 160)
probably refers to this camp.

SKILLCROFT, *Skyllecroft* 1252–3 FF, *Skill Croft* 1840 *TA*. The second
el. is *croft*. The first may be identical with that of Skilgate So. It is
suggested (DEPN, Elements I, 124–5) that this is a derivative of the
verb *scilian* 'to separate', which appears in late OE from Scandina-
vian, and that the meaning is 'boundary'. Skillcroft appears on the 6″
map as the name of a very small copse about a quarter of a mile from
the parish boundary, but it may originally have been the name of a
more extensive piece of land. Alternatively, *skil* might be used in a
sense similar to that of *several* in later place-names, denoting a piece
of land not included in the field-system. Professor Löfvenberg
prefers the ME surname *Skille*, but the el. might be expected to be in
the gen. if it were a pers.n. or surname.

All early forms in this section are from Bucklebury, except where
otherwise stated.

THE ALDERS.   THE ALLEY, ALLEY GULLY, *Alley Ground* 1840 *TA*.
ANDREW'S COPSE.   ASH PIECE.   BAZETT'S PLANTATION, 1791–2.

BEDDINGS GULLY, 1791–2.   BEENHAM HATCH, 1666, *Beneham Hatch Gate* 1583, *v.* hæcc-geat, and 150.   BERRY'S COPSE, *Berryes Wood and Gully* 1737, *Berry's Coppice* 1791–2, *Berrys Ground, Meadow and Pightle* 1840 *TA*, cf. Berry's Stile Cottages in Thatcham 189.   BLACKWELL COPSE, 1791–2, *Blackwells Orchard* 1839 *TA*. BLADE BONE INN, *Blade Bone Public House* 1791–2.   BOAR'S HOLE, 1761 Rocque.   BOOT P.H., 1840.   BRADFIELD GATE, 1791–2. BRIFF COPSE, 1791–2, *Brief Copse* 1817 OS, *Briffe Coppice* 1831. BRIFF LANE, 1791–2, *Brief Lane* 1754, cf. *Brief Meadows* 1840 *TA*. Cf. Brief, f.n. in Compton Beauchamp, Pt **2**.   BROCKS LANE, *Brokes Lane Gate* 1582, *Brookes Lane Gate* 1583, *Brocks Lane Gate* 1621, 1709, 1772, *Brix Meadow, Brox Meadow* 1791–2, *Brocks Pightle, Brocks Meadow or Brix* 1840 *TA*.   BROWN'S COTTAGES, 1791–2, *Browns* 1687.   BUCKLEBURY COMMON, 1761 Rocque.   BUCKLE- BURY COTTAGE AND PLACE.   BURGESS' COPPICE, *Burgess Wood* 1830 OS, *Burgess Hill* 1840 *TA*.   BUSHELL'S COPSE.   BUSHNELLS GREEN, 1675, 1840 *TA*, 1830 OS, *Bushenell, Busshendhill* 1565. BUSHNELLSGREEN GATE.   BUSHY COPSE, 1817 OS, 1846 Snare. BYLES'S GREEN, *Byles Green* 1826, *Biles Green* 1831.   CARBIN'S WD may be *terra qui vocatur terra kerebin* 13th *ReadingC*(2), possibly from a pers.n.   CARBINSWOOD LANE.   CHAPEL ROW, 1761 Rocque, *Chapel Rewe* 1617, *Chappel Row* 1698, *Chapell Row Hill* 1755, 1782, cf. *The Chapel* 1665, *v.* VCH III, 296, for the Magdalen Chapel, the ruins of which were removed in 1770, cf. also *Magdalin Hill infra* 162.   CHAPELROW COMMON, 1761 Rocque, 1791–2. CHAPELROW FM, 1791–2.   CHERRYORCHARD COTTAGE, 1791–2, *The Cherry Orchard* 1831.   COLE'S FM, 1823, *Colles* 1564, 1588, *Coles* 1565, *Colliss's* 1697, *Colses Farm* 1783.   COPYHOLD FM, 1846 Snare.   CRAY'S COPSE, 1791–2, *Crays Wood* 1822 OS, *Crays Barn Ground, Crays Meadow* 1839 *TA*.   LITTLE CRAY'S COPSE. THE DELL.   DODD'S SPRING, *Dods* 1830 OS, *Dods Barn Close and Meadow* 1840 *TA*.   DOLLIMERS COPSE, *Delamere's Coppice* 1698, *Dalmiores Coppice* 1737, *Dalemore Coppice* 1791–2. *Dollimers* 1840 *TA*.   DROVE LANE.   ELM COTTAGES, *Elm Cottage* 1831. FIRESIDE CLUB.   FIR TREES P.H., *The Firs* 1830 OS.   FISHPOND GULLY, *Fish Pond* 1812, *The Fishponds* 1831, *Fish Pond Pightle* 1840 *TA* (*v.* pightel).   THE FORTY, 1817 OS, *Green called The Forty* 1698, *v.* forð-ēg 'island in marshland', the site is a spur of land between two streams.   FRANKLIN'S COPSE, *Franklands, Franklands Wood* 1830 OS, *Franklins Coppice* 1840.   GEORGE AND DRAGON

P.H.   GRAVELLY HILL COPSE, *Gravelly Hill and Ground* 1840 *TA*.
GREEN'S OLD FM.   GREYS GULLY, cf. *Grey Croft* 1662, 1791–2,
Grey Close 1840 *TA*.   GUNNELLS FM.   GUTTER ROW, *Buckle-
bury Gutter Row* 1840.   HANGINGS COPSE, *Hangings* 1839 *TA*, *v.*
hangende.   HATCH LANE, 1671, *Hatch Croft* 1583, *Hatch Gate*
1604, *Hatch Meadow* 1840 *TA*, *v.* hæc(c).   HATCHMENTS SHAW,
Long and Short Hatchment 1839 *TA*, *Hatchmans* 1840 *TA*.   HATCH
PIGHTLE GULLY.   HAWKRIDGE WD, *Haukeridg Wood* 1622–3
RentSur, *v.* 154.   HEAD'S COPSE, 1840.   HEADS HILL COPSE.
HEATH COPSE, 1817 OS, *Heath Coppice* 1791–2.   HIGH COPSE,
High Wood 1830 OS.   HIGHCOTE COTTAGES.   HIGHLANDS.
HIGHWOOD COPSE.   HILLFOOT FM, 1830 ib, *Hillfoot* 1831, *Hill
Foot Homestead* 1840.   HILLHOUSE FM, *Hillhouse* 1662, *Hill Farm*
1830 OS.   HILLIERS, *Hilliers Fm* 1846 Snare.   HOCKETT WD,
Hockett Coppice 1791–2, *Hocket Wood* 1817 OS, *v.* 60.   HOLLY
FM AND WD.   HOLLY GROVE, HOLLY GROVE GULLY.   HOLLY
LANE.   HOMEFIELD COPSE, cf. *Le Homcrofte* 1316 *RecOffCat*, *Le
Home Close* 1591, *The Home Feilde* 1622–3 *RentSur*, *Home Field and
Ground* 1839 *TA*, *v.* 93.   THE HOMESTEAD.   HOPGOOD'S FM
AND GREEN.   HORN'S COPSE, 1817 OS, *Horne Coppice* 1737, *Horns
Coppice* 1791–2, 1840, cf. *The Horne* 1662, *v.* horn, the 400' contour
forms a projecting hill south of the Copse.   HORN'S GULLY (near
preceding).   HOUSE LEAS, *Howes Leaze Close and Copis* 1622–3
RentSur, *Houseleys Wood* 1830 OS.   HUNTERS HILL WD, 1830 ib,
Hunters Hill 1840 *TA*.   IRONMONGERS COPSE, *Ironmongers Cop-
pice* 1737, *Ironmongers Mead* 1840 *TA*.   JEWELL'S FM, JEWELL'S
SPRING, *Jewels* 1830 OS, 1846 Snare.   KING'S COPSE, *Kings
Coppice* 1768, *Kings Wood* 1830 OS, 1846 Snare.   LITTLE
CHOLSEYS COPSE, *Choseley Field* 1791–2, *Cholsey Field* 1830 OS, 1840
TA.   LITTLEFENCE WD.   LODGE COPSE (2 examples), cf. *Lodge
Coppice* 1737, 1791–2.   LONG GULLY, *Long Gullat* 1618, *v.*
goulet 'gully'.   LOWER COMMON, 1831, 1843.   MAGPIE FM.
MALTHOUSE WD, 1830 OS, *Malthouse Meadow* 1840 *TA*.   LITTLE
MALTHOUSE COPSE.   MANOR FM AND HO.   MARLSTON PIGHTLE.
MIDDLE WD, 1817 OS, 1846 Snare.   MILES'S GREEN.   MOUNT-
HILL COPSE, *Mount Hill* 1791–2, 1840.   MOUNT PLEASANT.
NEW BARN.   NEW COMMON.   NEW FARM GULLY.   NIGHT-
INGALE COPSE.   NIGHTINGALE'S GREEN, *Nightingales* 1840 *TA*.
NINE ACRE ROW.   NINE ELMS FM, 1830 OS.   NO MAN'S LAND
(near the parish boundary).   NUTTAGE COPSE AND GATE, *Nuttinges*

1583, 1743, *Nutings* 1668, *Nuttage Lane* 1696.   OAKEN COPSE, *Oaken Wood* 1830 OS.   OLD HANGERS, *Hangers Coppice* 1737, *Hangers* 1791–2, *Lower and Upper Hangers* 1840 *TA*, v. hangra. OLD ORCHARD WD, 1830 OS, 1846 Snare, *Old Orchard Grove* 1791–2. OSGOOD'S GULLY.   OVERALL COPSE, *Over Rails* 1791–2, *Overails Meadow* 1840 *TA*, second el. possibly ME reille, v. 281.   PEASE HILL, 1791–2, *Pease Hill Meadow* 1840 *TA*.   PIES COPSE. QUAVIES, *Little Quavies, Quavy Copis* 1622–3 *RentSur*.   RAMS-LANDS SHAW, *Rammeslond* 1407, *Rams Lands and Meadow* 1840 *TA*, v. hræfn, ramm, this is nearly 2 miles from Ramsbury (*supra*). RATCLIFFE SHAW.   READING'S GULLY.   REDHILL COPSE, *Red Hills* 1690, *Red Hill Coppice* 1695, 1840, *Red Hill* 1791–2, 1840, *Redhill Wood* 1830 OS.   RIDGE HILL WD, 1830 ib.   RIVER BARN, 1791–2.   ROSELANDS.   SADGROVE FM, 1817 OS.   SALT'S COPSE, LITTLE SALT'S COPSE, *Sauls Coppice* 1737, 1791–2, *Sols Copse* 1830 OS.   SANDPIT SHAW.   SCHOFIELDS FM.   SCOTLAND, 1831.   SCOTLAND PLANTATION, v. scot 'tax, payment'.   SER-MONS COPSE, *Sermons* 1583.   SHINGLETON.   THE SLADE, *Bucklebury Slade* 1761 Rocque, 1793, 1830, v. slæd.   SMITHCROFT COPSE, *Smythes Croaft* 1621, *Smith's Croft* 1791–2.   SPRING COTTAGE, 1831.   STONECROFT COPSE, *crofta que vocatur Stancroft* 1252–5 *FF*, 'stone croft', v. stān.   THORNCUTS COTTAGE, *Thorncut* 1840 *TA*.   THREE CROWNS P.H., 1817 OS.   TOM HAMPSHIRE. TOMLIN'S FM.   TURNER'S GREEN.   TYLER'S LANE, *Tyler's Barn* 1830 OS.   UPPER COMMON.   VANNERS, 1830 ib, *Vanners Coppice* 1737, *Fanners Coppice* 1739, *Vanners Meadow* 1791–2, *Vanners Lower Meadow and Pightle* 1840 *TA*.   VANNER'S BARN. WALNUT TREE COTTAGES.   WARREN PIT, *The Warren* 1791–2, 1840 *TA*.   WELLCROFT GULLY, *The Well Close* 1662, *Well Crofts, Well Meadow, Well Pound Meadow* 1791–2, *Well Close* 1840 *TA*. WESTROP FM AND GREEN, *Westip Farm and Green* 1761 Rocque, *Westrop* 1840 *TA*, possibly a late-recorded name in *prop*.   WEST-ROP GULLY AND HILL.   WESTROP WD, 1830 OS.   WEST WD, 1830 ib, *Weste Woode* 1571 *SpecCom, The West Wood* 1681. WHITMOOR COPSE, *Whitmore Leyton* 1583, v. hwīt, mōr, lēactūn. WINCHCOMBE FM AND LODGE.   WITHER'S FM (HOME FM on 1″ map).   WOOTTEN'S FM.   WORKHOUSE GREEN, *Workhouse Meadow and Pightle* 1840 *TA*.   WYNALLS COPSE, *Wynde Hill Close, Wynde Hill Copis* 1622–3 *RentSur, Wind Hill Wood* 1830 OS, *Wynals* 1840 *TA*.   ZINZAN PLACE.

FIELD-NAMES

Forms in (*a*) for which no date or source is given are 1840 *TA*, except those marked M, which are *Marlston TA*, 1839; those for which a date but no source is given are Bucklebury. Early forms for which no source is given are Bucklebury, except for those dated c. 1300, 1316, 1391, 1400, 1408 which are *RecOffCat*, and 1622–3 *RentSur*.

(*a*) Adams Bottom 1831 (cf. Adams Land Copse in Hampstead Norris); Angels Pightle (*Angell Corner* 1699, *Angels Piddle* 1791–2); Ash House, Ash House Breach; Avenal(l)s (*Avenalls Gutter* 1694, cf. Avenell's Copse in Thatcham 189); Barkers Pightle and Hill (*Barkers Piddle or Pightle* 1791–2, *Barkers Green* 1836); Barn Close and Ground (*Barn Close* 1791–2); The Beeches; Beenham Bourne 1831 (*v.* 150); Belchers Pightle (possibly *Belcheryng* 1407); Bottom Ground and Pightle; Bray Bones (*Brabans* 1589, *Brabons* 1670, *Brabants* 1687, 1743, *Bradbones* 1791–2, from the surname *Braban*); The Breach (also 1622–3, *v.* brēc); Brick Lane 1830; Broad Close and Fd (*Broadfield* 1674, *Broad Close* 1701); Broome Close, Broom Lands (*Bromelandes* 1544–5 Bodl, 1564, *Bromegrove* 1571 SpecCom, *Broomefeild* 1668, *Broom Lands* 1791–2, *v.* brōm); Butlers Pightle (also 1791–2); The Butts (*v.* butt², butte); Cart-house Pightle; Cate Mdw; Chalk Ground, Chalk Pit Ground M (*Chalk Platt* 1791–2); Church Closes and Lands (*Churchlands* 1689, 93); Clay Close M; Clay Pits Wood 1840; Coppice Close, Lower and Upper Coppice Ground (*Coppis* 1582, 1687, 1705, 1750, *Coppice Ground* 1791–2); The Corner Fd (*Cornersfeildgate, Cornersfeild* 1676); Corners Croft; Court Mdw (*Court Mead* 1685, *Court Meadow* 1765, *Court Gate* 1700, *v.* court); Cow Leaze, Little, Great and Rough Cow Leaze (*The Cowleazes* 1622–3 RentSur, *v.* lǣs); Crockers End Fm 1846 Snare (there is a slight possibility that this represents *Crochestrope* 1086 DB, *v.* 232); Culver Croft Mdw (*v.* culfre); Dean, Great and Little M; Dog Kennel Close 1840 (*Dog Kennel Piece* 1791–2); The Down; Duck Fd; Dunstan Close (*Dunsters Close* 1791–2, *v.* Dunston Park in Thatcham 190); Eales Downs (*Eelesdonne* 1662, *Eelsdowne* 1677, *Eelesdowne* 1677, 1683, *Eeles Downe Lane* 1679, *Yieldown Lane* 1693, *Yieldsdown Lane* 1697, *Elsdon Feild*, *Eelesdownefeild* 1706, *Eelesdown Lane* 1710, *Ellsdown Field* 1712, first el. probably the surname *Ely*); East Croft (*East Crat* 1674); Farthing Pightle (*Farthinges* 1583, 1593, probably from the surname *Farthing*); Fern Cote (cf. *Fern Croft* 1791–2); Flex Fd M (cf. (*on þa*) *fleax æcyres* 956 (c. 1200) BCS 919, *v.* fleax, æcer); Foot Path Ground; Fox Hole Pightle (cf. *Foxelandes* 1593); Furze Cover 1839 M; Gate Close; Gilberts Fd (*Gilbardesfeldes* 1565, *Gilbertsfeild* 1598); Goddards Ground (*Goddardes Grove* 1591); Great Ground; Green Close, The Green Lane (*The Green* 1752); The Grove (also 1662); Grub Ground (*Grubbs* 1791–2, *v.* 281); Ham, Great and Little (cf. *Hams Coppice* 1791–2, *v.* hamm); Hanging a long; Hawkeridge Green; Hay Fd; Hedges Ground; Herberts Ground (*Herbardys Lane* 1407); High Fd (*The Highfield* 1662, *Highfeild Gate* 1693); The Hill (*Le Hill* 1591, 1664); Hill Ground (also 1791–2); Hilly Piece; Hinds Lower Ground, Hinds Mdw

(*Hinds Ground and Meadow* 1791–2); The Hitch (also 1791–2, *v.* hiche); Hogstye Pightle; Hog Tub Ground; Hollidays (*Halydays* 1407, from the surname *Haliday*); Home Close, Ground, Mdw and Platt; Hop Pightle (also 1791–2, cf. *Ye Hop Kiln* 1775); The Hyde (*Hidehacch* 1348 Cl (p), *Hyde* 1485, 1791–2, *Hydelondes* 1512, *Hidelandes* 1565, *v.* hīd, hæc(c), land); Ingwell Pightle (*Ingewell* 1665, *Ingwell Spring* 1689, *Ingwell Pightle* 1791–2, *v.* Inkpen, Pt **2**, for a discussion of the p.n. el. **ing*); Kemp Lands; Kiln Ground, Close and Pightle (*Kiln Close* 1791–2); Kiln Ash; Kings Hill (1791–2); Kings Mdw, Lower Kings, Upper Kings Lane and Mdw (*Kings Meadow* 1791–2); Little Cote (*v.* cot); Little Ground (1791–2); Little Lane 1847; The Lodge 1831; Long Close, Croft, Ground, Mdw and Pightle (*Long Close* 1662, *Long Croft* 1791–2, *The Long Meade* 1672); Malm Close (*Maum Close* 1791–2, *v.* m(e)alm); Mead Close; Meadow, Lower, Middle and Upper, First and Second, Little (*Middle Meade* 1672, *The Meade* 1791–2); Meeting House Ground; Mill Pond Mdw (*The Millpond* 1662); The Moor, Moor Piece and Mdw (*Mormede, Le Morcroft* 1252–5 FF, *The More* 1564, *Moore Acre* 1621, *The Moors* 1791–2, *v.* mōr, mǣd, croft); Oak Lands; Old House Mdw and Orchard; Old Warren; Out Leaze (*v.* ūt, lǣs); Oxleys; Parsons Ground; Pebley Croft (*Pebley Hill* 1791–2); Peggs (*Peggesworth, Peggesworthe Lane* 1565, *Pegsworth* 1670, *Peggs, Peggs Land* 1840; *Peggesworth* appears to be identical with Pegswood Nb, 'Pecg's worð'); Picked or Peaked Close, Picked Pightle (*Picked Piece* 1693, *Pecked Close* 1791–2, *v.* pīced); Pightle (*The Pightle* 1791–2, *v.* pightel, a name found elsewhere in this parish); Pig Trough Ground (*v.* 284); Pikes (*Pike* 1791–2, *v.* pīc); The Plain (*v.* plain); Plantation Mdw; The Plat (*The Platt* 1791–2, *Platts Coppice* 1840, *v.* plat²); Pond(s) Close (*Pond Close* 1672, 1675); Potatoe Ground; Pound Close (*The Pound* 1565); Round Hill and Mdw (also 1791–2); Rye Close and Copse; Sand Fd (*Sandfeld* 1407, *Sandfeild* 1621, 1682, *Sandfeild Lane* 1694, *v.* sand, feld); Sawyers Mead (*Sawyers Meadow* 1791–2); Shaw (*Shaw-in-Warren* 1791–2); Shepherds Close and Fds (*Shepherd Feild* 1694, *Shepperds Close* 1791–2); Shilford Gate 1811 (*Shelford Gate* 1582, *Shilford* 1697, *Shelford Piece* 1791–2); Ship Hill; Short Lands (*Short Landes Closses, Short Lands Copis* 1622–3); Smallbone Close; Snells Ground (*Snells* 1582); Spring Pightle, Pond and Mdw (*Spring Pightle* 1791–2); Staff Close (*v.* 102); Stanford Fd, Mdw and Land (*Stufford* 1626, *Stanford Brook* 1699, probably stān, ford); Sweet Wells; Swilly Ground (*Swilling Piece, Swilly Close* 1791–2, *v.* 253); The T; Teggs Pightle (also 1791–2); The Thean; Thistley Close (also 1791–2); Three Corner Pightle (*Three Cornered Piece* 1791–2); Till Pightle; Totterdown Mdw (this appears from its position in the *TA* to have been in the same part of the parish as Ramsbury 155, and Totterdown could be from **tōtærn-dūn*, cf. the same name in Chieveley 244); Vetch Close (1791–2); Waring Hill (1791–2); Way Fd (*Wayelandes* 1564, *Waye Groundes* 1589, *Way Piece* 1791–2); Welford, Little and Great; Well Pightle, Great; West Close and Croft (*West Croft* 1791–2); West Lands, Lower and Upper, Westlands Mdw; West Moor (*Westmore Coppice* 1675); Wheat Close and Croft (*Wheatcrofte* 1565); Wheeldon Close; Wood Barn Ground and Croft; Workhouse Mdw and Pightle; Yard Pightle; Yew Tree Close (*Yew Tree and Clover Close* 1791–2).

(b) *Alburystreet* 1408 (possibly from Awbery's Fm in Beenham 150); *The Alder Gulley* 1683; *Argaston Houldes* 1582, *Argaston Hoald* 1588; *Banquetting House Ground* 1791–2; *Bean Croft* 1791–2; *Bernards Lane* 1699; *Berrettes Leyton* 1583 (*v.* lēac-tūn); *Birche Farm* 1623; *Blackerlowe* 1565; *Bochenell* 1407; *Boswills Greene* 1699; *Bottoms Kings* 1791–2; *Bowe Bridge* 1598 (*v.* boga, brycg); *Broad Lane* 1682, 1699; *Brook Mead* 1705; *Brouncroft* 1391 (*v.* brūn, croft); *Buckland* 1588, 1591, *Buckland Pittes* 1622 (*v.* bōcland, which occurs in f.ns. in Ca and Ess as well as in major names in southern England); *Burchen Close* 1591, 1664; *Burghildeburgemede* 1391 ('Bucklebury mead', *v.* mǣd); *The Burnt House* 1672, 1675, *Burnt House Ground* 1791–2; *Burnt Oak Piece* 1791–2; *Cetti Thomas* (a cottage) 1583, *Setty Thomas* 1671, *Cetty Thomas* 1701, *Citty Thomas* 1742, *City Thomas* 1750 (*v.* 284); *The Churchway* 1674, 1679, 1690; *Claret Myll* 1407; *Cliftland* 1593; *Coal Pit Piece* 1791–2; *Coldrupp* 1695 (possibly Colthrop in Thatcham 188); *Common Lane* 1582, *Common Meade* 1593, *Common Meadow* 1661, *Common Mead* 1772; *Corne Close* 1662; *Corner Cut* 1775 (*cut* appears to mean 'lot' in O, *v.* 281); *Cowdeane* 1622–3 (*v.* denu); *Dark Lane* 1751; *The Dean* 1791–2; *Dolehache Gate* 1565, *Dole Hatch Gate* 1583, 1589 (*v.* dāl, hæc(c)); *Le Dykedemede* 1252–5 FF, *Dikemed* 1267 *AddCh 19627* ('diked mead', possibly referring to drainage ditches); *The East Wood* 1683; *Elme Landes* 1589; *Elses Bridge* 1593; *Elyslond* 1407 (cf. Eales Downs in (*a*)); *Estend* 1408; *Ewe Close* 1662; *Fence Lane* 1691; *Foxburge* 1583, *Fookebridge* 1593, *Froxburge* 1671 (possibly 'frog bridge', *v.* frosc, brycg); *Free Hatch* 1683 (*v.* hæc(c)); *Le Frithe* 1565, *Le Frith* 1589, *Le Fryth* 1600, *Friths* 1661, *Frythes* 1686 (*v.* fyrhð); *Frith Coppice* 1598, 1731, 1783; *Le Frith Crofte, Frith Gate, Frythhouse* 1591, *Frith House Lane* 1670, *Freeth Lane* 1668, *Frith Lane* 1697, 1761; *Gander Lands* 1791–2; *Gennett Hilles* 1567, *Gemites Hill* 1591; *Gyddyall Lane* 1621 (*Gidihale* 1184 P (p), *la Gidihale* 1234–5 FF (p), *la Gydyhalle* 1252–5 *ib* (p), since all the early forms are from personal names, this may be a surname derived from Gidea Park, Ess 117–8, earlier *la Gidiehall*', *v.* gydig; the Ess name is first recorded in 1258, however, so the Berks name may be an independent example of the same compound); *Goose Close* 1791–2; *Great Gravel Pit* 1760; *Great Hill Ground* 1791–2; *The Great House* 1775; *Great Meadow* 1791–2; *Hackett Coppice, Hatchett* 1791–2 (probably hæcc-geat 'hatch gate', *v.* hæc(c)); *Le Hale* 1252–5 FF (*v.* h(e)alh); *Hall Piece* 1791–2; *Harlock* 1582, *Harlocke Hatch* 1583; *Head Acre* 1791–2; *Le Hether Gate* 1583; *Heycrofte(s)* 1407 (*v.* hēg, croft); *High Green Piece* 1791–2; *Hill Pidle, Hill Pidle Grove* 1668; *Le Hoke* 1316 (*v.* hōc); *Hotch Lane Piddle* 1791–2; *Hound Acre* 1791–2; *Hullepokestret* c. 1300, *Hullpockes* 1593, *Hulpecks* 1662 (probably a surname, *v.* strǣt); *Hundeshille* 1267 *AddCh 19627* (*v.* hund, hyll); *Julianelond* 1356, *Julianlond* 1408, *Julyanheys* 1407 (first el. probably the fem. pers.n. *Julian, v.* Reaney 185); *Kayd Hill Copis* 1622–3; *Kitchen Close* 1791–2; *Larkes Leyton* 1589, *Larts Leiton* 1672, *Laarts Leyton, Long Leton* 1687 (*v.* lēactūn); *Leg Acre* 1791–2 (*v.* Db 757); *Lewendene* 1252–5 FF (*v.* denu); *Lisbone* (a watercourse) 1589, *The Lysborne* 1591, *Lesborond* 1598 (*v.* burna, first el. possibly **lisc* 'reed' suggested in DEPN for Lyscombe Do); *Little Mead* 1682, 1701; *Longmore* 1675; *Long Piddle* 1675; *The Lott Mead* 1676, 1696, 1791–2, *The Lotts*

1772 (*v.* hlot); *Maudlin Hill* 1588, *Magdalin Hill and Well* 1676, *Marlin Hill* 1698, *Marling Hill* 1791–2 (probably from the Magdalen Chapel at Chapel Row, *v.* 156); *Mapell Bridge* 1665, *Maple Bride* 1715; *The Millpond* 1662; *The Mill Pownd* 1662, *Mill Pound* 1676; *Murihulle* c. 1300, *Muriehille* 1391, *Muryhil* 1400 ('pleasant hill', *v.* myrge, hyll); *New Coppice* 1791–2; *Newedik'* 1252–5 FF (*v.* nīwe, dīc); *New Way* 1750; *North Heath* 1691; *Oak Acre* 1791–2; *Orchard Pidle* 1662; *Peartree Close* 1791–2; *Picklemoor Croft* 1791–2; *The Piddle* 1791–2 (as elsewhere in this parish a variant of pightel); *Pitt Acre* 1791–2; *Place Meadow* 1791–2; *Porcok* 1252–3 FF; *Quorundone'* 1400, *Querendons Feld* 1407, *Querindons* 1582, *Quorendon* 1591, *Querundums* 1598, *Quarendons* 1665, *Cornedens Fild* 1564, *Corindons Gate* 1583 (probably a surname, e.g. from Quarlton La or Quorndon Lei); *Rack Close* 1791–2; *Ramsdale, Little* 1791–2; *The Reekyard* 1775; *Rough Halley Grove* 1791–2; *Roundslands Gully* 1791–2; *Shiphouse Bridge* 1698 (probably *sheephouse*); *Shop Pightle* 1791–2; *Smock Acre and Pightle* 1791–2 (*v.* 282); *Southefylde Pyke* 1544–5 Bodl, *Southfield Picks* 1742 Bodl (*v.* pīc); *South Hill* 1791–2; *Sparrow Meade* 1626; *Stanbrige* 1252–5 FF (*v.* stān, brycg); *Stanforland* 1391, *Stanfurlong* 1400 (*v.* stān, furlang); *Stareworke Close* 1668; *Sterts* 1670 (*v.* steort); *Stonylane* 1391, 1400; *Straight Acre* 1791–2; *Strandputcroft* c. 1300, *Stranputcroft* 1391, *Stanputcroft* 1400 (the name may be 'stonepit croft', with some corruption in the earlier spellings, but there was a Stephanus *de Strande* in the neighbouring parish of Hampstead Norris in 1231 (Bracton); *v.* strand, stān, pytt, croft); *The Three Gates* 1682, 1760; *Tythyngsman's Acre* 1604, *Tithingman's Acre* 1679 (a *tithingman* is either a parish peace-officer, or a collector of tithes); *Water-at-Readinge* (Pightle called) 1583; *Waterhouse* 1751; *Watry Lane* 1669, *Watery Lane* 1676, 1738, *Water Lane* 1697; *Weavers Hills* 1687, *Weabourn Hills* 1690, *Weybourn Hills* 1693; *Westchepe* 1591, *Westchepe Gate*, *Westcheape* 1598, *West Cheap Wood* 1737, *West Cheap Green* 1775, *West Cheap Coppice* 1791–2, *Westcheap Lane* 1793 ('west market', *v.* west, cēap); *Westend* 1408; *Whitehouse Corner* 1691; *Wollefrige Crofte* 1565; *Wood Gate* 1706, 1749; *Wordy* 1252–3 FF (*v.* worðig); *Yonside Closes* 1621.

Cholsey

CHOLSEY

Ceolesig, (to) ceolsige c. 895 (12th) BCS 565, *(to) ceolesige* 945 (12th) ib 810, *(æt) Ceolsige* c. 980 (e.11th) ASWills, *(into) Ceolesige* 1003–4 (c. 1240) ib, *(æt) Ceolesege* s.a. 1006 ASC D
Celsei, Celsea 1086 DB
Cealseia c. 1125 *AddCh 19575*, *Cealseiam* 1202 (1227) Ch
Chausi 1167 P *et passim* with variant spellings *Chaus(e)ia, Chausie, Chausy(a), Chausey(e), Chausee* to 1332 cl; *Schauseye* 1284 *Ass*
Chelseia 1176 P (p), *Cheleseia* l.12th ReadingC, *Chelseye* 1311–12 FF, 1327 SR, 1401–2 FA, *Cheleseye* 1318 Cl, *Chellesey(e)* 1396 AD
Chauweseia 1198 Cur

Cholsey 1316 FA, 1401 Fine
Cholsley 1761 Rocque

'Cēol's island', *v.* (ī)eg; the form dated 945 occurs in the bounds of Brightwell and Sotwell, and appears to refer to Cholsey Hill, which is a mile N.W. of the village. (ī)eg is here used in the sense 'dry ground in a marsh'.

The name occurs also in the phrase *Germanus Ceolesigensis æcclesiæ abbas* 997 (c. 1150) KCD 698 (the site of a monastery is shown on the 6″ map). The forms *Chausi* etc. gave the surname which occurs in Chazey Heath, Fm and Wd in Mapledurham O 60.

BUCKLANDS, *Boklande* 1294 Queen, *Boklonde* 1328 *ib*, *Boclonde* 1348 *ib*, *le Bokland* 1361 *ib*, *Buckland Feild* 1550 RentSur, *Bukelande* 1550 LRMB. OE bōcland 'land granted by charter', cf. the same name, Pt 2.

LOLLINGDON, *Lolindone* 1086 DB, *Lollindon'* 1220 Fees, *Lolledon'* 1241 *Ass*, *Lolindune* 13th *ReadingC*, *Lollingdon'* 1247–8 *Ass*, *Lollindon* 1271 Ipm, *Lollingdon* 1275–6 RH, *Lollyngdon, Lollyngton* 1327 Banco, *Lorington Farm* 1761 Rocque, 1790 Pride, *Loringdon Fm* 1830 OS. The name consists of dūn 'down', probably compounded with a personal name and -ing-. Stenton (40) suggests that the personal name is the well-recorded *Lulla*, and the -o- of the forms due to Norman influence. But since this development has not occurred in other place-names containing *Lulla*, such as Lullington Sx 417 which shows only a small proportion of forms with -o-, it might perhaps be safer to postulate on OE name **Lolla*.

UNHILL WOOD, *Unholt, Dunholt* 1241 *Ass* (p), *Donholte* 1275–6 RH, (*in bosco de Chauseye de*) *Hunhalt'* 1284 *Ass*, *Woode of Unholt, Wood called Unhold* 1550 RentSur, *Nonholte, Bosc' de Unholte, Bosc' voc' Unholde* 1550 LRMB; *Unwell Farm* is shown 1761 Rocque. The second el. is holt 'wood'. The first is uncertain, but it seems reasonable to assume that the original form was *Hun-*, and it might possibly be a plant-name, such as OE hūne 'hoarhound (*marrubium vulgare*)', found in Hound Ha (DEPN); cf. also Arundel Sx 136–7, which contains hār-hūne 'hoarhound'.

WINTERBROOK, *Winterbroc* Hy 3 Wallingford, *Wynterbrok'* 1284 *Ass*, *Wynterbrok* 1315 Pat, 1318, 1328, 1330 Queen, *Wynterbroke Syche*

1516–17 *Rent-Sur, Winterbrooke* 1550 *ib, Winterbrook* 1738 ArchJ 20, identical in meaning with the common name Winterbourne, for which *v.* 277. The form from 1516–17 has sīc 'small stream' added. Two references have been noted to a 'winter ditch' (*Winterdich* Hy 2 Wallingford, *Wynterdych* Ed 2 Wallingford) in contexts which suggest that it is the stream immediately to the N. of Winterbrook, which forms the boundary between Wallingford and Cholsey, and is marked Bradford's Brook on the 1″ map.

ABBEY BARN.   BAKER'S FM.   BLACKALL'S FM.   BOW BARN, 1841 *TA*, BOWBARN COTTAGES, BOW BRIDGE, 1830 OS, *v.* **boga.** BRADFORD'S BROOK (*v.* Winterbrook *supra*).   BREACH HO AND FM, *The Breche* 1550 *RentSur, v.* **brēc.**   BRENTFORD TAILOR INN. CARDYNHAM.   CAUSEWAY FM.   CHEQUERS INN.   CHOLSEY DOWNS, *Cholsey Down* 1840 *TA*, cf. *Downe Meade* 1550 *RentSur, The Down Mead* 1851 *TA*.   CHOLSEY HILL, 1830 OS, *Cholsley Hill* 1761 Rocque *v.* 163.   CHOLSEY FM.   CLAPS LANE.   CRANFORD HO.   CWICHELM.   DOWNS FM.   THE ELMS.   HALFPENNY LANE, 1830 OS, 1841 *TA, v.* 285.   THE HAZELS.   HEATHERCROFT FM, OLD HEATHERCROFT FM.   HIAWATHA.   HILLGREEN FM AND PONDS, *Hillgreen* 1761 Rocque.   HOLIDAY'S FM, *Holidayes* 1550 *RentSur.*   HONEY LANE, HONEYLANE FM, *Honey Lane Croft* 1841 *TA, v.* **hunig.**   KENTWOOD FM, *Kentwood Farme* 1550 *RentSur, Kentwoodferme* 1550 *LRMB*, named from a family surnamed *Kentwood* (doubtless from Kentwood in Reading 172), who held it in the late 14th cent. (VCH III, 298).   KINGSTANDING HILL, *Kings Standing Hill* 1830 OS, *v.* **standing.**   LA HAYE.   LOLLINGDON COPSE, LOLLINGDON HILL, *Lollington Hill* 1841 *TA* (*v.* 163).   MANOR FM.   MILL COURT, *Cholsey Mill* 1830 OS.   NAG'S HEAD P.H.   OFFLAND FM.   OLD BUTTS.   PANCROFT FM, *Pancotts Headlands* 1841 *TA*.   PAPIST WAY.   POUND FM. RECTORY.   RED LION P.H.   SHEEPHOUSE BARN, *Sheepehouse* 1550 *RentSur, Shepehowse Garden* 1550 *LRMB*.   STAR INN AND TERRACE.   THE THATCHED HOUSE.   UNHILL BOTTOM, NORTH AND SOUTH UNHILL BANK (*v.* 163).   UNION COTTAGES.   WEST END, 1830 OS, cf. *Le Westende Close* 1550 *LRMB, West End Croft* 1851 *TA*.   WESTFIELD NURSERY, *West Field* 1851 *TA*.   WHITE CROSS.

FIELD-NAMES

The principal forms in (*a*) are 1841 *TA*; early forms for which no date or source is given are 1550 *RentSur*.

(*a*) Above Mill Mere; Ambrose Croft; Aston Croft (cf. *Aston Moore*); Baldrood Furlong; Barn Piece; Bier Way; Bletchen Hill Furlong, Bletchen Slade Bottom; Bonnie Furlong; Bowslade (not near Bow Bridge *supra*, cf. *Bow Peace* 1550 *RentSur*, *v.* boga); Brewed Hill; Brook Furlong; Bush Acres (*Bush Close*); Chalk Pit Furlong (*Chalke Pytt* 1550 *LRMB*); Cheese Hill (*v.* 283); Clay Fd and Furlong; Cob Close; Crake Furlong; Croft Lands (*Le Croftes* 1328 *Queen*); Crooked Furlong; Crosslands; Crumps Corner; Dry Ditch Furlong; East Croft; Elder Furlong (*Elrefurlong* c. 1260 *Queen*, *v.* ellern); Frogpit (*Frogg Pitt*); Gardiners Furlong and Close (*Gardeners Meade* 1550 *RentSur*, *Gardiners* 1735 *PubLib*); God Speed Furlong (*v.* 283); Gore Furlong (*Gore*, *v.* gāra); Gossiter Furlong; The Grove; Hayway Furlong and Gate, Broad and Short Hayway; Headland; Hill Croft and Furlong (*Hellfeild*, *Hill Feild*, *Litlehell*, *v.* hyll); Holly Bush Piece; Idd Mead (*Idemeade*); Irregular Lands; Kiln Piece; Lanes Hedge Furlong; Lilsborough Hill; Loll Hill Furlong; Long Clot Furlong; Long Lands; Lot Mead; Malm Pit, Short Malm Way (*v.* m(e)alm); Mead Furlong; Meadow, Great and Little; Millham Mead (*Milnham*, *v.* myln, hamm); The Moors, East and West Moor (*Moore Ditch*, *Moore Lake*, *Moorehocks*, *Eastmore End*, *Westmore*, *v.* mōr); Owley Furlong; Picked Acres and Furlong (*v.* pīced); Pightle (*v.* pightel); Portway Furlong (*v.* portweg); Pudmore Croft (*Podmore Mill*, *Pudmore*); Quack Ditch; Ryeslade; Sandhills, Long and Short; Scotch Hedge; Shooting in the Downs; Short Furlong; Short Gravels; Smoke Furlong (*v.* 282); Sparrow Furlong; The String, String Furlong (*v.* 282); Way Furlong; West Croft Lands (*Westcroft*); Wet Furlong; Wheat Furlong; Wheathill; White Piece; Wigsbury Furlong; Winding Furlong; Woodlands.

(*b*) *Bloomes Grove*; *Broad Close*; *Dangreene Crosse* 1550 *RentSur*, *Dangeen Crosse* 1550 *LRMB*; *East End*; *East Street*; *Edsinn Meade* 1550 *RentSur*, *Edsam Mede* 1550 *LRMB*; *Henclose*; *The High Close*; *Highfeild*; *Hollynyden Feild*; *Home Croft and Feild*; *The Horse Croft*; *The Long Lease* (*v.* lǣs); *Lowenden* 1550 *RentSur*, *Lawnden* 1550 *LRMB*; *Monkendeane, Monkendon* (*v.* munuc, denu, there was a monastery at Cholsey); *Oakehanger* (*v.* āc, hangra); *Oldsham Meade*; *Pastmore*; *Petham* 1550 *RentSur*, *Retham* 1550 *LRMB*; *Pidle Close* 1550 *RentSur*, *Lower Piddle* 1701 *Bodl* (a variant of pightel); *Prestesforlang* 1318 *Queen* (*v.* prēost); *Sandfeild*; *Sharpenall Downe*; *La Smytheslonde* 1325 *Queen*; *Someheyst*; *South Mill Meade and More*; *Tadsey*; *The Thames Meade*; *Upstreete* (*v.* strǣt); *The Vineyard*; *La Vortie* 1325 *Queen*, *Forty House, Tythinge of Forty* (*v.* forð-ēg); *Westfeild*; *Winchurst* 1550 *RentSur*, *Wynchehurste* 1550 *LRMB* (*v.* wince, hyrst).

Grazeley

GRAZELEY

(*on*) *grægsole* (*burnan andlang burnan on*) *grægsole* (*hagan*) c. 950
(c. 1240) BCS 888

Greshull' 1198 P, 1269 *FF*

Greyshull' 1241 *Ass* (p), *Greishulle*, *Greysulle* 13th *ReadingC*,
Greyshulle 1294 *SR*, *Greysulle* 1327 *ib*, *Greyshall* 1539–40
ReadingA, *Greyshull* 1659 *PubLib*

Greseley, *Greshill'*, *Greynghull'* 1284 *Ass*, *Grasley* 1662–3 *PubLib*,
Gresly als Greshall 1758 ArchJ 14, *Grassley* (*Green*) 1761
Rocque, *Grazeley* (*Green*) 1790 Pride

'Badgers' wallowing-place', *v.* græg², sol. The second el. was
confused with hyll and lēah. The village of Grazeley is in Shinfield;
the civil parish (which does not include the village) owes its existence
to arrangements made in the 19th cent. (VCH III, 261, 276).

BELL PITS AND COPSE (near OLD BELL P.H.), *Lower and Upper Bell
Ground* 1846 *TA*.   BURNTHOUSE BRIDGE, FM AND LANE, *Burnt
House Pasture* 1846 *TA*.   BURGHFIELD BROOK.   FULLER'S LANE.
GRAZELEY MANOR FM.   KENT'S GREEN, *Kent's Common Pasture*
1846 *TA*.   RIDER'S LANE.

FIELD-NAMES

The principal forms in (*a*) are 1846 *TA*.

(*a*) Appletons Common Mdw; Balls Forehead (cf. The Forehead in
Stratfield Mortimer 217); Barley Croft; Bridgewater Ground; Broadway
Common Pasture; Chamberlain Common Pasture; Cooper Crutch; Coppice
Ground; Coppice Hale (*v.* h(e)alh); Downhams Pightle (*v.* pightel); Elms
Bottom and Broad; Hardage; High Fd; Home Close, Common and Mdw;
Hunts Pightle; The Lakes, The Lakes Mdw; Lanes Green Common; Long
Pightle; Long Slip (*v.* slipe); The Lotts (*v.* hlot); New Mdw; North Close;
Oat Harish (*v.* ersc); Palmers Pightle; Park Close; Pasture Piece and Slip;
Pear Tree Close; Pond Common Pasture; Pond Mead; Puss Close, Long
Puss; Railway Close; Round Mead; South Fd; Wallace Ground.

(*b*) *Holt Lane* 1761 Rocque (*v.* holt).

Pangbourne

PANGBOURNE

(*at*) *Peginga burnan, Pægeinge burnan* 844 (c. 1240) BCS 443
Pangeborne, Pandeborne 1086 DB, *Pangeburna* c. 1160 OxonCh *et
passim* with variant spellings *Pangeburne, Pangeburnia, Pange-
born', Pangeburn'*
Pankebourne 1412 FA
Pangbourn 1517 D Inc

'Stream of Pǣga's people', *v.* -inga-, burna, and 16.

PANGBOURNE STREET-NAMES

HORSHOE RD.   MEADOWSIDE RD.   THE MOORS *v. Moor Copse* 168.   READ-
ING RD.   RIVERVIEW RD.   THAMES AVE.

BERE COURT, 1761 Rocque, cf. *La Bere* 13th *ReadingC, Bere* 1305 Cl
(p), *The Bere* 1542 Leland, (*manor of*) *Beare* 1573 VCH III 303,
'swine pasture', *v.* bǣr².

BOWDEN GREEN, LOWER BOWDEN, LOWER BOWDEN FM, UPPER
BOWDEN FM, cf. *Pangbournebovedowne, Bovedowne, Bovedown Hethe*
1548 *LRMB, Pangborne Bovedowne* 1552 *LRMB, Bonedowne* 1667
*PubLib(Clayton), Lower Bowden Fm, Upper Bowden Fm, Bowden
Green* 1830 OS, 1846 Snare, *Lower Bowden* 1869 *PubLib*, 'above the
hill', *v.* bufan, dūn, identical with Bovingdon Bk 187-8. The land
slopes fairly steeply from here to the Thames valley at Pangbourne.

MAIDEN HATCH, MAIDENHATCH FM, *Madenhecka* c. 1175 *AddCh
19601* (p), *Madeh'* c. 1195 *AddCh* 7202 (p), *Madenhache* 1241 *Ass* (p),
Madenhacch' (p), *Madehach'* 1294 *SR, Madenhacche* 1327 *ib, Mayden
Hatche* 1552 *LRMB, Maidenedge* 1761 Rocque, 1790 Pride. The
second el. is hæc(c) 'wicket gate', referring either to a gate giving
access to a wood (if the name originally denoted the large house called
Maiden Hatch) or to a sluicegate on the R. Pang (if it belonged
originally to Maidenhatch Fm). The absence of any early forms with
Mayd- which certainly refer to this place is against the etymology
'maiden hatch', suggested by the modern spelling. (Cf. the spellings
for Maidencourt, Pt 2 and Maidenhead 53.) The first el. may be a
personal name *Māda*, which is postulated for Madingley C and
Madeley St and Sa, *v.* C 181.

ALDER COPSE.   BARE LEYS, *Bereleez* 1548 *LRMB*, *Bere Leaze* 1839
TA, *v.* bǣr², lǣs, this is not near Bere Court.   BARNARD'S COPSE,
Barnards Gritts 1839 *TA*, for Gritts *v. Grets* 169.   BARTHOLOMEW'S
BOTTOM PLANTATION, *Bartholomews Bottom* 1839 *TA*.   BARTHO-
LOMEW'S COPSE, *Bartholomew Copse* 1830 OS.   BEAR, GREAT AND
LITTLE, BERE PARK, these are near BERE COURT, *v.* 167.   BERRY'S
COPSE.   BLENHEIM BARN.   BOTTINGHAM SHAW, *Bottinghams*
1839 *TA*.   BOWRAM'S SHAW, *Bowram, Bowram Woode* 1548
LRMB.   BROADFIELD'S PLANTATION, *Broadfields Field* 1839 *TA*.
BROOMCLOSE PLANTATION, *Bromeclose* 1548 *LRMB*, *Broom Close*
1839 *TA*, *v.* brōm.   BROOMHILL PLANTATION, LITTLE BROOM
PLANTATION, *Great Broom Field*, *Little Broom Hill* 1839 *TA*.
CLAYESMORE SCHOOL.   COLERIDGE LANE.   COLLIER'S PLANTA-
TION, *Colliers* 1548 *LRMB*, 1839 *TA*.   COURTLANDS, COURTLANDS
HILL.   DARKLANE.   DARKLANE COPSE, 1830 OS, 1846 Snare.
FLOBRIGHAM'S COPSE.   FLOWERS FM (1846 Snare) AND HILL,
Flowers in the Marsh c. 1667 *PubLib*.   FRANKLIN'S COPSE, LOWER
FRANKLIN'S COPSE, *Frankeleyns, Copic' voc' Frankelyns, Nether
Frankeleyns* 1548 *LRMB, Franklands Woods* 1830 OS, from the
surname *Franklin*.   FULLER'S COPSE, 1830 OS.   GREENHILL
PLANTATION, *Greenhill* 1839 *TA*.   HANGING GROUND PLANTATION,
v. hangende.   HERRIDGE COPSE, *Herridges Moor and Pightle* 1839
TA.   HIGHGROVE WD, *Highgrove* 1548 *LRMB*.   HOARECROFT
SHAW, *Horecroft* 1548 *LRMB, Hoare Croft* 1839 *TA*, *v.* hār² 'grey',
the wood is not near a boundary.   HOGMOOR COPSE, *Hog Moor*
1839 *TA*.   WEST INHAMS PLANTATION, *Inholmes* 1548 *LRMB*,
West Inhams, East Inhams Sheep Croft 1839 *TA*, *v.* innām.   JES-
MOND HILL.   MAIDENHATCH FM (1846 Snare) AND BROOK, *v.* 167.
MARSH FM, *Pangborne Marsshe* 1548 *LRMB, Ye Marsh* 1667 *PubLib*-
(*Clayton*), *Pangbourne Marsh* 1839 *TA*.   MOOR COPSE, FURTHER
MOOR COPSE, *Le More, Moreclose* 1548 *LRMB, The Moor, Further
Moor* 1839 *TA*, *v.* mōr.   MOUNT COPSE.   NEW TOWN.
NORTHRIDGE BOTTOM PLANTATION, NORTHRIDGEHILL COPSE AND
SHAW, *Northrige* 1548 *LRMB*, *v.* hrycg.   GREAT OTWELL'S
PLANTATION, *Otwells* 1548 *LRMB*.   PEATMOOR COPSE, cf. *Peat
Mead Meadow* 1839 *TA*.   RUNDELLSFIELD PLANTATION, *Rundells
Field, Rundells Pit Field* 1839 *ib*.   SAWYER'S COPSE, 1830 OS.
SHEEP CROFT PLANTATION, *Shepecroft* 1548 *LRMB*.   SHOOTER'S
HILL, *Shoters Hill* 1548 *LRMB, Shooters Hill* 1667 *PubLib*(*Clayton*),
1761 Rocque, 1839 *TA*, *v.* scēotere, the same name occurs in K,

Nth, Wa. SOUTHWAY PLANTATION. STILE ACRE SHAW, *Stile Acres* 1548 *LRMB*, 1839 *TA*, v. stigel. THAMES VIEW. TURNER'S CLOSE PLANTATION. WAKEMAN'S COPSE. WALK COPSE. WELLFIELD WD AND GROVE. WEST END, *West End Ground* 1839 *TA*, *West End Ho* 1846 Snare. WILLIAM'S HEATH PLANTATION. WINLOED.

FIELD-NAMES

Principal forms in (*a*) are 1839 *TA*; early forms for which no date or source is given are 1548 *LRMB*.

(*a*) Barn Close (*Barneclose*); Belle Grave Dean (*Belgroves, Bell Groves, Belgrovedeane, v.* bēl[1], belle, grāf); Black Fd; Brixhams, Lower and Upper (*Brykesham, Brikham*); Brook Furlong (*Le Broke, Broke Closes, Brokefurlong, Broke Piddell, Brokes Felde, v.* brōc); Burgesses Fd; Butlers Broom (*v.* brōm); Chalk Pit Pightle (*v.* pightel, as freq. in this parish); Church Fd, Lower (*Churchefelde*); Cleaver Fd; Coopers Pightle; Down Fd (*Downefelde*); Dun Croft, Great and Little (possibly *Dongcrofte*, 'dung croft'); East Croft (*Estecrofte*); East Moor (*Estemore, v.* mōr); Elephant Moor; Garden Close; Great Ground; Home Close and Ground (*Home Close and Grove*); Keep Croft (*Kepe Crofte*, first el. possibly cȳpe, 'osier-basket', or OE *cēpe 'look-out place', *v.* Löfvenberg 32); Kiln Pightle; Lakard, Lower and Upper; Lambs Leys; Lane End Fd; Lyfords Lane Pightle, Lyfords Thorn; Malthouse Close; Marsh Mdw; Massledurham; Miles Fd, Great and Little (*Myles Croftes*); Mill Mead; The Moor; Mowing Dairies; Notts Pightle; Oaken Grove; Oak House Croft; Pangbourne Hill and Mdw; Pictons Pightle; Pitt Croft Boults (cf. *Pitclose, Pitheys*); Pound Ground; Powels Pightle; Ridge Bottom and Hill; Road Pightle; Row Pit Piece; Rye Fd; Stareley Fd (possibly *Steverleyhethe, v.* stæfer, lēah, hǣð); Stoneham, Great (*Stonehamfelde, v.* stān, hamm, feld); Thorn Close (*Thorne* 1341 NonInq (p), *Thorneclose, Thornehethe* 1548 *LRMB*, *Thorn Heath* 1761 Rocque, *v.* þorn); Tower Park (The Tower 1830 OS, 1846 Snare); Warren, Lower, Middle and Upper; Water Mead; Way Fd; Well's Pit; West Fd (*Le Westefelde*); West Moor (*Westemore*, cf. East Moor *supra*); Wheat Croft (*Wheatecrofte*); Wilders Grove (*Wilders More*); Yew Tree Hill Fd.

(*b*) *Agnes Crofte; Alwyns Deane; Bere Hatche Piddell, Esteberefelde, Middell Bere Felde, West Berefelde* (*v.* bǣr[2], hæc(c), and cf. Bere Ct *supra*); *Berymarsshe, Burymarshe, Bury Grove, Berygrove* (*v.* burh, mersc, grāf); *Billetts More; Blakebusshes; Blakepitts Piddell* (a variant of pightel, as elsewhere); *Le Breche* (*v.* brēc); *Brode Leez* (*v.* brād, lǣs); *Bromeheyse, Bromybere* (*v.* brōm, (ge)hæg, bǣr[2]); *Bulleys More; Bynemore; Calves Le(e)z* (*v.* lǣs); *Coppidhall* (*v.* coppede); *Cotts More; Cowecrofte, Cowlez, Cowe More, Cowe Perok* (*v.* cū, croft, lǣs, mōr, pearroc); *Dangeon Croft; Ferne Piddell; Gorlyngs; Grets, Over, Nether and Oken, Nether Greats* (*v.* grēot); *Grouecroft; Hillhowse, Hillhowse Garden; Hokerd Grove; How(e)-crofte, Grete and Litle* (*v.* hōh, croft); *Huwemede* 1255–8 *FF* (probably

'Hugh's mead'); *Le Hychynfelde, Hychyn Grove* (*v.* heccing); *Kents Piddell*; *Le Lambeclose*; *Langham* (*v.* lang, hamm); *Langemede* (*v.* lang, mǣd); *Le Laynes* (*v.* leyne); *Ley Crofts* (*v.* lǣge); *Long Acr*; *Mede Close*; *Millam Mede* (*v.* myln, hamm); *Mill Broke*; *Monken Mede* (*v.* munuc, mǣd); *Neckathorn* (possibly the same name as *Nachededorn* Hundred *infra* Pt **2**); *Newcroft, Newecrofte Grove*; *Okkeys*; *Oldeheyse* (*v.* (e)ald, (ge)hæg); *Overclose*; *Pakheys, Pekheyse, Pekehouse Mede, Pykeheysse* (*v.* pīc, (ge)hæg); *Le Peroke* (*v.* pearroc); *Piked More* (*v.* pīced, mōr); *Plomecrofte* (*v.* plūme, croft); *Rose Piddell*; *Le Ryde* (*v.* ryde); *Sares Copps*; *Seuerall Furlonge* (*v.* 282); *Shadwell* (probably 'boundary stream', cf. O 14); *Sharelands, Sherelande, Sherlande Close* (*v.* sc(e)aru); *Shepe Wasshing Piddell*; *Smallham* (*v.* smæl, hamm); *Southfelde*; *Spanyshe Busshe* (probably a plant or tree; the term is not in EDD or NED); *Tanhowse* (a building for tanning); *Thamyse More*; *Thelemede* (Theale 221 is not contiguous); *Totehill* (*v.* tōt-hyll); *Wade Meade* 1667 *PubLib*(*Clayton*); *Warwike*; *Wellclose*; *Westedole, Weste Dolls* (*v.* dāl); *Wheatecrofte*; *Whyte Acr*; *Woodheysse* (*v.* wudu, (ge)hæg); *Wydefelde, Wydegrove* (*v.* wid, feld, grāf).

Reading (including Caversham)

READING

(*to*) *Readingum* c. 900 (s.a. 871) ASC A, (*æt*) *Readingan* c. 980 (e.11th) ASWills, *in loco Readingon* c. 1000 Æthelweard,† *Readingan* c. 1025 HydeR, *Readin* c. 1047 Coin, *Readingas* c. 1100 *EgCh 2211*, *Readinges* l.13th Gerv

Rædigam 893 (e.11th) Asser, *Raedingcnensi æcclesiæ* 1130 (12th), *Raedingum* 1135 (12th) John of Worc

Readii c. 1044–6 Coin

Red(*d*)*inges* 1086 DB, *Reding*' 1152, 1153 BMFacs, *Redynges* 1295 FF *et freq* with variant spelling *Redyngges*; *Redyng* 1330 Fine *et freq* with variant spelling *Redinge*

Radinges 1152, 1153 BMFacs *et freq* with variant spelling *Radingas, Radingum, Radingges*; *Radinge* 1199–1200 MemR, 1224 (copy) Sar, *Rading* c. 1230 (copy) ib *et freq* with variant spelling *Radding*

Reyding' 1268 *Ass*

'The people of Rēad(a)', *v.* -ingas. *Rēad*(*a*) means 'the red one', *v.* Introd.

† This form can still be made out from the charred fragments of the MS of Æthelweard's Latin version of ASC.

READING STREET-NAMES†

ALL SAINTS' STREET (lost), *Vicus Omnium Sanctorum* 13th *ReadingC(2)*; for the chapel of All Saints, mentioned in connection with St. Mary's Church c. 1200, *v.* VCH III, 377

ARGYLE RD AND ST, *Argyll Road* 1875 *PubLib.*

BATH RD, 1738 *PubLib.*

BATTLE ST, cf. *Batal Lane* 1427, 1432 VCH III 366, *Bataylelane* 1427, 1429 AD, *v.* 175.

BLAGRAVE ST, John *Blagrave* of Southcot left part of the money with which *Blagrave's Piazza*, an arcade adjoining St. Lawrence's Church, was built in 1620. It was demolished in the 19th cent.

BOARDED LANE, *Rack Close Lane* 1805 *PubLib, Rack Close Lane als Boarded Lane* 1823 *PubLib.*

BREND LANE (lost), *Le Brendelane* 1332 (14th) *ReadingC(3), Brende Lane* Ed 6 *LRMB*, 'burnt lane', *v.* brende².

BRIDGE ST was earlier *Seven Bridges* (*Septem Pontes* Ed 1 (14th) *ReadingC(3), Seven Bridges* 1761 Rocque).

BROAD STREET, 1696 *PubLib.* The eastern part of this was occupied by two streets known as *Bocheria* 13th *ReadingAlm, Le Bocher Row* 1504 AD and *Chesrewe* 14th *ReadingAlm, Chese Rewe* 1520 ArchJ 5, 1552 *LRMB, Cheese Row* 1582 *PubLib. Cheese Row* later became *Fish Row* (*Fisher Row* 1689, 1799 *PubLib*).

BRUNSWICK ST, 1849 *Bodl.*

CASTLE ST, *Castelstrat* 13th *ReadingC(2), Castelstret* n.d. (14th) *ReadingC(3), Castelle-Streat* 1542 Leland, *Castle St* 1682 *PubLib.*

CASTLE HILL, 1846 Snare. For the castle, which was in existence t. Stephen, *v.* VCH III, 342.

CAVERSHAM RD, 1805 *Bodl.*

CHAIN ST, cf. *Chain Lane* 1761 Rocque.

CHURCH ST, 1805 *PubLib.*

COLEY AVE AND HILL, *v.* 176.

CROSS ST was earlier *Gotterlane* 13th *ReadingAlm, Guttereslane* 1313 (14th) *ReadingC(3), Le Gutterlane, Le Goturlane* 1490 AD, *Guttur Lane* 1512 AD, *Gutter Lane* 1552 *LRMB*, 'gutter lane'.

DUKE ST, 1761 Rocque. According to VCH III, 355, this name began to be applied to the southern part of High St about 1550, possibly with reference to the Duke of Somerset, who was given the manor and borough of Reading in 1548.

ERLEIGH RD, *v.* 93.

FOBNEY ST, *v.* 176.

THE FORBURY, *Forbyr'* 13th *ReadingC(2)*, n.d. (14th) *ReadingC(3), The Forbery, The Forbury* 1507 W. Harrison, *Medieval Man and his Notions*,

---

† The identifications in this article have mostly been taken from VCH III 336 ff. Further information may now be obtained from C. F. Slade's account of Reading in *Historic Towns*, 1 (1969).

Forbury 1552 *LRMB*, 1790 Pride. OE foreburg normally means 'outwork', but another sense occurs in the OE version of *Exodus*, which has *on ðæs geteldes forebirig* where the Vulgate has *in tabernaculi vestibulo*. In the Berks p.n. there can be no doubt that the term means 'forecourt', as it was originally used of the outer court of Reading Abbey (VCH III, 352). It is difficult to say whether this is a survival of the sense recorded in *Exodus*. Forrabury Co is also from OE foreburg (DEPN).

FRIAR ST, *Fryers Street* 1714,† 1805 *Bodl*, *Fryar St* 1758, 1775 *PubLib*, *Friar St* 1792 *PubLib*, from the former prior of the Grey Friars. The street was earlier *Nouus Vicus* 1224–5 *Ass*, 1240–1 *ib*, *Le Newstrete* 1490 AD, *Newstrete* 1512 ib, 1548–9 *RentSur*, *Newe Strete* 1552 *LRMB*.

GARRARD ST, *A New Road called Garrard Street* 1854 *Bodl*.

GRAPE PASSAGE, *Gropequeyntelane* 14th *ReadingAlm*, *Grope Lane* 1347 *ReadingAlm*, 1552 *LRMB*. A variant of the common *Gropecuntelane* (which occurs in Windsor 29), with *ME queynt* (NED *quaint* sb.) instead of the synonymous *cunte*.

GREYFRIARS RD, 1851 *Bodl*.

HIGH BRIDGE WHARF. The High Bridge, by which the High St crossed the Kennet, was the commercial centre of the medieval town. It is first mentioned by the name of *Altus Pons* in a document of c. 1230 (VCH III, 351), and was sometimes called *Magnus Pons*. It is *Le High Bridge* 1552 *LRMB*, *The High Bridge* 1836 *PubLib*. The High St crossed the Holy Brook by means of another bridge called *Le Smalebrugge* (VCH III, 351, *v*. smæl 'narrow', and cf. O 36).

HIGH ST, *Altus Vicus* 1240–1 *Ass*, 1310 (14th) *ReadingC(3)*, *Le High Strete* 1467 AD, *Hyghstrete* 1518 ib, *Le Highe Strete* 1552 *LRMB*, *High Street* 1761 Rocque. *Magnus Vicus* 13th *ReadingC(2)*, n.d. (14th) *ReadingC(3)* may refer to High St.

HOLYBROOK RD, *v*. 11.

HOLY WATER LANE (lost), *La Haliwatereslane* 1301 (14th) *ReadingC(3)*, *Halewatereslane*, *Holiwaterleslane* 1307 (14th) *ib*, *Le Holiwaterleslane* 1312 (14th) *ib*. The 'holy water' might be Holy Brook (11), presumably so named from its proximity to Reading Abbey.

HOSIER ST was earlier *Lortemere Lane* 13th *ReadingAlm*, *Lortemer'* 1347 *ib*, *Lortemerelane*, *Lurtemere Lane* n.d. (14th) *ReadingC(3)*, *Lurkemerelane* 1552 *LRMB*, *Lurknerlane* c. 1546 ReadingA. In VCH III, 351, this is stated to be a corruption of 'Loriners' lane'; but the early forms rather suggest the etymology 'dirty pool', *v*. lort(e), mere. *Loriner'*, mentioned 1347 *ReadingAlm* in the same list as *Lortemer'*, may refer to another part of the town.

KATESGROVE LANE, *Catesgrove Lane* 1715, 1722 *PubLib*, *Catsgrove Lane* 1743, 1750, 1797 *ib*, 1761 Rocque; probably named from *Kadeles Graua* 1158–64 *AddCh 19596*, *Cadelesgroue* 1335 (14th) *ReadingC(2)*, *Catelsgrove* 1539 VCH III 367, *Catellgrove, Catells Groue* 1552 *LRMB*. The second el. is grāf 'grove'; the first is possibly a pers.n. *Cadel from the recorded *Cada*. A name *Ceadela* occurs in a number of p.ns. The earliest spelling of this

---

† *Letters written by eminent persons in the 17th and 18th centuries*, published London 1813, containing an account of Reading taken from Hearne's MS Diaries.

name is perhaps too early for derivation from the surname *Caudell* (Reaney 63). Cf. also *Cadelesgroueslynch*' ?13th (14th) *ReadingC(3)*, *La Lynche iuxta Cadelesgroue* 1335 (14th) *ib*, *Catysgrovelynche* 15th *ib*, *v.* hlinc 'ridge, bank'.

LONDON ST, *vicus London*' 13th *ReadingC(2)*, 1310 (14th) *ReadingC(3)*, *Vic' Lond'* 1240–1 *Ass*, *Londonstrete* 1461 *AD*; cf. *Lundenisshelane* n.d. (14th) *ReadingC(3)*.

LOVE LANE (lost), *Louelane, Loue Lane* 1306 (14th) *ReadingC(3)* (p), *Love Lane* 1846 Snare, *v.* lufu.

MARKET PLACE, *Le Merket Place* 1552 *LRMB*, *Market Place* 1787, 1815 *PubLib*. On the east side of this was *Showemakers Rowe* 1552 *LRMB* (*Showemakerstrete* also occurs in this document), *Shoomaker Rewe* 1663 *Bodl*; cf. *Suter*' 1347 *ReadingAlm*, *Souterestrete* 1371 *Pat*, *v.* sūtere.

MILL LANE, *Mullelane* n.d. (14th) *ReadingC(3)*, *La Mellelane* 14th *Reading-Alm*, *The Myll Lane* 1536 *ArchJ* 1, *Le Myll Lane* 1552 *LRMB*.

MILMAN RD, *Milman Rd*, formerly *Grove Rd* 1886 *PubLib*.

MINSTER ST, *Munstrestrete* 13th *ReadingC(2)*, 1371 *Pat*, *La Munstrestret* n.d. (14th) *ReadingC(3)*, *Mensterestrete* 1332 (14th) *ib*, *Minstrestret* 1347 *ReadingAlm*, *Minster Street* 1548–9 *RentSur*, 17th *RecOffCat*, possibly referring to the Saxon nunnery known to have been in Reading, *v.* mynster. The top of Minster St was known as *Totehull*' 1310 (14th) *ReadingC(3)*, *Tothulle* 1314–15 (14th) *ib*, *Totehill*, 1552 *LRMB*, 'look-out hill', *v.* tōt-hyll.

THE MOUNT, *Bobs Mount* 1846 Snare.

ORTS RD, cf. *Le Orte Lane, The Orte, The Ortelands* 1552 *LRMB*, *Ort Lane now New St* 1817 *PubLib*. BLAKE'S BRIDGE over the Kennet in this part of the town was formerly *Orte Bridge*, but changed its name at the end of the Civil War, when the land adjacent to the bridge belonged to James *Blake* (ReadingA 2). Cf. also *Ye Orte Yate* Ed 6 *LRMB*, *v.* geat. *Orte Bridge* was at the S.E. corner of the Abbey's Firmary Garden (VCH III, 339). ort, from medieval Latin *ortus* 'garden', which may be the first el. of the word *orchard*, would suit the position and agree well with the form *The Orte* from 1552. No examples of this term as an independent English word are on record but Professor Löfvenberg draws attention to OFr *ort* 'garden' which could be the immediate source of this p.n.

OXFORD RD, 1827 *PubLib*. Cf. *Oxford Street or Oxford Place* 1836 *Bodl*.

PANGBOURNE ST, cf. *Pangbourne Lane* 1761 Rocque.

PIGNEY LANE (lost), 1761 Rocque, 1810 *Bodl*, *v. infra* 181.

QUEEN'S RD, 1893 *PubLib*.

REDLANDS RD, cf. *Redlands Ho and Fm* 1846 Snare.

ST. GILES CHURCH LANE (lost), *Vicus Sancti Egidii* 1343 (14th) *ReadingC(3)*, *St. Giles' Church Lane* 1746 *PubLib*, 1761 Rocque, *St. Giles' Church Passage* 1782 *PubLib*.

ST. MARY'S BUTTS, *St. Mary Butts* 1761 Rocque; each parish had its archery butts in Tudor times. This was earlier *Vetus Vicus* 1347 *ReadingAlm*, *The Olde Streete* 1619 *Bodl*, *Old St* (*now called Horn St*) 1797 *PubLib*, *Old St* 1804 *ib*. Part of this street was known as *La Wodestrete* 1333 AD, *Wodestret* n.d. (14th) *ReadingC(3)*, *Le Wodestret* 1404 AD, *Woodstrete* 1548–9 *RentSur*, 'street where wood was sold', cf. Ekwall, Street-Names 77.

SILVER ST, *Le Siuekarestret* 1311 (14th) *ReadingC(3)*, *Le Syuekarestret* 1326

(14th) *ib*, *Le Siuekerestret* 14th *ReadingAlm*, *Syvyor Strete*, *Syvyerstrete* Ed 6 *LRMB*, *Seyver St* 1545 *PubLib*, *Syvio' Strete* 1552 *LRMB*, *Siveiar Strete* 1554 *ReadingA*, *Sceivier St* 1661 *PubLib*, *Scrivyer St* 1689, 1692, 1700 *ib*, *Silver*, als. *Sievyer St*, *Scrivyer St* 1729 *ib*, *Scrivyer St* 1750 *ib*, *Silver St* 1775 *ib*, 1761 Rocque, *Silver als Scrivyer St* 1813 *PubLib*. 'Street of the sieve-makers' seems a likely etymology, but it is not easy to reconcile the earliest forms with ME *siuyere*, *syvyʒere* etc. It may be noted, however, that the spellings given for this word in G. Fransson, *Middle English Surnames of Occupation* (Lund 1935 p. 172) include *Le Siuegar* 1275 and *Le Siuiger* 1308. SOUTHAMPTON ST was earlier *Hornerestret* 1347 *ReadingAlm*, *Horn Street* 1761 Rocque, 1799, 1805 *PubLib*, 'street of the workers in horn'. Fransson, op. cit. p. 167, quotes surnames *Le Hornare*, *le Hornere* from the l.13th and e.14th.

SOUTHCOTE RD, v. 177.

SOUTHERN HILL, 1846 Snare.

THORN ST, *Thorn's Lane* 1827 *PubLib*, *Thorn St late Thorn's Lane* 1832 *ib*.

VASTERN RD, cf. *Vastern* 1233 Ch, 1846 Snare, *Le Vasterne* 14th *ReadingAlm*, 1552 *LRMB*, *Vastern or Fostern Meadow* 1805 *Bodl*, the name of the land given to the Friars Minor by the Abbot and Convent of Reading in 1233. It is identical with Vastern W 273, the source being OE *fæstern* 'stronghold'. Asser states that in 870 the Danes made a rampart from the Thames to the Kennet near Reading; this name could refer to a structure at the Thames end of the rampart.

VICTORIA RD, cf. *Victoria Street* 1849 *Bodl*.

WHITLEY ST, v. 177.

YIELD HALL LANE, cf. *Aula Gildena* 13th *ReadingAlm*, *Gildhall'* n.d. (14th) *ReadingC(3)*, *Le Olde Yeld Hall, the Newe Guildehall quond' voc' Le Friers, Le Newe Guylde Hall, Le Newe Yeildehall, Le Guildehall* 1552 *LRMB*, v. gild-hall. The lane (which connected the Guildhall to Minster St) was known from Tudor times as *George Lane* from the George Inn, built 1507.

ZINZAN ST, named from the house of a Mrs *Zinzan* who lived there in 1800 (*LHRS*).

The following street-names have not been identified: *Bredstret* 1548–9 *RentSur* (cf. Bread Street in London, Ekwall, *Street-Names* 72); *Cuthroat Lane* 1688 *PubLib*; *Flex Lane* 1552 *LRMB* (v. fleax): *Halfpenny Lane* 1772 *RecOffCat*; *Pottereslane* 1347 *ReadingAlm*, n.d. (14th) *ReadingC(3)*. *Back Lane, Carring Lane, Hog Lane* and *Rotton Row* (v. ratoun) occur 1761 Rocque.

No early forms have been found for the following Reading street-names: ABBATTOIRS RD, ABBEY ST AND SQUARE, ADDINGTON RD, ADDISON RD, ADELAIDE RD, ALBANY RD, ALBERT RD, ALEXANDRA RD, ALFRED ST, ALLCROFT RD, ALMA ST, ALPINE ST, AMHERST RD, AMITY RD AND ST, ANSTEY RD, ARTHUR RD, AUCKLAND RD, AUDLEY ST, AVON PLACE, BAKER ST, BEDFORD RD, BELLE AVE, BEECHAM RD, BELMONT RD, BERESFORD RD, BERKELEY AVE, BISHOP'S RD, BLAKE'S COTTAGES (v. 173), BLENHEIM RD AND GARDENS, BOULT'S WALK, BRIGHAM RD, BRIGHTON RD, BRISBANE RD, BROOK ST, BROWNLOW RD, BRUNSWICK HILL, BULMERSHE RD, CAMBRIDGE ST, CARDIGAN RD, CARNARVON RD, CAREY ST, CATHERINE ST, CHARLES ST, CHATHAM ST, CHEAPSIDE, CHESTER ST, CHESTERMAN ST, CHOLMELEY RD,

CHRISTCHURCH GARDENS, CINTRA AVE, CLARENDON RD, CLIFTON ST, COLLEGE RD, COLLIS ST, CONNAUGHT RD, CORK ST, COVENTRY RD, CRAIG AVE., CRANBURY RD, CRANE WHARF, CRAVEN RD, CRESCENT RD, CROWN ST, CUMBERLAND RD, CURZON ST, DE BEAUVOIR RD, DE BOHUN RD, DE MONTFORD RD, DENMARK RD, DERBY ST, DONNINGTON RD AND GARDENS, DORSET ST, DOVER ST, DOWNSHIRE SQUARE, EAST ST, EASTERN AVE., EDINBURGH RD, EDGEHILL ST, ELDON RD etc., ELGAR RD, ELM LODGE AVE., ELM PARK RD, ELMHURST RD, ESSEX ST, FATHERSON RD, FIELD RD, FILEY RD, FOXHILL RD, FRANCIS ST, FRANKLIN ST, FRESHWATER RD, GARNET ST, GEORGE ST, GLEBE RD, GOLDSMID RD, GORDON PLACE, GOWER ST, GRANGE AVE, GRANBY GARDENS, GREAT KNOLLYS ST, GREEN RD, GROSVENOR RD, THE GROVE, GUN ST, GURDAN PLACE, HAGLEY RD, HAMILTON RD, HATHERLEY RD, HENRY ST, HIGHGROVE ST, HILL ST, HOLMES RD, HOPE ST, HOWARD ST, JESSE TERRACE, JUBILEE RD, JUNCTION RD, KENDRICK RD, KENNET SIDE AND ST, KEN-SINGTON RD, KENT RD, KINGSGATE ST, KING'S RD, KING ST, LENNOX ST, LEOPOLD RD, LETCOMBE ST, LIEBENROOD RD, LINCOLN RD, LITTLE ST, LIVERPOOL RD, LORNE ST, LYDFORD RD, LYNMOUTH RD, LYNN ST, MAITLAND RD, MANCHESTER RD, MANSFIELD RD, MARLBOROUGH AVE., MASON ST, MEADOW RD, MELROSE AVE., MILFORD RD, MONTAGUE ST, MORGAN RD, MOUNT PLEASANT, MOUNT ST, MUNDESLEY ST, NEW RD, NEWPORT RD, NORRIS RD, NORTH ST, NORCOT RD, NORFOLK RD, NORTHFIELD RD, NORTHUMBERLAND AVE., NORTON RD, NORTHCOURT AVE., NORWOOD RD, ORCHARD ST, ORMSBY ST, PARKSIDE RD, PELL ST, PITCROFT AVE., PRINCE OF WALES AVE., PRINCE'S ST, PROSPECT ST, RADSTOCK RD, RANDOLPH RD, RECREATION GROUND, REGENT ST, ROSS RD, ROWLEY RD, RUPERT ST, RUSSELL ST, SACKVILLE ST, ST BARTHOLOMEW'S RD, ST EDWARD'S RD, ST GEORGE'S RD, ST JOHN'S ST, HILL AND RD, ST PETER'S RD, ST SAVIOUR'S RD, SALISBURY RD, SCHOOL RD, SHAFTESBURY RD, SHENSTONE RD, SHERMAN RD, SHERWOOD ST, SIDMOUTH ST, SOHO ST, SOUTH ST, SPRING GARDENS, SPRING GROVE, STANLEY GROVE AND ST, STANSHAWE RD, STARLANE WHARF, STATION RD, SUN ST, SURREY RD, SWANSEA RD, TALFOURD AVE., TILEHURST RD, TUDOR RD, VACHEL RD, VALENTIA RD, VALPY ST, VICARAGE RD, WALDECK RD, WANTAGE RD, WARWICK RD, WATLINGTON ST, WAYLEN ST, WATERLOO RD, WAVERLEY RD, WELDALE ST, WELLINGTON AVE., WEST ST, WEST HILL, WESTERN ELMS AVE, WESTERN RD, WESTWOOD RD, WILLIAM ST, WILLOW ST, WILSON RD, WILTON RD, WINCHESTER RD, WOLSELEY ST, WYKEHAM RD, YORK RD.

BATTLE FM, cf. (*messuagium apud*) *Bellum* 13th *ReadingC*, n.d. (14th) *ReadingC(3)*, *Maner' de Battell* Hy 8 *RentSur*, *Battle* 1601 *SpecCom*, *Battles Farm* 1747 *PubLib*, *Battle Farm* 1790 Pride. This may have been part of the estate owned by Battle Abbey in 1086 (VCH III, 366).

CAVERSHAM, *Caueresham, Cavesham* 1086 DB, *Kauersham* 1152–8 NLC, *Caueresham* 1155 ib *et freq* with variant spellings *Kaueresham, Kaveresham* to 1285 *Ass, Chauerisham, Chaueresham* 1173 P, *Keueresham* 1205 (13th) Os (p), *Cauersham* 1246–7, 1268, 1285 *Ass, Kawersham, Cawersham* 1268 *ib, Keveresham* 1275–6 AD, *Causeiham, shortly caullid Causham* 1542 Leland. The first el. is the pers.n. *Cāfhere*, which appears in Caversfield O 204. It is impossible to say whether the second el. is hām or hamm.

CAVERSHAM STREET-NAMES

ALBERT RD. ARDLER RD. BLENHEIM RD. BRIANT'S AVE. BRIDGE ST. CHALK PIT HILL. CHAMPION RD. CHESTER ST. CHICAGO RD. CHURCH RD AND ST. CLIFTON PARK RD. COLDICUTT ST. CONISBORO AVE. CROMWELL RD. DARELL ¦RD. DERBY RD. DONKIN HILL. GEORGE ST. GOSBROOK ST. GROSVENOR RD. HAMPDEN RD. HARLEY RD. HARROGATE RD. HEMDEAN RD, HILL AND RISE (*v. infra* 178). HENLEY RD. HIGHMOOR RD. ILKLEY RD. KIDMORE RD (from Kidmore O 76). KING'S RD. MARSAK ST. MATLOCK RD. MILL RD. MONTAGU ST. THE MOUNT (*Mounte Feld, Le Mounte* 1551-2 *Survey, v.* mont). NORTH ST. OAKLEY RD. OXFORD ST. PADDOCK RD. PATRICK RD. PEPPARD RD (leading to Rotherfield Peppard O 79). PIGGOTT'S RD. PRIEST HILL. PRIORY AVE. PROSPECT ST. QUEEN ST. QUEEN'S RD. RECTORY RD. RICHMOND RD. ST. ANDREW'S RD. ST. ANNE'S RD. ST. JOHN'S RD. ST. PETER'S HILL AND AVE. SEND RD. SHORT ST. SOUTH ST. SOUTH VIEW AVE. STAR RD. UPLANDS RD. VICTORIA RD. WASHINGTON RD. WESTFIELD RD. WOLSEY RD. WOODCOTE RD.

COLEY, *Colleia* 1173–80 *AddCh 19601* (p), *Colleia, Collai* c. 1195 *ib 7202* (p), *Collea* 1224–5 *Ass* (p) *et freq* with variant spellings *Collee, Colley(e), Colleya* to 1327 *SR, Celley* 1284 *Ass, Colle* 1341 NonInq, *Colye* 1596 *SpecCom, Coley House* 1790 Pride, *Coley House, Hill and Farm* 1846 Snare, 'charcoal clearing', *v.* col^1, lē(a)h, and cf. Cowley Db 244.

FOBNEY MEADOW, cf. *Vobeneye* n.d. (14th) *ReadingC(3), Vobney* 14th *ReadingC*, 1520 ArchJ 5, *Vobney Mede, Vobney Bridge* Ed 6 *LRMB*. 'Fobba's island', *v.* (ī)eg. The meadow lies between the main stream and a branch of the Kennet. For the pers.n. which is found in a number of p.ns., *v.* Ess 156, W 214.

KENTWOOD FM AND GROVE, cf. *Chanetwda* 1130–5 (14th) *ReadingC(3)* (p), *Kenetwida* c. 1180 A. H. Cooke, *The Early History of Maple-durham* (OxRecSoc 7) (p), *Kenetewuda* 1188 *et seq* P, *Kenetwude* 1198 ib, *Kenetwode* c. 1265 (c. 1450) Godstow (p), 1275–6 RH, *Kentwode* 1380 Gor (p), *Kentwood Pidle* 17th *PubLib(Clayton), Kent Wood Grove, Kentwood Common* 1761 Rocque, *Kentwood Common and Farm* 1790 Pride. 'Wood by the R. Kennet', *v.* wudu and 11–12 for the river-name. Kentwood Fm and Grove are actually about two miles north of the Kennet, and it must be supposed that a considerable area between that river and the Thames was known as 'Kennet wood'.

NORCOT FM, *Northcot'* 1327 *SR* (p), *Northcot* 1539–40, c. 1546
ReadingA, *Northecott* 1584 AD, *Norcott* 1608 *Dep*, *Northcott* 17th
PubLib(*Clayton*), 1761 Rocque, *Northcote* 1846 Snare, 'north
cottage(s)', *v.* **cot** and cf. Southcote *infra.*

SOUTHCOTE HO, *Svdcote* 1086 DB, *Sutcot*, *Sudcot* 1220 Fees, *Sukote*
1248–52 *FF*, *Suthcot'* 1284 *Ass*, *Suthcote* 1306 Cl, 1327 *SR*, *Suth-
cotes* 1337 Ch, *Southcote* 1445 Moulton, *Southcote House* 1846 Snare,
'south cottage(s)', cf. Norcot *supra*, the two places appear to be
named in relation to each other. CIRCUIT LANE is probably 'Southcote
Lane' with the same development as Circourt in Denchworth (Pt **2**).

WESTWOOD HO AND ROW, *Westwode* 1462 *Bodl*, *West-wood-row*
1539–40 ReadingA, *Westwood Row* c. 1546 ib, *Westwood Rewe* 1552
LRMB, *Westward Row* 1846 Snare, perhaps 'west of the wood',
with reference to Kentwood, *v.* **westan.**

WHITLEY, WHITLEY WOOD, WHITLEY PARK FM (2 examples),
Witelei 1086 DB, *Wytheleth* 1164–73 ReadingA, *Wythele* 1173–80 ib,
Wittelea, *Withelea* 1175 P, *Whythele* 1180–99 ReadingA, *Witheleia*,
Witeleia l.12th *ReadingC*, *W(h)iteleia* 1198 P, *Whytel'* 1252 Cl,
Witele(ye), *Witteleg'* 13th *ReadingC*, *Witele* 1275–6 RH, *Whytele(y)*,
W(h)ytelegh, *W(h)ytele*, *Wytteleyg'* 1284 *Ass*, *Whytele* 1279–80 *FF*
(p), 1294 *SR*, 1342 Pat, *Wytele* 1327 *SR*, *Whytlyngwode* 1309 Cl,
Whitele 1342 Pat, 1401, 1412 Fine, *Whitley Park* 1539–40 ReadingA,
Whytley Parke, *Whyteley Woode*, *Whitley Woodlands*, *Whitleywoode
Lande*, *Whitley Yeilde*, *Whitley Courte* Ed 6 *LRMB*, *Whitley Park*,
Whitley Wood Common 1790 Pride, *Whitley Park Fm*, *Whitley Manor
Fm*, *Whitley Wood* 1846 Snare. 'White wood or clearing', *v.* **hwīt**,
lē(a)h, and cf. the same name, Pt **2**. *v. infra* 182 for the Abbot of
Reading's park, which is referred to in the name Whitley Park Fm.

ANSLOW'S COT.   ARMOUR, 1846 Snare.   ASHCROFT, *Ascrofte*,
Ashecroft, *Asshecroftefeld* 1551–2 *Survey*, *Ash Croft* 1704 *Bodl*, *v.*
æsc and cf. other names which refer to ash-trees *infra* 181.   AYRES
FM.   BACK LANE.   BALMORE, *Balmers Field* 1687 *PubLib*.
BEECH WD.   BEECHAM HILL.   BIRD IN HAND P.H.   BLAGRAVE
RECREATION GROUND.   BLAKE'S BRIDGE, *v.* 173.   BLUNDELL'S
COPSE.   BROADOAK, *a certeyne brode oke* Ed 6 *LRMB*, the same
name occurs in Hurley 64.   CALCOT HANGER AND RISE, *v.* **hangra**
and 222.   CAVERSHAM BRIDGE, *pons de Caueresham* 1241 *Ass*, 1280

Os, *pons de Kauersham* 1273 (14th) *ReadingC(3), Causham Bridge* 1542 Leland, *Cauershambridge* 1551–2 *Survey*; it is referred to 1231 Cl as *Pons Rading ultra Tamisiam.*   CAVERSHAM HEIGHTS, HILL AND MILL.   CAVERSHAM PLACE PARK, *Caversham Park* 1846 Snare. CAVERSHAM RISE, 1846 Snare.   CHALK PIT HILL.   CHURCHEND, c. 1546 ReadingA, *Churche Ende* 1552 *LRMB*, *v.* ende, St. Michael's Church is in the centre of the hamlet.   CHURCHEND COPSE AND LANE.   CIRCUIT LANE, *v.* 177.   THE CLAPPERS (in R. Thames), *Le Clapper, Le Clopper* 1603–4 *Survey*, *v.* clapper 'bridge, stream-crossing'.   COCKNEY HILL, 1761 Rocque, *Coclehale* 1462, 1469 *Bodl, Cockney Hale Field, Cockney Hall Pightle, Cockney Hill* 1843 *TA* (Tilehurst), *v.* coccel 'tares', healh.   COLEY PARK, *v.* 176. THE COMMON.   COMPARTS PLANTATION, *Comparts* 1843 *TA* (Tilehurst).   COOMBE BANK.   COW LANE.   EMMER GREEN, *Ember Green* 1705 *PubLib, Emmer Wood, Emmir Green* 1840 *TA, Emmir Green* 1846 Snare.   FORD'S FM.   FRY'S ISLAND.   FURZE-PLATT (*v.* plat²).   GIPSY LANE.   GODDARD'S FM.   GRAVEL HILL.   GREENLANDS.   GRENADIER P.H.   GREY'S FM.   GROVE FM AND HILL, CAVERSHAM GROVE, *Grove Feld, Close and Land* 1551–2 *Survey, Grove Fm and Park* 1846 Snare.   GROVE HO (in Reading). GROVELANDS, *Grove Land* 1761 Rocque, *Groveland Fm* 1830 OS, *Grovelands Fm* 1846 Snare.   THE GUTTER.   HEMDEAN BOTTOM AND HO, *Hevendenefeld, Hevenden, Hemedeane, Hemondean, Hemden-feld, Hemeden(n)efeld* 1551–2 *Survey, Hem Dean* 1761 *Bodl*, probably 'level valley', *v.* efn, denu. There was a *Hevenemede* in Southcote (*infra* 183), but this must have been some distance from Hemdean in Caversham.   HILL SIDE.   HOME FM.   HONEYEND FM, 1802 *Bodl, Honeyden* 1675 Ogilby, *Honey End* 1830 OS, *v.* hunig.   HORN-CASTLE, 1830 OS, 1846 Snare.   IVY HOUSE FM.   JUNIPER PIT. KING'S MEAD, 1790 Pride, *Le Kings Mede* 1552 *LRMB*, cf. other 16th-cent. names in *Kinges- infra* 183.   LEIGHTON PARK SCHOOL. LITTLE JOHNS, *Little Johns Fm* 1846 Snare.   LITTLE LEA FM, *Little Lea Fm and Common* 1846 ib.   LONGBARN LANE.   LONG LANE.   LOUSEHILL COPSE, *v.* lūs.   MANOR FM.   MANSION HO.   MARSHALL'S HILL, *Marshalls Field* 1839 *TA*.   MERRY MAIDENS P.H.   MILKMAID'S BRIDGE (over R. Kennet), *Clapper Bridge* 1596 *PubLibDoc*, *v.* clapper and cf. The Clappers *supra*. MOCKBEGGAR, *Mock Beggar Fm* 1846 Snare; according to a note in *LHRS* by E. W. Dormer the name Mockbeggar first appears c. 1700, the farm being earlier known as *Aleyn's Farm* from Thomas *Aleyn* who was the Abbey's tenant there at the Dissolution. It is *Allen's Farm or Mockbeggars* c. 1833 ArchJ 35, *v.* 283.   MONKSBARN. THE MOOR.   THE MOUNT, 1761 Rocque, *v.* mont and cf. the same name in Caversham 176.   NEW TOWN.   NORRIS FM. OAKLAND HALL, *Oaklands Cottage* 1846 Snare.   OAK TREE FM. PALMER PARK.   PARK COTTAGES, south of Whiteknights Park 93. PARK FM AND LANE, near Calcot Park 195.   PEGSGREEN LANE, *Pig Green* 1675 Ogilby, *Pigs Greene Close* 17th *PubLib(Clayton)*, *Pegs Green* 1761 Rocque, *Pigs Green* 1830 OS, 1846 Snare, probably 'pig's green', the modern form being euphemistic.   PENHAMS SHAW, *Penhams* 1843 *TA* (Tilehurst).   PEPPER LANE, cf. *tenement called Pepyrs* 1539–40 ReadingA, *Peppar Fm* 1846 Snare.   PROSPECT PARK, *Prospect Hill* 1790 Pride, 1830 OS, *Prospect Hill Park* 1843 *TA* (Tilehurst).   PROSPECTPARK COTTAGES.   ROEBUCK HOTEL, *Roebuck* 1790 Pride.   ROOKERY POND.   ROPE WAY.   ROSEHILL, 1846 Snare, ROSEHILL COTTAGE.   ROUND COPSE.   ST. ANNE'S WELL, *Chapel of St. Anne in Le Temmes* 1551–2 *Survey*.   ST. BENET'S HOME.   ST. JOHN'S COTTAGES.   ST. MARY'S HILL. SCOURS LANE, *Northcote Scour Ten Acres* 1843 *TA* (Tilehurst), the lane leads to Norcot Scours in R. Thames.   SHIPNELL'S COTTAGES, *Shepnelle, Shypnelle, Shipnelle* 1551–2 *Survey*, possibly from **scypen** and **hyll**.   SOUTHCOTE COTTAGES AND MANOR FM, *v.* 177. SOUTHERN HILL, 1846 Snare.   STONEHAM COPSE AND HO. SURLEY ROW, 1733 *PubLib*, 1846 Snare.   TOOT'S FM, 1846 ib, *Toots* 1797 Davis, *Toot Fm* 1830 OS, in Caversham Heights, *v.* tōt. THE WARREN, 1846 Snare, *Warren Field, Meadow and Wood* 1840 *TA*, WARREN HO AND TOWERS.   WESTGROVE.   WESTWOOD FM AND KILN, *v.* 177.   WHITLEY HO etc., *v.* 177.   WOODSIDE COTTAGES.   WORLD TURNED UPSIDE DOWN P.H.

The following names of houses appear on the 6″ map in Reading and Caversham: CONSTANTIA, CRESSINGHAM, DALKEITH PLACE, DELLWOOD, THE DOWNES, ELM-HURST, THE ELMS (Caversham), THE ELMS (Whitley), THE FIRS, GRAYLANDS, HEATHFIELD, THE LAURELS, MANOR HO, MORLANDS, PARK HO, PARKHURST, PAXTON HO, THE PRIORY, ROOKWOOD, THE ROSARY, ROSIA, ROTHERFIELD GRANGE, SPRINGFIELD, STONEYCROFT, SUTHERLANDS, TURRET HO, THE VINEYARD, WALMER, WESTBOURNE, WEST DENE, WESTFIELD, WHITE HO.

FIELD-NAMES

Principal forms in (*a*) marked L are St. Lawrence parish *TA* 1847, M are St. Mary *TA* 1838, G are St. Giles *TA* 1839. Early forms with no date or source are 1551–2 *Survey* (Caversham); those dated 1182, a. 1184, c. 1185,

1216, ?13th, 1273, 1290, 1291, 1302, 1303, e.14th, 1331, 1353, n.d. (14th) are *ReadingC(3)* and are all (14th); 13th, 1253–4 (13th), 14th *ReadingC*; 1304–5 *DL*; 1490, 1515, 1516, 1548–9 *RentSur*; 1539–40, 1544, c. 1546 ReadingA; 1552, Ed 6 *LRMB*; 1596 *PubLibDoc* (Southcote).

(*a*) Alder Mead M (*The Allder* Ed 6); Aldridge Piece G (*Eldridge* 1601 *SpecCom*); Avenue Ground M; Back Lane G; Bank Mdw M; Barn Close G (*The Barne Close* Ed 6); Barnets, Barnets Mead M (possibly *Burnegats* Ed 6, *v.* bærnet(t)); Bingham Mead L; Black Jacks Fd G; Bleaching Ground Mdw M; Bridge Pightle M; Broad Close G; Broad Mead M; Broom Fd G (*v.* brōm); Bull Hern G (*Bulherne* Ed 6, *v.* bula, hyrne); Bull Mdw M; Butt Close G; Calf Lease G (*Calves Leaz* Ed 6, *v.* lǣs); Calvespit Farm 1830 OS (also 1761 Rocque); Chestnut Fd M; Church Mdw G; Cockshot Fd M (*Cokeshotte, Cokesettes, Cokesetours, v.* cocc-scyte); Corner Pightle M; Councils G (*Counsells Acres* Ed 6); Cowick Mdw G (*Cowyk'* 1302 (p), *La Couwyk* e.14th, *Cowick* 1539–40, *Cowyk, Cowickmeade* 1544, *v.* cū, wīc); Cow Lease G (*Cowelessowe* 1551–2 *Survey, Cowelease* Ed 6, *v.* cū, lǣs); Crapinum G (possibly *Crapoldes Inmone* 1309 Cl, *v.* innām, Dr O. von Feilitzen suggests for the first el. OFr *crapout, crapaud* 'toad' used as a surname); Daniels Lands G (*Daniells Lande* Ed 6); Deanes Mead M (*Deane, Greate and Parva Dene, Denne, Dene Crofte, Denehouse, v.* denu); The Devils Grandfather G (*v.* 283); Dewell M; Dipping Pond Mdw G; Dungcroftes G (*Dong(e)crofte* Ed 6, 'dung croft'); Easter Chalk Paddock M (*Easter and Wester Chalk Paddock* 1596, *v.* ēasterra, westerra; both terms occur several times in the f.ns. of this parish); Endhams and Mendhams M (possibly *Greate Mynhames, Litle Minhames* 1596, possibly from innām); Four Horse Shoe Fd G (*Horshoes* 1790 Pride, *v.* 283); Friars Crofts G; Fulbrook Mdw G; Furze Fd M; Gallows Ground G; Goslings Moor M; Grange Mdw G; Gravel Pit Fd G; Green Hill G; The Grove G (*The Grove* 1539–40, 1596, *Le Grove*); Hadsey, West M (*Easter and Wester Hadsey* 1596, *Hadsey Dytche* 1596 *SpecCom*, which may be *Herwardesl'* 13th (p), *Herewardesle* 1290, *Herewardesleie* 1331, 'Hereweard's lēah'); Hatch Fd G (*La Hache* 1248 *Ass, Hacche* 1377 Fine (p), *v.* hæc(c)); Hill Fd and Ground G (*Hillcrofte, Hill Close* 1551–2 *Survey*, Ed 6, *Hill Lande* Ed 6); Hogmoor G (*Hogemore, Gret and Litill* Ed 6, *v.* hogg, mōr); Home Close, Ground, Mdw and Pasture G (*The Homefelde, The Homegroue, Homeclose, Homelands* Ed 6, *Homecroft*); Homers Mead M (possibly *Holmans Mede* Ed 6); Honey Lease G, Honey Fd M (*Honye Lease* 1544, *v.* hunig); Horse Hill M (*Horsehill Meade* 1596); Horse Race G; Inhams G (*Litill Inholmes, Olde Inhomes, Olde Inhams* Ed 6, *v.* innām); Inland Mead and String M (*Inlands* 1596, *v.* inland); Kennet Moor M; Kiln Ground G; Lambs Leaze M (*Lambe Leaze* 1552, *v.* lǣs); Land Mdw G (*Landme* 1309 Cl, *Landemede* 1552, *Londemeade* Ed 6, *v.* land, mǣd); Lanterns G (possibly connected with *Lantherne Crate* 17th *PubLib-(Clayton)* in Tilehurst); The Lawn M; Lay Thrift G (*Lee* 1380 Fine (p), *Ley Close and Crofte, Leyfeld(e)* 1551–2 *Survey, The Lye Lands, The Lee Frithe* Ed 6, *The Lye or Line* 1771 Bodl, *v.* lēah, fyrhð); Lea Common G; Leys Mdw M; Lotmore G; Manhams M (*v.* Endhams *supra*); Man Moor G (*The Manmore* Ed 6, *v.* (ge)mǣne, mōr); Mattocks Vere G (*Mattocks Fere*

1552, *Mattocks Fyere* Ed 6, *v.* furh); Middle Fd G (*Middelfeld* 1304–5);
Milking Bridge Mead M; Mill Acre L, Mill Mdw M; Mislingstone G; The
Moor M (*Lez Moreplotts, Lez Morlands, Le Morsey* Ed 6, *The Moore Meade*
1596, *More Dytch* 1596 *SpecCom, Moreland* 1601 *SpecCom, v.* mōr); Mutton
Close and Fd G; New Leaze M (*Newe Leaze* 1552, *New(e) Lease, Easter and
Wester* 1596, *v.* lǣs); No Mans Common G (*Nomans Lande* Ed 6, *v.* mann);
North Fd M (*Northfeld* 1273, 1331, *La Northfelde* 1290, *La Northefeld,
Northefeldes* 1552); Outlet G; Ox Lease G (*The Ox Lease* Ed 6, *v.* lǣs);
The Paddock M (*Le Padoke, Lez Padokes* 1551–2 *Survey, Lez Parocks* Ed 6,
v. pearroc); Park G (*Parke Puddell, Park Closes* Ed 6, *The Parke Close* 1596,
there were several parks in Reading); Peggs Pit M; Peppard Park G (cf.
Peppard Rd 176); Picked Mead and Close M (*Piked Close* Ed 6, *v.* pīced); Pig
Post G; Pigney Mdw M (*Pigney Meadow and Bridge* 1761 Rocque); Pile Fd
M (*Pilefelds* 1552, *v.* pīl); Plat G (*v.* plǎt²); Plot M; Plots M; Plummery L,
Plumers Mdw M; Pottmanns Brook 1805 *Bodl* (*Portmanebrok* 1253–4 (13th),
Portmanebroc 13th *ReadingC(2), Portemanbrok'* 1273, *Portman Broke* 1552,
'burgess brook', cf. Port Meadow O 22; the Berks meadow belonged to the
merchant guild of Reading, *v.* VCH III, 344); Pound Fd G; Pump Fd G;
Red House Fd G; Red Lane House 1830 OS (also 1761 Rocque); Restraw
Mead M; Rough Pasture G; Round Hill G; Rushey Mdw, Rushy Close M;
Rye Fd (*Le Ryecroft* 1342 AD, *Ryeclose* Ed 6, *Reycrofte, v.* ryge); Sanfoin
Hill G (*v.* 282); Shipton Mdw (*Shipton* 1552); Shoulder of Mutton Piddle
G (*v.* 283); Slips G (*v.* slipe); Spring Wells G; Stable Ground G; Stewards
Mead M (*Stewardes Meade* 1596); Stoken Bridge Close and Mead M
(*Stoken Brydge* 1596, *v.* stoccen); String Mdw, The String M (*Easter and
Wester Stringe, Inlandes String* 1596, *v.* easterra, *wester; *string* 'a long
narrow strip' occurs in O, *v.* 282); Thames Mdw M; Twelve Acres G
(*Twelfacres* 1291, *Twelve Acr* Ed 6); Turnpike Ground M; Vistley Bit G;
Walkround G; The Wallet Mead M; Walnut Tree Ground M; Waterloo
Fd G (*v.* 284); Weigh Fd G (*Weycrofte, Wey Downe*); West Fd G (*Westfelde*
1544); Wiffity Mdw, Wiffity G (*Wevytre Mede, Wyvytre* Ed 6, this may be
identical with Wavertree La, 'a swaying or shaking tree', *v.* wǣfre); Wood
Thrift G (*The Woodfrithe* Ed 6, *v.* wudu, fyrhð, and cf. Lay Thrift *supra*).

(*b*) *Appull Durst, Appull Dores* (*v.* apuldor); *Ashemmeade* 1551–2; *Ashen
Grove* 1596; *Asshurst* 1304–5 (*v.* æsc, hyrst); *Asthen Parke; Averye; The
Back Brook* 1764 *PubLib; Backinge Grove; Banelandes* (*v.* bēan, land);
Barcrofte; Barlage; Barley Hedge; Le Barly Crofte Ed 6; *Barmasefeld,
Barnarsfeld, Burmansfeld, Barmarsfeld, Barmysfelde* 1551–2 *Survey, Barmers
Field* 1771 *Bodl* (it is not certain that all these forms relate to the same name);
Barnardes Felde, Barnardes Heye 1551–2 *Survey, Barners Feild* 1704 *Bodl;
Barne Crofte; Bastardescroft* e.14th (Will. *Bastard*' is mentioned 13th
ReadingC(2)); The Beare 1552 (*v.* bearu); *Le Beches* (wood called), *Le
Beache; Beacheam Crofte; Bechinge Grove Feld; Bensyde Lande; Berefeld*'
e.14th, *Burfield* 1539–40, *Borough Feld, Borowghfeld, Barrowefelde* 1551–2,
Longe Borough 1601 *SpecCom* (first el. probably beorg); *Berewerdishill* 1552
('bearward's hill'); *Berrybroke; Bottondene Feld, Botten Deane, Bottom Dell*
(*v.* botm, denu); *La Bournemed* 1182, *Burnemed*' 13th *ReadingC(2)* (*v.* burna,

mǣd); *Bovetowne* 1551–2 *Survey*, *Bovedowne* 1673 *PubLib*, *Bowedown* 1715 *PubLib* (probably 'above the hill', *v.* bufan, dūn); *Brackmansfeld, Brakemansfeld* (first el. possibly an occupational surname, from *brake* NED sb.[3]); *La Breche* 13th *ReadingC*(2), *Le Breche, Breache, Brechegrove, Le Brechefeld* (*v.* brēc); *Brewers' Meadows* 1544; *The Brickfelde* Ed 6; *Brode Croft*; *Brodefelde*; *Brode Leys* (*v.* brād); *La Broke* 1314 Ipm, *Brooke* 1596 (*v.* brōc); *Brokenboroughe, Brokenborough Lock* 1552 ('broken barrow', cf. the same name O 175); *Bromcroftes* 1309 Cl, *Brome Crofte, Bromeclose* 1551–2 *Survey*, *Bromyclose* Ed 6 (*v.* brōm, brōmig); *Brygede(a)ne*; *Bryghtwell*; *Buddes Oke*; *Bullheyse* 1552 (*v.* bula, (ge)hæg); *Burchencrofte* (*v.* bircen[2]); *Busshecroftes*; *The Busshe*; *Busshe Lyes, Busshye Lease* 1544, *Bushy Lease Meade* 1596 (*v.* lǣs); *Le Busshie Plotte, Busshie Piddles, Busshie Pitt* Ed 6; *Caldie Lane* Ed 6; *Calves Puddell* Ed 6; *Canon Mead, Cannons Close* 1601 *SpecCom*; *Capulle, Gret and Lytle, Dose Cabull*; *Causam Lott*; *Chakerland* (*v.* cheker); *Challam, Challans* (possibly from calenge, referring to disputed land); *Charlewood* 1601 *SpecCom* (*v.* ceorl, wudu); *Char Mead* 17th *PubLib*(*Clayton*); *Chawkesoneslandes*; *Churcheclose*; *Clayfield Coppices* 1716 *PubLib*; *Clerkenewellefeld'* 1291, *Clerkwelfeld* 1490, 1515, 1516, *Clerkenwell Field* 1520 ArchJ 5, *Clerkenwellfelde* 1552 (identical with Clerkenwell Mx 94–5, *v.* clerc); *Cley Close* Ed 6; *Cley Crofte*; *Cokenden*; *Cumba* Hy 2 (l.12th) *ReadingC, parcus . . . de Cumba* 1164–73 *AddCh 19599* (cumb 'valley', this was the Abbot of Reading's park at Whitley Pk Fm, *v.* D. M. Stenton, *English Society in the Early Middle Ages*, 104); *Comber Ditche* 1596 (the S.W. boundary of Southcott); *Conscyence Crosse Lane* 1596 (this ran north and south, east of Southcott Fm, cf. Weeping Cross O 396); *Copenhulle* 1331 (p) (*v.* hyll); *Corne Raye*; *Costowe, Costoue, Custowe, Costeu, Costowefeld, Costarde* 1551–2 *Survey*, *Costell Field* e.17th *Survey*, 1771 *Bodl* (*v.* cot-stōw); *Crockerelcrundele* 13th, *Cuxkerescrundele* 13th *ReadingC*(2), *Le Crondelfeld* 1331 (*v.* crundel); *Crown-field* 1539–40, *Le Crowne Feld* 1552; *Cudeford* (*als Farnham*) 1304–5; *Cueffold* 1304–5 ('cow-fold'); *Downe, parva Downe, Downe Landes* 1551–2 *Survey*, *Lez Downes* 1552 (*v.* dūn); *Le Drouelane* n.d. (14th) (*v.* drāf); *Drynkepenseclose* (perhaps a nickname 'drink pence' for an unproductive close, but the first el. may be a surname; a similar one is mentioned Reaney 101); *Dwoleslond* 1291 (first el. a surname, *v.* Reaney 104); *Dycons Lands* Ed 6; *Dysshemede* 1493 AD (probably 'ditch mead', cf. Dishforth YN 184); *Elme Grove* 1596; *Epeland*; *Erelles or Erles Wood*; *Estefeld* (*v.* feld); *Estmed* n.d. (14th), *Estmede* 1539–40, *Estemede* 1552 (*v.* ēast, mǣd); *Farmers Marche, Farmerse Felde, Farmersfeld*; *Faryngstone, Feryngstone*; *Le Fatt*; *Feldes Land*; *Flapp Yate* Ed 6 (cf. *flap* EDD, where the compound *flap-gate* is noted, meaning 'a small gate swinging without fastening between two posts'); *Le Forge Pidell* Ed 6; *Litill Formore* Ed 6 (*v.* fore, mōr); *Fortheye* 1314 Ipm, *Fortye* (*v.* forð-ēg); *Le Foxhills* Ed 6; *Foxle* 1291 (14th) (*v.* fox, lēah); *Frogmarsh* 1539–40, *Frogmersshe, Frogmarshe* 1552 (*v.* frogga, mersc); *Fuelmaresfeld* 13th, *Fuelmar'feld* 13th *ReadingC*(2) (*v.* feld, first el. possibly a surname from Fowlmere Ca or Fulmer Bk); *Furmustcrofte* ('foremost croft'); *Fyermedowe*; *Fyvemen Mede* Ed 6 (*v.* 285); *Gabull Loke* (possibly identical with *Capulle supra*); *Garstone* (*v.* gærs-tūn); *Gerdwicke Locke* 1596 *SpecCom*; *Le Gore* Ed 6 (*v.* gāra); *Gosewelles, Gosebroke* (*v.* gōs, w(i)ella, brōc); *Great Ham* 1687 (*v.* hamm); *Greenwell* 1704 *Bodl*; *Grene Ende* (*v.* grēne², ende); *Grimeshole* 13th (possibly 'devil's hollow', *v.* Grīm, hol); *Groseclose, Grosefeld*; *Goldescrouchesfeld* 1273, *Gull Crosse, Gull Crosse Feilde* 1552 (*v.* feld, the land was apparently marked by a cross, crūc³ being replaced by cros, first el. probably the surname *Gold*); *Hamse Stede, Hampstelles* (*v.* hāmstede); *Harehurst, Harewelle* 1304–5 (*v.* hara, hyrst, w(i)ella); *Hargorse; Harterige* 1552; *Haselmere, Haselmeredene* 13th, *Hawsemore Crofte, Hawezmore* (*v.* hæsel, mere, denu); *Hergyn Eiate* 1493 AD, *Argyng Heyatt, Hargyngayte* (*v.* ēgeð); *Le Hermitage* 1552; *Hethe Croft, Hetheclose, Hethynge* (*v.* hǣð); *Hevenemede* 1364 Ipm, 1365 Cl, (apparently 'heaven mead' but the first el. could be efn 'level', this was in Southcote); *Heydowne, Heygrove, Heyland, Heymeade, Heymedowe* (*v.* hēg, dūn, mǣd, the first el. of *Heygrove* may be (ge)hæg); *Heyle* 1314 Ipm (*v.* hēg, (ge)hæg, lēah); *Le Heys* Ed 6 (*v.* (ge)hæg); *Highe Feilde, Easter and Wester* 1596; *The Highway Close* Ed 6; *Holnesmede* 1364 Ipm, *Holmesmede* 1365 Cl (*v.* mǣd, first el. probably a surname); *Horsecroft, Hourse More, Horseleyes* 1551–2 *Survey, Horseleaze* 1552 (*v.* hors, lǣs); *La Horsengle* 1307 Ipm; *Horshott* 1552; *Lez Hundred Acr'* 1552; *La Hyde* 1305 Cl, *Le Hyde* (*v.* hīd); *Hyghen'sh* 1304–5; *Jeanecrofte; Jovey; Kentesput* 1273, *Kentesputtes* 1371 Pat (*v.* pytt, first el. either a surname or R. Kennet); *Kingesforlong, Kingesfeld; Kings Pounde* Ed 6; *Le Lake* 1552 (*v.* lacu); *Le Lane Piddell* Ed 6; *Langeneia* 1216, *Langeneya* 13th, *Langenheie, Langneya* n.d. (14th) (*v.* lang, (ī)eg, and cf. the same name O 27); *Lawntos Lande* Ed 6; *La Leyshecroft* 1342 AD; *The Litill Marsshe* 1552; *Longe Crofte; Longemerchs* 1273, *Longemarshe* 1552 (*v.* mersc); *Longeslande* Ed 6; *Le Longe Piddell* Ed 6; *Lytle Eres* (*v.* ersc); *Meade Platt; Medegrounde; Le Medstighele* 14th *ReadingAlm, La Medstyle* n.d. *ReadingAlm* (*v.* mǣd, stigel); *Meryhill; La Mersche* 1314 Ipm, *Le Mershe* (*v.* mersc); *Middeldeane* (*v.* denu); *Myddelland; Milne Barge; Le Morizene Gardyn* 1342 AD (*v.* morgen-gifu); *Morycrofte, Morydene; Mowe Meade* 1596; *Mulleweye* 1273 (*v.* myln, weg); *Muxenbrok* 1304–5 (*v.* mixen, brōc); *Mylfeld* 1544; *Mylestaks* Ed 6; *Mylke Close* 1596; *Mynster Mills* 1539–40, *Mynster Myll* 1552, *Mynskers Mille* 1576 *SpecCom, The Minster Mill Stream* 1764 *PubLib* (*v.* mynster, referring to the Abbey); *Nasshes* (*v.* atten, æsc); *Nethercrofte; Netherlands* Ed 6; *Netherclif Lande* Ed 6 (*v.* neoðera); *Newfield* 1694 *PubLib*; *Northams, Northame* Ed 6 (*v.* norð, hamm); *Northwode* 1314 Ipm (*v.* norð, wudu); *Noue Garstone* 13th *ReadingAlm* ('new enclosure', *v.* gærs-tūn); *Nyne Crofts* 1601 *SpecCom; Oldelandes; Oley Pitts* 1552; *Oselakemere* 13th (possibly 'Ōslāc's pool' *v.* mere); *The Ought Lands* Ed 6; *Overell Close* 17th *PubLib(Clayton); Le Ouergrove* Ed 6, *Ouerland* (*v.* uferra, grāf, land); *Owley; Oxemoremed* 1303, *Oxemore Mede* 1353 (*v.* oxa, mōr, mǣd); *Oystershells Bed* 1761 Rocque; *Pacchy Grove; Parsenychefeld* 1551–2 *Survey, Parson's Field* 1732 *PubLib* (*v.* feld, first el. *parsonage); Peishame* Ed 6 (*v.* pise, hamm); *Perrycrofte* (*v.* pirige, croft); *Plastersgrove* (first el. probably a surname from pleg-stow); *Pokefeld* (*v.* feld, first el. possibly pūca); *Le Poynt* 1331 (perhaps *point*, used of a projecting piece of land); *Prowefeild* 1704 *Bodl; Pryors Crofte* Ed 6; *Pugden; Puriham* 1309 Cl (*v.* pirige, hamm); *Pusecroft* 13th *ReadingAlm, Pease Crofte* Ed 6 (*v.* pise, croft); *Pydelles* 1544, *Pyddell, La Pedelle* 1551–2 *Survey, Le Puddells* Ed 6 (a variant of pightel, found elsewhere in this parish); *Pycke Croft, Pygge Crofte, Pygke Croft* (*v.* pīc); *Pykewell*; *Pytt Crofte*; *Pitclose* 1552; *Redyngmede or the Abbot of Redyng Mede* 1493 AD; *Reyley, Reyleyfeld*; *Le Roughe Deche* 1551–2 *Survey*, *Roe Ditch* 1632–3 *Bodl*, *Rowe Ditch* 1686 *PubLib* (*v.* rūh, dīc); *Rudden Lane* Ed 6; *Rugdeane*; *Rugende*; *Ruggeweye* 1273 (*v.* hrycg, weg); *Rushe Plate, Russhe Platte* 1551–2 *Survey, Russhe Piddell* Ed 6 (*v.* risc, plat²); *Rydings* Ed 6 (*v.* ryding); *Seynt Marie Crofte* (*v.* hlǣfdige); *Seynt Peters Hilles*; *The Seyntury Lande* 1576 *SpecCom* (cf. O 435); *Shepecotefelde* n.d. (14th), *Shepcotefeld* 1552; *Shepecrofte* Ed 6; *Sheremans Water*; *Shorte Roge*; *Smoke Acre* 1596 (*v.* 282); *Sote(n)ham, Olde Sotenham* 1304–5 (possibly 'Sutta's hamm', cf. Sotwell Pt 2); *Southmede* 1304–5 (*v.* mǣd); *Sowecrofte*; *Spyt(t)elfeld* 1490, *Spytylfeld* 1515, 1516, *Spittylfeld* Hy 8 AD, *Spittlefields* 1539–40, *Spitillfeld, Spetell Felde* Ed 6 (*v.* spitel, and cf. the same name Mx 152); *Stokinge, Stokynges, Stokingstyle* (*v.* stoccing, stigel); *Stoneycrofte*; *Stony Bottom, Norther and Souther* 1596; *La Stonyfeld'* 1273, *Litle and Greate Stony Feylde* 1596; *Stotescroft* Ed 6 (first el. stot 'horse, ox', or a surname derived from it); *Le Strake* Ed 6 (*v.* straca); *Suermedowe, Sewer Mede, Suermede* (*v.* sūr, mǣd); *Sutham* a. 1184, *Suthammesmed* ?13th (*v.* sūð, hamm, mǣd and cf. Northam *supra*); *Lez Swathe* (*v.* swæð); *Tanhousmede* 1539–40, *Tanhowse Mede* 1552, *Tounehouse Meade* 1576 *SpecCom* (a building for tanning); *Tanlock* (fishery) 1539–40, c. 1546, *Le Tanne Lock* 1552 (*v.* tān, loca, 'enclosure of stakes'); *Tenemer Well*; *Thachmed* 1314 Ipm (*v.* þæc, mǣd); *Thorny Mede* 1596; *Thorpe, West- and Est-* (*v.* þrop); *Trolls Croft* Ed 6; *Twelfacres* 1291, *Le Twelve Acr Felde* Ed 6; *Tyllehouse* 1551–2 *Survey, Tylecroft* 1552 (*v.* tigel, hūs, croft); *Tymber Heis* 1548–9 (*v.* timber, (ge)hæg); *Tythridge* Ed 6; *Uppclose, Uppcrofte* (*v.* upp); *Varneclose* (*v.* fearn); *Varyngworth Landes*; *Le Veronhill, Vernelle Grovefelde, Verenhille* (*v.* fearn, hyll); *Virge Lande*; *Vruyfeld*; *Wagball Hill* Ed 6; *Wakesham* a. 1184 (*v.* hamm); *Walcrofta* a. 1184, *Welle Felde and Crofte* (*v.* w(i)ella, feld, croft); *The Weste Ende Grene* Ed 6; *Westham, Vuer- and Nether-* 1290, *Vuere- and Nethere-* 1331, *Westhams* Ed 6 (*v.* uferra, neoðerra, west, hamm); *West Leye* (*v.* lēah); *Wheat Close* Ed 6; *Wheatehames* 1596; *Whethedge*; *Whitley West Ende, Whitley Hill* 1552 (*v.* 177); *Whyteclose, Whytclose, Wheteclose* 1551–2 *Survey, Wheat Close* Ed 6; *Wheat Croft Style* 1704 *Bodl* (*v.* hwǣte); *Whytestrete* 1342 AD (*v.* hwīt, strǣt); *Woodcrofte*; *Wood Downe*; *Woode Presse*; *Le Worthe* 1331 (*v.* worð); *Widenham* c. 1185, *Wydham* n.d. (14th) (*v.* wīd, hamm); *Wyke* (*v.* wīc); *Wynerdfeld* e.14th (*v.* wīn-geard); *Wyneteye* 1309 Cl; *Wyvelie Mede* Ed 6; *Yenderland* (possibly an error for *Yonderland*).

Sulhamstead and Sulhamstead Bannister

SULHAMSTEAD ABBOTS AND BANNISTER

Silamested' 1197–8 AC, *Silamesteda* a. 1202 *Queen, Silhamsted'* 1220 Fees, *Sillamsted'* 1224–5 *Ass, Sil(e)hamsted'* 1241 *ib*, *Sylhamsted'* 1242–3 Fees, *Silhamstede Banastre* 1297 Pat, 1313 AD, 1342 Pat, *Silhamstude, Sylhamstude* 13th *ReadingC, West-*

silhamsted', *Estsilhamsted'* 13th *ReadingC*(2), *West Silhamsted'*,
Est Silhamsted' 13th (14th) *ReadingC*(3), *Silhamstede Abbatis*,
Silhamstede Banastre 1317 (14th) *ib*, *Syllamstede Abbots*,
Syllamstede Banastre 1396 BM
Selehamsted' 1267–8 FF
S(*c*)*hylhamstede, Shilhamsted'*, *Shylhamstede abbatis*, *Sylhamstede
    Banastre* 1284 *Ass*
Syllampstede 1401–2 FA, *Selyhampsted Abbatis* 1463 Fine
Sulhampsted Banaster, Sulhampsted Abbatis 1535 VE, *Sulhamsted
    Bannister alias Michells* 1620 *PubLib, Sulhampstead Bannister als
    Mighells* 1662–3 *ib, Sulhamstead Banister als Michills* 1757
    ArchJ 14

v. hāmstede. Ekwall (DEPN) takes the prefix to be *sylh*, genitive
of sulh, 'narrow valley'. This is very probable, but formally it could
also be the word *siele, sele* 'sallow copse', suggested in DEPN for the
first element of Silchester (Ha) and Silton (Do), *v.* sele². There are
narrow valleys in the area, but the settlements are so widely scattered
that the topography of the original settlement cannot be evaluated.

The manor of Sulhamstead Abbots appears among the possessions
of Reading Abbey at the end of the 12th (VCH III, 307). Sulhamstead
Bannister derives its suffix from a family named *Banastre*, one of
whom gave land to Reading Abbey early in the 13th (VCH III, 431).
Michells or *Mighells*, used as an alternative suffix for Sulhamstead
Bannister, is from the church dedication to St. Michael.

According to VCH III, 430, the parish of Sulhamstead Bannister is
divided into two distinct portions, called the Upper End and the
Lower End. The Upper End is a long, narrow strip lying between two
portions of Sulhamstead Abbots parish. The Lower End is separated
from Sulhamstead by the southern part of Burghfield parish. On the
O.S. index map of civil parishes, only this latter portion is accorded
parochial status, giving the curious effect of a parish separated from
the village which gives name to it.

Sulhamstead†

SULHAMSTEAD WIDEMEAD LOCK, *Widemeda* 13th *ReadingC*, *Widemede, Wydemede* 13th *ReadingC*(2), *Wydemede* 1401–2 *RentSur*,
'wide mead', cf. Widmead in Thatcham 189.

† For names in Sulhamstead Bannister (which is in Theale Hundred) *v.* 221.

TYLE MILL, 1790 Pride, *Tyl(l)e Mylles* 1601 *Dep, Tile Mill* 1761 Rocque, *Tile Mill, Tile Mill Hatch* 1846 Snare, probably from a tiled roof, cf. Slate Mill O 415. In VCH III 308 this is identified with (*molendinum de*) *Russiford, Russieford', Rissieford'* 12th (l.12th) *ReadingC*, (*molendinum de*) *Russiford, Risiford* 13th *ib.* Other references to *Russeford* in the Reading Cartularies make it clear that it was near Widemead *supra*. Possibly 'rush island', *v.* risc, (ī)eg, to which **ford** has been added. Professor Löfvenberg prefers the adj. *rushy* (not recorded till 1382), and points to the f.n. *La Russipudel* in Burghfield 211.

THE BELLOWS, *The Billows* 1846 *TA*, this is a narrow belt of marsh. BENHAM'S FM, FIRS AND GULLY.   BOARMOOR WD, *Boar Moor Field* 1846 *TA*.   BOTTOM LANE.   BRAZENHEAD COPSE, *Brayen Head Field and Mead* 1846 *TA*; in VCH III, 43, reference is made to some cottages called Brazenhead Cottages from a brass knocker. BRISTOW'S COPSE.   FERN LODGE.   FIELD FM, *Fields Farm Close* 1846 *TA*.   FIRLANDS.   FISH HOUSE COTTAGE, cf. *Fish Pond Mead* 1846 *TA*, the 6″ map shows fish-ponds.   FOLLY FM, *v.* **folie**.   FORD BRIDGE.   FOUR HOUSES, 1846 Snare, *The Four Houses* 1761 Rocque, the modern 6″ map shows one house.   FOXES SPRING.   HOME FM, *Home Field, Meadow and Piddle* 1846 *TA*. JAQUES'S LANE, *Jakes's Ground* 1846 *ib.*   LITTLE NEW FM. MALTHOUSE COPSE, *Malt House* 1846 Snare.   MAYRIDGE FM, *Mare Ridge Fm* 1846 ib, possibly 'boundary ridge', *v.* **(ge)mǣre, hrycg**, it is on the parish boundary.   MAYS COTTAGE.   MEALES FM.   MILE HO, MILEHOUSE FM (1846 Snare) AND COTTAGES, this is a little over a mile from Theale.   MOATHOUSE COTTAGES, *Moat Ho* 1846 Snare.   OMER'S GULLY, *Omer Fm* 1846 ib.   PARR'S GULLY.   SHORTHEATH FIRS, *Short Heath* 1761 Rocque.   SOUTH SHRUBBERY.   SULHAMSTEAD BANNISTER UPPER END, *Sulhamstead Upper End* 1846 *TA*, *v.* 185.   SULHAMSTEAD GREEN, 1846 *ib.* SULHAMSTEAD HO, 1846 Snare.   TENNINGS'S COPSE.   THREE FIRS P.H.   THREE KINGS JACK'S BOOTH P.H., *Jack Boot* 1761 Rocque, *Jacks Booth* 1790 Pride, 1846 Snare.   TYLEMILL BRIDGE, LOCK AND LOWER BRIDGE, *v. supra*.   WHITE HO P.H.   WHITEHOUSE GREEN, *Whitehouse Green and Pasture* 1846 *TA*.   WHITE'S HILL.   WISE'S FIRS.   WOOLWICH GREEN, 1817 OS, 1846 Snare, *Woolwich, Woolwich Green* 1846 *TA*.   WOOLWICHGREEN FM. YEWTREE COTTAGES.

FIELD-NAMES

Except where otherwise stated, the principal forms in (a) are 1846 *TA*, which covers Sulhamstead and Sulhamstead Bannister; those marked M are modern names written on 6″ maps in Reading Public Library; early forms dated 13th, for which no source is given, are *ReadingC*, and those dated 13th (14th), n.d. (14th) are *ReadingC(3)*.

(a) Absend Close; Barrs Piddle; Bean Piddle, Bean Pightle (pightel, and the variant *piddle*, are common in the f.ns. of this parish); Bottoms (*v.* botm); Broad Croft; Brook Close; The Butts M (*v.* butte); Cart House Piece; Chalkam; Charcoal Mdw; Chatter Alley 1846 Snare, Chatterlly Common; The Chequers M (*v.* cheker); Church Close; Copid Cross M (*v.* coppod, coppede); Copper Close; Coppice Pightle; Copse Great Fd; Copyhold Fd; Corner Piece; Cow Moor; Crabtree Ground; Crooked Ley (*v.* lēah); Dingles Pightle; Dog Kennel 1846 Snare; The Down (*v.* dūn); Fire Drake (*v.* 285); Freelands; Furze Hovel Pasture; Glebe Ground; The Gore (*v.* gāra); Granary Pightle; Gravel Pit Ground; Great Lay; Greenfield; Hams (*v.* hamm); Hay Merch; Heath Close and Ground; Hill Bottoms and Ground; Honey Fd M (*v.* hunig); Hop Garden (*v.* hoppe); House Ground; Inhams (*v.* innām); Kings Grove; Kingslet M; The Lake (*v.* lacu 'stream'; the Kennet has numerous branches here); Layn Ground M (*v.* leyne); Lot Mdw (*v.* hlot); Match Wick Mead; Meadow Fd; Middleham M (*Mildha'* 1196 *FF*, *Middleham* l.12th BM, *Middelham* n.d. (14th), 13th, *v.* middel, hamm); Mongers Pasture; Moor; Mortimer Close (cf. Stratfield Mortimer 216); Muse, Great and Path; Navigation Mead (probably referring to the Kennet and Avon Canal); Nursery Ground; Oats Croft; Old Pond Tail (*v.* tægl); Orchard Close, Ground and Piddle; Paddock Fd; Pairtree Close and Ground; The Park; Parsons Piece; Pasture Piece; Peat Mead; Picked Close, Picket Ground (*v.* pīced); Pit Croft (*Putcroft* 13th *ReadingC(2)*, *v.* pytt, croft); Pond Pasture and Close; Popes Piddle; Pound Close and Mead; Puntfield Moor; Red Croft; Rides; Rye Close; Saw Pit Ground; Shop Close; Simmonds Marsh; Slab Mdw; Spring Close; Stoneham (*Stonham* 13th *ReadingC(2)*, *Stonehame* 1552 *LRMB*, *v.* stān, hamm); Stony Fd; Stream Close; Stump Mdw; Sulhamstead Park; Totterdowns (cf. 160); Town Land M; The Vines or Fynes M; Water Mead; Well Piddle; Wheat Field; Wheathams (*Wetham* 13th *ReadingC(2)*, *v.* hwǣte, hamm); Wickens Mead; Wide Moor; Wood Ground; Yew Croft.

(b) *Anketill' Dune* 13th *ReadingC(2)* (*v.* dūn, first el. a surname); *Benewell'* 13th *ib* (*v.* bēan, w(i)ella); *La Formore* 13th *ib* (*v.* fōr, fore, mōr); *Graue* 13th *ib*, *Grauam* 13th (14th) (*v.* grāf); *Hauekeresforde* 13th (*v.* hafocere, ford); *Langeforlong* 1313 AD (*v.* lang, furlang); *Merse* 13th *ReadingC(2)* (*v.* mersc); *Midemestedole* 13th, 13th (14th), *Midelmestedole* 13th (14th) (*v.* dāl, the first instance of *middlemost* in NED is a. 1300); *Ricardesdune Serle* 13th *ReadingC(2)* (*v.* dūn, *Ric. Serle* is mentioned in the charter); *Stodham* 13th, 13th (14th) (*v.* stōd, hamm); *Suthfeld* 13th *ReadingC(2)* (*v.* sūð, feld); *Wideham* 13th *ReadingC(2)* (*v.* wīd, hamm); *La Wlfhull'* 13th *ReadingC(2)* (*v.* wulf, hyll).

Thatcham

THATCHAM

Þæcham c. 954 (c. 1400) EHD, c. 971 (12th) ASWills
Taceham 1086 DB, *Taccheham* c. 1225 BM *et freq* with variant
spelling *Tacheham* to 1202 (1227) Ch, *Tacheam* 1168, 1170 P,
1202 (1227) Ch, *Tacham* 1224–5 *Ass*, 13th *ReadingC*(2), 1241,
1284 *Ass*
Thacheham c. 1125 BM, *Thacham* 1212 Fees *et freq* *Thatcham*
1224–5 *Ass*, 1316 FA, *Thacheam* 1342 Pat
Techam 1142–84 (l.12th) *ReadingC*, 1198 P, 1224–5, 1241 *Ass*
Thecham 1242–3 Fees, 13th *ReadingC*, 1284 *Ass*

A compound of þæc 'thatch' either with hām 'village' (referring
to the thatched roofs of the settlement) or hamm 'river-meadow'
(referring to a meadow where thatching material was obtained). Cf.
Thatcham Gl 3, 16. The forms show no sign of hamm, but the village
overlooks marshy ground by the Kennet, and the compound *þæcc-
hamm is well-attested elsewhere (cf. O 468–9).

Professor Löfvenberg comments that the only recorded form of the
first el. is *þæc*, and that the assibilated form found in Thatcham is
due either to influence of the verb *þeccan*, *þæccan or to the existence
of a side-form *þæcce.

THATCHAM STREET-NAMES

BROAD ST.   CHAPEL ST.   CHEAP ST, 1722 *PubLib*, *v.* cēap 'market'.

COLTHROP

Colethrop' 1220 Fees *et freq* with variant spellings *Colethrop(e)*,
Coletorp to 1242–3 Fees
Coldrop, Coltthrorp 1284 *Ass*, *Coldrop* 1294 SR, *Coldthrop* 1327 *ib*,
Colthrop 1402 AD, *Coulthroppe* 1618 *PubLib*, *Coldthorp, Coldrop
Farm* 1761 Rocque

'Cola's hamlet', *v.* þrop. Some of the forms suggest association of
the first el. with the word *cold*.

CROOKHAM

Crocheham 1086 DB, 1167 P, *Crokeham* 1170 *ib*, *Crokeham,
Crokam* 1517 D Inc

Crocham 1156 P *et passim* with variant spelling *Crokham* to 1415
Fine

Croukham 1228 BM, 1344 Cl, *Crookham (Heath)* 1713 *PubLibDoc*,
1761 Rocque

Probably a compound of crōc 'crook' with hām. Crookham Ho
and hamlet are a mile apart, and it is not clear where the original
nucleus of the settlement lay, but both places are on a ridge, the north
and south edges of which are marked by narrow indentations.
Crookham has previously (DEPN, Elements **1**, 113) been considered
to contain crōh² 'nook, corner', which might have been held to refer
to these gullies. The forms given above, however, definitely suggest
OE *Crōc-*, and the identification of Crookham with *croh hamme* in
the bounds of Brimpton (which lies behind the derivation from
crōh²) should probably be rejected, *v.* Pt 3. The charter-name is over
a mile from Crookham hamlet, and even further from Crookham Ho,
and the spellings for Crookham are inconsistent with an OE form
Crōh-. The R. Enborne, which flows immediately south of the
Crookham ridge, is marked by a striking series of small, sharp bends
in this stretch, and these could have been referred to as 'crooks'.
The first el. could be in the gen. pl. Crookham Ha (DEPN) may be
identical with Crookham Berks.

HENWICK FM, *Henewyk'* 1284 *Ass*, 1327 *SR*, *Henwick* 1408, 1601,
1610 *RecOffCat*. Probably identical with Henwick Wo 132, 'dairy
farm of the monks', from hīwan (gen.pl. hīgna) and wīc. Thatcham
was one of the original endowments of Reading Abbey.

WIDMEAD LOCK, *Widemede* 1225–6 FF, 13th *ReadingC(2)*, *La Wydemede* 1307 Ipm, *Wydemedesdrove* 1336 *RecOffCat*, *Wydmed* 1340 *ib*,
Wydemede 1547 LRMB, 'wide meadow' *v.* wīd, mǣd. The form
from 1336 has *drove* 'way along which cattle are driven', added.
The same name occurs in Sulhamstead (185).

ASHEN COPSE.   AVENELL'S COPSE AND COTTAGE, *Avenells* 1841 *TA*,
cf. Avenal(l)s in Bucklebury 159.   BANKS'S FM, *Banks Great
Meadow and Upper Mead* 1841 *ib*.   BARN GULLY, *Barn Close,
Barn Gully Meadow* 1841 *ib*.   BERRY'S STILE COTTAGES, *Le Bury*
1547 *LRMB*, *Lower, Upper and Hither Berry* 1841 *TA*, *v.* burh and
cf. Berry's Copse just over the parish boundary in Bucklebury 156;
there may have been an area called 'the Bury' N.E. of Thatcham.

BLACKLANDS COPSE, *Blacklands Wood* 1817 OS, *Blakelandes* 1547 *LRMB*, *v.* blæc (blacan), land.   BOAR'S GULLY.   BOND'S GULLY, *Bonds Ground* 1841 *TA*.   BRUSHWOOD GULLY.   BURDEN'S HEATH PLANTATION, *Burdens Heath* 1812 Bucklebury, *Great and Little Burdens* 1841 *TA*.   BURNELL'S FM.   CHAMBERHOUSE FM AND MILL, (manor of) *Chambirehous* 1446 Ch, *Chambrehous* 1450 Fine, *Chamberhouse Parcke* 1547 *LRMB*, *Chamber House* 1761 Rocque, 1817 OS, *Chamberhouse Mill* 1817 OS. Roger *de la Chambre* held land in Thatcham in the 13th cent. (VCH III, 316) and *Thomas de la Chambre of Crokham* is mentioned 1352 Pat; the house is mentioned in Ashmole (II, 326).   CLAPPER'S GREEN, 1841 *TA*, possibly dialect *clapper* 'rabbit-burrow'.   COLTHROP BRIDGE, COTTAGES, FM (*Coldrop Farm* 1761 Rocque) AND MILL (*Colthorpe Mill* 1547 *LRMB*), *v.* 188.   COMMON BARN, near Crookham Common.   COMPTON WOOD.   CONDUIT COPSE.   COOPER'S FM.   THE CORNER.   CROOKHAM COMMON, 1841 *TA*, *Crookham Heath* 1713 *PubLibDoc*, 1761 Rocque.   CROOKHAM END HO (on 2½″), *Crookham End Meadow* 1841 *TA*.   CROOKHAM HO, 1817 OS, *v.* 188–9.   CROWN ACRE COTTAGE, *Crown or Great Meadow, The Crown Acre in Beddals Field* 1841 *TA*.   DOGKENNEL COPSE, *Dogkennel Meadow* 1841 *ib.*   DUNSTAN HO AND LODGE, DUNSTON PARK, *Donstonefeld, Donstanefeld* 1547 *LRMB*, *Dunston Park* 1761 Rocque, *Donstan Field and Park* 1841 *TA*, the park was enclosed in the first half of the 18th (VCH III, 313); *Park Barn Ground* and *Park Meadow* 1841 *TA* probably refer to this.   DUNSTON WOOD.   EAST FIELD COPSE.   FOXHOLD, FOXHOLD FM, *Foxhole Coppice and Meadow* 1841 *TA*, *v.* fox-hol.   THE GABLES.   GEORGE'S FM (1830 OS) AND WOOD, *Georges Field and Meadow* 1841 *TA*.   GOLDFINCH BOTTOM.   GREAT WOOD.   GREEN LANE, *Green Lane Pightle* 1841 *TA*.   GULLY, BIG AND LITTLE.   HANGING LANDS GULLY, *Crookham Hangings* 1830 OS, *Hanging Lands* 1841 *TA*, *v.* hangende.   HART'S HILL, 1817 OS, HARTSHILL COPSE, FM (1817 OS) AND GULLY.   THE HASSOCK, cf. *Le Hassoke Mede, Hassokk Mede, Hassockemede Hassokefelde* 1547 *LRMB*. There are several copses with this name in Berks, and EDD records that in this county *hassock* is used of 'a wood usually of Scotch firs with much coarse rank grass'. NED gives a quot. from 1814 'The down is entirely spotted with small islets (the country people call them hassocks) of low trees and luxuriant underwood'. In f.ns. in other counties the word seems to mean 'a tuft of coarse grass', *v.* hassuc.   HEAD'S

HILL. HIGHFIELD COPSE, *High Field* 1841 *TA.* HOLLY COTTAGE. HOPGARDEN GULLY, *Hop Garden Ground* 1841 *TA.* HUNT'S GULLY, *Hunts Corner, Cow Leaze, Meadow and Pightle* 1841 *ib.* KEEPER'S HO. KENTON'S WOOD. KIRTON'S COPSE. LITTLE PARK FM AND HO, *Little Parcke Corner* 1620 *SpecCom*, this park can be traced back to the 13th, *v.* VCH III, 316. LONG COPSE. LONG GROVE COPSE, *Longe Grove* 1547 *LRMB, Long Grove* 1817 OS. LONGLANDS GULLY, cf. *Longe Lande, Le Longelandes, Le Langlandes* 1547 *LRMB, v.* lang, land. LOWER LODGE. MANOR ASH MOAT, *Manor Ash, Manor Ash Moat* 1841 *TA.* MANOR FM AND LANE. MONKEY MARSH LOCK. MOOR DITCH, cf. *Le Litill More* 1547 *LRMB, Thatcham Moor* 1722 *PubLib, Moor Common, Little Moor* 1841 *TA, v.* mōr. MORTIMER'S COTTAGES, *Mortimers Mead* 1841 *TA.* NEW GULLY. NEW TOWN. NORTHFIELD RD. OSIER GULLY. PARK COPSE AND FM (latter 1817 OS), near Dunston Park. PARK COPSE, PARK GULLY BRIDGE, near Little Park. PARK LANE, leading towards Dunston Park. PARK LODGE, PARKLODGE GULLY, near Chamberhouse Fm *supra.* PIPER'S FM, *Pipers Meadow* 1841 *TA.* THE PLANTATION (2 examples). POWELL'S COPSE. PRIOR'S MOOR DITCH. RAINSFORD FM. RAMSBURY COPSE AND CORNER WOOD (latter 1830 OS), *Ramsbury Meadow* 1841 *TA, v.* 155. ROBIN'S COPSE. THE ROOKERY, ROOKERY COTTAGES. ROUND COPSE. SAYER'S COPSE, *Sayers Meadow* 1841 *TA.* SHORTHILL COPSE. SIEGECROSS FM, *Seycrosse* 1547 *LRMB, Sedge Cross Farm* 1817 OS, *Sage Cross, Sedge Cross* 1841 *TA*, etymology uncertain, cf. Sage Croft f.n. *infra.* SHORTHILL COPSE. SOUTH LANDS. STONE HO, STONEHOUSE COTTAGES AND GULLY. SWAN INN. SYDNEY LODGE. THATCHAM FM AND HO. THATCHAM MARSH, 1761 Rocque. THORNFORD BRIDGE (1761 Rocque) AND GULLY, *Thornford Mead and Island* 1841 *TA*, the ford over R. Enborne is shown on 1″ map, *v.* þorn, ford. TRAVELLERS' FRIEND P.H. TURNPIKE COTTAGES. VOLUNTEER INN. WATERSIDE COPSE AND FM, *Waterside Mead* 1841 *TA*, the Fm is by R. Kennet. WESTCOMBE VILLA. WHITELANDS FM, *Whitelands* 1547 *LRMB, White Lands* 1841 *TA, v.* hwīt, land, cf. Blacklands Copse *supra.* WILDERS. WIMBLE'S FM, GULLY AND WOOD. WOODSIDE COTTAGES.

FIELD-NAMES

Principal forms in (*a*) are 1841 *TA*, and this award covers the modern parish of Cold Ash as well as that of Thatcham; early forms for which no date or source is given are 1547 *LRMB* (Colthrop); those dated 13th are *ReadingC-* (2); c. 1290, 1300, 1309, 1314, 1323, 1333, 1336, 1341–2, 1601, 1610 *RecOffCat*; 1450, 1499–1500 *RentSur*.

(*a*) Albourn Mead, Aldbourn Mdw (*Al(d)bourn* is R. Enborne 9); Albrays Fd; Alder Pightle; Arch Mdw; Bakehouse Ground and Mead; Bake Ground and Pightle (*v.* beak); Bandylands; Barn Fd and Ground; The Bates, Bates Mdw, Batts Mdw (*v.* bete²); Bean Croft; Benham Hill and Mdw (cf. Benham 267); Black Ground; Blanch Croft; Blew Close; Bodmin Acre; The Bourn (*v.* burna); Bowling Green; Brickford; Brick Kiln Ground; Broad Close (*Le Brodeclose*); Broad Croft (*Bradcrofte*); Broad Cut (*cut* is an occasional term for a piece of land, *v.* 281); Broad Lands; Broad Mdw (*Broad Meadows* 1706 *PubLib*); Broom Croft (*v.* brōm); The Budds; Bushey Park; Butchers Ground; Buttons Mdw; The Butts (*v.* butte); Calf Pightle; Carters Pightle; Carthouse Mdw; Chalk Ground; Chalk Pit Ground and Mdw; Cholsey Fd; Church Lands; Col(d)throp Marsh (*v.* 188); Colthouse Mdw; Commons Mdw (*Le Comen Mede*); Coppice Close and Ground; Costers (*v.* cot-stōw); Cot Mdw (*v.* cot); Cow Ground; Cow House Mdw; Cow Leaze (*Cowelez*, *v.* lǣs); Crab Tree Close; The Croft; Crow Fd; Cucko Pen (*v.* O 438); Curwell Leaze; Davids Mdw; Devils Den (*v.* 285); Dewberry Mdw (a type of blackberry, *v.* NED); Ditch Piece; Drying Ground; Dry Mdw; Ducketts; Dung Pookes; Eighteen Penny Mdw; The Farthings (*v.* fēorðung); Fidlers Ground; Fish Pond Piece and Mead; Five Acres (*Fifacre* 1225–6 *FF*, 13th, *Le v Acres*); Fodder Close; Fodder House Mead; Fort Pightle; Forty Platts (*v.* forð-ēg, plat²); Fox Pightle; Frenches Pightle; Frith (*Frythes Croft*, *v.* fyrhð); The Furlongs; Furze Close and Platt; Garden Piece; Gay Lands; Golden Leaze; Gratis (*v.* 283); Gravelly Ground; Green Fd; Grove; Gully Mdw; Gun Ground; Half Way Ground; Ham, Long and East (*Esteham*, *v.* hamm); Hanging (*v.* hangende); Hare Fd; Harrow Croft; Hart Mdw and Pightle (cf. Hart's Hill 190); Hay Croft; Haywards Half; Helens; Henleys (*Henley*); The Heron (*v.* hyrne); Hicks Bottom and Pightle; High Ground and Close; Hill Closes (*Hill Close*); Hill Croft (*Hullecroft* 1450, *Hullescroft* 1499–1500, *Hillcrofte*); Hilly Piece and Mead; The Hitch (*v.* hiche); Holbrook; The Holds; The Hollands, Hollands Mdw; Holly Grove; Home Close, Fd and Mead (*Le Home Mede*); Horse Leaze (*Horsselez*, *v.* lǣs); Horse Platt (*v.* plat²); Horse Pond; House Pightle; The Hyde (*v.* hīd); Irelands; Irish Fd and Hill (cf. Irish Hill in Hamstead Marshall, Pt 2); The Island (*Ilandes*); Jackmalls (*Great and Little Jacknells* 1713 *PubLibDoc*); Kill Hill and Mdw; Kiln Close, Kiln Ground Mdw; Kings Pightle; Kites Abbey Ground; The Lawn (*v.* launde) Leap Land Ground; Leates Ground and Mdw; Lee Close (*Le Lye*, *v.* lēah); Longwood Ground; Low Ground Mdw; Lucern or South Field Mdw; Malm Mdw and Pightle (*v.* m(e)alm); Malthouse Ground; Marks Acre;

Marsh Mdw (*Le Marsshe*); Mill Mdw (*Le Milhowse*); Minny Croft; Mow-croft Hill; Mulford Mdw; Muncle Marsh; The Muzzles; Nutmore Croft and Mead; Oak Crofts; Oakford Ground and Mead; Old Fd; Old Inclosure; Orchard Close and Mdw; The Paddock; Parish Land; Parsonage Pightle; Pear Tree Mdw; Peat Mead; Pebley Hill; Picked Close and Mdw (*Le Piked Close, v.* pīced); The Pightles (*v.* pightel, common in this parish); The Pills (*v.* O 462); Plat, Platts Mdw (*v.* plat²); Plot Mead; Plough Ground; Poffley Mead (*Pudfle Mede*); Poison Pightle; Pond Close; Poor Fd; Prince Fd; Princes Hold; Purgatory (*v.* 283); Puscott; The Query (*v.* 283); Racketts; Rag Ground Mdw; Red Lands; Reeds Pightle; Rickhouse Mead and Pightle; Rick Yard Mdw; Ripper Piece; Rough Patch; Round Ham, Hill, Mdw and Pightle; Runaway(s); Rushy Plat; Rye Furlong; Sage Croft (*Sagecrofte*, probably connected with Siegecross Fm *supra*); Sand Pit Ground; Sand Close; Scrubbs; Sellwood; Shaw Pightle (*Shaw Deane, v.* sc(e)aga, denu); Short Lands (*Shortelands, v.* land); Snipe Piece; Spring Mdw and Piece; Spur Croft; Squabbs; Square Pightle; Stable Mdw; Stone; Stone Cuts and Mdw; Stoney Lane Pightle; Straw Fd; The String (*v.* 282); Tadpoles Mdw; Tadslips Mdw (*Tadeslep* 13th, *v.* tāde, slǣp); The Tan House; Thamers Gore (*v.* gāra); Thistley Ham, Thistley Pightle; The Thongs (*v.* þwang); Three Corner Mdw and Pightle; Tree Lane Piece; Turn Croft; Vicarage Mead; Ware Ground; The Warren; Water Mdw; Way Mdw; Well Close; Wet Mdw; Wheelers Land and Pightle; White House Mead; Wood Ground; The Wood; Worthy Piece (*Le Worthy* 1309, *Wurthyfelde, v.* worðig); The Yards; Yates Pightle; Yellow Close.

(*b*) *Barnes Croftes*; *Bellemore*; *Bonnet Close*; *Bourestret'* 1341–2 (*v.* būr¹, strǣt, Thom. *atte Boure* is mentioned); *La Brecheacre* c. 1300, *La Breche* 1333 (*v.* brēc, æcer); *Brodefeld'* 13th (*v.* brād, feld); *Bushill Pidle*; *Busshy Close*; *Combefelde*, *Combe More* (*v.* cumb, feld, mōr); *Dederuding'* 1224–5 *Ass* (*v.* dēad, ryding); *Elforde*; *Englichecroft* 1336 (first el. probably the surname *English*); *La Estgrave* c. 1300 (*v.* ēast, grāf); *Gyles Land Mede*; *Hawecrofte* (*v.* haga¹, croft); *Hedefyld* 1450, *Hedfeld* 1499–1500 (*v.* hǣð, feld); *Le Hempefelde* (*v.* hænep, feld); *Heth(e)landes*; *Le Hillgrove*; *Le Horncroft* c. 1290 (*v.* horn, croft); *Inglesam Wayye* 1450 (Inglesham is in W); *Kewyke* 1450, *Kowyke* 1499–1500 (*v.* cū, wīc, the same name occurs in Reading 180); *Le Lane Close*; *Le Litelaker* 1309 (*v.* lȳtel, æcer); *Litill Mede*, *Litle Mede Plat*; *Lemmareshamme* 1336 (possibly 'Lēofmǣr's hamm'); *Longe Acr*; *Le Longecrofte*; *Lyteldon' field* 1341–2 (*v.* lȳtel, dūn, feld); *Medecrofte* (*v.* mǣd, croft); *Midleham* (*v.* middel, hamm); *Le Mydleclose*; *Le Mot(e)close* (*v.* mote, possibly connected with Manor Ash Moat *supra*); *Mulesfeld* c. 1300 ('Mūl's feld', cf. Moulsford, Pt 2); *Le Netherclose*; *Le Nethergrounde*; *Neweby* 1450; *Palmerslane* 1450, 1499–1500; *Parke Copice*, *Le Parke* 1547 *LRMB* (near Colthrop); *Pitfeldes*; *Ponsley Mede*; *Le Quon-hamene* 1314, *Le Quonham* 1323 (*v.* hamm, first el. obscure); *Le Rakheys* (*v.* hraca, (ge)hæg); *Rowe Close*; *Ryshamesacre* c. 1300, *Rixhamme* 1336 (*v.* risc, hamm); *Le Shepehouse Close*; *Smallege Mede* (*smallage* is used of wild celery or water parsley, *v.* NED); *Squyers Crofte*; *Stancrofte* (*v.* stān, croft); *Strowdes* (*v.* strod); *Sunhened* c. 1300; *Le Upperclose*; *Le Westeclose*; *Westeham* (*v.* west, hamm); *Le Whetecrofte* (*v.* hwǣte, croft); *Le Woode Crofte.*

Tilehurst

Tilehurst

Tigelherst 1167 P *et passim* with variant spellings *Tigelhurst'*,
   Tig(h)elhurst, Thigelhurst, Tyghelhurst to 1342 Pat
Tylhurst 1224–5 *Ass, Tyelhurst, Telhurst* 1284 *ib, Tyleherst* 1517
   D Inc, 1675 Ogilby, *Tilehurst* (*Common*) 1761 Rocque
Tygheleshurst 1295 Ipm

OE tigel 'tile' and hyrst 'wooded hill'. tigel occurs in a number of p.ns., usually in allusion to places where tiles were made. The charter no. 415 in Hurley is a grant dated 1348 by Roger *le Tyghelere* of *Tyughurst.* A *tegularia* near Whitley Park (Reading) is mentioned in a deed of 1182 in *ReadingC(3)*.

TILEHURST STREET-NAMES†

ARMOUR RD, *v.* 177.   LOWER ARMOUR RD.   BLUNDELLS RD (near Blundell's Copse).   CRESCENT RD.   KENTWOOD HILL, *v.* 176.   NORCOT RD, *v.* 177. RECREATION RD (near Blagrave Recreation Ground).   SCHOOL RD AND TERRACE. WESTWOOD RD, *v.* 177.   VICTORIA RD.

LANGLEY FM, *Langeleye* n.d. (14th) *ReadingC(3), Langley* 1552 *LRMB, Langley, Langl(e)y Mead* 17th *PubLib(Clayton), v.* lang, lē(a)h and cf. 251. This may be the unidentified DB *Lonchelei*, which was in Reading Hundred.

LENDHAM, *Lewdehammesweylet* 1462 *Bodl*, (way called) *Lewdehammesweylete* 1469 *ib, Lewdham Close, Field and Ground* 1843 *TA.* OE *weg-(ge)lǣte* 'road-junction', added to the gen. of a p.n. *Lewdehamm* 'Lēofede's hamm'; *v.* (ge)lǣt, and Feilitzen 322 for the pers.n. Lendham is near a cross-roads. The first el. may have been altered to avoid association with the word *lewd.*

ALDER COPSE.   BACK LANE.   BAREFOOTS BARN AND COPSE, *Bearfoot Fm* 1846 Snare; probably a surname, the name *Barefot*

---

† The settlement of Tilehurst is in the parish of Reading, but it seems desirable to
   list the street-names here.

occurs in Berks c. 1160 (F. M. Stenton, *The First Century of English Feudalism*, 278) and in the form *Barfot* 1331 Cl, 1348 Pat. None of these refs. is to land in Tilehurst, however, and another possibility is e.ModE *berefot* 'hellebore' given for Bearfoot Wood Gl **3**, 193. BEAL'S COPSE, FM AND PLANTATION, *Beals Ground* 1843 *TA*. BIRCH COPSE, GREAT AND LITTLE, *Burchen Coppice* 17th *PubLib(Clayton)*, *Birch Coppice Pightle* 1843 *TA*, v. bircen[1]. BOXGROVE COTTAGE AND WOOD. BROOMHILL. BUSHNELLS COPSE, *Bushnell's Coppice* 1817 *EnclA* (Theale). CALCOT PARK AND ROW, 1846 Snare, *Calcott Park* 1790 Pride, v. 222. CHURCHEND COPSE, *Church End Coppice* 1824 *PubLibDoc*, v. 178. THE CITY, a row of small houses beside a road, v. 284. CLAY COPSE, *Clay Croft and Pightle* 1843 *TA*. CORNWELL COPSE, *Cornwell* 1843 *ib*. CURTIS'S WOOD, *Curtiss Wood Ground or Upper Coppice Close* 1824 *PubLibDoc*, *Curtis's Wood Ground* 1843 *TA*. DARK LANE. DENEFIELD, *North Deenfield, South Deen Field Common* 1761 Rocque, v. denu, feld. GARSTON'S COPSE, *Garstons Mead* 1755 *PubLibDoc*, *Garston Coppice* 1824 *ib*, *Garstons* 1843 *TA*, v. gærs-tūn. HALL. HALL-PLACE FM, *Hall Place* 1817 *EnclA* (Theale). HALL'S COPSE. HAREFIELD COPSE, *Harrowfield Coppice* 1824 *PubLibDoc*. HIGH COPSE. HILDENS COPSE, *Hilldown Copse* 1846 Snare. KILN COPSE, *Kiln Coppice and Close* 1824 *PubLibDoc*, *Kiln Close and Pightle* 1843 *TA*. LANGLEY HILL, 1761 Rocque, v. 194. LITTLE HEATH, 1761 Rocque. LONG LANE. LONGLEAT may be *Longlete* 1535 VE. The name is apparently identical with Longleat W 169, 'long water-channel', but cf. Lendham 194, near the Tilehurst Longleat, the early forms for which contain *weg-gelæte* 'road-junction'. MAYBOUGH PIT, *May Bough Pit Ground* 1843 *TA*. MOUNT SKYVER WOOD. NABBS HILL. OLIVER'S COPSE, *Upper Oliver* 1817 *EnclA* (Theale), *Oliver's Coppice* 1824 *PubLibDoc*, *Olivers Grounds* 1843 *TA*. PINCENT'S FM (1846 Snare) AND LANE, *Pynsons in Tylehurst* 1552 *LRMB*, Edmund son of Gilbert *Pynceon* of *Tighelhurst* is mentioned 1316 Pat, and is called Edmund *Pynson* 1317 ib; for the history of the estate and family v. VCH III, 332. PINKCLOSE PLANTATION, PINK'S GROVE, *Pink Close* 1843 *TA*. SADLER'S FM. STONEHAM FM, 1830 OS, *Stoneham* 1824 *PubLibDoc*. TURNHAM'S FM, *Lower Turnhams* 1824 *ib*, *Lower and Upper Turnhams* 1843 *TA*. VICARAGE COPSE AND WOOD. WHITE HART P.H., *White Hart Ground and Pightle* 1843 *TA*, *White Hart* 1846 Snare. WITHY COPSE, *Withy Coppice* 17th *PubLib(Clayton)*.

FIELD-NAMES

Except for those dated 1824, which are *PubLibDoc*, the principal forms in
(a) are 1843 *TA*, which appears to cover the modern parish of Theale as well
as that of Tilehurst. Early forms dated 1300, 1302, 1320, 1322, 1325, 1328,
n.d. are *ReadingC(3)* and are all (14th); 1461, 1462, 1469 *Bodl*; 1539–40,
1544, c. 1546 ReadingA; and 1616, 17th *PubLib(Clayton)*.

(a) Bachelors Pightle (v. pightel, as elsewhere in this parish); Barn Pightle
and Close; Beach Fd; Best Leaze (v. lǣs); Bishams 1824, Bisham; Bitts
(v. bita); Blackbirds Pightle; Blackboy Mdw; Blackdicks; Blackham Allotment and Fd; Blind Stile; Blundells Coppice and Pightle; Bonny Fd and
Mead; Bottom Ground; Bowling Green; Bradfield, Broadfield (*Broad Field*
17th); Brickkiln Fd 1824; Brock Down; Brook Mdw; Broom Coppice
Ground; Broomham, Broomhams (*Bromham* n.d., v. brōm, hamm); Butter-
milk Hill; Chalk Pit Fd and Ground; Chapel Fd; Cherry Close (also 17th);
Choulham; Church Fd; Common Allotment and Pightle; Coppice Ground
and Close (*Coppice Close, Ye Coppice Place* 17th); Cottage Green; Cow
Moor; Crab Fd; Crow Lands; Crown Mdw and Pightle; Culver Croft (v.
culfre); Curlham Fd (*Culham* 17th); Curtains Pightle (Curtins Piddle 1817
EnclA (Theale)); Deadmoor Pond Piece; Dennets Hill (Dennett Hills 1817
EnclA (Theale)); Dickery Croft; Dog Kennel Mead; The Down (v. dūn;
Dunn Crofts; Dunts Lane Ground; Durnhams; Dwelling House Ground
and Pightle; Easter Croft; East Fd (*Estfeld* 1317 AD, v. ēast, feld); Elder
Bacon; Ell Mdw; Five Acres (*The Long Five Acres* 1755 *PubLibDoc*); Frontage
Allotment; Front Pasture; Fullers Hill; Gale Moor (v. mōr, first el. possibly
gagel); The Garden Ground; Garrett Pightle; Goodwins Pightle; Grange-
land; Granthams (*Grantham* 17th); Gravel Pit Piece (*Ye Gravell Pitts* 17th);
Green Pightle; The Grove (*La Graue, Le Grofcroft* 1320, *La Groue, Le
Grofcroft* 1328, v. grāf, croft); Ham, Great and Little, Ham Pightle, The
Hams (v. hamm); Hanging Downs (*Hangdowne* 17th, v. hangende); Har-
moor Ground, Mdw and Pightle; Harts Pightle; Haulham(s); Haw Croft;
Hawkins Pightle; Hazely Moor (*Haselmore* 1616, v. hæsel, mōr); Heath
Allotment (cf. *Tilehurst Heath* 1583 *Dep*); Highlands; Hill Ground, Down
and Pightle; The Hocket (cf. The Hockett in Bisham 60); Holly Wood
(*Holy Wood* 17th); Home Close, Ground, Mdw and Pightle; Homershams;
Hop Kiln Piece; How Croft; Kill Horse Fd (v. 283); Kinty Bottom; Kitchen
Pightle (v. cycene); Knapps Pightle; Lamb Ground and Pightle; Land
Field Allotment; Lane End Ground; Lane Mead and Pightle; Lawrances
Hill; Lay Croft; Leaze, High and Little (v. lǣs); Leekhams; Lock Mdw;
Lot Moor (v. hlot, mōr); Manorial Allotment; Man's Pightle; Market
Garden Ground; Market Lands; Marley Hall; Marshalls (also 1769
PubLibDoc); Martins Pightle; Meadly Gate Pasture; Mead Plot; Meggs
Coppice 1824; Mill Close and Fd (*Mill Orchard and Mead* 17th); Minnims
Sandy Fd; The Moor; Narcot Mdw, Northcot Mead (*Northcotfildes* 1584
AD, v. Norcot Fm 177); Nix Pightle; No Mans Land (v. 284); Oat Moor; Old
Hayes; Orchard Close; Oxlade (Oxlade's Close 1817 *EnclA*); Paddock,

North and South; Pasture Plot; Picked Close and Pightle (*The Piked Close* 17th, *v.* pīced); Pilots; Pinley Pightle; Pit Close (*Ye Pitt* 17th); Play Plot; Plot Pightle; Pond Close and Mdw; Poor Allotment (*v.* 285); Portlands; Post Ground; Pound Ground; Right Dean; Round Mdw and Pightle; Sandfield Allotment; Sand Pit Ground; Sandy Hill (*Sandhills* 17th); Sandy Close, Fd, Lands and Pightle; Shadwicks Pightle (*Shudwike* c. 1546, *Shadwyke* 1552 *LRMB*, *Shatwicks Close* 17th, *Shadwicke Tything* 1774 *PubLib*, possibly 'boundary wīc', *v.* scēad); Shallow Corner Homestall, Great Shallow 1824; The Shaw 1824; Sheep House; Sheets (*v.* scīete); The Slipe 1824 (*v.* slipe); Smooth Moor; Snells Pightle; Sparks Moor; Spring Close and Pightle; Stone Pit Allotment; Stop Lands; Strait Furlong (possibly strǣt, *v.* Streets *infra*); Stream Close; Streets, Great and Little, Streets Pasture and Pightle (*Longestrete* 1462, 1469, *v.* strǣt, no Roman roads are known in the area, but the Roman settlement at Reading presupposes one); String Close, The String, Strings (*v.* 282); The Stripe 1824 (*v.* strīp); Thames Mdw; Theale Mdw (*Le Thelemed* n.d., *v.* Theale); Thistley Croft; The Three Acres (3 *Acres Mead* 17th); Tilehurst Common (*Tylehurst Common* 1790 Pride); Tuckers Moor 1824; Turks Ground; Turnip Close; Turnpike Close; Upcrofts 1824; Upperhill Ground; Water Croft; Watery Croft; Way Lands; Way Moor; Well Close (also 17th); White Stiles; Wide Fd (*La Wydefeld* n.d., *v.* wīd, feld); Widows Pightle; Wood Close; Workhouse Pightle.

(*b*) *Anguey Meade* 1544; *Baglyes Gore* 17th (*v.* gāra); *Berlegh'* n.d. (*v.* bere, lēah); *La Breche* 1320, *The Breech* 1462, *The Breche* 1469 (*v.* brēc); *Brom Croft* 1462, *Bromecroft* 1469 (*v.* brōm, croft); *Bulle Crosse* 1544; *Church Piddle* 1755 *PubLibDoc* (a variant of pightel, cf. *Northpudell infra*); *Costenham* 1462, *Costeham* 1469 (*v.* hamm, first el. uncertain, but *v.* cost[1]); *The Dene* 1461, 1469 (*v.* denu); *Dog Pidle* 17th; *Gasum Mead* 17th; *Glidenheye* 1224–5 *Ass* (perhaps 'kite enclosure', *v.* gleoda, glida, (ge)hæg); *Greneshawe* 1462, *Grenesherde* 1469 (*v.* grēne[1], sc(e)aga); *The Hassacke* 17th (*v.* hassuc and cf. 190); *The Havedlond* 1462, *The Havedlonde* 1469 (*v.* hēafod-land); *Le Heygrof* 1322 AD, *Le Heygroue* 1322 (*v.* (ge)hæg, grāf); *Hodeshull'* n.d. ('Hod's hill', cf. Hodcott, Pt 2); *Holecroft* 1462, *The Holecrofte* 1469 (*v.* hol[1], croft); *Hop Garden* 17th (*v.* hoppe); *Kerton Pidle* 17th; *Lady Crofts* 17th (*v.* hlǣfdige); *The Little Barten* 17th (*v.* beretūn); *Litelpudell* 1462, *Litillpudell* 1469 (cf. *Northpudell infra*); *Longacre* 1462, *The Longe Acre* 1469; *La Longemerssh'* 1302 (*v.* lang, mersc); *Ye Midle Coppice* 17th; *La Middelfeld* n.d.; *Mote-hall* 1539–40 (*v.* mote); *Le Northfeld* 1300, *La Northfeld* 1302 (*v.* norð, feld); *The Northpudell* 1462, 1469 ('north pightle'); *Sandham* n.d., 17th (*v.* sand, hamm); *Shirlak'* 1325 (*v.* scīr[1], scīr[2], lacu); *Snontacre* n.d.; *Upper Downs* 17th; *Westmede* 1461, 1469; *Wodefeld, La Wodehouse* n.d. (*v.* wudu, feld, hūs); *Woodcocksacre* 17th; *Le Wydemed* n.d. (cf. the same name 189); *Yeldestrete* n.d. (possibly 'old street' with prosthetic y-, cf. Streets Pasture *supra*).

IX. THEALE HUNDRED

Thele 1238 Fees, *La Thele* 1241 *Ass et freq* to 1425 Ipm, *Thele* 1241 *Ass v.* Theale *infra* 241–2.

Aldermaston

<small>ALDERMASTON</small>

Ældremanestone, Heldremanestvne, Eldremanestune 1086 DB, *Aldremanneston'* 1178 P, *Aldremaneston'* 1220 Fees, *Aldremanston* 1296 Ipm, 1327 *SR*, 1340 Pat.
Aldermannestone c. 1160 OxonCh, *Aldermannestun* 1167 P, *Aldermaneston* 1229 Ch *et passim* with variant spellings *Alderman(e)ston'*; *Aldermanneston Achard* 1300 Cl
Audermaneston' 1235–6 Fees, *Ardemamston* 1284 *Ass*
Aldermaston 1405 Fine

'Farm of the (e)aldormann', *v.* tūn; Alderminster (Wo 184–5) is identical in origin, cf. also *Aldermanbury* (BdHu 11). *Achard* from the family of Robert Achard to whom the manor was granted by Henry I (VCH III, 388).

IMPSTONE PLANTATION, cf. *Merestone voc' Impstone* 1552 *LRMB*, *Nimph Stone* 1761 Rocque, *Nymph Stone* 1790 Pride, *Imp or Nymph Stone* 1846 Snare. The stone is on the Roman road west of Silchester (CALLEVA ATREBATUM), and may be a Roman milestone on which the letters IMP were visible at the beginning of the inscription. N- in the variant form may be from atten, or due to association with the word *nymph*. In VCH I, 200 n. 5, Haverfield states that there is no sign of any inscription now, but that the shape is not unlike that of a fragment of a Roman milestone. *Merestone* refers to the position on the county boundary, *v.* (ge)mære, stān.

ALDERMASTON BRIDGE, *pons de Aldermaneston'* 13th *ReadingC*(2). ALDERMASTON CT AND MILL.   ALDERMASTON PK, 1790 Pride, 1846 Snare, *Aldermason Park* 1761 Rocque, *The Park* 1839 *TA*.   ALDERMASTON WHARF, 1790 Pride, 1846 Snare.   ALMSWOOD COPSE. AQUA VITAE COPSE, 1846 Snare, *Acquavitae* 1839 *TA*, *v.* Padworth 156.   BARLOW'S PLANTATION.   BARNGROUND COPSE, *Barn Ground* 1839 *TA*.   BAUGHURST PLANTATION (Baughurst is in Ha).   BEST GULLY.   BIRCH COPSE.   THE BIRCHES (2 examples).   BLACK

PIGHTLE, 1839 *TA*.   BRICKKILN GULLY, *Brick Kilns* 1839 *TA*.
BROOM CLOSE.   BROOM COPSE.   BUDD'S PLANTATION.   BULL
PATE.   BURNHAM'S COPSE AND PLANTATION.   BURNTHOUSE SHAW,
Burnt House Ground 1839 *TA*.   BUTCHER'S COPSE.   CHURCH
FM.   CLAY CLOSE (2 examples).   CONQUEROR'S OAK.   CROSS-
LANE GULLY, *Cross Lane Ground* 1839 *TA*.   DEAD BOY PLANTA-
TION.   DECOY POND.   FISHERMAN'S COTTAGE AND LANE.
FORSTER'S FM, 1846 Snare.   FROUD'S BRIDGE.   FROUD'S FM,
1839 *TA*, 1846 Snare.   GRAVELLY GROUND COPSE, *Gravelly
Ground* 1839 *TA*.   GREAT FISHERS, *Fishers, Great and Little
Fishers* 1839 *TA*.   GUNTER'S PIGHTLE, *Gunters Lifehold* 1839 *TA*.
HARBOURHILL COPSE.   HARRIS'S COPSE AND GULLY, *Harriss Farm
and Platt* 1839 *TA*, *Harris Fm* 1846 Snare.   HILL CLOSE.   HIND'S
HEAD INN.   HITHER FURZE GROUND PIECE, UPPER HITHER FURZE
GROUND PIECE.   THE HORNETS.   JACOB'S GULLY.   KEEPER'S
BELT AND COTTAGE.   KEYSER'S PLANTATION.   KILN CLOSE, cf.
Kiln Meadow and Pightle 1839 *TA*.   LADIES' WOOD, *Lady Wood*
1523 Padworth, *Little Lady Wood* 1839 *TA*, *v.* hlæfdige.   LITTLE
HEATH, *Heath Allotment and Close* 1839 *TA*.   LITTLE PIGHTLE,
1839 *TA*, *v.* pightel, very common in this parish.   LONG CLOSE.
LOWGROUND COPSE.   MIDDLE CLOSE.   MOOR'S PLANTATION.
NEW PLANTATION.   NINE ACRE COPSE.   OAK PLANTATION (2
examples).   OLD COPSE.   OLD MALTHOUSE, *Malthouse Mead*
1839 *TA*.   MORRIS'S CLOSE.   OLD WARREN.   PAICE'S WD.
PARK FM.   PINE BELT PLANTATION.   PRIOR'S COPSE, *Priors
Coppice Ground* 1839 *TA*, cf. *Priorieesmede* 1451 *Queen*, in the
possession of Sherborne Priory.   PRIOR'S PIGHTLE COPSE.   RAG-
HILL, RAGHILL FM.   RED LANE, REDLANE HILL.   ROUNDWOOD
COPSE AND GULLY.   SEVEN ACRE COPSE.   SIX ACRE COPSE.
SIXTEEN ACRE GULLY.   SLADE'S HILL CLOSE.   SMART'S COPSE,
Smarts Lifehold 1839 *TA*.   SOKE PLANTATION, ALDERMASTON
SOKE, cf. *Soak* 1761 Rocque, 1790 Pride, *Aldermaston Soak* 1817 OS;
it is impossible to say whether this is OE sōcn, ME soke 'district over
which a right of jurisdiction was exercised' or *soce* dat. of soc
'sucking'. The area is not obviously marshy, so the first alternative is
probably to be preferred.   SPRING LANE.   STONY GROUND
COPSE, UPPER AND LOWER.   THREE CORNER PLANTATION (2
examples).   TULLSFIELD COPSE.   UPPER CHURCH FM.   UPPER
MOOR'S GULLY.   WATERMAN'S PIGHTLE.   UPPER WET PIGHTLE,
Wet Pightle, Lower Wet Pightle 1839 *TA*.   WITHY PLOT.

FIELD-NAMES

The principal forms in (*a*) are 1839 *TA*.

(*a*) Alder Mead; Ash House Mdw; Back Door Piece; Bare Lands, Bare Land Mead; Bottom Close; Bowling Green; Box Mdw (*Le Boxes* 1451 *Queen, v.* box); Bushey Leys, Bushy Close; Chalky Barn Ground; Church Close and Mead (not near Church Fm); Clinked Lands; Common Fir Plantation; Coppice Close and Pightle; Corner Ground; Cow Croft; Duck Mead; Earley Wood; East Mdw (*Estmede* 1451 *Queen*); Enclosed Mdw; Furze Ground; Furzey Close; Garden Ground and Mead; Gravels, Upper and Lower; Greethams Farm; Great Ground; Green Ground; Grubbed Coppice (*v.* 280); Gully; Hale Mdw (*v.* h(e)alh); Half Close; Half Furlong; Hamm Fd (*v.* hamm); Haskers Pightle; Hatch Gate Ten Acres (*v.* hæcc-geat); Hawcroft; High Fd; Hilly Ground; Hog Close; The Holloman; Home Close, Mdw and Pightle; Hop Garden and Pightle (*v.* hoppe); Howehead Mdw; Hunt Fd; The Land or Little Mead; Lawn, South and Front; Lees Moore; Ley Fd; Lye Fd Allotment; Lock Mdw; Lodge Ground and Pightle; Long Furlong and Ground; Madams Pightle; Mare Leys; Mays Down and Mdw; Milking Close; Mill Mead; Mire Close; Oak Close; Oxleys; Parish Croft; Pasture Pightle; Picked Five Acres (*v.* pīced); The Pightle (*v.* pightel, as elsewhere in the f.ns. of this parish); Pit Close; The Platt (*v.* plat²); Popes Hill Fd; Pound Close; Pyes Pightle; Rogerhams; Rough Ground; Round Fd, Mead and Pightle; Rowley Fd; East Rowney; Ruddle Fd; Rushy Close and Platt; Saint Johns; Shot Ground; Slipping; Small Pightle; Sparrow Mead; Spring Ground; Stoke Mdw; Turkey Light Mead; Vicarage Moore; Warf Fd; Walnut Tree Ground; Waterhouse Ground; Well Close; Woodcock Hill; Workhouse Mead(ow) and Pightle; Worting Mead.

Bradfield

BRADFIELD

(*in*) *Bradanfelda* 'c. 690' (c. 1200) BCS 74, *Bradanafel* '687' (c. 1200) ib 100, *Bradanfeltha* '699' (c. 1200), *Bradenfeld* '699' (c. 1240) ib 101, (*æt*) *Bradanfelda* 990–2 (contemporary) ASCharters
Bradefelt 1086 DB, *Bradefeld'* 1167 P *et passim* with variant spellings *Bradefeld, Bradefeud*; *Braddeffeld* 1420 Fine
Bredefeld' 1260–1 FF
Bradfelde 1316 FA, *Bradfeld* 1517 D Inc

'At the broad piece of open land', *v.* brād, feld. The same name occurs in Ess, Nf, Sf, YW. BCS 74, 100, 101 are spurious.

BUCKHOLD, *Bocholt* 1109–20 (13th), 1158 (13th) RSO, (*boscus de*) la *Bocholt* c. 1200 Rutland, (wood called) *Bokholde* 1348 Cl, *Bookholt*

1352 ib, (forest of) *Bokholt* 1356 (14th) Winchester, *Bokholte* 1410 Fine, *Buckall* 1687 *PubLib*, *East Buckholds* 1687–8, 1760 *ib*, *Buckhold* 1820 *PubLibDoc*, 'beech wood', *v.* bōc[1], holt.

FROGMOOR FM, LOWER AND UPPER, *Frogemore* 1267 *AddCh 19627* (p), *Ffrogemor* 1272–6 *FF* (p), *Froggemer* 1341 NonInq (p), *Lower and Upper Frogmore Fm* 1846 Snare, 'frog marsh', *v.* frogga, mōr. The same name occurs in Bk 193.

RUSHALL COPSE, RUSHALL MANOR FM, *Russehall'* 1240–1 *FF* (p), *Rushalls Fm and Wood* 1830 OS, 1846 Snare. The first el. is risc 'rush'. The early form suggests that the second is h(e)all 'hall', but this may be a corruption of earlier -*hale*, from h(e)alh 'nook', in which case the name would be identical with Rushall St. The farm lies in a shallow recess in a hill.

ACRES' FM. ADMOOR LANE, *Admore Lane* 1846 Snare, ADMOOR COPSE. AVENUE CLUMP. BACK LANE, BACK LANE PLANTATION. BARNELMS FM, *Barn Elms Fm* 1846 Snare. BEARD'S HILL, 1846 *TA*. BERRY'S FM, *Berries Fm* 1846 Snare, BERRY'S SHAW. BIRCHLANDS COPSE, *Birchland Wood* 1830 OS, 1846 Snare. BOOT FM, *Boot Pightle* 1846 *TA*. BOTTOMHOUSE FM, 1846 Snare, *Bottom Farm* 1830 OS. THE BOURNE, BOURNEFIELD FM, *v.* 8. BRADFIELD FM AND PLANTATION. BRADFIELD HALL, 1830 OS. BRADFIELD HO, 1761 Rocque, 1790 Pride. BROOMHILL COPSE, *Broom Hill* 1846 Snare. BROOMS. BUCKHOLD FM AND GRANGE. BUCKHOLD ROW, 1793 *PubLibDoc*, *Buckhold Rowe* 1661 *PubLib*, *Buckwell Row* 1761 Rocque, 1790 Pride, *Buckle Row* 1830 OS. BUCKHOLDHILL FM AND GATE, *v.* Buckhold *supra*. BUCKLEBURY COMMON WD GATE. BUSCOT, BUSCOT COPSE AND GULLY, *Biscot Wood* 1846 Snare. CHERRYORCHARD COPSE, *Cherry Orchard* 1846 Snare. CHICKORY PLANTATION. CLAY HILL, *Clay Close* 1846 *TA*. COCK LANE, 1846 Snare, *Cock Pightle* 1846 *TA*. COLLIER'S COPSE, LITTLE COLLIER'S COPSE, *Colliers Wood* 1830 OS. COPYHOLD FM, 1846 Snare. CRIPPS FM, 1846 ib. DINGLEY HILL. FIELD BARN. FISHER'S COPSE, LITTLE FISHER'S COPSE, *Fishers Wood* 1830 OS, 1846 Snare. FISH PONDS, *Fish Pond Mead* 1846 *TA*. FOLLY BRIDGE, 1846 *TA*. THE GRAVELS, 1830 OS, 1846 *TA*. GREATHOUSE COTTAGES, WALK AND WD; Bradfield House is shown here 1830 OS, not near Rushall Manor Fm, where it is now.

GREEN WD.   THE GROVE, 1846 *TA*.   HALL'S SHAW.   HAMBLIN'S COPSE.   HANGERS COPSE, 1846 Snare, *Hanger Copse* 1830 OS, *v.* **hangra.**   HARE PLANTATION, *Hareland Pit(t)* 1793, 1813 *PubLib Doc, Harelands* 1846 *TA*.   HEATH ROAD, *The Heath, Upper and Lower Heath* 1846 *ib.*   HERONS FM.   HEWINS WD, 1846 Snare, *Hewens Wood and Field* 1846 *TA*.   HEWINSWOOD COTTAGE. HILL PLANTATION.   HOG COPSE, 1846 Snare; Snare applies the name *Hogs Back* to the hill on which Hog Copse stands.   HOME FM.   HOP PLANTATION, *Hop Garden, Hop Ground Piece* 1846 *TA*. HORSE LEAS, *Horslease, Horseleys* 1846 *TA*.   HUNGERFORD LANE, 1846 Snare.   JENNETTS HILL, JENNETTSHILL WD, *Jennets Hill Wood* 1830 OS, *Jennetts, Jennetts Hill, Jennetts Hill Wood* 1846 Snare. KEEPER'S LODGE.   KILN COPSE, 1846 Snare.   KIMBER HEAD, *Kimberheads* 1830 OS, *Kimberhead Spring* 1846 Snare.   KNAPP'S WD, *Knapp's Hill* 1846 *TA*, *v.* **cnæpp.**   LAMDEN'S BOTTOM, *Lambdens* 1846 *TA*.   LONE BARN.   LONG COPSE.   LONG-MEADOW PLANTATION, *Long Mead* 1846 *TA*.   LYNCH'S COPSE, *The Lynches* 1846 Snare.   MALTHOUSE FM, *Malt House Ground* 1846 *TA*. MAPLETONS, *Mapletons Fm* 1846 Snare.   MEAD HO.   MIRAM'S COPSE, *Mirams Wood* 1830 OS, *Miriams Wood* 1846 Snare.   MODERN SIDE HO.   MONEY FM.   MOUNT'S HILL, *Mount Park* 1846 *TA*, *v.* **mont.**   NEW FIELDS.   OAKLANDS COPSE, *Oaklands Coppice* 1790 Pride, *Oakland Farm* 1830 OS, *Oaklands* 1846 Snare.   OLD HO. ORCHARD LODGE, *The Orchard* 1846 *TA*.   OWL PIT, OWLPIT COPSE, *Old Pit, Old Pit Wood* 1830 OS, *Owl Pit Field* 1846 *TA*. PITHER'S FM AND SHAW.   POMERANIA, 1846 *TA* (*v.* 284).   POND PIGHTLE.   POTASH FM, *Potash* 1846 *TA*.   RED HILL, 1761 Rocque, 1846 Snare.   ROTTEN ROW, 1846 ib, *Rotton Row* 1761 Rocque, 1790 Pride, *Rotten Close and Field* 1846 *TA*; this is a hamlet, *v.* **raton** 'rat'.   ROUND COPSE, 1846 Snare.   ROUNDMOOR COPSE.   ST ANDREW'S CHURCH AND WELL.   SANNYSFIELD COPSE, *Great Sannies, Sannys Field* 1846 *TA*.   SCRATCHFACE COPSE AND LANE.   SHERWOOD.   SLADE GATE, 1846 Snare, *Slades Gate* 1830 OS.   SLOW BOTTOM.   SNAKE COPSE.   SORREL COPSE.   SOUTH END, *Southend* 1648 *RecOffCat*, 1649 *et freq* to 1764 *PubLib*, 1846 Snare.   SOUTHEND FM.   STAIRS.   STAN-FORD WD.   STONE COPSE.   STROUD'S, *Strode* 1327 *SR* (p), *Strouds* 1830 OS, *Stroud Fm* 1846 Snare, *v.* **strōd** 'marshy land overgrown with brushwood'.   THUJA WD.   TRAVELLER'S REST P.H.   TUTTS CLUMP.   VILLAGE HO.   WALLINGFORD WD,

Wallingford Piece 1846 *TA*.   WAY ELLIOTT'S COPSE.   WAY-
LAND'S COPSE, *Weylands Field* 1846 *TA*, cf. Wayland's Smithy, Pt **2**.
WOODCOTE, *Woodcut Row* 1846 *TA*, John *de Wodecote* 1277–8 *FF*,
concerned with land in Newbury, may have come from this place, *v.*
wudu, cot.

FIELD-NAMES

The principal forms in (*a*) are 1846 *TA*, except where otherwise stated.

(*a*) Allams Pightle; Andrews Hill; Apple Tree Close; Aspen Stile Close;
Baileys Dean; Barelands; Barn Close; Beech Piece; Beeching Wood 1793,
1813 *PubLibDoc*; Betty's Pightle; Black Lake; Great Blundich; Bottom
Ground (possibly connected with Bottomhouse Fm *supra* 201); Bottom
Pasture; Breaches Ground (*v.* brēc); Brick Kiln Mead; Broad Close; Broom
Close (*v.* brōm); Browns Pightle; Buckleberry Close (*v.* Bucklebury 154);
Buckle Ground and Hill (cf. Buckhold 200–1); Butlers, Far and Near (cf.
Boterswode 1348 Cl, from the surname *Butler*); Calves Ley; The Cellar
Fds 1813 *PubLibDoc*; Chalk Pit Close and Pightle; Chapel Ground; Clarkes
Bottom; Cold Arbor (*v.* Sr 406–10); Colesalls Mead; Collins Wood 1846
Snare; Common Hill; Coney Close; Coomb, Lower and Upper, Coomb
Pightle (*v.* cumb); Coppice Fd; Cow Leaze; Cow Mdw; Long Cowes: Crab
Tree Close and Piece; Cross Lands; Dead Mouldy Fd (cf. Mouldy Hill
infra); The Dean, Pangbourne Dean; Dial Close (*v.* dial); Far Close; Farm
Yard Ground; First Fd and Pasture; Further Moore; Golds Pightle; Gorse
and Ling Piece; Goswells Pightle; Granary Close; Gravelly Ground;
Gravel Pit Ground; Great Fd, Ground and Mead; Great Mead Shaw;
Green Lane; Hale Fd (*v.* h(e)alh); Hall Pit Ground; Hangings, Great and
Little Hanging (*Hanging Close* 1813 *PubLibDoc*, *v.* hangende); Hares Piece;
Hazard; Hill Close; Hill Side Fd and Piece (not near Hill Plantation);
Hockleys Wood 1793, 1813 *PubLibDoc*, Hockley Wood 1830 OS; Holly
Wood Fd; Home Ground, Close and Mdw; Homestall Mdw; Kennel
Ground; Kings Lands; Lawn, Lower and Upper (*v.* launde); Ledge Hill
and Fd; Lime Pightle; Long Croft, Ground and Fd; Lower Yard; Mathern,
Lower and Upper, Walk Mathern; Mesopotamia (*v.* 284); Middle Close and
Pasture; Minnycuts; Mose's Pightle; Mouldy Hill (cf. NED **mouldy** *a*¹.
'of the nature of mould or fine soil'); Near Close and Fd; Norman Mead;
North Close; Old Lands; Old Warren 1846 Snare; The Park, Park Fd;
Parsonage Mdw; Path Close and Ground; Peaked Close, Pickett Ground
(*v.* pīced); Pightle (*v.* pightel, as freq. elsewhere in this parish); Pit Fd;
Pointers Pightle; Pond Ground, Close and Fd; Poor Folks Ground; Poors
Ground (*v.* 285); Posting Close; Pouch; Pound Pightle; Rack Close; Ram
Pightle; Rough Pasture and Mdw; Round Hill; Rushy Mead; Saffron Mead;
Sainfoin Fd; Sandpit Ground and Hill; Shaw Ground; Sling (*v.* 282);
Snells Hill; Spring Close and Ground; Stack Yard; Star Pightle; Stategate
Hanging (*v.* hangende); Steadmans Park; String or Spring Copse 1793, 1813
PubLibDoc; Swilly Hole ('swallow-hole', cf. EDD **swally** 2); Tan House
Mead; Tilehurst Green; Top Close; Twiners Heath Piece; Walnut Tree

Fd; Water Mdw; Well Close and Pightle; White Fd; Wingfield Mead; Wood Croft and Fd; Wood Side Fd; Yew Tree Close.

(b) *Ashmore* 1673 *PubLib*; *Catterslonde* 1348 Cl; *Clidehacchemore* 1272–6 *FF* (*v.* hæc(c), mōr); *Estrode* 1348 Cl (*v.* ēast, rod[1]); *Overgrounds* 1648 *RecOffCat*; *Puryefield* 1726 *PubLibDoc* (*v.* pirige); *Westecroft, Westmede* 1272–6 *FF* (*v.* west, croft, mǣd); *Westridge* 1721 *PubLib*; *Westrode* 1348 Cl (cf. *Estrode supra*); *Wilgrove* 1348 Cl.

Burghfield

BURGHFIELD

Borgefelle, Borgefel 1086 DB, *Boreghefeld'* 1219 FineR, *Borghefeld* 1300 Cl (p)

Burgefeld' c. 1160 OxonCh *et freq* with variant spellings *Burgefeld(e)* to 1316 FA, *Burghef'* c. 1200 AD (p) *et freq* with variant spellings *Burghefeld(e)* to 1365 Cl

Bergefelda 1167 P *et passim* with variant spellings *Bergefeld'*, *Bergefeld, Bergefeud*; *Bergafeld'* Sewali 1167 P, *Berchefeld* 12th (l.12th) *ReadingC, Bergeford, Berogeford'* 1202 P (p), *Beregefeld* 1205 ib (p), *Beregefeld'* 1212 Hunter Fines, *Berghefeld'* 1220 Fees, 1232 Cl, *Bereghefeld'* 1241 *Ass* (p), 1271 Fine (p), *Berghefeud'* 1284 *Ass*

Beruefeld 1185 RR (p), *Bereuefeld, Bereuf'* c. 1195 *AddCh 7207* (p), *Berwefeud'* 1260–1 *FF, Berwefeld* 1328 Banco

Bergfeld c. 1211 (e.13th) Thame

Buerghefeld 1212 Fees (p)

Burgfeld' 1224–5, 1241 *Ass, Burgfeld* 1294–5 AD (p), *Burghfeld* 1305 Cl *et freq, Burghfeld Regis et Abbatis* 1412 FA, *Burghfelde Regis* 1441 BM, *Burughfeld* 1474 Stonor, *Burghfeld Regis* 1517 D Inc

Burwefeld c. 1280 (c. 1444) BC (p), *Burwefelde* 1300 Ipm

Burrefeld 1343 Ch, *Burefelde* 1348 AD (p), *Burefeld* 1365 Cl

Burfelde 1393 Cl

Barfeild l.14th Gor

Birefilde 1393 AD

Berefeld 1433 AD

Buryfeld 1476 Cl

'Open land by the hill', *v.* be(o)rg, feld. Burghfield village lies on the lower slopes of a raised area, part of which is Burghfield Common. The name occurs also in the phrase *to Beorhfeldinga gemære* c. 950 (c. 1240) BCS 888 'to the boundary of the people of Burghfield'. There were two manors, known as *Burghfield Regis* and *Burghfield*

Abbas (VCH III, 400–1); the former passed to the Crown in 1459, and the latter was held by the Abbey of Reading; the former is said VCH III, 400, to have passed to the Crown in 1459, but it is called *Burghfeld Regis* in 1412 and 1441, when according to the VCH account it was held by the Mortimer family.

CARSWELL (lost), *Kersewella* Hy 2 (l.12th) *ReadingC*, *Karsewelle*, *Carsewelle* 12th (l.12th) *ib*, *Kerswell'* 1212 Cur, 1212–13 *FF*, *Kerswell*, 1229–30 *ib*, *Carswalle* 13th *ReadingC*(2), *Carswell* c. 1300 BC, *Carsewell* 1300 Ipm, 'cress stream', *v*. cærse, w(i)ella, a common name, of which there are three occurrences in this county.

HOSE HILL, *Hosa*, *La Hosa* 1211 Cur (p), *La Hose* 13th *ReadingC*(2) (p), (*crofta que vocatur*) *La Hose* 1349–50 *RentSur*, *Le Hose* 1401–2 *ib*. There is another example of this name in Hurley (*v*. 65 for forms), where it is said to be the name of a lane.

These two Berks examples must be considered in conjunction with a number of names in other counties. A f.n. *Hose* occurs three times in Ess (Ess 464), the forms being *La Hose* (14th), *Le Hose* (1487), *the Hose* (1534), and there is also a *Hosefeld* (1544) in the county. In D 294 a personal name *atte Hose* is associated with *Hosefenne* (modern Hawson Court) and *Hosebroc*, though it is not clear from the article whether the names occur in the same vicinity. Other examples occur in Ostbridge Gl **3**, 120–1, Horsebridge Ha (*Hosebrig* 1236 *Ass*), *hose graf* in Wickhambreux K (BCS 869), *Hos(s)ebrugge* 1535 and *Le Hose* 1540 in Tewkesbury (Gl **2**, 69), and various f.ns. in Gl (Gl **3**, 151, 157, 184, 191, 194).

In Ess 464 the source is said to be OE *hōs* 'bramble, thorn', which is the sense assigned to the word in BT. The meaning and form of this word are more accurately given in BTSuppl (*hos* sing., *hossas* pl. 'shoot, tendril').

The K, Ha, D and Ess names are cited under this word in Elements, and in PN Gl Ostbridge is interpreted 'bridge by the shoots'. Such an el. would be synonymous with hys(s)e, occurring in Hurstbourne Ha, Husborne Bd, Hycemoor Cu. It does not seem altogether satisfactory as the source of the simplex name, ME *Hose*, to which the definite article was frequently prefixed.

Other possible OE sources for these names given by Wallenberg, KPN 278, consist of *hōs* 'company, band' and *hosa* -*e*, 'covering for the leg: husk, sheath'. The first is formally unlikely, as none of the names has any ME spellings with *-ou-* or *-u-*. The second seems more promising, both formally and as regards meaning, and it is possible that it was applied in the sense 'stocking' to a long, thin object, such as a stream or, in the case of the example from Hurley, a lane. This use would be somewhat similar to that of pīpe, which occurs in charter bounds with reference to a small stream. The modern sense of *hose* 'flexible tube for the conveyance of water' is not recorded until 1495–7, when it occurs in Naval Accounts referring to hoses for ships' pumps. Another example of the p.n. may be Hose Wd St, 5 miles N.E. of Stone, which lies on either side of a small stream.

Professor Löfvenberg considers *hosa* 'stocking' a likely source of some of the p.ns. discussed here, but thinks that *hos* 'shoot, tendril', perhaps 'sapling' may occur in some of them. He suggests as another possibility an OE *hās*, which may have existed beside hǣs 'brushwood, a young wood of beech or oak'.

PINGEWOOD, *Punge* 13th *ReadingC(2)*, *Reading Alm* (*freq*), *Pinge Wood* 1727 *PubLib*, 1846 Snare, *Pingewood* 1761 Rocque, *Penge Meadow* 1842 *TA*. A marsh and a road *de Punge* are mentioned in the first reference. This name is cited in PN -ing (208) as a singular name in -ing of obscure etymology, possibly contracted from an earlier *Pyning*. It may, however, be a Celtic name identical with Penge Sr 14–15, from Pr Welsh *penn 'end', and *cēd 'wood'. The element *penno- sometimes occurs in OE place-names in the form *peon(n)* (cf. ASC *æt Peonnum*, Pen Pits W or Penselwood So, *æt Peonhó*, Pinhoe D), and this would account for the *-u-* of the early forms for Pinge. Penge Sr apparently contains pænn, another OE form of the word. Apart from the different vowel, the development suggested in Sr for Penge seems applicable to the Berks name, which would similarly be subject to strong Norman influence. Other examples of the compound, without this abnormal phonological development, are Penketh La, Penquit D, Pencoyd He, Penquite Co. The meaning is probably '(place at) the end of the wood'.

SHEFFIELD FM AND BOTTOM

    Sewelle 1086 DB
    Scheaffelda 1167 P, *Estschefeld* 13th *ReadingC(2)*, *Schefeld'* 1267–8
      FF et freq with variant spellings *Scheffeld*, *Schefeld* to 1350 Gor,
      Scheufeud 1284 BM

Scefeld' 1202 P

Sefeld', *Seofeld'* 1197–8 AC, *Suffeld* 1198 Cur, *Sefeld'* 1199 ib,
  Sufeld c. 1200, 1218–19 AD, *Seofeld* c. 1202 BM, *Suefeld* 1214
  AD, *Seffeld'* 1220 Fees, *Sefeldia* 1236–7 (c. 1250) Bract, *Sofeld*,
  Soeffeld, *Sefeld*, *Estsufeld* 13th *ReadingC*(2)

Shefeld' 1241 *Ass*, *Shefeud* 1284 *ib*, *Shefeld* 1329 BM, 1344 AD,
  Shiffeld 1409 BM, 1495 Gor, *Sheff(i)eld* 1609 *LRMB*

Cheffold' 1284 *Ass*

The first element is OE scēo 'a shelter', the second feld.

AMNER'S FM, (manor called) *Amenerscourte* 1490 *RentSur*, *Anniscourt*
1515 *ib*, *Amnerscourt* 1516 *ib*, *Amblers Fm* 1716 Rocque, 1790 Pride,
Ambers Fm 1846 Snare. It was suggested Sr 107–8 that this is named
from the almoner of Reading Abbey, but there was a local family
named *Anners*, whose surname could be responsible for the p.n.
Robert *de Anners* occurs 1252–5 *FF* in connection with land in
Wokefield, and Thomas *de Anners* witnesses a 15th-cent. deed in
ReadingC(2) (f. 51), concerned with land in Burghfield, *v.* court.
AMNER'S WD, *Ammers Wood* 1842 *TA*, *Amners Wood* 1846 Snare.
AUCLUM COPSE, LITTLE AUCLUM COPSE, cf. *Great Hakum* 1842 *TA*,
possibly 'at the oaks', *v.* āc (dat. pl. ācum). BEENHAM'S FM,
Benhams 1842 *TA*, *Beenham Fm* 1846 Snare. BENNETT'S HILL,
BENNETTSHILL COPSE, *Bennets Hill Ground* 1842 *TA*. BOLDRE-
WOOD. BRICKKILN COPSE. BROOKFIELD HO. BROOK HO.
BURGHFIELD BRIDGE, 1846 Snare, *Birfeldebrigge* 1490 *RentSur*, also
mentioned 1279 InqMisc I, this is probably *magnus pons* 13th
ReadingC(2), *Hybrugg'* 1386 *ReadingAlm*, *v.* hēah. BURGHFIELD
BROOK. BURGHFIELD COMMON, 1817 OS, *Burfield Common* 1761
Rocque. BURGHFIELD HILL, BURGHFIELDHILL FM. BURGH-
FIELD LODGE. BURGHFIELD MILL, 1846 Snare, *Molendinum de
Bergfeld* c. 1211 (e.13th) Thame, *Burnfield Mill* 1761 Rocque, *Bur-
field Mill* 1790 Pride. BURGHFIELD PLACE, 1846 Snare. BURGH-
FIELD SHAW. CLAY HILL, 1846 Snare. CLAYHILL BROOK.
CLAYHILL COPSE, *Clay Hill Wood Ground* 1842 *TA*. COTTAGE
LANE. CULVERLANDS, 1846 Snare, *The Culver Closes* 1659 *PubLib*-
(*Clayton*), *Culverlands Pasture* 1842 *TA*, *v.* culfre. CULVERLANDS
HOME FM. DEAN'S COPSE. DEVONGROVE. ESSEX COT-
TAGES. FIELD FM, 1846 Snare. FOLLY LANE, *Folly Pightle*
1842 *TA*, *v.* folie. FOX AND HOUNDS P.H. GREEN FM.
GROVE COPSE. GULLY COPSE. HATCH FM, 1846 Snare, *La*

Hacche l.13th *ReadingAlm* (p), *Hacche* 1348 Cl (p), *v.* hæc(c) 'gate'.
HERMIT'S HILL, *Armit or Hermit Field* 1842 *TA.*   HIGHWOODS.
HILLFIELDS, cf. *Hill Ground and Pightle, Little Hills* 1842 *TA.*   THE
HOLLIES.   HOME CLOSE.   HOSEHILL FM (*v.* 205–6).   JAMES'S
COPSE, *James Hill Ground* 1842 *TA, James Fm* 1846 Snare.   JUBILEE
POND.   KENNET COTTAGES.   KIRTON'S FM, 1846 Snare.   KNIGHT'S
FM, *Knights Mead* 1842 *TA.*   THE LAURELS.   LOVE'S FM,
Loves Meadow and Pasture 1842 *TA, Love Fm* 1846 Snare.   MANOR
HO.   MAN'S HILL.   MOATLANDS FM, 1846 Snare, *Moat Pightle*
1842 *TA.*   THE MOUNT, *Further, Lower and Middle Mount* 1842
TA, v. infra 210.   PILGRIMS.   PINCHCUT, *Pinchgutt* 1842 *TA,*
a derogatory nick-name, *v.* 283.   PONDHOUSE FM AND COPSE,
Pond House 1761 Rocque, cf. *Pond Piece, Close and Meadow* 1842 *TA.*
THE POPLARS.   RISING SUN P.H.   ROWGARSON COPSE, *Row-
garston* 1842 *TA, v.* rūh, gærs-tūn.   SCRATCHFACE, *Scratch Face*
1842 *ib.*   THE SCRUBBS, *Scrubbs Land, Scrubbs Long Pightle* 1842
ib, Burghfield Scrubbs 1846 Snare, *v.* scrubb.   SEARL'S FM, *Searles
Fm* 1846 ib, *Serles More* 1659 *PubLib(Clayton)*, Ric. *Serle* of Sulham-
stead occurs 13th *ReadingC(2)*, and Will. and Ask. *Serle* have land in
Burghfield 14th*ib.*   SHEFFIELD BOTTOM.   SHEFFIELD MILL, 1846
Snare, *Shefield Mill* 1761 Rocque, *v.* 206–7.   THE SHRUBBERIES.
SIMPSON'S FM.   SPRING WD.   SWAN INN.   TRASH GREEN,
1842 *TA,* 1846 Snare.   TRASHGREEN FM.   WALKER'S SHAW.
WELLMAN'S FM, 1846 Snare.

FIELD-NAMES

The principal forms in (*a*) are 1842 *TA,* except where otherwise stated.
Those marked M are modern names written on a 6″ O.S. map in Reading
Public Library; most of these occur also in the *TA*. Early forms dated 1197–8,
1218–19, 1294 are AD, 13th, 14th, 15th *ReadingC(2)*, l.13th, 1386 *ReadingAlm*,
1609, 1655, 1659, 1665 *PubLib(Clayton)*, and 1700, 1729 *PubLibDoc*.

(*a*) The Alder Moors; Alders; Arbor Fm 1846 Snare, Arbor Pightle (*v.*
here-beorg); Artrams; Ashen Close M; The Ashes, The Ashes Mead;
Asters; Aston Mead M, Astons Mdw; Baldones Moor M, Baldingsmoor
north, Baldings Moor south; Bell Fd (*v.* 285); Berry Hams (*v.* hamm);
Bishops Mdw M; Black Furlong; Bloxham Fd M; The Breaches M (*v.*
brēc); Brewers Moor; Brick Mead; Bridge Mead M, Little Bridge Pightle
(cf. *Briggheit* 1197–8, *v.* brycg, ēgeð); Broad Brooks; Broad Fd; Broadshoes
M; Brook Inhams (*v.* innām); Brook Mdw and Close; Bund Ground M;
Burghfield Green Mead; Burghfield Hill; Burnt Bridge Pightle; Burnt
House Ground M; Buscott Fd; Bushy Pightle; Busterfield Corner; Buttons

Grove; Calcot Mdw (*Calcote Meade* 1655, perhaps the same name as Calcot 222); Calves Lease (cf. *Chaluemede* 15th, *v.* c(e)alf, mæd); Carrot Pightle M, Carrot Beds and Pightle; Carthouse Pightle; Carters (cf. Rog. *le Cartere* 14th); Chalk Close; Chamberlains Pightle M (*Ye Widow Chamberlins Farme* 1665); Chapel Green 1846 Snare; Chapel Warden Waste; Charity Pastures; Cholsey Fd; Church Close; Clans Land; Cockley Ham M; Cockpit Pasture; Cockshots M (*v.* cocc-scyte); Common Pightle; Coppice Hill, Pightle and Mdw; Copyhold; Corner Ground; Cornwells; Costards M (*v.* cot-stōw); Cowlers Coppice Ground; Coxes Pightle; Crabtree Ground; Crickets; Crocks Pightle; Crows Nest M, Crows Nest Fm 1846 Snare, Crows Nest Fd (*v.* 283); Dead Horse Lane; Dewsland or Pay House Land M, Dews Lands; Drift Road; Dry Leaze M; Dung Close; East Mdw; Ferrex, Ferrex Moor M; The Fd; Fish Pond Mdw; Fishers Mdw; Fleet or Skittle Ground (*v.* flēot); Flowers Moor; Freeland Orchard M; Furze Fd; Garden Pightle and Close; Garston Mdw M, Gaston Mdw and Ground, Gaston Pound Ground (*Gastons* 1659, *v.* gærs-tūn and cf. *Newgarston' infra*); Giddy Webbs M; Goathurst Mead; Goats Pightle; Gosmoor M (*Gosmoore* 1655, *v.* gōs, mōr); Gravelly Pightle; Great Fd; Great Hill Ground; Green Close and Lane; Hams, Long, Little and Great M, Ham, Great and Little (*v.* hamm); Harts Mead, Hill and Valley; Haskins Pightle; Heavenly Mead (*Heauenly Mead* 1655, cf. *Hevenemede* in Reading 183); Hentleys Ground (cf. Rad. *Henteloue* 14th); Little Hercules; Hicks Hill; Highfield; Hillmans Ground (*Hillmanes Close* 1655); The Hockett M (cf. The Hockett in Bisham 60); Hog Moor; Holloways Pightle; Holybrook Mead (*v.* 11); Home Mdw and Moor; Honey Leaze and Pightle (*v.* hunig); Hop Garden (*v.* hoppe); Hothams; Kents Mead, Kents Path Ground; Kiln Plat; Kits Pightle (*Kitteslond* 1353 Black Prince, from the surname *Kitt*); Lady Lands M (*v.* hlæfdige); Lanes Mead; Leaches Pightle; Levinge or The Grante M, Lewings and Grante; Littenhams; Little Fd (cf. Great Fd *supra*); Lockwood, Lower; Long Coppice, Ground and Mead; Marsh Fd M; May's Land M; Mead Plot; Meadow Pightle and Strip; Mews Land; Middle Mead (*Middelmede* 1380 Gor, *v.* middel, mæd); Mill Fd M (cf. *Mulaker infra*); The Moor; Mouse Moor; Great Nettles M; New Inclosure; New Moor M; North Mead (*Northemed* late 13th, *Le Northmeade* 1609, *North Meade* 1700, *v.* norð, mæd); Nurtram Mead, Nurtrams; Oldbury M (*Ouldbury Coppice* 1655, *v.* (e)ald, burh); Old Ground M; Orchard Pightle; Ox Lease M; Park Ground; The Parlour; Parsonage Fd; Paynes Mdw; Pear Tree Ground; Pease Close (cf. *Pusecroft infra*); Perkins Mdw; Picket Close M, Picked Close and Fd (*v.* pīced); Pidgeon House Close; Pightle (*v.* pightel, as elsewhere in this parish); Pigstyes; Pilchers Green 1846 Snare; Pinks, Great and Little; Plumbs Pightle; Poors Fd; Pound Fd; Pudding Close (*v.* 284); Pug Pightle; Puss Grove, Lower (possibly 'hare grove'); The Rainbow (*v.* 281); Reads Green 1846 Snare; Reads Moor; Red Hall Court M; Rick Yard Pasture; The Ridges M; Round Ground; Rushy Plat M (*v.* plat² and cf. *Russipuddel infra*); Salters Pightle; Seers Pightle; Shaw Pightle; Sheep Moor (*The Sheepe Moore* 1655); Sheffield Mdw and Lane (*v.* Sheffield 286–7); The Ship; Skittle Ground M; The Slip (*v.* slipe); Smallbones; Smedneys Mdw M, Smidneys Mdw (possibly *Smitheshey* 13th *ReadingC(2)*, 14th *ReadingC(3)*, *v.* smið, (ge)hæg); Smiths Pightle; South Mead; Stable Ground; Star Close; Stoney Close M (cf. *Stonicroft infra*); Streakhams M; The Strings M (*v.* 282); Stubble Mdw M; Sturts Mdw M (*v.* steort); Three Corner Pightle; Thrift Mdws M, Thrift Coppice and Mdw (*Frithmore* 1231 Ch, *Frith, La Frithmor'* 13th, *Friþ* 14th *ReadingAlm, v.* fyrhð, mōr); Tile Croft M; Vetchey Lands; Vincents Mdw M; Viney Mead (*Vynheye* 1294, *Vyneye* 1365 Cl, *Vynee Mead* 1700, *Lower Vinee als Vinies Mead* 1729, 'vine enclosure', *v.* vine, (ge)hæg, or 'enclosure for heaping firewood', *v.* fīn and Löfvenberg 64); Walk Moor; Walnut Tree M, Walnut Tree Mdw; War Mdw; Warren M; The Watering Pightle; Webbs Fm and Moor; Wet Leaze M; White House Fm 1846 Snare; White Moor; Wickhams, Wickhams Mount, Mother Wickham (it is possible that this is another example of the p.n. wīchām, *v.* 24; it was adjacent to the Mount, on 6″ map at GR 667697; the course of the Roman road from Dorchester O to Silchester Ha is believed to be some 2 miles W. of this); Wincroft M; Withy Bed Grubb'd (*v.* 281); The Wipes M (perhaps a brushwood fence, *v.* EDD *wipe* sb²); Worsinghams; Worth Mead.

(b) *Adewell* 1229-30 *FF* ('Ad(d)a or Ead(d)a's spring or stream', cf. Adwell O 101); *Anketill'dune* 13th, *Asketillesdone* l.13th, *Askstilesdon'* 14th *ReadingAlm* (cf. Rob. *Asketyl'* 14th, *v.* dūn); *Backysdolle* 1515 *RentSur, Barksdale* 1516 *ib* (*v.* dāl, first el. probably a surname); *Berclingemed* 14th *ReadingAlm* (*v.* mǣd); *Berkemore* 1231 Ch, *Berkemor'* 13th, *Berksmor'* 14th *ReadingAlm* ('birch marsh', *v.* beorc, mōr); *Brocfurlong* 13th (*v.* brōc, furlong); *La Brok'londe* 13th, *Broclaunde* l.13th, *Broclond'* 14th *ReadingAlm, La Brocland* 15th *ib* (*v.* brōc, land); *Bucke Mead* 1655; *Buchacre, La Burchacre* 13th, *La Burchacre* 15th *ReadingAlm* ('birch acre', *v.* birce); *Burchefeldingefeld* 13th ('open land of the people of Burghfield', *v.* -ing, feld); *Buricrofta* 13th, *Buricroft* l.13th, 14th *ReadingAlm* (*v.* burh, croft); *Coppenham* 15th *ReadingAlm; Cunemede* 1197-8 ('cows' meadow', *v.* cū, mǣd); *La Dune* 13th (*v.* dūn); *Dynbroke* 15th (*v.* brōc); *Estcrofta, Estfeld, Estlandmed', Estelondemed'* 13th, *Estlonmed* l.13th, *Le Eastland Mead* 1609 (*v.* ēast, croft, feld, land, mǣd); *Feney* 1490, 1515, 1516 *RentSur* (*v.* fenn, (i)eg, but this may be another spelling for Viney *supra*); *Le Formede* 1380 Gor (*v.* fore, mǣd); *Gosebroke Med* l.13th, *Gosbrok'* 14th *ReadingAlm* (*v.* gōs, brōc, mǣd and cf. Gosmoor *supra*); *The Greate Mead* 1655; *Heathlands, Heathland Coppice* 1609; *Heggecrofte, Heggescroft* l.13th, *Heggescroft* 14th *ReadingAlm* (*v.* hecg, croft); *Heham* 13th (*v.* hamm, first el. uncertain); *Helwikemed* l.13th (*v.* mǣd, and cf. Halewick 71-2); *Hemeueld'* l.13th (*v.* feld, for the first el. cf. O 451-2); *Heyrescroft* l.13th, *Herescroft* 14th *ReadingAlm* (*v.* croft, first el. the surname *Ayer*); *Heywoods* 1659; *Horsehills* 1700; *Hulle* 13th (*v.* hyll, possibly Burghfield Hill *supra* 207); *Le Hurst* late 13th, *Hurst* 14th *ReadingAlm* (*v.* hyrst); *Husseiebrigge* 1197-8 (*v.* brycg, first el. the surname *Hussey*); *Inland Med* l.13th (*v.* inland, mǣd); *Kelerespuddel* 14th *ReadingAlm* (*puddel* is a variant of pightel, first el. probably a surname, *v.* Reaney s.n. *Kelman*); *Lamberts Hill* 1659; *Longbrok* l.13th (possibly 'along the brook'); *Lovedaysgarston'* 1380 Gor (*v.* gærs-tūn, first el. the surname *Loveday*); *Luereham* 14th *ReadingAlm* (*v.* hamm); *Lutelfriþ* 14th *ReadingAlm*

(v. lȳtel, fyrhð, cf. Thrift Coppice *supra*); *Morhacche* 13th *ReadingAlm* (v. mōr, hǣc(c)); *Mulaker, Mulnaker* 1197–8, *Melne Acre, Milne Acre* 1198 Cur, (v. myln, æcer); *Noua Garstona* 13th, *La Newgarston*, 14th (p), *Neusgarston'* 15th *ReadingAlm* (v. nīwe, gærs-tūn); *Punghacche* 13th *ReadingAlm* ('Pinge hatch- gate', v. 206); *Pusecroft(e)* 13th, *Pusecroft* l.13th (v. pise, croft); *Putacra* 13th (v. pytt, æcer); *La Rudinge* 13th, l.13th, *Ruding'* 14th *ReadingAlm, Ridings* 1659, v. ryding); *Rugheneie* 1197–8 (v. rūh, (i)eg); *La Russipuddel* 13th (v. pightel, first el. possibly *rushy*, v. 186); *Sarpacra* 13th (v. scearp, æcer); *Smalemed* l.13th, *Small Meade* 1659 (v. smæl, mǣd); *Stoken Bridge* Eliz ArchJ 41 (v. stoccen, brycg); *Stonicroft* 13th, *Stoniford* l.13th (p) (v. stānig, croft, ford); *Storkesham* 1218–19 (v. storc, hamm); *Strecchelane* l.13th (v. strecca, lane); *Thongs* 1659 (v. þwang); *Tothulle* l.13th (v. tōt-hyll); *Three Pingfeilds* 1659 (v. Pingewood *supra*); *Uluethemed'* l.13th ('Wulfgȳð's meadow', v. mǣd); *Westham* 13th, 15th *ReadingAlm* (v. west, hamm); *Whiteakers Farme* 1665; *Wieland* 1197–8, *Wicland'* 1197–8 AC (v. land, first el. uncertain); *Wlurone Cothstoe* 13th ('Wulfrūn 's cot-stōw'); *Le Writ* l.13th (possibly (ge)wrid 'thicket'); *Wytelemed* l.13th ('Whitley mead', from Whitley in Reading).

Englefield

Englefield

(*on*) *Englafelda* c. 900 (s.a. 871) ASC A

Inglefelle, Englefel 1086 DB, *Englefeldia* Hy 2 *AddCh 7200 et passim* with variant spellings *Englefeld(e)*, *Englefeld', Englef', Englefeud'*; *Engelfed* (sic) Hy 2 (13th) Gaimar, *Engilfeld, Engefeld, Englesfeld* 1284 *Ass, Eyngelfeld* 1330 AD

'Open land of the Angles', v. feld. The name was correctly translated by Asser 'Englafeld Anglice, Latine Anglorum Campus'. v. Introd.

WICKCROFT FM, *Wickcroft Close and Homestead, Wick Croft Moor* 1843 *TA*, cf. *Wyca* e.Hy 3 BM, *La Wike* 1281 AD, v. wīc.

WIGMORE WOOD, *La Wyde More* 1240 AD, *Widemoor Piece* 1843 *TA*, 'wide marsh', v. wīd, mōr. The *TA* name follows *Mays Field*, which survives in Maysfield Plantation, adjacent to Wigmore Wood, so the identification seems certain. The same name occurs near Malpas in Theale (222), about a mile away, and it may originally have been applied to the whole area.

ALDER COPSE.   ANDREW'S COPSE, PLAIN ANDREW'S COPSE, cf. *Andrewesplace* 1401–2 *RentSur, Andreislande* 1441 *ib, Andreweslond'* 1474–5 *ib, Little Wood Andrews* 1843 *TA,* from the surname *Andrew*.

BEECH HILL WD, *Beech Hill Piece* 1843 *TA*.   BENNETT'S COPSE
Benettsplace 1401–2 *RentSur, Beneteslond, Benettismor'* 1441 *ib,
Bentts More* 1474–5 *ib, Bennets Moor, Bents Ground* 1843 *TA*, from
the surname *Bennett*.   BOSTOCK LODGES, *Bostickefeild* 1596
SpecCom, Bostardfeld, Bostardefeild 1609 *LRMB, Bostockfield* 1843
TA.   CHALKPIT FM (1830 OS) AND COTTAGES, *Chalk Pit Ground*
1843 *TA*.   CHANTRY LANE, *The Chauntrye Lande* 1555 *RentSur,
Chauntry Field* 1843 *TA*; for the chantry of St Mary in Englefield
Church *v*. VCH III, 412.   CLAYS COPSE, OLD CLAYS COPSE,
Clayes 1609 *LRMB*.   COBBETYCROFT COPSE, *Coppyd Croft* Hy 8
RentSur, Coppid Croft 1596 *SpecCom, v*. coppede, possibly in the
sense 'provided with an embankment'.   COMMINS COPSE.
COMMON HILL.   CRANEMOOR LAKE, *Cranemer* Hy 8 *RentSur,
Cranemoor Pond* 1761 Rocque, 'heron pond', *v*. cran, mere, a fairly
common name, cf. *Cranford infra* 213.   DAINTY LAND.   LITTLE
DILHAM'S COPSE, *Great and Little Dilhams* 1843 *TA*.   DRAPER'S
OSIER BED.   DUNCROFT WD, *Dongcrofts* 1609 *LRMB, Dung Croft*
1843 *TA*, 'dung croft'.   ENGLEFIELD COMMON WD, *Common Wood*
1830 OS.   ENGLEFIELD HO, 1790 Pride.   ENGLEFIELD PARK,
1790 *ib*; according to VCH III, 408–9, this was known in the 17th as
'Englefield Park alias Highe Park', and represents two earlier parks,
known in 1588–9 as *Roo Parke* and *Hye Parke, v*. rā 'roe-buck',
hēah 'high'.   THE FISHERY.   HAM COPSE.   HAYWARDS FM,
possibly from the family of John *Le Haward*, mentioned 1349–50
RentSur.   HILLCLOSE WD.   THE LARCHES.   THE LAWN,
1843 *TA, v*. launde.   LOWER GROUND COPSE.   MAYSFIELD
PLANTATION, *Mays Field* 1843 *TA*, possibly *Marhillsfeild* 1609
LRMB.   OLD DEER PARK, OLD DEERPARK WD.   THE OVENS
(a small copse beside the R. Pang).   PARKER'S CORNER, *Parkers
Piddle* 1843 *TA*.   PENLOCK.   SANDPIT PLANTATION.   SIM-
MOND'S PIGHTLE COPSE.   SPRING PIGHTLE COPSE.   STONEPARK
PLANTATION AND WD.   TINKER'S PIGHTLE COPSE, *Tinkers Piddle*
1843 *TA*.   WEST CROFT, 1843 *ib, Westcrofte* 1543 *RentSur,
Westcrofts* 1609 *LRMB*.   WIMBLETONS, *Wimbleton Fm* 1830 OS,
Wimbledon Fm 1846 Snare.

FIELD-NAMES

The principal forms in (*a*) are 1843 *TA*. Early forms dated 1240, 1258–9,
1330, 1380, 1429 are AD, 13th *ReadingC*, 1349–50, 1401–2, 1441, Hy 6,
1474–5, Hy 8, 1543 *RentSur*, 1596 *SpecCom*, 1609 *LRMB*.

(a) Blackmoor; Bradfield Bourne Piece; Broom Close; Buckles Moor (this is mentioned before Hogmoor Bridge Mdw (v. 224), which suggests that it is on the line of the Roman road from Alchester O to Silchester Ha: the Bk and O sections of this were known as *Bogildestret, Buggestret* (O 241–2), and Buckles Moor may contain the same name applied to the Berks section); Burgamoor Piece; Bushey Moor; Copse Piddle; Corporation Fd; Duntsfield; Gravel Pit Piece; Haremoor Mdw (*Haremer Croft* Hy 8, v. hara, mere) Home Close (*The Holme Closes* 1596, *The Homeclose* 1609, v. hām (4) (a)); Home Piddle; Horns Piddle; How Croft; Huzzeys (*Husheys* Hy 6, the surname *Hussey*); Jordans Piddle; Mill Ground (*The Millplot* 1609); Neats Mdw (*Le Neats* 1609, v. atten, ēgeð); Parsley Ground; Petty Croft; Piddle (as elsewhere a variant of pightel); Pilgrim Close; Pipers Ground, Mdw, Moor and Piece (*Pypers* 1474–5); Polies Piddle; Pond Close; Poors Close and Piece; Punt Fd (*Poundfold* 1474–5, *Pynfold* Hy 8, *Pownfold* 1543, *Punfoldfeild, Punfallfeld* 1609, *Puntfield* 1761 Rocque, v. pund-fald, pynd-fald); Purfield; Rushey Plat; Simmonds Piddle; Stone, Little (not near Stonepark Wd).

(b) *Bareleg Acre* 1474–5 (probably a surname, v. Reaney s.n. *Barefoot*); *Bekforlong* 1330, *Bekfourlong* Hy 8 (possibly bæc 'ridge'); *Bisshopryche* Hy 6, *Byshoprich* 1474–5 (perhaps *bishopric* in the sense 'seat or residence of a bishop'; the Bishop of Coventry and Lichfield had the manor 1277–95); *La Blete More* 1240, 1258–9 (v. blēat 'wretched, bare', mōr); *Blundeleslonde* 1441, *Blondeles Lond* 1474–5, *Blundells* Hy 8 (v. land, first el. the surname Blundell); *Brianslese* Hy 6 (v. lǣs); *Le Brooke End* 1609; *Chappelfeild* 1609; *Chelleresse* 1429; *Clerkslond* 1401–2, *Clerkeslond* 1441–2, *Clerklond* Hy 8 (v. clerc, land); *Cokkyng'* 1441; *Crannford* 1240–1 FF, *Cranford* 1292 Ipm (v. cran, ford); *Cumbehome* 1609; *Dedecroft* 1380 (v. dēad, croft); *Denes Place* Hy 6; *Dente Lande* 1596; *Fernyforlong* 1380; *Fordley, Fordele Mulle* 1401–2, *Fordele Mille* Hy 6, *Farley Brooke, Farly Mill* 1609 (v. ford, lēah, myln); *Forscheter* 1441 (v. O 446); *Goldenesplace* 1401–2, *Goldene, Goldyws Place* 1441, *Goldyngs* Hy 8 (from the surname *Golden*); *Graue Leghe* Hy 2 AddCh 7200 (v. grāf, lēah); *Le Grenewey* Hy 8 (v. grēne[1], weg); *Hammerhatchfeld* 1609; *Hechynges* Hy 6, *Le Hechengs* Hy 8 (v. heccing); *Homecrofte* 1609; *Humeleg'* 1240–1 FF, *Homeleye* (alias *Humele*) 1292 Ipm (v. humele, lēah); *Jarwaiefeild* 1596; *Langfourlong* Hy 8 (v. lang, furlang); *The Leye* 1380, *Le Leye* Hy 8, *The Lye* 1543, *Little Leye* 1609 (v. lēah); *Longetonwe Croft* Hy 8; *Lotmede* 1543 (v. hlot, mǣd); *Lylyesleyghton* 1401–2 (v. lēactūn, first el. the surname *Lilley*); *La Medforlong* 1330 (v. mǣd, furlang); *Merse* 13th (v. mersc); *Middelcroft* 1255–85 PubLibDoc (v. middel, croft); *Moleslaghton'* 1441, *Moldesleythton'* Hy 6, *Moldes Leghton'* 1474–5 (v. lēactūn, first el. a surname); *Ochortfurlong* 1441 (v. orceard, furlang); *Peel Hill* 1609 (v. pēl); *The Ponds* 1609; *The Rothe* 1380, 1543 (v. roðu); *Rowsholt* Hy 6 (v. holt); *Saundresplace* 1401–2 (v. place, first el. a surname); *Sobbury* 1349–50; *Sylmyneslond* 1401–2; *Westmede* 1380 (v. west, mǣd); *Wildmore* 1609 (v. wilde).

Padworth

PADWORTH

(*æt*) *Peadanwurðe*, (*to*) *peadanwyrðe* 956 (c. 1240) BCS 984
Peteorde 1086 DB
Pedewrtha c. 1160 OxonCh *et freq* with variant spellings *Pedeworth*, *Pedewurða, Pedeworth'* to 13th ReadingC(2)
Pedwrth a. 1162 Queen, *Pedeworth* c. 1180–1200 *ib* (p), *Pedwrþe* 13th ReadingC(2)
Powrd' 1212 Fees, *Podewurth'* 1241 *Ass*
Padeworth' 1220 Fees *et passim* with variant spellings *Padewurth'*, *Paddewurth', Paddewrth, Padewrth', Padewurth, Padewrthe, Padeworthe* to 1395 Queen
Padwrth 1284 *Ass, Padworth* 1761 Rocque
Patheworth 1349 Cl

'Peada's worð'.

TOWNEY BRIDGE AND LOCK, (*seo mæd on*) *tun ege* 956 (c. 1240) BCS 984, *Towney Field* 1838 *TA*, 'island belonging to the tūn', *v.* (ī)eg, and cf. Borough Fm 133.

BREWERSLEES, *Brewer's Lease* 1840 Padworth. BRICKCROFT. CHESTNUT COTTAGE. THE CROFT. FIR COPSE. GRIM'S BANK, *v.* 5. HATCH FM, *Padworth Hatch* 1817 OS, *v.* hæc(c). HIGHWOOD COPSE, *Highwood* 1838 *TA*. LODGE FM. NEW PLANTATION. NORMOOR COPSE, *Normer Coppice* 1656 Padworth. OLD FM, 1846 Snare. PADWORTH BRIDGE AND HO, 1846 ib. PADWORTH COMMON, 1846 ib, *The Common* 1838 *TA*. PADWORTH GULLY AND LODGE. PARSON'S COPSE, *Parson's Close and Pasture* 1838 *TA*. POUND GREEN. SHOOTERSBROOK. UPPER LODGE. WHITE'S COPSE.

FIELD-NAMES

The principal forms in (*a*) are 1838 *TA*, except where otherwise stated; early forms for which no source is given are Padworth.

(*a*) Arable Piece; Bar Fd; Barn Close; Beachastes; Blackmore Close; Broad Close; Broom Close (*v.* brōm); Burvill, Great; Calves Leys (*Calves Lease* 1656, *v.* lǣs); Coppice Close; Cowderoys Long Barn Ground 1839 *TA* (*Aldermaston*) (*Coudreys Maner* 1464 Fine, late of Edward *Coudrey*); Cullmerwood; Damas Fd (cf. Damaskfield Copse in Hampstead Norris 251); Doiley Close; Drudge Close; Drying Ground; Duck's Nest; Dunston Fd;

Faulkner's Piddle; Furze Close; Green Hills; Halfpenny, Broad and Lower
(*Broad Halfpenny* 1817 OS, *v.* 285); Harris Pightle; The Hay Pit; Highfield;
Holly Coppice; Home Close and Mead; House Close; Kate's Pightle; Kiln
Close; Mam Hill; Mill Field and Mead (Padworth Mill 1817 OS, in 956
(*c.* 1240) BCS 984 there is mention of a *mylen stede* which belongs to Pad-
worth); Miry Pightle; Oaken Ground; Oar Close (*v.* ōra); The Park, Park
Close (*The Park* 1656); Pea Close; Picked Close (*v.* pīced); Piddle, Upper
(variant of **pightel**); Pleck, Little (*v.* **plek**); Pond Close; Round Mdw; Rush
Plot; Soverley; Staple Close; Tree Ground; Tyler's Pightle; Wallingford
Lands; Wood Pond Mead.

(*b*) *Brunts Stile* 1656; *Burrough Hill* 1656; *Carters Cross* 1656; *Coster Lane*
1656 (*v.* cot-stōw); *Farly Butts* 1656; *Ingmede* 1524; *Martins Orchard* 1656;
Notingmede 1523; *Oxenheath* 1663 (in 956 (c. 1240) BCS 984 there is mention
of an *oxena wic* 'oxen farm', belonging to Padworth); *Padworth Warren*
1663; *Pydmans Croft* 1524; *Silvers Hedge* 1656; *Streeam Dyche* 1524;
Sumerhedge 1656; *Le Yewtree* 1524.

Purley

PURLEY

> *Porlei, Porlaa* 1086 DB, *Magna Porlegh* 1284 *Ass, Porle maior*
> 1327 *SR*
> *Purleia* c. 1180 (c. 1200) Thame *et passim* with variant spellings
> *Purle, Purl', Purlye, Purlegh*; *Purle maior et Purle minor, Manga*
> *Purle, Parua Purle* 1284 *Ass, villata utriusque Purle* 1294 *SR,*
> *Little Purle* 1302 Pat, *Parva Purlee* 1401–2 FA, *Parva Purle,*
> *Porle Huscarle* 1428 ib
> *Pirlai* 1194 Cur (p)
> *Pourle, Pourleg'* 1297 CornAcc, *Much Pourle* 1456 ArchJ

'Wood or clearing frequented by the snipe or bittern', *v.* lē(a)h.
The first el. is OE pūr, found also in Purleigh Ess 222 and Purbeck
Do. Purley in Sr (Sr 54) is of different origin.

There were two manors, known as 'great' and 'little' Purley, the
former being once referred to as *Porle Huscarle*, from the family who
held it from the 12th to the 14th cent. (VCH III, 418–20).

BELLEISLE FM, *Belleisle House* 1830 OS.   BROOM COPSE.   HARRY
JAW'S WOOD, *Harry Jaes* 1839 *TA*.   PIKE SHAW, cf. *Pike* 1839 *ib,*
the 250′ contour forms a pointed hill in this part of the parish, *v.*
pīc[1].   PURLEY COPSE.   PURLEY HALL, 1761 Rocque, identified
VCH III, 420, with the manor of *Hyda* 1220 Fees, 1233 Cl, *La Hyde*
1313 Fine, 1333 Cl, *Hide* 1317 Ch; possibly from owners surnamed

de la Hide rather than from the size of the holding, *v.* hīd.
PURLEY LODGE.   PURLEY PK, 1846 Snare.   SALTNEY MEADOW,
Satney Mead 1839 *TA.*   SCRACE'S FM, *Scracys Acre* 1839 *ib.*
WESTBURY FM, 1846 Snare.

FIELD-NAMES

The principal forms in (*a*) are 1839 *TA.*

(*a*) Ash Piece; Block Piddle (*piddle* is a variant of pightel); Brier Hill;
Brook Furlong; Butt Acre and Piece (*v.* butte); Calf Lees; Calversham Mdw;
Catmore Piece; Chalk Piece; Churchams; Croft Moor; Elm's Piddle;
Elyham, Little (cf. Elyham House 1846 Snare); Farmers Piddle; Goodey
Down; Goosecroft; Gore Acre (*v.* gāra); Gravel Acre; Guntlings, Great and
Little; Hides, Upper (*v.* Purley Hall *supra*); Hill Piece; Hop Garden Piece
(*v.* hoppe); Ilsleys Piddle; Inhams (*v.* innām); Ivey Close; Luccam Piece;
Maggots Moor; Moors; Nippling Piece; Nut Moor, Little; Oathams;
Parsonage Piece; Pit Acre; Pond Acre and Mdw; Pound Mdw; Purley
Common Piddle; Purley Cross Piddle; Rick Yard Piddle; Russett Mdw;
Shepherds Piddle; Square Close and Pike (*v.* Pike Shaw 215); Streaks (*v.*
straca); Tea Piece; Veer, Lower and Upper (*v.* furh); Warren Park; West
Marsh; Wheathams Hill; Witches.

Stratfield Mortimer

STRATFIELD MORTIMER

Stradfeld 1086 DB
Stratfeld' Hugonis de Mortemer 1167, 1175 P, *Estratfeld* c. 1175
(c. 1195) ReadingA, *Stratfeld'* 1220 Fees, *Stratfeud'* 1239 Cl,
Stratfeud 1275–6 RH, *Stratfeld Mortim'* 1275–6 ib *et freq* with
variant spellings *Stratfeld'Mortimer, Stratfeld Mortymer, Strat-
feld Mortymar*; *Stratton' Morton, Stratfford Mortem', Stratfelde
Mortem'* 1284 *Ass*
Strafella 1173–82 (1328) Ch, *Strafeld'* 1190 P, *Straffeld* 1230 Ch
Stretfeld 1224–5 FF, *Strettefeld* 1284 *Ass*, *Stretfeld Mortimer*
1297 Pat

'Open land traversed by a Roman road', *v.* strǣt, feld. Stratfield
Mortimer and Stratfield Saye and Turgis in Hants are on either side
of the Roman road from London to Silchester (CALLEVA ATREBATVM).
The Berks place belonged to Ralf Mortimer in 1086, and his descen-
dants held it until the accession of Ed 4 (VCH III, 423). The manorial
addition has supplanted the place-name in local usage.

STRATFIELD MORTIMER STREET-NAMES

THE AVENUE.   RAVENSWORTH RD.   ST JOHN'S RD.   ST MARY'S RD.
VICTORIA RD.   WEST END RD (Mortimer West End is in Ha).   WINDMILL
RD (near Windmill Common).

THE FOREHEAD, *Forewode* 1305 Ipm, *Le Forewode* 15th VCH III, 422,
Le Forwood, Forewood 1552 *LRMB, Four Heads* 1761 Rocque,
Forward 1817 OS, *The Forehead* 1846 Snare, '(land) in front of the
wood', *v.* **fore, wudu,** and cf. Wa 243–4, where three other examples
of the name are cited.

ABBEYCROFT.   ADMIRAL'S COPSE.   BLACK'S HOLE, *Black Sole
Spring Piece* 1838 *TA, v.* **sol**[1] 'slough'.   BOUNDARY POND, *Boundy
Mede, Boundyfeld* 1552 *LRMB,* near the county boundary.   BRIAR
LEA.   BRIDGE'S FM, *Bridges Piddle* 1838 *TA.*   BUTLER'S LANDS
FM, *Butlers* 1552 *LRMB.*   CHURCH FM.   COLLEGE PIECE.
DRURY LANE, 1846 Snare.   FAIR GROUND, *The Fair Ground* 1838
TA.   FIVE OAKEN, *Le Fyve Oken Woode* 1552 *LRMB, Oken*
possibly from *ācum, v.* **āc.**   FURZE GROUND.   GIBBET PIECE.
GREAT PARK FM AND COPSE, LITTLE PARK FM, *Le Litlepark* 1305
Ipm, *Mortimer Parke* 1572 *SpecCom, Mortimer Great Park* 1761
Rocque, 1846 Snare, *Great Park Fm and Coppice, Mortimer Little
Park, Little Park Fm* 1846 ib. The parks are first mentioned in 1304
(VCH III, 426).   HEADLANDS FM, *Headlands Mead* 1838 *TA.*
HILL FM (near Mortimer Hill).   HOGS PLAT, *Hog Plat Piddle,
Hog Plot or Long Mead* 1838 *TA.*   HOLDENS FIRS.   HOME
WOOD, *Le Home Grove, Le Homes Coppice* 1552 *LRMB.*   KNOT-
MEAD.   LADYFIELD COPSE, *Ladyfelde* 1552 *LRMB, v.* **hlǣfdige.**
LITTLE COPSE (2 examples).   LOCKRAM BROOK, FM AND RD,
Lockram's Meadow, Lockram's Lane Ground, Inner Lockram's 1838
TA.   LONG MOOR, 1761 Rocque, *Le Longemore Slade* 1552
LRMB, v. **lang, mōr, slæd.**   LOVE'S ALLOTMENT.   LUKIN'S
WOOD, *Lukin's Mead* 1838 *TA.*   MANN'S FM.   MONKTON
COPSE, *Lower and Upper Monktons* 1838 *ib.*   MORTIMER COMMON,
1761 Rocque.   MORTIMERHILL, 1817 OS, Snare (1846) shows two
hills with this name.   MORTIMER HO (1817 OS), LAND AND LODGE.
MOWBRAY'S PIECE, *Mowbray Lodge* 1846 Snare.   NEW MOW
MEAD, 1838 *TA.*   NIGHTINGALE LANE, *Nightingales* 1552 *LRMB.*
PERREN'S FM, *Perrin's Meadow* 1838 *TA.*   PITFIELD LANE, *Pitte-
felde* 15th VCH III, 423, *Pitt Felde* 1552 *LRMB, Pit Field* 1838 *TA,*

v. **pytt, feld.**   PITT LANE FM.   SMITH'S COPSE, *Smith's Meadow,*
House Ground, and Piddle 1838 *TA.*   SPRATLEY'S BARN.   STAN-
MORE.   STARVEHILL PLANTATION, *v.* 283.   STEPHEN'S FIRS,
Stephyns 1838 *TA.*   TANHOUSE BRIDGE, *Tanhouse Mead and
Pightle* 1838 *ib.*   TICKLECORNER LANE, *Tickle Corner* 1846 Snare.
TOTTERDOWN HILL, *Totter Down* 1838 *TA*; this name often refers to
an Iron Age hill-fort (*v.* tōt-ærn), but nothing is marked here on
O.S. maps; it is at GR 665651.   TUN BRIDGE, *Tunbridge Ground*
1838 *TA.*   WARRENNESWOOD HO, *Warnes Wood* 1552 *LRMB.*
WHEAT'S FM, *Whits Land, Garden, Groue and Mede* 1552 *ib.*
WINDMILL COMMON, *Mortimer W. Mill* 1817 OS.

FIELD-NAMES

The principal forms in (*a*) are 1838 *TA*, except those dated 1846, which are
Snare. Some of the *TA* names may be in Mortimer West End, Ha. Early
forms dated 12th (l.12th) are *ReadingC*, c. 1227 *AddCh 19628*, 1295 (14th)
ReadingC(3), 1462, 1463 Brocas, 1652, 1662, 1703, 1729 *PubLib*, and 1761
Rocque; those for which no date or source is given are 1552 *LRMB*.

(*a*) Acre Piddle; Alcove; Alms Land; Apple Tree Ground; Bail Close,
Bailey, Bailey's Piddle; Balambs; Barn Close (*Barneclose*); Blacklands; Blue
Dick; Bottoms (*Le Botomes, v.* botm); Bounds Piddle; Bowlaway; Brawling
Stile Ground; Breache's Piddle; The Breach (*Le Breche, Le Breche Mede, v.*
brēc); Briary Close; Brickkiln Piece; Broad Close and Mead (*Le Brode Close
and Mede*); Broadmoor Fd (*Le Brodmore, v.* brād, mōr); Brockhill (*Brokehill,
v.* brōc, hyll); Brook Close; Broom Close, Brooming Close, Broomy Close
(*Le Bromecrofte* 1552 *LRMB, Broome Closes* 1662, *v.* brōm); Buck Close;
Burnt Hill; Bushel Leaze Mdw (*The Busshie Leaze*); Callow Strip; Cart-
house Piddle; Causeway Mead; Chalk Ground; Chimney Close; Church
Close; Common Piece; Cooper's Hall and Mead (*Cowpers Corner*); Coppice
Close, Ground and Piddle; Coster Fd (*Costowes, v.* cot-stōw); Cottage Mdw;
Court House Ground, Court Mead (*Courte Mede, v.* court, mæd); The
Croft; Dinniker Mead, Diniker, Dinneker; Doe's Piddle; Dog Kennel
Ground; Down, The Great (*Le Downe, Downe Grove, v.* 'dūn); Drove
Piece; Dry Mead; Dungeon Piddle; East Lands; Fisher's Fd and Piddle
(cf. *Fis(s)hewere*); Fish Pond Mead; Flat Close; Garden Ground and Piddle;
Goodwin Villa 1846; Granary Ground and Piddle; Gravel Pit Ground;
Grubbs, Grubbs Plot or The Wood (*v.* 281); Gully Middle; Halcomb; Hales
Green 1846, Hale's Corner, Heale Ground (*Le Hale Close, Hale Grove* 1552
LRMB, Hales Green 1761, *v.* h(e)alh); Hams Pasture (*Ham's House* 1652,
occupied by Alice *Ham*); Hanging Down (*v.* hangende, dūn); Hatherlands;
Hay Croft (*Hayecrofte* 1463); Heath Piddle (*La Hethe* 1295 (14th) (p), *Hethe
Closes, Hethes Mede, Le Hethe Crofte, v.* hǣð); Heaven (cf. 283); Hedge
Lands; Hill Bottoms, Ground and Pasture; Hoeman's Grove (*Le Hollmon
Busshe*); Hollow Hill; Holly Bush; Home Close (*Le Home Close*); Hoods

Green 1846 (also 1761); Hoods Piddle; Horse Ground and Plat; Hunters Park 1846; Hunts Mead; Inhams (*v.* innām); Kate's Piddle; Kiln Piddle; Kitchen Close (*Le Kechyn Crofte*, *v.* cycene); Knowles; Lain, The Little (*v.* leyne); Lambstone Copse 1846; The Lawn (*v.* launde); Leaping Bar Ground; Lime Close; Malthouse Ground; March Mdw; Mare Croft (*Marecrofts* 1729); Moon Lane Piddel; The Moor (*v.* mōr); Mount Ground and Piddle; Mouse Hill (*Mowshill*); Nutchers (*Le Noters Crofte*); Oaks Croft; Oak Slade (also 1761); Old House Ground; Old Wood; Orchard Close and Ground; (*Le Orcherde Crofte*); Ox Leaze and Close; Park Close and Drove (*Le Parke Close and Mede* 1552 *LRMB*, *Park Lane* 1761, *v.* Great and Little Park *supra*); Petty Croft; Picked Close (*Piked Croft*, *v.* pīced); Piddle (variant of pightel, as freq. in this parish); Pig Trough; The Plat (*v.* plat[2]); The Plot; Poison Piddle (*v.* 283); Pond Ground and Mead (*Le Ponde Close*); Pond Tail Mead; Poss Moor; Pound Close (*Le Poundes*); Pug Fd; Pump Pasture; Rag Piddle; Red Croft (*Le Red Crofte*); Red Meade (*Redemede* 1224–5 *FF*, *Redmede* c. 1227, *La Redmed* 12th (l.12th), *Redemede*, *v.* rēad, mǣd); Rickyard Ground; Rough Pasture, Piddle and Piece; Roundabouts (*v.* 281); Roundaway Strip; Round Mead; Rushey Piddle (the same name occurs in Burghfield 211); Rush Mead; Russell's Ground (*Russells Hills*); Ryass; Rye Ground; Sawpit Ground, Piddle and Piece; Sheepcot Fd; Shoemaker's Mead; Short Ground; Silchester Mount (Silchester Ha adjoins Stratfield Mortimer); Sluice Mead; Spring Piddle and Close; Stairs Piddle; The Stakes; Staniford's Mead; Stanfords 1846; Stonehams (*Stoneham*); The Street Ground; The Strip; Stroud's Coppice (*Le Strowds*, *v.* strōd); Suejays; Three Cornered Mead; Tile Barn Ground; Underwoods Lane; Upstair's Ground; Violet Mdw (*Violetts* 1552, *Violet Hill* 1761 Rocque, 1817 OS); Vitch Piddle; Water Roakes (*Wat at roks*); Well's Plat; Wheeler's Piddle; Whitbourne Mead; Whitburns; White Gate, White Hams; White House 1846 (*LHRS* says this is now Mortimer Lodge); Worden Piddle, The Wordens, Worne Field (cf. *Wordia* 12th (l.12th), *La Wortht* 1321 *ECR*, *Le Netherworthe et Le Upper Worthe* 1552 *LRMB*, *Worthine* 1571 *ECR*, (common called) *The Worthen* 1620 *ECR v.* worð, worðig, worðign).

(b) *Le Barton Close* (*v.* bere-tūn); *Beche Lande*; *Le Bevers Mede, Bevers Groue* 1552 *LRMB*, *Bever House* 1703 (Robert *Bever* mentioned); *Bramley*; *Le Brokes Down, Le Brokes Pidell*; *Byefeld Mede*; *Caplens Slade* (possibly connected with Chaplin's Copse, Mortimer West End, Ha); *Le Castell Close* 1552 *LRMB*, *Castle Place* 1652; *Le Chaldram, Le Litill Chaldram*; *Chalfgrove* 1305 Ipm (*v.* c(e)alf, grāf); *Chicheley Lande*; *Chuppinggesfrith* 1280 Ipm, *Cuppynggesfryth* 1300 Cl, *Kepingfrithe* ('Cypping's wood', *v.* fyrhð, and *v.* Feilitzen 221–2 for late OE and post-Conquest instances of the pers.n.; one of two thegns who held Stratfield Mortimer TRE was named *Cheping*, and a memorial stone in the church, described in VCH 1, 248, refers to *Ægelwardus filius Kyppingus*; possibly there was only one thegn of this name TRE, and the p.n. refers to him, or there may have been a local family in which the pers.n. recurs; it is not so common that the three instances can be unconnected); *Le Cliuerde*; *Culuerhouse Crofte* (*v.* culfre); *Edishe Close* (*v.* edisc); *Estoft*; *Evenhame* (*v.* efn, hamm); *Eyemore* 1305 Ipm (*v.* (ī)eg, mōr); *Faryscrofte* 1462; *Le Fere* (*v.* furh); *Le Ferny Crofte, Ferny Hills*; *Flete Brige, Les Flete Houses* (*v.* flēot, brycg); *Fore Mede* (*v.* fore, mæd); *Le Forgehouse*; *Frithes Mede*; *Le Gallant Crofte, Galland Mede* (possibly NED *gallant* a. and sb. 4, apparently the wild anemone or wind-flower); *Le Gret Feld*; *Le Grove Close*; *Le Hassock* (*v.* hassuc and 190); *Le Highefeld*; *Le Highewey*; *Le Hillclose*; *Hodcote*; *Holyfords Slade*; *Le Horse-leaze*; *The Litill Feld*; *Le Longeclose*; *Longecrofte*; *Longe Crosse* (cross called); *Le Longemede*; *Luffandesmed* c. 1270 AD, *Lovehame Mede* (*v.* mæd); *Le Marke Close*; *Le Marshe, Marshewood*; *Mayho*; *Le Netherhouse Mede, Le Nether Mede*; *New Pond* 1761; *Potters Oke*; *Pury Crofte* (*v.* pirige); *Le Racke Close*; *Le Realme*; *Reddelonde* 1462, *Le Red Lande Close, Le Redlande Coppice* (*v.* (ge)rydd, land); *Le Sares Croft*; *La Schete* c. 1227 (p), *La Scete* 12th (l.12th) (p) (*v.* scēat and cf. Sheet St 28); *Segemore* (*v.* secg[1], mōr); *Shipgrove*; *Spitts Acre*; *Le Stanke* (*v.* stank); *Le Thorn'* (wood called) 1224–5 FF, *La Thorne* c. 1227 (p), *bosc. de La Torne* 12th (l.12th), *Thorne* 1342 Cl (p) (*v.* þorn); *Le Viner* 1305 Ipm; *Le Woodlande*; *Wryeslade*; *Le Yate Crofte* (*v.* geat, croft); *Le Yondre Lande*.

Sulham

SULHAM

> *Soleham* 1086 DB, 1317, 1325 Cl, 1322 Fine
> *Suleham* 1142–84 (l.12th) *ReadingC et passim* to 1275–6 RH
> *Sulesham* 1241 *Ass* (p)
> *Sulham* 1284 *Ass*, c. 1290 Gor (p), 1294 *SR*
> *Soulham* 1305 Pat, Cl
> *Solham* 1333 Cl
> *Sullum, Sullam* 1535 VE

Probably a compound of sulh in the sense 'gully' and hām. The village is on a wooded slope, rising sharply from the stream which forms the west boundary of the parish.

NUNHIDE FM, *Nonnehyde* 1327 *SR, Sullam Ferme otherwyse callyd Nunhyde* 1535 VE, *Nunhyde* 1552 LRMB, *Nunhide* 1761 Rocque, 1790 Pride, *v.* nunne, hīd. An estate of one hide in Sulham was given to Goring Priory t. Hy 2 (VCH III, 430).

FURTHER AND HITHER CLAYHILL COPSE, *Clay Hill* 1840 *TA.*   LITTLE HORSEMOOR COPSE.   LONG PIGHTLE SHAW (*v.* pightel).   MOSS-HALL WOOD, *Moss Hall Groves* 1840 *TA.*   SLUICE COPSE.

FIELD-NAMES

The forms in (a) are 1840 *TA*.

(a) Barkers Pightle; Breach (v. brēc); Broad Croft; Charley Mead; Cocks Fd; Dean; Dog-Kennel Mdw; The Downs; Garden Close; Gravel Hill; The Great Ground; The Green; Hay Croft; Hop Ground; Kiln Close and Pightle; Long Lands and Pightle; Lovegroves Pightle; The Lynches (v. hlinc); Maple Croft; The Moors; The Park; Parsons Pightle (v. pightel); Ridings, Lower and Upper (v. ryding); The Rookery; Sandy Furlong; South Moor; The Strings, The Strings Lane (v. 282); Sulham Common; Sunny Pike (v. pīc¹); Swing Gate; Tickle Me Too (v. 285); Tree Moor; Warren, Lower and Upper.

Sulhamstead Bannister (for the parish-name, v. 184–5)

BROAD STREET, 1846 Snare.   BROOK COTTAGES.   BROOMFIELD HATCH, *Bloomfield Hatch* 1817 OS, 1846 Snare, and on 6″ map. CHANDLER'S FM.   CRICKETS WD.   GODDARD'S GREEN AND FM, *Goddards Green* 1846 Snare.   GORING LANE, *Goring Pasture* 1846 *TA*.   NEW LODGE AND RD.   OAKFIELD, *Wokefield Banastre* 1375 Cl, *Oakfield Green, Lo and Ho* 1817 OS, *Oakfield Lodge* 1846 Snare, this estate was part of the manor of Wokefield, v. 227–8. OSIER BED.   PALMER'S LANE, *Palmers Pightle* 1846 *TA*, v. pightel. RAPLEYS.   ROOKERY WD.   SAUNDERSCOURT FM.   WORKFIELD FM.

FIELD-NAMES

Some f.ns. listed under Sulhamstead (187) may belong here. The following are explicitly stated to be in Sulhamstead Bannister:

(b) *Burhforlong, Burhstret* 1313 AD (v. burh, furlang, strǣt); *Mulwey* 1313 AD (v. myln, weg); *Nephull'* 1409 PubLibDoc, *Nephulle, Est Nephulle* ?1422–3 AD (v. nēp, hyll).

Theale

THEALE

Teile 1208 (13th) RSO (p), *Thele* 1220 Fees, 1248–52 *FF*, *la þele* 13th *ReadingC*, *La Thele* 1272 (14th) *ReadingC*(2), *la Thel'* 1284 *Ass*, *Theale vulgo Dheal* 1675 Ogilby, *Theale* 1763 PubLib

v. þel 'plank', of which this is probably the pl. þelu. The same name occurs in So. The reference may be to a plank bridge across the Kennet, but Anderson (205) suggests that it could be to a structure used for the meetings of the Hundred. Dill Hundred Sx 435 appears to be named from such an erection.

CALCOT PLACE, *Caldecote* 13th *ReadingC*, 1284 *Ass*, *Colecote* 1325 Cl, *Caldicote*, *Calcote* 1552 *LRMB*, *Calcot* 1544 ReadingA, 1846 Snare, 'cold cottage(s)', *v.* c(e)ald, cot(e), and cf. 276.

MALPAS, *Maupas* 14th *ReadingC(3)*, *Mapers Meadow* 1840 *TA-(Sulham)*, *Mapus Mead* 1843 *TA*. The name occurs in *ReadingC(3)* at f. 158b, where a 14th-cent. hand has written *cuius vocatur maupas* over a reference to some pasture called *Wydemor* (*infra* 223), and has written *Carta de morelond et maupas* in the margin. It is a French name meaning 'bad passage', *v.* mal², pas. Other instances are Malpas Ch **4**, 38–40, Cu 347, Mon (NCPNW 239), YW **1**, 54, 138. DEPN states that there is an example in Co; and one near Bewdley Wo appears on the 1″ map. In the Berks, Cu and Mon names it seems certain that the reference is to marshy ground. To account for the frequent recurrence of the compound, it seems necessary to assume that *malpas* was a French appellative borrowed by English-speaking people. It is occasionally used with the definite article, cf. *le Maupas* 1373 YW I, 54, *y malpas* c. 1566 NCPNW 239, *le Malpas* c. 1195 Cu 347.

ARROW HEAD, 1842 *TA(Burghfield)*, *Langley Mead Arrow Head* 1843 *TA(Tilehurst)*; this may have been the name of the narrow, pointed strip between R. Kennet and Holy Brook; Holy Brook joins the Kennet at the point where the name is printed on the 6″ map. ASHES COPSE.   BATH COTTAGE.   BEANSHEAF FM, 1790 Pride, *Bensheves* 1390 Cl, *Bensheves*, *Bensheffes* 1416–17 Stonor, *Benesheves* 1474 ib, *Benschevys* 1494–5 Ipm, *Bean Sheafe Farm* 1761 Rocque, from the family of Robert *Benshef*, a juror in Reading Hundred 1241 *Ass*. Another Robert *Beneshef* is mentioned 1304–5 FF in connection with land in Tilehurst, and John *Benshef* appears 1316 Pat in connection with an offence at Tidmarsh.   BLOSSOMS END, BLOSSOMS-END FM, *Bloom End* 1761 Rocque, *Blossom End* 1790 Pride, *Blossoms End Fm* 1846 Snare, possibly from the family of Geoffrey *Blostme*, mentioned 13th *ReadingC(2)* in connection with Pangbourne. CALCOT GARDENS AND GRANGE, *v. supra*.   CALCOT MILL, 1755 *PubLibDoc*, *Calcott Mylne* 1596 *SpecCom*, *v. supra*.   COLLEGE COTTAGE.   DEADMAN'S LANE, 1830 OS, 1846 Snare.   FEEDING

MOORS, *Feeding Moore, Feading Moors* 1843 *TA(Tilehurst)*, probably referring to good pasture. THE FILBERTS, ('hazel nuts'). FORD'S FM. THE GRANGE. HOLY BROOK, *v.* 11. HORN'S COPSE, *The Horne* 1583 *Dep, Horns* 1843 *TA(Tilehurst)*, *v.* horn; the copse is in a narrow projection of the parish. HORSEMOOR WD. LIDLEY SHAW, *Lidley* 1843 *TA(Tilehurst)*. LITTLE COPPICE. MALPAS COPSE AND SHAW, *v.* 222. MEAD PLOT. NORTH ST, *Northstrete* 1441 *RentSur, Northestrete* 1555 *ib, venell' voc' North-streetlane* 1661 *LRMB, street* is used in the sense 'hamlet' and *north* refers to the position N. of Theale. THE POPLARS. RAILWAY HOTEL P.H. THATCHERS' ARMS P.H. THEALE GREEN. TRAVEL-LERS' FRIEND P.H. WIGLEY COPSE, *Wigley Mead* 1843 *TA(Tilehurst)*. YEWTREE COPPICE, *Yew Tree Pightle* 1843 *ib, v.* pightel.

FIELD-NAMES

The principal forms in (*a*) are 1817 *EnclA*, except where otherwise stated. For other 19th-cent. f.ns. *v.* Tilehurst 196.

(*a*) Barn Close; Bartholomew Mead; Cross Lane Ground; The Dean; Hole Piddle (*piddle* is a variant of pightel); Long Pightle; Oxlease Plot; Sandfield; Spire Mdw (*v.* spīr); Tuckers Green (also 1843 *TA (Tilehurst)*); Widmoor Common (*Wydemor, Widemora* n.d. (14th) *ReadingC(3), Wydmore, Wildmore* 1609 *LRMB, v.* wīd, mōr and *supra* 222, 211); Worldsend Ground 1843 *TA(Tilehurst)* (*Worlds End* 1761 Rocque, *v.* 284); Workhouse Common.

(*b*) *Hawkslade* 1516 *RentSur; Notmoor* 1790 Pride; *Pilhulle, Pilehulle* 1272 (14th) *ReadingC(2)* (*v.* pīl, hyll).

Tidmarsh

TIDMARSH

Tedmerse 1196 P *et freq* with variant spelling *Tedmers; Thedmers* 1213 OblR *et freq* with variant spelling *Thedmerch, Thedmersh, Thedmersche, Thedmersshe; Thed(e)merse* 1223 (c. 1250) Bract, 1241 *Ass, Tedemerse* a. 1280 *PubLibDoc*
Edmers' 1236–7 (c. 1250) Bract
Tydmers 1284 *Ass, Tydmerssch* 1412 FA, *Tydemershe* 1428 ib
Thudemers (p), *Tudemershe, Thudmers* 1300 Ipm, *Thudemersch* 1337 Gor (p)

Second el. mersc 'marsh'. The first might be OE þēod 'nation, people', found in Thetford (Nf), Tetford (L) and Ede Way (BdHu 122). The meaning could be 'common marsh'. Ekwall (DEPN) suggests a pers.n. *Tydda*, but more forms with *-u-* and with medial *-e-* might have been expected from such a base.

BARTON'S COPSE, *Lower and Upper Barton Meadow* 1839 *TA*. DAIRYPAIL SHAW.   FURTHERFIELD SHAW.   HARESCROFT COPSE, *Hare Croftes* 1544 AD, *Hares Croft* 1839 *TA*.   HOGMOOR BRIDGE (1843 *TA*(*Englefield*)) AND COPSE, *Hog Moor* 1839 *TA*(*Pangbourne*), *Hogmore Coppice* 1846 Snare.   HOME FM.   LEDGE PIT. MANOR HO.   MOOR COPSE, *Moor Coppice* 1846 Snare, cf. *The Moors* 1839 *TA*.   OXLEY'S COPSE AND SHAW, *Ox Leys* 1839 *ib*. PARK WOOD, 1830 OS, *Park Coppice* 1846 Snare, cf. *Park Meadow* 1839 *TA*.   PEATPITS WOOD.   SPARKMOOR COTTAGES, *Sparks Meadow* 1839 *TA*.   TIDMARSH FM AND GRANGE.   TIDMARSH MILL, cf. *Mill Ground* 1839 *TA*.   WITHY EYOT, *v.* ēgeð.

FIELD-NAMES

The principal forms in (*a*) are 1839 *TA*.

(*a*) Back Mdw; Bloom Hill; Burnice Mdw; Calves Leys; Chalsey Fd; The Crofts; The Dairies (possibly connected with Dairypail Shaw *supra*); Dunley Fd; Grass Moors; Green Mdw; Hailey Bottom; Henwoods Pightle (*v.* pightel); Great Hide (*v.* hīd); Hog Island (cf. Hogmoor *supra*); Home Mdw; Kiln Ground; The Linches (*v.* hlinc); Parsonage Ground and Mdw; Rack Close (*The Rack Close* 1612 *Dep*, belonging to a fulling mill); Sheep Croft; Shop Pightle; Tidmarsh Green; Yew Tree Piece.

(*b*) *Asshengarden* 1544 AD; *Brayle* (grove called) 1305 Ipm (*v.* lēah); *La Friht* Hy 3 AD (*v.* fyrhð); *Heghmore* 1305 Ipm (*v.* mōr); *Trescoteslese* 1255–8 *FF* (*v.* lǣs; for the first el. Dr O. von Feilitzen suggests an OE *þresc-cot 'threshing shed'); *Westmor* 1255–8 *FF* (*v.* west, mōr); *Wydemede* 1255–8 *FF* (*v.* wīd, mǣd and cf. 189); *Wynhird* 1305 Ipm (*v.* wīn-geard).

Ufton Nervet

UFTON NERVET

> *Offetvne* 1086 DB, *Offeton'* 1178 P (p), *Ofton' Roberd, Offeton' Nernut* 1284 *Ass, Ofton' Neremyt* 1294 *SR, Offeton Roberd* 1387 Fine
> *Vffetona* 1179 P (p), *Uftone* 1316 FA, *Uftone Robert* 1428 ib, *Uffeton Robert, Uffeton Richard* 1396 BM, *Ufton Nermyte, Ufton Robert* 1552 LRMB
> *Offentona* 12th (l.12th) *ReadingC, Offinton'* 1241 *Ass* (p), *Offintun'* 1242–3 Fees, *Offinton' Neyrnut* 13th *ReadingC*(2), *Offynton' Nernut* 1284 *Ass*

Uffinton' 1197–8 AC (p), 1220 Fees *et freq*, *Uffinton' Roberti* 1261–6 FF, *Huffinton'*, *Vffentun'* 13th ReadingC
Uffinton Richer, *Offinton Richer* 1275–6 RH, *Uffington' Roberd*, *Uffington' Nermyt* 1284 *Ass*
Ofton Roberd 1349 Cl

Probably 'Uffa's farm', identical with Uffington (Pt 2), although in this name the forms without the -*n*- of the genitive are earlier, and have given rise to the modern form.

There were two manors, Ufton Robert, so called from *Robert de Ufton* who held it in the 13th cent., and Ufton Nervet or Richard, which was held by Richard *Neyrnut* in the 13th cent. (VCH III, 440–1). For this surname, which means 'black night', *v.* DEPN s.n. Ufton Nervet. The modern *Nervet* is due to a misreading of -*n*- as -*u*-.

CULHAM SHAW, *Coleham in Neirmyt* 1401 Cl, *Cullum Copse* 1846 Snare. The second el. is hamm; the first could be col[1] 'charcoal', or, as Professor Löfvenberg suggests, a side form **cul*. This does not seem a likely compound, however, and a pers.n. *Cūla* is probably to be preferred, in which case the name is identical with Culham O 150–1.

MAY RIDGE, *Masrugia* 1142–84 (l.12th) ReadingC, *Marrug'* 1241 *Ass*, *Marruge* 13th ReadingC(2), *Marerugge* 1327 SR (p), *Marrug* 1341 NonInq (p), *Mare Ridges* 1761 Rocque, *Mare Ridge* 1846 Snare. Probably 'boundary ridge', *v.* (ge)mǣre, hrycg, in spite of the earliest form. Names with -*s(e)r*- normally keep the -*s*- till the 15th cent. or later (cf. Curridge 242 and Marridge W 288–9). 'Boundary ridge' is suitable topographically, the name being applied to the high ground in the extreme N. of the parish. Merridge So is identical.

TIDNEY BED (*Tidney, Tidney Mead* 1842 *TA*) may be named from (meadow called) *Tibney* 1391 Cl, *Tybbeneye* 1394 ib, 'Tib(b)a's riverside meadow', *v.* (ī)eg.

ARLETT'S PLANTATION.   ASHEN WD.   BIRCHEN HILL.   BRENT'S GULLY.   CHURCH PLANTATION, *Church Close and Pightle* 1842 *TA*. COLD HILL, *Coolhill* 18th *RecOff Cat*.   COWPOND PIECE.   COX'S WD.   GIBBET PIECE.   GOODBOY'S COPSE, *Goodboys Close* 1842

8   GPB

TA, Goodboy Copse 1846 Snare.   GRAVELLY PIECE, *Upper Gravelly Piece* 1842 *TA*.   HART'S LANE, *Harts Ground* 1842 *ib*.   HOLLY COPSE, 1846 Snare, *Holly Wood Six Acres* 1842 *TA*.   ISLAND FM. LAMBDEN'S FM (*Lamden Fm* 1846 Snare), HO AND WD.   LINLEY SHAW, *Four Acre Linley* 1840 Padworth, *Linley* 1842 *TA*.   LONG PLANTATION.   MAY'S LANE.   MIDDLE FM.   NANPIE SHAW. OLD PARK.   OVAL POND.   PEARTREE COPSE, *Pear Copse* 1830 OS, *Pear Tree Close* 1842 *TA*.   PENNSYLVANIA WOOD, *Pensylvania* 1842 *ib*, *v*. 284.   THE PINES.   POND SLADE.   POOR'S ALLOTMENTS.   RAVEN HILL.   ROUND OAK, 1790 Pride, ROUNDOAK PIECE, *Rownde Oake* 1656 Padworth, *Round Oak Close* 1842 *TA*. SEWARD'S GULLY.   SOMERWELLS, *Summerwell's* 1842 *TA*, *Summerwell Wood* 1846 Snare.   TETMOOR SHAW, *Tetemore* 1542 Padworth, *Tetmore* 1656 ib, *Great Titmore* 1840 ib, *v*. mōr.   UFTON BRIDGE. UFTON COMMON AND COURT, 1761 Rocque.   UFTON GREEN, UFTONGREEN FM, *Green Close* 1842 *TA*.   UFTON LOCK.   UFTON PARK, 1846 Snare, *Park Close* 1842 *TA*.   UFTON WD, 1817 OS. VICTORIA COTTAGE AND LODGE.   WEARY HILL.   WELL PIGHTLE, 1842 *TA*.   WEST MEADOW, *Westmede* c. 1210–30 *Queen*, *v*. mǣd, cf. *Eastmead* 1729 *PubLibDoc*.

FIELD-NAMES

The principal forms in (*a*) are 1842 *TA*. Early forms dated 12th (l.12th), 13th are *ReadingC*, 1346 (14th) *ReadingC(2)*, and 16th, 1709 VCH III.

(*a*) Appletons Pightle; Arston; The Avenue; Barn Close and Ground; Bowling Alley (*v*. 285); Bramley, Long, Bramleys, Great; Brandy Close; Breachmans Pightle; Broom Close; Bubble Pit Close; Burnt Oaks; Bush Hill; Bushey Mead; Calves Leys; Carrion Close; Carthouse Pightle; Cinquefoie Ground (for *cinquefoil, Potentilla reptans*); Coombs Pightle; Cottage Pightle; Crab-tree Close; Cuckoo Pightle; Dale Ground; Dog Mdw; Furzen Close; Gravel Ground; Gravel Pit Close (a number of gravel pits are marked on 6″); The Grove; Gully Close; Harlots Ground; Heath Close (*Hethlond* 1346 (14th), *v*. hǣð, land); Hill Close and Ground; Home Close; Honeycombs; Hop Garden Close (*v*. hoppe); Howcroft; Kates Mdw; Kiln Close; Lady's Mead (*v*. hlǣfdige); Lawn Pasture, The Lawn (*v*. launde); Lot Mdw (*v*. hlot); The Moor(s); Mount Sion (*v*. 283); Pightle (*v*. pightel); Pipsters; The Platt (*v*. plat²); Pond Close and Pasture (not near Pond Slade *supra*); Red Hills; Riding Mdw (possibly connected with the fishery called *Redings* 16th, *v*. ryding); Rookmoor, Rookmoor Mead (*Rockmore* 16th, 1709, *Rukemore* Jas I *SpecCom*, *v*. hrōc, mōr); Rushney Mead; Stony Fd; String Close (*v*. 282); Sunamer Moor; Trunk Close; Ufton Great, Little and Middle Fd; Walnut Tree Ground; Wood Close; Woodley; Yard Pightle.

(b) *Le Carpentereslond* 1346 (14th); *Clarissemor* 1346 (14th) (v. mōr, first el. the ME fem.pers.n. *Clarice*); *Maddemoure* 1378 Cl (v. mōr, first el. possibly mæddre); *Pole* 1340 Cl (p), (*manor of*) *Pole* 1396 VCH III, 442, *Le Pole* 1412 FA, (manor of) *Poleplace* 1512 Ch, *Polesplace* Jas I *SpecCom* (for this manor v. VCH III, 442; none of the people known to be connected with it are surnamed *Pole*, and it may be a genuine place-name, v. pōl); *Tarrin Veare* 1729 *PubLibDoc* (v. furh); *Wronkeshulle* 12th (l.12th) (v. hyll, first el. uncertain, but v. **wrang**).

Wokefield

WOKEFIELD

(æt) *Weonfelda* c. 950 (c. 1240) BCS 888
Hocfelle, Offelle 1086 DB
Wekefelda, Wechefelda 1167 P
Wogefeld' 1214 OblR, *Woghefeld'* 1242–3 Fees, *Wohfeld* 1325,
    1328 Cl, *Woghfeld* 1327 *SR*, 1337, 1338 Cl, 1354 Ipm, 1374 Pat,
    Woghefeld 1334 Cl
Weghfeld' 1220 Fees, 1269 *FF*, *Wegh'feld'* 1239 FineR, 1241 *Ass*,
    Weghefeld' 1242–3 Fees
Wocfeld' 1220 Fees, *Wocfeld* 1252–5 *FF*
Weoufeld(e) c. 1240 *ClaudiusBvi*
Wugefeld' 1241 *Ass*
Wogthfeld 1338 Cl
Wokefeld 1367 Fine, *Wookefeld* 1552 *LRMB*, *Wokefield* 1846 Snare

The *Weonfeld* of BCS 888 has not previously been identified with Wokefield. The grant is of 3 hides, and the boundaries include *grægsole burnan* and *hagan* (v. Grazeley 166), *fulan riþe* (i.e. Foudry Brook 10) and the boundary of Burghfield (204–5). This makes it clear that the estate included Wokefield and Sulhampstead Bannister, which two parishes form a triangular block of land between Foudry Brook, Burghfield and Grazeley. Two estates at Wokefield are described in DB, and are said to have been assessed at 1½ hides each T.R.E. This may be a historical reason for identifying the 3-hide estate of BCS 888 with Wokefield.

The linguistic history of the name is extremely difficult to interpret. It has generally been explained (DEPN, Skeat) as 'Wocca's feld', from the same pers.n., and probably the same man, as Woking (Sr 156) and Wokingham (139). These names may have influenced its development, but (even without the charter-form *Weonfelda*) it is very difficult to derive Wokefield, with its ME spellings in *Woge-*,

Wegh-, *Woh-*, from a base *Woccan feld. *Weonfelda* (without being associated with Wokefield) has generally been derived from *wēon-*, dat. of wēoh², adj. 'holy'. It is tempting to suggest that *Weonfelda* contains the inflected adjective, and Wokefield either the noun wēoh¹ 'heathen temple', or an uninflected form of the adjective. Unfortunately this last derivation does not seem possible, as a run of ME spellings like those for Wokefield only seems to occur when the base has *-hh-*, as opposed to the *-h* of wēoh. A partial parallel is provided by the forms for Beckenham K (KPN 212–13), the OE form of which was *Beohha hām*. A pers.n. *Weohha* would be a likely formation from names such as *Weohhelm*, *Weohhere*. *Wehha* occurs in the genealogy of the Kings of East Anglia. '**Weohha's* open land' is perhaps the likeliest etymology for Wokefield, but Dr O. von Feilitzen points out that the numerous and early *-o-* spellings presuppose shift of stress, *Weohha < Wohha*. The charter-form *Weonfelda*, which refers to the same estate, may have a different first el. or may be a poor spelling for *Weohhanfelda*. The scribe of *ClaudiusBvi* has written *Weoufeld(e)* in his heading and introductory remarks to the charter, which may indicate that he was trying to equate *Weonfelda* with 13th-cent. forms like *Wogefeld*'.

BURGHFIELD SLADE.   FERN LODGE.   GOODBOY'S LANE, *Little Goodboys* 1846 *TA*(*Sulhamstead*); cf. Goodboy's Copse in Ufton Nervet 225.   KEEPER'S LODGE.   LITTLE HEAVEN'S PLANTATION. PIERCE'S FM, *Pierses Grene* 1552 *LRMB*.   PITCHKETTLE WOOD. POND WOOD.   PULLEN'S POND.   SHEEPCOT LANE.   THREE FIRS P.H.   WOKEFIELD COMMON, 1846 Snare.   WOKEFIELD GREEN, 1846 Snare, *Le Grene,Wookefeld Grene* 1552 *LRMB*.   WOKEFIELD PARK.

FIELD-NAMES

The forms in (*b*) are 1552 *LRMB*.

(*b*) *Beche Lane* (*v.* bēce²); *Bromefeld* (*v.* brōm, feld); *Byehedge Lande*; *Le Culver Garden* (*v.* culfre); *Gilberts Coppice and Hedge*; *Hallfeld*; *Hatchelande* (*v.* hæc(c), land); *Hawkcome* (*v.* hafoc, cumb); *Haynes Grene*; *Hellmes Wood*; *Hidlande*; *Hill Close*; *Illesley*; *Le Longewood*; *Le Male Crofte*; *Meres Pidell* (*piddell* is a variant of pightel); *Le Merwood*; *Le More Copps*; *Mychaells Crosse*; *Myhills*; *Oxfeld Heathe*; *Rosewood* (*copic. voc.*); *Le Slade* (*v.* slæd).

Woolhampton

WOOLHAMPTON

Ollavintone 1086 DB, *Ullavinton'*, *Wllavint'* c. 1160 OxonCh, *Ullavinton* 1155–62 *Queen* (p), *Wollauintona* 1224–5 *Ass* (p), *Wu(l)lauinton'* 1242–3 Fees, *Wullauint'* 13th *ReadingC*, *Wolauinton'* 1294 *SR*, *Wellaventon* 1297–8 Ipm, *Wolavyngton* 1341 Pat *Hulaveton'* 1221 Cur, *Wllaueton'* 1284 *Ass*
Wullaminton 1275–6 RH
Wolhamton 1327 *SR*, 1517 D Inc, *Wilhampton* 1341 Cl, *Wolhampton* 1341 ib, 1378 Fine, *Wolamptone* 1428 FA, *Woolhampton vulgo Wollington* 1675 Ogilby

'Estate associated with Wulflāf', *v.* ingtūn. There has been confusion of the second el. with hāmtūn.

ANGEL'S COPSE AND PLANTATION, *Angle Copse* 1817 OS, *Angels Pightle, Old Angel Mead, Lower Angel Meadow* 1842 *TA*. BREAKNECK COPSE, *v.* 283. BUSHY PIGHTLE, 1842 *TA*, *v.* pightel. THE COURT. HALTON'S CORNER COPSE. HILL FOOT, *Hill Foot Piece* 1842 *TA*. KENNET ORLEY. KIFF GREEN, 1817 OS, 1846 Snare, KIFF GREEN FM, *Kiff Lands* 1842 *TA*. LONDON LODGE, *London Hill* 1842 *TA*. THE POPLARS. POPLEYHILL GULLY, *Pebly Hill Mead* 1842 *TA*. RADMAN'S GULLY. RISING SUN P.H. SHUTSDOWN PLANTATION, *Sluts Down* 1842 *TA*. TEMPLE GULLY, *Temple Field* 1842 *TA*, perhaps from a 'folly'; it is near the Court. WERNHAM'S WOOD. WICKHAM KNIGHTS BRIDGE, *Wickham Knight Meadows* 1842 *TA*; this may be another instance of the name *wīchām*, for which *v.* 24. The bridge is at GR 581663, exactly a mile from the Roman road from Silchester to Speen. *Knight* may be OE cniht, a word of some significance in association with *wīchām*, but there was a house of Knights Hospitallers in Brimpton, just over a mile away, and it may be a reference to these medieval 'knights'. WOOLHAMPTON COTTAGE, 1842 *TA*. WOOLHAMPTON FM, HO AND LODGE. WOOLHAMPTON PARK, *The Park* 1842 *TA*. UPPER WOOLHAMPTON.

FIELD-NAMES

The forms in (*a*) are 1842 *TA*.

(*a*) Ash Mdw; Barberry Mead; Breaches (*v.* brēc); Brick Kiln Ground; Bridge Close and Mdw; Chalky Barn; Church Acre; Costers (*v.* cot-stōw);

Dog Kennel Ground; Dry Ground; Englefield; Garden Mdw; Great Ground; Guinea Pightle (*v.* pightel); Hill Ground; The Hitch (*v.* hiche); Hog Pightle; Hop Garden (*v.* hoppe); Horse Head Pightle; The Lawn (*v.* launde); Leasemore; Margarets Mead; Mill Mdw; Money Mead; Monks Mdw; The Mount; Nursery Ground; Pound Fd; Rackett Mead; Rushy Mead; Rye Croft; Shrivery Well; The String (*v.* 28); Sunpiece.

(*b*) *Le Fleyhelne* e.14th VCH III; *Nuland* 1725–6 *Bodl* (*v.* nīwe, land).

X. FAIRCROSS HUNDRED

de Bella Cruce 1256 Pat *et freq*, *Fayrecrosse* 1535 VE, *Faircross* 1569 Anderson, *Faircrosse* 1610 ib.

For other meeting-places marked by a cross *v.* YW **1**, 261.

The name survives in Faircross Plantation and Pond in Chieveley (243), near Old Street (5). There is no record of the cross which must have marked the spot. Anderson (207) suggests that Meeting-house Copse in Chieveley also refers to the hundred meeting-place. This is at the junction of the three Domesday hundreds of *Borgelde-berie*, *Roeberg* and *Taceham*, which were amalgamated under the name of Faircross. The three original hundreds are mentioned separately as late as 1332. Forms for *Borgeldeberie* Hundred correspond closely to those given under Bucklebury (now in Reading Hundred 154). *Roeberg* Hundred is *Roeberg(e)* 1086 DB, *Ruggeberge* 1183 P, *Roeberge* c. 1200 *ClaudiusCix*, *Rugheburgh* 1220 Fees, *Roweberge*, *Ruweberg'*, *Roweburg'* 1224–5 *Ass*, *Rugheberg'*, *Rubergh'*, *Rugbergh'*, *Ruebergh* 1241 *ib*, *Rouberg* 1316 *FA*, *Rouborgh'* 1332 *SR*. 'Rough hill', *v.* rūh, be(o)rg; identical with the Hundreds of Roborough D 222, Rowbarrow Do and Rowborough W 242. The name survives in Rowbury Fm in Boxford (234), and Peake (VCH IV, 39) suggests that Courtoak Fm, about half a mile south, also refers to the hundred meeting-place. The remaining hundred is referred to as *Taceham* 1086 DB, *Tacham* 1175 P (from Thatcham, now in Reading Hundred 188). This hundred acquired a new name in the 12th cent., forms for which are *Gosefeld* 1169 P, 1184 *ib*, *Gosefeld'* 1177 *ib*, *Gossefeld* 1183 *ib*, *Gossetefeld*, *Gossefeld'* 1188 *ib*, *Goseflet* 1192 *ib*, *Gorsidhefeld* 1220 Fees, *Gosetefeld* 1224–5 *Ass*, *Gorsetefeld* 1224–5, 1248 *ib*, *Gosatteffeld'* 1241 *ib*, *Gossetefeld'* *ib*, 1275–6 RH, *Gorsatesfelde*, *Gorsetesfeld* 1248 *Ass*, *Gotsette(s)feud* 1261 *ib*, *Gottesfeld* 1275–6 RH, *Cotsetesfeud'*, *Gossetesfeld*, *Gotsetlesfeld'*, *Cossettefeld'* 1284 *Ass*, *Cottsettlesford* 1316 FA, *Cottesteffeld* 1327 *SR*, *Cotsetles-feld'* 1332 *ib*. Second el. feld 'open land'. Anderson (207) suggests a derivative, probably *gorsiht*, of OE gors(t), 'gorse, furze', for the first el. and this is convincing. Some of the forms show association with OE cotsetla 'cottager'. The site is not known. There is a f.n. in Chieveley, *Cotsetterfeilde*, *Cotcetterfeld* 1550 LRMB, *Cossiter Field*

1604 *RecOffCat*, which might preserve the name of the Hundred. There is also a *Gossacre Mede, Gossatur Mede, Gossatre Mede* 1547 *LRMB, Cossiter Meadow* 1780 *EnclA* in Speen, which appears to have the same first element.

The Hundred of Thatcham contained the lost DB manor of *Acenge*; this has not been identified, but *v.* Oakhanger 273–4. The Hundred of Bucklebury contained the lost DB manor of *Crochestrope* ('Crōc's þrop'); the only suggestion which can be offered for this is a 19th-cent. name in Bucklebury 159.

Beedon

Beedon

Bydene 965 (c. 1200) BCS 1171

Bedene 1086 DB *et passim* with variant spellings *Bedena, Beden', Bedone* to 1517 D Inc

Budene c. 1200 *ClaudiusCix*, 1284 *Ass et freq* with variant spellings *Buden', Budon', Buden; Budeney* 1316 FA, *Budon als Bedon* 1535 VE

Biddon 1574 Saxton

Beeden 1761 Rocque

The place is also referred to in the phrases *on beden weg* 948 (c. 1240) BCS 866 and *andlang byden hæma gemæres* 951 (16th) BCS 892. The name is OE **byden** 'vessel, tub', which was evidently used of the steep, narrow valley above which the village stands. Bidna D and Bidden Ha are identical, *v.* D 102.

STANMORE, (*æt*) *Stanmere* 948 (c. 1240) BCS 866, *Stanmere* 960 (contemporary) BCS 1053, 1412 FA, *Stanmore* 1761 Rocque. Cf. (*of*) *stanmeringa gemere* 916 (c. 1200) BCS 633, (*of*) *stanmeringa gemære* 1042 (c. 1240) KCD 762, 'boundary of the people of Stanmore'. 'Stone pool', *v.* **stān, mere**, identical with Stanmore Mx 65. A pool, probably the one in question, is shown on O.S. maps at the junction of Ball Pt Rd and Hailey Lane. In the bounds of Farnborough (BCS 633, 682 and 762) there are places called (*to*) *stanleage* and (*on*) *þone stanihtan weg*, which were near Stanmore and which were also named from the stony soil.

BALL PIT RD.   BARROW HILL, 1841 *TA*, from a tumulus, *v.* **beorg**. BEEDON COMMON, *Pillon or Beeden Common* 1761 Rocque.   BEEDON

FM, HILL (1830 OS) AND WD.   COLLEGE FM, cf. *College Inclosure*
1841 *TA*.   COMMON FM AND PLANTATION.   HALFPENNY CATCH
LANE.   OLD STREET LANE (*v.* 5).   PARK COPSE, cf. *Beedon
Park* 1830 OS, *Park Field* 1841 *TA*.   PURTON, *Purtons Allotment*
1841 *ib*.   RED LANE, *Redlane Barn and Wd, Red Lane Farm* 1761
Rocque.   ROSE COTTAGE.   ROUND COPSE.   WESTON'S FM.
WORLD'S END, *The Worlds End* 1830 OS, *v.* 284.

FIELD-NAMES

The principal forms in (*a*) are 1841 *TA*; early forms are *Queen*.

(*a*) The Acre and a half; Chalk Pit Lane; Church Mdw; Downsand
Grubbed Wd (*v.* 281); Drying Ground; Glebe Mdw; Greenhill Allotment;
Grubbings (*v.* 281); Home Fd Hill; Home Piece; Lady Close (*v.* hlæfdige);
Lambourne Close; Lance; Little Fd; Middle Fd (*Le Middiffelde* 1318, *v.*
middel); North Croft (*La Northcroft* 1341, *La Northcrofte* 1360); Oars Mead;
Picked Piece (*v.* pīced); Ploughed Piece; Ramridge, Great (*rammes hrycg* 948
(*c.* 1200) BCS 866, probably 'raven's ridge', *v.* hræfn, hrycg, and cf.
Ramsbury Pt 2, but the first el. might be *ramm* 'ram'; this is the ridge at
the edge of which Beedon village stands); Rylands (*v.* ryge, land); South
Fd; Stanmore Common and Fd; Stubs, Hither, North and South (*v.* stubb);
Swains Piece; Witch Piece.

(*b*) *The Horncroft* 1335 (*v.* horn, croft).

Boxford

BOXFORD

Boxora '821' (*c.* 1200) BCS 366, (*æt*) *Boxoran*, (*to*) *Boxorran* 958
    (*c.* 1240) ib 1022, *Boxoran* 960 (contemporary) ib 1055, 968
    (*c.* 1200) ib 1227, *Boxhora* 1167 P, *Boxore* 1199 Hunter Fines *et
    passim* with variant spellings *Boxora, Boxor'*; *Boxhore* 1241 *Ass*
    (p), 1401–2 FA
Bovsore, Bochesorne 1086 DB
Boxhole, Boxole c. 1180 (13th) Abingdon, *Boxhell'* 1199 Cur
Bockesoure 1198 P
Boxesore 1369–70 ObAcc
Boxforth 1517 D Inc
Boxworth 1535 VE, 1538 *RentSur*

'Slope or bank where box grows', *v.* box, ōra. The second el. has
been confused with worð and ford. Boxford Sf has ford as its
original final el. BCS 366 is spurious.

BRADLEYWOOD FM, *(on) bradan leage* 949 (contemporary) BCS 877, *Bradelaye, Bradele* 1340–1 *RentSur, Bradelewode* Hy 6 *RentSur, Bradley woode* 1547 *LRMB*. Probably 'at the broad wood', *v.* brād, lē(a)h, though the second el. could mean 'clearing'; *wood* was added later. Cf. the same name 80, 242.

COOMBESBURY FM, possibly *Colmeresbere* c. 1180 (13th) Abingdon, *Colemer* 1242–3 Fees. The forms are insufficient for a definite etymology. The earlier one suggests a name meaning 'cool pond' (*v.* cōl², mere, and cf. Colmore Ha), to which has been added bearu 'grove'. The O.S. maps do not show any pools near the farm.

HANGMAN'S STONE, *Hangmans Stone* 1761 Rocque. This is a boundary stone of the parishes of Boxford, Welford and Leckhampstead. *v.* Kelly 46 for a legend about the name, and cf. YW **1**, 76 for a parallel. Professor Smith suggests that such a boundary stone would be a place where felons were hanged. The bounds of Leckhampstead, 943 (c. 1240) BCS 789, run *of wines treowe on ðan readan hane*. It is tempting to identify this 'red stone' (*v.* rēad, hān) with Hangman's Stone, as Grundy does; but as *wines treow* occurs also in the bounds of Boxford and Welford, it appears that the tree, and not the stone, must have stood at the point where the three parishes meet, *v.* Pt **3**.

OWNHAM

> *Ouenham* c. 1180 (13th) Abingdon (p), *Ovenham* 1316 FA, 1340–1 *RentSur,* Hy 6 *ib, Ovenham, Ownham, Owenham* 1547 *LRMB Houeham* 1284 *Ass* (p)

Probably 'Ofa's homestead', *v.* hām. Formally the first el. could be ofen 'oven', but this is only postulated for names of later origin than this.

ROWBURY FM, *Roughborowe cop'* 1538 *RentSur, copic' vocat' the Rowborough* 1550 *LRMB, Rowbury Fm and Copse* 1830 OS. The 'rough hill' was the meeting place of one of the hundreds later merged in Faircross Hundred, *v.* 231. Rowbury Fm is situated on a gentle slope, and it is possible that the beorg was a tumulus, not a natural hill.

WESTBROOK, *Westebroc* 1316 Ipm, *West(e)broc* 1349 ib, *Westbroke* 1427 Fine, 1432 ib, 1453 ib, *Westbrook* 1761 Rocque. '(Place) west of the brook'. The same name occurs in Faringdon (Pt **3**).

WYFIELD MANOR FM, *Wyfeld, Wyfoldfelde, Wifoldfeld, Wynallde Felde, Wyvalde Hethe* 1550 *LRMB, Wyfols Fields* 1681 *RecOffCat, Wifehold or Wifield* 1761 Rocque. Robert son of Richard *de la Wyfolde* is mentioned 1309–10 *FF* in connection with land in the adjacent parish of Winterbourne, and it is very probable that the surname was derived from the place in Boxford. This is another example of the name found in Wyfold Court (O 46, lii), *Wyfold* Hundred (Pt **2**) and Wyvols Court in Swallowfield (109).

BASING'S FM.   BELL INN, *The Bell* 1830 OS.   BOROUGH HILL AND COPSE, *The Borough v.* burh; there is a hill-fort.   BOXFORD COMMON, *Boxworth Comen* 1538 *RentSur, Boxford Common* 1838 *TA.* BOXFORD FM, 1830 OS.   BUTCHER'S WD.   COURTOAK FM, 1830 OS, *Court Oak Common* 1838 *TA, v.* 231.   DEAN'S COPSE, possibly from a family surnamed *atte Dene* 1340–1 *RentSur, v.* denu.   GREEN LANE.   HIGHSTREET FM, on a road called HIGH STREET, *v.* hēah, strǣt.   HOAR HILL, *Hour Hill* 1761 Rocque, 1830 OS.   HUNT'S GREEN, HUNTSGREEN FM, 1830 OS, AND COPSE, possibly from the family of Peter *le Hunt* of Benham 1350 Pat.   IREMONGER'S COTTAGES, *Ironmongers* 1830 OS, *Ironmongers Ground* 1838 *TA.* KNAPP'S FM.   LEONARD'S PLANTATION, *Linniards, Lower Linniards* 1838 *TA*; this is at the head of the valley called *lindene* 968 (c. 1200) BCS 1227, *v.* Pt **3**; *lindene* is 'flax valley' and *Linniard* might be 'flax enclosure', *v.* līn, denu, geard.   MUD HALL COTTAGES, *v.* 283. NALDER PLANTATION (probably from atten and alder).   PRIDDLE'S FM.   PROSPECT COTTAGE.   ROWHEDGE COTTAGE.   SHEPHERD'S BORDER, *Shepherds Copse* 1830 OS.   UPPER FM, this may be the tūn which is mentioned in the bounds of Boxford, 958 (c. 1240) BCS 1022, *v.* Pt **3**.   WICKHAM HEATH, 1838 *TA, Wykeham Hethe* 1550 *LRMB*, from Wickham in Welford 274.   WILLIAMS'S COPSE, *Williams* 1550 *LRMB, Great Williams's* 1838 *TA.*   WOODMANS- FIELD COTTAGES, *Woodmanfeld(e)* 1550 *LRMB, Woodmans Field* 1838 *TA*, probably from a surname, but *v.* also wudu-mann.

FIELD-NAMES

The principal forms in (*a*) are 1838 *TA*; early forms for which no date or source is given are 1550 *LRMB*; those dated 1340–1, Hy 6, 1538 are *RentSur*.

(*a*) The Alders; Barn Close; Between the Rivers; Bin Marsh (*Byn Mershe, v.* binnan, mersc); Birch Close; Bottom Close (*Bottome Close, v.* botm); Broad Close (*Brode Close*); Browns Mead (*Brownes Close*); Butter

Mdw (*v.* butere); Calves Leaze (*Calfleys, v.* lǣs); Cockmoor Hill Furlong; The Common Marsh; Deal Close; Dores Close; Down Close, The Downs (*Le Downe* Hy 6, *Downeclose, The Doune Close, v.* dūn); Dunshot; Goose Furlong; The Grove(s); Harry Gate Furlong; Havin Mdw (*Halfene Medowe, Halfen Mede, Halfen, v.* mǣd; *Halfen* is possibly a compound of h(e)alh and fenn); Havocks Mdw; Holdways Fd; Home Close, Fd and Ground (*Home Close*); Honey Box (*v.* hunig); Horn Hill (*v.* horn); Horse Close; Hyde Mdw (*Hide Mede, Hyde Mede, v.* hīd); Jennings Meadow (*Jennyns Mede*); Jock Mead; The Lawn (*v.* launde); Loam Pit; Long Marsh Mead; Long Tows (*The Longtowe, Grete Longtowe Close*; Tows in Ludford L, *Towse* 1535 VE, may be another example of this name); Lords Mdw (*Lordes Mede*); Lower Ground, Land and Mdw; Ludlows Close; The Marsh (*The Mershe, Le Mershe Yate, v.* mersc); The Mdw (*The Medowe*); Middle Furlong; Mill Mdw; The Moor, Moor Close and Mdw (*The More, More Close and Mede, Morefelde, v.* mōr); Nower Hill Fd (*Nowerfelde v.* atten, ōra); Ownham Green (*v.* 234); Park Mdw; Peaked Close (*Pyked Close, Pikede Mede, v.* pīced); Pightle (*v.* pightel); Pine Hill Bottom; Pin Fold Bottom (*v.* pynd-fald, botm); Pit Mdw; Rye Piece; Sandy Piece; Sheep Down Furlong; Small Ground and Fd; South Close (*South(e)close*); Thornhanger (*Thorn(e)hangore, Thornhanger, Thornehongore, Thornehangfelde, v.* þorn, hangra); Upper Mdw and Ground; West Grove (*Westgroue, v.* grāf); White Mdw, Close and Croft (*White Close, v.* hwīt).

(*b*) *Abbots Mershe* (Boxford belonged to Abingdon Abbey); (*on*) *æsc meres* (*hammas*) 958 (c. 1240) BCS 1022, *Asshemer Cop'* 1538, *Asshe Moers, Copic' voc. Asshemershe* ('ash pool', *v.* æsc, mere; in the coppice-name the genitival -*s* has led to the second el. being confused with mersc; Grundy, in his discussion of the charter bounds of Boxford, says that the name Ashmore Coppice survives in the adjacent parish of Winterbourne, *v.* Pt 3); *Beche Close* (*v.* bēce[2]); *Bertoncroft* 1340–1, *Bartonemede* Hy 6 (*v.* beretūn, bærtūn, mǣd); *Le Breche* 1340–1, *Lez Breches* Hy 6, *Breche, Breache* (*v.* brēc); *Brodecrofte, Brodeland* (*v.* brād, croft, land); *Brokehell Cop'* 1538, *Copic' voc' Broke Well* (*v.* brōc, hyll); *Brome Close* (*v.* brōm); *Bryttaynes* (probably a surname); *Burchard*; *Busshelez* (*v.* busc, lǣs); *Butt Close, The Buttys Mershe* 1550 LRMB, *Buttes Meade* 1681 RecOffCat (*v.* butte, mersc, mǣd); *The Chalke Pitt Close*; *Cheuelesgrave* 1185 RR (p), 1241 *Ass* (p), *Chyvelsgrave* 1234–41 (l.14th) Chatsworth, *Cheveleys Grove, Childis Grove Crofte* ('grove belonging to Chieveley' 241–2); *Cony Close*; *Cowleis* (*v.* lǣs); *Le Crofte*; *Dede Close* (*v.* dēad, possibly used of infertile ground, in which sense it is noted 1577 NED); *The Foxbury*; *Fursecrofte* (*v.* fyrs); *Gracecrofte*; *Hake Dytche* (*v.* Chieveley field-names 245); *The Hallford Mershe* (*v.* mersc); *Hangre* (*v.* hangra); *Harde Mede* (*v.* heard); *Hawen Mede*; *Heath Close, Hethe Crofte* (*v.* hǣð); *Henne Close* (*v.* henn); *The Hichins* (*v.* heccing); *Hill Close*; *Home Mede*; *The Horsecrofte*; *Huddyfor*; *Kingestrete* 1248 *Ass*; *The Le Close*; *Long Crofte*; *Long Landis* (*v.* land); *Lowedenes* Hy 6 (*v.* denu); *Midle Grove*; *Myll Mershe* (*v.* mersc); *Le Neestone*; *Nether Close and Crofte*; *Le Nether Ende*; *The Nether Mershe*; *The Northe Hill*; *Orchard Close*; *Ote Close*; *Parocke Lane, Parrockis Mede, Little Parrok* (*v.* pearroc); *Pegeleys*

Thorne; *Pitleighton(e)* (*v.* pytt, lēac-tūn); *Le Purtockis*; *Pylle Mede* (*v.* pyll); *Rackheyes* (the same name occurs in Speen, Newbury and Welford, *v.* 261); *Saris Myll, Sares*; *Shyptone Yateclose*; *Some Leez* (*v.* lǣs); *The South Marshe*; *The Thiket*; *Tymber Crofte*; *Tymbers Close*; *Woodclose*; *Yonder Crofte*.

Brightwalton

BRIGHTWALTON

(*æt*) *Beorhtwaldingtune* 939 (c. 1240) BCS 743, *Bristoldestone* 1086 DB, *Bristwoldintona* 1087 BM, *Brichtwaldit'*, *Brichtwaldint'* William I (1312) Ch, *Brichtuuoldestun* c. 1100 *EgCh 2211*, *Brichtwaleston'* 1167 P

Bricthwalton' 1220 Fees, 1224–5 *Ass* (p), *Brichtwalton(e)* 1224 (copy) Sar, *Brig(h)twalton'* 1241 *Ass*, *Brictewalton'* 1242–3 Fees, *Brichtwalton* 1258 AD, *Bristwalton* 1268 ib, 1294 ib, *Brich-walton' Brychwalton'* 1284 *Ass*, *Bryght Walton* 1297 Pat, *Bryth Walton* 1301 Ipm, *Brightwaltone* 1316 Fa, *Bryʒtwalton'* 1327 SR, *Brytwalton* 1333–4 AD, *Brithwalton* 1338 Cl (p)

Bri(n)walton 1275–6 RH

Brickleton 1574 Saxton, *Brightwalton alias Brickleton* 1667 *PubLib*, 1755 ArchJ 15

Brightwaltham 1761 Rocque, 1830 OS

'Estate associated with Beorhtwald', *v.* ingtūn; the early forms show variation between connective *-ing-* and the *-es* of the gen. sing. According to ArchJ 36, p. 164, the pronunciation represented by the spelling *Brickleton* was still current locally in 1932.

BRIGHTWALTON HOLT, *Brightwaltham Holt* 1830 OS, cf. *Holte* 1283–4 Battle, *Greneholte* 1283–4 *AOMB*, Ed 1 *RentSur*, *The Holt* 18th ArchJ 10. *v.* holt 'wood'. One form has 'green' prefixed.

DUNMORE POND AND BARN (latter in Chaddleworth). The pond is (*to*) *dunian mere* 939 (c. 1240) BCS 743, *Dunmore* 18th ArchJ 10. The second el. is mere 'pond'. Toller (BTSuppl) suggests an OE *dūnig* 'on the downs' for the first. Professor Löfvenberg compares Dunny Grove Sr 386 (Will. *atte Donye* 1332, Thom. *atte Dunye* 1382), and considers that both names derive from an OE weak noun **dūni(g)e* of obscure origin and meaning, possibly a side-form of the plant-name *dȳnige*, which is also obscure.

HEMLEY COPSE, *bosco de Hemele* 1224 (copy) Sar, (wood called) *Hemele* 1294 Maitland, *Copp' called Hemley* 1557 *RentSur*. The second el. is lē(a)h 'wood'. The first is found in a number of names in O, v. O 451, where it is suggested that there was a ME *heme*, related to OE and modern *hem*, meaning 'boundary'. This copse is very near the parish boundary.

MANWOOD PIT, *Manewod'* 1261 Cl (p), *Comon called Manne Woode* 1557 *RentSur*, 'common wood', v. (ge)mǣne, wudu, identical with Manhood Hundred Sx 79, Man Wood Ess 495 and Manwood W 201.

TRINDLEY (lost). The wood appurtenant to Wickham in Welford, called *Trinlech* '821' (c. 1200), *Trindlæh* '821' (c. 1240) BCS 366, may be identical with *boscus voc. Trendale* 1294 Maitland, v. lēah. The first el. is possibly trendel, trindel 'circle', or *trind 'circular'. Alternatively Dr O. von Feilitzen points out that Tengstrand,† 285 ff., postulates an OE *trind 'stake for fencing', and 'wood where stakes are got' would be a meaningful compound. Professor Löfvenberg also prefers this etymology.

BLACK POND.   BOARDHOUSE PLANTATION, *The Boarded House* 18th ArchJ 10, *Boarded House Common* 1761 Rocque.   BRIGHT-WALTON COMMON, *Brightwaltham Common* 1830 OS.   BRIGHT-WALTON GREEN, *Grene* Ed 1 *RentSur* (p), 1283–4 Battle (p), 1327 *SR* (p), *Brightwaltham Green* 1830 OS, v. grēne[2].   BROWN'S LANE. COMMON LANE AND PLANTATION.   COOMBE FM, *The Comb Farms* 18th ArchJ 10, *Combe Farm* 1761 Rocque, the valley in which the farm lies is called *beocumb* 'bee valley' in the bounds of Farnborough 931 (c. 1200) BCS 633, v. Pt 3.   COOMBE HILL.   FOLLY FM AND COTTAGE, v. folie.   GRUBB'S WD COTTAGES.   HUNGERFORD RD COTTAGES.   LILLEY COPSE, *Copp' called Lyllyes* 1557 *RentSur*, v Pt 2.   LIME TREE FM.   LOVELL'S FM.   LOWER BARN, 1830 OS.   MANOR FM.   MARQUIS OF GRANBY P.H.   PUDDING LANE, 1838 *TA*, probably referring to mud.   SOUTHEND, *Suthende* 1327 *SR* (p), v. sūð, ende[1].   SPARROWBILL COPSE, *Sparrowbill* 1830 OS (a building south of the Copse); the name refers to the shape of the copse.   SPARROW'S COPSE, *Sparrow Copse* 1830 OS. TROUGH.   YEW TREE FM, *Yew Tree* 18th ArchJ 10, 1830 OS.

FIELD-NAMES

The principal forms in (*a*) are 1838 *TA*, except for those dated 1904, which are ArchJ 10. Early forms dated 1283–4 are Battle, 1294 Maitland, Ed 1 and 1557 *RentSur*, 18th ArchJ 10.

† E. Tengstrand, *A Contribution to the study of Genitival Composition in Old English Place-Names*, Uppsala 1940.

(a) Ash Close; Bailey's Hitching (v. heccing, and cf. *La Hechynge* in (b));
Barn Fd; The Beaches 1904; Bellows Nose (probably from the shape, v.
283); Blackneys, Great and Little; Breach Close, Hither and Further Breach
(*La Breche* Ed 1, v. brēc); Brick Down, Great and Little; Burgess' Mdw;
Butts Furlong *TA*, 1904; Chadmore Dean; Chapel Arch 1904; Common
Piece; Cooks Hill; Copton Bush 1904 (*Le Coppedeþorne* Ed 1, v. coppod,
þorn); Cornish Hill; Customs Mead; The Down (v. dūn); Dudshill *TA*,
Dutshill Piece 1904; Duns Breach (v. brēc); Ell Furlong (or Whitechester);
The Ford 1904; Grove End; Grubbed Ground (v. 281); Hawkridge Hill;
Hazelhanger 1904 (*Haselangforlong* Ed 1, v. hæsel, hangra); Hazells Hitch-
ing (cf. Bailey's Hitching *supra*); Heath Piece, Great and Long Heath (*Le
Hethe* Ed 1, v. hǣð); The Hill Ground; Home Close, Fd, Ground and
Mdw; Knights Close (*Knight's Cross* 18th); Lilley Hill (*Lilly Hill* 18th, v.
Pt 2); Long Dean (v. denu); Malthouse Ground; Oak Furlong; Park Quines
(*The Parks* 1557); Pilowth; Plantation Ground; Pond Ground; Rough
Down Bank *TA*, Rowdown Bank 18th, 1904; Rye and Pit Close (possibly
La Rede Putte 1294, v. rēad, pytt); Shelves, Western Shelves (v. scelf);
Stacun, Staycorn Barn 1904 (*Stacorn* 18th, *Stalkhorn* 1877–8 ArchJ 10);
Stanbrooks Hitching (cf. Hazells Hitching *supra*); Strop Mdw; Thicket
Lots 1904 (*Thickett, Thicket Lots* 18th); Town Fd; Townsend (*Le Toune-
sende* Ed 1, v. tūn, ende[1]); Twitching Piece (v. twicen(e)); Wards Ground
and Hill; Whitechester (or Ell Furlong); White Furlong; Whitelands 18th,
1904; Wolly Headge (v. Pt 2); Wood Breach (v. brēc).

(b) *Benacre* 1283–4 (v. bēan, æcer); *Westchirceweye, Estchirceweye*
1248–52 *FF* (v. cirice, weg); *Cow Lees* 1557; *Estfeld* 1294 (v. ēast, feld);
Eversolle n.d. AD, *Eversole* 1283–4 (p) ('boar's wallowing-place', v. eofor,
sol[1]); *Gilibertesbreche* 1224 (copy) Sar (v. brēc, first el. the pers.n. *Gilbert*);
Grasacra, Garsacra 1283–4 (v. gærs, æcer); *Gudeshull* Ed 1 (v. hyll, first el.
possibly the surname *Good*); *Haghecrofta* 1283–4 (v. haga[1], croft); *La
Hechynge* Ed 1 (v. heccing); *Hedacre* 1283–4 AOMB; *Holly Street Lane*
18th; *Holm* 1224 (copy) Sar (v. holegn 'holly'); *The Knole* 18th (v. cnoll);
Linoch n.d. AD; *Lower Post* 18th; *La More* 1283–4 (p) (v. mōr); *Nedacra*
1283–4 (v. nēd, æcer); *Otforlonge* Ed 1 (v. āte); *Stretend'* 1283–4 (v. strǣt,
ende[1]); *La Suth Breche* Ed 1 (v. sūð, brēc); *Westwode* 1283–4 (p) (v. west,
wudu); *La Whitecrofte* Ed 1 (v. hwīt, croft); *Wodemer* 1283–4 (v. wudu,
mere); *Wowelonde* Ed 1 (v. wōh, land).

Brimpton

BRIMPTON

(*æt*) *Bryning tune* 944 (c. 1240) BCS 802

Brintone 1086 DB, 1305 Ipm, *Brinton'* 1167 P, 1202 ib (p), 1235–6
  Fees (p), 1240–1 *FF*

Brimiton' 1177 P (p), *Brimton'* 1200 Cur *et freq* with variant
  spellings *Brimton(e)*, *Brimtona* to 1275–6 RH; *Brimton' de
  Ouwyle* 1241 *Ass*

Brunton' 1205 P (p)

Brimpton Hospitalium 1220 Fees, *Brimpton' de Ouwyle* 1238 ib, *Brimpton Douile* 1275–6 RH, *Brimpton'*, *Brimpton Dumle* 1284 *Ass*, *Brympton* 1412 FA, *Brymptone* 1428 ib

Brington' 1224–5 *Ass*

Brompton', *Brumpton'* 1284 *Ass*, *Brumpton'* 1311–12 *FF et freq* with variant spelling *Brumpton* to 1420 Fine; *Brompton* 1349 Cl, 1360 Ipm

'Estate associated with Brȳni', *v*. ingtūn. The same name has become Brington in Hu (BdHu 235) and Nth (Nth 79), and Brinton in Nf (DEPN).

There are two manors here in DB; one, later known as Shalford (*infra*), was given to the Knights Hospitallers by Simon *de Ovile*, a tenant of William de Roumare, Earl of Lincoln. Hence it is called *Brimton' de Ouwyle*, *Brimton Dumle*, *Brimpton Hospitalium*.

ROWNEY BRIDGE, *Roheney* 1329 Ch, *Rowney* 1620 *SpecCom*, 1713 *PubLibDoc*, probably '(at the) rough island', referring to land between branches of the Kennet, *v*. rūh, (ī)eg.

SHALFORD BRIDGE AND FM, (*on*) *scealdan ford* 944 (c. 1240) BCS 802, (*hospital' de, Hosp' Sancti Johannis de*) *Scaldeford* 1275–6 RH, *Schaldeforde* 1297–8 Ipm, *Shaldeford* 1316 FA, *Schawford* 1507 ArchJ 4. A well-recorded example of a common name meaning '(at the) shallow ford', *v*. sc(e)ald, ford. For the Hospitallers, who held this manor till their dissolution in 1540, *v*. *supra*.

ABLE BRIDGE, ABLEBRIDGE COTTAGES. ARUNDELL'S COPSE. BACK LANE. BANNISTER'S WD. BERRY'S COPSE. BLACKNEST, 1817 OS. BLACKNEST LODGE. BOOT FM, *Boot Field* 1839 *TA*. BORSON. BRIMPTON COMMON, 1761 Rocque. BRIMPTON LODGE. BRIMPTON MILL, *Brimpton Mille* 1620 *SpecCom*, *Brimpton Mills* 1817 OS. CHAPLIN'S WD, *Long Chaplins, Chaplins Berth* 1839 *TA*. SHORT AND LONG GULLY. THE HATCH. HIGHFIELD. HOCKFORD LANE. HOLDAWAY'S FM. HYDE END, *Hyde Ende or Hyde Place wherein the said John Hyde now dwelleth* 1620 *SpecCom*, *Hide End* 1761 Rocque; this estate was held by the family of *Hyde* from at least the 16th cent. (VCH IV, 54); Robert *de la Hide*, mentioned 1340 Cl in connection with land in Midgham, Woolhampton and Bucklebury, may have come from here, *v*. hīd. HYDE END

Fм, Fishery, Gully, Ho (*Hide End Ho* 1817 OS) and Wd. Inwood Copse, *Inwood Ground* 1839 *TA*. King's Bridge. The Lynch, *The Linch* 1839 *TA*, *v.* hlinc. Manor Fм, *Brimpton Farm* 1817 OS. Oak Cottage. Oakleigh. Paul's Hole Cottages, *Pauls Hole* 1839 *TA*. St. Peter's Almshouses. Shalford Bridge is *Sherbert Bridge* 1817 OS, *v. supra* 240. Three Horse-shoes P.H. Warren Fм, *Warren* 1761 Rocque, *The Warren*, *Warren Bank* 1839 *TA*. Water Lane.

FIELD-NAMES

The principal forms in (*a*) are 1839 *TA*, except where otherwise stated.

(*a*) Barn Close, Ground, Piece and Pightle; Bert Fd; Blacksmiths Mdw; Bramble Close; The Briffs (cf. Briff Copse in Bucklebury 156 and Briff's Copse in Hamstead Marshall, Pt 2); Broad Close; Broom Close (*v.* brōm); Burrows; Butchers Ground and Piece; Buttons; Calves Leaze (*v.* lǣs); Church Pightle; Copse Ground; Cow Leaze; Crooked Oak; Dicks Mdw; East Marsh; Forket Mdw; Grass Platt (*v.* plat²); Gravel Pit Ground; Green Fd; Great Ground; Gun Ground; Gutter Ground; Heath-side Farm 1817 OS; The Hillow Ground; Home Ground; Hop Garden (*v.* hoppe); Humfries Pightle; Hunts Hill and Pightle; Isle of Wight (*v.* 284); Jacks Mdw; John Alms Pightle; Marias Pightle; The Marsh; Mill Close, Fd and Mdw; The Moor; Old Ground; Park Ground; The Peaks (*v.* pīc¹); Peas Close; Picked Close (*v.* pīced); Pightle (as in other f.ns. in this parish, *v.* pightel); The Platt (*v.* plat²); Ponds Close; Rail Ground (*v.* 281); Rod Eyott (*v.* O 463); Rouning Ground; Rushy Pightle; Shalford Mead, Lower and Upper (*v.* 240); The Slip (*v.* slipe); Stone Pits; Stye Lands (*v.* stigu); Vady Mdw; West Lands; West Marsh and Mdw; Whistlestone Mdw; Lower Wigmore; Woods Pightle.

(*b*) *Barfoote* 1620 *SpecCom* (probably from a surname); *Hydemed* 1329 Ch (this was a meadow in *Roheney*, and as Rowney Bridge *supra* and Hyde End *supra* are not near each other it is uncertain whether *Hydemed* should be connected with Hyde End, *v.* hīd); *Longemeade* 1620 *SpecCom* (*v.* lang, mǣd); *Millfeilde, The Mill Meade* 1620 *SpecCom*.

Chieveley

Chieveley

(*æt*) *Cifanlea* 951 (16th) BCS 892, *Cifanlea* 960 (contemporary) BCS 1055, *Ciuenlea* 965 (c. 1240) BCS 1171
Civelei 1086 DB, *Civeleia* c. 1240 Abingdon
Chiuelai 1167 P *et passim* with variant spellings *Chiuele, Chyuelye, Chiuelye, Chiueleg', Chiuel', Chiveley, Chyuele, Chivele, Chyveley*

Chevel' 1261 Cl, *Chevelee* 1401–2 AD
Chiele, Chyele, Schiuele 1284 *Ass*

'Cifa's lē(a)h'. The pers.n. *Ceofa* is on record.

ARLINGTON

Harlingeden' 1203 Hunter Fines, 1220 Fees, 1224–5 *Ass* (p),
   Harlyngeden' 1268–72 FF
Herlingedon' 1203 Cur
Hurlingdon, Harlingdon 1547 *LRMB, Harlingdon* 1550 *ib*

'Valley of the people of Herela', *v.* -inga-, denu. This unrecorded
OE pers.n. occurs in a number of p.ns., *v.* BdHu 124, where it is
suggested that it went out of use at an early period, and also that the
distribution shows it to be definitely Anglian. The last suggestion
requires modification in view of its occurrence in this Berks name.

BRADLEY Ct, (*utðruht*) *bradanlea* 968 (c. 1200) BCS 1225, *Bradelea*
Hy 1 (c. 1200) *Claudius Cix*, 1167 P *et passim* with variant spellings
Bradelega, Bradelye, Bradele, Bradeleg(h), Bradeleye to 1364 Pat,
Bradele Gynmyng 1316 FA, *Bradley* 1398 Fine, *Bradley courte* Ed 6
LRMB, Great and Little Bradley 1757–8 ArchJ 14, *Bradley Farm*
1761 Rocque. '(At the) broad wood or glade', *v.* brād, lē(a)h. Thomas
de *Gimege* appears in this connection 1242–3 Fees.

CURRIDGE

Cusan ricge, (*æt*) *Cusan hricge* 953 (c. 1240) BCS 900
Coserige 1086 DB, *Coserug'* 1240–1 FF, *Cosrugg', Cosserugg'* 1284
   Ass, Coserugge 1305 Ipm, 1316 FA
Cuserugia 1147 BM *et passim* with variant spellings *Cuserig(g)e,*
   Cuseregge, Cuserug(g)e to 1310 Pat, *Chuserug'* c. 1170 (c. 1200)
   Thame, *Cusurugg'* 1275–6 RH
Cusrug 1230 Pat (p), *Cusrigge* 1281 Cl
Guserigg' 1275–6 RH
Currygge 1428 FA, *Currige* 1547 *LRMB, Courage* 1761 Rocque

'Cusa's ridge', *v.* hrycg.

OARE, (*æt*) *Oran* 968 (c. 1200) BCS 1225, *Ore* 1225 (c. 1250) Bract,
1242–3 Fees, 1316 FA, 1401–2 *ib, Orwe* (*sic*) *chapell* 1574 Saxton,
Oare 1761 Rocque, 'slope', *v.* ōra. The same name occurs in K and
W. An earlier reference to the Berks place occurs in the phrase (*on*)

orhæma gemære 951 (16th) BCS 892, 'boundary of the people of Oare', *v.* hæme, (ge)mære.

OGDOWN BARN, *Okdone* 1327 *SR* (p), *Okedown Cop'* 1538 *RentSur*, *Ockden, Okeden* 1547 *LRMB, Okedowne Wood, Okedens, Ogdene Mede* 1550 *ib, Ogdown* 1840 *TA*, 'oak hill', *v.* āc, dūn.

SNELSMORE (partly in Winterbourne and Shaw), *Snellesmore* 1242–3 Fees, 1401–2 FA, *Snelly's more* 1538 *RentSur, Snells more* 1547 *LRMB, Snelesmore* 1753 ArchJ 15, *Snelsmore, Snelsmore Heath* 1761 Rocque, 'Snell's marsh', *v.* mōr. *Snellesputte* 1234–41 (m.14th) *Lyell* was apparently a pit named from the same man.

ARLINGTON GRANGE FM, *v.* 242.   ASHFIELD'S FM, *Aysshefelde, Naysshefelde* 1547 *LRMB, Ashfield Fm* 1830 OS *v.* atten, æsc, feld. ASH ROW.   BAKER'S ROW.   BARRETT'S WD.   BASING'S COPSE. BEANS HILL, BEANS HILL COPSE.   BEECH COPSE.   THE BEECHES. BRADLEYHILL COPSE, BRADLEYHOME WD AND PARK (*v.* 242). BRAZIER'S FM.   BREACH ROW, 1830 OS, *Le Breche* 1550 *LRMB*, *v.* brēc.   BROOMDOWN FM, *Further Broom, Brown Down* 1839 *TA*. BUSSOCK WD (*v.* 277).   CARBROOK.   CHALKY LANE.   CHIEVE-LEY COTTAGE AND MANOR.   CHURCH FM.   COOMBE HO. COPYHOLD COPSE, *Copyhold Wood* 1830 OS.   COPYHOLD CLOSE AND FM.   CROSSROADS FM.   CURRIDGE HO AND FM (*v.* 242). DANECASTLE.   DEAN'S WD.   DOCTOR'S LANE AND ROW.   DOWN-END, 1749 ArchJ 20.   DOWN FM, HO AND LODGE, *Doune* 1327 *SR* (p), *Chyveley Down* 1538 *RentSur, Le Downe* 1550 *LRMB, v.* dūn. FAIRCROSS POND, 1761 Rocque, FAIRCROSS PLANTATION (*v.* 231). FOX AND HOUNDS P.H., 1830 OS.   FRESHFIELD.   GORSELANDS. GRANGE COPSE AND COTTAGES, *Le Grange* 1547 *LRMB, Grange Wood* 1830 OS.   GREEN'S FM, 1830 OS.   GRIGG'S COPSE, *Griggs, Griggs Heeth* 1547 *LRMB, Gryggs Crofte* 1550 *ib*, probably from a surname.   HARE AND HOUNDS INN.   HAZELHANGER, HAZEL-HANGER COPSE AND FM, *Hasyll Anger Cop'* 1538 *RentSur, Hasell Hanger, Hasellhangers Copps* 1550 *LRMB, v.* hæsel, hangra. HENRIETTA VILLA.   HIGH WD, *Highwood Mead* 1838 *TA*. HINDLEY'S PLANTATION.   HOLLY COPSE.   HOME FM.   HORSE-MOOR.   KEMPS COPSE.   KILN FM, *Kiln Meadow* 1839 *TA*. KITE'S ABBEY.   LANOLEE FM.   LITTLEDEANS WD.   LONG-CROFT WD, *Longcrofte* 1547 *LRMB*, 1550 *ib*.   MALTHOUSE WD,

Malthouse Fm 1830 OS.   MANOR FM.   MARSH LANE, *Marsh, Marsh Meadow* 1839 *TA*.   MEETINGHOUSE COPSE (*v.* 231). MIDDLE FM.   NEW FM.   NEWHOUSE FM.   NEW RD.   NOON'S COPSE.   OAKLANDS, OAKLANDS FM.   OAREBOROUGH HILL, COPSE AND LANE, OAREBOROUGH HILL COPSE, *Le Worborowhill* 1550 *LRMB*, this form is too late to be used with confidence, but it is possible that the original name of this prominent hill was OE *weard-beorg* 'watch hill' (cf. Warborough O 138, Warby Nt 240), the modern form being due to the proximity of Oare.   OARE COMMON, 1830 OS.   OLD KILN FM.   OLD STREET (*v.* 5).   ORCHARD COPSE, *Orchard Close and Meadow* 1839 *TA*.   OSMOND'S PIGHTLE.   THE PARSONAGE.   PHILLIP'S HILL, 1830 OS.   PRIOR'S COURT, 1761 Rocque.   PRIORSCOURT PARK, 1839 *TA*.   PRIORSCOURT FM AND WD.   RADNALL'S FM, 1830 OS, *Radnell(s)*, *Radnalls* 1547 *LRMB*. RECTOR'S COPSE.   RECTORY FM.   ROEBUCK WD, 1830 OS, also *Roebuck* (an inn).   THE ROOKERY.   ROUND COPSE.   SANDY ROW. SEVENACRES (Bird's Fm on 6″).   SMITHY COPSE.   SOUTHFIELD PIGHTLE, *Le Southefeld* 1550 *LRMB*, *v.* sūð, feld.   SPRING COPSE (3 examples, the one near Curridge is Spring Wd 1830 OS, the one near Hermitage is so named 1830 OS).   SUNHILL FM.   TOTTERDOWN, no early forms have been found, but in view of its proximity to a hill-fort this can safely be interpreted as 'hill with a look-out house' from tōtærn and dūn, cf. BdHu 140.   UPPER GRANGE COPSE.   WHEATSHEAF P.H.   WOODSIDE.

FIELD-NAMES

The principal forms in (*a*) are 1839 *TA* (for Snelsmore, Oare and Curridge); early forms for which no date or source is given are 1550 *LRMB*, those dated 1221–34 and 1234–41 are *Lyell* and are (m.14th), 1538 *RentSur*, 1547 *LRMB*.

(*a*) Ash Court; Ash Croft (*Aysshecrofte* 1547, *Asshecrofte*); Backet Fd; Barn and Will Down; Blackmore (*Blakemore Gate* 1547, Blackmoor Wood 1830 OS, *v.* blæc, mōr); Broad Close (*Le Brode Close* 1547); Brooms Close; Chalk Pit Close and Ground; Chapel Mdw; Cockshut (*v.* cocc-scyte); The Common, Common Fd and Lot (cf. *Le Comon Downe*); Coppice Close; Copse Piece; Cow Leaze (*Le Coweleaze, v.* lǣs); Crab Trees; The Croft; Dean, Great and Further (*v.* denu); Doskins Mead (*Dogskynnes*, possibly referring to shape); Furze Close (cf. *Le Fussenfelde* 1547 *v.* fyrsen); Gravelly Furlong; Gray Croft; Great Ground; The Green; Grubb Copse (*v.* 281); Harrington Fd (*Harrynton Heyth* 1538); Harrow Close; Hawkeridge Fd; Helens, East and West; High Court; Hill Close and Ground; Hollins Close (cf. *Hollons Corner, v.* holegn); Holly Bush Style; Home Close, Ground and

Mdw; Horse Shoe Ground (probably referring to shape); Knowl Hill (*Le Knoll, Knoll Feld, v.* cnoll); Lankets (*Lancots Wd and Pit* 1830 OS, *v.* 281); Long Lands; Long Mdw; The Lot, Lot Pightle (*v.* hlot); Mancroft (*v.* (ge)mǣne); Oare Chapel Pightle; Pease Hill; Picked Ground and Mdw (cf. *Piked Crofte, v.* pīced); Pidlands; The Pightle (cf. *Le Pidle* 1547, *v.* pightel as elsewhere in this parish); Pit Ground; Poors Land; Pound Close; Rag Pightle (*v.* ragge); Shepherds Close; Sling (*v.* 282); Small Mdw; Stub Furlong (*v.* stubb); Sturts, East and West (*v.* steort); The Tree Ground; Wall Close; Well Croft and Pightle; Wind Horns; Wind Mill Down; Witch Pit Ground (cf. Wych Pit in Hampstead Norris 253); Wood Ground.

(*b*) *Le Bakker Meade*; *Bedon Thropp Yate* (*v.* 232); *Bochecrofte*; *Brodehill* (*v.* brād, hyll); *Burycrofte* (*v.* burh, croft); *Le Busshyclose* 1547; *Le Butt* 1547 (*v.* butte); *Le Calf Leaze* (*v.* lǣs); *Chamons Crosse* 1547; *Cherrygorde*; *Churchefeld*; *Clyveld* 1547; *Cottsetterfeilde, Cotcetterfeld* 1550 *LRMB*, *Cossiter Field* 1604 *RecOffCat* (*v.* 231–2); *Cowdown* 1604 *RecOffCat* (*v.* dūn); *Crompelcroft* 1310 (l.14th) *Chatsworth* (*v.* croft, first el. possibly crymel); *ealdan byrig* 951 (16th) BCS 892, *Aldebir* (p), *Audebir'* 1221–34 (*v.* eald, burh, the reference is to the Iron Age hill-fort in Bussock Wood); *Elton Cop'* 1538 (*v.* 273); *Endelands* (*v.* ende¹); *Erles Copice* 1547; *Frethehorep' Frethorsseputte* 1221–34 ('horse pit' with an uncertain prefix, which may be fyrhð 'wood'); *Le Fryth* (*Copic' voc'*) 1547 (*v.* fyrhð); *Le Golly* 1547 ('gully'); *Gose Crofte* (*v.* gōs); *Le Grove Crofte, Le Grove*; *La Grutte* 1310 (l.14th) *Chatsworth* (possibly OE *grutt* 'an abyss, a gulf, a whirlpool', but Professor Löfvenberg prefers an OE **grytte* 'sandy, stony soil or land' for this and for ME surnames *atte Grutte* 1327 *SR*, Do and W); *Hakedic* 1221–34, *Hakediche, Le Hakediche Piddell* (probably 'hook ditch', *v.* haca); *Hasyll Wood Cop'* 1538; *Le Hitchyn, Le Hechyn* (*v.* heccing); *Hollingdon*; *Le Inlands* (*v.* in); *Iremonger(s) Gate*; *Langley Hatche* (*v.* 251); *Lippattysfelde, Lippattisfelde* 1547 (*v.* hlīep-geat, feld); *Lez Litill Launds* (*v.* launde); *Longefelde* 1547; *Lovelbury*; *Midlelitlefelde* 1547; *Le More, Lez Mores* (*v.* mōr); *Neweheathes*; *Northcrofte* 1547, 1550; *Okehangerfeild* (cf. Oakhanger 273–4); *Oken Crofte*; *Oley Hill*; *Le Over Closes* 1547; *Overhill* (*et Netherhill*); *Litill Ouerlands*; *Le Paroke* (*v.* pearroc); *Le Petycrofte* (perhaps French *petit* 'small', cf. Petty close Db 313, Petty Close Db 477); *Le Pyle* (*v.* pīl); *La Rendich(e)* 1221–34 (possibly 'border ditch', *v.* rend, dīc); *Rompney*; *The Shawe* 1538, *Shawe Crosse* 1547 (*v.* sc(e)aga); *Sheepdown* 1604 *RecOffCat* (cf. *Cowdown supra*); *Shepehouse Close*; *Shortehethes*; *Small Croftes*; *Le Southbrode Close* 1547; *Sowbury Pete*; *Wight Field*; *Woodakes Cop'* 1538; *Wooredown* 1538; *Wydemore Crofte* (*v.* wīd, mōr).

Cold Ash

This parish was formed for ecclesiastical purposes in 1865, out of the civil parish of Thatcham, and for civil purposes in 1894 (Kelly, 65). The name occurs on Rocque's map (1761). For 19th-cent. f.ns. *v.* Thatcham 192.

ASHMORE GREEN, 1761 Rocque.   ASHMOREGREEN FM.   BIG COPSE.   CARROTTY COW LEAZE, 1841 *TA* (Thatcham).   FURTHER CARROTTY COW LEAZE.   CHIVER'S GULLY.   CLAY HILL, 1841 *TA* (Thatcham).   COLDASH COMMON, 1830 OS.   COLDASH FM. CURRAGHMORE.   EASTON COPSE, *Easton Wood* 1830 OS.   ELM-HURST FM.   FISHER'S FM AND LANE, *Fishers Green* 1830 OS. GRIMSBURY FM (*v.* 252).   GROVE COPSE.   THE HANGINGS. HATCHGATE FM AND COTTAGES, *Hatchgate* 1841 *TA* (Thatcham) (*v.* hæcc-geat).   HENWICKLANDS COPSE, LITTLE HENWICK FM (*v.* 189).   HIGHFIELD HO.   HILLCREST.   HILLSIDE.   IVY HO, IVYHOUSE GULLY, *Ivey House Barn Ground, Ivey House Meadow and Pightle* 1841 *TA* (Thatcham).   LAWRENCE'S COPSE.   LITTLE COPSE.   LONG COPSE.   LONG LANE, LONGLANE.   LOWER BARN.   MANOR FM.   MESSENGER'S COPSE, cf. *Shaw Field late Messingers* 1841 *TA* (Thatcham).   MOUNT PLEASANT, *v.* 283. NOTHING HILL. POPLAR FM, POPLAR FM HO.   REDFIELD COT-TAGES, *Red Field* 1841 *TA* (Thatcham).   ROUND COPSE.   ST. FINIAN'S FM.   SETT COPSE.   SHAW FIELDS, *Shawfield* 1817 OS, *Shaw Field* 1841 *TA* (Thatcham).   STONE COPSE, 1817 OS. STONE COTTAGES, near preceding.   SUN IN THE WOOD P.H. SUNNYSIDE HO.   THIRTOVER, *Thurtover* 1841 *TA* (Thatcham). THORNEHILL.   WEAVER'S WD, *Weavers Wood* 1817 OS.   YATE'S COPSE.

Frilsham

FRILSHAM

> *Frilesham* 1086 DB, *Frillesham* 1203 Cur (p)
> *Fridlesham, Fridesham* 1174 P, *Fridelesham* 1188 ib (p), 1223 Cur, 1284 *Ass*, 1327 *SR*, *Fridlesham* 1220 Fees *et freq, Frydelsham* 1409 BM
> *Fretlesham* 1214 Cur, *Fritlesham* 1241 *Ass*
> *Fridetheyn* 1235–6 Fees
> *Friglesham* 1242–3 Fees
> *Ffrithelesham* 1248–52 *FF*
> *Finthelesham* 1284 *Ass*

'Friðel's homestead', *v.* hām. This unrecorded pers.n. is a strong form of *Friðela* found in Frilford (Pt 2).

BIRCH BARN AND COVERT.   BIRCH FM, 1761 Rocque, *Birche, Burch'* 1202 Hunter Fines, *Birche* 1327 *SR* (p), *v.* birce.   BURNT-

BUSH LANE. CHALKANGLES COPSE. COOMBEHURST. COOMBE WOOD, 1839 *TA, Combe Wood* 1830 OS, *v.* **cumb.** FRILSHAM COMMON, 1761 Rocque. FRILSHAM HO AND MILL. HATCHETS LANE, *v.* **hæcc-geat.** HOME FM. LONG GROVE, 1830 OS. MANOR HO. PARSONAGE FM. PIKES COPSE AND ROW. SULHAM'S COPSE.

FIELD-NAMES

The principal forms in (*a*) are 1839 *TA*.

(*a*) The Butts (*v.* **butte**); Chalk Pit Ground; Common Ground; Dry Mead; Herby's Hitch (*v.* **hiche**); Hill House Piece; Kings Wood (also 1830 OS); Littleworths; Mill Ham; Picked Piece (*v.* **piced**); Towns End Piece; Water Mdw; West Brook Fd; White Fd.

(*b*) *La Hide* 13th *ReadingC*(2), *La Hyde* ?14th *ib* (*v.* **hīd**).

Greenham

GREENHAM

> *Greneham* 1086 DB, 1248, 1284 *Ass*, 1517 D Inc
> *Grenham* 1185 RR (p) *et passim, Grenham Hospitalium* 1220 Fees

Probably 'green river-meadow', *v.* **grēne**[1], **hamm**, referring to land by R. Kennet. *Hospitalium* from the Knights Hospitallers, to whom the manor was granted in the late 12th cent. (VCH III, 319).

CAKE BALL, CAKEBALL COPSE, *Cakebull, Cakebullwoode, Copic' voc' Cakeball* 1547 *LRMB*. It is unfortunate that no earlier forms have been found for this name. It appears to be identical with Cakebole in Chaddesley Corbett (Wo 236), in which case it is possible that that name should be interpreted as a single topographical term, not as a combination of a pers.n. and **ball** 'rounded hill'. Cf. also Cakewood W 290, 12 miles W., which is *Cakewode* in 1362.

SANDLEFORD

> *Sandelford* c. 1150 HMC Var Coll VII 43, 1234 BM, 1242 Ch, 1275–6 RH, *Sandleford* 1220 Fees, *Sandleford'* 1241 Cl, 1242–3 Fees, 1284 *Ass, Scandelford* 1297 Pat
> *Sandraford* 1180 P, *Sanderford'* 1241 Cl, *Sanderford* 1246 Ch
> *Sanlesford* 1185 P, *Sandresford* 1234 Pat, *Sandlesford* 1340 ib, *Sondlesford* 1340, 1342 ib, *Sandelesford* 1349 Cl, 1378 Pat

Ekwall (DEPN) suggests 'sand-stream ford', with a compound of sand and w(i)ella as first el. Skeat (49) suggests 'Sandwulf's ford', but the element *Sand-* is not found in OE pers.ns., and Ekwall's etymology is more in accordance with the forms. These are too late for any degree of certainty. 'Sand-hill ford', *v.* **hyll**, is also possible. The ford over the R. Enborne is marked on the 6″ map.

ALDERN BRIDGE, 1547 *LRMB, Alder Bridge and Bottom* 1761 Rocque, *v.* **alren.**   ALDERNBRIDGE GULLY.   BALL'S HILL, BALLSHILL GULLY, *v.* **ball** and cf. Cakeball 247, which is about a mile N. BARNCLOSE COPSE, *Le Barne Close* 1547 *LRMB, Barn Close* 1840 *TA.* BARN COPSE.   BISHOP'S GREEN.   BOWDOWN HO, FM AND COPSE, *Bowdens, Bowdens Copice* 1547 *LRMB, Bowdown* 1840 *TA*, possibly manorial, from John *Bovedon* of Boxford, who died in 1450 seised of land in Boxford and Greenham (VCH IV, 45); but a meaning '(place) above the hill' (*v.* **bufan, dūn**) suits the site, and the family-name may be derived from this place.   BROWN'S POND.   BURY'S BANK, a linear earthwork, *v.* **burh.**   CLARKE'S GULLY.   CROOK'S COPSE.   DIRTY GROUND COPSE.   DRAYTON'S GULLY.   GORSE COVERT.   GREENHAM COMMON, *Greenham Heath* 1761 Rocque. GREENHAM LODGE.   GREYBERRY COPSE.   GROVE COTTAGE. HANDPOST GULLY, 'sign-post gully'.   HIGH WOOD.   HILL HO. THE HUT.   LITTLEMEAD REEVES, *Little Mead (Reeves)* 1840 *TA.* LODGE COVERT.   LOWER FM, 1761 Rocque.   NEWTOWN POND; Newtown is in Ha.   NOAH'S ARK, an isolated house on Greenham Common.   OAK PLANTATION.   ONE TREE COTTAGE.   PEAKED HILL, *v.* **pīced.**   PECKMOOR COPSE, *Pekmore* 1547 *LRMB, v.* **mōr.** PIGEON'S FM, *Pidgeon Fm* 1761 Rocque.   PILE HILL, 1761 Rocque, *Pilhill, Pilhill Heth* 1547 *LRMB.* The hill is the one climbed by the road to Greenham from the lower ground of Stroud Green. There may have been stakes (*v.* **pīl**) marking the route through the marshy ground.   PILEHILL COTTAGES.   REEVES'S Copse, *Reeves* 1840 *TA*, adjoining Littlemead Reeves *supra.*   SANDLEFORD COTTAGE, FM, PARK AND PRIORY, *v. supra*; the Priory was a small house of Austin canons, founded between 1193 and 1202 (VCH II, 86).   SLOCKETT'S COPSE.   STROUD GREEN, 1761 Rocque, *Strowde Grene* 1547 *LRMB, Strood Green* 1660 *Windsor, v.* **strōd** 'marshy land overgrown with brushwood'.   THE SWAN INN.   THORN BUSH.   WATER-LEAZE COPSE, *Waterleaze* 1624 *Windsor, v.* **lǣs.**   WELLMOOR COPSE,

Wellmore 1547 *LRMB*, *v.* w(i)ella, mōr.   WEST WOOD, 1840 *TA*,
Le Westewoode 1547 *LRMB*.   WESTWOOD FM.   WOODHOUSE
POND.   WORKHOUSE SPINNEY.   YOUNG COPSE.

FIELD-NAMES

The principal forms in (*a*) are 1840 *TA*; early forms dated 1235–6 are *FF*,
1547 *LRMB*.

(*a*) Bin Pightle; Black Mead and Gully; Bottom Mead; The Brow and
Gully; Calves Leaze Ground; Chapel Pightle (*Greenham Chapel* 1761
Rocque); Charles Pightle; Coach House Pightle; Cotmans Folly or Narrow
Drove; Crockers Pightle; Ell Close; Empole Plat (*Enpole Mede, Empole
Mede* 1547, *v.* pōl); Ham Fd, Marsh and Mead (*v.* hamm); Head Acre;
Hill Ground; Hilly Pightle; Hollybush; Home Ground and Piece; Hop
Garden (*v.* hoppe); The Island; Long Close and Ground; Lot Mdw (*v.*
hlot); The Meadow and Gully; Milk Furlong; Mill Mdw (*Greenham Mill*
1761 Rocque); Old Fd; Oldlands; Orchard Close; Ox Leaze (*v.* lǣs); The
Park; The Parsonage Pightle; Picked Ground and Piece (*v.* pīced); The
Pightle (*v.* pightel, as in other f.ns. in this parish); Plantation Ground; Plat,
Great and Little (*v.* plat²); Ploughed Ground; Poors Acre; Rough Mdw and
Moor; Round Close; Shepherd's Close; The Slip (*v.* slipe); Smithies; Steel
Hill (*v.* stigel); Stonylands; Tenny Piece; Top Mew; Wear Close.

(*b*) *Abbotts Golly* 1547 (an early example of *gully*, which is common in
minor names in this area); *Berediche* 1547 (*v.* bere, dīc); *Cleyhill Piddle* 1547
(*piddle* is a variant of pightel); *Le Courteheth* 1547 (*v.* court, hǣð); *Estfeud*
1235–6 (*v.* ēast, feld); *Le Gullet* 1547 (*v.* goulet); *Le Lungacr'* 1235–6 (*v.*
lang, æcer); *La Meredich'* 1235–6 (*v.* (ge)mǣre, dīc); *Meroweye* 1235–6
(*v.* (ge)mǣre, weg); *Poppley Crofte* 1547; *Wychemote* (*hethe voc'*) 1547.

Hampstead Norris

HAMPSTEAD NORRIS

Hanstede 1086 DB
Hamesteda Willelmi de Sifrewast 1167 P, *Hamestede* 1195 Cur
Hamsted' 1220 Fees *et passim* with variant spelling *Hamstede*;
　　Hamstede Cyfrewast', Hamsted' Ciffrewast, Hamstude Cyfrewast
　　1284 *Ass, Hamstede Ferres* 1401–2 FA, *Hamstedferreris* 1410–16
　　BM
Hampsted 1275 Fine, 1276 Ch, 1316 FA, *Hampstede Cyfrewast*
　　1351 Ipm, *Hampsted Ferrers* 1375 Fine, *Hampstedeferrerys* 1409
　　BM, *Hampstede Cifrewast* 1410 Fine, *Hampstede Norreys* 1517
　　D Inc

v. hāmstede 'homestead'. The descent of the manor is given in VCH IV, 74. William *de Sifrewast* was holding it in 1166–7. It passed to Thomas de Clare in 1269–70, and to Robert de Muscegros in 1276. The daughter of Robert de Muscegros married John, first Lord *Ferrers* of Chartley. In 1448 it was sold to the trustees of John *Norreys*.

BOTHAMPSTEAD

Bodeha'sted' 1199 Cur, *Bodenhampstede* 1317 Ch, *Bodemhamstede* 1335 ib

Botelhamested' 1237 Cl

Botenhamsted' 1241 *Ass*, *Botenhampstede* 1284 *ib*, 1328, 1349 Ipm, *Botenhampstede* 1338, 1349 ib, *Botenhampsted* 1345 Cl, *Bottenam-stede* 1391 ib

Bottom Hampsted 1593–7 AD

Bottompstead Green 1761 Rocque, *Bottomstead* 1830 OS

'Homestead in a valley', *v.* botm, hāmstede. DEPN discusses the name under the spelling Bottomstead, but the modern O.S. maps give Bothampstead. Bothampstead Fm (GR 505762) is on a flat shelf of land, not in a valley or hollow. The farm marked Trumpetts on 1″ map but Little Bothampstead on 2½″, about ½ mile south-east of Bothampstead Fm, is in a situation which suits the p.n. There is also Lower Bothampstead Fm, on the same shelf of land as Bothampstead Fm.

ELING

Elinge 1086 DB, 1241 *Ass*, 1247–8 *FF*, 1284 *Ass*, 1316 FA, *Elynge*, *Elinge*, *Yelinge* 1284 *Ass*, *Elynge* 1294 *SR*, 1300 Ipm

Eling' 1220 Fees, 1224–5 *Ass*, 1240 Cl, 1241, 1284 *Ass*, *Heling'* 1241 *ib*, *Eleng'*, *Yelingg'* 1284 *ib*, *Elyng'* 1297 CornAcc

Elinges (ter) 1224–5 *Ass*

Eling 1242–3 Fees, 1275–6 RH, *Yeling* 1246 Cl, *Elyng* 1327 *SR*, 1353 Cl, 1412 FA

PN -ing (44–5) gives this as a name in -ingas, from a pers.n. such as *Eli*, but the forms are more consistent with a singular name in -ing. There are a number of pools round the village, and the first element may be āel, 'eel'. *v.* Elements **1**, 289 for some place-names formed from -ing and an animal, bird or insect name, to which this would be analogous, and Gl **3**, 149–50, where derivation from āel and -ing is suggested for several lost names in Gl. Eling Ha (DEPN) and Ealing (Mx 90–1) are different names.

Spellings with *Y*- show the development of prosthetic [j] which is common before a front vowel.

HAW FM, *La Hawe* 1241 *Ass* (p), 1270 Pat, *Le Haghe* 1328 Ipm, *La Haghe* 1332 ib, *Hawe* 1516 AD, *Haw Farm* 1761 Rocque, *v.* haga[1] 'enclosure'. The same name occurs Gl **3**, 150. *Haghe* 1198 Hunter Fines may be this place.

LANGLEY, *Langelea* 1167 P, *Langelega* 1168, 9 ib *et freq* with variant spellings *Langelegh', Langel', Langele, Langeleye* to 1364 Pat, *Langle* 1316 FA, *Langley* 1398 Fine, 'long wood or glade', *v.* lang, lē(a)h, a common name.

WYLD FM, WYLD COURT FM, *Wille* 1086 DB, *La Wile* 1199 Hunter Fines, 1247–8 *FF* (p), *Wyl* 1220 Fees, *La Wyle* 1242–3 ib *et freq* to 1428 FA, *Wyle* 1284 *Ass*, 1294 *SR*, *Wile* 1410 Fine, *Wilde* 1517 D Inc, *Wild Court* 1761 Rocque, identical with Monkton Wyld in Do (Do 300). Ekwall (DEPN) suggests that the source is OE wīl 'trick', used of some mechanical contrivance. The addition of a parasitic -*d* after -*l* is common. The manor is wrongly identified in VCH (I, 357 and IV, 75) with Well House in this parish.

ADAM'S LAND COPSE, *Adams Lands, Adams Land Orchard* 1839 *TA*. ALLEN'S ALLOTMENT AND ROW, *Allens Field* 1839 *ib*. AMBROSE BARN, COPSE, POND AND ROW, *Ambrose Wood* 1830 OS, *Great and Little Ambrose* 1839 *TA*. BANTERWICK BARN, *Banterwick* 1830 OS. BEECH WD (1830 OS) AND LODGE. BIRCH COTTAGES, cf. *Birch Hill, Birch Nine Acres* 1839 *TA*, *v.* Birch Fm in Frilsham 246. BOTTOM FM. BOX COTTAGE. BOX WOOD, *Long Box Wood, Round Box Wood* 1830 OS. BREACH BARN AND ROW, *Breach Farm* 1830 OS, *The Breach* 1839 *TA*, *v.* brēc. BUTTONSHAW BOTTOM AND FM, *Buttons sawes* Ed 6 *LRMB*, *Buttons Haw* 1761 Rocque, possibly manorial, from the surname *Buttonshaw*, *v.* Reaney *s.n.* *Birkenshaw*. CHALKPIT PIECE, 1839 *TA*. LITTLE CHESERIDGE WOOD, *Little Chaseridge Wood* 1830 OS, *Chesridge* 1839 *TA*. CHURCH PIGHTLE, (*v.* pightel). CHURCH ST. THE COMMON, COMMON BARN AND FIRS, *Hampstead Common* 1839 *TA*. CUCKOO PITS. DAMASKFIELD COPSE, *Dormersfield Copse* 1830 OS, *Damask Field* 1839 *TA*, *v.* 285. DARK LANE ROW. DOWN ROW.

DOWN WOOD.   DROVE LANE.   ELING COMMON, FM AND GORSE, ELINGPARK COPSE, *v.* 250.   FENCE WOOD AND LANE.   FIFIELD FM.   THE FIRS.   FIRTREE FM.   FLOODCROSS COTTAGE, *Flood Cross* 1839 *TA*; *v.* flōde, used in Berks of an intermittent spring. The spring here is sometimes the source of the R. Pang.   FOLLY HILL, a round clump of trees, *v.* folie.   FOUR ELMS, 1830 OS, *Four Elms Piddle and Piece* 1839 *TA*.   FOX AND HOUNDS P.H. FURZE HILL, 1839 *TA*.   GRAVELLY PIGHTLE, *Gravelly Piddles, Gravelly Hill* 1839 *ib*, *piddle* is a variant of pightel.   GREEN HAMS LANE.   GRIMSBURY CASTLE, 1830 OS, AND WD, 'Grim's fort', referring to the Iron Age hill-fort; Grīm is a by-name of Wōden. HARBERT'S BOTTOM, 1839 *TA*.   HATCHGATE COTTAGE, *Hatch Gate Ground* 1839 *TA*, *v.* hæcc-geat.   HEATHER PIECE.   HERMITAGE, 1748 ArchJ 16, 1761 Rocque, *Le Eremytage Hedge* 1550 *LRMB*, *v.* ermitage.   HOLLINGSWORTH COTTAGE, *Great, Farther and Hether Hollingworth* 1622–3 *RentSur*, *Great, Picked and White Hollingsworth* 1839 *TA*. probably 'holly enclosure', *v.* holegn, worð, identical with Hollingworth Ch, La.   HORSLEYS ROW, *Horse Leaze* 1839 *TA*, *v.* lǣs.   LITTLE HUNGERFORD, 1761 Rocque, 1830 OS, cf. *Hungerford Meadow* 1839 *TA*, named from Hungerford Pt 2.   IVY COTTAGE.   LADIES HILL WOOD.   LAYCROFT WOOD, *Lay Croft Field* 1839 *TA*, *v.* lǣge, croft.   MALTHOUSE FM, *Malthouse Ground and Piece* 1839 *ib*.   MIDDLEFIELD BARN.   MILKHILL BARN, *Milk Hill, Milk Hill Bottom* 1839 *TA*.   MONEY'S ALLOTMENT. MUDGATE COTTAGES, *Mudgate Piece* 1839 *TA*.   NEW COPSE. NEW PLANTATION.   NINE ACRE ROW, *The Nine Acres* 1839 *TA*. NORTHFIELD ROW, *North Field* 1839 *TA*.   OAKHOUSE FM, 1830 OS, *Oak House* 1761 Rocque, *Oakhouse Lot* 1839 *TA*.   PARK WD, *Hampstead Park Wood* 1830 OS, *Park* 1839 *TA*.   PARSONS HILL ROW, *Parson Hill(s)* 1839 *TA*.   PARSONS PIECE.   PHEASANT HILL WD.   PICKEDCROFT ROW, *Picked Croft* 1839 *TA*, *v.* pīced, croft. PIMBUS SHAW, *Pinbus Shaw* 1830 OS, *Pummus* 1839 *TA*.   POUCH PIGHTLE, *v.* pightel.   POUNDPIT PIECE.   RAMSWORTH COTTAGES, *Ramsworth Barn* 1830 OS, *Ramoth, Ramoth Hill* 1839 *TA*. This is near Perborough Castle, a hill-fort in Compton parish, and may represent a name with hræfn as first el., *v.* 155.   RIDGE COPSE, GREAT AND LITTLE, *Ridge Wood* 1830 OS.   ROOK'S COPSE, *Rooks* 1839 *TA*.   ROUND HILL WOOD, 1830 OS.   SANDPIT COPSE, *Sand Pit Close and Piece* 1839 *TA*.   SPEEDWELL.   SPRING PLANTATION.   SLATES HILL WD.   SWALLOW HOLE (Swilly Pits *infra*, f.n., is not near this). TOWNSEND FM, *Townes End* 1622–3 *RentSur*, it is at the northern end of the village. WATER ST. WELLHOUSE, 1830 OS, WELLHOUSE FM, cf. *Well Meadow and Piddle, Wellhanger* 1839 *TA* (*v.* pightel, hangra), John *atte Welle* of *Hampsted Ciphrewas*, 1348 Cl, probably derived his name from this well. WELL LANE, leading to Wellhouse, *Well Lane Coppice* 1839 *TA.* WESTBROOK COPSE. WILD DUCK POND. WINDMILL HILL PLANTATION. WINTON HOUSE. WYCH PIT, this lies next to Cuckoo Pits *supra*; Witch Pit Ground occurs again as a f.n. in Chieveley 245, another instance is Witch Pits Fm Wa 296. YEW-TREE BOTTOM.

FIELD-NAMES

The principal forms in (*a*) are 1839 *TA*, except where otherwise stated; early forms dated 1622–3 are *RentSur.*

(*a*) Ashdown Bottom (*v.* botm); Awberry Hill; Badgers Piece; Ballings Moor; Bank Piece; Barn Close; Beech Close and Fd; Bellhinges Close; Brokas, Great and Little; Brood Fd; Broom Barley Fd; Broom Close and Fd (*v.* brōm); The Buck Lot; Buck Piddle (*Piddle* is a variant of pightel, as elsewhere in this parish); Burnlaked (probably an error for Burnbaked, *v.* beak); Bushey Hill; Calves Leaze (*v.* lǣs); Ceasars; Chalk Piddle; Clay Corner; Common Ground and Lot; Cooks Hill; Cow Common and Leaze; Cully Fd; The Dean (*v.* denu); Dennis Pightle; Down Fd; Dyche Fd; Elm Ground; Galloping Piece; Gas More; Granary Close; Green Close (*Grene Close* 1622–3); Green, Little and Great (*v.* grēne²); Grindstone Handle (*v.* 283); Hackney Bottom; The Hascock; Heath Fd; Herberts Piddle; Hill Ground; Hitchens; Home Fd, Hill, Ground, Piddle and Piece; Hookedge Piece; Keazey Fd; Kiln Ground; Langley Wood; The Lawn (*v.* launde); Lickfield; Louse Hill (*v.* lūs); Marling Heath; Marlstone Lot; Mill Fd; New Broke Lands; Old Down, East and West; Orchard; Oxford-shire; Parsonage Lot; Pendall Piece; Pens Mdw; Picked Fd, The Pikes (*v.* pīced); Pinfolds Pightle; Pit Hangers (*v.* hangra); Pitt Close; Pond Close; Portlucks; Ram Close; Ridge Fd, Great and Little; Rings Close; Rook Fd; Rowcroft Wood 1830 OS (possibly *Rughcroft* 1348 Cl in Yattendon, *v.* rūh, croft); Scorch Fd; Scottal Mdw; Shergood Coppice; Sladd (*v.* slæd); Slurts Coppice; Snipe Bottom; Spring Piddle; Stable Close; Stoney Close; The String (*v.* 282); Swansdown; Swilly Pits (cf. Swilly Ground in Bucklebury, both contain *swilly* 'gutter washed out of the soil', *v.* swelg); Thistley Fd Coppice; Tribute Fd; Velmer; Vicarage Close; Waley or Wayley Hill; The Walk; The Warren; Water Close; The Weals; White Lands; Woolly Coppice.

(*b*) *Heygrof* 1348 Cl (*v.* (ge)hæg, grāf); *The Homstall Orchard* 1622–3 (cf. Sandred 67–8); *Hucleseye* 1348 Cl ('Hucel's island', *v.* (ī)eg); *Little Mead Plott* 1622–3; *The More* 1622–3 (*v.* mōr); *The Seuerall Grounde* 1622–3 (*v.* 282); *Thornecraft* 1622–3 (*v.* croft).

Leckhampstead

LECKHAMPSTEAD

Lechamstede '811' (c. 1200) BCS 352, '821' (c. 1200) BCS 366, 956–9 (c. 1200) BCS 996, m.11th (c. 1200) ASWrits, *Læhham stede* '821' (c. 1240) BCS 366, (æt) *Leachamstede*, (æ) *lecham stede* 943 (c. 1240) BCS 789, *Lecanestede* 1086 DB, *Lechhamesteda* 1167 P, *Lekhamsteda, Lechamsteda* 1176 ib *et passim* with variant spellings *Lechamsted', Lekhamstede, Lechamsted(e), Lechamstud*; *Lekamsted'* 1220 Fees, *Leckhampsted* 1316 FA, *Lekhampstede* 1417–18 ObAcc, *Lekehamstede* 1517 D Inc
Leykhamstede 1286 Ipm, *Leychampsted* 1308 Ch
Lakamstede 13th Abingdon, *Lackhamstead* 1761 Rocque

v. hāmstede. The prefix, as in Leckhampstead Bk 43 and Leckhampton Gl **2**, 109, is lēac 'leek, garlic'. BCS 352 and 366 are spurious.

CHAPEL FM, this is near the site of the old church, which was pulled down in 1859. The modern church has amongst its plate a stand paten inscribed 'The gift of Mrs Eliz Hatt to Lackhampstead chapple A.D. 1737' (VCH IV, 67).   EASTLEY FM AND COPSE, (wood called) *Estele* 1348 Cl, *Esteley Wood* 1547 *LRMB*, *v.* ēast, lē(a)h; Henry de *Estleg'* 1235–6 Fees may have come from here.   EGYPT, 1830 OS, *Egypt Hill* 1841 *TA*, *v.* 284.   GOOSE LANE.   THE GREEN, *Leckhamsted Green* 1841 *TA*, *v.* grēne². GREENBANK. GROVE PIT.   GROVEPIT GREEN.   HIGHFIELD HO.   HILL GREEN, 1761 Rocque.   HILLGREEN HO.   LECKHAMPSTEAD MANOR. LECKHAMPSTEAD STREET, *Le Stret(e)* 1547 *LRMB*, *Leckhamstead Street* 1830 OS, *street* is here used in the sense 'hamlet'.   LECKHAMPSTEAD THICKET, *Le Thiket* 1348 Ipm, *Le Cowelease alias Le Thikket* 1547 *LRMB*, *Leckhamstead Thicket* 1761 Rocque, cf. Maidenhead Thicket 55.   LITTLE COPSE.   MALTHOUSE FM. MANOR FM.   NEW BARN.   NODMOOR CORNER, *Nonmore Corner* 1841 *TA*.   ROOKERY FM, *Rookery Piece* 1841 *ib*.   STAG P.H. STIRT COPSE, *boscum qui dicitur Stert* 1199–1200 Hunter Fines, *le Sterte* 1348 Cl, *Stirt Coppice* 1841 *TA*, 'tail of land', *v.* steort; there is no obvious tail-like feature here, so the reference may be to the shape of the wood.

FIELD-NAMES

The principal forms in (*a*) are 1841 *TA*; early forms for which no date or source is given are 1547 *LRMB*, those dated 1239–40 are *FF*.

(*a*) Barley Close (*Barley Close*); Barrell Hill; Black Pit; Blue Gate Piece; Bonners Lot; The Breach(es) (*Le Breche, Brecheclose, v.* brēc); Cart Close; Chalk Piece; Chalk Pit; Clay Pits (*Le Cleypitfelde*); Colycots (possibly *Cully Crofte*); Coppice Ground; Denclose (*Deneclose, v.* denu); Forwards; The Gravels; Great Ground; Green Drove (*v.* drāf); Heath Fd (*Le Hethefelde, Roughethfelde, v.* rūh, hǣð, feld); Holly Bush (cf. *Hollys, Grete and Litle*); Holt Piece; Home Fd and Ground (cf. *Homeclose*); Hopes Lot (*v.* hlot, frequent in this parish); Lady Bridge; Langman Hill (*Langnam, Langnamfeld*); Lay Fd, Layfield Hill (*Leyfelde, Leyclose, v.* lǣge); Little Lot; Long Down (*v.* dūn); Longlands; Milking Piece; Moorns Hill; Noys Ground; Nuttingtons (*Nuttenden*); Old Crofts (*Oldecrofte*); Old Lot; Park Fd (*Le Parkefelde, Lekehampstede Parke*); The Pightle (*Le Pidle, v.* pightel); Pond Ground; Pounds Close; Princes Ground; Reding Fd (*Reddamfelde*); Red Lot; Rough Down Piece; Small Mdw; Teg Pin; Wedges Lot; The Well Breaches (*v.* brēc); Well Piece; West Close Mdw (*Le Westeclose*); Wheat Close; White Croft Bottom; White Hill; Windmill Hill; Winters Lot (cf. *Wynterles*); Withey Bed Piece (*v.* wīðig, bedd); Yard Acres (*Yerde Acres*).

(*b*) *Baylesclyve* 1348 Ipm, Cl (*v.* clif, first el. the surname *Bail*); *Beche Breche* (*v.* bēce[2], brēc); *Blakegroves* (*v.* blæc, grāf); *Borelandes*; *Brodeclose*; *Calf Close*; *Churchefelde*; (*of*) *curspandic*, (*on*)*cyrspandic* 939 (c. 1240) BCS 743, (*on*) *crypsandic* 943 (c. 1240) BCS 789, *Cripsedich* 1239–40 ('curly ditch', first el. OE *cyrps*; this is an elongated, twisting hollow, visible in a field immediately west of the Newbury road, where it crosses the boundary between Leckhampstead and Brightwalton; the hollow runs north and south, athwart the boundary; Professor Löfvenberg prefers as first el. a pers.n. *Crypsa, cf. *Cripshill* O 87); *Le Downe(s)* (*v.* dūn); *Le Drove* (*v.* drāf); *Le Grove*; *Hill Close*; *Hoddes Green*; *Innerclose*; *Litle Close*; *Longclose*; *Merewey* 1239–40 (*v.* (ge)mǣre, weg); *Le Midleclose*; *Le Northerclose*; *Northfelde*; *Le Olde Felde*; *Le Ouer Close and Pudle* (*v.* uferra, clos and pightel); *Le Pitbreche* (*v.* brēc); *Pykedbrech* (*v.* pīced, brēc); *Le Shepehouse Pidle and Breche*; *Lez Springs* (*v.* spring, these are woods); *Streteleys* 1547 *LRMB, Streytleyse* 1550 *LRMB* (*v.* lē(a)h and cf. Leckhampstead Street 254); *Le Watercroft*; *Le Westegrene*; *Wheat Close*; *Wode* 1314 Cl (p) (*v.* wudu); *Le Woodcroft*.

Midgham

MIDGHAM

Migeham 1086 DB, 1220 Fees, 1254 Cl, 1547 *LRMB Miggeham* 1260–1 *FF*, 1284 *Ass*, 1327 Banco, 1341 Pat, *Myggeham* 1340 Cl, 1419 Fine

Micham 1169 P, 1241 *Ass, Micheham* 1184 P (p), 1224–5 *Ass,*
   1235–6 Fees, *Michham* 1337 Ipm
Migham 1199 Hunter Fines, 1220 Fees *et freq* with variant spelling
   Mygham to 1378 Fine
Midgham 1761 Rocque

Probably 'riverside meadow infested by midges', *v.* **mycg, hamm,**
but the second el. could be **hām.** The forms *Mighala* and *Miggehal,*
1156 and 1190 P, quoted in DEPN, probably refer to Midgehall W
(W 275), as the owners are the monks of *Fons Drogonis* (Stanley
Abbey) who owned the W place.

ALDERSHOT WATER.   BIDDEN'S SHAW, *Biddons* 1841 *TA.*   BUT-
TON COURT, Thomas *Butun* is mentioned 1260–1 *FF* in connection
with Midgham.   CHANNEL WD, *Chennets Wood* 1817 OS,
Chennits Wood 1846 Snare, possibly from Rad. de *Cheynduyt* men-
tioned 1306–7 *FF* in connection with Midgham, cf. *Channels Green*
1841 *TA.*   CHURCHILL HO.   COACH AND HORSES P.H., *Coach
and Horses Piece* 1841 *TA.*   COLLEGE COPSE.   COTTAGE
PLANTATION.   CRANWELL BRIDGE, *Crannels* 1841 *TA,* possibly
'heron stream', *v.* **cran, w(i)ella.**   EIGHT ACRE COPSE, LITTLE
EIGHT ACRE COPSE, *The Eight Acres* 1841 *TA.*   GARRET'S COPSE,
Great and Little Garratts 1841 *TA.*   GREAT MOUNTS COPSE,
Mounts Piece 1841 *ib, v.* **mont** and cf. The Mound *infra.*   HALL-
COURT FM AND SHAW, *Aula* 1326 Cl (p), *Halle* 1327 Banco (p), *v.*
heall, court.   HEALES LOCK.   HIGH WD, 1817 OS.   HOP-
GARDEN COPSE, *v.* **hoppe.**   KENNETHOLME.   KENT'S DOWN FM
AND GULLY.   KING'S FM.   MARSHALL'S CLOSE PLANTATION.
MIDGHAM BRIDGE, COTTAGE, GREEN AND HO.   MIDGHAM MARSH,
1761 Rocque, *North, South and East Marsh* 1841 *TA.*   MIDGHAM
PARK, *The Park* 1841 *ib.*   MORRIS COPSE.   THE MOUND, Great
Mounts Copse *supra* is on the side of the same hill.   NURSERY
COPSE.   OUZEL GULLY, *Owsells in Migeham* 1547 *LRMB,*
Woozalls 1841 *TA,* probably a surname from **ōsle** 'blackbird'.
OXLEASE BRIDGE.   PIGNELL'S GULLY.   QUAKING BRIDGE, *v.*
O 36 and PN St 7 for other examples of this name.   RIDING
PLANTATION.   ROWLAND'S WD.   SIX ACRE PLANTATION.   STONES-
FIELD GULLY.   WEBB'S FM.   WEBCROFT COPSE.   WESTEND
FM.

FIELD-NAMES

The principal forms in (*a*) are 1841 *TA*; early spellings dated 1449–50 are *RentSur*, 1547 *LRMB*.

(*a*) Balls Moor; Bottom Mead; Brocks; Butts Ground (*v.* butte); Calves Penn; Chandlers Pightle (*v.* pightel); Charity Land; Church Acre; Common; Coombe Fd (*Le Combe, Combe More* 1547, *v.* cumb, mōr); Dog Kennel Piece (cf. Kennel 1817 OS); The Down (*v.* dūn); Ewe Fd; Gravel Pit Fd; Great Ground; Ham Fd (*v.* hamm); Haven Fd; High Strings (*v.* 282); Home Close; Lye Fd; North Moor; Radmoor (*Rademore* 13th *ReadingC*, probably 'red marsh', *v.* rēad, mōr, and cf. Radmore St (DEPN)); Red Acres; Squires Croft (possibly *Spyers Crofte* 1547); Vady Mead; Water Mdw.

(*b*) *Estlegh* 1449–50 (*v.* ēast, lēah); *Hempefelde, Over and Nether* 1547 (*v.* hænep, feld); *La Sale* 1300 Cl (p) (*v.* s(e)alh); *Stredecrofte* 1449–50 (*v.* strǣt, croft, the Roman road from Silchester (CALLEVA ATREBATUM) to Speen (SPINAE) crosses the south of Midgham parish); *West Lands* 1694 *PubLib*; *Whatcrofte* 1449–50, *Le Whetecrofte* 1547 (*v.* hwǣte, croft); *Woodecroftes* 1547 (*v.* wudu, croft); *Wygemore* 1248 (1329) Dugdale (*v.* wigga, mōr and cf. Wigmore He).

Newbury

NEWBURY

Neuberie c. 1080 (copy) France *et passim* with variant spellings *Nubir', Neubir(e), Neubir', Neubyr', Nuibyr', Niuberie, Neubury, Neubery; Niweberiam* 1094–1100 France *et passim* with variant spellings *Niweberi, Nieweberia, Niwebir', Newebir', Niwebur', Newebyr', Niwebyr', Neuwebir', Neweburi, Newebury; Newbir'* 1219 FineR *et freq* with variant spellings *Newbiry, Nywbire; Nubre* 1401 Fine

'New market-town', *v.* nīwe, burh. Cf. Stenton 22 'Newbury — tells of the new borough founded by Arnulf de Hesdin, its Norman lord, at the point where the road from Oxford to Winchester crossed the Kennet'. For the earlier name of the manor, *v. Ulvritone infra* 259.

NEWBURY STREET-NAMES

ALBERT RD. ANDOVER RD. ARGYLE RD. BATH RD. BARTHOLO-MEW ST (*Bartilmewe Street* 1518 *Windsor, Bartholomew Street* 1639 BM, 1761 Rocque, *v. infra* 259). BEACONSFIELD TERRACE. BERKELEY RD. BLACK BEAR LANE. BLENHEIM RD. BOUNDARY RD. BROADWAY. BUCKINGHAM RD. CHALFORD RD. CHEAP ST (*Chepestrete* 1453 *Windsor, Cheap St* 1653 *PubLib*, cf. *Chepyngplace* 1376–7 *RentSur*,

Chepyngstrete 1439–40 *ib, v.* cēap, cēping).   CHESTERFIELD RD.   CLIF-
TON RD.   CRAVEN ST.   DONNINGTON SQUARE AND VILLAS.   EN-
BORNE PLACE AND RD.   ESSEX ST.   FAIR CLOSE.   FIFTH RD.
GLOUCESTER RD.   GREENHAM RD (cf. *Greenham Lane* 1677 *PubLib,
v.* 247).   HOWARD RD.   KENNET RD.   KINGSBRIDGE RD.   KING'S
RD.   LIVINGSTONE RD.   LONDON RD (in Newbury 10 a document of
1550 is cited which refers to 'the King's high waye, called Harrow Waye,
leading from Newbury to Reddinge'; the name is possibly transferred from
the ancient road called Harrow Way, some miles south of this).   MARKET
ST.   MARSH LANE AND RD (*Merschlane* 1376–7 *RentSur, La Mershelane*
1439–40 *ib,* cf. *le Mersshe de Neubury* Hy 6 *RentSur,* common called the
Marshe 1564 *Windsor, Newbury Marsh* 1761 Rocque, *v.* mersc).   MILL
LANE.   NEWTOWN RD (*Newton Lane* 1761 Rocque, leading to Newtown
Ha).   NORTHBROOK ST (*Northbrokstret* 1420–1 *RecOffCat, Northbroke-
strete* 1506 *Windsor, Northbrook Street* 1564 *ib,* 'street north of the brook',
i.e. the R. Kennet).   NORTHCROFT LANE AND TERRACE (*v. infra*).
OLD NEWTOWN RD.   OXFORD RD AND ST.   PARK TERRACE AND ST.
PELICAN RD.   PEMBROKE RD.   PORCHESTER RD.   PRIORY RD.
QUEEN'S RD.   RAILWAY RD.   ROCKINGHAM RD (possibly connected
with the f.n. *Rochynham infra* 261, but a number of Newbury streets are
named from towns in other counties and this may be from Rockingham Nth).
ROPE WALK.   RUSSELL RD (a place called *Russell* is mentioned in *Mul-
strete* Hy 6 *RentSur,* probably from the surname).   ST. JOHN'S RD.
SALCOMBE RD.   SHAW RD AND CRESCENT.   STANLEY RD.   STATION
RD.   WATERLOO TERRACE.   WEST MILLS.   WEST ST (*Weststrete*
1439–40 *RentSur,* it is west of Northbrook St).   WESTBOURNE TERRACE.
WHARF RD AND ST.   WINCHCOMBE RD.   WOODSPEEN TERRACE.
YORK RD.

The following street-names have not been identified: *Mery Hill* 1548–9
RentSur, Merryhill, Merry Hill Street 1739 *RecOffCat, Merry Hill* 1761
Rocque (a street), *v.* myrge 'pleasant', hyll; *Mortemereslane* 1439–40
RentSur, Roger de *Mortimer* had property in Newbury 1316 FA; *Mulstrete*
1439–40 *RentSur, v.* myln; *Sandleford Lane* 1661 *Windsor, v.* 247–8; *Shepe
Strete* 1548–9 *RentSur; Suttelane* 1376–7 *RentSur, Sottylane* 1499 *Windsor,
Satir Lane* 1564 *ib, Sotye Lane* 1661 *ib.*

GOLDWELL, *Goldewell'* 1376–7 *RentSur, Goldewell* 1542 *ib, watercourse called Goldwell, Gowldwell* 1570 *Dep, water course in Spineham-
land called goldwell* 1571 *ib,* 'stream or spring where golden flowers
grow', from OE golde and w(i)ella. For another example of this
name *v.* O 224–5.

NORTH CROFT, NORTHCROFT DITCH AND LANE, *Northcroft* 1252–5
FF, le Northcrofte 1439–40 *RentSur,* Hy 6 *ib, Northcrofte mead* 1567
Windsor.   NORTHCROFT LANE is *Northecroft lane* Ed 6 *LRMB,
Northcroft Lane* 1745 *ArchJ* 17, and possibly *Northcrosse lane* 1547

LRMB, *v.* norð, croft. This was the town meadow, and is north of the R. Kennet; presumably the meadow was named from a croft or enclosure here.

SPEENHAMLAND, *Spenamland'* 1220 Cur (p), *Spenhamelund'* 1225 FineR, *Spenehemelonde* 1241–59 AD, *Spenhamelond* 1243 Cl, *Spinhamland'* 1257 FineR, *Spenhamlond* 1275 Fine, 1374 Ipm, *Spenehamelond* 1276 Cl, *Spemhamlonde* 1285 ib, *Spenhemelond* 1295 Ipm, *Spenhamlonde, Spenehamlunde* 1297 ib, *Spenhemelonde* 1305 Fine, *Spenhamlaund* 1366 Pat, *Spinhamland* 1761 Rocque. The final el. is probably land 'property, estate', though the two early forms in -*lund'*, -*lunde* are unusual; hence 'land of the people of Speen', *v.* Speen (266) and hǣme.

ULVRITONE (lost). This is the name of the manor in DB, in which Newbury was included. The extent of the manor is discussed in VCH I, 313, 363, and IV, 134–5. Possibly an -*ingtūn* name with pers.n. in *Wulf-* as first el., but the p.n. does not occur again, and the DB form is insufficient for a safe etymology. By a strange coincidence there is a lost DB manor in Db called *Ulvritune*.

BARTHOLOMEW FM, *Bartilmewes in Newbury* 1547 *LRMB*, *Bartholomew Farm* 1567 *Windsor*, cf. Bartholomew St *supra* 257. The Hospital of St. Bartholomew is mentioned 1215 Ch and 1297 Cl. An account of its buildings is given in VCH IV, 132–3.   BRICKKILN COPSE, *Brick Kiln Close* 1840 *TA*.   CASTLE HOUSES, *Castle Inn* 1817 OS, not near Newbury Castle, which was south of R. Kennet.   CITY, a suburb, *v.* 284.   CORPORATION CLOSE.   DERBY ARMS P.H.   EAST FIELDS, *Estfeld* 1247–8 FF, *Le Estfeld* 1439–40 *RentSur*, *v.* ēast, feld, and cf. West Fields *infra*.   EYLES'S BUILDINGS.   FALKLAND FM AND LODGE, the Falkland Memorial is marked on 6″ map.   THE FOLLY, *The Folly Mead* 1840 *TA*, *v.* folie.   THE GORSE.   GUN P.H.   HAM BRIDGE, MARSH AND MILL, *Ham Marshe, Hame Marsshe, Ham Bridge, Le Ham Mille* 1547 *LRMB*, *Ham Mill, Ham Marsh* 1761 Rocque, *v.* hamm 'riverside meadow'.   HAMBRIDGE FM, HAM LOCK AND MANOR, near preceding.   THE LAWN. LOWERWAY FM, LOWER WAY LANE.   MARLBOROUGH HO. MONKEY LANE, 1761 Rocque.   ORMONDE HO.   PRIORY COTTAGES, probably named from Sandleford Priory 247–8.   REDFIELD HO AND COTTAGES, *Red Field* 1761 Rocque.   ROKEBY ARMS P.H.   SAND-

PIT HILL.   SPEEN CT.   WARREN COPSE, FM AND LODGE, *Warren Ground* 1840 *TA*.   WASH COMMON AND HILL, *Le Weshe, Le Este Comen als Le Washe, Le Washe Water* 1547 *LRMB, The Washe Lane* 1604 *Windsor, Wash Lane, Newbury Wash* 1761 Rocque. NED *wash* sb 7c 'a low-lying tract of ground, often flooded, and interspersed with shallow pools and marshes'.   WEST FIELDS, *Westfeld* 1252–5 *FF, Le Westfeld* 1439–40 *RentSur*, cf. East Fields *supra*.   WEST MEAD.   WHITE HORSE P.H.

The following house-names are shown on the 6″ maps in Newbury: ANDOVER HO, BATTLEDENE, BURLINGTON, CHERITON, DALRIADA, EDGECOMBE, THE FIRS, GLENDALE LODGE, GORSELANDS, THE LIMES, THE MOUNT, OAKDENE, PARK HO, PORTELET, SPRINGHURST, TETFIELD.

FIELD-NAMES

The principal forms in (*a*) are 1840 *TA*; early forms dated 1240–1, 1247–8, 1250 are *FF*, 1376–7, Hy 6, 1439–40, 1453, 1458, 1542, 1548–9, 1559, 1564–5 *RentSur*, 1540, 1567, 1586, 1593, 1619, 1661, 1715 *Windsor*.

(*a*) Baloon Mead; Barn Close and Ground; Black Stream Nursery; Camp Close (cf. *Campeden* 1376–7, *Campedene* Hy 6, identical with Campden Gl, *v.* camp, denu and Introd); Clay Close (cf. *Cleypyttes* 1453, *Cleyputtes* 1458, *Le Cleyputte, Le Clayepytts* 1542, *Cleye Pits* 1564–5, *v.* clǣg, pytt); Cow Fair Close; Crabtree Ground; The Crookspasture; Doctors Commons; Drapers Pightle (*v.* pightel); Garbage Furlong; Garden Close; Gravel Pit Furlong; Great Ground; Head Lands (*v.* hēafod-land); Hill Ground, Hilly Ground; Hog Trough; Home Mead; Horse Fair Close; Little Pightle; Malm Mdw Furlong, Malm or Lower Furlong (*Le Malme* Hy 6, 1439–40, *The Malme* 1593, *Malme or Mam Furlong* 1619, *v.* m(e)alm 'sand, sandy or chalky soil, soft stone'); The Marsh (near Wash Common); Mouse Furlong (*Musfurlong'* 1247–8, *Mussefurlonge* Hy 6, 1439–40, *v.* mūs); Picked Mead (*v.* pīced); Pig Trough Ground (cf. Hog Trough *supra*); Pond Close and Fd; Side Land Ground (*v.* 282); Slip (*v.* slipe); String Mdw (*v.* 282); Thrift Road Furlong (*Le Frithe* Hy 6, *The Frith* 1567, *Frythe Gate* 1593, *Frith Gate* 1619, *v.* fyrhð); Trundle Hill 1817 OS (also 1761 Rocque, *v.* trendel); Tydhams (*Tydeham* 1240–1 (p), Hy 6, 1439–40, *Tudeham* 1247–8 (p), *Tydhams* 1567, 'Tydda's hamm'); Water Mdw.

(*b*) *Bakehous* 1439–40 (a building where bread was made); *Bassotesmede* 1376–7 (*v.* mǣd, first el. the surname *Bassett*); *Bekelyscroft* 1376–7 (*v.* croft, first el. possibly a surname from Beckley O); *Brodegates* Hy 6, *Broad Yeate Mead* 1715 (*v.* brād, geat); *Brodemede* 1376–7 (*v.* brād, mǣd); *Bull's Close* 1661, 1715, *Bull Close Meadow* 1715; *Burgesye* 1453, *Burgs* 1559; *Castlemede* 1570 *Dep* (*v.* VCH IV, 133, for Newbury Castle); *Cattes Barn* 1548–9; *Le Conyngre* 1542, *The Coninger* 1564–5 (*v.* coninger); *Croune Mead* 1715; *Culuerhescrofte* 1458, *Culverhouse Piece* 1567, *Culverhouse Close* 1619 (*v.* culfre); *Dernefordesale* 1376–7, *Dernefordyshale* 1453, *Dernefordeshale*

1458 ('nook by the hidden ford', *v.* derne, ford, h(e)alh); *Dukes Meade* 1570 *Dep*; *Le Est Barre* Hy 6, 1439–40 (*v.* ēast, barre); *Estbury* 1458 (*v.* ēast, burh, possibly 'land east of the borough'); *Le Estende* 1542, *East End* 1564–5 (*v.* ēast, ende[1]); *Est Yate* Hy 6 (*v.* ēast, geat); *Farnesmor* 1376–7 (*v.* mōr, first el. apparently fearn, in the gen.sg., cf. Farnsfield Nt 163); *Fenchamlonde* Hy 6; *The Fludgates* 1567; *Gorford* Hy 6, *Garford* 1439–40, *Garfordes Furlong* 1567 ('dirt ford', *v.* gor, ford); *Goderd Londs* 1564–5; *Hammell'* 1250 (p) (apparently *hamel* 'hamlet', found also in a street-name in Oxford, O 39); *Hockhouse* 1548–9; *Le Hokes* Hy 6, 1439–40, *Lytle Hoke Meade* 1564–5 (*v.* hōc); *Horspolefeld* 1376–7, *Horspole* 1453, *Horsepolemede* 1458, *Horsepolefild(e)* 1542, *Horsepole* 1559, *Horse Poole* 1564–5 (self-explanatory); *Hurlebat* 1376–7 (presumably *hurlbat*, first recorded in NED c. 1440, a term for some kind of club; it may also have been a sport and the p.n. could refer to a place where it was played); *Kill-hill* 1567 (*v.* cyln, hyll); *Kings Ditch* 1567, 1619; *Lamborne Waye* 1542; *Langecroft* 1247–8 (*v.* lang, croft); *Leycestre* 1376–7; *Lott Meade* 1548–9 (*v.* hlot); *Lyllyshouse* 1542, *Lyllyes* 1559; *Maderlond* 1247–8 (*v.* mæddre, land); *The Manor Furlong* 1567; *Mantelysmede* 1453, *Mantelis Mede* 1458, *Mantellmede* 1542 (first el. the surname *Mantel*); *Marte Hay* 1548–9 (*v.* (ge)hæg); *Le Mores* Hy 6, 1439–40 (*v.* mōr); *Merewell* Hy 6, *Morwell* 1439–40; *Mylysmede* 1453, *Myles* 1458; *Neleshull'* 1247–8 (*v.* hyll, first el. probably the surname *Neal*); *Nepylls Mede* 1540, *Nepills alias Nepits Mead* 1604; *La Neulond* 1329 Cl, *La Nywelond* 1329 InqMisc (cf. Newland 126); *The Pounde* 1567; *Le Punfolde* 1376–7, *Pynfolde* 1458, *The Pynfold* 1559, *The Pynfolde* 1564–5 (*v.* pund-fald, pynd-fald); *Pykehornescrofte* 1376–7 (*v.* pīc, horn, croft); *Quechemede* c. 1260 PubLib, 1376–7, *Quychemede* 1439–40 (*v.* cwice 'couch-grass', mæd); *Rekhey* 1453, *Reckey* 1458, *Le Racke Heys* 1542 (possibly an enclosure with a rack, or manger); *Robwoodes* 1567; *Rochynham* Hy 6, *Rokynham* 1439–40 (*v.* hamm and cf. Rockingham St *supra* 258); *Safforn Close* 1559 ('saffron close'); *Le Sitcheside* Hy 6 (*v.* sīc, sīde); *Le Stalls* 1376–7 (*v.* st(e)all); *Sytehylle* 1453; *Tanbridge, Tainbridge* 1548–9; *Three Burrows* 1761 Rocque; *Treneke* 1240–1 (p); *Tymme* Hy 6; *Le Warres* 1569 Ashmole; *La Wetelond'* 1247–8 (*v.* wēt, land); *Wodehaye* 1458, *Le Woode Heys* 1542 (*v.* wudu, (ge)hæg); *Le Worthye* 1542, *The Worthe* 1548–9 (*v.* worðig, worð); *The Wythie Bed* 1586 (*v.* wīðig, bedd).

Peasemore

PEASEMORE

Praxemere 1086 DB

Pesemere 1166 (13th) RBE (p) *et passim* with variant spellings *Pesemera, Pesemer'*

Peselmera 1169 P, *Peselmere* 1187 ib

Pasemere 1229–30 FF

Pesmere 1385 Fine

Pusemere 1301 Ipm, 1316 FA, 1328, 1374 Ipm

Peysmer 1535 VE

The second el. is *mere* 'pond', the first *pise*, *peosu* 'pea', cf. Pusey Pt **2**. Ekwall (DEPN) suggests that the reference in this instance is to some wild plant resembling the pea. O.S. maps show a very small pond by the church.

GIDLEY FM ETC, *grove voc' Gydley, Gidleyfelde* 1547 *LRMB*. There may be a connection with *gyddan dene* 943 (c. 1240) BCS 789, on the E. boundary of Leckhampstead about three quarters of a mile away. The charter name means 'Gydda's valley', *v.* denu. This OE pers.n. is only recorded in p.ns. (*v.* DEPN s.n. Gedding). Gidley may mean 'Gydda's wood or clearing', in which case it is identical with Gidleigh D 439, *v.* lē(a)h.

BOLTON ROW. BUSHY LEAZE. CHALKPIT PLANTATION. CHAPEL WD. THE COTTAGE, *Cottage Piece* 1838 *TA*. DRAKE'S FM. EARL'S GROVE, 1838 *TA*. EBENEZER CHAPEL. EIGHT ACRE ROW, *Eight Acres* 1838 *TA*. FREELANDS, 1830 OS, 1838 *TA*. GIBBET COTTAGES. GIDLEY COPSE AND LANE, *v. supra*. HAILEY COPSE, LITTLE AND LOWER HAILEY COPSE, *Coppice called Haley* 1547 *LRMB*, *Hayley Copse* 1830 OS, cf. *Fern and Towne Hallyfelde* 1547 *LRMB*, *Hailey Field* 1838 *TA*, apparently identical with Hailey O 321, and several other names in O. The association with woodland suggests that an etymology 'wood with enclosures', first el. (ge)hæg, may be preferable to 'hay clearing' given in O and DEPN. HAILEY LANE. HEATH BARN, 1830 OS, *Peasemeareheth* 1547 *LRMB*, *The Heath* 1838 *TA*, *v.* hǣð. HUNHAM COPSE, 1830 OS. MANOR FM. MELL GREEN, 1830 OS, *Mill Green Piece* 1838 *TA*, possibly from a windmill; there is no stream. MUD LANE. PRINCE'S FM AND LANE. PRIOR'S SIDE AND WD, *Priors Woode* 1547 *LRMB*, *Priors Side* 1830 OS, from the Prior of Poughley, who was granted land in Peasemore in 1237 and in 1260–1 (VCH IV, 82). THE ROOKERY. ROUGHDOWN COTTAGES AND FM, *Rough Down Farm* 1761 Rocque, *Rough Down* 1838 *TA*. SHEEP LEAZE LANE, *Sheep Leaze* 1830 OS, 1838 *TA*, *v.* lǣs. WARRENDOWN ROW, possibly *weardan dune* 943 (c. 1200) BCS 789, cf. Worndown *infra* 263. WHITELANDS, probably *La Blanchetere* 1234–5 FF. WIDOW'S FM, *Widows Piece* 1838 *TA*. WILKINS'S BARN. WITNAM'S BARN AND COPSE, *virgate in Pesemere called Wycenam* (?*Wytenam*) 1288–9 Queen, *Wittenhams, Whytenhams, Wyttenhams* 1547 *LRMB*, *Wilnams Farm* (sic) 1761 Rocque, *Witnam* 1830 OS. This name and Hunham

Copse *supra* may contain **hamm** used (as in charter-bounds in this area) of a man-made enclosure, *v.* Pt **3**. First el. probably **hwīt** 'white'.

FIELD-NAMES

The principal forms in (*a*) are 1838 *TA*; early forms for which no date or source is given are 1547 *LRMB*.

(*a*) Barn Close; The Belchers; The Breach (*Litle Breeche, v.* brēc); Burland(s) (*Le Burne Landes, v.* burna, land); Collins Pit; Common Shot (*v.* scēat); Crabtree Piece; Cullimore Fd and Piece; The Down (*Peasemeare Downe v.* dūn); Drapers Piece; Ell Piece; Foot Path Fd; Ford Down Bottom; Ford Ground and Mdw; Frog Mdw (*Frogmede*); Gidley Hill (*v.* 262); Goodlands; Gravelly Fd; The Hearn (*Le Heron, Le Herron, v.* hyrne; *on þone ealdan hyrne weg* 948 (c. 1240) BCS 866, in the bounds of Stanmore, may be a road leading to this place); High Elms; Hill Common; Home Close and Mdw (*Le Home Close*); Horse Close; Kiln Close; Lilly Hill (*v.* Pt **2**); Mackerill Close; Middle Fd (*Le Midlefelde*); Picked Acres (*v.* pīced); Pit Piece; South Fd (*Southfelde*); Stockwell Piece; Town Plat (*v.* plat²); Wood Piece; Worndown (probably *weardan dune* 943 (c. 1200) BCS 789, in the bounds of Leckhampstead, *v.* Pt **3**).

(*b*) *Aysshelande* (*v.* æsc, land); *Le Comen Downe*; *Le Ferme Homefelde*; *Le Forge*; *Hamedone* 1329 Ch (*v.* dūn); *Herlesdun'* 1234–5 *FF* (possibly 'Herel's dūn'); *Hundegrave* 1329 Ch (*v.* hund, grǣf); *Le Netherclose*; *Le Northfelde*; *Le Overclose*; *Le Parsonage Barne*; *Pors Ferme* (*v.* 285); *Suston, Le Sutton*; *Suthleshe* 1234–5 *FF*, *Suthlye, Suley* (wood called) 1329 Ch, *Sowle* (*v.* sūð, lēah); *Le Westefelde*; *Le Wildewaye* (*v.* wilde, weg); *Wytecroft* 1329 Ch (*v.* hwīt, croft).

Shaw cum Donnington

SHAW

> *Sagas* c. 1080 France, *Essages* 1086 DB, *Shage* 1167 P *et freq* with variant spellings *Shaga, Shaghe, Shagh'* to 1327 *SR*; *Sages* 1186 P (p), 1231 (c. 1250) Bract, *Saghe* 1199 Hunter Fines *et freq* with variant spellings *Sagh', Sagh,* to 1275–6 RH; *Sagnes* 1203 P, *Shawes* 1241 *Ass* (p), 1343 Fine, *Sawe* 1242–3 Fees, *Shaue* 1284 *Ass*, 1363 Fine, *Schahe* 1294 *SR*, *Shagwe* 1306 Ipm

v. sc(e)aga 'small wood, shaw'. The final -*s* of a number of forms should probably be disregarded for the etymology, cf. Barnes Sr 11–12, Staines Mx 18–19.

DONNINGTON

    Deritone 1086 DB, *Derinton'* 1253 Cl
    Dunintona 1167 P, *Duninton'* 1215 ClR, 1220 Fees, *Dunynton* 1334 Ipm
    Doniton' 1229 Cl (p), 1235–6 Fees
    Dunyton', Dodynton', Dunyeton', Donygtone 1284 *Ass, Duniton'* 1294 *SR*
    Dunyngton 1300 Ipm, 1316 FA
    Donyngton 1300 Ipm, 1389 Ch, 1394 BM
    Dynynton 1307 Ipm
    Donynton' 1327 *SR*

'Estate associated with Dun(n)', *v.* ingtūn; identical with various Doningtons and several other Donningtons, for which *v.* DEPN. Some forms show Norman French confusion of -*n*- with -*r*-.

ANGEL'S HILL.   ASHPIECE COPSE.   ASH PLANTATION.   BRICK-KILN WD, *Brick Kiln Coppice* 1761 Rocque.   CASTLE INN. CASTLE HO AND WD, cf. *Castle Houses* 1817 OS, *Castle Mead* 1838 *TA*, *v.* Donnington Castle *infra*.   THE CEDARS.   THE COTTAGE. DALBIER'S MEAD.   THE DEAN, *Deane Landes* 1547 *LRMB, The Dean, Dean Field* 1838 *TA*, *v.* denu.   DOLMANS, *Dolmans Ground* 1838 *TA*.   DONNINGTON CASTLE, 1761 Rocque, *Denyton Castle, Don(n)ington Castle, Denington Castle* 1675 Ogilby, the Castle was built in the 14th cent.   DONNINGTON GROVE, *Le Grove* 1547 *LRMB*.   DONNINGTON HURST, HOLT AND LODGE.   THE DURNALS, *v.* Snelsmore Ho *infra*.   FAIRVIEW.   GRANGE FM, *Le Grange Ferme* 1547 *LRMB, Grange Field* 1838 *TA*; this was a virgate of land in Shaw which was sold to the Abbot of Waverley in 1199 (VCH IV, 90).   THE GULLY.   THE HAYES.   HIGH WOOD, 1761 Rocque, *Le Highwoode* 1547 *LRMB*.   HIGHWOOD VILLA.   HILIKA. HILL FM.   HILL'S PIGHTLE.   HONEY BOTTOM, HONEYBOTTOM FM, *Honey Bottom Ground* 1838 *TA*, *v.* hunig, botm.   IVY COT-TAGES.   KILN COPSE.   LOVE LANE.   MERLEBANK.   MOUSE-FIELD FM, *Mousefeldes* 1547 *LRMB, Mousefield* 1761 Rocque, *v.* mūs, feld.   NEW FM.   NOTHING HILL.   PACKER'S COPSE. THE PRIORY, on the site of the Priory of Crutched Friars, *v.* VCH IV, 94.   SHAW BRIDGE, *Shawbridge* 1758 ArchJ 14.   SHAW DENE HO, *Shaw Dean Farm* 1830 OS.   SHAW HO AND MILL.   SMITH'S

CLOSE ROW.   SNELSMORE HO (THE DURNALS ON 6"), *Durnywells*
1547 *LRMB*, possibly 'hidden springs', *v.* d(i)erne, w(i)elle.
SOUTHCOTE.   SPOUT DITCH, *Le Spowte* 1547 *LRMB*, a branch of
the R. Lambourn followed by the parish boundary, *v.* spoute 'spout,
gutter, mouth of a water-pipe', which perhaps implies that part of
the stream had been encased in piping.   SWILLY COPSE, cf.
Swilly Ground in Bucklebury 160 and Swilly Pits in Hampstead
Norris 253.   WHITEFIELD FM, 1761 Rocque, *Whytefelde* 1547
LRMB, *v.* hwīt, feld.

FIELD-NAMES

The principal forms in (*a*) are 1838 *TA*; early forms for which no date or
source is given are 1547 *LRMB*.

(*a*) The Braids (*Bredes Copies, v.* brǣdu); The Breach (*v.* brēc); Common
Fd; The Cow Leaze (*Cowelease, Cowemede*); Day Mead (*v.* dey); The Dells;
Dry Mead; Fern Ground; Fortys, Little and Home (*v.* forð-ēg); Gravel
Hill (*Gravelhill Close*); Great Fd (*Greatefelde*); Great Ground; Grove Mead;
Heath Ground; Home Close (*Le Home Close*); Hospital Mead; Long Close
(*Longclose*); The Mealies; Mill Mead; Park Mead and Piece (*Le Parke Feld*
1547 *LRMB, Donningeton Parke* 1591 *DL, v.* VCH IV, 94); Parsonage Mead;
Pound Acre; Purgatory (*v.* 283); Red Farm Pightle; Rough Piece; The
Runaways; Rushy Mdw; Shaw Mead (*Shawe Mede and Woode*); Tanners
Pightle (*v.* pightel); Three Corner Piece; Vetch Close; The Warren; Water-
house Piece; Water Piece; West Fd (*Le Weste Felde*); White Ground.

(*b*) *Barney, Barneyclose, Le Barne Close; Beikpitacr; Le Beneclose, Bene-
crofte* (*v.* bēan); *Birds Grove; Blakdiche* (*v.* blæc, dīc); *Le Bonny Mede;
Brodecrofte* (*v.* brād, croft); *Le Bromycloses, Le Bromehill, Bromehill Close*
(*v.* brōm); *Le Bussheylez* ('bushy meadow', *v.* lǣs); *Chalkepit Yateclose;
Cleyclose; Cokerells Copis; Cornecroft* 1547 *LRMB, Cornecrofte* 1592 *RecOff-
Cat; Donnyngton Brige; Le Este Felde; Este Mede; Fursy Close* (*v.* fyrs);
Le Grasse Heyes; Gratten; The Hale Close (*v.* h(e)alh); *Hatche Piddell* (*v.*
hæc(c)); *Herlington Hethe* ('Arlington heath', *v.* 242); *Hetheyate Close, Heth
Yate* (*v.* hǣð, geat); *Hikmans Mede; Hokeyat* (*v.* hōc, geat); *Le Horsseley*
(*v.* hors, lēah); *Hychyn, Hichins* (*v.* heccing); *Inholmes* (*v.* innām); *Kings
Pidell* (*v.* pightel); *Lady Close* (*v.* hlǣfdige); *Lampeacrfelde* 1547 *LRMB,
Lamp Acre Field* 1696 *RecOffCat, Lampe Lande* 1548–9 *RentSur* (*v.* 285);
*Le Lane Close; Litlefelde; Longecrofte; Le Longelane; Longhedowne; Lords
Mede; Lotmede* (*v.* hlot); *Milkehill* (*v.* meoluc, hyll); *Le Millers House; Le
Milne Pounde; Le Ouer Copice* (*v.* uferra, copis); *Oxleaz* (*v.* lǣs); *Le Pite
Close; Pokelande, Pokelmede Grove, Pukland Barrs, Poklande Grove* ('goblin
land and mead', *v.* pūcel); *Le Pople Close, Popleyclose, Pop(p)ley Crofte*
(*v.* popel); *Pors Mede* (*v.* 285); *Prior's Grove* 1640 *RecOffCat* (this was part
of the Priory of Crutched Friars, *v.* 264); *Purtoke; Roughdowne; Le Safron
Close; Seuerall* (*v.* 282); *Le Shepehouseclose; Showte Mede; Smertes Lande
Smythes Barne; Somerlez* (*v.* sumor, lǣs); *Le Stone; Strowde Grene* (*v.* strōd);

Tudhill; *Le Welclose, Wellclose*; *Le Westmede*; *Le Westewoode*; *Weylandes*; *Whitleyfelde*; *Le Worthy* (*v.* worðig); *Wydemede* (*v.* wīd, mǣd); *Wynterburne Crosse* (*v.* 277).

Speen

SPEEN

Spene '821' (c. 1200) BCS 366, 1208 P *et freq, Chirchespene* 1445 AD, *Churchspene* 1460 AD, *Manor of Church Spene, otherwise called Spene* 1489 Ipm, *Churchespene* 1555 BM, *Speen als Church Speen* 1751 ArchJ 15
Spone 1086 DB
Spenes 1167 *et freq* to 1242–3 Fees, *Spienes* 1199, 1201 P, *Spenis* 1224–31 (c. 1280) S

There is an authoritative discussion of this name by Professor K. Jackson in *Britannia* I (1970), p. 79. Speen represents the *Spinis* of the Antonine Itinerary, but the English form cannot be derived directly from the Latin one. The latin name means 'at the thorn-bushes'. The English appear to have confused this (or the PrWelsh version of it) with an OE word which may be related to the recorded word spōn 'chip, shaving', which occurs in a number of p.ns.

Speen is mentioned in BCS 366 as the name of a wood—'silva integra quae dicitur Spene Pohanlech et Trinlech'. If there was an OE word derived from spōn, this may have been substituted for the Latin name by popular etymology because it was appropriate to the woodland which had apparently taken the place of the Roman settlement.

Professor Jackson points out that Ekwall's suggestion of an 'Old Welsh' **spian* must be disregarded; the word Ekwall had in mind was **sbiðad*, which does not suit.

Professor Löfvenberg comments that if the OE name is a derivative of spōn 'chip, shaving', perhaps also 'shingle', its OE form will have been *Spēne*, as is indicated by the charter form. It may have denoted a place (wood) where wood-chippings were left or shingles were made (cf. Spoonley Gl 2, 27). For the formation cf. OE **selte*, **sælte* 'salt-pit, salt-working' in Salt St, OE **sende* 'sandy place' in Send Sr (Sr 146).

BAGNOR, *Bagenore* 1086 DB, 1199 Cur (p) *et passim* with variant spelling *Bagenor'* to 1404 Fine, *Bag(g)enore* (p), *Bagenhore* 1241 *Ass*, *Baggenor'* 1247–8 FF (p), *Bag(g)enore* 1284 *Ass*, 'river-bank frequented by badgers', *v.* **bagga**, ōra. The first el. may be in the gen.pl. The village lies on the bank of the R. Lambourn.

MARSH BENHAM, *Bennahamme, (æt) Bennanhamme* 956 (c. 1240) BCS 942, *Bennanham* 960 (contemporary) BCS 1055, *Ben(n)eham, Benham* 1086 DB, *Benneham, Bennaham* Hy 1 (c. 1240) Abingdon, *Benham* 1160 P *et passim, Bennham* 1212 Fees, *Marsh Benham* 1761 Rocque, 1817 OS, 'riverside meadow belonging to Benna', *v.* **hamm**. The pers.n. cannot be the recorded OE *Beonna*, as BCS 1055 is a contemporary parchment. Except for Hoe Benham and Benham Burslot the settlements with this name are on the marshy N. bank of the R. Kennet. The other settlements are: BENHAM BURSLOT (Welford parish), *Benham Buslot* 1830 OS.   HOE BENHAM (Welford parish), *Holebenham* 1220 Fees, 1242–3 ib, *Hole Benham* 1235–6 ib, *Halebenham* 1242–3 ib, *Holbenham, Ole Benham* 1284 *Ass, Lobbenham* 1401–2 FA, *Hoobenham* 1547 *LRMB, Holt Benhame* 1619 *Dep, Hoe Benham* 1761 Rocque. The prefix is holh 'hollow'; the place lies at the head of a valley.   BENHAM VALENCE, *Estbenham* 1275–6 RH, 1284 *Ass, Benham Valences* 1284 ib, *Benham Valence* 1316 Ipm, 1327 *SR*, 1360 AD. The gift of the manor to William de *Valencia* is recorded 1251 Ch. *Est-* because E. of Marsh Benham *supra*. BENHAM LOVELL (lost), *Benham Lovell* 1385 Cl, 1427, 1432 Fine, 1619 *Dep*, 1665 *PubLib, Benhamlovell* 1453 Fine. The family of *Lovell* held the manor in the 13th cent. (VCH IV, 106).

WOODSPEEN, *Wodespene* 1275 Cl *et passim* with variant spelling *Wodespen'; Wode Spene* 1325 Cl, *Wodespeyne* 1316 Ipm, *Woodspene* 1316 FA, *Woodyspene* 1547 *LRMB*. The prefix is wudu 'wood', added to distinguish this settlement from the main village, which was known as *Church Spene* (*v.* 266).

THE ALDERS.   ALLOTMENT PLANTATION.   BACK WD, *Backwood Coppice* 1665 *PubLib(Clayton)*.   BAGNOR BRIDGE, BAGNOR MARSH, 1830 OS, BAGNOR WOOD, *Bagnor Copse* 1830 ib, *v. supra*.   BARNETT'S LOCK, *Barnetts Meadow* 1780 *EnclA*.   BELL MOUNT (near Five Bells P.H.).   BENHAM GRANGE, GRANGE FM.   BENHAM LODGE PLANTATION.   BENHAM MARSH FM, *Benham Mershe* 1547 *LRMB, Beneham Marshe* 1549 *ib, Benham Marsh* 1665 *PubLib(Clayton)*, 1761 Rocque.   BENHAM VALENCE PARK, *Beneham Parcke* 1547 *LRMB, Mannor and Park of Benham Valence* 1619 *Dep*, cf. 'Willelmo

de Valenc' — ad parcum suum de Benham' 1252 *Cl*, *v.* 267.
BERKELEY PLANTATION.   BRADFORD'S GORSE.   BRICKKILN WD.
BROOMCLOSE BORDER.   BROOM COVERT, *v.* brōm.   BURGHLEY.
CHAPEL ALDERS.   COKES PLANTATION.   COLLEGE COPSE.   COOK'S
FIRS.   COPSE FM.   DEAN WD, DEANWOOD, *Deane Woode*,
Denewood 1547 *LRMB*, *Deans Wood* 1817 OS, cf. William atte *Dene*
1327 *SR*, *v.* denu.   THE DISMALS, a small wood.   DRAYCOT
PLANTATIONS.   ELMORE HO AND PLANTATION, *Elmore, Elmore
Feild* 1591 *DL*, *Ellmore Field* 1780 *EnclA*.   THE FIRS.   FIVE
BELLS P.H.   FOLEY FM AND LODGE.   FURZE HILL, 1817 OS,
Furzen Hill 1780 *EnclA*, cf. Le *Furseys* 1547 *LRMB*, *Furssen Woodes*,
The Fursy Close 1549 *ib*, *v.* fyrs, fyrsen.   THE GABLES.   GRAVEL
HILL, cf Gravel Close etc. in f.ns. 269   GROVE FM AND RD,
Spene Grove 1547 *LRMB*, *The Grove* 1780 *EnclA*.   HOLMBY.
HOME FM.   JANAWAYS.   JUBILEE PLANTATION.   KNIGHT'S
FM.   LADY WELL.   LAMB'S PLANTATION.   MAGDALEN PLAN-
TATIONS.   MANOR FM.   MANOR HO.   MAY'S LANE.   MILK-
HOUSE RD.   MOUNT HILL, *v.* mont.   NALDERHILL COPSE, 1780
EnclA, *Nalder Hill in Benham Vallens heathe*, *Nalders Hill als Longe
Crosse* 1591 *DL*, *Nalder Hill* 1817 OS, *v.* atten, alor.   NALDERHILL
HO AND RD.   NEWTON'S LANE.   OAK COPSE.   OLDFIELD WD,
The Old Feild 1591 *DL*.   PEEWIT FM.   PLAIN PLANTATION, *v.*
plain, here 'a piece of flat meadowland'.   RACK MARSH, possibly
connected with *Rackehaies* in f.ns. 270.   RYOTT'S PLANTATION.
SCOTCH WD, 1817 OS, *Scotts Wood* 1591 *DL*, William *Scot* is
mentioned 1366 Pat.   SHEPHERD'S FM AND PLANTATIONS.   SHEP-
PARD'S COPSE.   SPEEN FM, HO, HOLT AND LODGE.   SPEEN HILL,
Spenehulle 1340 *RentSur*, *v.* hyll.   SPEEN MOOR PLANTATIONS,
Spene More 1547 *LRMB*, *Spene More*, *Spynne More* 1591 *DL*, *v.*
mōr.   SPRING WD.   STARVEALL PLANTATIONS, *v.* 283.   STOCK-
CROSS, 1817 OS, *Stok(e)crosse*, *Stokcrosse Close* 1547 *LRMB*.
TOOMER'S PLANTATION.   TOP SHRUB, a hill-top plantation.
WHITE LODGE.   WHITTLE COPSE, *Whyttellfilde* 1542 *RentSur*,
Whitlefeld, *Whiteleyfelde* 1547 *LRMB*, *Whittle Feild* 1591 *DL*, 1780
EnclA.   WICK WOOD, Le *Wyk(e)woode* 1547 *LRMB*, *Weeke Woode*
1591 *DL*. There was also a *Wikemede*, *Wykemede* 1340 *RentSur*, John
atte *Wyke* being mentioned in this reference, and *Wycroft* n.d. AD,
Adam de *Wika* being mentioned. There was probably a lost place
called *Wick*, *v.* wīc, wudu, mǣd, croft.   UPPER WOODSPEEN FM,
v. 267.   WORKHOUSE POND.   WYFORNE, *Wyvorns* 1547 *LRMB*.

FIELD-NAMES

The principal forms in (*a*) are 1780 *EnclA*; early forms for which no date or source is given are 1547 *LRMB*; those dated 1340, 1340–1, Hy 8 are *RentSur*, 1549 *LRMB*, 1591 *DL*, 1665 *PubLib(Clayton)*.

(*a*) Blasters Coppice (*Blasters* 1549, 1665); Boulters Cross Fd (*Bulters Crosse, Bolters Crossefeyld* 1591); Broad Close (*Brodeclose*); Castle Mdw (*Castelmede* 1340–1, *Castelmead* Hy 8, *Castell Meade* 1549, *Castle Meade* Jas 1 *SpecCom*, 1619 *Dep*, 1665, possibly named from Sham Castle in Hamstead Marshall, it was in the south-west of the parish, *v.* Pt **2**); Clay Pit Fd (cf. *Claye Crofte* 1591); Conigre (*v.* coninger); Cossiter Mdw (*Gossacre Mede, Gossatur Mede, Gossatre Mede* 1547 *LRMB, Coriter Meade, Coryter Meade* 1591, these forms show some resemblance to those for *Gorsetefeld* Hundred 232); Cow Leaze (*Le Cowlees* 1547 *LRMB, The Cowleaze* 1665, 1787 *Bodl, v.* lǣs); Edycroft Fd (*Idewcrofte, Idowe Crofte, Idyote Crofte*); Fields Coppice; Goose Plot; Gravel Close (*The Grauell Pittes* 1591, *Gravell Close* 1665); Harwell Close; Hatchett Mdw (*v.* hæcc-geat, it is not possible to connect this with (*on þæt*) *hæcget* 956 (c. 1200) BCS 942, *v.* Pt **3**); The Hook; Horsepool Fd (*Horspolefelde*); Isle of Wight Mdw (*v.* 284); Long Mdw; Lott Mdw (*v.* hlot); Marsh Furlong (*Mershefurlong, Le Marsshefurlonge*); Pitchlade (*Piksladesfeld* 1331–2 *AE, Pycheslade* 1340, *Pincheslad* n.d. AD, *v.* slæd, first el. uncertain); Speen Lawns (*Speen Lawn* 1761 Rocque, possibly identical with *Spenelayne, Spene Leyne* 1547 *LRMB, Spinnye Lane* 1591, *v.* leyne, launde); Speen Marsh (*Spenemarsshe*); Traitors Mdw; Whitchurch Close and Mdw (*Whitechurche*); Wickham Heath Common (*v.* 274); Woodspeen Marsh; Worly Marsh; Worthy Fd (*Le Worthy, Le Wurthy, Le Worthie* 1547 *LRMB, The Worth(e), The Worthey* 1591, *v.* worðig, other probable references to this place occur in Enbourne and Newbury f.ns.).

(*b*) *Barley Close* 1549; *Barneclose; Barreclose* (*v.* barre); *Barton' Crofte, Barton Close and Meade* (*v.* beretūn); *The Bayardes* 1591; *Bells Croft, Bellycrofte* 1549; *Beneclose* 1549 (*v.* bēan); *Benham Hethe* (*v.* 267); *Bidwell Close* 1549; *Blacke Moore, Blakehedge* (*v.* blæc, mōr, hecg); *Bradley Downe* 1549 (cf. Hamstead Marshall fields, Pt **2**); *Braycrofte* 1549; *Breche* n.d. AD, *Le Breche* (*v.* brēc); *Brodecrofte* (*v.* brād, croft); *Brode Waters Mede* 1549; *Burycroft* 1340–41, *Bury Acr* (*v.* burh); *Bushey Acr; Busshey Close* 1549; *Buttes Leaze* (*v.* butte, lǣs); *Bywestethewenewey* 1340 (possibly 'west of the two ways', *v.* twēgen); *Le Carte Sherde* (*v.* sceard); *Cattesflodesforlong* 1340 (*v.* cat(t), flōd, furlong); *Chalcrofte, Chalcrofte Corner* 1549; *Churchefield* 1340; *Clappender Iland* 1549; *Contemede, Countemede* 1340; *Cornes Mede; Court Bridge* 1591; *Le Dead Water; Deyes* 1445 AD; *La Doune* 1331–2 *AE* (*v.* dūn); *Drawe Crofte; Dudmills; Edith Crofte* 1591; *Estfeld* 1331–2 *AE, Le Este Felde* (*v.* ēast, feld); *Farme More* 1591; *Frebery Mead* 1752 *PubLib; Frogge Lane* 1591; *Gardinereslond* 1340 (from the surname *Gardiner* and land); *Giggs Pitts* 1549; *Godewynesyate* 1340 (*v.* geat), *Godewyns Mille* 1445 AD, *Goodwyns Mill and Meades* 1547 *LRMB, Goddines Mill Meade* (from the surname *Go(o)dwin*); *Goldyngham* 1340 (*v.* hamm); *Grenehill* 1547 *LRMB,*

The Greene Hills, The Grene Hill 1591; *Le Grene Lane*; *Grenelanemarsshe*; *Le Grene Wey*; *Gretes* (*v.* grēot); *Greybury Close*; *Hakkers Bridge* 1549; *Harefeldes*; *Heathe Close* 1591; *Hech(e)croft, North- and South-* 1340 (*v.* hiche); *Hedehulf* 1476 VCH IV; *Le Hethe* 1549 (*v.* hǣð); *Le Homefelde, Homeclose*; *Le Horseland Furlong*; *Ilemore, Ilemore Wood, Ylemore* (*v.* igil, mōr); *Le Kechyn Close* (*v.* cycene); *The Kell Crofte* 1591; *Lang Crofte*; *Le Long Acre*; *Longe Crosse* 1591; *Lordes Mede, Lordes Lake*; *Le Lye* 1547, *Lye Poole* (*v.* lēah); *Marshehouse Mede*; *Mathewes Lane*; *Le Mede Close*; (*on*) *meosbroces* (*ford*) 956 (c. 1200) BCS 942, (*on*) *meos broces* (*heafod*) 958 (c. 1240) BCS 1227, *Mersshebrokes Deane* 1547 LRMB, *Mesbroke Deane* 1550 LRMB (*v.* mēos, brōc, denu and Pt 3); *Le Middlefelde* 1547 LRMB, *The Middle Field* 1787 *Bodl*; *Midle Wood* 1665; *Mill Mede, Over- and Nether-*; (*copic' voc'*) *Newlands*; *Newmans Grove*; *Le Oldelond* 1331–2 AE, *Eldeland* n.d. AD (*v.* (e)ald, land); *Olmer Acr'*; *Olyuers Close* 1547 LRMB, *Olivers Woode* 1591; *Otecroft* 1340–1, *Oteclose* (*v.* āte); *Ouerclose*; *Ouermede* (*v.* uferra); *Parkfeld* 1331–2 AE, 1340, *Parkemead* Hy 8, *Le Parke Mede* 1549, *The Park, The Parke Mead, Upper Parkhill, The Park Lawnes* 1665; *The Parocke* (*v.* pearroc); *The Peaze Close* 1591 (*v.* pise); *Perygrove, Perrygrove* (*v.* pirige, grāf); *Pitt Close* 1591; *Le Pors Close, Pors Copies* (*v.* 285); *Queenshows* 1476 VCH IV; *Le Rackehaies* (the same name occurs in Newbury, and the two places may be identical, *v.* 261); *Reymede* (cf. Ray in Maidenhead 55); *River Furlong* 1787 *Bodl*; *Rok(e)ley Hills* 1547, *Ruckill Hills* 1591; *The Rowtie Close* 1591; *Schephousforlong* 1340, *Schepusberton, Schepyncberton* 1340–1 (*v.* scēap, hūs, beretūn), *Little Shepehouse* 1550 LRMB; *Shepe Acr'*; *Shillinge Valle* 1591 (possibly connected with *scilling hangran* 949 (contemporary) BCS 877, *v.* Pt 3); *Skittyshe Leighton* (*v.* lēactūn); *Somerlese* 1340 (*v.* sumor, lǣs); *Sorthwet Lande* n.d. AD; *Southward Acre* 1787 *Bodl*; *Spenehethe, Spene Mill*; *Steresclose*; *Stoke Crofte*; *Swiston' Diche*; *Thechingfeld*; *Le Thistellcrofte*; *The Tyle Close* 1591; (*on*) *Eoccenford* 956 (c. 1200) BCS 963, *Ukkefordysmede* 1476 VCH IV, *Ucford Meadow* 1591 (this name presents difficult problems, which are discussed in Pt 3; the charter-name is not certainly identical with the f.n. in Speen, but both mean 'ford on the R. Ock'); *Vicaredge Close* 1591; *Le Water Furlong, Le Water Mede*; *Weepingcross Closes* 17th and 18th *RecOffCat* (*v.* O 396) *Were Iland* (*v.* wer); *Westfeld* 1331–2 AE, *Le Westefelde*; *Westlese, Westmede* 1340–1, *West Mede* 1547 LRMB, *The Weste Meade* 1591, *Westmead* 1665; *Wey Close*; *Le Whitefeld, Whitecrofte* (*v.* hwīt); *Wymershe*; *Wynyerde* 1340 (*v.* wīn-geard); *Yonderclose*.

Stanford Dingley

STANFORD DINGLEY

Stanworde 1086 DB, *Stanford' Willelmi* 1220 Fees, *Stanford'* 1235–6 ib, *Staunford'* 1241 Ass (p), *Stamford' Cancelar'* 1242–3 Fees, *Staunford', Stamford' iuxta Bradef'* 1284 Ass, *Stanford* 1316 FA, *Staneford Deanly* 1535 VE, *Standford Dingley* 1744 ArchJ 16, *Standford* 1761 Rocque

'Stony ford', a common name which occurs several times in this county. Here it refers to a crossing-place on the R. Pang. Robert *Dyngley* appears in this connection 1428 FA. *Willelmi* from William de Stanford, who held land here in 1224–5 (VCH IV, 111). *Cancelar'* in 1242–3 is unexplained.

THE BUILDINGS.   BULL P.H.   COOK'S COPSE, *Cooks Acre* 1838 *TA*, *Cooks Wood* 1846 Snare.   COXLANDS.   THE FIRS.   GRAVEL COPSE, *Gravels* 1838 *TA*.   LITTLE HERN, *Hide and Hern* 1838 *ib*, *v.* hyrne.   LOCK'S MOOR, 1838 *ib*.   MANOR FM.   MAZELANDS COPSE, *Mazelands* 1838 *TA*, possibly from a turf maze, *v.* O 235. OXLEY'S SHAW, *Oxleys* 1838 *TA*.   PANGFIELD (Field Fm on 6″). QUILL COPSE.   RUSHDENS, *Rusdens* 1830 OS, *Rusden Ground and Hill* 1838 *TA*, cf. VCH IV, 112, 'there was a house called Rushdens in this parish in the 16th and 17th centuries'.   TANNER'S COPSE, *Tanners Wood* 1830 OS.   TIMBER COPSE, *Timber Wood* 1830 ib, 1846 Snare.   UPPERLANDS COPSE, *Upland Wood* 1830 OS, *Upper Lands Wood* 1846 Snare.

FIELD-NAMES

The principal forms in (*a*) are 1838 *TA*, except for those dated 1846, which are Snare.

(*a*) The Acre Piece; Andrews Hill; Barn Close; Bottom Piece; Chosley Fd; Common Mdw; Coppice Ground; Cottage Pightel (*v.* pightel, as elsewhere in this parish); Cow Leaze (*v.* læs); Cripses Pightel; Culver Croft (*v.* culfre); Ducketts Mdw and Pightle; Edgelands Copse 1846; Furze Hills; Freelands Copse 1846; Gate Piece; Gatewick; Great Fd; The Hall; Hay Croft; Hill Ground; The Hitch (*v.* hiche); Little Half; Mungy Fd (perhaps dialect *mungy*, used of soft, over-ripe fruit); Over Ground; Park, Lower and Upper; Pit Piece; The Pound; Sandy Acre; Several, Further and Hither (*v.* 282); Shepperds Pightle; Stablish Piece; Stile Piece; Water Lane 1846; West Moor.

(*b*) *Helises Grofue* 1281 BM.

Wasing

WASING

> *Walsince* 1086 DB
>
> *Wawesing'* 1186 P (p), *Wauesing* 1224–5 *Ass*, *Wawesenge* 1235–6 Fees, *Wausynge* 1316 FA
>
> *Waghesing, Waghesing'* 1220 Fees, *Wahesinge* 1242–3 ib
>
> *Wasinges* 1235–6 Fees, 1297 Pat

Wakesing', Wausing' 1241 *Ass, Waysingg', Wausingg', Waysing* 1284 *ib*
Wasinge 1242–3 Fees, *Wasing* Ed 6 *LRMB*

This name is unexplained. The evidence is clearly in favour of its being a singular name in -ing, and it may originally have been the name of the stream which flows from Wasing Wood to the Enborne. If so, it could be a stream-name of the same type as Wantage 17–18, Lockinge 13 and Ginge 10, in which the first el. is probably a derivative of a verb which describes the stream; there is, however, no verb on record which would explain the spellings. Ekwall (DEPN) suggests an -ingas formation from a word meaning 'ploughshare', but this is based on the incorrect statement that Wasing lies in a tongue of land between the R. Kennet and R. Enborne. The parish is to the south and east of both rivers, not between them, and the most distinctive feature of the topography appears to be the stream mentioned above.

BIRCH COPSE.   BREACHES GULLY.   DAIRY COPSE, *Lower Dairy*, *Upper Dairy Meadow* 1848 *TA*.   GARDEN PIECE.   HASSOCK COPSE, probably dialect *hassock* 'a wood usually of Scotch firs with much coarse, rank grass', *v.* 190.   HOWELL'S WD.   OLD WARREN COPSE.   PAICE'S GULLY.   SUNDAY'S HILL COPSE. WASING CORNER, FM, LOWER FM, LODGE, PARK, PLACE AND WD.

FIELD-NAMES

The principal forms in (*a*) are 1848 *TA*.

(*a*) Back Door Ground; Baileys; Home Ground; Knights Mdw (cf. Wickham Knights Bridge 229, in the adjacent parish of Woolhampton); Lawn Park, Lower and Upper; Lodge Lawn Park (*v.* launde); Mud Close; Picked Fd (*v.* pīced); Saw Pit Ground; Waterhouse, Waterhouse Mdw.

Welford

WELFORD

Weliford '821' (c. 1200), *Wælingford* '821' (c. 1240) BCS 366, (*æt*) *Welig forda*, (*to*) *Weligforda* 949 (contemporary) ib 877, (*æt*) *Weligforda* 956 (c. 1200) ib 963
Waliford 1086 DB, *Walifort, Waliford* Hy 1 (c. 1200) *ClaudiusCix*, *Wali(g)ford* c. 1200 *ClaudiusCix, Waleford'* 1284 *Ass*

Weliford' 1167 P, *Weleford'* 1178 ib (p), *Welif'* 1220 Fees, *Weliford*
1230 Pat, *Welleford'* 1272 Os, 1284 *Ass*, *Weleford* 1275–6 RH,
1284 *Ass*, *Weleforde* 1316 FA
Welford 1386 Fine

'Willow ford', from **welig** and **ford**. The place is on the R.
Lambourn. BCS 366 is spurious.

EASTON, *Eastune* c. 1180 (13th) Abingdon, *Eston'* 1220 Fees *et freq*
with variant spellings *Eston(e)* to 1401–2 FA, *Aston'* 1284 *Ass*, *Easton*
1761 Rocque, 'east farm', cf. Weston 274. This is probably the
Eastun of BCS 366, a spurious charter which confirms a number of
places to Abingdon.

HUGMAN'S WD, (*boscus de*) *Uggenham* 1313 (l.14th) *Chatsworth*,
Ogenham 1392–3 *RentSur*, *Huggenham* (*alias Henggenham*) 1342 (l.
14th) *Chatsworth*, *Hugnam Cop'* 1538 *RentSur*. Cf. *Hugman Field*
1837 *TA*. The second el. is probably **hamm**, which in this area
probably means 'woodland enclosure', *v.* Pt **3**; the first might be a
pers.n. *Ugga*, *v.* DEPN s.n. Ugborough.

ELTON

    Elfledestona c. 1130 Oxford Charters
    Alflintona 1220–32 Os, *Alfyntona*, *Alflynton'* 1272 ib
    Elphinton Ade et Galfridi 1220 Fees, *Elfintona* 1222 Os, *Elfington*
    (p), *Elfinton* 1275–6 RH, *Elfenton'* (p), *Elfeton'* 1284 *Ass*,
    Elfynton' 1297 CornAcc
    Elfeton', *Elfreton'*, *Elfleton'* 1241 *Ass* (p), *Elfreton'* 1242–3 Fees
    Ailfleton' 1244 *AddCh 10604* (p)
    Elflintona c. 1280 Os, *Elflynton* 1389 ib
    Elfton 1340 Cl
    (*molendinum de*) *Elstone* 1432 Os
    Elfyngton alias Aylton 1509–10 Os
    Elton Farm 1761 Rocque

v. **tūn**, **ingtūn**. The first el. is a pers.n., but it is difficult to say
which. Dr O. von Feilitzen suggests that the base was OE **Æðel-
flǣdingtūn*, the earliest spellings having -*es*- by analogy with other
p.ns. formed from a masc. pers.n. and **tūn**.

OAKHANGER HO, *Akhangre* 1219 *FF* (p), *Akhanger* 1238–9 *ib* (p),
Akhengre, *Hakangre*, *Okhangre* 1241 *Ass* (p), *Okhangre* 1315 Pat,

1327 *SR*, 1332 Ipm (p), 1417–18 ObAcc, *Oakhanger* 1761 Rocque, 'oak wood on a slope', *v.* āc, hangra. Formally this might be the unidentified DB *Acenge* (cf. DB *Hertange* for Hartanger K), but the identification is very doubtful, as *Acenge* was in Thatcham Hundred, and Welford was in Rowbury.

ROOD HILL, *Rodehull'* 1241 *Ass*, 'hill with a cross', *v.* rōd². The reference may be to a crucifix or to a gallows.

SOLE FM, 1806 *RecOffCat*, *The Sole* 1550 *LRMB*, 1761 Rocque, *v.* sol 'miry place', used of a wallowing place for animals, cf. Grazeley 166. This is probably a shortened form of the name *Blakesole* 1243 (m.14th) *Lyell*, 1243–4 *FF* (p), which is identical with Blakeshall Wo 257, *v.* blæc.

WESTON, *Westun* 1086 DB, *Westuna* Hy 1 (*c.* 1200) *ClaudiusCix et passim* with variant spellings *Weston*, *Weston'*; 'west farm', cf. Easton 273.

WICKHAM, *Wicham* '821' (c. 1200) BCS 366 (a spurious charter), 1167 P *et freq* with variant spellings *Wickham*, *Wycham*; *Wikeham* 1550 *LRMB*. *v.* Wickham Bushes 24. No actual Roman buildings appear to be on record here, but the 6″ map marks 'Roman Coins found' and 'Roman Pottery and Coins found' on either side of the Roman road, very close to Wickham, *v.* also *Medieval Archaeology* XI (1967), p. 89. *Capell de Wykeham*, *Capell' de Wickham* and *Wykehamhill* are mentioned 1550 *LRMB*.

ALDER'S COPSE.   BARN COPSE, *The Barne Groue* 1550 *LRMB*, *v.* grāf.   BAYDON RD, this is the Roman road called Ermine Street, a stretch of which is named from Baydon W, through which it passes. BENHAM BURSLOT, *v.* 267.   BENHAM BORDER, GRANGE AND FM, *v.* 267.   BLINDMAN'S BORDER.   BOARD LANE.   BREACH BARN, *Le Breache* 1550 *LRMB*, *v.* brēc.   BUCK'S COPSE, *Bucks Field Bottom* 1837 *TA*.   EASTON COPSE, *Easton Grove* 1830 OS, *v.* 273. ELTON LANE, 1830 ib, ELTON WD, *v.* 273.   FIELD'S COPSE, 1830 OS.   FIVE BELLS P.H.   FRANCIS COPSE.   GLEBE FM.   GREY'S COPSE, 1830 OS, *Grays*, *Grays Close* 1837 *TA*.   THE GROVE, GROVE BORDER, *Le Groue*, *The Groue Close* 1550 *LRMB*, *Grove Corner* 1830 OS, *Grove Barn Hill*, *Grove Corner and Field* 1837 *TA*, *v.*

grāf.   HALFWAY, HALFWAY FM AND P.H., *Half way House* 1675
Ogilby, *Halfway House* 1761 Rocque; it is approximately half-way
between Newbury and Hungerford.   HARROD'S BARN AND BORDER.
HELL PIT.   HIGHWOOD COPSE, *Hyethwood Cop'* 1538 *RentSur*,
Le High Wood, *Le Hiewood Groue*, *The Highwood Coppes* 1550
LRMB, v. hēah, wudu and copis; the last el. is frequent in this
parish.   HOE BENHAM, HOE BENHAM LANE, v. 267.   HOME
FM, *Home Close* 1550 *LRMB*, *Home Close and Meadow* 1837 *TA*.
KING'S BARN.   MANTCLOSE BARN AND COPSE, *The Man Close(s)*
1550 *LRMB*.   MILTON LODGE.   NEW BARN.   NEWGROUND
BORDER.   NINNOCK'S BORDER, *Nynehoks*, *Nyne Hokys*, *Le Nyne-
hokis* 1550 *LRMB*, *Ninnicks Ground* 1837 *TA*, apparently 'nine
hooks', v. hōc.   PAINE'S COPSE.   POUND'S BORDER.   QUEEN'S
PLANTATION.   RED HO.   THE ROOKERY.   ROYAL GROUND
BORDER.   RUBBISH BORDER, *Rubbish Ground* 1837 *TA*.   RYE-
LANDS BORDER, *Rylands* 1837 *TA*, v. ryge, land.   SCROGGIN'S
COPSE.   SHIRLEY'S COPSE.   SHOWELLS, *Showels* 1830 OS.
SOLE BORDER, COMMON AND PLANTATION, v. 274.   SOUTH BARN.
STOGDALE COPSE.   STONY CROFT.   TITHE BARN.   TULLOCK
FM, 1761 Rocque, TULLOCK BORDER AND BOTTOM.   WADLING'S
BORDER.   WELFORD FM, 1830 OS.   WELFORD PARK, 1830 OS,
The Park 1761 Rocque, 1837 *TA*.   WELFORD WDS, 1830 OS.
WESTON FM AND MILL, v. 274.   WICKHAM GREEN, 1761 Rocque,
WICKHAMGREEN FM, v. 274.   THE WILDERNESS, 1837 *TA*.
WOODLANDS BARN.

FIELD-NAMES

The principal forms in (*a*) are 1837 *TA*. Early forms for which no date or
source is given are 1550 *LRMB*; those dated c. 1180 (13th) are Abingdon,
c. 1225–30, 1313, 1342 *Chatsworth* (l.14th), 1374, 1392–3, Hy 6, 1538 *Rent-
Sur*, 1662 *PubLib(Clayton)*.

(*a*) Barn Close (*Barne Close*); Bells Mdw; Birch Close; Black Close; The
Blackney Piece; Blacksmiths Mead; Blondy Mdw; Bottom, Long, Middle
and Upper (v. botm); Broad Close (*Brodeclose*); Broom Fd (cf. *The Brome
Close*, v. brōm); Burrough Fd; Butters Piece; Cockle Croft (v. coccel);
Coppice Close (*Coppes*); Cox Hill, North and South; Cunnygaw Hill (*Ye
Conygree* 1662, v. coninger); Dean Close (*The Den Close*), Dean, Long, Little
and Great (*The Long Deane*, v. denu); Door Close; Dry Mdw; East Fd
(*Le Estfelde*); Farm Ground and Mdw; Furze Ground; Gravel Close (*The
Grauell Close*); Gravel Pit Lot; Green, Little and Middle; The Grubbed
Ground (v. 281); Haycot, Haycot's Piece; Hill Beans; Hog Plot; Holly
Bush; Inn Mdw (*Inmede, Inne Mede*, v. in); Jail Bird (v. 283); Key Close

(*Keiclose, v.* cǣg and Journal 1, 14); Kiln Ground; Kites Hill (*The Keites*); Lane Close (*The Leane Close*); Long Leach (*v.* lǣc(c)); Lime Tree Piece; Lot, Upper (*v.* hlot); Longwood Green; Luckeridge(s); The Marsh (*Mersshe* Hy 6 (p), *The Mershe, v.* mersc); Milk Close; Mill Close (*Mill Close,* cf. Ralph atte *Mulle* 1350 Pat, *v.* myln); North Fd (*Le Northfelde*); Old Lane; Old Peat Mdw; Old Sainfoin Piece (*v.* 282); Ox Leaze (*Oxlease* 1662 *v.* lǣs); Parkgate Marsh; Parsons Piece; Partridge Piece; Pear Tree Close; Pit Close (*La Pette* c. 1180 (13th), *Le Putte* 1392–3, *v.* pytt); Pond Plot; Pound Close; Red Lands; Red Lands Hill; River Pasture; Round Close; Sadlers Hill; South Croft (*Southcrofte*); South Fd (*The Southfelde*); Water Mdw (*Watermede*); Wernham Grounds (cf. Wernham Furlong in Kintbury, Pt 2); Western Bottom; Western Mdw; West Fd (*Le Westfelde*); White Close and Fd (*White Close, Whitefelde, v.* hwīt); Willow Bed Mead.

(*b*) *Andros Breche* (*v.* brēc); *Aucke Groue*; *The Beche Close*; *Brandies Mede*; *Brians*; *The Brode Downe, Brode Groue, The Brode Mede* (*v.* brād, dūn, grāf, mǣd); *The Broke Close*; *The Bryerye Groue* (*v.* brērig, grāf); *The Busshe Groue and Close*; *The Busshey Lez* (*v.* lǣs, the same f.n. occurs in Shaw cum Donnington 265); *Le Cattesmarshe, Cattesmershe Mede* (*v.* cat(t), mersc); *Chaldecote* Hy 6, *Chalcote Corner* (*v.* ceald, cot); *Chalkecroft Cop'* 1538, *Chalkcrofte, The Chalkecrofte* (*v.* cealc, croft); *The Claper* ('rough bridge', *v.* clapper); *The Cowe Close*; *Cowlese* (*v.* lǣs); *Depeclose*; *Donts Close*; *Downe, Greate and Litle* (*v.* dūn); *Est Mede* (*v.* ēast, mǣd); *The Ferney Close*; *The Furdermede* ('further mead'); *Fursy Lease Close*; *Galdcrofte, Gallcrofte* (*v.* galla, croft); *The Greate Mede*; *Grenche Slade* 1538 (*v.* slæd); *Hard Meade* 1662; *Hemparock, Hemperocke, Hem Downegroue, Hem Downe, Hemdowne Felde, Hemperock Felde* (probably 'border paddock and down', *v.* hemm, pearroc, dūn); *Le Hethe, The Hethe Close, The Hethe Hill* (*Brueria* c. 1180 (13th) (p), *v.* hǣð, bruiere); *Hill Crofte*; *The Hitchyng, The Hychine* (*v.* heccing); *The Home Mede, Homegroue*; *Horse Heyse, The Horse Mede, Horselees*; *Hulleacr'* 1374 (*v.* hyll, æcer); *Hurde Welle, Hurdwell Close, Howrdwell, Greate and Litle* (*v.* hirde, wielle); *Le Ilandis*; *The Inner Mershe*; *June Mede*; *The Kerdeclose*; *Kettis Close*; *Kytchine Close* (*v.* cycene); *The Landewe* (*v.* 282); *Lande Mede*; *Litle Downe*; *Le Litle Feld*; *The Litle Mede*; *The Litle Groue*; *Locklynche* (*v.* hlinc); *Long Close*; *The Long Groue*; *The Long Mede*; *The Malte Close*; *Martens Close and Groue*; *The Mawry*; *Mede Close*; *The More Mede* (*v.* mōr); *Morye Cop'* 1538; *The Nells*; *The Nether Close*; *Northclose*; *The Northe Groue*; *Le Northwode* 1392–3 (*v.* norð, wudu); *Okeland Cop'* 1538; *Okes* c. 1225–30 (*v.* āc); *Okes Coppes*; *The Over Close*; *Poghole* 1313 (*v.* hol[1]); *The Pounde* (*v.* pund); *Racke Heyse* (*v.* 261); *Rawlyns Grove*; (*on ðan*) *readan hane* 943 (c. 1240) BCS 789, *Redhone Cop'* 1538, *Coppies voc' Redhone* ('red stone', *v.* rēad, hān); *Ristone*; *Roundewell*; *Rugworth Cop'* 1538; *Russheparrock* (*v.* risc, pearroc); *Southdoune* 1342 (*v.* dūn); *Southwode* 1342 (cf. *Le Northwode supra*); *Le Stewe* (*v.* stewe); *Still Close*; *Le Stitche, Le Stittches* (*v.* sticce); *Stonan Coppies*; *Stonye Cop'* 1538; *Stuble*; *Sydweye* 1374 (*v.* sīd, weg); *Triks Worth*; *Walands*; *Webhey*; *Welclose*; *Welford Butts* (*v.* butt[2], butte); *Westclose*; *Westlande Mede*; *Le West Mede*; *Wewescrofte* 1374 (*v.* 282); *The Whe(a)te Close,*

Wdefold c. 1225–30 (*v.* wudu, fold); *Le Wood, The Wood Groue, Le Wood Grene; Yerden, Muchel-, Mildel-, Litel-* 1342 ('great, middle and little yard', *v.* micel, middel, lȳtel, geard); *The Yardes, The Yardes Close; The Younder Medowe, The Younder Yardes, The Yondre Grove, The Yonder Close*.

Winterbourne

WINTERBOURNE

Wintrebvrne, Wintreborne 1086 DB, *Winterburn*' 1178 P (p) *et passim* with variant spellings *Winterburn(e), Wynterburn(ia), Wynterburne, Wynterbourn; Wintreburn*' 1220 Fees, *Wynterburn' Danvers, Wynterburn' Mayn* 1310–11 *FF, Wynterburne Mayne* 1394 BM, 1412 FA, *Wynterborne Mayne, Wynterborne de Anvers* 1428 FA, *Wynterburne Mayne, Wynterburne Davers, Wynterburn Danvers, Wynterborn Gray, Wynterborn Mayn* 1476 AD, *Winterbourne Davers* 1752 ArchJ 15

'Stream dry except in winter', a very common name, for other examples of which *v.* DEPN. The place is also referred to in the phrase *Winterburninga gemære* 951 (16th) BCS 892, 'boundary of the people of Winterbourne'.

Before the Norman Conquest there were three manors in Winterbourne, which appear to have been united before the end of the 15th cent. The descent of these is discussed in VCH IV, 62–5. Winterbourne *Gray* is so called from the family of Sir Robert *Grey* of Rotherfield (O), who married into the family holding this estate in the early 14th cent. Winterbourne *Danvers* from the family of that name who had a large estate here in the 13th cent. The manor of Winterbourne Grey passed to William Danvers in the early 15th cent. Winterbourne *Mayne* from an owner whose Christian name was *Maen*, who died in 1260–1 seised of this manor. The site of the manor of Winterbourne Mayne was known as Bussock's Court (*infra*) in the 16th cent (VCH IV, 65).

BUSSOCK, BUSSOCK CT AND WD, BUSSOCK MAYNE, *Bussokke* 1394 BM, *Bussok(k)s, Bussok Homefelde* and *Mede, Bussocks Felde, Downe, Mede* and *Copice, Bussoks Copice* 1547 *LRMB, Bussocke Court* 1590, 1624 Moulton, *Bussock Court* 1752 *PubLib, Bushook* 1761 Rocque. Probably an OE *buscuc* 'place overgrown with bushes', from **busc** and **-uc**. A close parallel is *riscuc* 'place overgrown with reeds', from which Rushock Wo 255 is derived.

AZURE.   BLUE BOAR INN.   THE BUNGALOW.   THE ELMS.
THE FORD, 1830 OS, *Le Forde, Ford Close* 1547 *LRMB*.   HOP
CASTLE, 1830 OS.   KIMBER'S COPPICE AND POND.   LOWER FM.
MAPLEASH COPSE, *Mapleheys* 1547 *LRMB*, *Maplehay Copse* 1830 OS,
Maple Ash Piece 1840 *TA*, v. mapel, (ge)hæg.   NEW INN P.H.
NORTH HEATH, 1752 ArchJ 15, 1761 Rocque, cf. *Northhetche, South
Hethe* 1547 *LRMB*, John *atte Hethe* appears 1327 *SR*, v. hǣð.
NORTH HEATH FM.   PEBBLE LANE, cf. *Poppley Yate infra* 279.
PENCLOSE FM AND WD, *Penne Close, Copic' voc' Penclose* 1547 *LRMB*,
Penclose 1761 Rocque, *Penclose Fm and Copse* 1830 OS, v. penn².
PIT KING FM, *Pit Kings* 1840 *TA*.   POPE'S WD.   SNELSMORE
COMMON, v. 243.   VAUXHALL COPSE, *Vauxhall* 1840 *TA*, v. 284.
WARD'S COPSE, *Wards* 1547 *LRMB*.   WITHY COPSE, 1830 OS.
WYFIELD COPSE, *Wyvel Close, Copic' voc Wyvolds* 1547 *LRMB*, v.
Wyfield Manor Fm 235 and copis.

FIELD-NAMES

The principal forms in (*a*) are 1840 *TA*; early forms for which no date or source is given are 1550 *LRMB*.

(*a*) Boar Ground; Bottom Lot; Bow Croft (*Bowecrofte, v.* boga, croft); Breach, Old, Hither and Further (*Breche, Este et Weste, v.* brēc); Brokeless Piece; Broom Close (*v.* brōm); Chalk Pit Ground and Piece; Church Piece; Cinque Foin Piece (*v.* 282); Crabtree Ground; Crouch Hill (*v.* cruc¹); Great Fd; Great Lot; Green Hill; The Hales (*v.* healh); Hill Lot; Hilly Ground, Little and Great; Hitchen, Hitchin (*Le Hychyn, v.* heccing); Hollow Lot; Home Fd and Mead; Honey Bottom (*v.* hunig); The Hook (*Le Hoke, v.* hōc); Horse Leaze (*The Greate Horsseleez, v.* lǣs); Lay Close (*The Leyclose, v.* lǣge, clos); Little Lot; Longlands; Long Mdw; Lot Mdw (*v.* hlot); Lower Mdw; Malthouse Piece; Moor Acre; New Close (*Le Neweclose*); North Heath Common (*v. supra*); The Park; Parsons Lot; Penfolds; Picked Lot (cf. *Pikked Close, v.* pīced); Pig Pen Piece; Pond Close; Pot Style; Rollhouse Piece; Ruin Mdw (*Rewen, Rewande, Rewen Piddle*); Shepherds Fd; Silas; Water Mdw; White Close (*Le Wheteclose, v.* hwǣte); White Hill; Winstanley; Wood Lot Piece; Worridge Gate.

(*b*) *Ayssheclose, Aysshcrofte* (possibly identical with Ash Croft in Chieveley 244, *v.* æsc); *Barneclose, Le Barne Medowe*; *Battyscroft* (probably from the surname *Batty*); *Bechyn, Litle and Greate*; *Blakedyche* (*v.* blæc, dīc); *Bowds Corner*; *The Brodeclose*; *Busshycroft, Busshy Leaz* (cf. 265, 276), *Lez Busshes*; *Castel(l)holde*; *Churchefelde*; *Cowlease* (*v.* lǣs); *Crokdell, Crokwell Yat* (*v.* geat); *Davers Woode* (perhaps belonging to the *Danvers* family, *v.* 277); *Dongpot Close* (possibly *dung-pot* 'tub in which manure was carried', *v.* EDD); *Downe*; *Estebroke* (*v.* ēast, brōc); *Foxes Grove*; *Giffords Felde and*

Wood, Giffords Foxbury, Giffords Ponde, Gyffords Garden; *Le Grasseclose*; *Le Greate Barley Close*; *Le Grove* (*v.* grāf); *Harrys, Great and Litill*; *Haywards Wood*; *Hempeclose*; *Hethecrofte* (*v.* hǣð, croft); *Heynolds*; *Homeclose, Homecrofte*; *Kechyn Grove* (*v.* cycene); *Kings, Litle and Greate*; *Kings Copps*; *Le Lande*; *Litle Mede*; *Loke* (pasture called) 1234–5 *FF*; *Maffull Grove, Maple Grove*; *Marden Felde*; *The Medeclose, Le Medeplott* (*v.* mǣd); *Midlecrofte*; *Moreclose*; *Mylbanke*; *The Netherclose*; *Le Northfelde*; *Oteclose* (*v.* āte); *Le Overcrofte*; *Pereclose, Peremede* (*v.* peru); *The Pertaunce* (wood called); *Pidle, Greate and Litle, The Pidells* (*v.* pightel); *Pocoks* (coppice called); *Poppley Yate* (*v.* popel, geat); *Le Redd Lande*; *Romeys*; *Russheclose*; *Le Rye Close*; *Safron Close*; *Sengecrofte*; *Smythescrofte*; *Le South Felde*; *Stonemede*; *Threhampfeld*; *Watercrofte*; *Welcrofte*; *Whytefelde*; *Wood Crofte*.

Yattendon

YATTENDON

Etingedene 1086 DB, *Hetingedon'* 1177 P (p), *Yetingeden'* 1220 Fees, *Jetingedon'* 1223 Cur, *Yetingedene* 1224–5 *Ass* (p), *Etingeden'* (p), *Yetingeden'* (p), *Wetingeden'* 1241 *ib*, *Yetingeden'* 1242–3 Fees, *Etyngeden* 1258 Ch

Yetingden 1242–3 Fees (p), *Yetyngden* 1352 Pat

Gettendon' 1195 P, *Chetingdon* 1284 *Ass* (p)

Jatingden 1232 Pat (p), *Yattingden'* 1241 *Ass* (p), *Yatyngdon* 1253 Ipm, *Yatingden* 1252 Ch *et freq* with variant spellings *Yatingden, Yatyngdene* to 1348 Pat; *Yatinden* 1274 Fine (p), *Yatindene* 1316 FA, *Yatyndon, Yatendone* 1517 D Inc, *Yattington* 1574 Saxton, *Yaddington* 1813 *PubLibDoc*

Watindeden', Watingeden' 1235–6 Fees, *Iating(e)den'* 1241 *Ass* (p), *Yatingeden(e)* 1242–3 Fees, *Yattingeden'* 1272 Cl, *Yatingedon* 1273 Fine (p), *Yatyngeden'* 1327 *SR*

Probably 'valley of the people of Gēat', *v.* -inga-, denu, and cf. Eaton Sr 88. *Geatingas* could mean 'the dwellers by the gate', but no feature of the topography supports this. Alternatively, the pers.n. could be *Ēata*, with the development of prosthetic [j]. The village is on a plateau, and it can only be suggested that denu refers to the valley which rises from the R. Pang to this higher ground, immediately west of the village.

EVERINGTON HO

Eurinton' 1176 P, 1241 *Ass* (p), *Yeurinton'* 1220 Fees, *Effrinton'* 1241 *Ass* (p), *Eurinton* 1252 Ch

Euerinton' 1180 P (p), *Euerigton'* 1185 RR, *Everington'* 1247–8 *FF*, 1272 Cl, *Everington* 1761 Rocque

'Estate associated with Eofor', *v.* ingtūn.

AXE AND COMPASSES P.H.   BLACKGROVE COPSE, *Black Grove* 1830 OS, *Blackgrove Corner* 1844 *TA*.   BRICK CLOSE ROW, *Brick Close* 1844 *ib*, cf. Brick Yard 1830 OS.   BROADFIELD COTTAGES, *Broad Field* 1844 *ib*.   BUSHY COPSE.   CALVESLEYS FM, *Calvesleys* 1844 *TA*.   CLACK'S COPSE, 1830 OS.   CLAY LANE.   COSTARD'S COPSE, *Costards Wood* 1830 OS, *costard* is sometimes from cot-stōw. ENGLANDS, *England Field and Piece* 1844 *TA*.   EVERINGTON BARN, HILL AND LANE, *v. supra*.   GRAVEL PITS, GRAVELPIT COPSE. LARCH COPSE.   MANOR HO.   MANSTONE FM AND LANE, *Manstone* 1761 Rocque; Symo de *Manestune*, mentioned 1220 RSO in connection with a chapel at Sindlesham, may have come from here, but he is perhaps more likely to have derived his surname from one of the better-documented places called Manstone in Do, K and YW. The name means 'Man(n)'s farm'.   MUMSGROVE COPSE, *Mums Grove* 1844 *TA*.   OAKEN COPSE, 1830 OS.   OLD PARK.   ROW PIT, *Rowpit Ground* 1844 *TA*, *v.* rūh 'rough'.   WITHY COPSE, cf. *Withey Close* 1844 *TA*, *v.* wīðig.

FIELD-NAMES

The principal forms in (*a*) are 1844 *TA*.

(*a*) Ashampstead Lawn (*v.* launde); Barn Spring; Birch Plat (*v.* plat[2]); Bowling Alley Close; Burnthill Allotment; Catherine Close; Church Mdw; Coppice Ground; Culvert Close; Dove House Close; Gravel Close (not near Gravelpit Copse *supra*); Green Ditch; Grove House Close (*Grouehouse* 1517 D Inc, *v.* grāf); Hillberry; Hillbottom; House Park; Long Ground; Pightle (*v.* pightel); Meal Close; Middle Lawn; The Moor; Oak Field Lawn (*v.* launde); The Park, Park Fd; Picketts (*v.* pīced); Pitfields; Place Mead; Pound Piece; Row Court; Rush Plot; Sandy Hill; Slow Pightle (*v.* pightel); White Close.

(*b*) *Braiesgrove* 1348 Cl (*v.* grāf, first el. probably a surname from Bray 43–4); *Lampe Acre* 1548–9 *RentSur* (*v.* 285).

GLOSSARY OF SOME TERMS IN MINOR NAMES AND FIELD-NAMES

The following terms are discussed here because they are not included in Elements:

cut, ModE, a piece of land, possibly one assigned by lot (O 438). Occasionally in f.ns., e.g. Broad Cut, Stone Cuts (Thatcham).

drift, ModE, a similar term to drāf, but only noted in modern names. Occasionally in minor names and f.ns., in such terms as Drift Road, Driftway.

grub(s), grubbed, grubbing, ModE, probably referring to land which has been cleared of trees or weeds (O 448). Common in f.ns., e.g. *Grubbs* 1791–2 in Bucklebury, Grubbed Coppice in Aldermaston, *Grubbinge Mead* e. 17th in Winnersh.

handpost, ModE, 'sign-post'. Occasionally in minor names and f.ns., e.g. Handpost Fm in Swallowfield, -Gully in Greenham, -Pightle in Winnersh.

Lammas, ModE, referring to land which was under particular cultivation till harvest and reverted to common pasture from Lammastide till the following spring. Occasionally in f.ns., e.g. *Lamas Piddell'* 1606 in Binfield, Lamas in Windsor.

lanket, ModE, dialect term for a long, narrow field, Lankets (f.n.), Chieveley.

rainbow, ModE, referring to fields where the ploughing follows a curving boundary. (The) Rainbow, Burghfield, Sandhurst.

reille, ME, 'fence, railing' (Db 746). In minor names, Bear's Rails in Windsor (from 1607), Snaprails in Sandhurst (from 1613), Overall Copse in Bucklebury (from 1791–2), 19th-cent. f.ns. in Brimpton, Shinfield, Finchampstead, and two earlier f.ns., *Rayles Lane* 1641 in Wokingham, *The Rayles* 1607 in Sunninghill. Bear's Rails in Windsor is the name of a small, rectangular earthwork. All the names are in wooded country.

roundabout, ModE. The Roundabout, Winnersh, and occasionally in f.ns., where the forms include The Roundabout, Roundabout(s). The meaning probably varies from name to name. The Roundabout in Winnersh is a piece of land almost surrounded by lanes. Other examples may refer to a field surrounded by a wood, or a field with a clump of trees in the middle (O 440).

sainfoin, ModE, common in O f.ns. (O 464), but very rare in Berks. Cf. Sanfoin Hill Reading, Sainfoin Fd Bradfield, Old Sainfoin Piece Welford. Cinque Foin Piece in Winterbourne probably refers to sainfoin, but it is uncertain whether sainfoin or the weed cinquefoil is referred to in Cinquefoie Ground, Ufton Nervet. Lucerne is another crop referred to occasionally in f.ns., e.g. Lucerne Piddle Barkham, Lucern Mdw Thatcham.

several, ModE, referring to land in private ownership, especially enclosed land as opposed to common land. F.ns. in Hampstead Norris (1622–3), Pangbourne (1548), Remenham (*TA*), Shaw cum Donnington (1547), Stanford Dingley (*TA*).

sideland, ModE, the headlands of a ploughed field. Side Land Ground (f.n.), Newbury.

sling, ModE, 'a long, narrow field, a strip of land'. F.ns. in Bradfield and Chieveley. **slang** (discussed by J. McN. Dodgson, *Notes and Queries*, Spring, 1968), f.n. in Winkfield.

smoke, ME, referring to land held by payment of a money-tax in place of tithewood. Occasionally in f.ns., e.g. Smoke Acre Piece in Blewbury, Smock Acre and Pightle in Bucklebury, Smoke Furlong in Cholsey, *Smoke Acre* (1596) in Reading.

string(s), ModE, a long, narrow strip, often woodland, especially in a valley by a stream. F.ns. in Burghfield, Cholsey, Hampstead Norris, Midgham, Newbury, Sulham, Thatcham, Tilehurst, Ufton Nervet, Woolhampton. In 6 instances the name occurs as The String(s).

RECURRING MINOR NAMES AND F.NS., NOT FULLY EXPLAINED, NOTED IN BERKS AND OTHER COUNTIES

Cuckoo Pen (O 438, Gl **4**, 60). Swallowfield, Thatcham (f.n.), Winkfield. Cf. Cuckoo Nest (f.n.), Winkfield, Cuckoo Pits, Hampstead Norris, Cuckoo Pightle (f.n.), Ufton Nervet.

Dimmings Dale (Db 169, YW **6**, 108). Swallowfield (f.n.).

Landew (O 457). *The Landewe*, 1550 Welford.

Mount Scipett. Bray.

Noah's Ark. Cookham, Greenham, Swallowfield.

Weeping Cross (O 396). *Weepingcross Closes* 17th, 18th, Speen.

Wewe (O 290). *Wewescrofte*, 1374 Welford.

SPECIAL CATEGORIES OF FIELD- AND MINOR NAMES

(a) *Nicknames for poor land or unpleasant places:* Beggar's Bush (Sunninghill), Beggar's Hill (Woodley and Sandford); Breakheart Hill (Windsor); Breakneck Copse (Woolhampton); Cold Harbour (Hurley, Shottesbrooke), Cold Arbour (Bradfield); The Devils Grandfather (Reading), possibly Dick's Devil (St Nicholas Hurst); Dungeon Piddle (Stratfield Mortimer); Great Goings Out (Hurley); Hopeless Ground (Winnersh); *Idellstartes* (Sonning); Jail Bird (Welford); Kill Horse Fd (Tilehurst); Lick Pots (Easthampstead); Littleworth(s) (Easthampstead, Frilsham); Lousy Hill (Cookham); Mockbeggar (Reading); Mud Hall Cottages (Boxford); Pinchcut, earlier *Pinchgutt* (Burghfield); Poison Piddle (Stratfield Mortimer), Poison Pightle (Thatcham); Poor Pightle (Wokingham); Poor Man a Peny (Cookham); Purgatory (Shaw cum Donnington, Thatcham); Sorry Bargain (Waltham St Lawrence); Starveall Plantations (Speen), Starvehill Plantation (Stratfield Mortimer); The Wilderness (5 examples).

(b) *Nicknames for productive land or pleasant places:* Butter Croft (Warfield), Butter Mdw (Boxford); Butter Pightle (Waltham St Lawrence), Buttersteep (Sandhurst, Winkfield); Cheese Hill (Cholsey); Feeding Moors (Theale); God Speed Furlong (Cholsey); Gratis (Thatcham); *Hevenmede* (1364 Reading), Heavenly Mead (Burghfield), Heaven (Stratfield Mortimer); Mount Pleasant (5 examples); Mount Sion (Beenham, Ufton Nervet, the reference may be to godliness rather than pleasantness); *Paradis* (1309 Earley), Paradise (Beenham, Binfield, Waltham St Lawrence).

(c) *Nicknames referring to shape or location:* Bellows Nose (Brightwalton); Cowstail Pightle (Swallowfield); Crows Nest (Burghfield); *Dogskynnes* (1550 Chieveley); possibly Four Horse Shoe Fd (Reading); Grindstone Handle (Hampstead Norris); Half Moon (Binfield, Wokingham); *The Harpe* (1635 Binfield); Highcockett (Wargrave); Hogshead Hill (St Nicholas Hurst); Leg Acre (Bucklebury), *Legg Croft* (1609) Cookham; Pauls Foot and Leg (Cookham); Leg of Mutton (Barkham); *Long Neck* (1607 Wargrave); The Query (Thatcham); Ragaback Close (Cookham); Shoulder of Mutton (5 examples); Sparrowbill Copse (Brightwell); Spectacles (Shinfield); The T (Bucklebury); The Triangles (Shottesbrooke); *Twotayles* (Bray); Waistcoat Piddle (Ruscombe); Welsh Harp Piece (Woodley and Sandford). Hog Trough (3 examples), Pig Trough (Newbury), Hog Tub Ground (Bucklebury) could belong here, but could simply refer to the presence of a feeding trough.

(*d*) *Nicknames for small plots or settlements:* Handkerchief Ground and Piece (Arborfield, Shinfield); Wren Park (Easthampstead). *City* occurs occasionally in modern f.ns. and minor ns., apparently used sarcastically of a small settlement. Cobbler's City in Woodley and Sandford is a row of small houses, so is the City in Tilehurst. City in Newbury is a suburb. It is possible that the cottage in Bucklebury called *Cetti Thomas* 1583, *City Thomas* 1750 belongs here. Other instances occur in Pt 2. The 1″ map, sheet 168, shows a tiny cluster of buildings E. of Ashmansworth Ha called The City (GR 4357).

(*e*) *Transferred place-names*, (1) *Foreign;* Belleisle (Purley); Botany Bay (Ruscombe, White Waltham); Calcutta (Shinfield); California (Wokingham Without), cf. also California in England on 2½″ map on the boundary between Barkham and Finchampstead; Cape Farewell (Wargrave); The Chantilly Gardens (Earley); China Island (Sunninghill); Denmark Cottages (Woodley and Sandford); Egypt (Leckhampstead); Finland (White Waltham); Formosa Place (Cookham); Gibraltar (Cookham); Mesopotamia (Bradfield); New American Garden (Earley); New England (4 examples); Newfoundland (Bisham, St Nicholas Hurst); Pennsylvania (Ufton Nervet); Pomerania (Bradfield); Waterloo (Cookham, Shinfield, Wokingham Without). (2) *English:* Great and Little Brittain (Remenham); Little Hungerford (Woodley and Sandford); Isle of Wight (3 examples); London Lo (Woolhampton); Piccadilly (St Nicholas Hurst, Winnersh); Vauxhall Copse (Winterbourne).

(*f*) *Names referring to sticky soil:* these contain *honey*, as in minor ns. Honeyhill (Wokingham Without), Honey Lane (Cholsey Hurley), Honeyend Fm (Reading), Honey Bottom (Shaw cum Donnington), and several f.ns.; or *pudding*, as in Pudding Acre (Cookham), Pudding Close (Burghfield), Pudding Hill (Hurley), Pudding Lane (Arborfield, Brightwalton), Plum Pudding Fd (Waltham St Lawrence). Cf. also Porridge Bottom (Finchampstead), Featherlands Copse (Swallowfield).

(*g*) *Names for land on a boundary:* (1) *No Man's*, as in No Man's Land (6 examples), *Nomans Eight* (1636 Bray), No Man's Green (Wargrave), No Mans Mow (Waltham St Lawrence). The earliest forms noted are for *Nomans Land* in Shinfield and Reading, 1550 and Ed 6. (2) *World's End*, Beedon, Earley, Sunningdale, Theale. Some of the names in (*e*) refer to position on a boundary.

(*h*) *Recreation:* Bowling Alley (Yattendon, Ufton Nervet), Skittle Ground (Burghfield), possibly *Hurlebat* (1376–7 Newbury).

(*i*) *Names referring to objects found*: Brickbatts (Waltham St Lawrence); Horsenails (Waltham St Lawrence), *Horsenayles* (1603–4 Sonning); *Oystershells Bed* (Reading).

(*j*) *Folk-lore*: Devil's Den (Thatcham), Devil's Lane (Winkfield); Fire Drake (Sulhampstead); Robin Hood's Arbour (Maidenhead), Robin Hood Lane (Winnersh). *v.* also **Grīm** and **pūca** in List of Elements (Pt **3**).

(*k*) *Land for* (*1*) *Church or* (*2*) *Charitable use*: (1) Bell Fd (Burghfield), *Bellfield* (1607 Bray); *The Chauntrye Lande* (1555 Englefield), *Chauntrygrove* (1640 Winkfield); *Lampe Acre* (1547 Shaw cum Donnington, 1548–9 Yattendon); *The Seyntury Lande* (1576 Reading). *v.* also **hlæfdige** in List of Elements (Pt **3**). (2) Poors- as in Poors Garden (Ruscombe), *Poureslond* (1420 Arborfield), *The Poor's Land* (1739 Sandhurst) etc.; Charity-., as in Charity Pastures (Burghfield), Charity Piece (Wokingham) etc.

(*l*) *Miscellaneous unexplained: Banquetting House Ground* (Bucklebury, possibly belongs in (*b*), cf. Banquetting Field O 443); *Conscyence Crosse Lane* (1596 Reading, possibly a variant of Weeping Cross O 396); Damas Fd (Padworth), Damaskfield Copse (Hampstead Norris); Elephant Moor (Pangbourne); *Fyvemen Mede* (Ed 6 Reading, perhaps referring to the number of mowers required); Halfpenny Catch Lane (Beedon), Halfpenny Lane (Cholsey), Halfpenny (Padworth), The Halfpenny (Hurley); Jack's Bridge, Queen's Bridge and King's Bridge (Wokingham Without); Leapfrog Mdw (Cookham); Little Hercules (Burghfield); The Parlour (Burghfield, cf. Puppy's Parlour O 444); *Le Realme* (1552 Stratfield Mortimer); Smallbones (Burghfield); Three and odd (St Nicholas Hurst); Three Sisters (Windsor); Tickle Me Too (Sulham); The Wallet (Finchampstead), Wallet Mead (Reading); Witch Pit (Chieveley), Wych Pit (Hampstead Norris).

INDEX OF PARISHES IN PART I